ADOLESCENCE

Continuity, Change, and Diversity

SECOND EDITION

ADOLESCENCE
Continuity, Change, and Diversity

SECOND EDITION

Nancy J. Cobb
California State University, Los Angeles

Mayfield Publishing Company
Mountain View, California
London • Toronto

Library of Congress Cataloging-in-Publication Data

Cobb, Nancy J.
Adolescence : continuity, change, and diversity / Nancy J. Cobb.
    p.   cm.
Includes bibliographical references and index.
ISBN 1-55934-392-3
1. Adolescence.   2. Adolescent psychology.   3. Teenagers—United
States.   I. Title.
HQ796.C596   1995
305.23′5—dc20   94-29682
                                                                              CIP

Manufactured in the United States of America
10   9   8   7   6   5   4   3   2   1

Mayfield Publishing Company
1280 Villa Street
Mountain View, California 94041

Sponsoring editor, Franklin C. Graham; *developmental editor,* Barbara Armentrout; *production editor,* Merlyn Holmes; *copyeditor,* Ruth Letner; *text designer,* Jeanne M. Schreiber; *cover designer,* Steve Naegele; *cover art,* © 1994 Adam Peiperl; *illustrators* Willa Bower, Robin Mouat, and Mark Schultz; *photo researchers,* Melissa Kreischer and Larisa North; *manufacturing manager,* Aimee Rutter. The text was set in 10/12.5 Galliard by CRWaldman Graphic Communications, Inc. and printed on 45# Somerset Matte (an acid-free paper), PMS 157, by R. R. Donnelley & Sons.

Text and photo credits appear on page 673, which constitutes a continuation of the copyright page.

To Joshua and Jenny
Love,
Mom

Brief Contents

PART ONE FOUNDATIONS OF ADOLESCENT DEVELOPMENT 2

1 A Lifespan Perspective on Adolescence 4
2 Theoretical Foundations of Adolescent Development 40

PART TWO CONTINUITY AND DIVERSITY IN ADOLESCENT DEVELOPMENT 88

3 The Biological Context of Development: Puberty 90
4 Cognitive Development: Processes and Transitions 144
5 Adolescents in the Family 208
6 Adolescents and Their Friends 254
7 Adolescents in the Schools 290

PART THREE CONTINUITY AND CHANGE IN IDENTITY CONSOLIDATION 334

8 Defining the Self: Identity and Intimacy 336
9 The Sexual Self: Close Relationships in Late Adolescence 384
10 Careers and College 430
11 Facing the Future: Values in Transition 488
12 Atypical Development in Adolescence 528
13 Studying Adolescence: Research Methods and Issues 586

Contents

To the Instructor   xxi

To the Students   xxvii

PART ONE   **Foundations of Adolescent Development**   **2**

1   **A LIFESPAN PERSPECTIVE ON ADOLESCENCE**   **4**

Adolescents in a Changing Population   7

The Many Faces of Adolescents   9

    One Face or Two? Sex and Gender Differences   9

    The Colors of Change: Ethnic and Racial Differences   11

    Research Focus   Archival Research: Racial Socialization—Survival Tactics in a White Society?   14

Defining Adolescence   17

    A Biological Definition   18

    A Psychological Definition   20

    Research Focus   Interviews: A Job? Marriage? Kids? Don't Rush Me—I'm Only 16!   22

    A Sociological Definition   26

The Lifespan Approach   27

    Lifespan: Change and Continuity   27

    New Ways of Looking at Development   28

Life Stages Throughout History   30

    A Time Before Childhood?   30

    The Creation of Adolescence   32

    A New Age: Youth   33

    Adulthood in Change   33

    An Era of Unisex and Uni-Age   34

Adolesence: A Unique Age   36

SUMMARY   38

KEY TERMS   39

2   THEORETICAL FOUNDATIONS OF ADOLESCENT DEVELOPMENT   40

Models and Theories   **42**
A Model Defined   42
A Theory Defined   43
The Environmental Model   45
The Organismic Model   48
The Psychoanalytic Model   51
Environmental Theories   **55**
Focus on the Biological: Havighurst   55
Focus on the Personal: Skinner   56
Focus on the Interpersonal: Bandura   58
Organismic Theories   **59**
Focus on the Biological: Hall   59
Focus on the Personal: Piaget   61
Focus on the Interpersonal: Gilligan   64

Research Focus   Projective Measures: If Shakespeare Had Been a Woman, Romeo and Juliet Might Have Survived Romance   70

Psychoanalytic Theories   **70**
Focus on the Biological: Freud   70
Focus on the Personal: Horney   75
Focus on the Interpersonal: Erikson   77

Research Focus   Erikson's Psychohistorical Approach: A Clinician's Notebook from the Dakota Prairies   78
Focus on the Interpersonal: Chodorow   80
SUMMARY   **84**
KEY TERMS   **86**

PART TWO   Continuity and Diversity in Adolescent Development   88

3   THE BIOLOGICAL CONTEXT OF DEVELOPMENT: PUBERTY   90

The Endocrine System   **92**
Hormonal Activity   93
The Timing of Puberty   94

The Physical Changes of Puberty   **97**
    Recollections of an Adolescent Girl   98
    Recollections of an Adolescent Boy   99
    The Growth Spurt   102
    The Reproductive System   104
    Menarche and Spermarche   108

    Research Focus   An Experiment: A Cure for "The Blahs" Before
    They Begin?   110

    The Secular Trend   113
The Psychological and Social Implications of Puberty   **115**
    Two Explanations of the Effects of Physical Change   115
    The Timing of Change: Early and Late Maturers   116

    Research Focus   Longitudinal Design: Body-Image Satisfaction—Mirror,
    Mirror, on the Wall   120

    Body Image   122
Eating Disorders   **124**
    Dieting   124
    Bulimia and Anorexia   125

    Research Focus   Bias and Blind Controls: Eating Disorders   126

    Obesity   128
Making Sexual Decisions   **129**
    Problems Adolescents Face   129
    Sexual Attitudes and Practices   130
Contraception Use   **135**
    Lack of Information   136
    Inability to Accept One's Sexuality   137
    Cognitive-Emotional Immaturity   137
Sex Education: What Adolescents Need to Know   **138**
    Sources of Information   138
    The Effectiveness of School Programs   139
SUMMARY   **141**
KEY TERMS   **142**

4   **COGNITIVE DEVELOPMENT: PROCESSES AND
TRANSITIONS   144**

How Adolescents Think   **148**
    Thinking Abstractly   148
    Thinking Hypothetically   148

Research Focus   Correlational Research: Do Fairy Tales
                      Come True?   150

Thinking Logically   152

Piaget's Stage Theory of Intelligence   **154**

Sensorimotor Thought   154

Preoperational Thought   155

Concrete Operational Thought   156

Formal Operational Thought   156

Do Adolescents Think the Way Piaget Says They Do?   158

A Psychometric Approach to Intelligence   **163**

Intelligence: What Is It?   164

A Closer Look: The WAIS-R   165

Does Intelligence Change with Age?   169

Research Focus   Cross-Sectional and Sequential Designs: Does Intelligence
                      "Slip" with Age?   172

*Are There Social-Class, Ethnic, and Racial Differences
in Intelligence?*   174

Are There Gender Differences in Intelligence?   176

Beyond IQ: Information Processing   **179**

Sensory Memory   180

Short-Term Memory   180

Long-Term Memory   181

Sternberg's Componential Intelligence   **183**

Three Components of Intellectual Functioning   184

Gardner's Seven Facets of the Mind   **185**

Practical Intelligence   189

Thought and the Adolescent   **189**

Pseudostupidity   189

An Imaginary Audience   190

New Emotions   192

Arguing   192

Doubt and Skepticism   193

Understanding Others   194

Adolescents in the Classroom   **196**

Inductive Reasoning   196

Deductive Reasoning   197

Minority Adolescents in the Classroom   197

Can Adolescents Think Like Scientists?   200

Study Skills and Knowing What You Don't Know   *204*
Metaphors and Meaning: When is a Ship a State?   *204*
SUMMARY   **205**
KEY TERMS   **207**

5   **ADOLESCENTS IN THE FAMILY**   **208**

Changing Relationships with Parents   **210**
Turmoil and Change   *210*
Calm and Continuity   *212*
Change and Continuity   *213*

Research Focus   Internal and External Validity: Family Fights   **217**

Parents and Adolescents   **218**
Styles of Parenting   *218*

Research Focus   Direct Observations: Parenting Styles—Like Father, Like Son?   **221**

Whose Identity Crisis? Parents and Middle Age   *222*
Adolescents' Identity Crisis: Gaining Sense of Self   *223*
Autonomy and Individuation   **224**
Autonomy   *225*
Individuation: The Developmental Process   *225*
Family Interaction and Adolescents' Individuation   *229*
The Family Paradigm   *236*
Families and Ethnicity   *239*
Siblings   *242*
Families in Transition   **243**
Changing Family Structures   *243*
Changing Work Roles: Dual-Earner Families   *250*
SUMMARY   **252**
KEY TERMS   **253**

6   **ADOLESCENTS AND THEIR FRIENDS**   **254**

Friendships During Adolescence   **256**
Friends and Self-Esteem   *257*

Research Focus   Sampling: How Do You Feel at This Moment?   **258**

Changes in Friendships with Age   *259*

Friendship Patterns   **263**

    What Girls Want in a Friend   *264*

    What Boys Want in a Friend   *266*

    Peer Interactions   *267*

    Interracial Friendships   *268*

The Peer Group   **271**

    Cliques and Crowds   *271*

    Research Focus   Naturalistic Observation: "Hanging Out"—Cliques and Crowds   *274*

    Popularity   *275*

    Dating   *278*

Adolescents, Parents, and Peers   **280**

    Conformity   *280*

    Values and Peer Pressure   *282*

    Deviant Behavior and Peer Pressure   *284*

    The Generation Gap: Is It Widening?   *286*

SUMMARY   **287**

KEY TERMS   **289**

7   **ADOLESCENTS IN THE SCHOOLS**   **290**

Secondary Schools Today   **292**

    Academic Tracking   *293*

    School Size   *297*

    School Climate   *298*

    Teachers' Attitudes   *298*

    Research Focus   Dependent Variables: Beauty and the Best—Are Looks and Grades Related?   *299*

    School Violence   *300*

    Teaching Peace   *303*

    Preparing for High School: Junior High or Middle School   *304*

Adolescents at School   **306**

    Literacy, Television, and Homework   *306*

    Patterns of Achievement   *309*

    Gender Differences and Achievement   *311*

    High School Dropouts   *313*

Adolescents at the Edge   **317**
  Gifted Adolescents   *317*

    Research Focus   Case Studies: Educating the Gifted Adolescent   **318**

  Adolescents with Learning Disabilities   *322*
Culture and Gender in the Classroom: Education for All   **324**
  Gender Stereotypes in Teaching Materials   *324*
  Multicultural Education   *326*
  Overcoming the Differences   *328*
SUMMARY   **331**
KEY TERMS   **333**

PART THREE   **Continuity and Change in Identity Consolidation**   **334**

8   **DEFINING THE SELF: IDENTITY AND INTIMACY**   **336**

Identity: The Normative Crisis of Adolescence   **338**
  Identity Defined   *340*
  The Process of Identity Consolidation   *340*
Variations on a Theme of Identity   **342**
  Identity Statuses   *343*
  Identity and Personal Expressiveness   *346*
  Identity Styles   *347*

    Research Focus   Operationalizing Concepts: You Are How
                          You Think   348

Identity: Gender and Ethnicity   **351**
  Gender Differences in Identity Formation   *351*
  Contributions of Ethnicity to Identity Development   *356*
The Self   **361**
  Self-Concept: Who Am I?   *361*
  Self-Esteem: Do I Like Myself?   *363*
Intimacy: The Self Through Relationships   **368**
  Intimacy with Oneself   *369*

    Research Focus   Path Analysis: Too Young for Intimacy?   370

  Intimacy with Others   *371*

Intimacy and Identity: Different Paths to Maturity?   **372**
    Development in Adolescence   375
    Development in Females   376
    Dimensions of Relatedness   377
    Gender Differences in Relatedness   378
    A New Definition of Maturity   380
SUMMARY   **382**
KEY TERMS   **383**

9   **THE SEXUAL SELF: CLOSE RELATIONSHIPS IN LATE ADOLESCENCE   384**

Gender Stereotypes: The Meaning of Masculine and Feminine   **386**
    The Masculine Gender Role   388
    The Feminine Gender Role   388
    Androgyny: A New Alternative   388
Sexuality and Intimacy   **390**
    Love and Romance   390
    Dating and Sexual Activity   395

    Research Focus   Between-Subjects Design: Date Rape   396

Sexual Orientation   **398**
    Homosexuality   400
    Biological and Psychosocial Bases of Sexual Attraction   401
Sexual Functioning: Fact and Fiction   **403**
    The Sexual Response Cycle   403

    Research Focus   Matched-Subjects Designs: Initiation of Sexual Activity   404

    Myths and Misconceptions   406
Teenage Pregnancies and Parenting   **409**
    Teenage Mothers   409
    Teenage Fathers   410
    Adolescents and Abortion   411
Sexually Transmitted Diseases   **414**
    Chlamydia   415
    Gonorrhea   415
    Genital Warts   416
    Genital Herpes   417

Syphilis   417

Pubic Lice   418

Risks and Precautions   418

HIV Infection and AIDS   419

Research Focus   Ethics: AIDS Prevention Research—What You Can't Say
Can Kill You   426

SUMMARY   **427**

KEY TERMS   **429**

10   **CAREERS AND COLLEGE**   **430**

Adolescents at Work   **433**

Part-Time Employment   433

Dropouts and Employment   438

Choosing a Vocation   **440**

Social-Cognitive Theory   441

Ginzburg: Vocational Stages   443

Super: Careers and the Self-Concept   445

Holland: Personality Types and Work   446

Joining the Workforce   **448**

Job Availability   448

Women and Work   450

Minorities and Work   454

Intervention Programs: Strategies for Change   **457**

Counselors as Change Agents   457

Research Focus   Quasi-Experimental Designs: Precollege Programs for
Minority Youth   458

Irrational Beliefs and Maladaptive Myths   459

Adolescents and College: Thinking About Ideas   **461**

New Solutions to Old Problems: Structural Analytic Thinking   461

Research Focus   Factorial Designs: Career Indecision—Don't Push Me;
I'm Still Thinking   462

How College Changes the Way Adolescents Think   465

Gender Differences in Intellectual Development   467

Research Focus   Theory-Guided Research: How Sexist
Is Our Language?   470

Adolescents as Experts   **472**
 Experts and Novices   *472*
 Knowledge of One's Culture: Everybody's an Expert   *474*
Putting Knowledge to Work   **476**
 Active Knowledge   *476*
 Inert Knowledge   *477*
 Thinking as Problem Solving   *479*
Creativity   **479**
 Characteristics of Creativity   *479*
 Origins of Creativity in Adolescents   *480*
Adolescent Decision Making   **482**
 Personal Effectiveness   *482*
 Dealint with Everyday Problems   *483*
SUMMARY   **485**
KEY TERMS   **487**

11   FACING THE FUTURE: VALUES IN TRANSITION   **488**

The Values of Adolescents   **490**
 Values and Identity   *491*
 A Developing Morality   *497*
Social-Cognitive Theory and Moral Development   **497**
 Internalizing Standards   *497*
 Considering Intentions   *497*
 Questioning Values   *498*
 Acting Morally   *498*
 Critique of Social-Cognitive Theory   *499*
Kohlberg and Moral Development: Morality as Justice   **501**
 Preconventional Moral Reasoning   *503*
 Conventional Moral Reasoning: Internalizing Standards   *505*
 Postconventional Moral Reasoning: Questioning Values   *505*

 Research Focus   Surveys: Death of a High School Basketball Star   *506*

 Critique of Kohlberg's Theory   *508*
Gilligan: An Ethic of Care   **510**
 Level 1: Caring for Self (Survival)   *511*
 Transition: From Selfishness to Responsibility   *512*
 Level 2: Caring for Others (Goodness)   *512*
 Transition: From Conformity to Choice   *513*

considers developmental theory in the light of what is known about class, ethnic, racial, and sex differences.

The Lifespan Perspective

Our understanding of the psychological, biological, social, and historical forces that shape individual development throughout life has grown immensely during the 1980s. Yet few textbooks seek to integrate these multidisciplinary findings into a cohesive portrait of adolescence within the lifespan. This book views adolescence as a period of both the consolidation (continuity) of developmental tasks and the establishment of new foundations (change) for the future of the maturing adult.

Organization

Part One provides the foundation for the study of adolescence. Chapter 1 introduces the basic definitions and then places adolescence in historical context. Adolescence has not always existed as it does today in technological societies; even in today's world, there are cultures in which only two stages of life are recognized: childhood and adulthood. Chapter 2 introduces theories and models of adolescence and relates these to the broad developmental issues discussed throughout the book.

Most textbooks on adolescence introduce the topic of research methods at the very beginning, when students are least interested, and then ignore the topic for the rest of the course. This book treats research methods in special "Research Focus" boxes in every chapter, as the methods become pertinent to specific problems, and then more comprehensively in a final chapter. Each Research Focus box starts with a practical problem and illustrates how researchers used a particular approach to solve it. A list of the Research Focus boxes appears at the end of the table of contents. Taken all together, the boxes present the full range of topics important for an understanding of the methodologies employed by developmental researchers.

Parts Two and Three are the core of the textbook. Part Two opens with puberty (Chapter 3) and traces the changes adolescents undergo intellectually (Chapter 4), within their families (Chapter 5), with peers (Chapter 6), and at school (Chapter 7). These chapters provide a foundation for understanding adolescents in the various contexts of their lives. Part Three opens with a chapter on identity (Chapter 8), in which the changes covered in Part Two are examined in light of the central task of adolescence, that of identity formation. The next three chapters examine the various aspects of identity separately: gender roles and intimate relations (Chapter 9), vocational choices or preparation for these through college

(Chapter 10), and developing values and beliefs (Chapter 11). Part Three closes with a chapter on atypical development and one on research methods.

Learning Aids

Each chapter begins with a personal vignette that provides insight into how adolescents perceive their world or deal with its challenges. These vignettes are intended to engage the reader and focus attention on themes within the chapter.

In addition, each chapter ends with a summary and a list of key terms. Key terms appear in bold type in the chapter and are defined in the glossary at the end of the book. To clarify and reinforce essential points, the text is also illustrated extensively with charts, tables, drawings, and photographs.

Supplemental Teaching Aids

A Resource Book for Adolescent Development provides suggestions for teaching about gender and ethnic diversity, additional readings for each chapter, lists of audiovisual and online resources, and exercises that can be used in group or individual projects. Also included are handouts about how to read a journal article on adolescence and how to write a paper on adolescent research as well as review charts of the core theories and models of development. The resource book also contains transparency masters to supplement class lectures.

An extensive test bank, by Dr. Andrea Weyerman of Augusta College, is available in printed form and on computer disk in the Brownstone Diploma II testing system for IBM compatibles and in Chariot for Apple Macintosh. For each chapter, there are multiple-choice items, true/false questions, fill-in or short-answer questions, and essay questions.

Acknowledgements

So many people have contributed to the writing of this book. I am especially grateful to Frank Graham, Sponsoring Editor at Mayfield, for expecting the best and having little patience with anything less. His confidence in the project made it possible to write about the field of adolescence in new ways, and many of his ideas appear throughout the manuscript. To Barbara Armentrout, Developmental Editor, special thanks for the creative energy and time she put into this book. Special thanks, too, are due Sharon Montooth and Merlyn Holmes, Production Editors at Mayfield, for the care and competence with which they saw this book through the production phase. Thanks also go to Jeanne Schreiber, designer; Pam Trainer, Permissions Editor; and to the copyeditor, Ruth Letner, for all their work.

The reviewers who contributed countless helpful comments and suggestions at varying stages in the writing of this book also deserve a note of thanks. Those who helped in reviewing the manuscript for the first edition include

Mary Ann Drake, Mercer University
Daniel Fasko, Morehead State University
Gregory T. Fouts, University of Calgary
Larry Jensen, Brigham Young University
Alan Krasnoff, University of Missouri–St. Louis
Judith Rae Kreutzer, Fairmont State College
David S. Moshman, University of Nebraska–Lincoln
Christine (Coco) Readdick, Florida State University
Lee B. Ross, Frostburg State College
Toni Santmire, University of Nebraska–Lincoln
Lisa Smulyan, Swarthmore College
Debra C. Steckler, Mary Washington College

Reviewers whose comments have helped to shape this new edition include

Terry Bontrager, Rhode Island College
Stephanie Clancy Dollinger, Southern Illinois University at Carbondale
G. Alfred Forsyth, Millersville University
Peggy Forsyth, Millersville University
Nancy Kalish, California State University, Sacramento
Lissa Mathews, Arizona State University
Merle McElroy, Southeastern Oklahoma State University
Debra Steckler, Mary Washington University
Frank Vitro, Texas Women's University

Even with all their help, this book would not have been written were it not for the love and support that came from friends and family. To all my friends at First Pres in Burbank, thank you for your prayers and your support, and to Abba, Father God, thank you for the gracious, and often surprising, ways You answered them. To Mom, for believing I could do anything; to Bill, for an endless supply of video tapes and humor columns; to Michael, for countless discussions, witty and wise, and your belief in me; and to Joshua and Jenny, for making adolescence more real than I could ever have imagined—and more outrageous and wonderful—my love and my thanks!

To the Student

Think about adolescents you know. Or try to remember yourself as an adolescent. If your experience of adolescence is recent, your perspective may still be fresh and somewhat subjective. If your own adolescence is a number of years behind you, your vision may be more objective but may also have blurred with the passage of time. Whether thinking about adolescents you know or of your own adolescence, one thing is certain: you cannot recapture the excitement, the anguish, or those many "firsts" you experienced then. As adults, our perspective is different, balanced by having "firsts" followed by seconds and thirds. Because we recognize that our adult perspective is so different, we have a new appreciation for the special contexts of adolescent development. Today, we have a better appreciation for the context of adolescence, a context simultaneously shaped by the forces of continuity, change, and diversity.

This perspective allows us to see that, despite frequent similarities between adolescents and adults in speech and appearance, striking differences often separate our understanding of the world from theirs. The differences can be dramatic:

A 14-year-old, when asked by her mother why she's been acting so dreamy lately, replies, "You wouldn't understand, Mom, you've *never* been in love!"

A 15-year-old who occasionally experiments with drugs and knows others who have overdosed with the same substance tells himself, "It can't happen to me—I'm different."

A frightened 16-year-old tells his mother that because he hadn't had sex "enough times" with his girl, that he didn't think she could get pregnant. "Girls just don't get pregnant that way, not by having sex just once, just that one time!"

A gifted 17-year-old who can think circles around most adults still feels like a child inside and becomes anxious at the thought of leaving home for college.

Thoughts and feelings like these point to the very deep differences in the ways adolescents and adults perceive and relate to their worlds. This textbook examines the many contexts of adolescent experience and development: the physical changes brought on by puberty, the growth of intellect and logic, relations with family and friends, sexuality, and the larger worlds of school and work. The goal is to present information in a way that helps the reader appreciate the complexity of adolescent interactions with adults and others. Only through understanding what is meaningful in adolescent development can we become positive influences in the lives of today's adolescents and tomorrow's adults.

A Focus on Meaningful Differences

Just as we distinguish phases of childhood and adulthood, such as toddlers from school-age children, or young adults from middle-aged adults, we also can distinguish early adolescents from late adolescents. Early adolescents' first steps take them out of childhood. Late adolescents stand at the threshold of adulthood. Early adolescents struggle with the changes of puberty, a new awareness of their sexuality, and with changing parental and peer relationships. Late adolescents grapple with the challenge of achieving an identity, preparing for adult roles by taking a first job or continuing their education, and integrating sexuality into their relationships.

Increasing your understanding of the many aspects of adolescent behavior is the objective of this textbook. Yet many questions will remain unanswered. The study of adolescent development is a young field and has not been investigated as extensively as other developmental periods, such as infancy or early childhood. Many interesting questions have not even been asked, let alone identified, and you will probably find that you want to know more than developmentalists can answer.

Some of your questions will remain unanswered for another reason. To obtain answers one would have to study adolescents in ways that are simply not possible. Many factors interact to make adolescents the individuals they are. Some factors are undoubtedly inborn; others are shaped by the contexts of their lives—by families, friends, schools, and communities. Many of the research methods that contribute to our understanding of adolescence isolate a behavior for closer study and then extrapolate from the findings to other developmental contexts. Although isolating behavior in order to study it increases our knowledge, it can also lead to distortions, because a person's behavior always assumes a somewhat different form in each different context. Compensating for such distortions is at best an inexact science. In the chapters that follow, you will find information that increases your understanding of adolescent behavior, but you are cautioned that such knowledge is subject to future revision as more research is conducted and applied.

Other questions cannot be answered because of ethical limitations. For instance, does assignment to a lower academic track lead to poorer learning and increased risk of dropping out of school? To answer such a question, we would have to assign adolescents at random to either a lower or higher track, and compare their academic performance. Most parents would naturally object to arbitrary assignment of their children to classes that might limit their academic achievement.

Also, investigators who believe that assignment to a lower academic track might adversely affect learning could not ethically conduct such a study. Researchers have therefore chosen to study naturally occurring groups instead. But they face still other problems when they do. For example, some unknown factor could be the cause of the differences between groups. Consequently, there are many questions for which we do not have—and are unlikely to get—definitive answers.

Extending Knowledge to Practical Outcomes

Many who read this textbook will become teachers, nurses, social workers, or counselors. Almost all will establish families of their own, if they have not done so already, and will face the immensely important challenge of raising adolescents. One way or another, all will come into contact with adolescents who will affect their lives. This textbook will help you make connections between learned concepts and everyday situations. Throughout each chapter, adolescent development is discussed within the context of practical applications. The examples used to establish these connections illustrate in concrete ways the situations faced by adolescents of different ages, sexes, and cultural backgrounds.

Finally, it is important to stress that research can have meaningful applications to the lives of adolescents. The Research Focus boxes that appear in each chapter isolate recent studies that warrant special attention. These boxes will help you to distinguish between various kinds of research and to become familiar with the kinds of issues researchers face. In addition, each piece of research is discussed in terms of practical applications that can make a difference in the lives of adolescents.

The Place of Values

Developmentalists attempt to study adolescents in a value-free context in order to objectively observe and record what they see. Yet values affect their observations if only through their choice of what they consider important enough to observe. Observations that confirm our expectations are usually not subjected to the same critical tests, or followed up with further observations, as are those that are unexpected. Such expected observations often reflect gender and ethnic stereotypes, however unintentionally. Thus, when research finds that males use rules more effectively than females to regulate and prolong their play, few questions are asked. Similarly, studies finding that minority adolescents are more likely to be in noncollege than college tracks in high school are not questioned. Each finding reflects an expected outcome.

But when we look beneath the surface of studies such as these, we often find that other conclusions are equally supportable. Take the case of the use of rules. Is it simply a matter of males being "better" at using rules than females? Hardly. But it takes a different set of values to alert researchers to look for other answers. When they do, they find that females interpret the need to settle their differences through rules as a sign that the friendship is in jeopardy, and they tend to end the game to protect their relationships. Similarly, a closer look at the relatively larger numbers of minority students in noncollege tracks supports alternative conclusions. Research controlling for background variables, such as minority status and intelligence, finds that students assigned to noncollege tracks still do more poorly than those in the college tracks. Assignment to the track itself, rather than ability or minority status, appears to be the key factor in determining a student's investment in learning.

It is only fair to point out that this textbook is not free of values. It makes a deliberate effort to take a second look, to determine whether expectations concerning gender and ethnicity contribute to the conclusions researchers make. Many psychological theories have been formulated on the basis of data collected only from males. Others implicitly assume a male perspective. And nearly all theories assume the perspective of the dominant culture. This book explicitly points out these shortcomings when they occur and organizes the coverage of topics within chapters to include issues of gender and ethnicity.

Even so, an additional set of values will color what you are reading. These are your own values. They operate in much the same way as those of the developmentalists who collected the initial observations. As a student, you need to be a discerning reader. Think about how you are reacting to what is stated and what the research implies. You may be surprised to find that many of your assumptions about adolescents run counter to what you are reading.

Your understanding of adolescence will have increased immensely by the time you finish the final chapter of this textbook. For those of you planning to work or share some part of your lives with adolescents, the knowledge you gain will be both meaningful and practical. Above all, you will have gained a sense of the immense richness of diversity in the human experience.

ADOLESCENCE
Continuity, Change, and Diversity

SECOND EDITION

PART ONE

FOUNDATIONS OF ADOLESCENT DEVELOPMENT

Metamorphosis, change, transition. Adolescents experience all of this. In just a few years, nearly everything changes, from the way they think to how they look and feel. At times, it may seem as if sorcery is involved. Or perhaps it is a mystery of nature. For like caterpillars, adolescents shake out their wings and fly when the time arrives.

Even with the many changes adolescents experience, there is also continuity to their lives, both in their physical growth and in the general patterns to their development. Adolescents remain the same individuals, in fundamental ways, that they were when children and will be when adults. Whether it's coping with stress, solving a problem, daydreaming, or planning, the approach they adopt and the outlook they take bears a characteristic stamp that identifies each as an individual, whether at 6, 16, or 63. The adaptive mechanisms that individuals acquire in childhood are generally the ones through which they cope as adolescents and adults.

As a group, adolescents live with more diversity than did their parents or grandparents. The number of ethnic and racial minorities in the United States has been increasing steadily over the past several generations. Two generations ago, minorities made up approximately 10% of the population. Before this generation of adolescents reaches its twenties, that figure

will be just under 17%. All adolescents are affected by increasing cultural diversity: The experiences of majority as well as minority adolescents will be colored by the diversity that marks our culture.

Change, continuity, diversity. Each of these characterizes the lives of adolescents today. Each is also a theme of this textbook, guiding our study of adolescence.

Chapters 1 and 2 set the stage for the study of adolescence. Chapter 1 introduces the central characters, the adolescents themselves, and the supporting cast, their families and the bit players appearing around them in the culture. It also introduces the production end of things: the research that illuminates our understanding of adolescence. Chapter 2 is a behind-the-scenes look at the critics: the theorists who interpret the drama of adolescence.

The major themes of the text are introduced in Chapter 1. The first of these—achieving a sense of oneself—threads its way through each of the chapters and highlights significant gender differences where these exist. A second theme of the text spotlights the increasing cultural diversity that characterizes our society. The ethnic composition of the United States is changing rapidly; differences that distinguish ethnic and cultural groups affect the lives of adolescents in a multitude of ways. A third theme organizing the text, a lifespan developmental perspective, places the age-specific changes of adolescence within the context of developments throughout the life cycle. A fourth and final theme distinguishes early and late adolescence as two distinct periods of development. Parts Two and Three examine the major developments within each of these stages.

Chapter 2 introduces the developmental theories that guide research in adolescence. Many theories have focused on males, assuming their experiences are normative for both sexes. Current research increasingly shows this assumption needs revision. Chapter 2 presents alternatives to prevailing developmental theories, as well as established developmental thought.

The first of many Research Focuses appears in these opening chapters. These boxes highlight procedures that developmentalists use when conducting research on adolescence. Each Research Focus opens with a practical problem, then examines the particular approach taken by those who studied this problem. Together, they cover the full range of topics one would expect to find in an in-depth treatment of developmental methodology. Separate Research Focuses cover the many types of research, discuss issues unique to developmental research, and present issues common to all research.

ADOLESCENTS IN A
CHANGING POPULATION

THE MANY FACES
OF ADOLESCENTS
One Face or Two? Sex and Gender
    Differences
The Colors of Change: Ethnic and
    Racial Differences

■ RESEARCH FOCUS   Archival
Research: Racial Socialization—
Survival Tactics in a White Society?

DEFINING ADOLESCENCE
A Biological Definition
A Psychological Definition

■ RESEARCH FOCUS   Interviews:
A Job? Marriage? Kids? Don't Rush
Me—I'm Only 16!

A Sociological Definition

THE LIFESPAN APPROACH
Lifespan: Change and Continuity
New Ways of Looking at Development

LIFE STAGES THROUGHOUT
HISTORY
A Time Before Childhood?
The Creation of Adolescence
A New Age: Youth
Adulthood in Change
An Era of Unisex and Uni-Age

ADOLESCENCE: A UNIQUE AGE

SUMMARY

KEY TERMS

CHAPTER ONE

A Lifespan Perspective on Adolescence

Each culture has its stories. They offer a way of understanding ourselves and our lives. Most of us accept the stories our culture tells us—stories we've heard since childhood. It is daring to live lives that are too different from these. But in adolescence, one may dream the daring. Listen to the story told by a Chinese American girl who dares to dream for herself the exploits reserved for boys—initiation into the rites of a warrior.

> *After I returned from my survival test, the two old people trained me in dragon ways. . . . Tigers are easy to find, but I needed adult wisdom to know dragons. "You have to infer the whole dragon from the parts you can see and touch," the old people would say. Unlike tigers, dragons are so immense, I would never see one in its entirety. (Kingston, 1977, p. 34)*

So Maxine Hong Kingston describes the fantasies of a Chinese American girl who dreamed of avenging her people as a fierce and beloved warrior.

Adolescents still dream of dragons. Fantastic? Of course. But in another sense, dragons are made of common stuff. They are what looms large when life seems small. So, too, with dreams. This girl's dreams were not that different from those of other adolescents. Dreams and dragons alike are personal. The dragon was spun from remarks surrounding her youth: "Better to raise geese than girls. . . ." "When you raise girls, you're raising children for strangers." The dream, of course, was to slay the dragon—and prove them wrong.

Each culture offers up its dragons. The Chinese are no different in this respect. The trick is to recognize a dragon when one finds it. As Maxine Hong Kingston tells us, they are too large ever to be seen. In studying the youth who pursue them, though, we will have occasion to examine some of their parts. These are rarely the same from one culture to the next, or even within the same culture when it is as diverse as ours.

All cultures have one part of the dragon in common. They hold up one set of stories for females and another for males: All offer a different set of experiences to their youth depending on their sex. As a result, females and males are likely to follow different developmental paths. These paths give rise to important differences

Adolescence spans the years from 11 to 19, a time of dramatic physical, emotional, and intellectual changes. Some of the cast members in this school play still look like children, and others seem nearly adult.

in personality development, as well as different definitions of maturity. In tracing these differences through the chapters of this text, we must question prevailing definitions of maturity along the way. A central theme of the text is the impact of these differences on adolescent development.

A second theme of the text spotlights the increasing cultural diversity that marks our society. Adolescents reflect their cultural heritages; we will frequently look at their families and often at their cultural and ethnic backgrounds. Although most readers of this text live in the United States and Canada, these cultures are themselves highly diverse. These differences affect the lives of adolescents in intimate and pervasive ways.

A lifespan developmental perspective—a third theme—organizes our study of adolescence. The lifespan reveals continuity as well as change with the years. Traditionally, developmentalists have not allowed themselves this broad a view of their field. Until fairly recently, we have lifted a particular span of years out of the life cycle for closer observation. But in doing so, we often missed the similarities it held with other ages. The lifespan perspective, since it is multidisciplinary, provides several perspectives from which to view adolescence. Psychology, sociology, education, history, and anthropology all bring insights to this field of study.

A fourth and final theme of the text distinguishes two distinct periods in adolescence. Early adolescents must contend with puberty, changing gender roles, developing more autonomous relationships with parents, and more mature relationships with peers. Late adolescents face the need to integrate their sexuality into their relationships, prepare for adult work roles, arrive at a set of values to guide their behavior and, through each of these, achieve a sense of their own identity.

Chapter 1 begins our study by examining the many faces of adolescents. We look first at differences between the sexes then turn to cultural and ethnic differences. Various concepts have shaped attitudes toward cultural diversity. The melting pot concept first served as a metaphor for cultural diversity in the United States. Most recently, cultural pluralism has guided thinking in this area.

Adolescence itself is not easy to define. Think for a moment of a 17-year-old boy who has just graduated from high school. He's as tall as his dad and can beat him in arm wrestling. He has a driver's license but isn't allowed to drink alcoholic beverages in his state. He's old enough to enlist in the Army, but can't vote for another year. It's clear that he is no longer a child, but is it just as clear that he is an adult? Even though he can drive a car and carry a gun, he is not old enough to vote or drink. Adolescence abounds with paradoxes such as these. We will look at biological, psychological, and sociological definitions of adolescence.

The chapter moves to a consideration of the lifespan developmental perspective. Several features distinguish this approach; each brings an advantage to the study of adolescence. A glance at life stages at different points in history informs us that adolescence has not always existed as we know it today; nor, for that matter, has childhood or adulthood.

Despite the tremendous diversity of experience among adolescents today, all face the task of gaining a sense of themselves. Adolescence is frequently discussed as a transitional stage. The lifespan perspective suggests that adulthood is equally transitional, as are other developmental periods. We look to adolescents and parents, and their parents, for similarities and differences in developmental issues. Perhaps we can think of adolescence—like every other age—as a developmental lens that focuses the past onto the future.

ADOLESCENTS IN A CHANGING POPULATION

There are over 13 million 11-to-15-year-olds and another 13 million 15-to-19-year-olds in the United States. Adolescents make up approximately 10% of the population. Many of these adolescents are the children of the "baby boomers" who were born in the years following the Second World War, from 1946 to 1964. As their parents' generation has been squeezing its way through the population, the population has been ever so slightly aging with it. The median age for the population in 1982 was 30.6. By 1990 it had risen to 32.9; by the year 2000, this

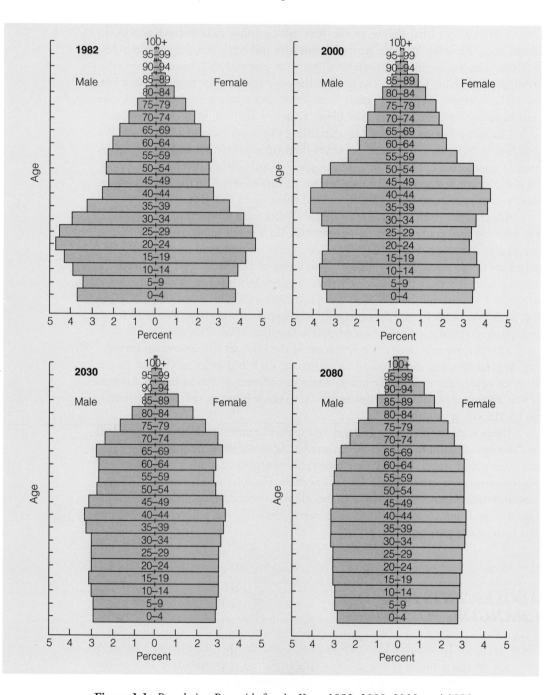

Figure 1.1   Population Pyramids for the Years 1982, 2000, 2030, and 2080.

Source: U.S. Bureau of the Census. (1984). Current population reports, Series P-25, No. 952, Projections of the population of the United States by age, sex, and race: 1983–2080. *Washington, DC: U.S. Government Printing Office.*

figure should be 36.3, and by 2030 it will reach 40.8 and continue to climb (U.S. Bureau of the Census, 1992a). We can see these trends in the population pyramids shown in Figure 1.1. The pyramid for 1982 was still a bit bottom heavy, that is, relatively youthful. By 2000 the baby boomers will all be over 35, and the nation's median age will lift appreciably.

Such population changes can affect adolescents more immediately than one might think. As the number of 18-to-24-year-olds declines, colleges and universities will welcome students to bolster enrollments. Similarly, young workers will be in demand as their numbers proportionately drop in the workforce. Demographer Ben Wattenberg anticipates a downside to these trends as well. He points out that our declining birth rate, or the "birth dearth" as he calls it, will also result in fewer buyers and a generally slower economy. Today's adolescents may face higher prices and a lower standard of living than their parents did (Wattenberg, 1987).

Family characteristics are also changing. More families are headed by single parents. In 1990 approximately twice as many children under 18 lived with a single parent as a generation ago (U.S. Bureau of the Census, 1992a). This figure is even higher for minority children and adolescents, approximately 28% for Hispanics and 54% for blacks (U.S. Bureau of the Census, 1992b). By far, most single parents are women. These figures contain a hidden dimension for many adolescents—poverty. One-third of the families maintained by single women qualify as poor. Approximately 20% of 10-to-15-year-olds live below the nation's poverty level, as do 17% of 15-to-19-year-olds. The difficulty of making it on one's own while maintaining a family has, in part, accounted for other changes in families. Many single parents live with a relative, usually one or both of their parents, to make ends meet. As we turn the corner to the twenty-first century, it may be with a grandparent at the wheel and mom and the kids in the back seat (U.S. Bureau of the Census, 1992c).

THE MANY FACES OF ADOLESCENTS

One Face or Two? Sex and Gender Differences

Few differences are more important to adolescents than those associated with being male or female. Yet few are as likely to be misunderstood. Misunderstandings arise from a basic confusion—that of sex with gender (Unger, 1979). Sex refers to whether one is biologically female or male and is determined at the moment of conception. **Sex differences** are biologically based. Examples include differences in the reproductive systems of males and females, or differences in the average height and body proportions of each sex. Gender refers to the distinctions a culture makes in what it considers masculine or feminine. **Gender differences** are socially determined. For example, our culture expects males to be strong and rational and females to be intuitive and helpful. One is *born* female or male, but one is *socialized* to be feminine or masculine.

Why are so few girls in advanced science and math classes? Are boys naturally better at these subjects, or are they simply behaving according to gender stereotypes?

A quick tour through a high school reveals many differences between students of either sex. It also reveals the difficulty we face in interpreting these differences. Walk into a math class, such as trigonometry or calculus, and you'll see more males than females. Why? Is the male brain better suited to math than the female brain, or are males expected to be better in math and simply live up to that expectation? In other words, is this a sex difference or a gender difference? Continuing the tour, we'd probably find more females than males in a home economics class. You might ask, "Is it in one's genes to be domestic?" (a sex difference). Or "Are females encouraged to be domestic in ways that males are not?" (a gender difference).

Gender stereotypes are the beliefs most people hold concerning what is a "typical" male or female. These stereotypes encompass traits, roles, and occupations. For the most part, characteristics perceived as typically masculine are the opposites of those seen as feminine (Constantinople, 1973). Males, for example, are thought to be independent, active, and rational. Females, on the other hand, are perceived as dependent, passive, and emotional. As a result of this either/or approach, gender stereotypes can be problematic for adolescents, when their being different from the stereotype of their own sex brings them closer to the stereotype for the other sex. Consider a boy who approaches situations intuitively rather than rationally. Not only is he seen as less masculine than boys who adopt rational approaches, he is also seen as more feminine (Lips, 1993).

On a more positive note, gender roles are more flexible today than in the past, allowing adolescents to express both feminine and masculine qualities. Adolescents of either sex can be sensitive and assertive, gentle and self-reliant. These adolescents are called **androgynous** ("andro" for male and "gyno" for female). However, fashioning one's own gender role in this way usually occurs in late adolescence since it requires a degree of self-knowledge and confidence beyond the reach of most early adolescents.

Whether based on sex, race, or even age, stereotypes usually reflect differences due to status as well. In our society, males frequently have positions of higher status than females. Behaviors of females and males that are attributed to their gender can often be explained by differences in their status. The masculine stereotype, for instance, includes qualities such as independence, decision-making skill, and risk-taking. The confusion of status differences and gender differences becomes clear when we think of reversing the roles typically held by females and males. When status roles are reversed, as in the case of a male secretary and a female boss, the differences attributed to their gender often disappear. Who is more likely to make decisions, and who to be helpful? Or who will likely take risks, and who will be more dependent? Differences between the sexes exist in a social context, and this context will affect our interpretation of them (Lips, 1993).

Before leaving this discussion of gender differences, one final point is important. Gender differences are much smaller than individual differences. That is, the differences that exist *between* adolescents of either sex are much smaller than those that exist *among* adolescents of the same sex (Lips, 1993).

Social context gives rise to another difference facing adolescents: their cultural backgrounds. Increasing numbers of adolescents in the United States belong to ethnic and racial minorities. All adolescents—those within the majority as well as those in minorities—are affected by increasing cultural diversity.

The Colors of Change: Ethnic and Racial Differences

Adolescents of both sexes are coming of age in a culture that is ethnically and racially diverse. The proportion of ethnic and racial minorities in the United States has been steadily increasing. In 1950 minorities made up 10.7% of the population. By 1970, this figure increased to 12.4%, and by the turn of the century it should be just under 17%. By the year 2080, one out of every four people in the United States will belong to a racial or ethnic minority (U.S. Bureau of the Census, 1992a).

Ethnicity and race can affect adolescents in many ways. Just how they do depends first on whether adolescents have minority or majority status. Adolescents who belong to a minority are more aware of the racial or ethnic differences that distinguish them than are those who belong to the majority. Majority adolescents may even be unaware that they are members of a racial group. Thomas Kochman (1987) found that whites distinguished each other in terms of ethnicity, but not race. They would, for example, refer to themselves as Irish or Polish, never as "white." The terms "minority" and "majority" are relative, of course. Whites are actually in the minority throughout the world, though in the majority in the United States. Similarly, within this country, white adolescents can experience minority status if they live in a community or attend a school in which some other ethnic or racial group predominates (Phinney & Rotheram, 1987).

Ethnic groups can be distinguished in a number of ways: by country of origin, sometimes by race, by language, by religion—any one of these, or any combination. What is important is that individuals belonging to the group are seen by others, and by themselves, as a separate group within society for whom their common heritage continues to be a significant part of their lives. Thus ethnicity is more than ancestry; it almost always involves culture, or the socially shared values, beliefs, and norms that determine one's way of life and that are passed on from one generation to the next (Betancourt & Lopez, 1993).

Most ethnic groups are also considered minorities, though they need not always be. For example, in Canada, English-speaking and French-speaking people are both members of dominant groups, yet each is a different ethnic group (Phinney & Rotheram, 1987). At this point, the term "minority" deserves closer attention. It might seem, for example, that members of the majority would always outnumber those of a minority. Yet such is not always the case. In certain areas of the United States people of one race outnumber those of another yet are not considered part of the majority. In some counties of Mississippi, the ratio of blacks to whites is three to one, yet the latter are considered the majority. It could be argued that the majority status of the whites is determined not by local ratios, but by those for the country as a whole. Yet a look at other countries suggests that qualifiers other than sheer numbers are involved in determining majority status. The British, for example, while vastly outnumbered in India, retained their majority status, as have whites in South Africa (Simpson & Yinger, 1985).

Minority status has less to do with numbers per se than it does with the distribution of power within a society (Simpson & Yinger, 1985). It also signifies, for one reason or another, a failure to be fully assimilated into the dominant culture. Louis Wirth (1945) defines a **minority** as

> a group of people who, because of their physical or cultural characteristics, are singled out from the others in the society in which they live for differential and unequal treatment, and who therefore regard themselves as objects of collective discrimination. The existence of a minority in a society implies the existence of a corresponding dominant group with higher social status and greater privileges. Minority status carries with it the exclusion from full participation in the life of the society. (p. 347)

Minorities can be set apart by race, religion, nationality, or other defining features (see Box 1.1). In fact, the above definition of a minority could also include women, the elderly, the disabled, or adolescents themselves. Several models characterize relationships that can exist between minorities and a dominant culture. We will look at assimilation, acculturation, and cultural pluralism.

BOX 1.1

Socializing Afro-American Children

When strangers stop me on the street or at airports, often it is to comment on the essays I write about my family. Those about life in our old home in Brooklyn provoke the most response. "It is obvious," a nun in a brown habit said one day, "that yours was a house of joy." I loved the phrase, but it troubled me.

It was not, I started to say to her, always so joyful. In fact, there were times that were painful, as there might be in any family. Some of our dinner-table discussions touched sensitive subjects. For example, our parents often struggled to help us understand and battle racial rejection. It was not always easy for them, proud immigrants in a new land.

One of the heroes of our family in the late 1940s was Dr. Ralph J. Bunche. He was then this nation's highest-ranking black diplomat. He was also a leading academic. His field at Harvard had been international organization, a subject of special interest to our family. It was at the time of the formation of the United Nations. There must have been a dozen pictures of Dr. Bunche around our home. We owned at least one copy of everything published under his name.

The difficult time came the night of Dr. Bunche's public humiliation. He was denied entry to the Forest Hills Tennis Club, then the scene of the most prestigious matches in the world of tennis. Dr. Bunche's rejection became our own. . . .

The idea that it would reject the hero of our family meant it had rejected each of us. . . .

As one of my three sisters, a tennis player, began to put her troubled thoughts into words, tears welled up in her eyes, and she stopped talking. My mother's eyes met my father's. I could tell they had been discussing this between themselves.

"I want you children to understand what you are seeing here." He pointed across to a side table where the *New York Daily News* lay. The story of Dr. Bunche's rejection was prominently displayed. "I know you feel sorry about Dr. Bunche, but I tell you my prayers tonight are for those men who have humiliated them. . . .

"People who create special rules of exclusiveness think they are showing the rest of us what great status they have achieved. In fact they are telling us the very opposite. . . ."

"The very opposite." My mother repeated my father's last phrase for special emphasis. They often reinforced each other's points by repeating a few of the exact words.

"In fact," my father continued, "when people need racial exclusiveness in their social lives, it is usually to prove to others they have 'arrived.' But that's not how I read such men. I read them as socially insecure. Have you ever noticed that truly confident people walk and work among all with ease? The strong do not need that sort of status; the wealthy but weak do."

"Dr. Bunche," my mother said with a wry smile, "is fortunate he will not have to associate with such people." At last we laughed.

Source: Adapted from Robert C. Maynard. (1990, August 5). An example of how Afro-American parents socialize children. The Oakland Tribune.

Archival Research: Racial Socialization—Survival Tactics in a White Society?
With Michael Wapner

Parents reflect the values of their society, and in doing so, pass them on to their children. Psychologists refer to parents as socialization agents. As "agents" of society, they also communicate the statuses and roles that make up the social order, and prepare their children to participate accordingly as adults. So far so good.

So what's the bad part? Minority parents face a special problem when they encounter societal values that can diminish the self-esteem of their children and, if internalized, could prevent them from realizing their potential. How do minority parents prepare their children for entrance into a society that frequently views their group negatively?

In a sense, they become "double agents." In addition to socializing their children into the values of the broader society, minority parents interpret that society's values in ways that shield their children from harm. By explicitly speaking against negative stereotypes, by serving as models themselves, and by exposing their children to cultural experiences that reflect the strengths of their own background, they inculcate feelings of worth and group pride. In black society, this process is termed *racial socialization*.

The way black parents perceive society, and communicate those perceptions to their children, should reflect their own position in it. Yet we know little about the influence of demographic variables on racial socialization. Frequently a single study lacks the scope to address such issues. Tapping into existing databases, often collected from national samples, offers a useful alternative. *Archival research* does just that: It uses existing information to obtain answers to research questions.

Archives exist in many forms: vast databases collected from national samples, written records such as books or newspapers, and publicly maintained records are examples. The databases maintained by the U.S. Census Bureau are an obvious source of archival information, illustrating the first of these forms. How might one use books or newspapers to answer research questions? Consider, for example, the question of whether school materials reinforce traditional sex-role stereotypes. To answer, one might sample textbooks and analyze their content for the frequency of female and male characters, their activities, and the settings in which they appear (e.g., home or work). Is living together prior to marriage more common today than a generation ago? One can look at marriage license applications for common addresses, to determine an answer.

An obvious advantage to archival research is *accessibility:* The data have already been collected. An-

(continued)

Cultural Assimilation: The Melting Pot. Through **cultural assimilation**, it was once assumed that minorities would lose their distinctive characteristics and become indistinguishable from others in the culture. This loss would presumably occur either through rejection of these characteristics by the dominant group, along with subtle coercion to adopt its own norms, or through acceptance by the minority group of the dominant group's norms and rejection of their own. To the extent that immigrants did not assimilate, the public school system took on the responsibility of "Americanizing" the second generation. Since parents often retained their foreign ways, the second generation children frequently experienced conflict over the resulting cultural duality they experienced. The assimilation model was at the heart of the melting pot concept that dominated cultural thought until the mid-1950s. This concept assumed that our culture was formed of diverse elements

other advantage is that many archives, such as the U.S. Census data, are more complete than any data that could be collected in a single research study. Another advantage is that the measures are *unobtrusive*. Subjects do not know they are being studied and therefore do not change their behavior or their answers to questions (as they might, for instance, if asked whether they are living together). Unobtrusive measures are *nonreactive:* They do not change the behavior they are measuring.

Disadvantages to using archival data also exist. Information may be lost over time. The quality of record keeping can change with time, causing unsuspecting researchers to infer that changes have occurred when in actuality none have. Computers, for example, allow better record keeping by police. As a result, crime may appear to have increased, whereas in actuality it is only being recorded more precisely.

What does archival research tell us about racial socialization? Do most black parents act as "double agents" to shield their children from harm by the larger society? Michael Thornton, Linda Chatters, Robert Taylor, and Walter Allen (1990), analyzing data from a national survey of black Americans, found that they do. Nearly two-thirds of all black parents engage in some racial socialization. What demographic variables predict racial socialization? These investigators found that sex, age, marital status, and region of the country all predict the likelihood of racial socialization. Mothers are more likely than fathers to prepare their children for the realities of minority status. So, too, are older parents, those who are married (versus never married), and those who are more educated. Regional differences also predict socialization approaches. Black parents living on the Northeast, more so than those in the South, engage in racial socialization.

For most black parents, race is a salient issue in the socialization process. Most feel the need to prepare their children for the minority experience of living in our society. Yet just like jewelers refining a precious metal, they may find that gold appears beneath the surface dross. The dross? Children learn of racially based restrictions, such as job and housing discrimination. And the gold? They learn that they must work hard, get a good education, and, above all, be proud of who they are.

What other groups can you name in which children and adolescents need "corrective" socialization? Can you think of any groups where it is needed but not generally available? Who teaches gay adolescents how to deal with negative stereotypes? Their heterosexual parents? What can mentally handicapped or intellectually gifted adolescents learn from their parents of average intelligence? Who socializes adolescents in more androgynous sex roles? Traditional parents?

Reference: M. C. Thornton, L. M. Chatters, R. J. Taylor, & W. R. Allen. (1990). Sociodemographic and environmental correlates of racial socialization by black parents. Child Development, 61, 401–409.

---

that lost their uniqueness as they blended into the whole. Each contributed to the overall cultural "flavor," like a stew in which the tastes of individual herbs are no longer identifiable (Rollins, 1981).

In actuality the melting pot concept was a myth. Although it implied that new groups would change the culture's flavor, the groups that assimilated took on the characteristics of the dominant group. To do so they had to be Protestant, Anglo-Saxon, and white. By those criteria, only some groups could in fact assimilate—the Scotch-Irish, for example, German Protestants, Swedes, or Norwegians. In each case, the dominant culture was changed little. Groups whose addition would in reality change the culture were not assimilated.

In a similar way, our culture expects adolescents to assimilate into adult society. They are expected to give up their denims and Big Macs and to "dress for

On school days, dual-culture adolescents blend in with the mainstream teenage culture of their friends, but with their family they partake of traditional customs and may even speak a different language.

power" and speak authoritatively. In other words, they are expected to take on adult ways and responsibilities. But just as with other minorities, adolescents are not admitted into adult society by simply adopting the protective coloration of adults. They must wait until they reach the age of adulthood—21, in most cases—and even then they may be regarded as "kids" by those who are older. Others may go through life without ever assimilating into fully adult roles. And some may find the values of the dominant society so contrary to their own experiences that they experience validation only by assimilating into a subculture such as a gang.

Acculturation: Behind the White Picket Fence.   The concept of assimilation fails to distinguish between what people value and what they will do to fit in; it fails to distinguish between cultural and social systems (Parsons, 1961). Cultural systems refer to the values, language, and ways of a people. Social systems define interrelations among people. Thus it is possible for people to assimilate to a social system while still maintaining a separate cultural identity—that is, their original language and customs. This pattern is known as **acculturation**. Acculturation, not assimilation, characterizes the socialization process for many minorities.

Acculturation assumes that people will adopt the ways and customs of the dominant culture while retaining their ethnic group as a primary reference group. Acculturation differs from assimilation in important ways. One can become acculturated, for example, without being accepted by the majority culture; one cannot assimilate without being accepted. One can also become acculturated without valuing or identifying with the majority culture, as one must do in order to be assimilated. Thus many adolescents who are fully acculturated in their speech, dress, and other observable behaviors can continue to live in ethnic communities, listen to their own radio stations, and celebrate their own holidays. The persistence of an ethnic identity, then, is as much a psychological phenomenon as it is a sociocultural one. Ethnic identities give individuals a sense of continuity with their past as well as a definition of themselves in terms of the people from whom they came (Rollins, 1981).

Cultural Pluralism: Milkshakes and Sushi. **Cultural pluralism** is one step removed from acculturation. In a pluralistic society, minorities are invited to coexist with the majority, participating fully in its political and economic systems while retaining their cultural, linguistic, and religious diversity. Cultural variability is the norm. Perhaps Switzerland is the best example of a pluralistic culture; its population is made up of three distinct people: the French, the Italian, and the German Swiss. All retain their linguistic and cultural differences, yet all are unified politically and economically. The United States is becoming a more pluralistic culture; religious pluralism is now a fact, and cultural pluralism is gaining acceptance. Whether this diversity is a true reflection of pluralistic ideals or more a reflection of failed assimilation can be debated. The goal of pluralism is cultural coexistence, that of assimilation is the "Americanization" of new groups (Rollins, 1981; Simpson & Yinger, 1985).

Just as with gender differences, differences due to ethnicity or race per se contribute less to the overall variability among adolescents than do differences among individuals within any ethnic or racial grouping. In other words, adolescents from different racial groups are far more alike than they are different. In fact, analyses of group differences in terms of race account for only approximately 10% of the variability among individuals (Betancourt & Lopez, 1993).

DEFINING ADOLESCENCE

It is not an easy task to define adolescence. A single definition is either hopelessly inadequate or much too complex. If we settle for more than one definition, we need to link them to some common theme. And, since adolescents themselves change so rapidly, each stage of adolescence—early and late—carries with it special conditions that any definition needs to address. Fortunately, most developmental experts accept a common set of definitions for studying adolescence: biological,

Although these middle-school students may all be the same age, they're not necessarily all adolescents yet. The start of adolescence is signaled by puberty rather than by a particular chronological age.

psychological, and sociological definitions. A particular aspect of adolescent life is examined within each definition and compared to the other definitions. To construct a working set of definitions, let's begin with the most basic and obvious one, the biological and physical basis of adolescent life.

A Biological Definition

The *biological* and physical changes of **puberty** quite literally transform children into sexually and physically mature adults (Hyde, 1990). These changes occur in all adolescents no matter what their culture and are, in fact, the only universal changes of adolescence. They are caused by a heady hormonal cocktail served up by mother nature herself. Sometimes increasing by as much as twentyfold with the onset of puberty, hormones account for puberty's dramatic events.

Beginning in early adolescence, puberty takes anywhere from 2 to 4 years to complete. Several growth processes are involved, each one regulated by different hormones and frequently occurring at different rates, resulting in **sexual dimorphism,** a term for the physical differences between males and females. These include differences in height, weight, and body proportions, as well as differences in the reproductive system itself (Strong & DeVault, 1994).

Some changes, such as growth of the ovaries or uterus, go unnoticed. Other changes, such as the appearance of facial hair or breasts, though of less reproductive significance, are more dramatic. By age 10 or 11, nearly all preteens begin to look for signs of change in themselves. The events most closely associated with puberty—menstruation in girls and ejaculation in boys—actually occur fairly late in the process. Which changes will occur first and just when they will happen is hard to say for any one person. Wide variations exist in the timing and sequence of development from one individual to the next. Also, development is not necessarily even; some functions mature at a faster rate than others. However, some general statements can be made about the most likely course of events.

The physical growth spurt, one of the first noticeable changes for girls, is a period of accelerated growth beginning just after age 10 and peaking at about age 12. Boys begin to grow approximately 2 years later, peaking at about age 14. During this period girls grow approximately 3½ inches a year and boys slightly more. Growth in height is accompanied by a corresponding gain in weight and an increase in the rate of muscular development. Body proportions also begin to change, as girls' hips widen and boys' shoulders become broader.

Changes in the reproductive system and the appearance of secondary sex characteristics can also be charted. For boys, changes in the testes and scrotum and the appearance of pubic hair are among the first noticeable changes. For girls, the growth of breast buds and pubic hair typically coincide with growth of the uterus and vagina. Development of the external genitalia also typically occurs in the first year of puberty. Midway through puberty most girls begin to menstruate, usually coinciding with a peak in the growth spurt. Also midway through puberty boys will first experience ejaculation, which may or may not be accompanied by orgasm. Most adult males usually experience orgasm at the same time as ejaculation; however, these are independent processes and may occur separately. Boys, in fact, typically experience erections and sometimes orgasm well before the time they first ejaculate (Hyde, 1990).

Toward the end of puberty, secondary sex characteristics find full expression. Some are long awaited, such as breasts in girls and facial hair in boys; others less so, such as the development of sweat glands and oil glands in the skin, which can be responsible for embarrassing odors and acne. Related to the production of the hormone androgen, these latter events affect boys and girls alike, although boys suffer more than girls because of the higher levels of androgen in their systems.

Even though puberty serves as a convenient, if somewhat imprecise, marker for the onset of adolescence, the changes we have described are completed well before adolescence ends. The task of specifying an end to adolescence is more difficult, and we must turn to psychological and sociological definitions.

A Psychological Definition

Imagine, for the moment, the world of a 15-year-old boy. Video games, comics, and friends fill after-school hours. Old toys and a skateboard are scattered about his room; two pet rats sleep in a cage on the bureau. A notice about a summer program in math for the college-bound is pinned to a bulletin board. He hates math, doesn't know if he wants to go to college, and can't imagine working. His childhood seems to be slipping away, and adulthood remains impossibly distant.

How do adolescents maintain a sense of themselves when faced with changes such as these? The answer gives us a *psychological* perspective on adolescence. Each adolescent reaches a point when it is not possible to continue living out the same life patterns he or she did as a child. The task facing adolescents is to forge a stable identity, to achieve a sense of themselves that transcends the many changes in their experiences and roles. Only then will they be able to bridge the childhood they must leave and the adulthood they have yet to enter.

The task arises naturally from forces present in adolescence: puberty, cognitive growth, and social expectations. The first force to make itself felt is usually puberty. In addition to visible changes in height, weight, and body proportions, puberty brings an inner world of sexual stirrings. These bodily changes are accompanied by adolescents' new awareness of themselves and others' reactions to them; the period is marked by rapid cognitive as well as physical growth. Social expectations subtly change as well. Parents and others expect a new maturity from adolescents. They expect adolescents to begin planning for their lives and thinking for themselves. In short, they expect them to be more responsible—to be more adult.

The convergence of physical maturation with changing personal and social expectations confronts adolescents with new **developmental tasks**. These tasks represent our culture's definition of normal development at different points in life (see Table 1.1 on page 37). Since our sense of ourselves comes in part from our awareness of how others see us, cultural norms give shape to personal standards. Biological maturation contributes more heavily to some tasks, such as adjusting to an adult body, while cultural norms contribute more to others, such as developing social skills.

Adolescents face eight developmental tasks. The first four are primarily the concern of early adolescence, the latter of late adolescence. Each, however, can be thought of as a facet of one central task: achieving a continuing and stable sense of self (Havighurst, 1972).

1. *Achieving new and more mature relations with age-mates of both sexes.* Physical maturation plays an important part in this developmental task. Whether adolescents keep pace with age-mates in physical development or fall behind can affect their friendships and influence membership in social groups. Those who ma-

Adolescents develop a stable identity by trying out new roles and relationships, such as taking part in a neighborhood cleanup project.

ture much slower, or faster, will be dropped from the group. The groups themselves function as a sort of social laboratory in which adolescents try out and learn new ways of being with others, ways that are more adult. Approval by the others in the group and by age-mates in general becomes especially important as adolescents experiment with new forms of behavior.

2. *Achieving a masculine or feminine social role*. Although puberty provides the biological basis for this task, cultural expectations are equally important in determining behaviors regarded as masculine or feminine. Well-defined gender roles await adolescents, reflecting our culture's view of characteristic male and fe-

RESEARCH FOCUS

Interviews: A Job? Marriage? Kids? Don't Rush Me—I'm Only 16!
With Michael Wapner

As a teenager, would you have imagined yourself as you are today? How do adolescents envision their lives as future adults? Do they think of who and what they will be at 25? At 50? At 64? *Is* there life after 30 for most adolescents?

The only way to get answers to questions such a these is to ask teenagers themselves. A. L. Greene (1990) interviewed tenth- and twelfth-graders and college sophomores and seniors to find out how adolescents and young adults anticipated the course of their lives, that is, the events and experiences they expected to have by certain ages.

Interviews, along with questionnaires, are a type of *survey research.* (See Chapter 14, Research Focus: Surveys.) Surveys rely on self-reports rather than direct observations of behavior, resulting in several important advantages. The researcher can sample a broader range of experience than is permitted by direct observation. Researchers also have access to experiences and behaviors they could not easily observe—attitudes, beliefs, prejudices, and opinions, as well as many private behaviors, such as sexual practices, substance abuse, and family violence.

Interviews provide rich sources of data. Rather than a simple yes or no, they often yield highly personal and complex responses. They are flexible instruments in the hands of a skilled interviewer; the use of *probes* allows the interviewer to follow up on brief responses and gain insights into attitudes and behaviors that would otherwise be missed. The establishment of *rapport,* a comfortable relationship between the subject and the interviewer, increases the likelihood that the interview will reveal information that otherwise might be withheld.

Interviews can reach individuals who might not otherwise respond to a questionnaire. Subjects who cannot read, because they are either too young or illiterate, can nonetheless respond to an interviewer's questions. Also, many subjects who just "wouldn't have the time" to fill out and send back a questionnaire are willing to be interviewed.

Interviews also have a number of disadvantages. Along with questionnaires, they suffer from problems of inaccuracy. Untruthfulness, selective memory, intentional or unintentional withholding of information, and distortion due to social desirability or interviewer bias all potentially contaminate the data. *Social desirability* refers to the tendency of subjects to answer questions in such a way that they "look good" to the interviewer (and to themselves). *Interviewer bias* arises from the many ways in which the interviewer's personality and expectations influence the answers given by the subject. Interviewers can also bias answers by subtly communicating that some answers are better than others—for example, by following certain answers with probes until they conform to expectations and leaving others as they are given.

What do interviews of adolescents tell us about

(continued)

male behavior. Most adolescents will conform in large measure to these expectations. Most, too, will tailor their gender roles, taking a tuck here or there, to achieve the best fit. Our culture expects males to be strong, active, assertive, and independent, and females to be the weaker, passive, and dependent sex. Every Tarzan, in other words, needs a Jane. Fortunately for both Tarzan and Jane, as well as the rest of us, these roles have become more relaxed over the last several decades.

RESEARCH   FOCUS (*continued*)

their expectations for the life course? Greene asked individuals to identify the events and experiences they thought would occur in their future. He also asked them to indicate how old they would be when each occurred. Greene *coded* each of their responses according to four event categories: Achievement (buying a home, job promotion), Relational (getting married, becoming a parent), Experiential (being middle class, traveling), and Existential (being happy, becoming wise).

How conventional (or idiosyncratic) are adolescents' expectations for their lives? Will they be any different than the adults they see around them? And can they imagine life after 30? In answer to the first question, adolescents' projected life courses are more idiosyncratic than those of older college students. The expectations of college students conform to cultural norms for getting a job, marrying, becoming a parent, being promoted, and so on. Adolescents' trajectories into the future still follow individual paths.

When asked to think of their futures, can adolescents think of themselves as young adults, middle-aged, or old? Not easily, it seems. Adolescents' views of their futures are truncated: The future events they envision are more likely to occur in the near than the distant future. This tendency is especially true of females. Adolescent males project themselves further into the future than do females, and think about events and experiences as more evenly distributed throughout their lives.

Why might males project themselves more easily than females into the future? What cultural experiences contribute to this gender difference? Simple answers are not forthcoming. Adolescent females are just as likely to anticipate professional achievement as their male counterparts, and few gender differences emerged in other comparisons aside from the frequency with which females anticipated role conflict between work/school and childbearing. Cultural images of males and females throughout the lifespan may contribute to this gender difference. Are these images more positive for older men than women of the same age? Do males remain attractive longer than females? Does sexuality, attractiveness, power, or personal effectiveness extend further into the life course for males than females?

As with much good research, one ends up with as many questions as answers. If you were the investigator, how would you begin to look for some of the possible answers? What questions would you include in the next interview?

What ethnic or racial differences would you expect to find in adolescents' life-course projections? Consider this brutal reality: Black males have a shorter life expectancy than white males, and at all ages more are in jail, addicted to drugs, or dead from violence than age-mates from the dominant culture. If you were a black adolescent, would these realities influence how you envision the rest of your life?

Reference: A. L. Greene. (1990). Great expectations: Constructions of the life course during adolescence. Journal of Youth and Adolescence, 19, *289–306.*

Patterns of work, marriage, and child care are changing rapidly for women. We can see corresponding changes in their gender roles as they move out of the home and into the workforce, combining careers with more traditional roles. The socially defined role for men has changed less rapidly, although they, too, face adjustments if only because the roles for women are changing, and the roles of each sex are defined in relation to the other.

3. *Accepting one's physique and using the body effectively.* Puberty again provides the biological basis for this task, as it transforms the bodies of adolescents into those of adults. Girls are slightly ahead of boys in this respect, maturing about a year or two earlier. Tremendous variations characterize physical maturation, both within and between individuals. This variability gives puberty a special mystery for the adolescent, who is "the fascinated, charmed, or horrified spectator that watches the developments, or lack of developments, of adolescence" (Tanner, 1972, p. 1).

The cultural basis for this task is given by well-defined stereotypes of the "perfect" body for females and males. The ease with which adolescents come to terms with their bodies will in part reflect the degree to which they match these images.

4. *Achieving emotional independence from parents and other adults.* Puberty plays a less well-defined role in this task, although increases in physical size and strength are undoubtedly important. Children derive much of their strength by internalizing, or taking on, their parents' attitudes and values. The strength provided by having their parents within them enables them to step out into the world. An implication of the process, however, is that at some point each of us must redefine our sources of personal strength. Adolescence is the time when most of us do.

As adolescents become responsible for more areas of their lives, they experience new personal strengths. Redefining responsibility, however, redefines their relationships with parents. Both parties are likely to greet these changes with mixed feelings. In return for self-reliance, adolescents must trade in a comfortable dependence. Parents must in turn trade a final say in things for trust in the adolescent's judgment. The process is painful for both; it is difficult to shed familiar roles when new roles are not well defined or fully understood.

5. *Preparing for marriage and family life.* Although most adolescents will eventually marry and have children of their own, marriage today is more of an option than it has been in the past. At present, there are more single adults in the United States than ever before (U.S. Bureau of the Census, 1992a).

Sexual maturation provides the biological basis for this developmental task. Although sexual maturation usually takes place in early adolescence, most individuals do not achieve a fusing of genuine intimacy with sexual feelings until late adolescence or early adulthood.

6. *Preparing for an economic career.* Perhaps nothing better signifies adult status than being able to support oneself. This developmental task has become increasingly problematic for adolescents today because of the many years of education required prior to assuming many kinds of jobs. The President's Science Advisory Committee has commented, "As the labor of children has become unnecessary to society, school has been extended for them. With every decade, the length of schooling has increased, until a thoughtful person must ask whether society can conceive of no other way for youth to come into adulthood" (Coleman, 1974, p. vii).

Adolescents typically are torn between the desire for emotional and financial independence from their parents and the reluctance to give up the comforts of dependence.

7. *Acquiring a set of values and an ethical system as a guide to behavior—developing an ideology.* Thought undergoes profound changes in adolescence. Adolescents can consider abstract principles and hypothetical situations that are beyond the grasp of children. These changes make it possible for adolescents to think of their beliefs and values as part of a larger system that they can evaluate in terms of new principles. Some psychologists believe that the development of conscience and moral thought parallel intellectual development. Others point to important sex differences in moral thought.

8. *Desiring and achieving socially responsible behavior.* Adolescence is a stepping-off point. Children view the world from the window of the family; adolescents and young adults from their places of work and new social roles. So, too, children know themselves primarily through their relationships within the family; adults through their status within the community. Once adolescents achieve emotional independence from parents and become economically independent, whether through occupation or marriage, they become members of a larger community.

Each of these eight developmental tasks confronts adolescents with the larger task of achieving a sense of themselves. A new independence from parents, preparation for adult roles of work and family, and formation of a set of values by which they can relate to their communities are necessary steps into adulthood. Even teen-agers who master these steps, however, find the gateway to adulthood locked and must wait for someone to come along with the key. The lock is sprung not by biological or even psychological maturity. The final tumbler is keyed to a socio-logical definition of adolescence.

A Sociological Definition

Sociologists define individuals in terms of their status within society, reflected in large measure by their self-sufficiency. From a *sociological* perspective, adolescents emerge as individuals who are neither self-sufficient, and hence not adult, nor com-pletely dependent, and thus not children. Adolescence becomes a transitional pe-riod whose end is marked by legislation specifying age limits for the legal protection of those not yet adult. David Bakan (1971) suggests that complex social conditions require the prolongation of childhood or, rather, the delay of entrance into adult-hood. These conditions can be traced to the way this nation produced its goods.

The United States remained an agrarian and rural society well into the first half of the nineteenth century. With industrialization, both of these conditions changed. Mills and factories drew people like magnets to growing urban centers. Many were new immigrants drawn to the country by a recent labor shortage. Rising numbers of immigrants and unrest in new urban centers focused attention on the need for government to oversee the education and socialization of individuals into a new way of life. Three social movements surrounding industrialization contrib-uted to the emergence of adolescence as a distinct new age group.

Compulsory education laws were introduced for children between ages 6 and 18 on a widespread basis in the United States in the late nineteenth century. Previously, children attended school, or did not, as their parents saw fit. Just as children had worked alongside their parents on farms and in fields when additional hands were needed, they now accompanied them to the factories. Their presence in the factories created certain problems. The hours were long and jobs were in-creasingly scarce, as the nation found that machines could indeed do the work of ten people. The cheap labor of children became an economic liability to the adults in the labor force. Compulsory education laws ensured basic skills among future workers—and also protected the jobs of adults in the workforce.

Similarly, **child labor laws** specifying minimum ages for different types of work restricted the numbers of children who could hold full-time jobs. In 1832, 40% of the factory workers in New England were children. These young factory workers became a liability to the nation rather than an asset, as industrialization solved the labor-shortage problem. Child labor laws ensured humane working con-ditions for children, but at the same time they protected the jobs of adults in the workforce (Bakan, 1971).

Finally, laws instituting separate legal proceedings for juveniles, giving us a separate system of **juvenile justice**, were introduced at about this time. These laws were intended to free the courts from punishing children as adults, and to allow them to offer corrective measures instead. Bakan points out, however, that these laws also suspended important legal rights guaranteed to adults, such as due process and the presumption of innocence. This legislation, just as that governing child labor and education, specified an age group. Each social movement targeted the population to which it applied in terms of age. Adolescence emerged as a period in life bounded at one end by puberty and at the other by legal age requirements.

Each of the three definitions of adolescence that we have considered is incomplete by itself, but together they give us a fairly good sense of adolescence in total. Adolescence is a period in life that begins with biological maturation, during which individuals must accomplish certain developmental tasks, and that ends when they achieve a self-sufficient state of adulthood as defined by society. With this definition in hand, let us now turn our attention to the approach this text will take in studying adolescence: the lifespan developmental approach.

THE LIFESPAN APPROACH

The lifespan offers a unique perspective from which to view adolescence. Issues that arise in adolescence can be traced back to childhood and followed into adulthood. Issues of autonomy and competence, for example, are immensely important to adolescents. Both are also significant issues facing two other age groups: the elderly and toddlers. We can see continuities such as these, and also note the more obvious changes that occur within the age category itself. The lifespan approach studies adolescent development from several perspectives.

Lifespan: Change and Continuity

The lives of a teenager and a grandparent appear, and are, very different, yet beneath the surface each person may be coping with similar issues. The teenager, for example, may be trying to get the keys to the family car, while the grandparent may be facing the need to surrender them after a lifetime of use. The issue for both is the same: independence. If we were to study either of these ages apart from the other, we would miss the important developmental threads that weave their way through the fabric of life.

Similarly, adolescents and middle-aged parents must cope with changing body images. An adolescent boy and his father will both experience changes in physical development. The adolescent is experiencing rapid muscular development, noticing a new "buffed" look, and pulsing with vitality. His father may be noticing signs of aging: a slight paunch around the middle and the tendency to become winded faster than he remembers. Despite the differences in their ages and in the particular changes they encounter, there are similarities in their experiences as well. Subtle changes in strength and energy level create a new awareness of their bodies and themselves and a need to integrate these changes into the self that each has always known.

New Ways of Looking at Development

The lifespan approach views development from a number of perspectives. Four of these are especially helpful for understanding adolescence: the biological, psychological, sociological, and historical perspectives.

Biological Perspective.   **Development** is the orderly set of changes that occur over time as individuals move from conception to death. Three features characterize these changes: growth, differentiation, and complexity. Adolescence is a time of rapid development with respect to each.

Growth is the result of a metabolic process in which proteins are broken down and used to make new cells. Gains in height of several inches each year are a striking example of growth during adolescence. Although growth this rapid may feel chaotic to adolescents and parents, it is still an orderly process.

Development progresses from the general to the specific. This aspect of growth is known as *differentiation*. At puberty, for example, hormones act on the testes in boys, causing sperm cells to appear, and on the ova in girls, causing them to divide and mature.

Differentiation brings new *complexity*, and with it, a need to organize new cells into a functioning whole. During adolescence, the endocrine system accomplishes much of this integration through the action of hormones. Hormones govern everything from dramatic changes in height to delicate changes within the reproductive system. Adolescents will attest, however, that the integration they achieve is less than perfect. A girl can have the figure of a woman before she ever begins to menstruate, and a boy can be inches taller than his father and have not a wisp of hair on his chin.

Psychological Perspective.   The significance of biological changes should not be confused with inches, pounds, curves, or hairs. The real significance of biology, even when it is one's own, is determined by others. Biological change is always interpreted. Does muscular development signal a new maturity or the burden of adult responsibility? Does the onset of menstruation mean that a girl has become a woman, or has lost her childhood? A psychological perspective on development considers the impact of changes such as these on adolescents' sense of who they are.

The "buffed" adolescent mentioned earlier knows it's just a matter of time before he develops his full strength and, with this strength, gains new responsibilities and privileges. His father, too, may fear that it is just a question of time before his eyesight and memory will go the way of his sagging waistline. Just how confi-

As adolescents grow and develop physically and cognitively, they feel increasingly confident about taking on adult roles and responsibilities.

dent, optimistic, independent, or assertive each feels reflects his sense of mastery over his body and surroundings. These feelings change with age in predictable ways.

Sociological Perspective.   Seen from this perspective, development involves a change in social roles. The sociological perspective views development in terms of the progress people make in passing through social institutions. One's roles in the family, in school, or at work change with age. Individuals move from role to role and enter and leave institutions in response to societal expectations for different ages. This pattern of change is known as age-grading.

Each society has its own timetables governing its passages. In our society, we are expected to start school at 5 and graduate by 18, to have a job by 21, and to retire at 65. Timetables can become difficult to follow as the schedule of arrivals and departures overlap. Each of us fills many roles: child, parent, friend, student, employee, boss. The conflicting demands of these roles can leave us unsure as to when we have passed from one role to another.

Historical Perspective.   Societies, like individuals, change with time. Our society has changed in significant ways even within our lifetime. These changes affect us at every stage of the lifespan. Adolescence, or, for that matter, any life stage, is as much a product of our society as video games or personal computers. For one thing, adolescents today are growing up in an aging society. Couples are having fewer children and adults are living longer than ever before. The percentage of the population 65 and older has more than doubled in the last 80 years. If these trends continue, half the population will be middle-aged or older by the year 2100 (U.S. Bureau of the Census, 1992a).

Even though the pattern of growth is the same for each generation, people age in different ways depending on when they are born. Their year of birth defines their **cohort** group. Members of a cohort group undergo similar experiences in the course of their development, experiences they share and that frequently set them apart from other cohorts. One group may experience war, another economic depression, and another prosperity. Such societal changes in turn affect the availability of jobs or scholarships, the number of potential mates, the quality of schools and housing, and innumerable other life circumstances.

LIFE STAGES THROUGHOUT HISTORY

How many different ages are there in life? That was the riddle of the Sphinx: "What walks on four legs in the morning, on two at noon, and on three in the evening?" We all do, according to Homer. However, as with many questions, the answer one gets depends on who one asks. Homer divided the lifespan into three ages: infancy, youth, and old age. Shakespeare gave us six: "the infant mewling and puking . . . the whining schoolboy . . . the lover, sighing like a furnace . . . a soldier, full of strange oaths . . . the justice, in fair round belly . . . the sixth age shifts . . . with spectacles on nose . . . turning again toward . . . second childishness." Infancy, childhood, adolescence, young adulthood, middle age, and old age. Our conception of aging has expanded distinctly over the centuries.

A Time Before Childhood?

Philippe Aries, a French historian, traces changes in attitudes toward various age groups by noting the words by which a group has, or has not, been identified. He notes that at certain points in history there were no words to refer to childhood. In the Middle Ages, a single word served for infancy, toddlerhood, childhood, and adolescence. Aries maintains that the absence of specific words for different ages implies that people did not feel it necessary to distinguish between them (Aries, 1962).

Barbara Hanawalt (1986) argues that Aries's view of children stepping immediately into adulthood is too starkly drawn. According to Hanawalt's analysis of

Although historians are not all in agreement, life stages seem to have been defined in different ways in different periods. As the clothing of the children in this 17th-century Dutch family indicates, childhood has not always been a clearly different stage of life.

the Middle Ages, "The patterns of work and play, the rather late age of majority, and premarital sexual flirtation all point to teenage years not unlike our own" (p. 188).

Even though a period separating childhood and adulthood may have been recognized, the ages of life nonetheless were defined quite differently. For instance, English laws in the 16th century defined "young people" as single people below the age of thirty. Similarly, in colonial America, although youth was distinguished from childhood and adulthood, this period could last well into one's twenties or even thirties, ending only when one married. Even then, one might not be considered fully adult until the death of one's own parents. Until then even married children were only marginally independent (Moran, 1992).

Neil Postman (1982) argues that childhood became a recognizably distinct stage in life only when conditions prompted a re-definition of adulthood. Postman argues that childhood was born in the mid-1400s, to strange parents: a goldsmith named Gutenberg and a converted winepress. If the invention of the printing press created childhood, it did so by default. What it really created, maintains Postman, was adulthood. Adults came to be defined as those who could read the new documents, maps, charts, manuals, and books that were quickly becoming available. The concept of adulthood was based on reading competence, and childhood on reading *in*competence. Before this time, adulthood directly followed infancy, which was considered to end at about age 7, when children mastered spoken language. Postman adds:

> In a literate world to be an adult implies having access to cultural secrets codified in unnatural symbols. In a literate world children must *become* adults. But in a nonliterate world there is no need to distinguish sharply between the child and the adult, for there are few secrets, and the culture does not need to provide training in how to understand itself. (p. 13)

Printing brought about the concept of authorship, and with it, a new awareness of individuality. Postman believes this heightened sense of individual importance was critical in the development of childhood. "For as the idea of personal identity developed, it followed inexorably that it would be applied to the young as well" (Postman, 1982, p. 28). Prior to this point there was a striking lack of individuality, compellingly illustrated by the frequent practice of calling children within a family by the same name. Four sons might all be named John and distinguished only by order of birth.

The "knowledge gap" that developed with printing—something like eight million books were printed in the first 50 years—created the need for schooling. Improving economic conditions made it possible for more families to send their children to school, and a new age group emerged in societies throughout Europe (Postman, 1982).

The Creation of Adolescence

In a similar way, adolescence emerged from childhood in the middle of the nineteenth century. This time industrialization gave birth to the new age group. As we read earlier in the chapter, David Bakan (1971) suggests that adolescence emerged as a response to social conditions that required the prolongation of childhood. The machines of an industrialized society demanded skills as well as physical strength, and the entrance of young workers into the workforce was delayed until they had acquired those skills (Kett, 1977).

Other conditions sped the arrival of adolescence. Industrialization created a shift in the rural/urban population distribution. Large numbers of youths of the same age became concentrated in one place, a phenomenon unheard-of in the days of the one-room schoolhouse. It became possible to have separate classes for youths of different ages. Finally, much as with the arrival of childhood, a growing middle class made it possible for parents to send their children to school in order to secure for them the better jobs that were becoming available. The first high schools were formed in these urban centers in the early 1900s, and the youths who attended them became a noticeable new age group.

A New Age: Youth

Kenneth Keniston (1970) points out that more recently another age group has emerged for much the same reason. This group spans the years between adolescence and adulthood. Postindustrial technology has increased the demand for education, and prosperity has enabled parents to support their children longer. Consequently, the entrance of many young people into the workforce has been further delayed. These young people are no longer adolescents but not yet adults. They are no longer struggling with the problems of achieving a personal identity, yet they have not yet assumed the commitments of marriage, parenting, and a career. Keniston uses the term **youth** to refer to this group.

Adulthood in Change

Views of adulthood are also changing. Until fairly recently, adulthood was regarded as a continuous stretch of time lasting from the end of adolescence through old age. We now distinguish three phases of adulthood—early, middle, and late—with different experiences common to each. Young adults establish intimate relationships, usually—though not always—by marrying and having children. For men, and for many women as well, the twenties and thirties are devoted to career advancement. In the midlife years—the late thirties, forties, and early fifties—adults experience nearly as much change as they experienced in adolescence. Such terms as "midlife crisis" and "male menopause" reflect the transitional nature of this period. Higher levels of health and widespread prosperity have prolonged the period of middle adulthood and have delayed the onset of old age. Adults in the middle years begin to look back and question how well they are prepared to face the future.

Attitudes toward old age have changed as well. Until relatively recently in history, most people did not live beyond their fifties; the age of 40 was considered old. Today, reaching 40 merely signals the passing of youth. Prior to the 1800s, only 2 percent of the U.S. population reached the age of 65. Not until the 1900s did substantial numbers of people live into their sixties. Now many people live healthy lives well into their seventies and eighties (Aries, 1962).

Increased numbers of pension plans have led to earlier retirement for millions of workers. In 1900, two out of three men who were 65 or older were still working. By 1960, only one out of three worked, and in 1980, one out of five. With increased longevity, individuals will spend approximately one-quarter of their adult lives in retirement (Riley, 1986). As fewer older adults stay in the workforce, new norms of work and leisure are established, contracts are changed, and expectations for achievement are reshaped.

An Era of Unisex and Uni-Age

Some of the voices that chronicled the arrival of childhood and adolescence predict that these ages may soon disappear. We will always have 4- and 15-year-olds, to be sure, but we may lose the developmental markers by which they are distinguished.

Childhood exists when there are separate domains for adults and children. The business of children, in other words, is to prepare themselves for adulthood. Postman (1982) suggests that just as the printing press created separate domains, a more recent invention has begun to merge them. The Gutenberg of our times is Dr. Samuel Morse, inventor of the telegraph (Postman, 1982).

The telegraph ushered in the age of electronic communication and, with this, a parallel revolution from print to images. Images, unlike books, are readily available to those of any age. They require no interpretation and no years of preparation for their mastery. The "knowledge monopoly" that previously separated children and adults was broken. Postman writes:

> The essential point is that TV presents information in a form that is undifferentiated in its accessibility, and this means that television does not need to make distinctions between categories of "child" and "adult." . . . This happens not only because the symbolic form of television poses no cognitive mysteries but also because a television set cannot be hidden in a drawer or placed on a high shelf, out of the reach of children; its physical form, no less than its symbolic form, does not lend itself to exclusivity. (1982, pp. 79, 80)

Television, movies, and home videos disclose secrets that were previously the domain of adults. For that matter, printed books did much the same thing 500 years ago when they broke the monopoly of the privileged few who could read and write. The difference is that literacy also established an obstacle that could only be overcome by years of preparation, as children learned to read and understand ever more complex forms of written expression. Television, however, tells all to anyone who may be watching; its images are self-explanatory. This point becomes important if one believes that groups are defined in significant ways by the exclusivity of the information available to their members. Lawyers are distinguished from doctors, students from teachers, or, in this case, children from adults by what they know. If the authority of adults derives, in part, from their ability to initiate children into their secrets, adult authority is diminished to the extent that there are no secrets (Postman, 1982).

David Elkind (1984) also notes that many of the visible markers that distinguish age groups are fading. A generation ago, children, adolescents, and adults dressed in characteristically different ways. Jeans and sneakers marked the appearance of adolescence just as suits or high heels marked adulthood. Today, designer jeans and name-brand gym shoes are worn by people of all ages. Even infants wear designer labels and babies can outgrow their first Reeboks before ever taking a step. Transition markers, such as short to long pants for boys or knee-highs to stockings for girls, are gone.

Preteens enjoy the same types of music and entertainment as adolescents. Similarly, team sports that were once the domain of adolescents, signifying their movement into adulthood, are organized for children. In the past, children would practice in back lots to "make the team" in high school. Now they have their own teams, complete with umpires and uniforms. Beauty pageants for toddlers and martial arts for elementary schoolers similarly blur age distinctions (Elkind, 1984).

Another marker of maturity that is quickly disappearing is access to sexual information. While information about sex is more available than ever before, its availability to children as well may lessen its significance for adolescents. So, too, with violence, once reserved for the mature (Elkind, 1984).

To the extent that adolescence and childhood are becoming less distinct as life stages, loss of markers for adulthood may follow. Ages are given definition in relation to each other. Current media images of parents are noticeably different from those of a generation ago, as in the "child-adult," a carefree, irrepressible, parent to a competent and responsible child or adolescent. This adult need only be compared with TV images of adults in the 1950s, such as in "Leave It to Beaver" (Elkind, 1984).

A look at cultures other than our own assures us that wide differences can exist in the organization of the life course; life stages are socially constructed. Whether age has become more or less important in regulating the transitions between stages, however, is still in debate. Some assert that life stages are more clearly demarked and passages are more tightly organized by age than ever before. Others argue that age is less relevant to life experiences now than in the past. Increases in technology and gains in the sophistication of information require periodic retraining. Career paths structured by age do not hold up to rapid technological change. The information explosion, when coupled with increasing longevity, can lead to changes in our existing pattern of education, work, and retirement. It can also lead to reversals in age-grading as the young get ahead of older workers, especially in information technologies such as the computer and entertainment industries (Held, 1986).

Family roles also structure the life course, but recent trends suggest that these roles are less closely related to chronological age than before. There is greater variation in age when marrying, remarrying, and having children in a first or second marriage. Age-grading may remain relatively tight in public roles, whereas in private family roles it is becoming looser. This asynchrony poses interesting questions. One can only wonder how each of these sectors, public and private, will contribute to individuals' senses of themselves. We may be approaching a time when the private sector of marriage and children defines one not so much through social roles with a semipublic identity as through a set of experiences that allow one to explore the self (Held, 1986).

Although the age categories we presently identify within the lifespan are tied to changing social and historical conditions, development throughout the lifespan reveals consistencies as well. In the section that follows we will look for continuities in the experiences of adolescents and their parents and grandparents.

ADOLESCENCE: A UNIQUE AGE

Table 1.1 lists Havighurst's (1972) developmental tasks for different ages in life. The sheer length of the columns for adolescence and middle childhood show these stages to be active times of change. A second look, however, shows middle age to be nearly as active, just one task short of adolescence. Parents may believe stress stalks in the form of adolescence, but it is just as likely to assume the form of middle age.

Interesting parallels exist between the tasks of both adolescents and their parents. Adolescents must accept their physical types (or physiques, to use Havighurst's term), while their parents must come to accept and adjust to the physiological changes of middle age. Adolescents face the tasks of achieving emotional independence from parents and other adults; a parallel task for parents is assisting their teenage children to become responsible and happy adults, while simultaneously adjusting to the needs of their own aging parents. A task of adolescence is to prepare for marriage and family life; that of middle age is to relate to one's spouse as a person. Just as adolescents face the task of preparing for an economic career, their parents face the task of reaching and maintaining satisfactory performance in their occupations. Adolescents must achieve socially responsible behavior, while their parents face the need to achieve civic responsibility.

No cause for surprise, then, that relationships between adolescents and parents are occasionally tense. But despite sources of potential tension, most adolescents report surprising levels of satisfaction with their parents. Most agree with the way they have been parented and report that they hold many of the same values as their parents (Youth Indicators, 1993).

Parallels exist for adolescents and grandparents as well. Both groups must come to terms with rapidly changing bodies and the resulting changes to their sense of themselves. Both, too, face the need to redefine the self in terms of an occupation. For adolescents this task assumes the form of commitment to a career, and for grandparents, adjustment to retirement, often from a job that has been an important source of self-definition. Similarly, the issue of economic independence faces both groups. Adolescents may have to postpone work while they continue education; recently retired grandparents often face radically reduced incomes. Most adolescents are looking forward to marriage at a time when grandparents begin to worry about losing a spouse. Both face the task of adapting social roles to changing life circumstances. Finally, both face the need to establish satisfactory living arrangements, a problem for many adolescents who continue to live at home while they pursue their education, as well as for grandparents who may not be able to maintain a separate residence of their own and face moving in with their children.

TABLE 1.1

Developmental Tasks

Infancy and Early Childhood	Learning to walk Learning to take solid foods Learning to talk Learning to control the elimination of body wastes Learning sex differences and sexual modesty Forming concepts and learning language to describe social and physical reality Getting ready to read
Middle Childhood	Learning physical skills necessary for ordinary games Building wholesome attitudes toward oneself Learning to get along with age-mates Learning appropriate masculine or feminine social roles Learning fundamental skills in reading, writing, and calculating Developing concepts necessary for everyday living Developing conscience, morality, and a scale of values Achieving personal independence Developing attitudes toward social groups and institutions
Adolescence	Achieving new and more mature relations with age-mates of both sexes Achieving a masculine or feminine social role Accepting one's physique and using the body effectively Achieving emotional independence from parents and other adults Preparing for marriage and family life Preparing for an economic career Acquiring a set of values and an ethical system as a guide to behavior—developing an ideology Desiring and achieving socially responsible behavior
Early Adulthood	Selecting a mate Managing a home Learning to live with a marriage partner Getting started in an occupation Starting a family Taking on civic responsibility Rearing children Finding a congenial social group
Middle Age	Assisting teenaged children to become responsible and happy adults Achieving adult social and civic responsibility Reaching and maintaining satisfactory performance in one's occupational career Developing adult leisure-time activities Relating oneself to one's spouse as a person Accepting and adjusting to the physiological changes of middle age Adjusting to aging parents
Later Maturity	Adjusting to decreasing physical strength and health Adjusting to retirement and reduced income Adjusting to the death of a spouse Establishing an explicit affiliation with one's age group Adopting and adapting social roles in a flexible way Establishing satisfactory physical living arrangements

Source: R. J. Havighurst. (1972). Developmental tasks and education. New York: David McKay.

Although adolescents have the longest list of developmental tasks, people at every age—childhood, middle age, old age—must adapt to developmental changes.

The many developmental tasks of adolescence confirm it to be a transitional period. However, to see adolescence just, or even primarily, as a transition is to miss the point: Transition characterizes every age. It is, in fact, what allows us to distinguish each age from the preceding one. Middle age is no less a transition, nor is later maturity. To view adolescence as a transition is to fail to see adolescents themselves. Adolescents are not just in the process of becoming someone else. They are individuals in their own right.

SUMMARY

Adolescents in a Changing Population

Adolescents make up approximately 10% of the nation's population. The median age of the population itself has been increasing, a change that has far-reaching effects on adolescents. Adolescents today comprise a relatively smaller percentage of the population than they did a generation ago.

Family characteristics are also changing. With increasing numbers of divorces, more families are headed by single parents. Adolescents in single-parent families are more likely to experience economic hardships than those in dual-parent homes.

The Many Faces of Adolescents

Sex and gender differences, though vitally important to adolescents, are frequently confused. Sex differences are the physiological differences associated with being female or male. Gender differences are the cultural expectations that surround each sex. Gender stereotypes are important components of gender; these are shared beliefs that some qualities characterize one sex and others characterize the opposite sex.

Increasing numbers of adolescents in the United States belong to ethnic and racial minorities. Several relationships can exist between minorities and the dominant culture. The assimilation model assumes that members of a minority lose their distinctive characteristics as they adopt those of the dominant group. The acculturation model recognizes that minorities may adopt the behaviors of the dominant group while maintaining a separate cultural identity. Cultural pluralism acknowledges the coexistence and coparticipation of individuals from distinct cultures.

Defining Adolescence

Three sets of definitions together are needed to give a comprehensive view of adolescence. A biological definition emphasizes the events of puberty that transform the bodies of children into those of sexually and physically mature adults. A psychological definition distinguishes adolescence in terms of the developmental tasks to be accomplished. Each of the tasks adolescents face relates to the central task of achieving a stable personal identity. A sociological definition defines adolescents in terms of their status within society. Specifically, this approach views adolescence as a transitional period between childhood and adulthood.

The Lifespan Approach

The lifespan gives us a unique perspective on adolescence. One can see that many of the issues arising in adolescence are common to other ages as well. Continuities in developmental experience, as well as the more obvious differences, emerge.

The lifespan approach looks at development from four perspectives: biological, psychological, sociological, and historical.

Life Stages Throughout History

Our conception of age has changed distinctly over the centuries. During the Middle Ages, individuals did not distinguish childhood from adulthood. Childhood as a distinct age may have emerged with widespread literacy and the need for schooling. Adolescence occurred with the industrial revolution in response to social conditions that required the prolongation of childhood. A new age of youth has recently emerged with the prolongation of education and the postponement of the commitments of adulthood. Adulthood also has recently undergone change. We can distinguish three distinct phases: early, middle, and late.

Many of the developmental markers distinguishing different ages in the lifespan are disappearing. As age distinctions blur, adolescents face a more difficult task in establishing markers signifying their more mature status.

Adolescence: A Unique Age

Parallels exist between the developmental tasks of adolescents and their middle-aged parents. Both must come to terms with changing bodies. As adolescents face the task of unraveling their emotional dependence on their parents, their parents must adjust to the changing needs of their own aging parents. Similar parallels exist for adolescents and their grandparents.

KEY TERMS

Sex Differences	Acculturation	Child Labor Laws
Gender Differences	Cultural Pluralism	Juvenile Justice
Gender Stereotypes	Puberty	Development
Androgynous	Sexual Dimorphism	Growth
Minority	Developmental Tasks	Cohort
Cultural Assimilation	Compulsory Education Laws	Youth

MODELS AND THEORIES
A Model Defined
A Theory Defined
The Environmental Model
The Organismic Model
The Psychoanalytic Model

ENVIRONMENTAL THEORIES
Focus on the Biological: Havighurst
Focus on the Personal: Skinner
Focus on the Interpersonal: Bandura

ORGANISMIC THEORIES
Focus on the Biological: Hall
Focus on the Personal: Piaget
Focus on the Interpersonal: Gilligan

RESEARCH FOCUS   Projective
Measures: If Shakespeare Had Been a

Woman, Romeo and Juliet Might
Have Survived Romance

PSYCHOANALYTIC THEORIES
Focus on the Biological: Freud
Focus on the Personal: Horney
Focus on the Interpersonal: Erikson

RESEARCH FOCUS   Erikson's
Psychohistorical Approach: A
Clinician's Notebook from the
Dakota Prairies

Focus on the Interpersonal: Chodorow

SUMMARY

KEY TERMS

CHAPTER TWO

Theoretical Foundations of Adolescent Development

A theory is like a bridge that connects an island of understanding to the mainland of life. In this case, the island is adolescence and the mainland is the whole of human life. Imagine the limitations in going to and coming from such an island if there were but one theory to connect adolescence to the rest of development. But there are many theories, and each theoretical bridge approaches adolescence from a particular direction. Depending on which theory you take, different landforms appear. Some theories reach deep within the personality, others drop you off at the shores of behavior. Still others feed into the traffic of thought and intellect. Taking just one approach would give a limited view of adolescence. Together, they provide access to a panorama of thoughts, feelings, and behaviors. This chapter is like a number of short trips into adolescence, each one crossing a different bridge. Crossing all of the theoretical bridges will give us as complete a picture of adolescence as is possible at the present time.

Like bridges, theories are functional. The first section of the chapter looks at the functions theories serve and at the models that generate them. Beneath the surface of every scientific theory are the beliefs we hold about the world we live in. We believe, for instance, that males and females *are* different. Many of us believe that there *has to be* a difference. Many of us believe that without differences the human species would be less viable than it is. Although we hold many beliefs, only a few belief systems have produced developmental theories. When a belief system does produce a complete model of behavior, it is given a name. Thus, we have in adolescent development the environmental, organismic, and psychoanalytic models. From these three it is possible to view the whole outline of what we know about adolescence.

Once the three developmental models are discussed, the theories that guide our view of adolescent development are treated in some detail. It is important to keep in mind that not every theory focuses on the same aspects of development.

41

Each theory has its own view of what influences are most important and least important to our behavior. For instance, some theories stress the importance of feelings and personality development, while others emphasize thought and judgment. Also, a single theory may fail to cover all the things one might want to understand about adolescents. Almost no theory, for example, allows us to chart the development of females as well as males. And while many theories acknowledge the influence of culture on personality development, few have explored its implications for particular ethnic or racial minorities.

MODELS AND THEORIES

A Model Defined

Models are the bedrock on which theories rest. Scientists build their theories around basic assumptions, or models, about the nature of human functioning. These assumptions can be so fundamental that they go unnoticed, yet they exert powerful influences on the theories they generate. For one thing, assumptions determine which questions appear reasonable and which seem foolish. If a scientist assumes that human behaviors are primarily reactions to events in the environment, then it makes sense to inquire how the events differ that immediately precede different behaviors. If another scientist assumes that behavior reflects goal-directed decisions, then it is reasonable to ask people about their goals and how they make their decisions. Notice that the first scientist—we can use the label behaviorist— is likely to observe what people do and what's going on around them when they do it. The second—a cognitive psychologist—is likely to ask people *why* they do what they do. In each case, the beliefs that direct scientific investigation are collectively called a **model**. It is important to know just what a model is and how it serves our understanding of adolescence.

You might think that only scientists have models of human behavior. Actually, we all do. Do you think behavior is rational and goal-directed, or does it simply reflect past reinforcements? What motivates us? A succession of rewards and punishments? Inner goals? How much are we influenced by our biology? Do hormones and genes shape our interests and drives? Or do our interests and drives reflect acquired tastes and passions?

Not all of us share the same model. Models are easiest to see when the differences between them are extreme. Consider a teenage babysitter putting a young child to bed. The child lost a tooth that day and insists on placing it under his pillow. The child's belief system (model) includes tooth fairies. The babysitter's does not. What would the babysitter think if the child were to run up to her later with money in his hand and explain that he found it under the pillow? The teenager would question her sanity before admitting to anything like the tooth fairy—and with good reason. Scientists and teenagers alike base their theories on assumptions about what is real and what is not, and most adolescents assume that fairies are not real (Kuhn, 1962; Reese & Overton, 1970).

Models are useful because they generate theories. But models themselves are too general and often too vague to test. Theories, on the other hand, are specific explanations of particular phenomena that can be confirmed or disconfirmed. The babysitter dismisses the child's explanation because she assumes that a person, not a fairy, must have put the money under the pillow. We can even imagine her reviewing each alternative: "The money was there all along . . . I put it there and forgot . . . His mom or dad put it under the pillow before leaving . . . He took the money from his piggy bank just to put one over on me!" Each possibility reflects a model in which *people* put money under pillows, a model that bestows reality on some events—whether they be people, quarks, or electromagnetic fields—and nonreality on others.

A Theory Defined

Mention the word "theory" and many people mentally close up shop and take a walk. The word sounds too abstract to suggest any help with day-to-day problems. Images of bespectacled academics come to mind. Yet each of us comes up with any number of "minitheories" every day. In its simplest form, a theory offers an explanation by relating something that we don't understand to something else that we do.

Theories reflect the models from which they derive. A look at our example shows us why. A **theory** consists of statements arranged from the very general to the very specific. The most general statements derive directly from the model and are called **axioms**; they are the assumptions one never thinks to question. An axiom that might be derived from the teenager's belief system would be that only things occupying space and existing in time are real. This axiom would exclude all but the most substantial of fairies. A **law** is at the next level. Derived from axioms, laws state relationships that are either true or false. Careful observations inform us of the validity of laws. A law from the above example might be that inanimate objects (such as teeth) remain stationary unless moved by some external force. Laws make it possible to predict specific events. We might predict that a tooth placed under a pillow would be there the next morning unless someone moved it.

All developmental theories have one thing in common: Each is an attempt to explain the constancies and changes in functioning that occur throughout the life course. Rather than embrace all aspects of functioning, developmental theories have limited themselves to particular aspects. Some, for instance, are concerned with personality development, others with social or intellectual development, still others with moral and ethical development. Whatever their focus, each theory looks at the similarities and differences that occur with age and attempts to explain them in terms of their sources or causes (Lerner, 1986).

How much are our interests and abilities due to inherited traits, and how much are they due to our environment? Comparisons of the life course of twins have provided important information but no definitive answers about the relative influences of nature and nurture.

Questions concerning the source of development have traditionally divided theorists into two camps. The division reflects their position on the **nature-nurture controversy**: Is nature—that is, heredity—primarily responsible for development, or is nurture—that is, the environment—responsible? Those who view nature as organizing developmental variables emphasize the importance of factors such as genetic inheritance and maturation. Developmentalists who look to nurture for explanations emphasize conditions such as the home environment and learning.

A second issue, following from the first, also distinguishes developmental theories. This issue concerns the nature of the developmental laws that relate behavior to either source: the **continuity-discontinuity issue**. Can one explain behavior at any, and every, point in the life cycle without formulating new sets of laws? Do the same laws apply to other species as well (continuity)? Or do lawful relationships change with age and across species (discontinuity)? Developmentalists who stress the importance of genetic inheritance and maturation typically assume that different sets of laws are needed for species with different genetic endowments, and within a species, at different points in development due to maturation. These theorists see development as occurring in discrete stages. Conversely, those who trace development to environmental sources are more likely to see these forces as exerting the same influence independent of age or species (Lerner, 1986).

Finally, developmentalists differ in the assumptions they make when explaining the occurrence of new behavior. Those who assume that the same set of laws are sufficient to describe behavior at all points in the life cycle believe in **reductionism**, which is an attempt to explain complex behavior by reducing it to its simpler components. Developmentalists who assume that new laws are needed at different ages argue from the standpoint of **epigenesis**, holding that new complexities in development emerge that cannot be predicted from earlier forms (Lerner, 1986).

Differences in these sets of assumptions characterize two models of behavior: the environmental and the organismic. The first considers the environment to be the primary source of behavior, assumes continuity to developmental laws, and is reductionist in nature. The second looks to genetic or maturational forces—that is, nature—to explain development, assumes a noncontinuity position, and views development as epigenetic. All the theories deriving from a model bear a strong "family resemblance." Even so, you will find in reading through this chapter that the degree to which they reflect the assumptions characterizing the model will vary. Some theories reflect each of the model's assumptions perfectly; others are only a good approximation.

One organismic theory, the psychoanalytic theory of Freud, is sufficiently broad in scope, and has spawned enough offshoots, that it is given separate treatment as a model. The psychoanalytic approach gives importance to environmental as well as biological forces. This model adopts a compromise position with respect to continuity of developmental laws, and assumes certain relationships to hold at all developmental periods and others to be specific to each particular period (Lerner, 1976).

The Environmental Model

The environmental model traces development to environmental forces. These forces affect behavior in lawful ways; the laws are assumed to apply at all levels of development. The assumption of continuity to behavioral laws underlies a strong reductionist approach in environmental theories. Since everything from silicon chips to bones and brain tissue is made of atoms and molecules, the laws that describe their actions should describe the functioning of humans as well as the workings of a computer. To explain vision, an environmentalist would speak of the amount of light necessary to stimulate receptors in the retina, or of the exchange of sodium and potassium ions across the membrane of a neuron as the impulse is propagated along the neural fiber. Everything from a toddler taking first steps to the virtuosity of a concert cellist playing a Bach fugue is understood as a sequence of simple reactions, each prompted by the completion of the last, and all traceable to an external force. In other words, "there is nothing special about the complex pattern of events we call psychological functioning. In the final analysis these events involve the functioning of the very same atoms and molecules that are involved in the workings of a liver, a kidney, or a shooting star" (Lerner, 1986, p. 45).

Reductionism reduces psychological phenomena to simple components that operate, in principle, no differently than those in a machine. The metaphor of a machine is helpful in understanding the environmental model, because it translates otherwise abstract assumptions into an everyday example. Based on what we know about the example, we can predict certain outcomes and events that otherwise might remain unclear.

In order to get a machine to work, you have to start it; a machine does not start on its own. You have to plug it in, push a button, or whatever. This sets off a chained sequence of events that takes the same form each time it unfolds. As long as the parts bear the same relationship to each other, tripping one will set the next in motion. Machines do only what they are constructed to do. Vacuum cleaners do not give off light, and refrigerators don't suck up dirt. But if you know what kind of machine you have, and just what point in the sequence is unfolding, you should be able to predict what it will do next.

Is human behavior as predictable? The environmental model assumes it is— ideally. In actuality, it is difficult, if not impossible, to specify the myriad parts that make up the human machine. Even if one could, must our actions be started by something external to ourselves, or are we capable of self-initiated behavior? The environmental and organismic models give us different answers (Reese & Overton, 1970).

If the model of the machine is correct, behavior is always a response to an external event. Actions are *re*actions to forces external to us. The environment becomes the source of our behavior. We, like machines, remain quiescent until something stimulates us to act. Does an engine fail to start because it doesn't "want" to? Intention and desire are reduced by the environmentalist to links in the chain of human behavior. The burden for explaining and changing behavior remains with the environment. Is an adolescent disruptive in class? Look for the events in the classroom that cause this behavior. Is a teenager anxious in new situations? Have that person list situations from the most to the least anxiety-producing, then tackle the easiest. Success will make the next one more approachable. While it is often difficult to trace behaviors to the events that occasion them, it is infinitely easier than it would be if organisms could, at any moment, choose to alter what they were doing just because they felt like it. Human behavior is, at least in the abstract, predictable for those who hold to this model.

For most environmentalists, behavior is linked to external events through simple associations, formed through respondent and operant conditioning. Books have been written about these simple forms of learning. Here we can explore only the outlines of each. However, it is important to understand each form of learning, in order to fully comprehend the environmentalist position.

Respondent Conditioning.   Respondents are reflexes that occur involuntarily, in response to particular stimuli. Food causes one's mouth to water. Tapping sharply beneath the knee causes the knee to jerk. Respondents can be brought under the control of other environmental stimuli through **respondent conditioning**, also known as classical conditioning. Ivan Pavlov, a Russian physiologist, was the first to study this simple form of learning. He noticed that his laboratory animals began salivating at the sounds of their evening meal being prepared. Many of us have probably noticed the same thing when feeding a pet. To a physiologist, salivation in response to a sound is not expected, because salivation is a reflex that should occur only when triggered by its own stimulus. The trigger is a chemical reaction caused by food touching the membranes lining the mouth. Pavlov's dogs were salivating *before* food ever reached their mouths (Pavlov, 1927).

Pavlov identified four elements in respondent conditioning. The food that triggers the salivation is the **unconditional stimulus (UCS)**; reflexive salivation to the food is the **unconditional response (UCR)**. The food-preparation sounds are the **conditional stimulus (CS)**, and salivation in response to the sounds, the **conditional response (CR)**. To make sure you have the components of respondent conditioning down pat, try analyzing the following example for the UCS, UCR, CS, and CR.

A 16-year-old who had difficulty waking for school in the morning solved his problem by placing an alarm clock inches away from his pillow. Each morning, as the first rays of light appeared through the blinds, the alarm went off and he was startled awake. He was especially annoyed during Spring Recess to find that at the first rays of light, he continued to awaken even though he had not set the alarm. What are the UCS and the UCR in this example? Can you identify the CS? The CR? (The answers appear at the end of the chapter, after the footnote on p. 84.)

Operant Conditioning.   Most human behavior is not reflexive. B. F. Skinner, an American psychologist, referred to most actions as operants, to distinguish them from respondents. He pointed out that operants frequently do not have identifiable stimuli to elicit them. Instead, they are emitted. Examples of operants might be reading a book, eating a meal, or choosing to wear a purple shirt. You might say that one is prompted to read a book by seeing it. Yet there are also numerous times when one notices a book and does not read it, or when one will look for a book that one has not seen. Operants, just as respondents, can be brought under the control of environmental events. Skinner studied this simple form of learning— **operant conditioning**—extensively (Skinner, 1938, 1953, 1961).

Operant conditioning occurs when a behavior produces consequences that affect the frequency of its future occurrence. Some consequences are pleasant. When they follow a behavior, the behavior becomes more frequent; this procedure is called **positive reinforcement**. Other consequences can be unpleasant, and behavior that *removes* them becomes more frequent; this procedure is called **negative reinforcement**. Positive and negative reinforcement have powerful and pervasive effects on behavior. Skinner successfully used operant conditioning in laboratories, classrooms, and mental hospitals. The breadth of his successes supports his conviction that the environment exerts a pervasive influence on human behavior. Together, these two forms of learning tie many aspects of behavior to environmental sources. Reflexive responses ranging from behavioral reflexes to emotional responses (the involuntary nervous system is involved in emotional expression) can be respondently conditioned, and nonreflexive actions, whether a simple tap of a finger or Van Cliburn playing Chopin, can be explained in terms of operant conditioning (Skinner, 1953).

Before leaving this model, we will look at how it explains the way we perceive our world. The environmental model holds that knowledge is a direct copy of reality. Copy theory holds that we do not need to interpret our sensations or in any other way try to make sense of experience. Our sensory systems do this for us. You recognize the letters in this sentence through receptors in the retina that fire in a pattern corresponding to the physical configuration of the letters. In a sense, the retina can be thought of as a film that retains the patterns of light to which it was exposed. Receptors carry the physical pattern of the letters through neural pathways to appropriate centers in the brain. All you need to do is keep your eyes open and make sure there's enough light to "expose the film."

For those of you who think you take a more active role in defining your world, read on. The organismic model differs sharply from the environmentalist position.

The Organismic Model

The organismic model takes the living, biological system as its metaphor for human behavior. This model explains human development in terms of variables closely tied to the nature of the organism and governing its growth. Organismic theorists differ sharply from environmentalists, practically point by point, in their views of human nature (see Table 2.1).

Three points summarize these differences. Organismic theorists view the human organism as active rather than passive. They believe this activity to be internally organized, and not just a reaction to external events. Finally, they understand behavior as the unfolding of genetically programmed processes, which produce discontinuous development, marked by qualitatively different stages. Environmentalists, on the other hand, view developmental change as continuous, with ever more complex behaviors being constructed from the same simple building blocks (Lerner, 1986; Reese & Overton, 1970.)

TABLE 2.1

Comparison of Developmental Models

	Environmental	Organismic	Psychoanalytic
Organism is	Passive	Active	Active
Behavior is	Reactive, involuntary	Organized, voluntary	Organized, determined
Development is due to	Behavioral conditioning	Environmental-genetic interactions	Environmental-genetic interactions
Focus on	Behavior	Cognition, perception	Intrapsychic dynamics
Stages	No	Yes	Yes

The Active Organism.   Organismic theorists point out that environmental events become clear only when we respond to them. It takes an action from us to define the conditions that will then be perceived as events. Noam Chomsky (1957), a psycholinguist at MIT, has pressed this argument effectively (John Dewey made the same argument in 1896). Chomsky argued that many sentences appearing to have a single meaning actually have many. They appear clear because we have *already* assumed a context in which they are unambiguous. Consider the sentence, "They are eating apples." Seems clear enough. What are they doing? They are eating apples. Yet if the sentence is a response to the question "What kind of apples are those?" its meaning changes. There are different kinds of apples. Some are for cooking and others for eating. And what are those? They are eating apples.

Organized Activity.   Perhaps the description of a simple experiment will illustrate the point best. Individuals heard a click every 20 seconds for several minutes. With the first click, heart rate, brain-wave activity, sensory receptivity, and electrical conductance of the skin changed. These changes make up the orienting response, a general reaction to novel events. With each recurrence of the click, the orienting response decreased until it barely occurred at all (Sokolov, 1963). When **habituation**, or decreased response, had been pretty well established, the click was stopped, and everyone reacted with a full-scale orienting response. What was the stimulus for their reaction? Could it have been the *absence* of sound? The same silence, however, did not produce a reaction before the procedure began.

The phenomenon of habituation tells us that organisms detect regularities in their surroundings and anticipate them. Events that match, or confirm, their anticipations provoke no further reaction. Those that do not conform prompt a reaction. Notice that our definition of a stimulus has changed. The stimulus is no longer an external event. Nor is it simply an internal event. It is a product of both. The stimulus is the match, or mismatch, of input with what is anticipated. As such, the original meaning of stimulus, as a goad or prod to action, is lost (Miller, Galanter, & Pribram, 1960).

Developmental Stages.   Organismic theorists argue that as we age, we organize experience in different ways than we did during the preceding period of development. Each period is a separate **stage** with its own characteristics. For example, Jean Piaget, a Swiss developmentalist, described several stages in the development of thought, the last of which begins in adolescence. In the first stage, infants do not have symbols through which they can represent their experiences, and thought in the absence of symbols is very different from the symbolic thought of adults, or even of slightly older children. When language first develops, young children organize their experience in very personal ways, not according to the linguistic categories used by older children or adults (Piaget, 1952, 1954).

You can see this difference for yourself with a simple procedure. Just ask a preschooler and an adolescent to say the first word that comes to mind after hearing each of two words. To "fork" the preschooler is likely to say "eat"; the adolescent will most likely say "spoon." To "chair" the preschooler will likely respond "sit"; the adolescent "table." Preschoolers organize experience in terms of what they do with things. They answer with functional categories: One eats with a fork and sits on a chair. Adolescents organize experience in terms of linguistic categories: "Fork" and "spoon" are both utensils and "chair" and "table" are furniture.

A final point before leaving this model concerns the way we know our world. Recall that the environmental model views perception as a passive copy of reality. The organismic model maintains, predictably enough, just the opposite—that perception is an active, constructive process. In order to perceive the letters that make

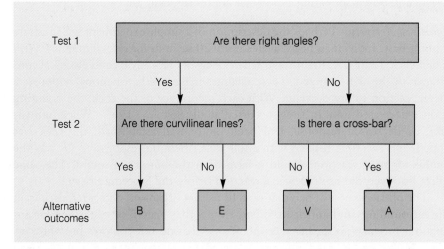

Figure 2.1 Letter Recognition.

Figure 2.2 The Same Physical Arrangement of Lines That Form the Letter B Also Forms the Number 13.

up this sentence, we scan them to see whether certain features are present. Are there right angles? Could that letter be a B, or an E? An E has the same number of right angles as a B, but lacks curvilinear lines (Figure 2.1). Are there curvilinear lines? Research on letter recognition lends substantial support to this type of analysis. Confusion errors in tasks calling for individuals to quickly identify letters flashed on a screen confirm that the more features two letters have in common, the more likely they are to be confused with each other (Neisser, 1967).

Now look at the example in Figure 2.2. The same lines that formed the first letter in the earlier example appear here. But now they follow a sequence of numbers. The letter B easily becomes the number 13.

Is perception simply the stimulation of sensory receptors, as copy theory asserts? If so, you should not have seen the same physical configuration first as a B and then as 13. Organismic theorists argue that context—whether a succession of clicks or a series of numbers—establishes an expectancy that directs the extraction of information. Put a slightly different way, they are saying that we actively "construct" the events to which we respond (Neisser, 1967, 1976).

These two models have generated a lively debate in the scientific community. The third model offers yet another perspective, and along with it, fuel for more debate.

The Psychoanalytic Model

Psychoanalytic theories, like many other organismic theories and some environmental ones such as social-cognitive theory, combine elements of both approaches. They hold that development is organized around stages that take form as maturation enables the organism to interact with its surroundings in new ways. Like environmentalists, they emphasize the way the environment contributes to the personal experiences that focus inner organization. Freud, for example, assumed that young boys experience horror when they first see a little girl naked, believing that she has been castrated. Their reaction to this experience both reflects and redirects inner psychic forces. Freud (1925) would argue that maturation has brought them to a stage in which sexual tensions receive genital focus and also involve them in a dangerous rivalry with their fathers. To protect themselves from a fate similar to the girl's, boys must repress their sexual fantasies, thus resolving the Oedipal complex and moving them into the next stage of development. (The Oedipal complex is further discussed later in this chapter.)

For psychoanalytic theorists, life is a battle, and we are all on the front lines. Two opposing forces, one within us and the other outside, fight for control. Since each is an integral aspect of our personalities, the victory of either one means a sure defeat to the individual. This model emphasizes both inner processes and external events.

Adolescents typically invest themselves in honing new skills—from pottery to running competitively. According to the environmental model, a combination of practice and negative and positive reinforcements is the prerequisite for acquiring new skills.

The psychoanalytic model stresses a balance between strong biological instincts and social constraints. We achieve this balance only with time and at some personal cost. As in any war, there are casualties. True spontaneity may be the first to go. The second takes the form of compromise: We learn to make do with lesser delights to avoid the anxiety provoked by indulging our first instincts. There are victories as well. We gain control over instinctual urges that otherwise, these theorists say, could destroy us and our civilization (Hall, 1954).

Like organismic theorists, psychoanalytic theorists believe that development occurs over distinct stages that unfold in different zones of the body, focusing the expression of psychic energy. This energy, which Freud termed **libido,** takes different forms depending on the body zone through which it is channeled. Expression of the libido moves from the region of the mouth in infancy (*oral stage*), to the sphincters in toddlerhood (*anal stage*), to the genital region in early childhood (*phallic stage*). Because genital expression of the libido in early childhood is associated with tremendous anxiety, it goes underground (*latency stage*), so to speak, and does not arise again until it emerges full-force with puberty (*genital stage*), once again pressing for genital expression (Freud, 1954).

Different aspects of the personality express or inhibit these instincts. The **id** demands immediate gratification of the biological impulses which it houses. It operates according to the pleasure principle. The **ego** attempts to satisfy impulses in the most diplomatic way without getting the organism into really deep trouble. It operates according to the reality principle. Even so, reality for most of early childhood does not include issues of right and wrong, only what one can get away with without getting punished. Moral concerns arise when the **superego** emerges, and with it the conscience. This part of the personality internalizes social standards and comes about when the child identifies with the parent of its own sex. (The emergence of the superego is discussed later in this chapter.)

Although Freud included both biological and environmental forces in his theory, he embodied each in a separate aspect of the personality: biological forces in the id and social standards in the superego. The ego, like a clever general, is given the job of leading the weary troops between these warring factions. The functions of the ego—such as planning, comparing, and evaluating—emphasize the active role we take in structuring our experiences, another similarity between organismic and psychoanalytic theorists. Perhaps because the psychoanalytic model does not require us to choose between environmental and biological influences, it has remained immensely popular. And since it is willing to address unconscious motives and thoughts, it permits us to explain much of human behavior that otherwise would remain obscure (Hall, 1954).

Is the psychoanalytic model better than the others for these reasons? Or perhaps the environmental model is more "scientific," because it focuses on behaviors that can be observed and precisely measured? Comparisons all too frequently lead to evaluations, and someone usually ends up holding the short end of the theo-

According to the organismic model physiological and cognitive readiness is the key. The psychoanalytic model also acknowledges the importance of developmental readiness but in addition emphasizes psychic motivations.

retical stick. Comparisons can also be misleading. Each model addresses different aspects of human functioning. We need all three to begin unraveling the knotty problems of adolescence. The psychoanalytic model helps us understand motives and feelings that otherwise would never see the light of day. The environmental model gives us objective and easily testable theories of behavior. The organismic model offers sophisticated approaches to cognition and perception. Unless we are willing to settle for theories about adolescents who act but don't think and feel, or teenagers who think and feel but can't act, we need the insights each model offers.

But what about the developmental theories spawned by these models? Remember, a single model can parent many theories. We will look at several theories for each. Examining more than one theory should help distinguish the assumptions of the model from the particular form they take in a theory. Our consideration of theories will parallel the organization of the text itself, focusing first on theories with a biological, then a personal, and finally an interpersonal perspective on adolescence. Of course, a biological focus will take a different form when spawned by an environmental model, than by an organismic or a psychoanalytic one. The same is true for those with a personal or interpersonal focus.

ENVIRONMENTAL THEORIES
Focus on the Biological: Havighurst

Robert J. Havighurst, an educator from the University of Chicago, stressed the importance of learning in giving shape to development. "One learns to walk, talk, and throw a ball; to hold down a job, to raise children; to retire gracefully. . . . These are all learning tasks. To understand human development, one must understand learning" (Havighurst, 1952, p. 1).

Havighurst maintained that each of us masters a succession of tasks throughout our lives. These tasks reflect social expectations for more mature behaviors as we age. Physical maturation frequently sets the pace for what is expected of us. For example, we expect children to be toilet trained once they develop control over the sphincter, the muscle used in elimination. We don't expect infants to stay dry through the night, or to let us know when they will soil a diaper. Similarly, we don't expect adolescents to hold down full-time jobs and be self-supporting. Yet we do expect them to develop more mature relations with age-mates once puberty confers mature bodies and interests (Havighurst, 1952).

Havighurst called these learning experiences **developmental tasks.** (These tasks are listed in Table 1.1. on page 37). He defined a developmental task as "a task which arises at or about a certain period in the life of the individual, successful achievement of which leads to . . . happiness and to success with later tasks, while failure leads to unhappiness in the individual, disapproval by the society, and difficulty with later tasks" (Havighurst, 1952, p. 2). Thus the successful mastery of each task lays the foundation for the next.

Despite the importance he gave to learning, Havighurst recognized that we can only master a new skill when we are physically ready to perform it. He spoke of "the teachable moment." Biological maturation prepares us for certain experiences that will have an optimal impact only if they occur when we are ripe to receive them. The very same experiences will have practically no effect at all if they come too early or if the moment is lost by their coming too late.

A second environmental theorist, B. F. Skinner, considered every moment to be teachable.

Focus on the Personal: Skinner

Skinner's ideas have influenced countless psychologists and educators and infuriated others, for the same reason: Skinner reduced the nuances and complexities of human behavior to the events that follow it rather than to what might have preceded it. His approach is a radical departure from the way most people understand their behavior. Most of us think that what we do is a response to inner states, to our feelings and thoughts. Skinner told us our behavior is under the control of external events. He called his approach radical behaviorism.

Skinner said it is senseless to talk about inner states such as motives and intentions. We can't measure or observe them. He believed we can only understand behavior by describing the conditions under which it occurs. When antecedent conditions cannot be identified, he suggested looking at what follows the behavior. When we do, lawful relationships emerge.

Skinner's first subjects were rats. He constructed a small box with a metal lever protruding from one wall, and selected a simple behavior—pressing the lever—for study. Since there was little for an animal to do in such a small space, its explorations soon brought it near the lever. Skinner waited until the animal touched the lever, then dropped a food pellet into a chute that ended in a dish beneath the lever. Each time the rat pressed the lever, a pellet of food dropped into the dish. In no time the rat began to steadily press the lever. Skinner had

Radical behaviorist B. F. Skinner (1904–1990) contended that behavior is determined solely by external forces and can be explained only in terms of what can be actually observed. The subconscious urges described by Sigmund Freud have no place in Skinner's theories.

brought a voluntary behavior—putting a paw on a metal lever and depressing it—under the control of its consequences. By making food contingent on lever pressing, he controlled the frequency with which the rat pressed the lever (Skinner, 1938).

Critics reacted by saying that humans are different from animals, or at the very least different from rats. Our behavior reflects motives and intentions, not contingencies. Skinner's reply to these objections was that our intentions reflect our reinforcement histories. Consider a teenager who has a favorite color—purple, for instance—and buys many of her clothes in that color. Skinner would explain this preference for purple in terms of past reinforcements when wearing purple. She may have worn a purple skirt one day and received several compliments. When next shopping for clothes, she tried on several items that were purple, finally buying one. She spent a few extra minutes with her appearance the day she wore her new clothes and once again received several compliments. Skinner would suggest that this history of reinforcements shaped her preference for purple.

We can analyze many social interactions in terms of positive and negative reinforcement. Sometimes such an analysis seems especially appropriate with adolescents and parents. Let's look at an exchange between an adolescent and his mother. She has just told him to pick his clothes up from the living room floor. He responds "Sure, Mom," with a slightly sarcastic edge to his voice. She reacts quickly and sharply, with more animation than he has seen all day. He picks up his clothes and carries them off to his room.

Now take a closer look at what has just taken place. The mother reinforced her son when she allowed herself to become "engaged" by his sarcasm. She paid more attention to him than she had all day. Attention is a powerful reinforcer. Even though this may not be the kind of attention the teenager, or anyone, seeks, if it is more than he usually gets, and if he is frequently sarcastic when his mother scolds, she is very likely reinforcing a behavior that in fact annoys her.

Also notice that *he* reinforced *her* scolding. By picking his clothes up when she scolded (removing something that displeased her), he negatively reinforced her scolding—the very behavior that maintains his sarcasm. We can analyze many parent-adolescent interactions in terms of the reciprocal effects of positive and negative reinforcement. Adolescents frequently develop the very behaviors their parents find most objectionable. According to behaviorists such as Skinner, this is no accident. Those are the very behaviors parents are most likely to notice.

Reinforcement is a powerful force in shaping and maintaining behavior. But must we actually do something or receive reinforcement in order to learn? Critics of radical behaviorism point out that we can know *what* to do before we ever do it. Many actions are novel, yet they unfold in smooth, successful sequences, not in the on-again, off-again manner one would expect if trial and error governed their performance. Language itself is perhaps the most intricate of all human activity, and the most difficult for Skinner to explain. We produce endless numbers of novel sentences each day. Has each been shaped through reinforcement? How is radical behaviorism to account for each of these?

Albert Bandura, a psychologist at Stanford University, stresses the social nature of learning; his approach is called social-cognitive theory.

Focus on the Interpersonal: Bandura

Bandura believes that most human learning is **observational learning,** not conditioning, and occurs by *observing* what others do and *imitating* what one sees. One need not actually perform the behavior oneself. Inner processes such as attention and memory focus behavior. This theory departs from strict environmentalist assumptions by emphasizing inner, cognitive processes by which individuals interpret their experiences. Bandura supported his position in a dramatic study of aggression in children.

Young adolescents learn new behaviors by closely watching how other people behave and trying out those new behaviors themselves, either in actuality or in their imagination. For social-cognitive theorists the most important element of learning is observation; for behaviorists, it is performing the behavior.

over and again in her research, whether she is studying morality and choice, descriptions of the self, or interpersonal dynamics (Gilligan, 1982).

Notice the way two of Gilligan's subjects, an 11-year-old boy and 11-year-old girl, describe themselves, as shown in Box 2.1.

Jake describes himself at length. He first identifies himself by his age and name and then his status within his community. We never know what his mother does, but we know that doesn't contribute to his sense of position as does his

BOX 2.1

Self-Descriptions of Two Adolescents

How would you describe yourself to yourself?

JAKE: Perfect. That's my conceited side. What do you want—any way that I choose to describe myself?

AMY: You mean my character?

What do you think?

Well, I don't know. I'd describe myself as, well, what do you mean?

If you had to describe the person you are in a way that you yourself would know it was you, what would you say?

JAKE: I'd start off with eleven years old. Jake [last name]. I'd have to add that I live in [town], because that is a big part of me, and also that my father is a doctor, because I think that does change me a little bit, and that I don't believe in crime, except for when your name is Heinz; that I think school is boring, because I think that kind of changes your character a little bit. I don't sort of know how to describe myself, because I don't know how to read my personality.

If you had to describe the way you actually would describe yourself, what would you say?

I like corny jokes. I don't really like to get down to work, but I can do all the stuff in school. Every single problem that I have seen in school I have been able to do, except for ones that take knowledge, and after I do the reading, I have been able to do them, but sometimes I don't want to waste my time on easy homework. And also I'm crazy about sports. I think, unlike a lot of people, that the world still has hope. . . . Most people that I know I like, and I have the good life, pretty much as good as any I have seen, and I am tall for my age.

AMY: Well, I'd say that I was someone who likes school and studying, and that's what I want to do with my life. I want to be some kind of a scientist or something, and I want to do things, and I want to help people. And I think that's what kind of person I am, or what kind of person I try to be. And that's probably how I'd describe myself. And I want to do something to help other people.

Why is that?

Well, because I think that this world has a lot of problems, and I think that everybody should try to help somebody else in some way, and the way I'm choosing is through science.

Source: C. Gilligan. (1982). In a different voice. Cambridge, MA: Harvard University Press, pp. 35–37.

father's occupation. He then identifies his abilities and interests. He ends with a description of an important physical characteristic. We get the impression of a distinct personality from this description. Gilligan agrees. Jake has described himself in terms of the things that distinguish him from others. His self-description emphasizes his uniqueness and separateness.

Amy's description of herself is brief. We know only that she enjoys school and wants to be a scientist. Otherwise she describes herself in terms of her relationship with others. We know nothing about Amy apart from the qualities she believes will allow her to help others. Short, tall, freckled, funny, well-off, or disadvantaged—things that set her apart from others receive little attention. Gilligan stresses that this sense of responsibility for and connectedness to others frequently

---

BOX 2.2

*Choosing Between Responsibility to Self
and Responsibility to Others*

When responsibility to oneself and responsibility to others conflict, how should one choose?

JAKE: You go about one-fourth to the others and three-fourths to yourself.

AMY: Well, it really depends on the situation. If you have a responsibility with somebody else, then you should keep it to a certain extent, but to the extent that it is really going to hurt you or stop you from doing something that you really, really want, then I think maybe you should put yourself first. But if it is your responsibility to somebody really close to you, you've just got to decide in that situation which is more important, yourself or that person, and like I said, it really depends on what kind of person you are and how you feel about the other person or persons involved.

Why

JAKE: Because the most important thing in your decision should be yourself, don't let yourself be guided totally by other people, but you have to take them into consideration. So, if what you want to do is blow yourself up with an atom bomb, you should maybe blow yourself up with a hand grenade because you are thinking about your neighbors who would die also.

AMY: Well, like some people put themselves and things for themselves before they put other people, and some people really care about other people. Like, I don't think your job is as important as somebody that you really love, like your husband or your parents or a very close friend. Somebody that you really care for—or if it's just your responsibility to your job or somebody that you barely know, then maybe you go first—but if it's somebody that you really love and love as much or even more than you love yourself, you've got to decide what you really love more, that person, or that thing, or yourself.

appears in girls' and women's descriptions of themselves. It is, she notes, a very real difference between most women and men.

We see this difference clearly when Jake and Amy are asked how one should choose when responsibility to oneself and responsibility to others conflict (Box 2.2). Jake believes we are mostly responsible to ourselves. Being independent means taking care of ourselves and making sure that our actions don't hurt others ("If you want to kill yourself, use a hand grenade instead of an atom bomb so you don't take your neighbors with you!"). Jake starts with the assumption that individuals are separate and proceeds with the need for rules to protect each person's autonomy. Thus for Jake, responsibility is not doing certain things.

BOX 2 . 2 *(continued)*

Choosing Between Responsibility to Self and Responsibility to Others

And how do you do that?

Well, you've got to think about it, and you've got to think about both sides, and you've got to think which would be better for everybody or better for yourself, which is more important, and which will make everybody happier. Like if the other people can get somebody else to do it, whatever it is, or don't really need you specifically, maybe it's better to do what you want, because the other people will be just fine with somebody else so they'll still be happy, and then you'll be happy too because you'll do what you want.

What does responsibility mean?

JAKE: It means pretty much thinking of others when I do something, and like if I want to throw a rock, not throwing it at a window, because I thought of the people who would have to pay for that window, not doing it just for yourself, because you have to live with other people and live with your community, and if you do something that hurts them all, a lot of people will end up suffering, and that is sort of the wrong thing to do.

AMY: That other people are counting on you to do something, and you can't just decide, "Well, I'd rather do this or that."

Are there other kinds of responsibility?

Well, to yourself. If something looks really fun but you might hurt yourself doing it because you don't really know how to do it and your friends say, "Well, come on, you can do it, don't worry," if you're really scared to do it, it's your responsibility to yourself that if you think you might hurt yourself, you shouldn't do it, because you have to take care of yourself.

Source: C. Gilligan. (1982). In a different voice. Cambridge, MA: Harvard University Press, pp. 35–37.

Carol Gilligan, a psychologist at Harvard University, has focused her research on female development and challenged the definition of developmental stages by Kohlberg and other developmentalists whose theories are based primarily on the experiences of male subjects.

Amy's answer is much longer than the one she gave in describing herself. She puts her responsibility to others first. Not always, of course; but she differs in an important way from Jake in her view of responsibility. Amy sees responsibility as an action, as a positive response. She assumes a connectedness with others. She talks about people and caring, all on a very personal level, whereas Jake mentions the community and seems to imply a need for rules to regulate the actions of its members.

Amy and Jake have taken different paths through childhood. They are likely to follow different paths into adulthood. Amy experiences herself in terms of her connection with others, Jake through his separateness. Each is also developing different strengths: Amy in interpersonal relations, Jake in functioning autonomously. At this point, the strengths of one are the weaknesses of the other.

Susan Pollack and Gilligan (1982) noticed unusual violence in men's fantasies about seemingly peaceful, intimate scenes. When asked to tell a story about a couple seated on a bench, over one-fifth of the men described some act of violence—murder, rape, kidnapping, or suicide. None of the women did. Gilligan reminds us that men, from an early age, define themselves through their separateness and uniqueness. Intimacy and closeness with others pose threats to their sense of themselves, and they react to this danger with themes of violence.

Women experience themselves through their relationships with others, and experience danger in impersonal settings. Gilligan points out that 20 years earlier Matina Horner (1968) had noted unexpected themes of violence from women who were asked to complete a story about a young medical student, Anne, who finished the term at the top of her class. Women reacted to her success with fear. The tough competition of medical school that ended with Anne's success also signaled failure for others. Would the other students react with anger, ostracizing Anne? Isolation is a dangerous consequence of success, to the extent that it sets women apart from others and can trigger fears of isolation and rejection.

Gilligan brings a new awareness to the study of personality. She identifies two unique perspectives on human experience, each more dominant in one sex than the other. The first is individualistic, defining the self in terms of its uniqueness and separateness. Relationships with others are governed by a consideration of individual rights, rules, and the application of an impartial justice. Gilligan finds this approach more characteristic of males. The second perspective reflects a sensitivity to and connectedness with others. The self is defined through interpersonal relationships. Rather than rights and rules governing relationships, a sense of responsibility toward others arising out of one's connectedness with them shapes relationships. An ethic of care—rather than abstract justice—dictates personal responsibility in dealings with others. This second approach is more characteristic of females.

Gilligan's theory has generated considerable interest and debate. Its strength lies in giving us a more complete picture of the human condition, one that gives equal attention to the experiences that organize a characteristically female perspective. Its weakness, to date, is in the equivocal support it has received from the research it has stimulated (e.g., Walker, 1984, 1986; but see Baumrind, 1986).

Before leaving Gilligan's approach, let's go back to a point raised earlier when discussing Piaget: the differences he observed between girls' and boys' use of rules. Gilligan cites research by Janet Lever (1976, 1978), which found that boys' games occur in larger groups, are more competitive, and last considerably longer than girls' games. Of special interest is the fact that although boys quarreled throughout the games, they never let the quarreling disrupt their play. They were always able to settle their disputes through the rules of the game. Girls play in smaller, more intimate groups, usually with a best friend. When disagreements occur among girls, they tend to stop the play.

On the face of it, these findings seem to support Piaget's contention that boys' moral (and social) development outpaces girls'. Gilligan interprets the data differently. She points to different priorities in the play of either sex. The game has first priority for boys, and rules enable them to continue it. With girls, the relationship comes first, and the need for rules to negotiate play signals danger. Girls will end the game in order to preserve the relationship.

RESEARCH FOCUS

Projective Measures: If Shakespeare Had Been a Woman, Romeo and Juliet Might Have Survived Romance

With Michael Wapner

Picture a couple sitting quietly beside a river. The spires of a town rise in the distance. What thoughts run through their minds in this peaceful setting? Homicide? Betrayal? Death? Stabbing? Rape?

Impossible?

Yet when late adolescent males were asked to tell a story about a scene such as the one above, over one-fifth spoke of violent acts such as these; very few females did. What are we to make of this violent imagery—or its absence?

Explanations of gender differences in aggression have typically assumed that females repress "normal" levels of aggression, that is, the levels seen in males. Susan Pollack and Carol Gilligan (1982) suggest another explanation for this gender difference. They suggest that differences in aggression reflect the way individuals of either sex perceive social realities. Males and females alike will respond with violence when they perceive danger, but each perceives danger in different settings.

Males are socialized to be independent and self-sufficient. Settings that limit their independence, by involving them in emotional connections with others, can challenge their sense of self. Will males see danger in situations that involve affiliation? Females are socialized to be interdependent and form connections with others. Will females perceive danger in situations in which they are isolated from others? Would settings of competitive achievement arouse fears of isolation by setting females apart from the group?

Deep-seated feelings such as reactions to danger are often difficult to observe and measure. Pollack and Gilligan used a *projective measure*—the Thematic Apperception Test (TAT)—to get at these feelings. This measure consists of a series of ambiguous pictures; subjects are asked to tell a story about each. It is assumed that they will project themselves into the situation they are describing and actually tell about their own thoughts and feelings.

Projective measures such as the TAT give a rich, complex record of an individual's feelings. Often the individual is unable to verbalize these feelings

(continued)

Is this a less-developed sense of morality? Surely not. But it *is* a very different dynamic, one that has been addressed by only a handful of developmental theorists to date. Freud, for instance, offers little by way of understanding differences such as these, despite his towering genius in other matters. In fact, he muddies the waters even more.

PSYCHOANALYTIC THEORIES

Focus on the Biological: Freud

As a young physician with a private practice in neurology, Sigmund Freud might have been more surprised than anyone at the direction his career would take. Were it not for some of his patients who complained of mysterious ailments, he might have remained an obscure but successful Viennese doctor.

RESEARCH FOCUS (*continued*)

and may even be unaware of them. Since individuals respond to their interpretations of events rather than to the events themselves, projective measures have an additional advantage in that they let us see these interpretations.

TAT measures have a number of disadvantages as well. Extensive training is required before one can interpret the responses. Reliability and validity for these measures are frequently low; that is, the measure does not necessarily give the same "reading" each time it is used, and may not always tap what it was designed to measure. These problems are common with subjective measures such as the TAT, in which there is always a danger that the investigator may be reading his or her own feelings into the subject's answers.

Pollack and Gilligan used two TAT cards that portrayed affiliation and two portraying achievement. Individuals wrote stories to all four cards. When the investigators analyzed the stories, they found that males wrote many more violent stories to the affiliation cards than to the achievement ones—more than three times as many. The opposite pattern emerged for females; nearly three times as many females wrote violent stories to the achievement cards as to the affiliation ones.

These findings support the hypothesis that males and females perceive danger in different settings. More specifically, the very relationships females seek in order to protect themselves from isolation—a setting they regard as dangerous—are the ones that males perceive as dangerous, because they involve connection with others.

William Shakespeare foresaw only doom and death in the adolescent love affair between Romeo and Juliet. Had Juliet taken the pen from his hand, we might have had a happier ending.

Are adolescents still writing scripts that reflect these gender-specific fears? Or have changing sex roles spelled the end to this particular gender difference? Do the purveyors of popular culture know how males' fears differ from females'? Do they use them? Movie and television producers may not have read Pollack and Gilligan, but when was the last time you saw a movie where the heroine chose career over love or the hero walked away from worldly success to start a family? If you do recall such a film or TV show, was it a commercial success? Would you pay to see such a movie?

Reference: S. Pollack & C. Gilligan. (1982). Images of violence in Thematic Apperception Test Stories. Journal of Personality and Social Psychology, 42, *159–167.*

The mysterious symptoms were no different from those he saw daily, such as numbness and paralysis from damaged nerves. But the nerves in these patients were unaffected; he found only healthy neural tissue when he examined them. How could patients suffer neurological symptoms with no physical damage? Fortunately, a Frenchman named Jean Charcot had just concluded a series of studies in which healthy people were told under hypnosis that they would awake with physical symptoms (among those suggested were numbness and paralysis). When they awoke, they had no memory of the suggestion, yet they exhibited the symptoms, just as Freud's patients did (Thomas, 1979).

The Unconscious.   Freud eventually solved the mystery, but only by tossing aside current notions about the mind. He asserted that we have an active mental life of which we remain completely unaware, an unconscious that affects our actions in very direct ways. Thoughts, feelings, or problems that are too disturbing to face or

Sigmund Freud (1856–1939), the founder of psychoanalysis, defined five stages of psychosexual development. These particular stages have been subject to much debate, but many theorists have built on his general concept of developmental stages.

that cannot be solved immediately are pushed out of the conscious mind, repressed to the unconscious realm of thought. Although **repression** momentarily reduces the distress, it does not get rid of the problem. The thoughts and feelings continue to exist and continue to push for expression, like a teapot that has been brought to a boil: If you cover the spout, the pressure within continues to build until the steam is released through some other opening, perhaps by blowing off the lid. The repressed ideas and feelings escape in many ways—in dreams, actions, or even physical symptoms, as with Freud's patients. The only requirement limiting their expression is that the person remain unaware of their true meaning, thereby protected from the distress they occasion. The treatment that Freud eventually devised involved discovering the unconscious source of the patient's distress and bringing it to light in the safe atmosphere of therapy (Freud, 1954).

Freud formulated his theory of personality development while treating these unusual symptoms. He believed that they resulted from an inner war between conflicting aspects of the personality. Although Freud first noticed these aspects of the personality in his patients, he believed them to be present in all of us.

Three Facets of the Personality.   For Freud, all thought and action is motivated. He termed the life force that motivated these the libido (introduced earlier in the chapter). Different aspects of the personality control the expression or inhibition of libido. Its expression is highly pleasurable (assuming a sexual nature even in infancy), and the pressure resulting from its blockage is painful. The facet of the personality that seeks immediately to satisfy the libido's expression is the id. Present from birth, the id has limited means for gratifying libidinal impulses. The infant can only cry its displeasure or fantasize about the food and comforts it desires.

The ego soon emerges as a means of realistically satisfying these instinctual impulses. The ego can distinguish the id's fantasies from actual goals, and can negotiate the realities of the environment. It also realizes that while some forms of expression will be tolerated, others will bring more pain than they're worth. The ego seeks to gratify as many of the id's demands as possible without bringing on the wrath of parents, peers, and society. It operates according to the reality principle, both facilitating and blocking the expression of the libido.

A final aspect of the personality, emerging from the ego when the child is about 4 or 5, contains the moral values acquired from our culture and dictates what we should and should not do. Freud called this the superego. It has two aspects, the conscience and the ego-ideal. The conscience embodies the "should-nots," those thoughts and actions for which we have been punished in the past; the ego-ideal represents the "shoulds," the positive values we have learned as children. These two aspects of the superego gradually assume the controls that once had to be exercised by parents and others, so that with the ego, behavior becomes self-regulated. The superego also introduces us to the human drama that Freud believed lay the foundation for adult sexuality, and his view of the differences between men and women (Hall, 1954).

Formulation of Gender Differences.   Freud called this drama the **Oedipal complex** after the Greek myth of a young man who murdered his father and married his mother. Freud believed that every boy falls in love with his mother, and every girl with her father. The resolution to this love triangle lays the foundation, according to Freud, for fundamental differences between the sexes. We shall look at the Oedipal complex in boys first, since Freud framed his theory around the male experience.

During the phallic stage, the third of Freud's stages of personality development, the libido seeks expression through the genitals. The young boy derives sexual pleasure from masturbating. This activity imbues his penis with such significance that when he first notices a girl without one, he is horrified and assumes she has been mutilated. He also thinks that the same could happen to him if he is not careful. Before you think he is overreacting, consider the reason for his fears. His feelings for his mother transform his father into a rival. Castration would be a fitting punishment for his sexual longing for his mother. Freud believed the boy's fear (termed castration anxiety) to be so great that he represses his sexual desire for his mother. In yielding to his father, he identifies with him, and in the process, takes on his values. Thus the boy's fear of castration motivates him to move beyond his incestuous desires, repressing these and identifying with the father. The superego that emerges from this process is strong, since it reflects the power that the boy sees in his father.

The girl falls in love with her father and views her mother as a sexual rival. For her the Oedipal, or Electra, complex revolves around a different set of motives. Instead of anxiety, she experiences longing and inferiority. She sees that she has "come off badly" in comparison with boys and feels inferior because she does not have a penis. She wants her father to give her one, too. Of course, these longings (which Freud calls penis envy) cannot be satisfied, and are finally replaced by a compensatory wish: that her father give her a baby. Freud writes, "Her Oedipus complex culminates in a desire, which is long retained, to receive a baby from her father as a gift—to bear him a child" (Freud, 1925, p. 124). Freud believed that the girl's longings for a penis and a child intermingle in the unconscious and prepare her for her future roles of wife and mother.

Notice that the girl never cleanly resolves the Oedipal complex; she retains a lingering longing in the unconscious that imbues her personality with its essential feminine features, one of which is a feeling of inferiority. Freud believed that the woman moves from feelings of personal inferiority to contempt for all women. Once she realizes that her lack of a penis is not a personal form of punishment for something she has done, but is shared by all women, "she begins to share the contempt felt by men for a sex which is the lesser in so important a respect" (Freud, 1925, p. 253).

Freud was ahead of his time in many ways in his acceptance of women. He freely admitted women into his analytic circle and frequently referred patients to women analysts (Tavris & Wade, 1984). However, his theory of the feminine personality is uniquely uncomplimentary. Freud believed females to be masochistic, vain, and jealous. The masochism (deriving pleasure from pain) stems from their frustrated longing for their fathers. The vanity and jealousy he attributed to penis envy. "If she cannot have a penis, she will turn her whole body into an erotic substitute; her feminine identity comes to depend on being sexy, attractive, and adored. Female jealousy is a displaced version of penis envy" (Tavris & Wade, 1984, p. 182).

Finally, Freud believed that the female superego is not as strong as that of men; the implication is that females are less moral. Two things account for their weaker superegos. Females are never as highly motivated as males to resolve Oedipal issues, since they literally do not have as much to lose, and they identify with a weaker figure than do males: The mother is more nurturant, and less threatening and powerful, than the father.

Anna Freud, his daughter, extended Freud's theory by focusing on the unique demands which adolescence places on the ego. She contended that the adult sexual drives which emerge with puberty strain the child's organization of the personality and require new and stronger defenses against the incestuous threats which these drives reintroduce. She noted that intellectual developments in adolescence make such defenses possible, namely in the form of *intellectualization*, or the ability to

RESEARCH FOCUS *(continued)*

of possessions. Generosity, because it reflected a more basic harmony with their surroundings, was a virtue. Conversely, the Yurok value thrift and a meticulous management of resources. They live in settlements along the Klamath River. Once a year, when the salmon return to breed, they experience the abundance that the Sioux lived with in every season. For the rest of the year, they must cautiously manage that brief harvest to avoid hunger and need.

These particular differences are less important than the common function served by the communal practices of either group. Ritual ways of living provided each with a group identity. It is from this group identity that members of the community derived a sense of their own identity. Erikson arrived at this observation after noting what he referred to as a "cultural pathology" among the present-day Sioux Indians. He traced this problem to their inability to find "fitting images to connect the past with the future" (Erikson, 1963, p. 117). The Sioux's lifestyle had been tied to the buffalo, the provider of meat for food; pelts for clothing and shelter; bones for needles, ornaments, and toys; and even dried droppings for fuel. The destruction of the buffalo herds by white settlers resulted in the destruction of the Sioux's way of life—and of the group identity from which new generations could derive a sense of themselves. Speaking of the present generation of Sioux, Erikson noted that

the majority of them have as little concept of the future as they are beginning to have of the past. This youngest generation, then, finds itself between the impressive dignity of its grandparents, who honestly refuse to believe that the white man is here to stay, and the white man himself, who feels that the Indian persists in being a rather impractical relic of a dead past. (1963, p. 121)

If Erikson's theory is correct, that without "fitting images to connect the past with the future" young people are lost, what are the images that performed this function for you? Is there any single or even small set of recurrent experiences that anchor you in your community and physical environment the way the buffalo anchored the Sioux? Is it possible that American civilization at the end of the twentieth century has no such single image? Perhaps these images belong to subgroups rather than the culture as a whole. For instance, is the "gang" for the East Los Angeles gang member in any way analogous to the buffalo for the Sioux? What functions would the "gang" have to fulfill for its members to qualify as an "image"? If it is an image in the Eriksonian sense, then what will it take to discourage gang membership in East Los Angeles and similar urban communities?

References: Robert Coles. (1970). Erik Erikson: The growth of his work. *Boston: Little, Brown. Erik Erikson. (1963).* Childhood and society. *New York: Norton.*

and on his stages of psychosexual development. Yet he differed from Freud in several important respects. Perhaps the most significant is Erikson's emphasis on the healthy personality. Erikson stressed the social functions of the ego that allow individuals to cope successfully. These functions assume central importance in adolescence, as adolescents question who they are and where they are going.

Identity is a central aspect of the healthy personality, reflecting both an inner sense of continuity and sameness over time and an ability to identify with others and share in common goals, to participate in one's culture. Erikson (1963) believed that identity develops as adolescents assume commitments to future occupations, adult sex roles, and personal belief systems. It is no accident that identity assumes importance as individuals step from childhood into adulthood and, with this, into their culture. It is also no accident that identity emerged as a central concern to a young artist in search of himself.

Psychosocial Stages of Development. Erikson (1963) believed that new aspects of the person emerge through inner growth, making new types of social encounters possible. As with other stage theorists, he assumed that development occurs in the same set sequence for all, reflecting an internal ground plan in which each stage has its own period of ascendence, a time in which the individual is especially vulnerable to certain influences and insensitive to others. (This assumption is known as Erikson's **epigenetic principle**.) Society challenges us with new demands as we age. We experience these as crises. Each takes a slightly different form and gives each age its unique characteristics. Table 2.3 presents and describes each of Erikson's life stages.

Each of the first four crises equip adolescents to meet the central challenge of achieving an ego identity. Trust establishes the confidence in themselves and in others that is needed to begin the task. Autonomy gives self-direction and purpose, the ability to follow goals that one sees for oneself rather than those set by others. Initiative allows adolescents to explore the options that open up with adolescence, and industry allows them to realistically evaluate these options and select the ones they will commit themselves to (Erikson, 1963, 1968).

The establishment of identity involves the individual in a succession of commitments to life goals that serve to define the self. The young adult faces the crisis of sharing that self with another—of intimacy, first with a mate and then, for most, with children. Middle adulthood extends the adult's concerns beyond this intimate group to others in the community. Older adults face a final crisis of reviewing their lives and accepting the decisions they have made. Erikson calls this last crisis one of personal integrity.

Like Freud's, Erikson's theory reflects a male bias. Erikson considers the achievement of identity to be the central crisis of adolescence, even though he asserts that a different sequence exists for females. Most females resolve the crisis of intimacy, which Erikson places in early adulthood, *before* they complete identity issues. Their sense of themselves derives more from their relationships than from commitments to work and ideology. Although Erikson notes these differences, he does not change his sequence of life stages; that is, he equates the male experience with development in general (Bardwick & Douvan, 1971; Gilligan, 1982).

Focus on the Interpersonal: Chodorow

Another theorist, also influenced by Freud, gives us a very different view of development. Nancy Chodorow offers an alternative to the universal developmental

T A B L E 2 . 3	

Erikson's Developmental Stages

Stage	Psychosocial Crisis
Birth to Adolescence	
Infancy	Trust vs. mistrust. Realization that needs will be met leads to trust in others and self.
Toddlerhood	Autonomy vs. shame and doubt. Physical maturation gives sense of being able to do things for self.
Early childhood	Initiative vs. guilt. Increasing abilities promote exploration and expand experience.
Middle childhood	Industry vs. inferiority. Accomplishments and skills provide basis for self-esteem.
Adolescence to Old Age	
Adolescence	Identity vs. identity diffusion. Biological and social changes of adolescence occasion a search for continuity of self.
Early adulthood	Intimacy vs. isolation. Sense of self provides the basis for sexual and emotional intimacy with another adult.
Middle adulthood	Generativity vs. stagnation. Concern for children and future generations reflects need to leave something of oneself.
Late adulthood	Integrity vs. despair. Acceptance of one's life as having meaning gives one a sense of dignity.

Source: E. Erikson. (1963). Childhood and society. *New York: Norton.*

sequence charted by Erikson. Chodorow (1978) attributes psychological differences in the makeup of women and men to the social fact that for most children the first intimate relationship is with a woman—their mother. This initial relationship has very different consequences for girls than it does for boys.

Chodorow asserts that infants experience themselves as continuous with the mother. They live within the boundless security of her presence, little caring which smile is theirs or whose hand reaches out to the other, all of it part of the same encircling awareness. Mothers, too, empathically relate to their infants and experience a continuity with them.

> In a society where mothers provide nearly exclusive care and certainly the most meaningful relationship to the infant, the infant develops its sense of self mainly in relation to her. Insofar as the relationship with its mother has continuity, the infant comes to define aspects of its self . . . in relation to internalized representations of aspects of its mother. (Chodorow, 1978, p. 78)

Nancy Chodorow's research challenges Freud's and Erikson's assumptions of a universal development sequence. Because boys must define themselves outside their relationship with their mother but girls define themselves within that relationship, the course of identity development is fundamentally different for the two sexes.

Important to Chodorow are the necessary differences in the way children of either sex develop beyond this point. Girls can continue to define themselves within the context of this first relationship. Mothers, as well, can see their daughters as extensions of themselves. Girls can experience a continuing attachment to the mother while still defining themselves as females. None of this is possible for boys. They must separate themselves from the mother much earlier than girls in order to develop as males. Mothers, too, experience their sons as separate and different from themselves, unlike their daughters. Thus, boys embark on a developmental path marked not by attachment but by separation and increasing individuation.

Chodorow argues that since the primary caregiver is the same sex for girls, there is less need for the girl to differentiate herself in terms of ego boundaries. Chodorow brings us to a point made earlier by Freud: The personalities of women are frequently less differentiated than those of men, and are more closely tied to

A growing body of research can describe the differences in identity development for these two students due to their gender. Few researchers, however, have explored differences in identity development for various racial or ethnic groups.

their relationships. But she sees this difference as an asset, as a strength rather than a weakness. Girls can experience continuity with others and relate to their feelings. Chodorow points to the heavy costs males pay for their greater individuation. In curtailing their emotional attachment to the mother, they also limit their ability in general to relate empathetically to others. Thus, differences in ego boundaries lay a foundation for a greater capacity for empathy in females. In fact, Chodorow sees the capacity for empathy to be a core part of the feminine personality, giving them a sense of connectedness with others (Chodorow, 1978; Gilligan, 1982).

　　Taking up Chodorow's point, Gilligan suggests that because of the difference between females' and males' capacities for empathy, males should experience more problems with relationships and females with individuation. Since human development is charted, to date, in male terms—that is, in terms of increasing separation and individuation—when women have problems with individuation, these are seen as a sign of developmental immaturity. Men's problems with relationships, however, do not evoke a parallel interpretation. Gilligan pointedly notes that "women's failure to separate then becomes by definition a failure to develop" (Gilligan, 1982).

Gilligan points out that science has not been neutral. Our theories reflect "a consistent observational and evaluative bias." We tend to interpret "different" as either better or worse, since we have a tendency to work with a single scale. Since most scales are also standardized in terms of male development, male behavior is taken as the norm and female behavior as a departure from the norm. This approach is perpetuated by the fact that most research is done by males, with many important studies using only males as subjects (Gilligan, 1982; Yoder & Kahn, 1993).

Gilligan offers us a challenge: Can we see human behavior from other than this single perspective? She dares us to ask not only why women's feelings "get in the way" of their reasoning when thinking about others (a quality she does not regard as a weakness), but also why men's feelings do not.[1] Instead of asking why more women than men have problems with individuation, we need also to ask why more men have problems with intimacy and relationships. Until we begin to ask and find answers to all of these questions, our psychology of human development will remain incomplete.

---

[1] Freud's (1924) observation that females have a lesser sense of justice than males and are more influenced by their feelings received later support by Kohlberg and others in that females' moral judgments were more likely to reflect interpersonal concerns and males' to reflect abstract principles (Kohlberg & Kramer, 1969).

Answers to Respondent Conditioning Example on p. 47:
    CS: The first rays of light.
    UCS: The alarm.
    UCR: Waking to the alarm.
    CR: Waking to the first rays of light.

SUMMARY

Models and Theories

Models are sets of assumptions about the nature of reality. These assumptions are too general to be tested; however, theories, which derive from models, are more specific explanations of phenomena, and can be confirmed or disconfirmed. Theories serve four major functions: (a) They serve as a guide to formulating questions; (b) they describe phenomena by allowing one to relate isolated facts to a body of knowledge; (c) they make it possible to predict new behavior based on explanations of previous actions; and (d) they suggest ways for changing the behavior they describe by allowing one to identify antecedent events.

The assumptions that make up a model can frequently be expressed as a metaphor. The machine is a popular metaphor for human behavior, and models based on this metaphor assume that behavior is as predictable as that of a machine. Such models, however, allow no room for self-initiated action. Three models of human behavior are the environmental, organismic, and psychoanalytic models.

The environmental model views humans as passive and sees their actions as *re*actions to environmental events. People are assumed to remain quiescent until something stimulates them to act. Behavior is linked to external events through simple associations; these are formed through respondent and operant conditioning.

The organismic model takes the living, biological system as its metaphor for human behavior. Theories derived from this model assume that variables tied to the nature of the organism structure development. These theorists assume that the human organism is active and does not passively await stimulation, and that activity is internally organized instead of structured by environmental events. Behavior is seen as an unfolding of developmental stages, each of which is qualitatively different from the last.

The psychoanalytic model emphasizes both inner processes and external events in explaining behavior. Freud, the major theorist for this model, assumed that biological impulses are housed in the id and social standards in the superego; the ego balances the demand for expression of the id against the realities of social constraints.

Environmental Theories

Robert Havighurst traces development across a succession of developmental tasks that reflect social expectations for more mature behavior with age; physical maturation sets the pace for these expectations.

The theory of B. F. Skinner is a radical departure from the way most people understand their behavior. Skinner assumes that behavior is under the control of the events that follow it instead of reflecting preceding motives or intentions. Skinner refers to these antecedent events as reinforcers.

Albert Bandura also emphasizes the importance of learning in development, but believes that most human learning occurs through observing others rather than through direct conditioning. Inner processes such as attention and memory are important in Bandura's social-cognitive theory.

Organismic Theories

G. Stanley Hall assumed that stages of development mirrored evolutionary changes from earliest times to the present. Even though his own theoretical assumptions were not supported, Hall laid the foundation for a scientific study of human development.

Jean Piaget succeeded where Hall had failed. Piaget, too, extended Darwin's theory of evolution to human development. He viewed intelligence as a means of adapting to one's environment only those forms of thought that promote adaptation surviving with increasing age. Piaget viewed intelligence as biologically based. He assumed that knowledge, rather than being a simple copy of reality, is an active construction of what we know of the world. He also assumed that these experiences are organized in qualitatively different stages with age.

Carol Gilligan focuses on the interpersonal aspects of development. She notes striking gender differences in the ways individuals of either sex define themselves. Males tend to view themselves as separate from others; females typically describe themselves in terms of their relationships with others.

Psychoanalytic Theories

Freud assumed that all thoughts and actions are motivated; he termed the life force motivating these the libido. Different aspects of the personality control the expression of the libido. The id, present from birth, has limited means for gratifying libidinal impulses. The ego, next to develop, seeks to gratify as many libidinal impulses as possible within social constraints. The last aspect of the personality to develop, the superego, contains the moral values of one's culture and dictates what one should and should not do.

Karen Horney considered the development of a healthy personality in terms of the ability to value oneself and see that one is valued by others. Horney placed less emphasis than Freud on biological instincts and more stress on the impact of one's culture. Though she, like Freud,

considered early experiences important, she did not view them as having the determining effect on later personality that Freud did. In particular, Horney reinterpreted Freud's analysis of the feminine personality as a reflection of living in a male-dominated society and of women's economic dependence on men.

Erik Erikson assumed, as did Freud, that personality develops through a sequence of stages, but he carried these through the lifespan. He assumed that society challenges us with new demands as we age and that we experience these as crises. Each crisis takes a slightly different form and gives each stage its unique characteristics. Achievement of a personal identity is the central crisis of adolescence; this involves adolescents in a set of commitments to life goals that give definition to the self.

Nancy Chodorow builds on a foundation provided by Freud but attributes gender differences to the social fact that for almost all children the first intimate relationship is with a female—the mother. Girls can continue to define themselves within the context of this first relationship, but boys must separate themselves in order to develop as males. As a consequence, girls' development is characterized by attachment, and boys' by separation and individuation.

KEY TERMS

Model	Reductionism	Conditional Stimulus (CS)
Theory	Epigenesis	Conditional Response (CR)
Axiom	Respondent Conditioning	Operant Conditioning
Law	Unconditional Stimulus	Positive Reinforcement
Nature-Nurture Controversy	(UCS)	Negative Reinforcement
Continuity-Discontinuity	Unconditional Response	Habituation
Issue	(UCR)	Stage

Libido

Id

Ego

Superego

Developmental Task

Observational Learning

Reflective Abstraction

Assimilation

Accommodation

Equilibration

Repression

Oedipal Complex

Identity

Epigenetic Principle

CONTINUITY AND DIVERSITY IN ADOLESCENT DEVELOPMENT

Part Two begins, as does adolescence itself, with puberty. The years of early adolescence from 10 through 14 differ in important ways from those of late adolescence, from 15 through 19. Whether we consider physical and intellectual changes, relationships with family or with friends, or the extended social world of adolescents, clear differences between early and late adolescence emerge.

Early adolescents are adjusting to changing bodies, new intellectual skills, a new school setting, and changing relationships with parents and friends. While they approach greater autonomy in their relationships with parents, they're also moving toward heterosexual relationships with friends. In contrast, by late adolescence, the wrinkles of puberty have ironed themselves out, the need for autonomy has been supplanted by the more pressing need to consolidate a personal identity, and decisions about college and jobs that seemed distant indeed to early adolescents press for resolution. Early adolescents are just stepping out of childhood; late adolescents stand on the threshold of adulthood.

The chapters in Part Two—Chapters 3 through 7—follow an "inside-out" approach in tracing the changes of adolescence. We begin by considering changes within the individual, both biological and intellectual, then discuss the interpersonal worlds of family and friends, and finally focus on the extended interpersonal context of the school.

Pubertal changes clearly set early adolescence apart as a distinct time of life. These changes start a year or two earlier in girls than boys. Sometime around the fifth grade, most girls begin to notice the first signs of puberty: wisps of pubic hair and breast buds. Girls begin a growth spurt that peaks somewhere around the age of 12, at approximately the age that boys notice their first pubertal changes: wisps of pubic hair and a slight enlargement of the scrotum. All through middle school and junior high, girls will be taller than boys and ahead of them in physical development. Between the ages of 12 and 13, most girls will have their first period. Boys will experience their first ejaculation approximately 2 years later when they reach 14, at about the time their voices begin to change. Throughout early adolescence, each sex adds subcutaneous fat and muscle, relatively more of the former in girls and more of the latter in boys. These changes transform their bodies into those of adults. Puberty is just the beginning, but one that's hard for adolescents to miss. Chapter 3 traces the sequence of these physical developments and considers their implications for young adolescents.

The intellectual changes that take place in early adolescence are, in their own way, as dramatic as the biological ones. Early adolescents begin to think in ways that are more like adults than like children just a few years younger. They can imagine the impossible, dream about the future, and entertain all manner of thoughts about the simplest of everyday situations. They are no longer limited to thinking about actual, concrete experiences. Adolescents can think in the abstract and possess a new self-awareness. Their ability to examine their thoughts and to imagine the thoughts of others contributes to this process. Chapter 4 looks at the intellectual changes of adolescence.

Changing relationships with parents also contribute to adolescents' new sense of themselves. An increase in autonomy and a greater role in decision making are common in early adolescence. Chapter 5 looks at the characteristics of families that facilitate the development of autonomy and lay a foundation for the development of identity. Families themselves are changing in our society. Increasing numbers of adolescents experience divorce, single parenting, and step-parenting, and more live in homes in which both parents are wage earners. This chapter examines the effect of these trends on adolescents.

For adolescents, friendships and school are the primary social settings outside the family. Friends contribute to early adolescents' developing sense of self. Close friends are the emotional supports to whom adolescents turn; in larger numbers, peers are socialization agents, guiding adolescents into more adult roles. Early adolescent friendships differ in distinct ways from those of late adolescence; these differences reflect the tasks adolescents face at each age. Chapter 6 looks at adolescents and their friends.

The everyday world of early adolescents expands at school, as they leave the comfortable familiarity of elementary school and enter a middle school or junior high. They have different teachers throughout the day, and can not always count on having a close friend in class with them. Having options in the classes they can take emphasizes the larger issues of defining their own goals and arriving at workable plans for their lives. Chapter 7 covers these issues, closing the section on biological, intellectual, and social changes of adolescence.

THE ENDOCRINE SYSTEM
Hormonal Activity
The Timing of Puberty

THE PHYSICAL CHANGES
OF PUBERTY
Recollections of an Adolescent Girl
Recollections of an Adolescent Boy
The Growth Spurt
The Reproductive System
Menarche and Spermarche

RESEARCH FOCUS An
Experiment: A Cure for "the Blahs"
Before They Begin?

The Secular Trend

THE PSYCHOLOGICAL AND
SOCIAL IMPLICATIONS OF
PUBERTY
Two Explanations of the Effects
  of Physical Change
The Timing of Change: Early
  and Late Maturers

RESEARCH FOCUS Longitudinal
Designs: Body-Image Satisfaction—
Mirror, Mirror, on the Wall

Body Image

EATING DISORDERS
Dieting
Bulimia and Anorexia

RESEARCH FOCUS: Bias and
Blind Controls: Eating Disorders

Obesity

MAKING SEXUAL DECISIONS
Problems Adolescents Face
Sexual Attitudes and Practices

CONTRACEPTION USE
Lack of Information
Inability to Accept One's Sexuality
Cognitive-Emotional Immaturity

SEX EDUCATION: WHAT
ADOLESCENTS NEED TO KNOW
Sources of Information
The Effectiveness of School Programs

SUMMARY

KEY TERMS

has sometimes been called the body's master clock, because it serves as a control center for biological rhythms, including the ones of puberty. The **pituitary**, an endocrine gland, hangs from the hypothalamus by a slender stalk (the infundibulum). The pituitary has two lobes, or sections. The one closest to the nose is the anterior (front) lobe. The one farthest is the posterior (back) lobe.

The hypothalamus is actually very small, just one three-hundredths of the brain's total size. Yet it is involved in many aspects of bodily functioning and plays a central role in regulating the events of puberty. Most of what we know about the hypothalamus comes from experiments with laboratory rats. For example, if the blood supply from the hypothalamus to the pituitary is cut off, a rat's reproductive organs soon begin to wither and the animal becomes sterile (Restak, 1984). But what is this important substance carried in the blood?

Research has shown that the hypothalamus secretes a hormone called gonadotropin-releasing hormone (GnRH), which tells the anterior pituitary to manufacture gonadotrophic hormones, which act directly on the gonads. The **gonads** are the sex glands, the ovaries in females and the testes in males. Two gonadotrophic hormones—luteinizing hormone (LH) and follicle-stimulating hormone (FSH)—stimulate the gonads to produce their own sex hormones, estrogens in females and androgens in males. The whole system acts sort of like a row of dominoes. Knocking the first one over trips the second, which affects the third, and so on. In the laboratory rats, when the blood supply from the hypothalamus failed to reach the anterior pituitary, the anterior pituitary stopped producing the hormones that stimulate the gonads. When the gonads were no longer stimulated, they shut down and withered, reverting to an earlier state (Restak, 1984).

The hypothalamus functions like a clock by measuring out its signals in rhythmic pulses. A single pulse of GnRH normally reaches the anterior pituitary each hour. The timing of these pulses is critical. If the pulses decrease to one every several hours or even increase, the mechanism breaks down and the anterior pituitary fails to release its gonadotropins into the bloodstream; gonads will not develop (Knobil, 1980; Kulin, 1991a).

Both LH and FSH circulate through the bloodstream in low levels during childhood. Levels of each increase prior to puberty, starting at about age 8 or 9 in girls. By the beginning of puberty, pulses occur more frequently during sleeping than waking hours, especially for LH. Figure 3.2 illustrates the marked difference in prepubertal and pubertal LH release, with the sleep-associated release occurring only during puberty. By the end of puberty and throughout adulthood, LH is again released evenly over waking and sleep cycles. (Cotman & McGaugh, 1980; Cutler et al., 1983; Knobil, 1980).

A Feedback System.   The level at which hormones circulate in the bloodstream is controlled by a delicate feedback system involving the hypothalamus, the anterior pituitary, and the gonads, as shown in Figure 3.1. A feedback system sends information from one point in a sequence back to an earlier point, thereby regulating

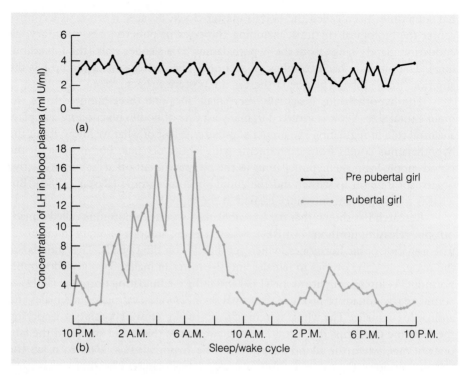

Figure 3.2　Release of LH During Waking and Sleep Cycles in (a) a Prepubertal Girl and (b) a Pubertal Girl.

Source: Adapted from M. P. Warren. (1983). Physical and biological aspects of puberty. In J. Brooks-Gunn & A. C. Petersen (Eds.), Girls at puberty: Biological and psychosocial perspectives. *New York: Plenum Press.*

later activity. A gonadostat, much like the thermostat controlling the heat in your home, is located in the hypothalamus. Instead of sensing temperature, it senses the presence of circulating hormones. When the levels drop too low, the hypothalamus signals the anterior pituitary to increase production of gonadotrophic hormones, which in turn stimulate the gonads to produce more sex hormones. As levels of sex hormones increase, the hypothalamus decreases its signals to the anterior pituitary.

During childhood, the gonadostat is set at a low level. This makes the feedback system especially sensitive to circulating hormones. Even small amounts prompt the hypothalamus to cut back its signals to the pituitary. This low set-point keeps the prepubertal level of circulating hormones low. Late in the prepubertal period, the hypothalamic gonadostat is reset, allowing the levels of circulating hormones to increase (Kulin, 1991a).

THE PHYSICAL CHANGES OF PUBERTY

Puberty brings about the physical differences that distinguish females and males. Differences in the reproductive system itself, such as growth of the ovaries in females and the testes in males, constitute **primary sex characteristics**. Other changes, such as the growth of pubic hair, the development of breasts in females and facial hair in males, represent **secondary sex characteristics**. Not all of these changes occur at once, of course, and not all are viewed as equally important by adolescents. The changes that occasion most fascination, such as menstruation in girls or facial hair in boys, are not usually the first to occur, although the timing of these changes varies considerably (Petersen, Crockett, Richards, & Boxer, 1988).

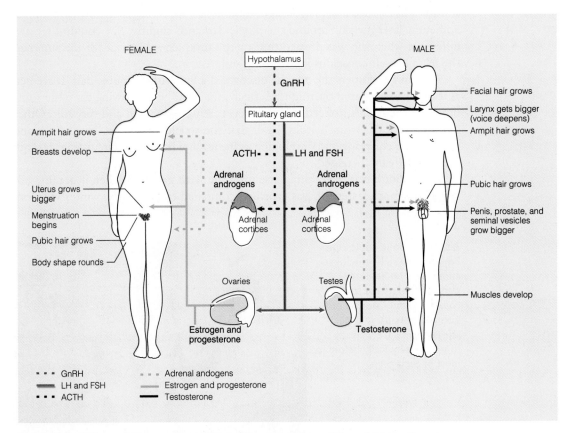

Figure 3.3 Effects of Hormones on Physical Development and Sexual Maturation at Puberty.

Source: Insel & Roth. (1994). Core concepts in health (7th ed.). Mountain View, CA: Mayfield, p. 103.

The sequence of changes varies less than their timing. One adolescent can be almost fully matured before another has begun to develop, yet each will experience the events of puberty in roughly the same order (Tanner, 1974).

The changes of puberty are easiest to follow if we chart them separately for each sex (Figure 3.3). Girls are generally 2 years ahead of boys. We will start with them first, as nature has done. A fictitious adolescent named Sarah will serve as our model.

Recollections of an Adolescent Girl

Sarah reports that the first change she noticed was in her breasts. She was in the fifth grade at the time, not quite 11 years old. It was such a small change that she almost didn't notice it at first. A slight mound had appeared just below each nipple. Sometime later the skin around the nipple darkened slightly. She couldn't see any difference when she was dressed, but by the time school let out for the summer, she felt a bit self-conscious in a bathing suit.

Sarah remembers the day she discovered a few wisps of pubic hair. It seemed as if they had appeared overnight. Actually, they had been growing for quite some time, but she hadn't noticed because they were unpigmented and very soft. Other changes were occurring within Sarah that she would never see. Her uterus and ovaries were enlarging and developing as the level of hormones circulating through her bloodstream increased.

She didn't notice anything else until the sixth grade. By then it became obvious how much faster she was growing, compared to before. By winter vacation,

Although young adolescent boys may be self-conscious about their bodies if the signs of puberty are late in coming, young adolescent girls are more likely to feel self-conscious if they start to mature physically before most of their peers.

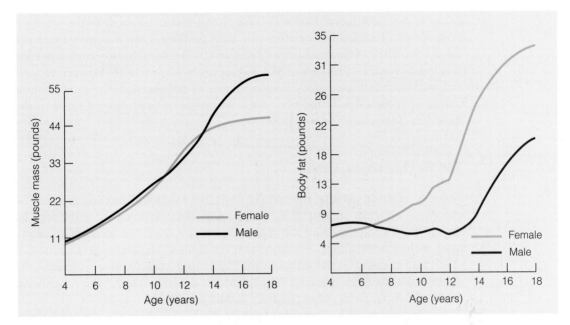

Figure 3.4 Development of Muscle Mass and Body Fat for Females and Males.
Source: Adapted from D. B. Cheek. (1974). Body composition, hormones, nutrition, and adolescent growth. In M. M. Grumbach, G. D. Grave, & F. E. Mayer (Eds.), Control of the onset of puberty. *New York: Wiley.*

Body proportions begin to change even earlier. About 1½ years before the growth spurt, girls' legs start to grow faster than their bodies, giving them a long, "leggy" look. Most of the early gain in height is due to a lengthening of the legs. The shoulders also widen before the actual growth spurt. Somewhat later, during puberty itself, the hips widen. These growth patterns give young adolescent girls a characteristic look: relatively long legs, slender bodies, wide shoulders, and narrow hips—our present standard of beauty. Puberty changes all this (Faust, 1983).

Males. The growth spurt can begin anywhere from age 10½ to age 16 in boys. Boys grow for a longer time than girls, reaching their peak rate in growth 2 years later than girls reach theirs. The average height of boys prior to the height spurt is 58 inches. They add another 12 to 13 inches during the growth spurt. Most of this increase is due to a lengthening of the trunk, since the legs began to grow earlier.

Striking sex differences begin to appear in muscle mass and body fat. Figure 3.4 shows the dramatic increase in muscle mass that accompanies the height spurt in males, and the corresponding increase in body fat for females (Petersen, Crockett, Richards, & Boxer, 1988). In addition to obvious differences in muscle mass, males also develop larger hearts and lungs; they have higher systolic blood pressure, can carry more oxygen in their blood, and can dispose of the chemical by-products of exercise more efficiently than females. They also have more red blood cells. These differences are not necessarily inherent in the two sexes, however. It is just as possible that they reflect differences in activity levels between females and males that become more pronounced during adolescence. The most obvious change is in the shape of the body itself: In males, the hips widen relative to the shoulders (Petersen & Taylor, 1980).

The Reproductive System

Females.   During puberty, the uterus, ovaries, and vagina all increase in size. The **uterus** is a muscular sac shaped like an upside-down pear, enclosed at the neck by the **cervix**, which opens into the vagina. Some girls think the uterus is an empty space within them. Figure 3.5 shows that the walls of the uterus lie against each other; they remain this way unless pushed apart by a fetus. During pregnancy, the uterus holds the fetus. The length of the uterus doubles during puberty, growing to about 3 inches at maturity (McCary & McCary, 1982).

The **ovaries** flank either side of the uterus. Each is about the size of a walnut. They have two major functions. The first is to house the immature eggs, or **ova** (singular **ovum**), which each infant girl stores from the time of birth. The second function is to produce estrogens and progesterone. The ovaries begin to grow at

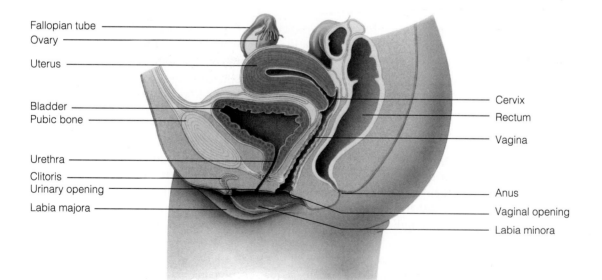

Figure 3.5   Female Reproductive System.
Source: Insel & Roth. (1994). Core concepts in health (7th ed.). Mountain View, CA: Mayfield, p. 100.

a slightly faster rate at about the age of 8. About a year before any of the visible signs of puberty, gonadotropins from the anterior pituitary stimulate the ovaries to accelerate their production of estrogens. These gonadotropins—FSH and LH— also stimulate the follicles, individual chambers housing each ovum, to develop.

The **fallopian tubes** feed into either side of the uterus from the ovaries. Each tube is approximately 4 inches long, and is lined with tiny hairs called cilia that move in a sweeping motion and set up currents within the fluid in the tubes. These currents catch the mature egg as it is released from the ovary and sweep it into the oviduct, where it is carried to the uterus. If live sperm are present to fertilize the egg, fertilization will take place at the top of the oviduct. If no sperm are present, the egg passes outside the body along with the lining of the uterus, which is prepared monthly for a fertilized egg.

The **vagina** is a muscular tube leading to the uterus. During puberty it lengthens to its adult length of 4 to 6 inches, and becomes more flexible, developing a thick lining. Two glands on either side of the vaginal opening, Bartholin's glands, also develop during puberty. These secrete a lubricant during sexual arousal. The walls of the vagina touch each other (just as do those of the uterus), unless they are separated by something such as a tampon, a penis, or a baby during birth.

Many girls mistakenly think of the vagina as a hollow tube leading to an even larger space inside. This misunderstanding can cause some teenage girls to be fearful of "losing" tampons in some vast, unknown space within. In actuality, the vagina is closed off at the inner end by a tight, muscular gate, the cervix. Menstrual fluids or semen can pass through, but the cervix must be dilated (opened) for anything larger to pass.

The opening to the vagina is partially covered by a fold of skin called the hymen, sometimes referred to as the "cherry." This delicate membrane is frequently torn or stretched during childhood. Activities ranging from bicycle riding to using tampons can stretch the hymen. Folklore holds that first intercourse ruptures the hymen, causing some bleeding and discomfort, and that an intact hymen is a sign of virginity. Relatively few females today survive their active childhoods with the hymen intact. Even when it remains, stretching the hymen through intercourse rarely produces discomfort.

The **clitoris**, not the vagina, is the primary source of sexual stimulation. The clitoris is similar to the penis; both have a glans, a shaft, and a prepuce. The **glans** is supplied by an extensive network of nerve endings, making it the most sensitive part of the clitoris. Hidden beneath the skin and connected to the glans is the **shaft**. Numerous blood vessels, which develop during puberty, feed into the shaft. During arousal, these become engorged with blood, causing the clitoris to become erect. A thin covering of skin, the **prepuce**, covers the glans.

Males.   The epididymis, vas deferens, seminal vesicles, prostate gland, and Cowper's gland form the internal male sex organs (see Figure 3.6). The **epididymis** is a long, oval mass sitting near the top of each testis that receives the sperm produced by the testis. The epididymis leads into the **vas deferens,** long, coiled tubes that

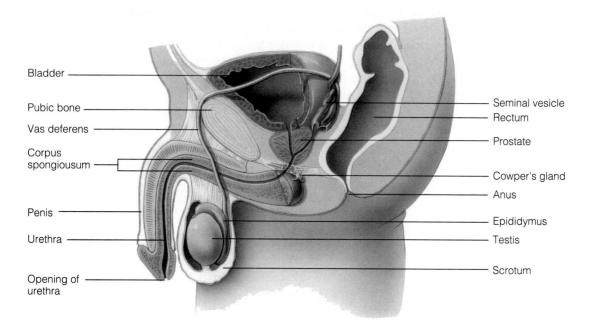

Bladder

Pubic bone

Vas deferens

Corpus spongiousum

Penis

Urethra

Opening of urethra

Seminal vesicle

Rectum

Prostate

Cowper's gland

Anus

Epididymus

Testis

Scrotum

Figure 3.6   Male Reproductive System.
Source: Insel & Roth. (1994). Core concepts in health (7th ed.). Mountain View, CA: Mayfield, p. 101.

carry the sperm to the **seminal vesicles** where they are stored. Tiny hairlike cilia line the walls of the epididymis and the vas deferens, just as they do the fallopian tubes in females, and move the immature sperm on their way to the seminal vesicles.

Both the seminal vesicles and the **prostate gland** produce **semen,** a milky white fluid in which the **sperm** are suspended. This fluid is ejaculated during an orgasm. The prostate gland begins to develop at around 11 years of age, at about the time the testes begin to develop. Sperm can be found in the urine of boys by about the age of 14 (Kulin, 1991b). A single ejaculate of approximately 3.5 cc contains upwards of 400,000,000 sperm. It has been estimated that an adult male will release a billion sperm for every egg released by a female (Arey, 1956).

The **Cowper's glands** begin to mature at about the same time as the prostate. These glands secrete a lubricating fluid that facilitates passage of the sperm through the urethra and also protects them from the acidic environment of the urethra. This fluid appears at the opening of the glans of the penis during sexual arousal, and frequently contains some sperm. Intercourse, even with no ejaculation, can result in pregnancy just from the presence of sperm in the lubricating fluid (McCary & McCary, 1982).

At puberty, increases in FSH, LH, and prolactin (the same hormones that stimulate the ovaries to develop and produce estrogen) stimulate the testes to develop and produce testosterone. Levels of circulating testosterone increase twenty-

RESEARCH FOCUS *(continued)*

purposely treated differently than the other, the *control group*. In all other respects the two groups are equivalent. If the groups differ afterward, we can assume the difference is due to the way they were treated. In order to be confident about this assumption, however, we must be sure that the groups are the same at the outset. The simplest way to ensure this would be to start with identical groups. But since no two individuals are ever the same in all respects, such a tactic is impossible. An equally good approach is to make sure the groups don't differ in any *systematic* way. We can accomplish this by assigning individuals at random to either condition. If each person has the same chance of being assigned to either group, and if we assign enough people to each, the differences among the people would balance out between the groups. *Random assignment* will distribute any initial differences more or less evenly between the groups.

Klein and Litt followed this procedure. After an initial interview to determine possible contraindications to the use of aspirin, they randomly assigned subjects to either an aspirin or a no-aspirin condition. These conditions represented their *independent variable,* the variable that is manipulated by the investigator to determine its effect on behavior. Investigators *manipulate* a variable by randomly assigning subjects to its conditions. This can

be done by tossing a coin, pulling numbers out of a hat, using computer-generated random sequences, and other such means. Because assignment to conditions is random, the groups should not differ in any systematic way before the experiment begins.

Half of the adolescent girls took 600 mg of aspirin four times a day for 3 days prior to their expected period. The other half took an identical *placebo* containing no aspirin. To determine whether aspirin had an effect, the investigators asked the girls to rate the severity of symptoms when their periods occurred. These ratings were the *dependent variable*. Do the girls' reactions "depend" on how they were treated? In this experiment they did. Taking aspirin significantly reduced dysmenorrhea compared to the placebo control.

Before you rush to tell your friends about this treatment for "the blahs," keep in mind that aspirin is a drug, and a powerful one. Its use is medically contraindicated for many people, such as those with asthma, some allergies, or ulcers (its slows blood clotting). Medication, including the lowly aspirin, should be taken only under proper supervision.

Reference: J. R. Klein & I. F. Litt. (1983). Menarche and dysmenorrhea. In J. Brooks-Gunn & A. C. Petersen (Eds.), Girls at puberty. *New York: Plenum Press.*

to their fathers, whereas a small sample of fathers who were interviewed said they would be comfortable talking with their daughters. It is interesting that girls who tell their fathers, or who know their mothers have told them, report fewer menstrual symptoms such as cramps or other discomfort. This inclusion of the father may reflect a more open, relaxed attitude about menstruation or perhaps a more open attitude at home in general (Brooks-Gunn & Ruble, 1983).

The source of a girl's information is related to her experience of menstruation. Different sources may give different types of information and communicate different attitudes about menstruation. Girls who are informed by their mothers generally have fewer symptoms. Mothers may be more positive, stressing menarche as

Although they may not share their feelings with friends, some girls may feel ambivalent about menarche, while others accept it as a natural part of maturing. The difference is due in large part to how parents prepare their daughters for the physical changes of puberty.

a sign of growing up, and friends may be more likely to discuss the "hassles" of menstruation. No matter how well prepared a girl is, however, she is invariably surprised by menarche (Brooks-Gunn & Ruble, 1983).

Spermarche. **Spermarche** is the term for a boy's first ejaculation of seminal fluid, which usually occurs early in his teens, by about 13 (Kulin, 1991c). For some, it will occur spontaneously in a **nocturnal emission** (also known as a "wet dream"); for others, through masturbation or intercourse. Relatively few boys are likely to have anyone explain all this to them. Peers and books or magazines are the most likely sources of information. From the subject matter taught in health classes, boys may be better informed about menarche than about ejaculation. The small amount of current information available on boys' reactions to this important event comes from a small sample of white, middle- to upper-middle-class boys attending a private school. Despite their relative lack of preparation, most of the sample were not alarmed, though they did admit to being surprised and a little scared. Generally, their reactions were very positive. They reported feeling very excited, grown up, happy, and proud (Thornburg, 1975; Gaddis & Brooks-Gunn, 1985).

Boys are not likely to discuss their experience with friends or with their fathers. This reaction to ejaculation contrasts sharply with that of girls to menarche, most of whom tell their mothers immediately and share their new status with friends several months later (Ruble & Brooks-Gunn, 1982). The difference may reflect the closer association of first ejaculation with masturbation for boys. Neither boys nor girls seem to discuss masturbation. For girls, the lack of any association of menarche with masturbation may account for their greater willingness to discuss it. Or it may be that they have had discussion modeled for them by their mothers, since most are prepared for menarche, whereas most boys have not been prepared for first ejaculation by their fathers (Gaddis & Brooks-Gunn, 1985).

Most adolescent boys receive considerably less information than girls about the reproductive nature of pubertal changes. Few fathers explain nocturnal emissions to their sons, and neither parent is likely to explain menstruation. A survey of college males found that many had gotten much of their information about menstruation as young adults from female friends, once the security of early adulthood permitted such discussions (Brooks-Gunn & Ruble, 1986). Perhaps because of inconsistency in the way males get their information about menstruation, this information more frequently reflects negative cultural beliefs.

The Secular Trend

Quite a bit of evidence indicates that puberty begins earlier today than it did in the past. This downward shift in age is called the **secular trend**. The greatest changes occurred from the mid-1800s to the mid-1900s. The trend appears to have leveled off. The average age for menarche in the United States is about 12½. In Britain during the mid-1800s, menarche occurred between 15½ and 16½ years (Frisch, 1983). Figure 3.8 shows a striking drop in age at menarche over a period of 130 years for a number of countries. Age at menarche has dropped by about 3–4 months every 10 years (Tanner, 1991).

Adolescents not only begin puberty earlier than in previous generations, they also grow faster. We have only scanty records from earlier centuries, but the pieces fit a predictable pattern. In the nineteenth century in Britain, females reached their adult height at about 21. Adolescent girls stop growing today by 16 to 18. British men in the nineteenth century continued growing well into their mid-twenties, reaching their adult height at 23 to 25 years. Adolescent boys today reach their adult height by 20 to 21 (Frisch, 1983).

Adolescents also grow to be larger than they once did, girls growing half an inch to an inch taller than their mothers and weighing about 2 pounds more. For boys these differences could be even greater. Generational differences are startling when we make comparisons across centuries. American sailors during the War of 1812 were probably just an inch or two over 5 feet tall, since the decks of the USS

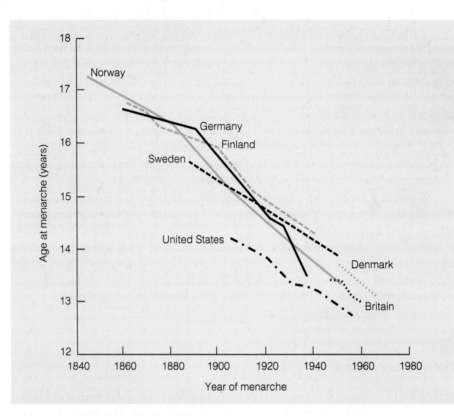

Figure 3.8 Trends in the Age of Menarche.
Source: Adapted from J. M. Tanner. (1968). Earlier maturation in man. Scientific American, 218, 26.

Constitution were only 5′6″ high. Similar evidence from medieval armor, old clothing, and antique furniture all point to a dramatic increase in stature over the centuries. The seats of the La Scala opera house in Milan, for example, built in 1776, were 18 inches wide. Most seats today are 24 inches wide (Muuss, 1975; Tanner, 1991).

A number of conditions probably contribute to the secular trend. Improved nutrition is almost surely an important cause of the accelerated growth patterns. Despite the prevalence of fast foods and junk foods, diet today is immeasurably better than in the past. Rose Frisch (1983–1991) suggests that the earlier age for menarche today is due to the faster rate at which children grow; they simply get bigger sooner today. She argues that menarche occurs when girls reach a critical weight, and they reach this weight sooner today than in centuries past. She adds that the secular trend should level off as nutrition and child care reach optimal levels. This may be happening now (Wyshak & Frisch, 1982).

THE PSYCHOLOGICAL AND SOCIAL IMPLICATIONS OF PUBERTY

In a widely cited study, Stanley Schachter and Jerome Singer (1962) gave individuals enough adrenalin to produce a rush. Those who had not been told they would experience any symptoms interpreted their physical state in terms of the events happening around them. If they were with someone who was angry, they experienced their arousal as anger; if with someone who was happy, they interpreted the same state as happiness. The physiological source of their emotions was the same, yet the psychological effect depended on who they were with.

Adolescents, like the individuals in Schachter and Singer's study, frequently interpret their changing chemistries by looking to others. Hormones increase dramatically during puberty. How do these changes affect adolescents? Can we assume they work in simple and direct ways? Or are even the most powerful chemical forces at times dependent for their psychological effect on the interpretations that adolescents and others give them?

Two Explanations of the Effects of Physical Change

Direct-effects models propose direct and immediate links between inner states and psychological effects. Are increases in testosterone, for example, related to increases in aggressiveness? Does maturation of the reproductive system occasion more frequent sexual arousal? Petersen and Taylor (1980) summarize the evidence for direct hormonal effects as "less than overwhelming," but point out that as experimental methodologies become more sophisticated, they may reveal relationships previously missed.

Mediated-effects models emphasize the importance of variables either within or external to the adolescent that mediate the effects of physical changes. Biological changes can speak through many voices: Thoughts and feelings about the meaning of changes, cultural standards of attractiveness, individual coping strategies, how acceptable one feels or needs to be, how one feels about growing up or about adults, parental conflict concerning pubertal changes, and social pressures for normative behavior are all possible mediators for the effects of physical changes (Petersen & Taylor, 1980).

Each of the above mediators of biological change provides alternate routes along which a single event may travel. Different outcomes are possible with the same event. Menarche can lead to enhanced self-esteem through the perception of oneself as more adult, or to monthly tensions through cultural beliefs of menstrual distress. Similarly, the growth spurt can lead to a positive perception of the self through increased peer acceptance or to renewed conflict in the family, as power relations with parents are negotiated. Mediated-effects models allow us to formulate complex relationships between events, and give importance to biological events while acknowledging the contribution of the adolescent's and others' perceptions of these events.

Often it is not easy to disentangle cause from effect in developmental research, whether mediated or direct. For instance, Terrie Moffitt, Avshalom Caspi, Jay Belsky, and Phil Silva (1992) noticed that girls from stressful homes, defined as those in which the fathers were absent and there was family conflict, were more likely to reach menarche at an earlier age. At first glance, it would appear that environmental "stressors" prompted earlier maturation in these girls. These investigators offer an alternative which is less obvious but more direct: that heredity is largely responsible for age at menarche. We know, for instance, that mothers and daughters tend to have similar ages of menarche. We also know that early maturers tend to be sexually active and marry earlier than late maturers, and that early marriages are more likely to end in divorce. It may simply be that mothers who themselves were early maturers have early maturing daughters who, because their mothers married early, are more likley to experience the stress of divorce—that is, conflict and father absence (Moffitt, Caspi, Belsky, & Silva, 1992).

Some of the most interesting effects have less to do with the source of the changes that take place than with their timing. A large and growing body of knowledge concerns the advantages and disadvantages of being early or late in the developments of adolescence. This research represents the best tradition of the mediated-effects model.

The Timing of Change: Early and Late Maturers

Differences in the timing of pubertal change from one adolescent to the next, or within any adolescent, are collectively known as **asynchrony**. Asynchrony simply means that all changes do not occur at the same time. For adolescents who believe changes should occur together, the fact that they haven't, or that they occurred together but at the "wrong" time, can have enormous implications. Many changes receive cultural as well as personal interpretation. These interpretations affect the way adolescents feel and think about themselves. Change can be difficult enough when all goes according to schedule, but when adolescents develop faster or slower than their friends and classmates, or at obviously uneven rates within their own lives, differences can be hard to ignore.

It is common for adolescents to experience asynchrony today. In fact, our society seems to foster asynchrony on adolescents. Most adolescents are biologically and intellectually mature by their mid- to late teens, yet many remain emotionally and socially dependent on parents while they obtain the education they need to succeed in an increasingly technological society. Little information exists on the possible effects of these asynchronies on personality development. Certainly, we need more research on this important topic, because it affects the lives of millions of adolescents and their parents.

We know most about the effects of asynchrony as it concerns differences in the rate of maturation between adolescents. Even here, the findings are not easy to interpret. Probably the most influential set of studies comes out of research conducted at the University of California, Berkeley, in the 1950s and 1960s by Mary Cover Jones, Nancy Bayley, and Paul Mussen. Looking at the relationships between the timing of maturation and personality measures, they observed some important differences (Jones, 1957, 1958, 1965; Jones & Bayley, 1950; Jones & Mussen, 1958; Mussen & Jones, 1957).

Early and Late Maturing Boys. The Berkeley research found that boys who matured early appeared more adult and more attractive to their peers and to adults than boys who matured later. Early maturing boys were also more popular and achieved more recognition in activities ranging from captain of the football team to class president. Personality measures showed further differences between early and late maturing boys. Early maturers were more self-confident and less dependent. The late maturers often appeared more rebellious and more concerned with rejection. Some differences persisted into adulthood. These, too, favored the early maturers, who by then were men in their thirties.

Other investigators report similar findings, suggesting that early maturation offers distinct advantages, and that late maturation may even handicap boys in

Early maturing boys often show off their strength at the expense of smaller, later maturing boys. Will their different rates of maturation affect the development of self-image in these two boys?

relatively permanent ways. These beliefs have received little challenge, despite the fact that in some studies only a few of the comparisons between early and late maturers are statistically significant, and even these do not support the notion of a handicap (Stevens-Long & Cobb, 1983).

Research by Harvey Peskin (1967, 1973) challenges these pictures of early and late maturing boys. His data give us an alternative perspective on the effects of timing. Peskin is one of the first to suggest that early maturation may have its own disadvantages. Recall that adults and peers react to early maturing boys as adults much sooner than they do to late maturers. Early maturing boys may feel pressured into prematurely committing themselves to goals and life choices in order to live up to the expectations of others, whereas their late maturing cohorts have more opportunity to explore personal alternatives. Perhaps late maturers can better reflect on their feelings, both positive and negative, maybe leading to greater insight as well as a heightened awareness of negative feelings—for example, the rejection and rebellion frequently found in later maturers in earlier studies (Stevens-Long & Cobb, 1983).

The work of John Clausen (1975) gives us yet another way to interpret differences between early and late maturing males. Clausen suggests that the importance of early maturation may be greater among working-class boys, but that more general differences in body type, height, and intelligence better predict personality differences than timing per se. He suggests, for instance, that adults as well as peers tend to look to boys with muscular bodies (mesomorphs) as leaders, and are more likely to perceive boys who are especially thin (ectomorphs) as timid and less assured.

Just how important is rate of maturation or body type to personality development? Efforts to disentangle the effects of such factors are complicated by the fact that the significance of physical characteristics can change even within a culture from one ethnic group to another or from one generation to another. An attribute such as body type may not be equally valued by all segments of society. The stereotype of the computer "hacker" may be as popular to one group as that of the varsity linebacker is to another.

Early and Late Maturing Girls.   Clear gender differences exist in the effects of timing. Early maturing girls do not share the advantages of early maturing boys (Brooks-Gunn, 1991). Many are self-conscious about their adult bodies, and lack the poise of late maturing girls. Their height, menarcheal status, and developing breasts can be sources of embarrassment among classmates who have the bodies of children. The picture brightens with junior high. Early maturing girls are no longer set apart by their adult bodies. They enjoy a new prestige and, with this, frequent popularity. Socioeconomic status appears to be important in mediating the effects of timing for girls as well. Early maturation is a more positive experience for middle-class girls than for working-class girls (Clausen, 1975).

Several factors contribute to the difficulties generally experienced by early maturing girls. For one thing, early maturing girls are less likely to be prepared for pubertal changes than late maturers since most will begin to menstruate before they learn of menstruation either from their mothers or in a health class. They are also less likely to have close friends with whom they feel comfortable discussing the changes they are experiencing. In general, early maturers have more negative attitudes concerning menstruation, poorer body image, and more eating problems. The latter may be due to being somewhat heavier in a culture that values thinness (Brooks-Gunn, 1991).

Some effects persist into adulthood for females, just as they do for males. Researchers have found that early maturing girls are more introverted and experience more emotional conflict as young adults. Early maturing females appear to come into their own in middle adulthood, when they surpass late maturers on many measures of mental health (Peskin, 1973; Petersen & Taylor, 1980).

Explaining the Differences. Several hypotheses explain the psychological effects of timing, each of which takes a mediated-effects approach. The *deviance hypothesis* suggests that timing has a psychological impact by changing the adolescent's status relative to his or her peers. Adolescents who mature either way ahead of or way behind their peers become deviants. According to this position, early maturing girls are the most deviant and experience more disadvantages. Girls generally mature several years ahead of boys. Thus, girls who mature the earliest are the most anomalous group among their age-mates. Late maturing boys are the second most deviant group, since they are at the other end of the developmental parade. Early maturing girls and late maturing boys do in fact have the hardest times (Petersen & Crockett, 1985).

A second explanation suggests that early maturers do not have as much time as other adolescents to complete the developmental tasks of middle childhood. The *stage termination hypothesis* predicts more difficulty for those facing the demands of adolescence first, that is, early maturing girls. A positive note for these adolescents is that they have more time to complete the tasks of adolescence. The early years of adolescence, however, can be expected to be rough, as early maturers cope with new experiences, expectations, and feelings when they have not yet completely resolved the problems of middle childhood (Peskin & Livson, 1972).

A third explanation, the *adult status hypothesis,* suggests that the advantages or disadvantages of early and late maturation depend on the status that awaits adolescents when they become adults (Block, 1978). Adult males generally enjoy a higher status in society than females. They are frequently the decision makers within the family and have positions of greater power and influence in society. Early maturing boys enjoy the higher status afforded males when they attain the adult bodies of males. Movement toward adulthood for girls does not carry the clear advantages it does for boys. At best, the advantages are mixed. Girls can anticipate the greater independence enjoyed by adults, but female adult models are frequently financially and emotionally dependent on males. Physical maturation has more of a sexual meaning for girls than boys, perhaps because adult women traditionally

RESEARCH FOCUS

Longitudinal Design: Body-Image Satisfaction—Mirror, Mirror, on the Wall
With Michael Wapner

How do adolescents feel about their bodies? Are they satisfied? Concerned? How well do they accomplish the developmental task of accepting the changes that puberty brings? Does a 14-year-old who thinks her nose is too big enter adulthood with the same concern?

Even though one's nose is disproportionately large at one point during adolescence, things even out with continued growth. Because growth proceeds in a *cephalocaudal* direction—from head to toe—the nose grows before the bottom half of the face fills out. As adolescents contend with changes such as this one, we might expect body-image satisfaction to change as well. Does it? How could a researcher discover whether body-image satisfaction changes or remains the same with age?

The simplest procedure would be to ask adolescents of different ages how satisfied they are with their bodies. Simple as this may sound, a few methodological complexities exist. But let's start at the beginning and see how one investigator obtained her answers. Maijaliisa Rauste-von Wright, a psychologist at the University of Helsinki in Finland, studied a group of approximately 100 adolescents over a 7-year period. She first questioned them when they were 11, and last when they were 18. This investigator used a *longitudinal* design. In this type of research, one studies a single *cohort,* a group of individuals all the same age, and repeatedly observes its members as they age. Rauste-von Wright selected four *times of measurement,* observing the adolescents when they were 11, 13, 15, and 18 years old.

By following the same individuals over time, we can see patterns to development that we might otherwise miss. And since we are comparing the adolescents with themselves at each age, we minimize the problem of having equivalent samples. Are there any problems with this type of research? Unfortunately, the answer is yes. To understand what these problems are, we must define three terms: age changes, time of measurement differences, and confounding.

Age changes are the biological and experiential changes that always accompany aging. They occur in all cultures and all points in history. We assume that age changes have a biological basis (although we are not always able to identify them), and should therefore be universal; that is, they should occur in all people no matter what their social or cultural background. A good example of an age change is menarche, the growth spurt, or any of the many changes of puberty that will occur in any adolescent regardless of culture (e.g., Finland or the U.S.) (Rauste-von Wright collected her first observations in 1969).

Time of measurement differences reflect social conditions, currents of opinion, and historical events that are present when we make our observations and that can affect attitudes and behavior. When we study age changes by repeatedly observing the same group of individuals over time, we can mistake time of measurement changes for age changes. It's always possible, for example, that researchers today are more conscious of staying fit than they were in 1969 and would interpret an adolescent's answers to questions about being overweight differently than those asking the same questions 20 years ago. (Not since the 1920s, for example, have people been as concerned with their weight as they are now.)

Confounding occurs when observations reflect systematic differences in more than one variable, with the result that we can not separate the effects of one from those of the other. Longitudinal research confounds age changes with time of mea-

(continued)

RESEARCH FOCUS *(continued)*

surement differences. It is impossible, in other words, to conclusively separate the effects of age from those due to time of measurement. Do changes in body image satisfaction reflect differences due to age, or to currents of opinion existing at the time that might have affected adolescents' satisfaction with their bodies?

Longitudinal research suffers from other problems as well. It is difficult to keep in touch with individuals over the years. Maintaining elaborate records, and the staff required for this bookkeeping, can be expensive. Longitudinal research is also time consuming. We must wait while individuals age. And there is no guarantee that we will outlive them. A more serious problem than any of these is the nearly inevitable loss of subjects over time (Rauste-von Wright started with 105 and ended with 90). People move away, die, or for other reasons are not available for study. This loss is called *subject mortality,* and is almost always systematically related to age. In other words, the individuals who remain in the study are not necessarily representative of those their age in the general population, because the less healthy and otherwise less fortunate are the first to leave the sample. (Perhaps adolescents with very negative body images do not want to be reminded of their feelings and drop out.)

With these cautions in mind, let's go back to Rauste-von Wright's observations to see what they tell us about body-image satisfaction among adolescents. Satisfaction drops in mid-adolescence but rises again and increases to an even higher level by the age of 18. Adolescents appear to master the developmental task of coming to terms with their changing bodies. At all ages, however, males are more satisfied with their bodies than females, appearance being more important to females' sense of themselves than it is to males.

When we wish ourselves to be taller or shorter, thinner or more "buffed," we invariably imagine only the positive results—the admiration, the acceptance, or perhaps the anonymity of more con-ventional features. But we rarely figure on the stresses on identity that even highly desirable changes can bring about.

Almost everyone is dissatisfied with some aspect of his or her appearance. But appearance is also a large and important component of identity. The continuity of "you-ness" depends on the fact that whatever changes in appearance do take place are sufficiently minor and gradual that they rarely affect our recognizability as the same person who existed before the change. But what if appearance changes were so radical and rapid that accompanying challenges to identity were equally radical? For instance, suppose that for every change in appearance there was an accompanying loss of memory of all events associated with the former feature? The overweight boy, for example, who is now thin would have no memory of how it felt to be fat. He would no longer remember the fantasies that gave him solace, the empathy (or impatience) he felt with other overweight people, the interests and abilities he cultivated to compensate for his appearance. Similarly, suppose his friends and family no longer associated him with those feelings of sympathy or impatience they felt for his previous bulky self?

It may be that your unhappiness with that hated featured of your own body is so great that even this imaginary scenario is an acceptable price to pay for change. But it does, you must admit, give your appearance fantasies a different feel.

Actually, the scenario is not so imaginary. There was a time when your body was so small, for instance, that the adult-sized world that loomed over you was, without question, not the world you knew. And yet most of us have little or no recollection of that world and the feelings that came with it. In some ways, that little person who used to exist was indeed someone else.

Reference: Rauste-von Wright, M. (1989). Body-image satisfaction in adolescent girls and boys: A longitudinal study. Journal of Youth and Adolescence, 18, 71–83.

have been defined through their roles as wife and mother. Maturity does not move them into positions of leadership, financial independence, and physical prowess.

Is this what life is all about? Perhaps not, but such are the values of society. Consequently, the adult status hypothesis can explain why early maturation is more advantageous for middle-class than working-class girls. More of the former can expect to achieve positions of independence and prestige as adults (Block, 1978).

Body Image

Just how satisfied adolescents are with their bodies depends a lot on the reactions of others. Few adolescents can be objective when it comes to evaluating their bodies. For that matter, few adults can be objective either. Adolescents' and adults' self-images reflect the attitudes of others, or their perceptions of these attitudes, as well as their own evaluations of how attractive a particular trait may be. Body images are caught by social mirrors and always reflect comparisons with others.

These images can get pretty distorted at times, especially in adolescence, when bodies change in so many ways. In early adolescence, physical changes contribute heavily to adolescents' senses of themselves. Adolescents' self-images are strongly

Between the ages of 10 and 14, girls are usually taller than boys of the same age. Because girls reach physical maturity earlier than boys, social interactions between them can be awkward at times.

tied to their body images; this is true for both sexes. Furthermore, just how satisfied adolescents are with their bodies roughly predicts their levels of self-esteem, especially for girls. Superficial or not, this relationship reflects something of a social reality, since peer acceptance is related to body type (Tobin-Richards, Boxer, & Petersen, 1983; Stiles, Gibbons, Hardardottir, & Schnellmann, 1987).

In general, boys have more positive body images than girls. Girls tend to be critical of the way they look, believing themselves to be heavier than they are and wanting to be thinner. Boys, on the other hand, are content with their appearance, wanting, if anything, only to be somewhat more muscular. Girls' tendency to overestimate their weight declines after mid-adolescence; however, their dissatisfaction with their bodies continues to increase through late adolescence (Phelps, Johnston, Jimenez, Wilczenski, Andrea, & Healy, 1993).

Among boys, early maturers have more positive body images; however, among girls, the opposite is true: Late maturers feel more positive about their bodies and more attractive than early maturers. The one exception to this rule concerns the development of breasts. Girls with better developed breasts have more positive images of themselves.

Girls are most satisfied with their bodies when they perceive themselves as being slightly underweight. Their body image is very negative if they see themselves as overweight. Weight clearly contributes to a sense of oneself in different ways for girls than boys. Boys feel best about their bodies when they are average in weight, and they feel equally bad when they are either underweight or overweight. Perhaps the need to see oneself as thin accounts for the negative body image that many postpubertal girls develop. The addition of subcutaneous fat that precedes menarche dramatically alters the thin, long-legged look, one of our culture's ideals for women. Or perhaps it is movement toward the status of adulthood itself that precipitates a drop in body image for females. In any case, postpubertal girls have lower body images and feel less attractive than boys (Brooks-Gunn, 1991; Duke-Duncan, 1991).

Fitting a new body-image into a sense of self is an important developmental task of early adolescence, and girls experience more difficulty than boys. In a longitudinal study of over 600 adolescents, Roberta Simmons and Dale Blyth (1987) found consistent gender differences in body image and self-esteem during early and mid-adolescence. Girls are less satisfied with their weight, their general body type, and consider themselves less attractive than do boys. These differences appear as early as the sixth grade and persist into the tenth. Perhaps not surprisingly, girls have lower self-esteem than boys at each of these grades and are more self-conscious. Even as girls evaluate their looks more negatively than boys, they place more value on personal appearance than do boys.

Just what adolescents make of physical appearance is another thing. Are the pounds they add simply excess fat from the Big Macs, Jumbo Jacks, fries, and shakes they consume, or are they the muscle and subcutaneous fat that will transform their bodies into those of adults?

EATING DISORDERS

Some adolescents mistake the natural changes of maturation for unwanted fat, and diet to regain their former shapes. Others, perhaps unsure whether they are ready for adulthood, delay its appearance by literally starving themselves. Still others turn to food when stressed and become obese.

Dieting

Most adolescents do not have eating disorders; however, problem eating behaviors are fairly common. Most females believe they are too fat and place themselves on diets (Howat & Saxton, 1988; Ledoux, Choquet, & Manfredi, 1993; Phelps et al, 1993). One study of ninth-graders found that 25% of the girls were currently on diets, and 75% reported having been on a diet at some prior time. Many skipped breakfast and ate salads as their main meal. All knew which foods were high in calories and stayed away from them. Boys were untroubled about their weight; 80% said they had never tried to lose any weight (Leon, Perry, Mangelsdorf, & Tell, 1989).

To the extent that dieting leads to inadequate nutrition, it can interfere with growth. Little information related to dieting and growth exists. At the very least one can conclude that rapid or significant weight loss during periods of rapid growth are not advisable (Parr, 1988). Adolescents at greatest risk from dieting are girls. Cultural messages on the importance of being thin are clear—females need to be thinner than do males in order to be considered attractive. One survey found that nearly three-quarters of the female characters on television were actually underweight. Most of the males were of average weight (Silverstein, Perdue, Peterson, & Kelly, 1986). Those most susceptible to this message are girls who are dating and are also early maturers; because of their pubertal status, they are less likely to be thin than late maturers (Smolak, Levine, & Gralen, 1993).

Television is not unique in communicating to females the importance of being thin. Silverstein, Perdue, Peterson and Kelly also sampled advertisements in popular women's and men's magazines for messages about body shape. Ads for diet products in women's magazines outnumbered those in men's magazines 60 to 1. Despite the clear message to stay thin, women's magazines contained over 1,000 advertisements for food; 10 appeared in all the men's magazines.

Adolescent females today face a standard of beauty that is considerably thinner than in the past. Models of feminine beauty—whether actresses, performers, or individuals advertising products—are thin indeed, compared to curvaceous counterparts of generations past. The flapper era of the 1920s was the only other time during this century when the popular images of women were as thin as they are at present. Developmentalists note with some alarm that eating disorders became epidemic among young women then, and warn that, with respect to eating disorders, history may be repeating itself.

Bulimia and Anorexia

Both bulimia and anorexia have increased significantly over the past 10 to 15 years, and both are more common among females than males (Tobias, 1988). **Bulimia** is characterized by binge eating: consuming large amounts of food in a short time, usually in less than 2 hours. Binges are usually accompanied by the fear that one cannot stop oneself and are followed by self-deprecating thoughts. They tend to be done in secret and usually end only because of abdominal pain or falling asleep.

Anorexia is a disorder in which individuals severely limit their intake of food, dieting to the point of actual starvation. Actual starvation has mental and emotional, as well as physical, effects, and anorexics can be apathetic and irritable. Due to the loss of body fat, anorexics frequently become amenorrheic, ceasing to have menstrual periods.

Most bulimics are aware that their eating patterns are abnormal, and most make continued attempts to lose weight through highly restrictive diets, self-induced vomiting, and use of laxatives or diuretics. Anorexics deny that they have any problem and reject help (*DSM-IIIR*, 1987).

Less than 5% of high school students are thought to be bulimic; the percentage of those who are anorexic is even smaller. Whereas anorexia is more com-

Anorexics severely limit their intake of food; some lose up to 25% of their body weight. However, they usually have a distorted body image; even though they look dangerously emaciated to friends and family, to themselves, they still do not feel thin enough.

RESEARCH FOCUS

Bias and Blind Controls: Eating Disorders

"You always shut yourself off in your room," her mother said, somewhat angrily.

"I just want to be left alone," she pleaded, the hint of a whine in her voice. The teenager was 17, and her dark eyes communicated a sulky resentment.

The research assistant on the other side of the one-way mirror quickly coded the girl's response: "asserting," "appeasing," "separating," and "interdependent."

"Some message!" he thought, as he watched the family in front of him.

The girl was trim, neither overweight nor underweight. He couldn't tell from her appearance which type of disorder she suffered from; he only knew that this project was about adolescents with eating disorders. For all he knew, she could be part of the control group.

Why keep this graduate student in the dark about the families he is observing? Why not assume that the more he knows, the better he'll understand and more accurately record their behavior? Investigators have found from painful experience that their expectations all too often influence what they see—sometimes even causing them to read things into a person's behavior that just aren't there. Their expectancies can *bias,* or systematically alter, the results of the study.

Whenever investigators know the condition to which a subject is part, they can bias the outcome of the research either by unconsciously treating subjects in that condition differently or by interpreting—that is, scoring—their behavior differently. If, for example, this graduate student believed that the parents of girls with a certain type of eating disorder were harsh and demanding, he might read hostility into their remarks even when it wasn't there, or perhaps be less friendly with them when introducing them to the experiment. The latter difference might lead to tensions in family interactions that otherwise would not be present, thus unintentionally confirming initial expectations.

(continued)

mon in young adolescents, bulimia is more common in older adolescents and young women (Howat & Saxton, 1988; Johnson, Steinberg, & Lewis, 1988).

Though bulimics can be of any weight, they are rarely fat (Ledoux, Choquet, & Manfredi, 1993). Usually their weight fluctuates widely, sometimes by as much as 20 to 30 pounds over a period of just several months. Anorexics are excessively thin, frequently losing up to 25% of their body weight.

Anorexia and bulimia are closely related disorders. Both involve an obsession with food and a morbid fear of being fat. Both also share an obsessive need to be thin. Many anorexics engage in binging and purging, and many bulimics start with an initial anorexic phase. Most bulimics usually begin self-induced vomiting approximately a year after they start binging (Fairburn & Cooper, 1982). Due to the large numbers of calories bulimics consume, they can only maintain their weight by alternating binges with highly restrictive diets, or by purging what they have eaten through self-induced vomiting, laxatives, or diuretics.

Bulimics are likely to live with the disorder for a number of years before seeking help. During that time they suffer physical as well as emotional symptoms,

RESEARCH FOCUS (continued)

Investigators can eliminate experimenter bias by conducting the experiment "blind." In a *single blind control* procedure, such as the one above, the investigator is unaware of the condition of which each subject is part; expectations cannot contribute to any of the observed differences. A single-blind control is adequate in many experiments. Some, however, require a *double-blind control,* in which both the subjects as well as the experimenter are ignorant of which condition each subject is in. Double-blind controls are frequently used in drug studies in which it is necessary to control for the patients' as well as the doctor's expectations that they will get better if they take an experimental medication. In double-blind drug studies, *all* subjects are given a pill, but half receive a *placebo,* or sugar pill.

Let's get back to the other side of the one-way mirror. Do families of girls with different eating disorders interact in characteristically different ways? Laura Humphrey (1989) observed 74 adolescent girls with their parents. Sixteen were *anorexic,* 16 were *bulimic,* 18 were both *bulimic and anorexic,* and 24 were normal controls. All of those in the first three categories were patients who had been hospitalized long enough so that one could not distinguish the anorexics by their appearance.

Parents of anorexics were both more nurturing and comforting *and* more ignoring and neglecting than were those of bulimics or controls. The anorexic girls were the most submissive of the group when they were with their parents. Bulimics and their parents were more likely to engage in mutual grumbling and blaming and to exchange disparaging remarks. Interactions of normal controls and their parents were characterized more by helping, protecting, trusting, and simple enjoyment of each other.

These findings underscore the importance of treating the family as a whole, as well as working individually with the adolescent when treating eating disorders. Most eating disorders are associated with a pattern of disturbed family interactions.

Reference: L. L. Humphrey. (1989). Observed family interactions among subtypes of eating disorders using structural analysis of social behavior. Journal of Consulting and Clinical Psychology, 57, *206–214.*

such as fatigue, weakness, and constipation. Dental caries and erosion of the enamel of the teeth are also common from frequent contact with stomach acids through self-induced vomiting (Johnson, Steinberg, & Lewis, 1988). Anorexics have a distorted body image and are not likely to seek help even when they become emaciated through self-starvation.

Bulimics often have low self-esteem and a history of depression (Ledoux, Choquet, & Manfredi, 1993). These adolescents are likely to feel self-conscious around others, be sensitive to rejection, and have difficulty expressing their feelings directly. Both bulimics and anorexics are likely to have high standards and expectations for themselves and be overly critical when they fail to meet them.

Both disorders are more common among adolescents from middle-class, upwardly mobile homes who are typically "good girls" seeking approval and love by pleasing others. Both disorders require professional intervention. Each is a serious threat to health and reflects underlying emotional problems that need treatment (Tobias, 1988).

Eating Disorders and Family Conflict.   Eating disorders hide deeper, underlying problems in which family experiences play an important role. Four characteristics of families that lead to the expression of psychological problems as physical symptoms frequently characterize the families of anorexics and bulimics (Minuchin, Rosman, & Baker, 1978; Tobias, 1988). *Enmeshment* exists when boundaries between family members are not clear. In enmeshed families, everyone is involved in everyone else's life, making it difficult to be independent or autonomous. *Overprotective* families show an inappropriate concern for the welfare of family members. Families characterized by *rigidity* have a need to maintain the status quo and are unable to face change. These qualities make adolescence, a time of many changes, especially difficult. Finally, families in which there is *inadequate conflict resolution* avoid conflict, with the result that differences are never cleanly resolved and members continue to impinge on each other. An eating disorder may be the only way in which adolescents from such families can gain a sense of maintaining control over their lives (Tobias, 1988).

Obesity

Physical appearance is perhaps never more important than during adolescence. Body image contributes significantly to self-image for most adolescents. Those who are obese have less-positive self-images and lower self-esteem than adolescents of average weight. **Obesity** is defined as being 20% above the average weight for one's height. Approximately 15% of all adolescents meet this criterion; this figure makes obesity the most common eating disorder of any age (Grandjean, 1988).

Obesity has multiple causes. The likelihood of a genetic component is strong in that obese children tend to have obese parents. This relationship is difficult to interpret in any simple way, because parents and children share eating habits and lifestyles as well as genes. Also, the eating patterns of obese adolescents differ from those who are of average weight. Obese adolescents are more likely to eat irregularly, missing meals and snacking. These habits make it difficult to maintain a balance between hunger and satiation. Obese adolescents are also more likely to eat rapidly, to eat somewhat larger portions, and to eat food that is denser in calories (Lucas, 1988).

Perhaps the biggest difference between obese adolescents and those of average weight is in how active they are, not how much they eat. Obese adolescents are considerably less active than their peers of average weight. A low level of activity can contribute as much to obesity as excess eating. Once again, separating cause from effect is difficult. Are obese adolescents less active because of their weight; that is, are they less likely than their peers to be chosen for the team or to be good at sports? Or do adolescents who are inactive simply run a greater risk of becoming obese (Lucas, 1988)?

The relationship between obesity and inactivity highlights the importance of exercise in weight reduction programs. Exercise increases the body's metabolism,

Because most junior high school students are in transition from concrete operational thought to formal operational thought, they need a lot of hands-on activities in the classroom.

The ability to think about thought allows adolescents to arrive at possibilities they could never reach otherwise. We can see this quality of formal thought at work in one of Piaget's tasks, a game in which balls are shot onto a gameboard with a spring launcher. The balls differ in size and in the smoothness of their surfaces. Eventually each stops rolling, the larger and rougher ones first. Piaget asks adolescents to explain why they stop. At first adolescents identify wind resistance and friction as important. But they soon realize something else: that the balls would roll forever if neither of these was present. This conclusion can be reached only through thought, because the conditions under which the event would occur are never actually present (Flavell, Miller, & Miller, 1993; Ginsburg & Opper, 1988).

Do Adolescents Think the Way Piaget Says They Do?

Few developmentalists object to the way Piaget describes thought at any age; the differences he notes are clear. Not as clear is what accounts for these differences. Piaget attributes changes with age to the emergence of stages, each one unique and different from the last, each abruptly ushering in a new form of thought when new mental structures mature, and each making its appearance in all individuals despite differences in their backgrounds. However, research has not supported these assumptions—that age changes are more than quantitative, that they are abrupt, and that they occur in all individuals despite their other differences. Each of Piaget's assumptions is discussed below.

Is There a Qualitative Difference?   Piaget believed that the changes he chronicled were not simply due to learning, but became possible only with the biological maturation of underlying mental structures. Yet quite a bit of evidence exists to the contrary. For instance, Lavee Artman and Sorel Cahan (1993), working with large numbers of fourth-, fifth-, and sixth-graders, found that schooling contributed more to their success on certain Piagetian-type problems than did age.

Piaget assumed that formal thought was necessary to understand certain types of logical relationships. However, not only can younger children think in ways Piaget believed only adolescents could, but adolescents frequently think in ways characteristic of earlier ages (Flavell, 1992). In the syllogism below, for example, one has to use deductive reasoning to decide the validity of the third statement:

1. Lestat is a vampire.
2. All vampires are immortal.
3. Lestat is immortal.

Deductive reasoning presumably emerges with formal thought. Yet preschool children can also solve syllogisms requiring this type of logic. J. Hawkins, R. D. Pea,

RESEARCH FOCUS (*continued*)

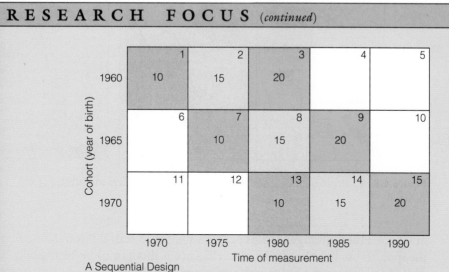

A Sequential Design
The cells are numbered in the upper-right hand corner. The numbers in the centers of the cells are ages.

in 1970, 1975, or 1980). If all we had were the diagonals, we couldn't say anything about the relationship of intelligence to age.

But sequential designs give us more. We have vertical and horizontal means as well. The first of these, the column means, allow us to estimate differences due to time of measurement, and the second, the row means, the effect for cohorts. Comparing performance measured in 1975 (cells 2 and 7), with performance measured in 1980 (cells 3, 8, and 13), with that in 1985 (cells 9 and 14) provides an estimate of the amount of variability in intellectual functioning that is contributed by time of measurement. Differences among row means allow us to estimate the size of a cohort effect. By subtracting each of these estimates from the diagonals, we end up with an estimate of age effects.

Does intelligence "slip" with age? Sequential designs find that age effects are minimal. Simply put, adolescents can expect to hold on to their "smarts" as they enter adulthood. But what shall we make of the cross-sectional data indicating (erroneously as it turns out) that intelligence declines in adulthood? Obviously, some measures of intelligence confound the period in which one lives, the historical context, with attributes of the individual. The result of that confusion is to stigmatize older people. Sound familiar? This problem is reminiscent of similar complaints that intelligence tests penalize ethnic and racial minorities because they confound cultural and economic conditions with attributes of the individual.

Reference: A. Anastasi. (1988). Psychological testing (6th ed.). New York: Macmillan.

Figure 4.8 Example of a Type of Item in the Picture Arrangement Subtest of the WAIS-R.

in school. **Fluid intelligence** taps people's abilities to reason through situations on the spot, to use their heads. Fluid intelligence is thought to be biologically based and declines more markedly with age in adulthood than does crystallized intelligence, which reflects cultural learning (Schaie & Willis, 1993).

We began our discussion of intelligence with a warning that intelligence tests have an arbitrary quality to them. The questions they contain don't only tap the capacities with which one is born; they also tap a general knowledge gained by living in a culture. People from different cultures, though theoretically just as able, will not do quite as well as those from our own. If different questions were included, ones that reflected their particular cultural experiences, their performance would improve, while that of the average North American would drop slightly.

Are There Social-Class, Ethnic, and Racial Differences in Intelligence?

Imagine the following scene of a teenager taking the Picture Arrangement subtest of the WAIS-R. She is Japanese American. The examiner places a set of four cartoon drawings on the table in front of her and tells her to arrange them so that they tell a story (see Figure 4.8). One drawing shows a man fishing by a river. A second shows a woman pointing at a garden while the man looks on. The third shows the man digging and discovering a worm, and the fourth shows him getting out the gardening tools. The girl tries first one arrangement, then another. None seems right to her. Finally the time runs out. You are puzzled. Why was this difficult for her? You quickly arrange the pictures mentally in this order: the second, the fourth, the third, the first. The story? The man has been told by his wife to garden, gets out the tools, discovers a worm as he works, and, reminded of more pleasant pursuits, goes off fishing. It's easy for most North Americans—unless they happen to be of Japanese descent. In Japan, wives don't give chores to their husbands. This girl knew that, and the pictures made no sense to her (Wechsler, 1981).

Will standardized performance tests fully reveal this young woman's abilities? Many researchers believe that such tests may be weighted with questions based on experiences of the dominant culture and that the scores from such tests may not accurately represent the capabilities of adolescents from nondominant cultures.

Performance on measures such as the one above reflect not only a person's ability but also the extent to which that person's background is similar to that of the dominant culture. If one belongs to certain minorities, one is not as likely to do as well as someone from the dominant culture. Differences exist even among individuals within the same culture but from different social classes. Adolescents from lower-income homes can score as much as 15 to 20 points below their age-mates from the middle class. Ethnic and racial differences can be equally as large, and the latter have prompted considerable debate.

Arthur Jensen (1969, 1985) argues that up to 80% of one's intelligence is determined by heredity, and that racial differences in intelligence are largely genetic. Most other experts place the contribution of heredity considerably below this figure, estimating its contributions to be about equal to those of one's environment. These investigators maintain that enriched environments should actually raise a child's IQ and impoverished ones should lower it. Scarr and Weinberg (1983), for instance, report that black children born to lower-income parents and adopted by white upper-middle-income parents scored an average of 20 points higher than children who remained in lower-income homes. Even if the genetic component of intelligence *were* closer to Jensen's estimate than most experts believe, cultural differences could still account for very large differences in IQ. A fictitious adolescent with an IQ of 100 (up to 80% of which Jensen believes to be inherited) would be expected to have an IQ as high as 120 if reared under the best of conditions, or as low as 80 under the worst—a difference of 40 IQ points due to environment!

Thomas Sowell, a behavioral scientist at Stanford University, points out that the performance of minorities today closely resembles that of other minorities in the early 1900s, whether of European or non-European descent, before they assimilated into the culture (Sowell, 1978). Sowell focuses on black Americans, highlighting three distinct patterns that characterize their performance. He notes first that they do most poorly on the most abstract items on the tests. Investigators have concluded from this pattern that lower performance is genetically based, since abstract items should not reflect information specific to a culture. Sowell notes that white ethnic groups experienced a similar difficulty with abstract items when they immigrated to this country. Yet when members of these same ethnic groups were tested several generations later, they performed no differently from the population in general on the same items.

Sowell identifies a second pattern in the test performance of black Americans: a decline in the intelligence of children as they age. Again, this decline occurred among children of European immigrants. Finally, Sowell compares the performance of black women with that of women from white ethnic groups when they first immigrated. All scored higher than the men in their ethnic groups. This pattern exists even though intelligence does not differ appreciably between men and women for the population in general. Gender differences in intellectual functioning among early immigrants shows the same pattern: higher scores for women. Recent comparisons with Mexican Americans and Puerto Ricans also show the same trend.

Sowell suggests that degree of assimilation, not racial or ethnic differences, best predicts a group's level of functioning on measures of intelligence. Those groups that are upwardly mobile—one of our best indices of assimilation—show marked increases in intelligence from one generation to the next. Groups that assimilate more slowly do not show an equivalent increase with time.

One last set of differences deserves our attention before we leave this approach to intelligence. These differences concern the sexes. It is only natural to ask whether males and females differ in their intellectual functioning.

Are There Gender Differences in Intelligence?

Does intelligence differ in females and males? Popular belief holds that it does. We hear, for instance, that males are more logical and females more intuitive, that males are better at numbers and females at language. We expect females to be good at simple, repetitive tasks requiring fine motor coordination, and males to have little patience or ability for such tasks. Some differences have been noted, but they are not large nor are they always the ones stereotypes would lead us to expect (Lips, 1993).

Before we look more closely, keep in mind that there are no gender differences in overall intelligence. In fact, intelligence tests are constructed so that there will not be. Questions that are answered more accurately by females are balanced by other questions that favor males. There is also no evidence linking intellectual functioning to specific biological factors, such as prenatal hormones or the presence of the X or Y chromosome, that would differ for either sex (Lips, 1993).

Several specific gender differences exist. The first of these is verbal ability. Females do somewhat better on measures of verbal reasoning and fluency, comprehending written passages, and understanding logical relations. This difference first appears in infancy as children learn to speak. Boys soon catch up, and the difference disappears by about age 3. Performance during the grade-school years shows no differences. By early adolescence, girls again perform better on measures of verbal ability. This difference persists throughout the remainder of adolescence and adulthood. Despite the consistency of the findings from one study to the next, the difference attributable to gender is always quite small, accounting for less than 1% of the variability between scores (Hyde, 1981).

Gender differences in spatial ability also exist. Males do better on tests that require one to mentally manipulate things or remember a visual figure in order to find it in a more complex figure (Schaie & Willis, 1993). Most research has found this difference to be small, accounting for less than 5% of the variability among individuals. A recent comparison of males' and females' spatial abilities found some measures to account for 15% of the variability among individuals of either sex (Krasnoff, 1989). However, none of the published differences are large enough to explain the preponderance of males in professions that might tap these abilities, such as engineering or architecture (Hyde, 1981).

A third gender difference favors males: math. Differences do not appear until early adolescence; then boys begin to do better than girls on measures of quantitative ability. The overall difference, once again, is small, accounting for 1% to 5% of the variability among adolescents. Despite the slight advantage held by boys, girls may still get better grades in math at school. Some studies have found that among the very most able students in mathematics, those with the higher scores are more likely to be boys. Their findings are dramatic, yet they should be interpreted with caution. Comparisons at the very highest levels of ability often involved only small numbers of adolescents (Benbow & Stanley, 1980, 1982, 1983). Carol Dweck (1986) interprets these differences to reflect gender differences in motivational patterns that occur when adolescents encounter new and initially confusing material (see Chapter 7). Schaie and Willis (1993) report differences in adulthood, although only on some measures.

Are males more logical and females more intuitive? Are males better at numbers and females better at language? Does any difference between males and females, or between any two individuals regardless of sex, matter when it comes to mastering the computer?

Being good at math is expected more of adolescent males than adolescent females in this culture. Differences in mathematical ability emerge in adolescence, when individuals become aware of cultural sex roles. Also, gender differences disappear when prior mathematical experience is controlled. Of course, it is possible that by limiting comparisons to samples of girls who have had as much mathematical experience as boys, one is drawing samples that are not representative of girls in general. Nonetheless, the overall difference between males and females is so small as to be negligible, and certainly does not allow one to predict success or failure in mathematics courses in school or, later, in a mathematics-related profession on the basis of gender. One authority on gender differences pointedly asks,

> Has it been our intent to divide the population into the pinks and the blues and to develop one set of cognitive skills in the pinks and another set in the blues? If this is not our intent, the educational and social practices that have occurred "naturally" will need reexamination. (Sherman, 1978, p. 66)

The psychometric approach to intelligence has done much to further our understanding of intelligence. A more recent approach, to which we turn next, has contributed considerably to our understanding of the processes that underlie intellectual functioning in all individuals, regardless of sex or culture.

BEYOND IQ: INFORMATION PROCESSING

Have you ever caught yourself missing what someone just said after hearing your name mentioned in another conversation? Or have you ever asked a person to repeat something, only to find you know what that person said before hearing it again? How many times have you repeated a phone number until you could write it down, or noticed that you know what you *don't* know in addition to what you *do* know?

Robert Siegler (1991) summarizes two fundamental characteristics of cognition that are studied by information-processing theorists: thinking is both quite limited and quite flexible. Simply put, we are limited in just how much we can attend to at any point in time, as the examples above illustrate; and we are very good at adapting the way we think to the demands of the task or the moment, also illustrated above. With age, we develop increasingly efficient processes for overcoming these cognitive limitations.

Information is processed in stages, each of which is a separate aspect of memory. These memory systems, the *structural characteristics* of the information-processing system, exist at all ages. We see little change in them from one type of task to the next or from one person to the next. Other aspects of information processing vary with the task and with the person, reflecting the particular *processes* that may or may not be carried out.

Just as computers differ in capacity, speed, and in the types of software they can handle, information processing theorists think of intellectual functioning as changing with age in comparable ways. Four factors thought to contribute to developmental change are (1) basic processes, such as the speed with which information is processed, (2) the use of strategies, (3) metacognitive skills, such as knowing what one knows or needs to know, and (4) knowledge, or the actual information that is stored (Brown & DeLoache, 1978; Siegler, 1991).

R. C. Atkinson and R. M. Shiffrin (1968) distinguish three memory systems: a **sensory memory,** a **short-term** memory, and a **long-term** memory. Sensory memory is very brief, lasting for half a second or less. This is the memory that allows you to reconstruct that lost "snippet" of conversation you asked someone to repeat.

Short-term memory, though longer, is also brief for memory (lasting under a minute) and also limited in how much it can hold. You can manage only about seven items—about the size of a phone number—without losing some. Long-term memory lasts from a minute to a lifetime. Because of the vast information it contains, we need to categorize. Scanning the categories allows us to know what we know and what we don't.

Research suggests that few important changes occur with age in the structural aspects of memory, whereas age has a dramatic effect on the processes involved with memory (Siegler, 1991).

Sensory Memory

Sensory memory appears to have the same capacity and duration limitations for people of all ages. And since it is so brief, with little time to consciously process information, few developmental changes occur in sensory memory (Siegler, 1991).

Short-Term Memory

Information that is deciphered from sensory memory enters short-term memory or is lost. Information is held for less than a minute, unless one does something to keep the material alive, such as repeating it over and over to oneself. This procedure is called **rehearsal** and illustrates the use of a memory strategy. As one might expect, given the limits of how many items one can repeat without losing track of some of them, short-term memory is only helpful in remembering a few items at a time. Unlike either sensory or long-term memory, we are usually aware of the items in short-term memory.

Strategies are not equally effective at all ages. Young children, for example, are not likely to repeat items in order to remember them. Even older children do not rehearse as effectively as adolescents, but tend to repeat each item to be remembered in isolation from the others. Adolescents repeat each new word with the last few in the list. The latter strategy leads to much better recall (Ornstein, Naus, & Liberty, 1975).

In addition to strategies, changes in basic capacities, such as speed of processing, account for differences in cognition. As children get older, they get faster at retrieving items from short-term memory (Hale, Fry, & Jessie, 1993; Kail, 1991). Speed of processing, in turn, influences the effectiveness of strategies such as rehearsal, making it possible for more words to be refreshed before returning again to the first (Kail, 1992). We can see such an age difference in Figure 4.9. We know a lot about the way individuals search short-term memory from a simple experimental procedure. Subjects see a set of items followed by a single item called a probe; they must say whether the probe was a member of the set they just saw (Sternberg, 1966). As set size increases from one to five items, reaction time, or how quickly one gives one's answer, also increases (see Figure 4.9). This finding tells us that people check items against the probe one at a time in a *serial search*. (They do this whether or not the probe is a member of the set.) One could stop

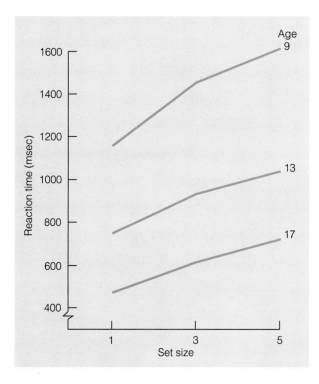

Figure 4.9 Search Time Through Short-Term Memory for 9-, 13-, and 17-Year-Olds.

Source: D. P. Keating & B. L. Bobbitt. (1978). Differences in cognitive-processing components of mental ability. Child Development, 49, 155–167.

the search with a positive probe once the item has been found. The fact that they search through all the items and only then stop to make a decision as to whether the probe was among them suggests that decisions take longer than scanning.

The slope of the function for reaction time gives us the rate at which people check the contents of short-term memory. This rate increases with age, shortening the time required to find a specific item. Each additional item adds approximately 85 milliseconds (msec) to the search time for the youngest children, but only 60 msec for the 17-year-olds. Notice, though, that even with sets of a single item, the difference in reaction times for 9- and 17-year-olds is larger than this 20-msec difference. The reaction time for a single item also reflects the time it takes to encode the item and respond to it. Adolescents need less time to recognize the item they are looking for and to respond to it than do children (Keating & Bobbitt, 1978).

Long-Term Memory

Information in short-term memory is either transferred to long-term memory or lost. **Encoding** is the process by which information is transferred from one stage to another. To encode information for long-term memory, one must relate it to

As adolescents grow older, they can retrieve items from memory more quickly, use memory strategies more effectively, and because of greater content knowledge, assimilate new information more readily.

things one already knows. Even though long-term memory has no time or capacity limitations, there is no guarantee that one will always be able to use the information that is encoded in it. Retrieving information is the biggest problem. Imagine misplacing a book in a large city library. How likely are you to recover it if you can't remember which part of the library you were in when you put it down? The book is still there, but you can't retrieve it without using the system by which it was coded.

We also find age differences in long-term memory, a number of which reflect speed of processing, in this case, how quickly one can reach and retrieve information as it is needed. Items stored in long-term memory are encoded according to meaning; in other words, they are named and stored by category. In one experiment, 11- and 19-year-olds responded to pairs of letters that appeared on a computer screen by indicating whether they were the "same" or "different." The letters could differ either in name or in appearance, that is, whether they were typed in uppercase or lowercase. Subjects who were told to respond according to the physical appearance of the letters had to perceptually scan their features—Are they the same size? Do they both have right angles?—but did not need to locate them in memory by name. Subjects who were told to respond to the letters categorically, according to name regardless of how they were typed, had an additional step that involved retrieving information (the letters' names) from long-term memory. It takes longer to respond on the basis of a name (or category) than on physical appearance. Since this step involves retrieving information from long-term memory, it also shows that older subjects needed less time to retrieve information from long-term memory than younger ones (Hale, Fry, & Jessie, 1993).

Age differences in long-term memory also include knowledge about one's memory. Early adolescents know more than children about their memories, and they use their knowledge to monitor what they do. This knowledge is called **metamemory**. Adolescents know the limits of their memories; for example, just how long a passage can be before they must reread it in order to remember it, or whether they are familiar with a name and hence likely to recall information about it. They know what strategies work best for them, are aware of using them, and realize how much they help. In contrast, younger children must often be told to use a strategy and then must be shown how it has helped in order to continue to use it (Siegler, 1991).

In addition to developmental changes in strategies, basic processes, and metacognition, content knowledge also changes with age. Adolescents simply know more than younger children. This knowledge provides a context for assimilating new information, increasing the likelihood that relevant features will be processed and encoded. Because information can be related more easily to what one already knows, it has more meaning and is more easily remembered.

STERNBERG'S COMPONENTIAL INTELLIGENCE

Adolescents function more intelligently than younger children at many tasks involving memory. They process information faster and use more intelligent and efficient strategies. They also know more about the limitations of their memories, and adapt their strategies to compensate for anticipated failings. Robert Sternberg, a psychologist at Yale, has developed a theory of intellectual functioning that accounts for these differences, as well as others. He analyzes intellectual functioning into *components*, or processes that operate on information. A component might translate perceptual information (e.g., the lines, angles, and curves of letters) into a concept (such as a name). Or it might translate one concept into another, or into an action. Sternberg identifies three kinds of components: metacomponents, performance components, and knowledge-acquisition components (Sternberg, 1984). Figure 4.10 illustrates the relation of these components.

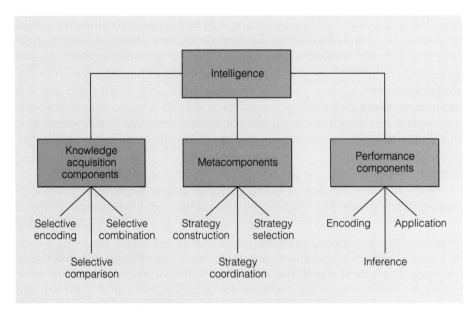

Figure 4.10 Sternberg's Components of Intellectual Functioning.
Source: R. Seigler (1991). Children's thinking. (2nd ed.), Englewood Cliffs, NJ: Prentice-Hall.

Three Components of Intellectual Functioning

Metacomponents allocate and coordinate the resources that are available for processing information. They decide when more information is needed and whether a particular strategy should be used or another one constructed, and monitor and keep track of one's progress. *Performance components* carry out the actual procedures selected by the metacomponents. If metacomponents are the supervisors, performance components are the actual workers. Performance components might decipher information in sensory memory, encoding this as names of letters. They might compare elements, inferring similarities or differences, or apply a procedure completed in one domain to another aspect of the problem. *Knowledge-acquisition components* acquire new information as it is needed. They sift through information, picking out that which is relevant to the problem and integrating it with what one already knows, giving it new meaning.

We can apply this analysis to the way people solve problems. Sternberg studied analogies because they reveal interesting age differences. An example of an analogy is the following: "Swift is to *Gulliver's Travels* as Pope is to: (a) the *Baedecker*; (b) 'The Rape of the Lock'; (c) the Vatican." To construct an analogy, one must choose the term that completes the second pair so that the two terms bear the same relationship to each other as the terms in the first pair.

To begin, one must encode each item: Does "Swift" refer to speed, or is it someone's name? (Encoding is a performance component.) The word "Travels" suggests the first alternative, and you know that the *Baedecker* is a travel guide. But then what is Pope? You may decide at this point that you need more information (a metacomponent) and search your memory for anything related to travel. You remember that *Gulliver's Travels* is the name of a book; then Swift could be the name of its author. Notice that one uses inference (another performance component) to determine the relationship between the first two terms. Encoding Swift as an author's name would mean that Pope is the name of an author. This last step has involved another performance component, mapping, or using the relationship between the first two terms to establish a relationship between the last two. Thus the fourth term must refer to something that Pope wrote. This extension rules out the Vatican, and since the *Baedecker* travel guide bears the name of its author, you are left with "The Rape of the Lock." You justify your selection by noting that the terms are all capitalized, as they would be in a title, and respond with alternative (b).

People of all ages use the same components to construct analogies, but spend different amounts of time on each (Sternberg & Rifkin, 1979). Adolescents and adults spend proportionately more time encoding the items than doing any of the other steps, while children spend relatively little time encoding. How does this fact relate to the characteristics of adolescent thought we reviewed earlier? Recall that adolescents tend to think of all the possible forms something might assume before they begin to work with any of them. They generate a world of possibilities, whereas children latch on to the first thing that comes to mind, their time for encoding being relatively brief. Sternberg also finds that with age, people spend much more time planning how to solve a problem than actually carrying out the steps (Sternberg, 1981, 1984). Once again, this difference reflects the tendency of adolescents to generate a strategy, and contrasts with the tendency of children to jump right in and move things about.

Notice, too, that analogies might be difficult for children because they require one to find the appropriate class for each term and then map the relationship between the classes of one set to those of the other. This higher-order, or abstract, form of thought awaits adolescence. Most children have as much success with analogies as they do in relating horses to goldfish (Sternberg, 1984).

Sternberg's componential analysis gives us an expanded view of intelligence. Rather than ranking one person relative to another in terms of a single number, such as IQ, we get a picture of intelligence at work: setting priorities, allocating resources, encoding information, monitoring feedback, and so on. But is it a single intelligence that works for us, or does intelligence take more than one form?

GARDNER'S SEVEN FACETS OF THE MIND

Howard Gardner, a psychologist who has written extensively on the development of intellect and creativity, proposes not one but seven forms of intelligence: musical, bodily-kinesthetic, logical-mathematical, linguistic, spatial, interpersonal, and in-

According to the research of Howard Gardner, these adolescents are demonstrating different types of intelligence. Gardner has identified seven forms of intelligence, including not only the logical-mathematical domain measured by IQ tests but also interpersonal, bodily-kinesthetic, and spatial intelligence.

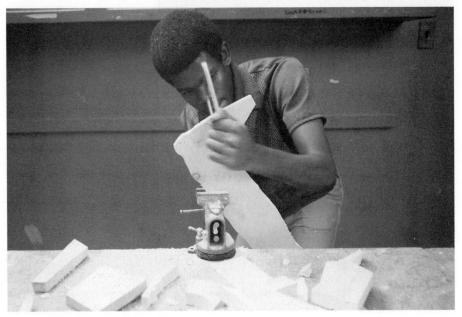

trapersonal. Gardner, like others, defines intelligence in terms of one's ability to solve problems as they arise, but the range of problems that he accepts as legitimate for the study of intelligence is much broader than it is for others (Gardner, 1983).

Gardner points out that most measures of intelligence tap a limited range of abilities, which he identifies as logical-mathematical. Since these measures are also good at predicting success at school, they continue to be used. But what about problems that don't call for logical-mathematical analysis? How do we find our way back to a parking lot in a new area of town, or recognize the composer of a piece of music? Do these tasks call upon intelligence? Do musicians, athletes, or surgeons have more of some talent in common than the rest of us? Gardner would answer Yes to both.

T A B L E   4 . 2

Gardner's Seven Forms of Intelligence and Corresponding Potential Professions

Form of Intelligence	Potential Professions
Musical	Musician Music teacher
Bodily-kinesthetic	Dancer Athlete
Logical-mathematical	Scientist Mathematician Teacher
Linguistic	Interpreter
Spatial	Artist Architect Landscape designer
Interpersonal (understanding others)	Psychologist Counselor
Intrapersonal (understanding the self)	Poet Writer

Source: H. Gardner. (1983). Frames of mind. New York: Basic Books.

Of course, one could list endless problems or talents and claim a separate intelligence for each one. Gardner uses several criteria to isolate legitimate intellectual domains. He points out that a domain must be universal to all humans and should show development with age. Each intelligence should be capable of being expressed in its own symbol system, for example, words for language, equations for mathematics, or notes for music (Walters & Gardner, 1986).

Evidence for separate intellectual domains also comes from child prodigies, idiot savants, and people who have suffered brain damage. In each case we can see an uneven profile of abilities. Prodigies such as Mozart or Yehudi Menuhin showed musical genius at an early age, yet remained quite ordinary in other domains. Cases have been reported of autistic children who could perform rapid mental calculations yet not be able to carry on a conversation or dress themselves. Similarly, people who have suffered brain trauma may have some areas of functioning spared (Gardner, 1983). Table 4.2 shows Gardner's seven forms of intelligence and corresponding potential professions.

Gardner anticipates objections to labeling these domains as intelligence. But he replies that nothing is sacred about the word "intelligence." His choice of the term over other equally suitable ones, in fact, is deliberate. It emphasizes his point that present measures of intelligence are limited because they place logical-mathematical and linguistic abilities "on a pedestal" above other abilities, such as musical and interpersonal ones. In doing so, our measures of intelligence reflect our culture's bias in favor of logical and verbal abilities over abilities such as kinesthetic or artistic ones. Gardner argues that to call one type of ability "intelligence" and another "talent" reflects this bias. He challenges us to consider them all "talents" or to consider them all "intelligences" (Gardner, 1983).

Practical Intelligence

Gardner is not alone in viewing present measures of intelligence as overly narrow and related more to academic than real-life experiences. Some psychologists speak of a *practical intelligence*, which they distinguish from the academic intelligence tapped by intelligence tests. Neisser (1976) defines this type of intelligence as "responding appropriately in terms of one's long-range and short-range goals, given the actual facts of the situation as one discovers them" (p. 137). He points out that the problems one must solve on tests that tap academic intelligence share a number of features: They are designed by someone else, are usually not very interesting, and have nothing to do with daily experience. Also, most test problems are well defined; they have a single answer and only one way of arriving at it (Wagner & Sternberg, 1986). In contrast, practical intelligence applies when one must discover the problem, instead of having it defined by someone else. Another difference is that finding the solution is frequently pleasurable. Finally, usually a number of approaches will work, each leading to a slightly different solution.

How much has our view of intelligence been influenced by the tests we use to measure it? Probably too much. Even though these tests can predict academic success, they often have little or no connection to other areas of life. Nothing illustrates this last point better than adolescents themselves, who may reach a pinnacle of intellectual achievement as measured by tests of intelligence, only to be pulled up short by the simplest of life's situations. Despite arriving at the cutting edge of thought, adolescents frequently nick themselves in the process.

THOUGHT AND THE ADOLESCENT

Pseudostupidity

Many of the intellectual advances of early adolescent thought have their down side. The ability to hold a problem in mind and consider it from all possible perspectives occasionally leads teenagers to make things more complicated than they actually are. David Elkind (1978), a psychologist who writes extensively on thinking in childhood and adolescence, suggests that frequently teenagers fail to see the obvious not because the task is too hard for them, but because they have made a simple task more complicated than it actually is. He refers to this tendency as

pseudostupidity. While a teenager is mentally ticking off all the oddball but none-theless possible alternatives, someone else usually comes up with the obvious. Teen-agers can feel stupid, asking themselves, "Why didn't I think of that?"

Early adolescents also frequently read complex motives into situations where none exist. A simple request such as, "Would you hand me the paper on your way out?" can be viewed with skeptical eyes. The teenager may wonder, "Is this just another attempt to control?" To avoid being controlled, the adolescent may con-sider refusing, but may also suspect that the need to refuse is merely another re-sponse to control. Neither able to comply nor to refuse, the teenager shoots back an angry remark to the effect that the news isn't worth the ink it takes to print it and storms out, leaving the parent to wonder what would have been done with something as loaded as "How was your day?"

An Imaginary Audience

One of the hallmarks of adolescent thought is the ability to think in the abstract, and nothing is more abstract than thought itself. Adolescents can think about thinking, not only their own thoughts but those of others. This ability can bring its own problems. Elkind (1967; 1985) assumes that this ability underlies a new form of egocentrism in adolescence. Early adolescents frequently lose perspective as to what concerns them and what concerns others. Since so many of their con-cerns focus on themselves, they can have the feeling that others, too, are thinking about them. Elkind refers to this loss of perspective as the **imaginary audience**. Adolescents can have the feeling that every eye is on them and every thought is about them. The imaginary audience may explain adolescents' exaggerated feelings of self-consciousness, as well as their intense need for privacy.

Very few of us command the type of attention that adolescents feel they capture. Those who do are special; they are political figures, athletes, entertainment personalities, or in some other way notable. The imaginary audience gives adoles-cents this same feeling of specialness. Elkind (1978) calls this feeling the **personal fable**. It is a belief that we are different and special, and that what happens to others won't happen to us. Elkind reminds us that this story we tell ourselves isn't true.

The personal fable can have some very personal consequences for adolescents. One is a confusion over what they have in common with others and what is gen-uinely unique to themselves. Confusions such as this lead to the belief that no one else can understand your feelings, because you are the only one to have ever felt this way. It's not unusual, for example, for early adolescents to tell their parents that they couldn't possibly understand how it feels to be in love!

Another consequence is a mistaken assumption that everyone else shares their concerns. Jim may feel that his nose is too big for the rest of his face and not want to go anywhere because he's afraid he'll be kidded about it. In fact, no one else notices his nose or particularly cares what size it is. Convincing him of this, how-ever, may be next to impossible. Adolescents caught in this form of the personal

Adolescents assume that everyone is as preoccupied with them as they are with themselves. This self-focused perception often leads to extreme self-consciousness and an intense need for privacy as well as a feeling of being unique and special.

fable are not dissuaded by reasoning. Elkind suggests agreeing with them. If one were to agree with Jim that his nose was too big, he might end up defending himself.

Elkind (1978) suggests that the personal fable explains many of the tragic cases of adolescents who appear to be self-destructive. Their behavior may not be motivated as much by a desire to destroy themselves as by their belief that what they see happening to others won't happen to them; that because they are unique, they are invulnerable to the events that touch others' lives.

The capacity of adolescents to catch glimpses of themselves in the eyes of others may be important to gaining a sense of themselves. Erikson (1968) speaks of identity formation as a process by which adolescents come to see themselves as individuals and at the same time as members of a social group. Even while assessing their individual worth, adolescents use the standards and norms shared by members of their social group. How they see themselves will reflect the way they measure up in the eyes of others. The ability of adolescents to examine their thoughts and to imagine the thoughts of others underlies a new awareness of their own separateness from others and of what they have in common with others through shared values and behaviors.

New Emotions

How one feels depends on the interpretations one gives to experience. "Did that person just brush me off, or simply fail to notice that I was going to say something?" Depending on which interpretation one gives, the encounter can occasion either feelings of irritation or no feelings in particular. Intellectual development in adolescence makes it possible for teenagers to react emotionally in new ways. Children focus on the immediate elements of the situation: To a compliment they react with pleasure; to a present, with happiness. Adolescents do all this and more.

Adolescents can consider what a situation might mean as well as the way it appears. By being able to turn something around in their minds, they can assign more than the obvious meaning to social encounters. Adolescents do not always complicate life in this way, but they do so more than children and also more than most adults. A compliment can be the occasion for anger if seen as an attempt to win a favor. Or a present can cause depression if seen as an emotional bribe. Adolescents also experience emotions that are relatively foreign to children; they get high on themselves, moody, depressed, or elated (Hirsch, Paolitto, & Reimer, 1979). Unlike children, adolescents relate their feelings to their experience of themselves as well as to the events that may prompt the feelings, adding an extra level of magnification to their view of the world.

Arguing

The ability of adolescents to consider the possibilities in any situation affects more than their emotions. An immediate consequence is that adolescents can argue better than children can. Carrying out an argument, whether in a debating class at school or with a parent in the kitchen, rests on the ability to test one thought against another. Adolescents are not limited, as are children, to testing their thoughts against facts; they can test them against other thoughts. (Remember the experiment with the green and white poker chips?) This new ability makes it possible for adolescents to argue for or against an idea regardless of whether they actually believe in it. The test of the argument is whether it has an inner logic. Children are limited to arguing either for things they believe in or against those they do not. The only test they can apply is to compare what they say with how things really are for them—how they feel, or what they believe.

Because of their literal approach, children cannot consider that a statement could mean something other than it says it does: It's simply taken at face value. A father's complaint, "If we had no dandelions, this would be a fine lawn" will bring a response of "But we have lots of dandelions, Dad," or "I like our lawn." Adolescents can consider statements about things that are contrary to the way they presently are or about things that don't exist. They can imagine a lawn that is free of dandelions, or even a lawn of *nothing but* dandelions. Perhaps this ability to

One evening during a dinnertime discussion, parents may suddenly realize that their adolescent's arguments are better constructed and more difficult to refute. His improved ability at argumentation may at times be frustrating, but it is also a sign that he is learning to manage his emotions.

divorce thought from fact, to think in ideals, even when these are counter to fact, provides the basis for the new ability of adolescents to plan and to gain new perspectives on themselves, their families, and their friends.

Doubt and Skepticism

Prior to formal thought, children believe that knowledge comes simply with exposure to the facts, never considering that "factual" information can be interpreted in more than one way. As a consequence, differences of opinion are treated as one person being wrong and the other one right. With formal thought, adolescents realize that what they have regarded as "truth" is simply one fix on reality, and that other equally compelling interpretations are possible. The result can be a profound skepticism in which they come to doubt the possibility of ever knowing anything in this "newly created world of wholesale uncertainty" (Boyes & Chandler, 1992).

T A B L E   4 . 3

Selman's Levels of Social Understanding

Number	Name	Age
0	*Egocentric Viewpoint*	Early childhood
1	*Social-Informational Level*	Ages 6 to 8
2	*Self-Reflective Level*	Ages 8 to 10
3	*Mutual Level*	Ages 10 to 12
4	*Social and Conventional System*	Ages 12 to 15 and older

Source: R. L. Selman. (1980). The growth of interpersonal understanding. *New York: Academic Press.*

Understanding Others

Adolescents gradually become better able to understand others as they become able to consider another person's perspective. Robert Selman (1976, 1980), outlines several levels in the development of **social understanding** (see Table 4.3), reflecting differences in one's ability to infer the views of another and to coordinate that view with one's own (Small, 1990). At the highest level, level 4, one can infer how another might be thinking *and* anticipate how that person will react to one's reactions to them. An adolescent, for example, might get angry with her friend upon hearing that the friend used cocaine after swearing he'd stay off it, but may keep her anger to herself, guessing that her friend is also afraid and angry with himself and will not confide in her in the future if she loses her temper. Compare that type of understanding with that of a young child at the first of these levels, level 0, who would unthinkingly assume that others feel and think as she does.

Considering the perspective of another person reflects more general role-taking abilities. Selman speaks of these as understanding "the self and others as subjects, . . . [reacting] to others as like the self, and . . . to the self's behavior from the other's point of view" (Selman & Byrne, 1974, p. 803). Prior to being able to consider another's perspective, young children do not realize that others' thoughts and feelings are different from their own. Nor do they understand the relationship between a person's actions and that person's feelings. Selman calls the lack of perspective that characterizes early childhood an *egocentric viewpoint* (level 0).

As thought becomes more flexible (from age 6 to 8, with the beginning of concrete operational thought), older children realize that another person might view a situation differently than they do, but they cannot imagine that the other person could understand how they feel. Children at this level assume that they would have to tell the other person how they feel for the other to know. At this level, they can observe themselves or the other, but are not aware that the other can also observe them. Selman calls this initial awareness the *social-informational* level, level 1.

KEY TERMS

Sensorimotor Thought
Object Permanence
Schemes
Assimilation
Accommodation
Preoperational Thought
Centration
Conservation
Reversibility
Egocentrism

Concrete Operational
   Thought
Mental Operations
Formal Operational Thought
Intelligence
WAIS-R
Crystallized Intelligence
Fluid Intelligence
Sensory Memory
Short-Term Memory

Long-Term Memory
Rehearsal
Encoding
Metamemory
Pseudostupidity
Imaginary Audience
Personal Fable
Social Understanding
Inductive Reasoning
Deductive Reasoning

CHANGING RELATIONSHIPS
WITH PARENTS
Turmoil and Change
Calm and Continuity
Change and Continuity

■ RESEARCH FOCUS   *Internal and*
External Validity: Family Fights

PARENTS AND ADOLESCENTS
Styles of Parenting

■ RESEARCH FOCUS   *Direct*
Observations: Parenting Styles—Like
Father, Like Son?

Whose Identity Crisis? Parents and
   Middle Age
Adolescents' Identity Crisis: Gaining a
   Sense of Self

AUTONOMY AND
INDIVIDUATION
Autonomy
Individuation: The Developmental
   Process
Family Interaction and Adolescents'
   Individuation
The Family Paradigm
Families and Ethnicity
Siblings

FAMILIES IN TRANSITION
Changing Family Structures
Changing Work Roles: Dual-Earner
   Families

SUMMARY

KEY TERMS

CHAPTER FIVE

Adolescents in the Family

TANYA: *"Why don't we visit Grandma and then go someplace exotic like the Everglades?"*

WILLIE: *"Do you know how hot it is in Florida in August? I vote to skip the family visit this year and go to Acapulco. That's a real vacation."*

DAD: *"I could sure use some time on a beach."*

WILLIE: *"Right, Dad, but you don't want to share it with a crocodile, do you?"*

TANYA: *"They're alligators, not crocodiles, Surfer Joe."*

MOM: *"I'd like to see the pyramids in Mexico. We could stop off at Acapulco on the way."*

TANYA: *"Hmm."*

DAD: *"How far inland are they?"*

MOM: *"I don't know, but I could call a travel agent."*

WILLIE: *"Get real, Mom. Do you think you can get us to sweat a path through the jungle once we've seen the sands of Acapulco?"*

TANYA: *"Willie'd die in the heat there, too."*

DAD: *"Maybe we should think of a winter vacation."*

TANYA: *"All right, let's vote on this."*

WILLIE: *"Okay, let's vote."*

It would be great if we all had the choices open to this family—sandy beaches, the Everglades, Acapulco, the pyramids of Mexico. In a sense we do. You see, this family is participating in a research project in which they have been asked to make plans for an imaginary 2-week vacation, the cost of which is no problem. The researchers aren't interested in where the family finally decides to go; Grandma might still get lucky. They are studying how members of families interact with each other, and how these relationships affect adolescent development (Grotevant & Cooper, 1986). We will, too, as we consider adolescents and their families in this chapter.

Does adolescence necessarily bring turmoil to families? Is conflict unavoidable? What does current research tell us? The first section of this chapter evaluates recent findings on adolescent-parent relationships.

We will look at parenting styles before focusing on parents and then on adolescents. Adolescents gain a sense of themselves as they discover which aspects of

209

their behavior reflect their own and which reflect their parents' ways and attitudes. Resolving these issues is easier in some families than in others. Which dimensions of family interaction facilitate psychological growth? Do these patterns differ with ethnicity? A section on individuation in the family provides tentative answers. Communication becomes especially important during times of change, and some ways of communicating are much more effective than others.

The structure of families has changed dramatically in a single generation. Increasing numbers of adolescents experience divorce, live with a single parent, or have a stepparent join the family unit. Family relationships can be problematic even at their best; some require more coping skills than others. We discuss the changing conditions of family life, and the ways adolescents and their families cope with them.

Yet another change involves maternal employment. Most adolescents have mothers who work outside the home. What effect, if any, does maternal employment have on adolescents and their families? A review of recent research offers some insights.

CHANGING RELATIONSHIPS WITH PARENTS

Laurence Steinberg, at Temple University, notes that the adolescent's family has become the focus of intense research following a period of mysterious neglect. He suggests that developmentalists stopped studying the family because they could not make sense of what they saw. You might wonder what observations could be so perplexing that investigators would need to re-focus their approach. Actually, it was what developmentalists did *not* see that caused the confusion: They did not see a period of "storm and stress" within the family once children reached adolescence. Most expected to, and maintained that emotional turmoil is inevitable, even desirable (Steinberg, 1987b).

Turmoil and Change

Is turmoil necessary for healthy development? Does adolescence so disrupt one's sense of self and one's relationship to the rest of the world that emotional tumult, mood swings, and unpredictable behavior inevitably result? Psychoanalytically inclined developmentalists answer yes. They maintain that adolescents must separate from their parents in order to develop as their own persons, and that this separation is inevitably conflictual. These developmentalists believe that adolescence involves such a momentous upheaval that it is impossible to maintain one's emotional balance. Adolescents who do not experience turmoil are viewed with concern, in the belief that they are failing to take the steps necessary to develop as healthy individ-

Are disagreements between adolescents and their parents an inevitable part of growing up? Research says they are, but also that most adolescents and parents stay close in spite of conflict.

uals. Anna Freud (1969) felt so convinced that emotional turbulence was a natural consequence of adolescence that she considered it abnormal for adolescents to maintain their emotional balance.

Is turmoil inevitable? According to psychoanalytic theorists, it is. Sigmund Freud believed that dramatic increases in hormones during adolescence reactivate earlier incestuous feelings (see Chapter 2). He felt that the only way adolescents can defend against these repressed Oedipal impulses is to distance themselves from their parents. This distancing creates the emotional separation necessary for further psychological growth (Blos, 1967, 1979; S. Freud, 1954).

The psychoanalytic view has received considerable support from clinical psychologists who work with troubled adolescents, and also from those working with adult patients who, during the course of therapy, refer to problems they experienced as adolescents (Blos, 1967, 1979; A. Freud, 1969). Very little research was done with normal adolescents until the 1960s. Most developmentalists simply assumed that they could generalize clinical data to a normal population—that all adolescents experienced emotional turmoil. Theoretical support for such assumptions was strong, since prevailing theory maintained that adolescence was a time of intense conflict. Why *not* study troubled adolescents for insights into this time of life?

Calm and Continuity

Surveys of normal adolescents give us a different picture of adolescents' relationships with their parents. These studies point to continuing, close relationships (Douvan & Adelson, 1966; Kandel & Lesser, 1969; Offer, 1969; Offer, Ostrov, & Howard, 1981). Even though conflicts become more frequent in adolescence, they do not prevent adolescents and parents from remaining close. Adolescents who are the most autonomous are also most likely to say that their parents remain an important influence in their lives, and that they continue to seek their advice (Fuligni & Eccles, 1993).

Daniel Offer and his associates found little evidence of emotional turmoil in the adolescents they studied, or of conflict in their relationships with their parents. Most adolescents described themselves positively, as happy and self-confident. The majority did not feel that there were any major problems between themselves and their parents. They reported feeling close to their parents and believed their parents were proud of them. These investigators point out that adolescents' positive feelings toward their parents appear to be extensions of similarly positive feelings as children. Summarizing their findings concerning adolescents and their parents, they state that their "most impressive findings . . . are that eighteen out of nineteen items strongly indicate that the adolescents have positive feelings toward their families" (Offer, Ostrov, & Howard, 1981).

Change and Continuity

Can both of these characterizations of parent-adolescent relationships be true? Are some changes so significant that to deny them is to deny what adolescence is all about, and do most adolescents remain close to their parents while going through these changes? Recent research answers yes. Relationships with parents remain important in adolescence, *and* these relationships are renegotiated (Baumrind, 1991a). Both change *and* continuity characterize adolescents' relationships with their parents. Relationships between parents and younger children are relatively one-sided in their distribution of power and responsibility, even in families where parents involve the children in family decisions. Several conditions cause adolescents to press for change in this family arena.

One condition is adolescents' new awareness of themselves. The ability to think abstractly contributes to this awareness (see Chapter 4). Teenagers can imagine how someone else might see their interactions with others. They can get a feeling for how their actions and intentions are seen not only by the person they are with, but by others in general. This ability sharpens their sense of themselves as separate from others. They begin to appreciate the many ways they are different, even though they do the same things, share the same tastes, and have similar preferences as their friends.

The very same ability that allows teenagers to see themselves through the eyes of others also allows them to see themselves with their parents in a new light (Eisert & Kahle, 1986). They see how their relationships with their parents differ from the ones they have with their friends (Eccles, Buchanan, Midgley, Fuligni, & Flanagan, 1991). The latter are egalitarian and mutual; friends arrive at decisions jointly. James Youniss (1980) suggests that adolescents become conscious that they live in two very different social worlds; one with friends, in which they participate on an equal footing, share in decision making, and negotiate differences; the other with parents, in which they have little power, make few decisions, and conform to parental expectations. Adolescents face the need to achieve a single sense of themselves that holds across *all* the social situations they enter; as a first step, they press for fuller participation in relationships within the family. As adolescents move toward a more equal relationship with their parents, communication can become difficult. Box 5.1 offers suggestions for improving family communications.

Perhaps at no time are their changing roles more evident than when parents and adolescents discuss their perceptions of family conflicts. Judith Smetana and Rusti Berent, at the University of Rochester, asked seventh-, ninth-, and eleventh-grade adolescents and their mothers to respond to vignettes describing typical conflicts that occur at home, such as those involving household chores, keeping one's room clean, or personal appearance. Each conflict was presented both from the parent's perspective and the adolescent's, by giving justifications each might use in appealing to the other (see Table 5.1).

BOX 5.1

Strategies for Better Family Communication

Central to any effective communication is one's acceptance of the other person. Frequently, there isn't any need to offer help or give advice; all that's needed is simply to listen. Parents' comments are usually motivated by good intentions: they only want to help their children learn new skills ("Here's how you should do that") or to prevent them from making unnecessary mistakes ("Watch out for that car in the intersection"). However, such comments communicate nonacceptance, letting the adolescent know that the parent's way is better. Active listening offers an alternative.

Listening to Adolescents: Active Listening

Active listening is a way of drawing people out and helping them explore their feelings by feeding their message back to them. In the process, you find out if you have understood what they said. Consider the following example:

Allen: Do I have to get up? [He has just been told it's nearly time to leave for a baseball game.]

Father: You don't feel like playing baseball today?

Allen: I'll miss messing around with my friends.

Father: You'd rather mess around with your friends than play baseball?

Allen: Yes. We have fun together.

Father: It's not fun to play baseball?

Allen: No. Sometimes the other guys razz me when I don't get a hit.

Father: You don't like being teased?

Allen: It makes me feel like I'm not a very good player.

Father: You'd like to be good at baseball?

Allen: Yes, I felt terrific that day I got that base hit.

Father: Would you like to practice before the game?

Allen: Hey, Dad, that'd be great. I'll get dressed.

Notice how this boy is able to discover how he really feels when his father actively listens. Notice, too, that the father does not offer a solution, give advice, or do anything other than feed back what his son is saying.

An essential ingredient to active listening is communicating acceptance to the other person. The paradox in accepting people as they are is that as they feel accepted, they are free to change. Many parents, and adolescents for that matter, communicate nonacceptance, believing that if you want someone to change, you must let the other person know

(continued)

BOX 5.1 (*continued*)

Strategies for Better Family Communication

what needs improvement. Telling adolescents, or parents, that they need to improve communicates that they are not all right the way they are. This communication puts the person on the defensive—and closes off the conversation.

Active listening takes time. Each must be willing to let the other feel his or her way through a problem. If you don't have the time, it is important to say so and arrange some other time to talk. Parents must also genuinely want to let the adolescent find a solution to the problem, and not use active listening merely as a way to get her or him to do what they think should be done. They must accept the problem as the adolescent presents it and accept the adolescent's feelings about it. Parroting back words without reflecting feelings is not active listening. You need to feed back all of the message, and feelings are an important part of it.

Talking to Adolescents: You-Messages and I-Messages

Let's turn the situation around and look at how parents can talk so that adolescents will listen to them. The simplest approach would be to let adolescents know how they feel, but parents rarely do that. Instead, they are likely to tell adolescents what to do ("Pick up your clothes"), warn them what will happen if they don't ("If I have to tell you one more time, you've lost your clothes allowance"), moralize ("You should contribute your share of the work around the house"), or make a suggestion ("Why don't you put your clothes in the hamper when you take them off?"). Each of these approaches is usually met with resistance. After all, who likes being told what to do, warned, or made to feel wrong?

The parental comments in the preceding paragraph are examples of **you-messages**. They communicate that parents do not expect adolescents to be helpful unless they are told to be. And by offering a solution without letting adolescents help in defining the problem, such remarks subtly communicate that parents don't think adolescents can help or are willing to find a solution.

An **I-message** tells the adolescent how his or her actions make others feel. Adolescents can hear such messages as a fact about the parent, not as an evaluation of themselves, and thus they have little need to be defensive. A parent who says "I can't hear what she's saying to me when you interrupt" communicates a different message than one who says "It's rude of you to interrupt." I-messages let adolescents know how their behavior affects others. These messages also communicate to adolescents that parents trust them to find a solution, and put the responsibility for change with the recipient. Because I-messages do not accuse, suggest, or warn, they are easier for adolescents to hear.

Source: Adapted from T. Gordon. (1972). Parent effectiveness training. New York: New American Library.

T A B L E   5 . 1

*Differences in Parents' and Adolescents' Attempts
to Resolve Conflict*

The examples below are responses to a typical conflict:
Mother wants Anne to wear something else, but Anne doesn't want to.

	Type of Justification	Example
Parent	Conventional	Reference to behavior standards, arbitrarily arrived at by family members, e.g., "I'd be embarrassed if any of my friends saw you looking like that."
	Pragmatic	Consideration of practical needs or consequences, e.g., "You'll catch a cold."
	Authoritarian	Reference to authority and punishment, e.g., "I'm your parent, and I say you can't dress like that."
Adolescent	Conventional	Reference to standards of behavior shared with peers, e.g. "My friends would think I'm weird."
	Pragmatic	Consideration of practical needs or consequences, e.g. "I'm comfortable in these clothes."
	Personal	Portraying the issue as one of maintaining personal jurisdiction in an area, e.g. "The way I dress is an expression of me and my personality."

*Source: J. G. Smetana & R. Berent. (1993). Adolescents' and mothers' evaluations of justifications for
disputes.* Journal of Adolescent Research, 8, 252–273.

Perhaps not surprisingly, given their responsibility for maintaining family ways, mothers considered conventional justifications to be more adequate in resolving conflict than did adolescents. Adolescents, on the other hand, saw this type of reasoning as a source of conflict. This was especially true of mid-adolescent 9th graders, for whom family conflict is likely to have reached a peak as gains in autonomy are won by questioning parental authority.

Mothers also considered appeals to authority and threats of punishment to be more effective in getting adolescents to comply with their wishes than did adolescents, a difference that increased with the adolescents' age. Adolescents, on the other hand, appealed to practical considerations, perhaps because such arguments are less likely to be challenged by parents. Smetana has found that, although adolescents may believe their position can be justified by appeals to personal jurisdiction ("It's my room and I can keep it as I like"), they will use pragmatic reasons ("It doesn't matter if it's messy; I can find whatever I need") when arguing with a

RESEARCH FOCUS

Internal and External Validity: Family Fights

How much do adolescents fight with their parents? John Hill and Grayson Holmbeck (1987) asked parents and their seventh-grade teenagers to fill out a questionnaire concerning family disagreements. They found fewer disagreements than they had expected given that seventh graders are entering mid-adolescence, a time when conflict between parents and adolescents frequently peaks. They wondered why this was.

These investigators had gone to the homes of families from whom they collected data and waited while parents and adolescents filled out the questionnaires. They did this to make sure that everyone returned the questionnaire. Everyone did. But adolescents and parents may have been less willing to admit to conflict under such conditions than if they had filled the questionnaires out in private. In short, there was more than one possible explanation for the findings. When research fails to provide an unambiguous answer to the question it was designed to address, we say that it lacks *internal validity*.

A second type of validity is *external validity*. Does the answer we get apply only to the people we have observed, or can we generalize the findings to others? Just how representative are the findings? We can look at another study of parent-adolescent interactions to see the importance of this second type of validity. Raymond Montemayor and John Brownlee (1987) found that as they move into middle adolescence, young people spend less time with their fathers but about the same amount of time with their mothers as they did in early adolescence. This is an interesting finding, but it may not hold for all families. Over two-thirds of the families in this study were members of the Mormon Church, and all were white and middle class. Though the results of the study are likely to be accurate for white, middle-class, church-going families, we cannot say whether they hold for families in general. In fairness to these investigators, much research fails to establish representative samples.

External validity can also be affected by the very conditions that are necessary to achieve internal validity. Consider a hypothetical experiment in which adolescents and their parents are brought to a laboratory to study the effects of stress on adolescent-parent conflicts. As they arrive at the laboratory, families are assigned at random to either of two groups to distribute differences among them evenly across two conditions: Families in one group will be made to experience stress in some way, while those in the other group will not be. Investigators will observe the interactions of family members in each group.

Let's say we see no difference in the frequency or severity of conflict among stressed and nonstressed families. Is it safe to conclude that stress is unrelated to the frequency of conflict? Isn't it just as likely that all families could be restrained in their interactions, knowing they are being observed? Even though laboratory research affords investigators more control over conditions that could influence their observations, it also may yield data that are unrepresentative of the way people would normally react. In this case, the best place to make observations would probably be in the family car going home!

References: J. P. Hill & G. N. Holmbeck. (1987). *Disagreements about rules in families with seventh-grade girls and boys.* Journal of Youth and Adolescence, 16, 221–246. R. Montemayor & J. R. Brownlee. (1987). *Fathers, mothers, and adolescents: Gender-based differences in parental roles during adolescence.* Journal of Youth and Adolescence, 16, 281–291.

parent. Parents are not as likely as adolescents to view the behaviors in question as rightfully within the adolescent's purview (Smetana, Braeges, & Yau, 1991).

Adolescent appeals to social convention in resolving family conflict are likely to generate more conflict than they settle, usually because the conventions referred to are those of their peers, perhaps already a sore point for many parents.

Parents themselves initiate some of the changes that take place in their relationships with their adolescent children. They expect adolescents to be more assertive and independent than when they were younger. They think teenagers should get around more on their own, whether going to the library or to a part-time job, and have ideas of their own, from what to wear to how to study for a test. Even so, many parents react with ambivalence to adolescents' bids for independence. For some adults, the sense of themselves is strongly tied to their parenting roles, and to include adolescents in more family decisions, they must redefine those roles.

PARENTS AND ADOLESCENTS

People learn to parent not from reading books or taking courses, though both can be helpful, but from the way *they* were parented. As such, we should find the characteristics of parents to be related to those of their children.

Styles of Parenting

Diana Baumrind (1971, 1975a), at the University of California, Berkeley, identified three styles of parent interaction with their children (see Table 5.2). **Authoritarian parenting** stresses obedience, respect for authority, and traditional values, and engages in little give and take with the children. **Authoritative parenting** stresses self-reliance and independence, and maintains an open dialogue with the children, giving reasons for discipline. Authoritative parents value independence in their children, yet are willing to assert their own authority, and do so by consistently enforcing their standards. **Permissive parenting** (also called *laissez-faire* parenting) is accepting, uses little punishment, makes few demands for responsibility, and exercises little control or power.

Both authoritarian and authoritative parents provide strong models, but in different ways. Authoritarian parents attempt to control their children, authoritative ones to guide them. In line with this difference, the latter place greater value on autonomy and self-discipline and the former on obedience and respect for authority. Both types of parents define limits and set standards. Authoritative parents, however, are more willing to listen to reasons and arguments, tending to draw the line around issues rather than set absolute standards.

TABLE 5.2

Parenting Style and Social Competence

Parenting Style	Characteristics	Adolescent Social Behavior
Authoritarian	Punitive, restrictive, controlling	Ineffective social interaction; inactive
Authoritative	Encourages independence; warm and nurturing; control with explanation; adolescent expresses views	Social competence and responsibility
Permissive (*laissez-faire*)	Lack of involvement; nonpunitive; few demands; adolescent has a lot of freedom	Immature; poor self-restraint; poor leadership

Source: Adapted from D. Baumrind. (1971). Current patterns of parental authority. Developmental Psychology Monographs, 4, 1.

Authoritative parents, in contrast to authoritarian and permissive ones, try to balance tradition with innovation, cooperation with autonomy, and tolerance with firmness. The children of such parents tend to be socially competent and responsible.

Baumrind considers authoritative parenting to be superior to the other types. She stresses, however, that this type of parenting is not simple, nor is it stress-free. In fact, parenting authoritatively seems to be distinguished by the presence of tensions produced by the need to balance opposing forces: tradition with individualistic innovation, cooperation with autonomous behavior, and tolerance with principled firmness.

At times it may seem easiest to simply appeal to authority or threaten punishment, both characteristic of authoritarian parenting. Smetana and Berent (1993) found that, although each of these alternatives has the short-term payoff of being effective in achieving compliance, adolescents and parents alike see them as having the potential for causing conflict, especially with older adolescents. William Cook (1993), at the University of Texas at Austin, characterizes this conflict as a downward spiral in which coercive attempts to get adolescents to behave in desired ways result in greater negativity among adolescents, causing parents to feel even less in control of the situation than before.

As a group, children of authoritative parents are more competent and independent, and are less likely to be rebellious, than those of other parents (Baumrind, 1991b). Their parents have stressed self-reliance and have paved the way for independence by involving their children in decision making from early childhood on. Interestingly, the conditions that lead to rebelliousness in adolescence, or childhood, are not necessarily rigorous demands, but arbitrary ones. Parental strictness per se does not appear to be the issue; rather it is the willingness, or lack thereof, to give adolescents a voice in decision making (Fuligni & Eccles, 1993). Andrew Fuligni and Jacquelynne Eccles, at the University of Michigan, found that early adolescents who perceive their parents as unwilling to relax their control or allow them to participate in decisions often turn to friends for support and advice, even when maintaining such relationships involved some personal cost. Parents encounter rebelliousness, it seems, when they fail to leave room for autonomy, do not give reasons for their actions, or are inconsistent in their punishment. Inconsistency can also take the form of different parenting styles from each parent, as when one parent is authoritative and the other permissive. This type of inconsistency is associated with lower self-esteem and lower school achievement in adolescents (Johnson, Shulman, & Collins, 1991).

Parenting styles vary little with the gender of adolescents, but they do change with their age. In a study of nearly 8,000 high school students, Dornbusch, Ritter, Leiderman, Roberts, and Fraleigh (1987) found that authoritarian parenting decreases as adolescents get older; similarly, permissiveness increases. Interestingly, authoritative parenting does not vary with adolescent age. The reason, Dornbusch and his associates suggest, is that authoritative parenting reflects an ideological commitment on the part of parents and is not a simple response to what adolescents do.

Parenting styles also differ somewhat with ethnicity. Asian, black, and Hispanic families are somewhat more authoritarian and less authoritative than white.

RESEARCH FOCUS

Direct Observations: Parenting Styles—Like Father, Like Son?

If an adolescent cut class to comfort an upset friend, which of the following should a parent do?

- Refuse to listen to any excuses and dock the adolescent's allowance for cutting school.
- Talk with the adolescent about the friend and then work out an agreement in which he or she speaks with the teacher and makes up missed work.
- Shrug your shoulders and say, "Kids will be kids!"
- Probably not want to hear about it.

The alternative a parent selects is likely to reflect his or her parenting style. How do parenting styles differ? Is one better than another?

Diana Baumrind did not rely on paper-and-pencil measures like the example above to assess styles of parenting and their effects. She trained assistants to observe parents and adolescents in structured family interactions. The families were videotaped and later coded according to dimensions believed to have developmental significance.

These dimensions suggest important behaviors that differentiate styles of parenting. *Responsiveness* reflects sensitivity, support, and a willingness to be engaged. *Demandingness* refers to maturity demands, amount of supervision, and willingness to confront adolescents when necessary. Together these provide the connectedness and individuality important for personality development. High to low scores for each of these dimensions distinguish different styles of parenting with children (see the figure).

Direct observation, as the term suggests, involves directly observing behavior as it unfolds in a situation, classifying and coding it. *Coding* systems allow researchers to categorize behaviors. Instead of everything parents do, for instance, only specific behaviors are recorded. This approach makes it easier to detect relationships. The behaviors to be coded are arrived at beforehand. Frequently, observers work from a checklist. As each type of behavior occurs, they simply note its occurrence. Soon patterns emerge showing the frequency of different types of behavior in different settings or with different people.

Observing behavior directly has a number of advantages. All the potential biases inherent in the use of surveys—selective memory, intentional distortions, the influence of social desirability, and so on are eliminated. When observations are carried out in a natural setting, such as in Baumrind's research, an additional advantage is the increased *external validity* of the research, or the likelihood that the behavior being observed is representative of the way people actually behave in that setting. The use of a coding system increases the *reliability* of the observations, or the degree to which the two observers working independently of each other agree in their observations. Data analysis is also easier.

Are there any disadvantages? Direct observation is time-intensive; observers must be trained to identify behaviors accurately, and this takes time. The actual data collection also takes more time in a natural setting than in the laboratory. In a sense, one stands in a stream of behavior with a net, ready to catch (record) certain specimens of interest—but there is no way to speed up the rate at which the behaviors flow by.

Is one style of parenting better than another? Are some actually harmful? Authoritative parents consistently have adolescents who are personally competent and maintain close relationships with their parents. Democratic parenting is nearly as consistently effective. Both these styles are highly responsive and highly to moderately demanding, dimensions that contribute to connectedness and individuality. Adolescents with authoritarian parents are also competent, but are more conforming. Baumrind notes that "good-enough" parents, while adequate for sons, may not be good enough for most daughters; low self-esteem and alienation were frequently observed. Finally, unengaged parents have adolescents with frequent problems.

References: D. Baumrind. (1991a). The influence of parenting style on adolescent competence and substance use. Journal of Early Adolescence, 11, 56–95.

With respect to permissiveness, blacks are less permissive than whites, and Asians and Hispanics more so (Dornbusch et al., 1987).

Parenting styles are related to academic achievement in adolescents. Students with authoritative parents get better grades than those with authoritarian or permissive ones. This is especially true for Hispanic girls, who usually do significantly better than their male peers, except when reared in authoritarian homes (Dornbusch et al., 1987). Steinberg (1989) found that each of the components of authoritative parenting—parental acceptance, psychological autonomy, and firmness—contributed to academic achievement.

In general, parents who are responsive, consistent, willing to listen, and willing to give adolescents a voice in decision making will have healthy relationships with their adolescents. All this may sound good in theory; however, many parents may be at a point in their own lives in which responsiveness, consistency, and a willingness to listen—let alone sharing responsibility—are especially difficult, if not outright problematic. They, too, are facing a crisis—that of middle age.

Whose Identity Crisis? Parents and Middle Age

Middle-aged parents face the downward side of the developmental curves their adolescent children are climbing. Each of the developmental tasks facing adolescents comes up for review again in the middle years. Table 1.1 lists these tasks, along with those of middle age.

Just as puberty marks the beginning of adolescence, physical changes alert parents that they are entering middle age, and many find these changes difficult to accept. Perhaps the first sign of aging for most adults appears when they step on the bathroom scales. Middle age brings an increase in body weight and a change in its distribution. The face becomes thinner, as do legs and arms. But what is lost in the extremities is gained through the middle (Stevens-Long, 1992). Bob Hope once quipped that "Middle age is when your age begins to show around your middle." Changes such as these are difficult at any age, but the kicker for most parents is the timing: Most adults begin to experience these changes just when their adolescent children are developing beautiful bodies and fantastic physiques.

How might these and other physical changes affect the willingness of parents to listen to or share responsibility for decision making with adolescents? An everyday example such as buying clothes provides some insights. While bathing suits are merely "swimwear" to parents of preteens, to parents of adolescents they can raise issues of sexuality, promiscuity, or just unfair competition. Adolescents' arguments that suits of the same style are worn by young children go unheard, if parents are alarmed by their adolescent's obvious physical maturity, or their own feelings of physical decline and undesirability.

Middle-aged parents face another assault on their egos. The functioning of the reproductive organs begin to decline, marking a period of life known as the **climacteric.** Women experience **menopause,** a cessation of menstrual periods, somewhere between ages 48 and 52. Unlike menarche, menopause is a gradual process that takes many months, and for some women, several years (Masters, Johnson, & Kolodny, 1988). The body also decreases its production of estrogens. As the level of circulating estrogen decreases, the genital tract is affected, sometimes impairing sexual function as a result (Stevens-Long, 1992).

The climacteric in men is not as noticeable as in women, though it does affect them as well. Middle-aged men are likely to experience a change in sexual functioning. Erections and orgasms take longer to achieve. For both sexes, there may be a slight diminishment of the intensity of orgasm (Masters, Johnson, & Kolodny, 1988).

Just when their children reach sexual maturity, middle-aged parents face a sexual identity crisis—or at least a serious inventory taking. Changes in sexual function can affect parents' sense of themselves as sexually desirable partners. For increasing numbers of middle-aged adults, these changes come at a time when they face the loss of a marriage partner through divorce and the doubts and anxieties raised by dating. Parents may view their adolescents' dates and romantic involvements with more concern—or perhaps vicarious pleasure—than they would if their own sexual functioning and prowess were not as salient a concern to them.

Similarly, just when adolescents begin to think about future careers, many middle-aged parents begin to review their own careers and question whether the jobs they have been pursuing all these years have been worth the effort they have put into them. Many adults may face the realization that they will never advance beyond their present position. This realization can be especially painful if they see opportunities for their children that offer more promise than the jobs they presently have. Listening to plans about the future can be difficult as they face hard facts about their own present realities.

Each of these areas of change is a source of stress in the lives of parents and adolescents. The fact that the changes experienced by one generation complement those experienced by the other so neatly almost guarantees that relationships will be more stressful.

Adolescents' Identity Crisis: Gaining a Sense of Self

Many adolescents mistakenly assume, as they begin to get a sense of themselves, that they are unique—completely different and separate from others. The mistake, actually, is in stopping there. They *are* unique, and this highlights their separateness. But uniqueness comes out of their most intimate relationships and can only be experienced fully when relating to others. Adolescents share commonalities with others that are as important as their differences—the need to feel good about themselves, to feel a sense of accomplishment, to be loved. Separate? Yes, but only when their sense of connectedness with others gives them the security to explore themselves.

Adolescents' search for the truth about themselves begins when the separate worlds in which they live begin to pull apart. Adolescents begin to see themselves as more than their parents' children, to question where the skills they are acquiring in school will take them, to ask who they will be living with in the future. Erik Erikson (1968) suggests that the search ultimately leads to a sense of "sameness and continuity" that allows adolescents to transcend the differences they experience in their many roles—full-time student, part-time employee, daughter, son, friend, neighbor, and so on.

Gaining a sense of themselves almost seems to require the tools of a magician, or an actor: mirrors, sleight of hand, impressive costumes. Adolescents frequently find themselves playing out roles that are just a bit too big for them or not quite right. They try on these roles because the comfortable ones of childhood no longer fit. Adolescents find themselves looking inward and outward all at once, one eye on the inner self and another on those around them. They are well aware others may be judging them in terms of the cultural images they both share, but also in terms of how well the others have achieved precisely what they themselves are attempting to do (Erikson, 1968).

AUTONOMY AND INDIVIDUATION

The drama of gaining a sense of themselves unfolds on a well-known stage: at home as adolescents interact with parents, pressing for greater autonomy. In winning new responsibilities, they discover strengths that are uniquely theirs and that distinguish them from their parents, a process known as individuation.

A messy room and a busy phone may be signs of a young adolescent moving toward autonomy rather than of innate sloppiness or irresponsibility.

Autonomy

One of the major issues confronting early adolescents is to become more autonomous. **Autonomy** involves independence and being responsible for one's actions. Adolescents press for greater inclusion in decisions; they ask to be treated as more adult. The number of decisions they make by themselves increases with age from early to late adolescence; decisions they share with parents or that are made by parents alone decrease with age. These trends are more pronounced for males than females (Dornbusch, Ritter, Mont-Reynaud, & Chen, 1990).

Bids for greater autonomy might be expected to occasion some conflict with parents, and they do. Most conflicts are over household routines, such as picking up after oneself, doing homework, and chores. And most of these involve mothers, since they are more immediately involved in maintaining the household than are fathers (Steinberg, 1987a, 1989). Parenting style, especially that of mothers, is particularly important for girls' autonomy. For boys, age is the single most important determinant of increasing independence (Bartle, Anderson, & Sabatelli, 1989).

Autonomy is a much larger issue for early adolescents than for older ones. Arehart and Smith (1990) found that concern with questions of autonomy accounted for nearly half of the variability among early adolescents' answers to a measure of psychosocial maturity. By the end of high school, autonomy issues have been resolved and new issues appear.

Parents can either facilitate or hinder the growth of autonomy (Pardeck & Pardeck, 1990). As adolescents vie for a say in and eventual control over the decisions that affect them, some conflict with parents may be inevitable (see Box 5.2). Not all parents react the same to these demands. Some are able to turn over increasing responsibility to their children; others, threatened by bids for greater autonomy, react negatively. The less conflict in the family, the greater the adolescent's movement toward psychosocial maturity (Gavazzi & Sabatelli, 1990). Not all of the difficulty comes from parents. Adolescents contribute to some of the conflict themselves. In order to achieve autonomy, adolescents must go through a psychic housecleaning known as individuation.

Individuation: The Developmental Process

Adolescents must undo one of their major accomplishments as children. They must disassemble and rebuild the psychological structure they have lived in through childhood. They do this by examining their feelings, attitudes, and beliefs, in order to discover which are really theirs and which are their parents'. Because children uncritically assume for themselves their parents' attitudes and ways, this examination process is a necessary step for early adolescents. It may be that the only way children can feel strong enough to step out on their own and explore the world for themselves is to carry some of their parents' strengths along with them. The

B O X   5 . 2

An Interview with Anne Petersen:
Adolescents and Their Parents

What Is Important for Parents of Adolescents To Know?

The societal view of adolescents is negative. I collect cartoons, and they portray an extreme view of adolescents as having hormone attacks, being difficult, impossible.

This belief in our country that adolescents are difficult and want to be independent is one of the biggest pitfalls for parents. We know that though adolescents want to be autonomous, they need parents. We know that young adolescents are argumentative, sometimes obnoxious. Parents throw in the towel, and that is the worst thing they can do. Adolescents need to know that parental support is there. There have been historical changes in the family, increasing the possibility for kids to be independent with cars and to have more time away from home; all these changes have exacerbated the trend toward independence and separation. Too much freedom is detrimental to adolescents' development.

Parents need to know that when you ask adolescents, especially young adolescents, who is more important to them, they say the parents, even if the parents are reporting conflict. We find, then, that parents are less positive about their adolescents than their adolescents are about them. Adolescents' off-putting behavior—telling parents to get lost because the adolescents are mature—is not really the message they want to send. They are asking for a little more space; they are asking for help in becoming autonomous and interdependent rather than independent.

Research shows that conflicts are about little things, not big things. The conflicts are not about values, but largely about doing dishes, taking out the garbage. They are a way of relieving tensions. Parents ought to be a safe source for venting tensions. If they cease to be a safe source, then young adolescents are really lost; they have no one.

Parents sometimes believe that they need to be their child's buddy, but that's not true. They need to be parents. They need to provide unconditional love, firm guidelines, and strong expectations.

Puberty, with all the change that accompanies it, is a difficult time for boys and girls, especially when they have to change schools. It seems to work slightly differently for boys and girls. In general, boys seem less influenced by what is going on with parents, but basic support is pretty important. If parental support is not there, it is very bad for girls. Those girls who have a lot of family conflict or lack support are the ones who become the most depressed.

very internalizations that promote autonomy in childhood are the ones that adolescents must get beyond in order to grow, and this process is termed **individuation** (Josselson, 1980, 1988).

Adolescents accomplish this growth in ordinary ways—by making decisions for themselves, and by living with the consequences of these decisions. The major decision all adolescents face is who is going to make the decisions, but because decisions take many different forms, this point is easily missed. Adolescents find

BOX 5.2 (*continued*)

An Interview with Anne Petersen:
Adolescents and Their Parents

How Would You Say Your Own Research Has Influenced
the Way You Rear Your Children?

I think it has changed a lot of things. That my daughter rebelled was a big shock. I remember vividly the day she refused to do something. There was no door banging, but she said she would not do something I had just assumed she would do. I immediately had the stereotypic reaction, "Oh my heavens, what is going on here?" All of a sudden I realized that this was what I had been talking about for a long time. Knowing all the data, why should I be surprised that my kid goes through this too?

It helped a lot to know what could be effective in dealing with this. We had a family conference. What she was saying was, "How about taking my needs into account?" She was upset that we just assumed she would be a part of some activity. It is enlightening to realize that we don't treat an adult, a colleague, or a friend like that. It makes sense to change your behavior toward young adolescents. Well we worked it out. There are still occasional lapses of communication, and that's where the problems really are. Somebody assumes that somebody else is going to do something, and there is either a conflict of schedules or wishes. But at least saying, "Yes, you are right, you ought to have an increasing role in family decision making" and have a forum within which to do it made a lot of difference to her. She did not have to explode. She could put her two cents in.

When there is a good reason, we change our plans to meet her needs. It is important for us to show that we do not need to be controlling things, that we do respect her views, that she does have a voice. I am sure if you were to ask both our children, they would say they do not have as much say as they would like. That is because we still do believe that we are the parents and there are some things we need to decide.

We believe that it is important to let them see how we are thinking about things and to understand decision-making processes. So, we talk in the family about money and about vacation plans, and we really try to include them—not just out of respect for them to increasingly become a part, but also to let them see how we think about things so they have the benefit of knowing how adults make decisions. That seems to work pretty well.

Source: Adapted from J. Brooks. (1991). [*Interview with Anne C. Petersen, Dean*
of the College of Health and Human Development, Pennsylvania State University].
In J. Brooks, The process of parenting *(3rd ed.). Mountain View, CA: Mayfield.*

themselves arguing about who they can go out with, how tight is too tight for jeans, how late they can stay up, when they do their homework, or who gets to say what courses they can take in school. Much of the process is repetitive. Decisions made one day must be renegotiated the next, as the same issues continue to come up in different forms.

Perhaps the process is repetitive because it involves learning in a real-life situation instead of in a classroom. In the classroom, principles are stated explicitly,

Individuation is the process of distinguishing one's own attitudes and beliefs from those of one's parents. Adolescents who successfully complete this process can maintain a comfortable closeness with their parents and not fear they will lose their newfledged identity.

frequently apart from any context, and adolescents must relate these principles to real-life situations. Just the opposite occurs when learning outside the classroom. Outside their classes, adolescents learn by doing and by experiencing the consequences. No one is there to help identify which principles operate in that situation. As a result, it is often difficult to separate the elements that remain constant across situations from the situations themselves. Are adolescents really arguing about how loud their music can be, or about who gets to decide how loud is too loud?

There is another reason why adolescents tend to repeat the decision-making process. Frequently what they learn from their decisions has very personal consequences, which they may not be ready to accept. Discovering how to solve an algebraic equation has little bearing on life outside math class; algebra is "safe" knowledge. But discovering that you are the only one who can make decisions for yourself, and that there is no one to blame or praise but yourself, is something else again. Understanding is rarely just an intellectual matter; it also reflects one's emotions and beliefs, and some things can be understood only when one is prepared to let go of old beliefs. Sometimes adolescents, or adults for that matter, cannot allow themselves to understand until they can live with the consequences of that understanding. They may prefer to live with isolated actions, not seeing how one fits with another to form a larger picture (Wapner, 1980).

Even though the daily decisions adolescents make often seem trivial, the process itself never is; it is a way of separating themselves as individuals. The process is also frequently lonely. Rejecting parental attitudes and values can often leave adolescents with an empty feeling; they've discarded old ways before developing new ones of their own. Ruthellen Josselson (1980) suggests that emotions help adolescents with this transition. The very intensity of their emotions lets them know there is still someone inside. This function may account for some of the emotional intensity of early adolescence. Older adolescents have become surer of their decisions, and much of the earlier emotional overkill drops out. By late adolescence most have disentangled their needs and ideas from those of their parents and have a sense of being in charge of their lives. They no longer need emotion to fill a psychic void or to convince themselves, or others, that they are in control.

Throughout the individuation process, adolescents attempt to preserve a sense of sameness of their inner selves and of what they mean to others. The identities that emerge must be continuous with their past and also allow them to project themselves into the future. Adolescents who successfully sort through their own and their parents' attitudes and beliefs can maintain a comfortable closeness with their parents, without fearing a loss of their own individuality. (See Box 5.3.) This closeness is an important source of continuity in their lives. Adolescents do not need to discard old relationships or adopt completely new lifestyles in order to be their own person (Mazor & Enright, 1988). Individuation involves both a growing independence from parents, such as in managing daily events or needing less support, and positive feelings about one's independence. The latter, at least for late adolescents, appears to be a better index of individuation than the more concrete changes, as it can predict such things as easier adjustment to college (Rice, Cole, & Lapsley, 1990).

Family Interaction and Adolescents' Individuation

The family has a critical role in the personality development of adolescents. But how do families exert their effect? Are parents models for the behaviors adolescents acquire, or do these behaviors develop in the context of interactions among family members?

Individuality and Connectedness in the Family. Harold Grotevant and Catherine Cooper (1986), developmentalists at the University of Minnesota and the University of California at Santa Cruz, identified dimensions of family interaction that contribute to the development of individuation. They used a deceptively simple approach to study family interactions: They asked families to make plans for an

BOX 5.3

The Joys of Parenting Early Adolescents

"Seeing him care for younger children and babies is a great pleasure. He's a great nurturer with small children. He has endless patience."—*Mother*

"He is a talented athlete, and his soccer team got to a championship game. He scored the winning goal, and when he took off with the ball down the field, I was very proud of him. It was a unique feeling of being proud that someone I had helped to create was doing that. He had felt a lot of pressure in the game, so to see how incredibly pleased he was gave me great joy."—*Father*

"Now that they are older, they bring new skills into our lives. I did not learn algebra in school, but to help him with problems now and then, I learned algebra from the book. I am very pleased to be able to help."—*Mother*

"It is gratifying to me to see him learn the rules. He makes sure his homework is done, and he does it on his own steam."—*Mother*

"I like that he does things I did, like play the trumpet. He started at the same age I did and since he took it up, it has rekindled my interest and I started practicing again. This last weekend, we played together. He also brings new interests, too. Because he likes sailing, I have started that and really like it."—*Father*

"She is in that dreamy preteen state where she writes things. She wrote a poem about the difference between being alone and loneliness. She has a real appreciation of time on her own and how nice being alone can be. I like that because I had that at her age."—*Mother*

"It's nice just being able to help them, feeling good because they are being helped out and benefitted."—*Father*

"It's nice to see her being able to analyze situations with friends or with her teachers and come to conclusions. She said about one of her teachers, 'Well, she gets excited and she never follows through with what she says, so you know you don't have to take her seriously.' "—*Mother*

imaginary vacation, and analyzed the communication patterns that developed within the family. They looked for patterns that evidenced two qualities they believed to be critical for the development of individuation: individuality and connectedness. **Individuality** is the ability to have and express one's own ideas (*self-assertion*) and to say how one differs from others (*separateness*). **Connectedness** reflects one's openness to others' opinions (*permeability*), and one's respect for their ideas (*mutuality*). Box 5.4 analyzes the vignette that opened this chapter for statements that illustrate each of these four factors.

Adolescents in an individuated relationship have a clear sense of themselves as distinct from other people yet feel emotionally connected with them. They have their own ideas, which they can express, and are open to those of the person they

B O X   5 . 3 (*continued*)

The Joys of Parenting Early Adolescents

"I really enjoy being in the scouts with the boys. Once a month we go on a camping weekend, and I really look forward to that."—*Father*

"I was so impressed and pleased that after the earthquake, he and a friend decided to go door to door and offer to sell drawings they made of Teenage Mutant Ninja Turtles. He raised $150 that he gave for earthquake relief. I was very proud that he thought this up all by himself."—*Father*

"I was very happy one day when I found this note she left on my desk. It said, 'Hello!!! Have a happy day! Don't worry about home, everyone's fine! Do your work the very best you can. But most important, have a fruitful life!!' I saved that note because it made me feel so good."—*Mother*

"He enjoys life. He has a sense of humor. He's like a butterfly enjoying everything; eventually he'll settle in."—*Mother*

"He's very sensitive, and his cousins two years older than he ask his advice about boys. They may not take it, but they ask him even though he's younger."—*Father*

"It's very rewarding to see them in their school activities. My daughter sings in the school chorus, and I enjoy that, and my son is in school plays."—*Father*

"I am very pleased that she is less moody now than she used to be. We used to refer to her lows as 'Puddles of Frustration,' but she's gotten past that now."—*Mother*

"Well, they have their friends over, and we have ping pong, pool, cards, and we stressed having these things available. I enjoy playing all these games with them."—*Father*

Source: Adapted from J. Brooks. (1991). The process of parenting (3rd ed.).
Mountain View, CA: Mayfield.

are with. In a sense, individuation allows them to respect each person as an individual—including themselves. Equally important, individuated relationships allow adolescents to experience their connectedness with another person and still see how they are different. Research on individuation suggests that adolescents who achieve high levels of individuation can remain close to their parents without feeling a loss of their own distinctiveness. The research also supports the view that parent-adolescent relationships continue to be close as they move toward greater mutuality (Mazor & Enright, 1988; White, Speisman, & Costos, 1983).

Adolescents do not have to have an individuated relationship with both parents. A single relationship in which there are moderate to high degrees of separateness and permeability makes individuation possible. Adolescents who achieve

BOX 5.4

Communication Patterns That Foster Individuation

Individuality

Self-Assertion: The ability to have one's own ideas and express them.
"I'd like to see the pyramids in Mexico."

Separateness: The ability to say how one differs from others.

1. Requests action:
   "All right, let's vote on this."
2. Directly disagrees:
   "Get real, Mom. Do you think you can get us to sweat a path through the jungle once we've seen the sands of Acapulco?"
3. Indirectly disagrees:
   "Do you know how hot it is in Florida in August?"
4. Irrelevant comment:
   "They're alligators, not crocodiles, Surfer Joe."

Connectedness

Permeability: Openness and responsiveness to the opinions of others.

1. Acknowledges:
   "Hmm."
2. Requests information or validation:
   "How far inland are they?"
3. Agrees with another's ideas:
   "I could sure use some time on a beach."
4. Relevant comment:
   "Maybe we should think of a winter vacation."
5. Complies with a request:
   "Okay, let's vote."

Mutuality: Sensitivity and respect for others' ideas.

1. Indirect suggestion of action:
   "Why don't we visit Grandma and then go someplace exotic like the Everglades?"
2. Compromise:
   "I'd like to see the pyramids in Mexico. We could stop off at Acapulco on the way."
3. States other's feelings:
   "Willie'd die in the heat there, too."
4. Answers request for information/validation:
   "I don't know, but I could call a travel agent."

Source: C. Cooper, H. Grotevant, & S. Condon. (1983). Individuality and connectedness in the family as a context for adolescent identity formation and role-taking skill. In H. D. Grotevant & C. R. Cooper (Eds.), Adolescent development in the family. *San Francisco: Jossey-Bass.*

Warm and loving relationships within the family help adolescents individuate and develop self-esteem. Without family members who believe in them and stand by them, teenagers may lose faith in themselves and drop out of school long before graduation day.

the highest levels of individuation, however, are likely to come from families in which members delight in examining their differences yet experience connectedness with each other.

Adolescents low in individuation typically have families who avoid disagreeing with each other and are so responsive to others' opinions that they cannot form a differing opinion of their own. Families with few disagreements communicate one important message to their members: that it is important to agree. Adolescents from these families must express the family point of view in order to voice anything at all. Doing so reassures others that they agree with them. As an extreme example, when the mother in one family asked where they should go on their vacation, each member responded by repeating the father's suggestion of going back to Spain. When asked for more suggestions by her father, the adolescent daughter could not elaborate and fumbled an "I don't know," indicating her father should offer more suggestions. It was hard for this adolescent to explore issues outside her family's belief system, even when they only involved choices for an imaginary family vacation (Grotevant & Cooper, 1986). Adolescents who can experience their separateness from other members of the family are freer to develop their own point of view. Even so, their explorations take place in an emotional context of connectedness, which provides the security that allows them to examine ideas.

To develop a point of view, adolescents must be able to see how their ideas differ from those of others. Interactions that focus on differences and similarities provide important developmental experiences; they can also involve conflict. Conflict itself isn't necessarily bad. In the context of clarifying a position, it can help adolescents gain a sense of what they believe. For adolescents to have their ideas challenged without experiencing this as criticism, a supportive family atmosphere is important (Powers, Hauser, Schwartz, Noam, & Jacobson, 1983; Shulman, Seiffge-Krenke, & Samat, 1987). In fact, adolescents' experience of support is generally unrelated to conflicts with parents (Barrera, Chassin, & Rogosch, 1993).

Ego Development of Parents and Children.   Measures of ego development of parents and adolescents find complex relationships between the level of development in parents and that of their children. Stuart Hauser, Emily Borman, Alan Jacobson, Sally Powers, and Gil Noam (1991) found that parents' ego development, especially that of mothers, predicted ego development in adolescents, as measured by the coping strategies adolescents used. These investigators suggest that coping styles in parents, just as in adolescents, reflect the level of their ego development. By observing and interacting with their parents, adolescents adopt coping styles that reflect the interactional patterns that characterize their family life.

Supporting these observations, research finds that ego development in adolescents relates to the parents' use of cognitively stimulating behaviors and to their supportiveness. Adolescents with the highest levels of ego development are most likely to come from families with a high degree of noncompetitive sharing of perspectives and support. There is little distortion (inaccurate portrayal of another's view or the task) or avoidance (distracting attention from the problem) and little rejection (trying to close off discussion without exploring differences) (Powers et al., 1983).

How might such a family operate when faced with a problem? First, they might not see the problem as having a single solution and are likely to "agree to disagree." This approach should not be confused with a dismissal of the problem. Each person thinks carefully about his or her own position and the positions of others. But if they cannot resolve their differences, they are comfortable letting things rest there. They are likely to openly discuss their differences without criticizing each other's remarks. As a result, they aren't defensive with each other. The stress is on clarifying one's position relative to another when differences arise. Members of the family listen a lot to each other, though they are not necessarily swayed from their own ideas. There is also obvious emotional support for each other.

Parents are genuinely proud of adolescents for knowing and standing by what they believe (Powers et al., 1983).

We can compare the above family's approach with that of a family in which adolescents are likely to have low ego development. We also see much noncompetitive sharing of perspectives, but there is also high avoidance, distracting attention from the problem. Even though family members may share opinions, they avoid discussing them; they are not able to explore their differences long enough to reach an understanding of each other's position.

Self-Awareness and Support. Other investigators have found similar dimensions of family interaction to be important for the development of individuation. David Bell and Linda Bell (1983) emphasize the importance of self-awareness and support. They find that adolescents with high degrees of self-awareness are more accepting of themselves. Accepting oneself means that one can be aware of needs and motives that one might otherwise feel a need to deny or distort, sometimes by attributing them to others. Thus, self-awareness clears the way for more accurate perceptions of others. Self-aware adolescents are also in a better position to appreciate their own complexity, and to acknowledge complexity in others. Insight into themselves and others makes it possible for them to validate the other person's experiences. Others, in turn, are more likely to validate theirs. Being able to communicate that you have heard another person, for example, allows that person to relax and listen to you. This process of mutual validation promotes self-awareness in each person by providing accurate feedback to each (Bell & Bell, 1983).

A negative converse to this bright picture exists for other adolescents. The inability to understand one's own complexities makes it likely that one's approach to others will be simplistic. Adolescents who do not understand their own actions will make inaccurate observations about the reactions of others. Motives unrecognizable in themselves will color their perceptions of others. Neither the adolescents themselves nor those with whom they interact are likely to receive validation through their encounters with each other, further perpetuating this negative cycle.

Family Climate. Bell and Bell believe that supportive—that is, warm and loving—relationships within the family are central to the development of positive self-regard, and hence of individuation. It is possible, of course, for families to be supportive and yet not be validating. Such families might be warm and loving, for example, but not comfortable with their differences. Because they are threatening, differences of opinion are avoided. Validating another person merely requires that one be aware of and comfortable with differences between oneself and others, making it possible to listen without the expectations that reflect one's own needs. One can hear what the other is saying more accurately. An accurate reading of another person does not, however, signal agreement, or even liking: A family can be validating yet not supportive.

To test their ideas, Bell and Bell observed adolescent girls and their families interact in a "revealed differences" task, in which differences in the way members of a family answered questions on a scale were revealed (e.g., "We fight a lot in our family," or "We really help and support one another"). As family members tried to reach agreement on items on which they had disagreed, a research team coded their exchanges for support and acknowledgment of what each person said.

These investigators found, as had Powers and her associates, that the effect of parental ego development on adolescents' ego development is not direct, but is mediated by a family climate characterized by accurate interpersonal perception. Thus parents' ego development is positively related to an accurate perception of others, which in turn is related to adolescent ego development. It is the family *process*, not a modeling of parental behavior, that promotes ego development in adolescence. The best climate is one in which people accurately read their own and others' actions, in which they are not excessively concerned with others' reactions, and in which there is little covert conflict. Both parental ego development and family comfort with differences facilitate the development of such a climate (Bell & Bell, 1983). However, even with optimal family climates, parents can still wish at times that they had known more about adolescence (see Box 5.5).

The findings of studies such as these emphasize the need to consider the family system as a whole rather than focus on individuals. Parents' personalities do not directly affect adolescent development; it is the family system that mediates the effect of parental ego development and parental self-regard. However, individual characteristics of parents can contribute to the family climate, which then affects the parents' behavior and the adolescent's personality (Bell & Bell, 1983).

The Family Paradigm

The way a family experiences the world reflects its **family paradigm**, the core beliefs held by members of the family about their environment. A family might believe, for example, that the world is orderly and that one need only persist in order to discover the ground rules that operate in any situation. Other families might see their world as chaotic or even hostile. Thus some families will be optimistic and open to new experiences, while others will be pessimistic and retreat into themselves (Constantine, 1987).

One can study family paradigms by observing families as they solve a problem, with the assumption that their approach to the problem will reflect their more general views of the world. Two dimensions that distinguish families are especially important in this context. Families can be distinguished by the degree to which they think through a problem (problem analysis) and the extent to which they work together in coming up with a solution (working together). Families characterized by a high degree of problem analysis look for complexity, revealing their belief that the problem need not be simple to be solvable. Families low in problem analysis tend to come up with superficial answers, perhaps reflecting their belief

BOX 5.5

What Parents Wish They Had Known About Adolescence

"They seem to get caught up in fads in junior high. They do certain things . . . to be part of the crowd. I wish I'd known how to handle that. At what point are these fads okay, because it's important to identify with your peer group, and at what point do you say no? If they are really dangerous, then it's easy; but with a lot of them, it's a gray area, and I wish I'd known what to do better."—*Father*

"I wish I had realized that she needed more structure and control. Because she had always been a good student and done her work, I thought I could trust her to manage the school tasks without my checking. But she lost interest in school, and I learned only very gradually that I had to be more of a monitor with her work than I had been in the past." —*Mother*

"I wish I had known more about the mood swings. When the girls became thirteen, they each got moody for a while, and I stopped taking it personally. I just relaxed. The youngest one said, 'Do I have to go through that? Can't I just skip that?' Sure enough, when she became thirteen, she was moody too."—*Mother*

"I wish I'd known how to help the boys get along a little better. They have real fights at times, and while they have a lot of fun together and help each other out, I wish I knew how to cut down on the fighting."—*Father*

"I wish I knew what to expect. They are all so different, and they don't necessarily do what the books say. Sometimes, I'm waiting for a stage; now I'm waiting for adolescent rebellion, and there is none."—*Mother*

"I wish I had known about their indecisiveness. He wants to do this; no, he doesn't. He gets pressure from peers and from what we think is right, and sometimes he goes back and forth. I am more patient about that now."—*Mother*

"I wish I had known that if we had dealt with some behaviors when they were younger, we would not have had a problem from 11 to 14. He was always a little stubborn and hardheaded, wanting to do what he wanted. But right now, I wish we had done something about the stubbornness because it is a problem. He does not take responsibility, and it gets him into trouble at school. Looking back it has always been a problem, but we did not deal with it."—*Mother*

Source: Adapted from J. Brooks. (1991). The process of parenting (3rd ed.).
Mountain View, CA: Mayfield.

that most problems are insolvable. Similarly, families that work well together pay attention to what each person is doing and coordinate their efforts; those at the other end of this dimension talk little among themselves and come up with individual answers (Reiss, Oliveri, & Curd, 1983).

By classifying families according to these two dimensions, we can describe four types of families, each with a distinctive approach to solving problems. David

Problem analysis

		High	Low
Working together	High	Members focus on the problem and work cooperatively, usually coming up with several possible solutions: *Cooperative Problem-Solving Families*	Members focus primarily on the thoughts and feelings of the group, only secondarily on the problem. They are often so sensitive to each other that they can miss much of what goes on outside the family: *Enmeshed Non-Solving Families*
	Low	Members perceive themselves as having to work alone, with little group experience. Each sees the problem as difficult yet solvable: *Disengaged Problem-Solving Families*	Members are isolated from each other as well as from those outside the family. There is little exploration or understanding of the problem they face: *Isolated Non-Solving Families*

Figure 5.1   Family Types Distinguished by the Way They Analyze Problems and Work Together

Source: Adapted from D. Reiss, M. E. Oliveri, & K. Curd. (1983). Family paradigm and adolescent social behavior. In H. D. Grotevant & C. R. Cooper (Eds.), Adolescent development in the family. *San Francisco: Jossey-Bass.*

Reiss, Mary Ellen Oliveri, and Karen Curd (1983), developmentalists specializing in family relations, give us descriptions of each type of family (Figure 5.1).

Individuals from various types of families differ in characteristic ways. Autonomy characterizes adolescents from cooperative problem-solving families (those high in both problem analysis and working together) as well as those from isolated non-solving families (those low in both problem analysis and working together), but for different reasons. Members of cooperative problem-solving families explore their surroundings as a team; their approach to problems is optimistic. Members of isolated non-solving families are more pessimistic; they do not approach each other or those outside the family for help even when they face a solvable problem. The high autonomy of adolescents from these families probably reflects their lack of connectedness with other family members. Blind clinical observations of parents and adolescents from each family type confirm these observations. In isolated non-solving families, parents appear worn and confused, and the adolescents depressed and self-destructive. In cooperative problem-solving families, the parents are involved, and the adolescents are assertive and sociable. Findings such as these strongly suggest that a family's paradigm has important implications for adolescent social behavior (Reiss, Oliveri, & Curd, 1983).

Reiss, Oliveri, and Curd suggest that the interactions of any family member with those outside the family not only reflect the core beliefs of the family, but also serve to stabilize the family paradigm, that is, to confirm it. The behavior of adolescents, as well as that of other members of the family, functions to maintain the family's view of the world. Thus the high engagement of adolescents from cooperative problem-solving families not only reflects their belief that most problems can be solved; their stance also makes it likely that they will confirm this belief by sticking with problems until they are solved (Reiss, Oliveri, & Curd, 1983).

A family's racial or ethnic background contributes to the family paradigm by affecting the way it experiences the world.

Families and Ethnicity

Over the past two decades, the number of minority families in the United States has increased dramatically. Twenty percent of all children under the age of 17 belong to a minority group. By the twenty-first century, one-third of all those in school will be Asian, Black, Hispanic, Native American, or a member of some other minority (G. Miller, 1989). As a group these adolescents have certain problems in common: They experience more poverty, poorer living conditions, inferior education, more unemployment, and higher dropout rates than age-mates from the dominant culture. They are also more likely to experience intergenerational conflict, as they become acculturated into the ways of the majority culture more rapidly than their parents, who frequently remain committed to the traditions of their native culture (Feldman, Mont-Reynaud, & Rosenthal, 1992; Yau & Smetana, 1993). Despite the tensions this can create within the family, adolescents whose parents maintain warm and caring relationships with them weather the stresses of dual-cultural membership (Chiu, Feldman, & Rosenthal, 1992).

Ethnicity is an important factor contributing to the impact of the family on adolescent development. The organization of the family system often takes typically different forms in families with differing cultural backgrounds.

Asian American Families.   Less than 1% of adolescents in the United States are Asian American, most of whom are of Chinese and Japanese backgrounds, although Vietnamese, Korean, and Filipino groups are growing in number. Asian traditions emphasize the importance of the group rather than the individual, and Asian American adolescents feel strong loyalties to their families. Roles are more rigidly defined than in Western families, and relationships are vertically, or hierarchically, arranged, with the father in a position of authority at the top. Family relationships reflect the roles of members more than in individualistic, Western cultures. An aspect of the children's role is to care for their parents. This sense of responsibility to the family characterizes Asian American adolescents (Huang & Ying, 1989; Nagata, 1989).

Traditional socialization practices in Asian American families stress duty, control of emotions, and obedience to elders. Asian American adolescents may continue to express strong loyalties to family, but in most other respects adopt the ways of the dominant culture.

Socialization practices emphasize duty, maintaining control over one's emotions and thoughts, and obedience to authority figures within the family (Nagata, 1989). Chinese-American adolescents, for example, indicated, when asked, that they would meet parental expectations rather than satisfy their own desires when these conflicted. However, many of those responding to such questions cited practical reasons for doing so in addition to respect for cultural traditions, saying it would increase the likelihood that they would be given permission to do something else they might want to do (Yau & Smetana, 1993).

Black Families.   Approximately 14% of adolescents in the United States between the ages of 10 and 19 are black (U.S. Bureau of the Census, 1992). In 1991, 63% of all black families were maintained by a single parent, nearly all of these by the mother (U.S. Census, 1992). The median income of black families is approximately 60% that of white families, and usually both parents must be employed for a black family to have middle-class status (Gibbs, 1989). Tremendous diversity exists in income levels, and in associated educational attainment and other indices of well being, among blacks. Despite the massive inroads made against discrimination in

Since divorce is more common today than in previous generations, adolescents are less likely to experience any stigma associated with it. Many of their friends have gone through a similar experience, and natural support groups exist in which adolescents can air their feelings and gain perspective on their situation.

Even so, adolescents whose parents are divorced are less likely than peers from intact homes to adopt mature coping strategies, especially when they feel threatened. This is true even though they may recognize that the strategies they use—such as escape, avoidance, confrontation, or self-blame—are not particularly effective. They are also more vulnerable to stress, in that they are not as likely to see themselves as potentially controlling the situation or managing a successful outcome. Perhaps experiencing a divorce, which is an event beyond their control, makes these adolescents less likely to feel in control of other stressful situations. Or it might be that the degree of control they perceive themselves to have in a situation is related to their self-esteem, which is lower in these adolescents (Irion, Coon, & Blanchard-Fields, 1988).

Marital conflict rather than divorce per se contributes heavily to the stress adolescents experience. Conflict most likely affects adolescents by affecting the quality of parent-child relationships (Fauber, Forehand, Thomas, & Wierson, 1990). Adolescents are more likely to experience problems when their parents divorce relatively late rather than early, when they were children (Needle, Su, & Doherty, 1990; Smith, 1990). Adolescents whose parents divorce late experience more years of marital conflict. A 3-year longitudinal study of over 1,000 seventh-, ninth-, and eleventh-graders found that conflict within the family, not divorce, was associated with negative effects such as depression, anxiety, and physical symptoms. Adolescents from intact homes with high levels of conflict showed lower levels of well-being than those in low-conflict divorced homes on all measures that were used (Mechanic & Hansell, 1989). A full 25% of the adolescents reported that their parents' divorce was a positive change. Other studies find even higher agreement among adolescents on the preferability of divorce to their previous conflict-ridden lives (McLaughlin & Whitfield, 1984). As the conflict surrounding a divorce becomes more openly expressed, some adolescents report experiencing greater feelings of personal control (Proulx & Koulock, 1987).

Adverse effects of divorce appear to be minimal as adolescents reach early adulthood. T. J. Barkley and M. E. Procidano (1989) found no difference between late adolescents from divorced and intact families on measures tapping their sense of control, mood, interpersonal dependency, or perceived social supports. In other ways, the increasing divorce rate in society may affect all adolescents. Perhaps the issues facing this generation of adolescents will be to find meaning in relationships and institutions that previous generations accepted as givens. The prevalence of divorce, even when not personally experienced, raises issues of intimacy and family relationships for all adolescents.

Single-Parent Families.   Most of the adolescents who live in single-parent families do so because of divorce; most of them live with their mothers (Buchanan,

Maccoby, & Dornbusch, 1992). One of the most noticeable differences between these adolescents and those from intact homes is their economic well-being. Approximately half of all families headed by a single female parent live below the poverty level, compared to only 10% of two-parent families (McLanahan & Booth, 1989). For many adolescents, this income level is a dramatic change. One year following a divorce, a single mother's income is likely to have dropped to 67% of the total household income before divorce, whereas the father's income is likely only to drop to 90%. The initially lower earning capacity of most women, along with frequent lack of child support and little state support, contributes to this pattern. On average, single mothers working part-time earn approximately 30% of what married fathers earn, and mothers employed full-time earn 60% as much

Responsiveness, consistency, and a willingness to listen and to give adolescents a say in decision making are all characteristics of parents who have a healthy relationship with their children. Achieving this kind of parenting can be a challenge for reconstituted families, however, because the relationships are new and complex.

(McLanahan & Booth, 1989). Economic hardship contributes to adolescents' distress in intact families as well. In this case, however, it does so primarily by undermining the marital relationship which then affects the way each partner relates to the adolescent (Ge, Conger, Lorenz, Elder, Montague & Simons, 1992).

Adolescents in single-parent families face the need—some for the first time—to take on part-time jobs to pay for things they previously took for granted. There are advantages and disadvantages in this situation, as in almost any other. On the positive side, adolescents stand to gain in autonomy and independence through being more responsible. Hetherington (1989) finds that adolescents are given greater responsibility, have a greater role in family decision making, and are given more independence than in intact families. Potential disadvantages can result when responsibilities exceed adolescents' capabilities or keep them from normal activities, such as schoolwork and social participation.

Many adolescents face additional changes immediately after a divorce. Thirty percent of adolescents move within the first year following a divorce; for many this means adjusting to a new neighborhood and a new school, and making new friends. Less-frequent contact with old friends is an additional loss. Frequently, divorced mothers will change their employment within the same time period, adding to the general level of stress within the family. Divorced mothers report lower levels of psychological well-being and more concerns than mothers in two-parent families. Adolescents living with divorced mothers are likely to enjoy the same family support as before, yet they typically have less contact with their neighbors than those living in two-parent families. Most divorced mothers, however, are relatively successful in establishing the social supports they need (McLanahan & Booth, 1989).

On the positive side, relationships between adolescents and mothers often become stronger in the process of coping with these conditions; relationships become closer and less hierarchical. Mothers and daughters especially are likely to find these relationships satisfying, with the exception of early maturing girls, for whom family conflict increases. Adolescents living with their mothers may also develop more liberal attitudes regarding work and gender roles. Daughters living with their divorced mothers report high expectations from their mothers for them to attend college. Divorced mothers may see a need for their daughters to be economically and socially independent, in case of similar circumstances (McLanahan, Astone, & Marks, 1988; Sessa & Steinberg, 1991).

Buchanan, Maccoby, and Dornbusch (1992) compared adjustment in adolescents living either with their mothers, their fathers, or part-time with both. They found, in contrast to previous research (e.g., Hetherington, 1989), that it was relatively unimportant for adolescents to live with the same-sex parent. Boys, in fact, adjusted just as well, if not better, when living with their mothers as with their fathers. Of course, comparisons of this sort are problematic since fathers usually get custody only when the mother has psychological or emotional problems, which in themselves can affect an adolescent's adjustment.

An increasing number of divorced fathers receive custody of their children, although this arrangement is still relatively uncommon. Buchanan, Maccoby, &

Dornbusch (1992) found that 19% of the 517 adolescents they interviewed lived with their fathers, in comparison to 70% living with their mothers, and only 10% part-time with both. Perhaps because of the special circumstances under which fathers are likely to be awarded custody, more experienced difficulty. For instance, hostility between parents remained higher when the father had custody; fathers with custody also worked more hours per week than did mothers with custody, and residential arrangements changed more frequently following the divorce than in the other two types of custody arrangements.

Other things being equal, however, fathers have been found to adjust to their custodial role well. A survey of over 1,000 single fathers found them to be relatively comfortable in their roles. Those who were most comfortable were the ones who had been at it the longest; presumably they had worked out the kinks and developed their own successful routines over the years. Those who were satisfied with their social lives also reported more satisfaction with their roles, as did those who had higher incomes and rated themselves high as a parent (Greif & DeMaris, 1990).

Remarriage and Stepparents.   Parents who divorce are likely to remarry and to introduce a stepparent into their children's lives. Close to 20% of children under the age of 18 live with a stepparent, who in most cases is a stepfather. Remarriage usually occurs soon on the heels of the divorce, typically within 3 years. Many stepparents bring a stepsibling or two (residential or weekend) in the process. For adolescents, this series of events comes on top of the changes introduced by puberty, moving to a new type of school, and rapidly changing social relations. Fewer changes would still be enough to disrupt anyone's equilibrium. Yet many families weather the stresses of these new relationships, and some even thrive (Giles-Sims & Crosbie-Burnett, 1989a; Glick, 1989).

We don't have much information about the conditions that facilitate or hinder healthy stepfamily relations (Giles-Sims & Crosbie-Burnett, 1989a). Yet some general statements can be made. Perhaps the first is to underscore the importance of **role clarity,** the understanding among family members regarding each person's role and how it affects the others (Giles-Sims & Crosbie-Burnett, 1989a; Visher & Visher, 1989). Adolescence introduces its own confusions into roles and issues; for example, child versus adult, dependence, independence, autonomy, and emotional connectedness. The addition of stepparents to this combustible mix creates great potential for human drama. An adolescent who bridles at suggestions from his mother can refuse to even listen to a stepfather. If a 6-foot tall, strapping, 15-year-old male is confused about his role as a "child" to a biological parent, magnify that confusion by an order of ten when you add a stepfather who is 3 inches shorter, 20 pounds lighter—and an emotional rival.

Adolescents' reactions to stepfathers vary considerably with their gender, frequently improving conditions at home for boys, and just as frequently worsening them for girls (Hetherington, 1989; Needle, Su, & Doherty, 1990). The transition is easiest for boys. Boys in remarriages have been found to differ little in their behavior at home or at school from boys in intact families. Girls remain antagonistic and disruptive. In addition to gender differences, the timing of the remarriage is also important. Boys adjust best in remarriages when their mother remarries prior to adolescence. Adolescents of either sex show behavior problems even in remarriages that have lasted for several years if their mother remarried after they had reached adolescence (Hetherington, 1989).

Ordinary family problems are magnified in stepfamilies. Who makes the decisions? Are stepparents responsible for the children of their spouses? Can they tell them what to do? Discipline them (Fine, 1989)? The most successful families establish clear guidelines for interactions. Families with the most ambiguity in roles are those with a stepmother and at least one child in common (Pasley & Ihenger-Tallman, 1989). The difficulties facing stepmothers are especially acute, because they are likely to oversee the management of the household, a role that can bring them into direct conflict with stepchildren who may resent their presence. For families experiencing problems, support groups and counseling can help establish guidelines for daily living, such as who supervises homework, who disciplines, buys clothes, cleans up, and so on. Mundane matters can easily become explosive unless defused with professional help (Visher & Visher, 1989).

A recent study of nearly 90 stepfather families with at least one adolescent gives us some answers to questions concerning patterns of decision making and the types of problems different members of the family are likely to experience (Giles-Sims & Crosbie-Burnett, 1989b). Most of the adolescents' problems centered around issues of discipline and authority. Views such as that expressed by the following adolescent were common:

> I resent it when he tries to discipline me, but I realize the bad comes with the good. I *don't* feel he has as much control as my natural father, but in this home it is mostly my mom who disciplines me. We both realize that my stepfather could never take the place of my natural father in my mind and heart. (p. 1071)

Adolescents also said that they would tell other adolescents to think about moving out if they had problems with a stepfather. As one said, "See what things might change, try and get along with him. If it doesn't work out and it is possible, move in with your father, but only as a last resort" (p. 1071).

Mothers' concerns also reflected issues of discipline, but included concerns about financial support and responsibility as well. For stepfathers, as for adolescents, discipline and authority were central concerns (Giles-Sims & Crosbie-Burnett, 1989b). Stepfathers interviewed for the study said things like the following:

> I rarely feel comfortable disciplining . . . maternal instincts are very strong here . . . because early attempts to discipline resulted in her becoming quite defensive about their behavior.

> She is at an age where any authority is threatening to her and she is resentful of my discipline. (p. 1071)

With respect to the major decisions made in these families, the adults felt that the mother had the most power, the stepfather next, and adolescents the least. Adolescents also felt their mothers had the most power, but saw themselves as having more than their stepfathers. Power was distributed more equally with respect to everyday decisions, with no one member having that much more say than the others. Adolescents had their way as often as either adult in these everyday matters. These findings parallel those of other studies which find that stepfathers are less authoritative than fathers in nondivorced families (Hetherington, 1989).

Adolescents themselves may contribute heavily to the success or failure of remarriages (White & Booth, 1985). Giles-Sims and Crosbie-Burnett (1989b) suggest that their ability to do so comes from the relative power they hold in reconstituted families. They note that 12% of the adolescents in their sample had decision-making power equal to or greater than the parents. As the family reorganizes with time, power relationships change. Adolescents in families that had been together longer had less power than in newly constituted ones.

Not all studies find that the age of children in remarriages affects the quality of family life. A comparison of stepfather families with young children, school-age children, or adolescents found marital satisfaction to be unrelated to the age of the child (Kurdek, 1990). The average length of the marriage in this study was 8½ months, a period perhaps not long enough for serious difficulties to develop.

What contributes to the success of reconstituted families? Successful families are those that establish rituals. These can range from everyday routines, such as walking the dog and doing the dishes, to family traditions and celebrations, such as serving breakfast in bed when it's someone's birthday or backpacking on weekends (Whiteside, 1989). Rituals provide for shared experiences and also contribute to role clarity.

Changing Work Roles: Dual-Earner Families

The number of women in the work force has increased substantially over the last several decades. Nearly three-quarters of women between ages 25 and 54 work outside the home (Orthner, 1990). What effect does maternal employment have on adolescents? Research addressing this question has yielded inconsistent findings, suggesting that *whether* mom works is not as important as the *conditions* that are present when she does (Joebgen & Richards, 1990).

A. M. Joebgen and M. H. Richards (1990), for example, periodically contacted adolescents and parents throughout the day (they wore beepers) to sample their activities and their moods. They found the match between the mother's level of education and her employment to be most predictive of her self-esteem and well-being. This in turn related to well-being in adolescents. Maternal employment per se was not important; what mattered in terms of both her well-being and the adolescent's emotional adjustment was the match between the mother's interests and abilities and the work she did during the day—whether inside or outside the home.

Studies of working mothers and their adolescents find no consistent relationship between maternal employment and such important indicators of adjustment in adolescents as academic achievement, emotional development, or social competence (Armistead, Wierson, & Forehand, 1990; Bird & Kemerait, 1990; Keith, Nelson, Schlabach, & Thompson, 1990). When trends do emerge, they suggest that maternal employment has a more beneficial effect on daughters than on sons (Orthner, 1990), although some research suggests a reversal of this relationship (Paulson, Koman, & Hill, 1990). Similarly, job-related stresses of employed mothers do not seem to spill over to their relationships with their adolescent children or to affect the latter's psychosocial adjustment (Galambos & Maggs, 1990).

Despite the absence of any consistent negative effects associated with maternal employment, many families have come to expect that dual-income families will suffer as a result of the mother's employment. N. L. Galambos and J. L. Maggs (1990) quote from an article in *Time* magazine as follows:

> A motif of absence—moral, emotional, and physical—plays through the lives of many children now. . . . To support a family, buy a house and prepare for a child's future education, two incomes become essential. (Morrow, 1988, p. 27)

The effects of mom's joining the workforce appear to be more positive than negative. Maternal employment has a liberalizing effect on gender roles in the household. In single-earner families, with the traditional model of fathers as "breadwinners" and mothers as "homemakers," fathers spend more time with their sons than their daughters, while in dual-earner families, they spend equivalent amounts of time with each (Crouter & Crowley, 1990). Even though traditional, single-earner families expect daughters and sons to spend equal amounts of time doing household chores, they assign work in gender-stereotypic ways. Girls, for example, might be expected to clear the table, do dishes, or watch younger siblings, boys might mow the lawn, wash the car, and take out the garbage. In other respects, dual-earner families mirror for daughters the social realities facing employed mothers. Just as the work load of employed mothers increases when they work outside the home (since they continue to be responsible for work within the home), daughters actually do 25% more work in dual-earner homes than in traditional families (Benin & Edwards, 1990).

Maternal employment may affect the mother's sense of well-being more than the children's during adolescence. A study of over 100 families with adolescents between ages 10 and 15 found that parents who were positively invested in their jobs weathered the stresses of adolescence better than those who were not (Silverberg & Steinberg, 1990). As adolescents enter puberty, begin dating, and engage in more activities outside the home, parents face midlife identity issues and frequently a drop in self-esteem. Midlife concerns, self-esteem, and life satisfaction among parents suffer when teens start to date. Parents who are involved in their work roles, however, show increases in self-esteem and life satisfaction and have fewer midlife concerns when their children start to date (Silverberg & Steinberg, 1990).

Maternal employment can relate to well-being in yet another way. As adolescent autonomy increases, conflicts with parents increase, especially with mothers (Smetana, 1988; Steinberg, 1987a). The stability of work roles outside the home, in which established patterns of authority and decision making are not questioned, can buttress parental self-esteem in the face of changing relationships at home.

SUMMARY

Changing Relationships with Parents

Relationships with parents change during adolescence. Psychoanalytic theory expects this change to bring about emotional turmoil and distancing from parents.

Large-scale studies of normal adolescents find that even though conflicts increase, adolescents continue to maintain close relationships with parents. These relationships are renegotiated as adolescents press for more mutuality and fuller participation in family decision making.

Parents and Adolescents

Three styles of parenting have been identified: (a) Authoritarian parents stress obedience and respect for authority and traditional values. (b) Authoritative parents stress self-reliance, maintain open communication, and consistently enforce family rules. (c) Permissive parents use little punishment and make few demands. Authoritative parenting fosters competence, independence, and academic achievement.

Just when adolescents reach puberty, most parents face middle age. This particular combination of developmental changes can heighten the tensions within families with adolescents.

Autonomy and Individuation

Adolescents become more autonomous as they become more independent and responsible for their actions. Frequently these changes bring conflict with parents over household routines, more frequently with mothers than fathers. Parenting style, especially of mothers, is related to girls' autonomy. Age is the best predictor of increased autonomy for boys.

Increased individuation accompanies autonomy as adolescents sort through values and views to discover which ones reflect the way they think. This discovery involves making decisions for themselves and living with the consequences.

Individuation gives adolescents a set of attitudes and ways of acting that are genuinely their own; however, they must still put these together into a working whole that reflects an inner sense of self. Family characteristics of individuality and connectedness facilitate the process of identity achievement. Individuality refers to having and expressing ideas of one's own and being able to say how one differs from others. Connectedness reflects one's openness to others' opinions and respect for their ideas. These qualities of family life help adolescents explore options while feeling emotionally supported even when family disagreements arise.

The quality of adolescents' interactions with their parents, as well as personality characteristics of the parents themselves, are important to ego development in adolescence.

The way a family experiences its world reflects

its family paradigm: core beliefs held by family members about their environment. Two dimensions distinguish different family paradigms: the degree to which a family analyzes the problems it faces, and the extent to which members of the family work together in solving these problems.

Ethnicity contributes to the impact of the family on development. Adolescent-parent relationships typically take different forms in families with differing cultural backgrounds.

Family size also affects adolescent development. Over three-quarters of adolescents have at least one sibling. Most develop close bonds of affection despite the inevitable conflicts. Older siblings serve as models for younger ones; they are also likely to serve as caretakers. Siblings provide friendship and company for each other.

Families in Transition

Nearly half of all adolescents will experience divorce. The impact of divorce depends on conditions in the adolescent's life, such as age, gender, amount of marital conflict, support from family and friends, and economic stability.

The effectiveness of parenting drops in the first several years following divorce, and both parental self-esteem and adolescents' coping strategies suffer. Marital conflict, rather than divorce itself, contributes heavily to the stress adolescents experience.

Most adolescents in single-parent families live with their mothers. Daughters fare better in single-parent families than do sons. With remarriage, daughters experience more problems than before, whereas those of sons eventually lessen. Stepparents, usually stepfathers, report that most difficulties center around issues of authority and discipline. Role clarity facilitates interaction in stepparent families.

The number of women in the work force has increased substantially over the last several decades. The effects of maternal employment on adolescents are mediated by several factors, one of the most important being the mother's satisfaction with her work. Maternal employment may liberalize gender roles in the family and increase a parent's sense of well-being.

KEY TERMS

Active Listening	Permissive Parenting	Individuality
You-Message	Climacteric	Connectedness
I-Message	Menopause	Family Paradigm
Authoritarian Parenting	Autonomy	Role Clarity
Authoritative Parenting	Individuation	

FRIENDSHIPS DURING
ADOLESCENCE
Friends and Self-Esteem

■ RESEARCH FOCUS   *Sampling:
How Do You Feel at This Moment?*

Changes in Friendships with Age

FRIENDSHIP PATTERNS
What Girls Want in a Friend
What Boys Want in a Friend
Peer Interactions
Interracial Friendships

THE PEER GROUP
Cliques and Crowds

■ RESEARCH FOCUS   *Naturalistic
Observation: "Hanging Out"—Cliques
and Crowds*

Popularity
Dating

ADOLESCENTS, PARENTS,
AND PEERS
Conformity
Values and Peer Pressure
Deviant Behavior and Peer Pressure
The Generation Gap: Is It Widening?

SUMMARY

KEY TERMS

THE PEER GROUP

A Malayan proverb counsels that one should trumpet in a herd of elephants, crow in the company of cocks, and bleat in a flock of goats. This pretty much sums up the behavior of adolescents with their peers. The peer group is one of the most important socializing forces in the lives of adolescents, regulating the pace as well as the particulars of the socialization process. Adolescents who fall behind their friends in social skills are dropped from the group, just as are those who move ahead too quickly. Similarly, those whose tastes and attitudes fail to match the group's are likely to be considered "nerdy," "geeks," or just "out of it." The cost of bleating when others are crowing can be high.

The peer group assumes special importance in adolescence for a number of reasons. Adolescents are moving toward greater autonomy and independence, and peers provide much needed emotional and social support. Adolescents also learn many social skills with peers that they would not learn from parents or teachers. Peers reward each other with potent reinforcers: acceptance, popularity, and status (Muuss, 1990).

Cliques and Crowds

Most adolescents move in two types of groups: the clique and the crowd. A **clique** consists of the close friends with whom adolescents spend most of their time. A clique can be as large as ten or as small as three. Friends in the same clique are usually in the same class in school, the same sex and age, share the same ethnic background, and live close to each other. Since they live in the same neighborhood, their socioeconomic backgrounds are also similar (Brown, 1989).

A **crowd** is larger than a clique and more impersonal. Crowds usually number about 20. Not all the members of a crowd are close friends, but each is someone adolescents feel relatively comfortable with. Crowds consist of the friends in one's clique along with adolescents from several other cliques. It is nearly impossible for an adolescent to be a member of a crowd without belonging to one of these cliques; however, many adolescents belong to a clique and not to a crowd (Dunphy, 1963).

The functions of cliques and crowds differ. Crowd events provide the settings in which adolescents try out new social skills. Clique activities provide feedback about the success of these skills and advice when skills fall short. If the crowd has a single purpose, it is to help adolescents move from same-sex to mixed-sex interactions. Many adolescents need all the help they can get.

Adolescents spend most of their time talking about crowd activities when they are with members of their clique, either planning the next event or rehashing the last one, gathering valuable information from such "pregame" and "postgame" analyses. The feedback comes from specialists—other adolescents who know just how difficult a social maneuver can be, and who can recommend something that has worked for them in similar situations.

At crowd events, such as high school football games, where various cliques mingle, adolescents can practice new social skills and new roles with new people.

If clique activities are coaching sessions, crowd events are the game itself. Adolescents enter the field ready to try out new social moves. Reflecting their specialized nature, crowd and clique activities take place at different times during the week. Crowd events, just like actual games, occur on weekends, and clique activities, like other coaching sessions, take place throughout the week (Coleman, 1980).

Developmental changes occur in the structure of peer groups just as they do with friendships. Both cliques and crowds evolve as adolescents face different issues; so does the importance of being in a group. Belonging to groups is most important to early and middle adolescents, and less so for preadolescents, for whom they are not yet needed, or late adolescents, who no longer need them (Gavin & Fuhrman, 1989). As shown in Figure 6.1, five stages emerge, marking the transition from same-sex to mixed-sex groups.

The first two stages characterize interactions of early adolescents. Adolescents move in isolated, same-sex cliques in stage 1. There is no crowd at this stage; members of one clique have little to do with those of another. The first movement toward heterosexual encounters occurs in stage 2 with the emergence of the crowd.

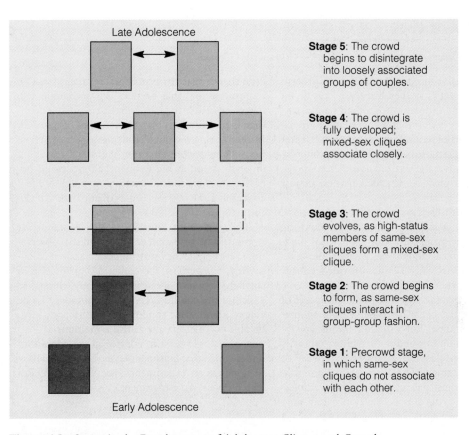

Figure 6.1 Stages in the Development of Adolescent Cliques and Crowds.
Source: Adapted from D. C. Dunphy. (1963). The social structure of urban adolescent peer groups. Sociometry, 26, 230–240.

Members of unisex cliques get together in crowds made up of cliques of both genders. Adolescents consider these initial interactions to be daring and only engage in them in the safety of groups (Dunphy, 1963). The author can attest to the accuracy of this observation. At a party given by her sixth-grade daughter, one of the girls hung some mistletoe. Within minutes the boys had fled the house and milled about in the yard in the dark, returning only after the mistletoe had been removed. Yet reports that filtered back over the next week indicated the boys had had a *great* time and wanted to know when there would be another party.

Stages 3 and 4 appear during mid-adolescence. In stage 3, heterosexual cliques emerge among the more popular adolescents as dating begins. These adolescents still retain their membership in their same-sex cliques, thereby involving other members in mixed-sex interactions. In stage 4, previously same-sex cliques reorganize into mixed-sex cliques for after-school activities. Adolescents in both of

RESEARCH FOCUS

Naturalistic Observation: "Hanging Out"—Cliques and Crowds

One of the purest forms of research is to observe adolescents directly, as they live their lives doing what they would ordinarily do in their natural settings. Researchers who follow this strategy are using the method of naturalistic observation. Dexter Dunphy (1963) studied adolescent peer groups by observing friends as they walked home from school, met for sports practice, attended parties, or just "hung out" together.

Dunphy identified two types of peer groups: the clique, a small group of intimate friends; and the crowd, a larger group of about 20. Crowd functions serve as social laboratories where adolescents try out new social skills. Cliques provide feedback about the success of these skills.

Naturalistic observations carry the advantage of assuring that the behaviors observed are spontaneous and genuine. But wouldn't having an observer like Dunphy around put a damper on many of the things adolescents would ordinarily say or do? Yes, but after a while he becomes so commonplace that he's just part of the backdrop. Adolescents find they don't especially notice him anymore. Since naturalistic observation places few, if any, restrictions on the conditions of observation, little chance of artifice exists; that is, there is

little chance that any procedural restriction will be responsible for what occurs. This technique also makes it possible to study behavior in greater depth than is possible with many other types of research. Instead of singling out a particular aspect of behavior, such as a score on a test of abstract reasoning or one's mood at the moment, all aspects of behavior are there for observation. A wealth of ideas concerning the possible causes of any behavior can come to mind.

This last point illustrates both an important strength and a weakness of naturalistic observations. Although they provide a rich source of hypotheses concerning the conditions giving rise to any behavior, they also offer few, if any, clues as to which of the conditions is the actual cause. To be able to identify one condition as a cause, one must be able to rule out alternative conditions. To do this, one would need to control all the conditions under which that behavior occurs. One would have to conduct an experiment. (See Chapter 3, Research Focus: An Experiment.)

Reference: D. C. Dunphy (1963). The social structure of urban adolescent peer groups. Sociometry, 26, 230–240.

these stages continue to associate with same-sex friends while they are at school (Montemayor & Van Komer, 1985).

The crowd becomes more important by mid-adolescence and is fully developed and at its strongest by stage 4. By stage 5 (late adolescence) the crowd has fulfilled its primary function and is no longer needed. Adolescents are comfortable with others of the opposite sex, and the crowd disintegrates into loosely grouped cliques of couples who are "going together." Cliques also become less important with age. The number of adolescents belonging to a clique declines from the sixth to the twelfth grades. Similarly, the number of adolescents identified as "liaisons," individuals whose primary ties are with members of other cliques, increases during these grades (Brown, 1989).

All crowds are not created equal. Ask any adolescent. Some are more prestigious than others. A "leading crowd" exists at most schools (Coleman, 1961;

Brown & Lohr, 1987). Students in this crowd are held in high regard by others, sometimes even to the point of envy. Almost always the members of this crowd feel good about themselves as well, having higher levels of self-esteem than students in less-prestigious crowds (Brown & Lohr, 1987). All the students at any school know what it takes to be a member of the leading crowd. For boys, being good at sports is important; for girls, it is being a social leader. Students in the leading crowd are also likely to be leaders in the school and even to have teachers look to them for help with extracurricular activities (Brown & Lohr, 1987).

Other crowds form a loose status hierarchy below the leading crowd. Adolescents receive constant reminders at school of their status. Who they sit with in the cafeteria, who can cut in front of whom in line, which clubs and activities are open or closed to them—all confirm the loose pecking order that reflects the relative prestige of their particular crowd. One might think that the only ones to escape with their self-esteem intact would be those from the leading crowd. However, adolescents from other crowds appear to fare just as well if they like the crowd to which they belong. This suggests that although peer group membership is important for adolescents, it is a sense of belonging rather than the status of the group itself that is critical (Brown & Lohr, 1987).

Popularity

Which adolescents are popular? Research on popularity consistently shows that for boys, being good in sports contributes significantly to popularity, and for girls, being a social leader is important. For both, physical attractiveness is also a significant factor (Coleman, 1961; Williams & White, 1983). In addition, personality characteristics such as being comfortable with oneself, enthusiasm, and friendliness relate to popularity (Coleman, 1980; Sebald, 1981).

Determinants of Popularity.   In a classic study of popularity, students at ten different high schools were asked to identify which of their classmates were the most outstanding athletes, social leaders, "brains," and so on. For boys at every school, the best athletes were also considered to be the most popular with girls. Athletes were twice as likely to be in the leading crowd as were "brains." Perhaps not surprisingly, when boys were asked how they would most like to be remembered, 44% of them said as an "athletic star." For girls, being a leader in school activities contributed most to popularity and was the way most of them wanted to be remembered (Coleman, 1961).

This picture has changed little over the years. J. M. Williams and K. A. White (1983) replicated the earlier study and found that 43% of the adolescent males they interviewed wanted to be thought of as good in sports. Being an athletic star carries as few advantages for adolescent females as it did a generation ago (Kane, 1988). Just like their mothers, the most popular girls are leaders in school activities (Coleman, 1961; Williams & White, 1983). One noticeable change is that adolescent females value good grades more than they did a generation ago (Butcher, 1986).

Even though most adolescents think good looks are important for popularity, physical attractiveness may not be as important as they believe. Physical appearance probably contributes to popularity only for those adolescents at either extreme. For those in between—and this would be most adolescents—other factors are more important (Cavior & Dokecki, 1973). Conversely, academic achievement is probably more important than most research has suggested. Part of the difficulty in interpreting the findings on academic achievement may be due to the way questions have been worded. When asked, "How would you like to be remembered?" boys say as an athletic star and girls as a leader in activities (Coleman, 1961). But when asked, "How would you rank the following in importance to you?" most adolescents put getting good grades above being good in sports or being a social leader (Butcher, 1986).

The importance of athletic ability, school activities, and academic achievement for popularity also vary from one school to another. Athletic ability tends to have more importance, for example, in rural communities and in schools drawing from lower socioeconomic levels, whereas in urban settings, or in communities with more highly educated parents, it is less important (Eitzen, 1975).

Social Competence.   Several dimensions of **social competence** have been found to be important for popularity among children. Although these dimensions almost surely remain important social skills, we know considerably less about adolescents (Allen, Weissberg, & Hawkins, 1989). The skills involve assessing the situation, responding to it, and adopting a process approach to relationships.

The first component of social competence, assessing the situation, is to see what's going on and adapt one's behavior accordingly (Putallaz, 1983). In a sense, joining a social group involves some of the same skills adolescents learn when driving. One has to judge the speed of the ongoing activity, accelerate, then move into the thick of things. Pulling onto a freeway at 10 miles per hour requires everyone else to slow down to your speed: It doesn't work.

When adolescents "pull into the fast lane" with a remark such as "What are you doing?" they're asking others to stop for them, an unlikely response if they are enjoying themselves. Entry remarks that call attention away from the ongoing activity are likely to be rebuffed. Similarly, remarks about oneself are usually unsuccessful ways of getting a group's attention. Instead, fitting into a group appears to be a matter of figuring out what the group is doing. Those who are better at this are more popular. Simply put, one needs to be able to know what the group is doing in order to join in (Putallaz, 1983; Dodge, 1983).

The second dimension of social competence is responding appropriately to others' behavior. Those who are popular are distinguished not as much by their own initiation of encounters as by their positive response to the initiations of others. In fact, popular individuals approach others infrequently; but they *are* better at keeping things going, and others appear to have a better time with them (Dodge, 1983).

Joking around with casual acquaintances—other players in a pickup baseball game, for instance—doesn't come easily to every adolescent. For most, however, social competence increases with age and experience.

The third dimension distinguishing social competence is adopting a process approach to relationships. Popular individuals recognize that relationships take time to develop, they wait before entering a group. Apparently they understand the best way to reach a goal is sometimes an indirect one. For example, instead of directly asking, "What are you doing?" they might ask someone over after school or suggest going to the library to study together (Asher, 1983).

Research with adolescents supports the observation that making friends is a matter of social competence, and not luck. Prosocial behaviors, such as sharing and being cooperative, are related to peer acceptance, as is knowing which strategies are appropriate for making friends and which ones aren't (Wentzel & Erdley, 1993). In fact, one of the best correlates of loneliness in mid-adolescence is perceiving oneself as having poor social skills (Inderbitzen-Pisaruk, Clark, & Solano, 1992).

Even in close friendships, social skills are important to the relationship. What form these skills take depends in part on the power adolescents see themselves as wielding vis-à-vis that of their friend. Not until about mid-adolescence do same-sex friends see themselves as balanced in power (Furman & Buhrmester, 1992).

Power-balanced relationships are important for the types of strategies adolescents use when resolving differences with others; when equally powerful, one can bargain or negotiate; when not, one is reduced to nagging or simply going along with what the other wants (Hartup, 1993).

Dating

Dating is so much a part of the cultural scene one might assume it has always been practiced. Yet it is a relatively recent phenomenon. Prior to the early 1900s, couples dated primarily to determine their suitability for marriage. Before that, girls were given in marriage by their families to suitable partners; young couples had little say over the choices of their prospective mates.

Dating today serves a number of functions, of which the selection of marriage partners is only one. A very important function for adolescents when they first begin to date is simply recreation: Dating is fun—or at least it's supposed to be. Adolescents also report feeling nervous and apprehensive. Dates can have awkward moments. Many adolescents fear rejection and are uncertain as to how to act on a date. Should the male or the female open the car door? One girl explained, "You just sort of walk along and if he walks the other way, you know you have to open it yourself." Should the male help a female on with her coat? "I act like I'm having problems, and if he doesn't notice, I forget it," suggested one teenager (Place, 1975). Yet despite the uncertainties, most adolescents find dating enjoyable.

When Dating Begins.   Adolescents start to date between the ages of 12 and 16. Girls go out on first dates somewhat earlier than boys (they also enter puberty earlier). Most girls start to date by age 14, although age itself is not the only indicator. One can better predict whether an adolescent is dating by knowing whether friends have begun to date than by knowing the adolescent's age or even sexual maturity (Dornbusch, Carlsmith, Gross, Martin, Jenning, Rosenberg, & Duke, 1981). Parents seem especially subject to a form of peer pressure all their own in this respect. As one adolescent girl remarked when she explained how she got her parents to consent to letting her go on a date, "If your girlfriends are not going out, forget it. I just gave examples of who was going out." Another ice-breaker was a strategy learned from childhood:

DAUGHTER: Dad, can I go to the movies with Eddie?

FATHER: I don't know; ask Mom.

DAUGHTER: Mom, Dad said Eddie and I can go to the movies if you say it's okay.

MOTHER: Okay, then, you can go.

DAUGHTER: Dad, Mom said it's okay.

The peer group regulates the pace of socialization into more adult roles. Adolescents who don't begin dating when their friends do may be dropped from

When they are just beginning to date, most adolescents worry about awkward moments and fear rejection. Once they do date someone regularly, however, the self-consciousness diminishes and they can relax and have fun.

their peer groups. Adolescent girls frequently report friction with their friends when they begin moving into opposite-sex relationships. These conflicts often involve concerns of disloyalty and competition. Boys, on the other hand, do not experience the same difficulties (Miller, 1990).

Crushes. Even before dating begins, adolescents go through a stage in which they develop crushes. A crush involves an idealized fantasy about another person, and it is rarely reciprocated (Adams-Price & Greene, 1990). The other person remains distant, even if it's someone just two seats away in the same class. The absence of reciprocity and the distance factor in crushes are important features, because they allow adolescents to explore heterosexual role possibilities at a safe distance (Erikson, 1950, 1968).

Multiple Dating. Once dating begins, most adolescents practice multiple dating: going out with many different partners. Multiple dating often involves adolescents in superficial relationships in which each partner plays out a well-defined role. Important personality characteristics can be missed in these brief encounters. Characteristics such as loyalty or integrity may never become apparent, because multiple dating involves non-exclusive relationships that limit the commitment between partners. Instead of making it easier for teenagers to meet many different people, multiple dating may bring them up against the same role played out, in somewhat different form, by each. Paradoxically, by dating many different partners, they may have less chance to learn objective ways of assessing the personalities of others than if they got to know one or two people better (Husbands, 1970; Stevens-Long & Cobb, 1983).

Multiple dating may also reflect a quest for the impossible "ideal" date—the "perfect" person who can surely be found if one meets enough people. Many adolescents enter relationships the way they enter a supermarket: with a shopping list in hand. They want someone who is good-looking, intelligent, and has a sense of humor. The problem with looking for someone with specific attributes is that the same characteristics may not fit one's interests and needs in ten years. This approach to finding "Mr. Right" or "Ms. Perfect" assumes that relationships are static and do not change with time. But does one stay the same despite one's involvement with another person? The quest for the ideal date assumes that happiness is a function of being with the right person, and that if one is unhappy, one should look for someone else (Stevens-Long & Cobb, 1983).

Another approach to relationships emphasizes the way they affect the process of personal growth. The relationship becomes a medium for exploring the self and developing one's potential. Well-being is a function of what one brings to the relationship. Other people make one neither happy nor unhappy; satisfaction and happiness reflect a state of self-actualization. How does this relate to dating? The "ideal" date may be like the unicorn: sought by all but found by none (Stevens-Long & Cobb, 1983).

ADOLESCENTS, PARENTS, AND PEERS

Conformity

Friends draw adolescents into realms beyond the family that highlight differences between themselves and their parents. These differences become important ways of organizing their individuality; however, they can leave adolescents with feelings of loneliness. Peers provide the emotional support that contributes to feelings of self-worth (O'Brien & Bierman, 1988). Peer expectations for well-defined standards of speech and dress also establish outward behaviors that define the group and establish a sense of belonging among its members. Adolescents consider it a bargain to give up some of their individuality for the security that comes with belonging to a group (Gavin & Furman, 1989).

Conformity peaks in early adolescence when adolescents begin to experience their separateness from their parents. Studies of conformity show that early adolescents are most influenced by others' judgments, sometimes even changing their answers when they are obviously right to conform to those of the group. By mid-

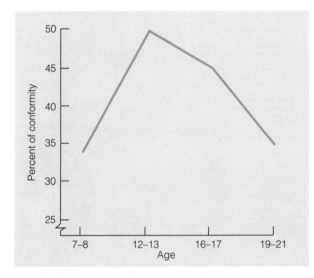

Figure 6.2 Changes in Percent of Conformity with Age.

Source: P. R. Costanzo. (1970). Conformity development as a function of self-blame. Journal of Personality and Social Psychology, 14, *366–374.*

adolescence, conformity has already begun to decrease (Gavin & Furman, 1989). Figure 6.2 shows this trend.

Conformity isn't limited to adolescence; it characterizes behavior at every age. Nor is conformity necessarily bad. It is simply a tendency to go along with the standards and norms of one's group. Trends in fashion, food, and recreation are as apparent among 50-year-olds as 15-year-olds. We notice conformity, however, when the norms for one group run counter to those of another, as sometimes occurs with adolescents and their parents. Different behaviors and skills contribute to acceptance more by peers than by adults. These differences increase with age in early adolescence (Allen, Weissberg, & Hawkins, 1989).

Not all adolescents are equally likely to conform to the opinions of others. Those who have high status in their peer group are less likely to show conformity. The same is true for adolescents who have a well-developed sense of themselves. In general, adolescents who have a firm sense of who they are, and are held in high regard by others, are less influenced by others' opinions. The same has been found to be true for adults (Harvey & Rutherford, 1980; Marcia, 1980).

Conformity also reflects adolescents' relationships with their parents. Parents who have encouraged adolescents to take part in responsible decision making within the family, who provide reasons when disciplining, and who encourage a verbal give and take with their children—that is, authoritative parents, as discussed in Chapter 5—have adolescents who show the least conformity. Adolescents from these homes have more positive self-concepts and a better developed sense of self. Further, they have learned from childhood to live with the consequences of their decisions, even when these have been as simple as deciding not to clean their rooms and choosing to be "grounded" instead. They have also learned that even when

Every generation of adolescents creates a culture that seems wholly foreign to older generations. And yet, in spite of their untraditional tastes, adolescents' values remain surprisingly similar to those of their grandparents' generations.

their parents disagree with them, they still have their emotional support (Cooper, Grotevant, & Condon, 1983).

However, even authoritative parents can worry that peers will have more influence than they on their children's values and activities. Adolescents are beginning to spend more time with their friends than with their families. Perhaps, too, parents realize that the decisions adolescents make can affect their futures in ways decisions rarely do for children. Even so, adolescents report that parents are the best all-around source of support, whether emotional or informational, in the form of advice (Reid, Landesman, Treder, & Jaccard, 1989).

Fashion fads such as shaved heads, black lipstick, and oversized jeans do little for parents' fears that they have lost their children to an alien culture. But even flagrant differences such as these do not mean that parents no longer influence their children's values. If they did not, adolescents would not have to go to such extremes to assert their individuality. Nor do obvious differences in taste, as in music and clothes, reflect a shift in underlying values. This is not to say that adolescents are not influenced by their peers. They are. But the extent to which they are and the way this occurs cannot be thought of simply as an "either-or" contest between the values of parents and those of peers.

Values and Peer Pressure

Adolescents experience **peer pressure** as a pressure to think and act like their friends. The price of belonging to a group is to maintain the ways of the group.

This pressure changes with age. One of the primary functions of the peer group is to help adolescents gain their footing as they step outside the family. As adolescents become more sure of themselves, pressures to maintain the norms of the group lessen. Peer pressure is strongest in early adolescence, when adolescents most need the support of a well-defined group. Conformity is also greatest then. As adolescents become more sure of themselves, the peer group becomes less important. As a result, the need to define group membership through rigidly prescribed standards of dress, speech, and so on lessens (Clasen & Brown, 1985).

With age, too, adolescents become more comfortable in thinking for themselves and arriving at their own decisions. They are less likely to look to their parents *or* their friends for advice, and when they do seek advice, they are better able to weigh the opinions of others and arrive at their own decisions. This confidence reflects a new level of security in their values and how they arrived at them (Josselson, 1980).

Most adolescents spend more time talking with their friends than with their parents and are more influenced by their friends about day-to-day decisions. But the background and the values of an adolescent's friends tend to be similar to those of the adolescent's parents.

If anything, the values of peers and parents are likely to complement each other rather than conflict. Friends typically share similar experiences; they live nearby, come from families of about the same income level, and are likely to share the same ethnic background. As a result, friends' values are likely to be similar to those of the adolescent and his or her parents (Tolson & Urberg, 1993; Youth Indicators, 1991).

Of course, some differences between parents and peers can be expected. And when they occur, the reference group that adolescents turn to will depend on a number of factors, one of which is the type of decision to be made. Adolescents generally look to their friends for short-term decisions, such as whether to go to a party, or what clothes to buy. They turn to their parents for decisions about their futures: plans for education or marriage, or choosing an occupation. Thus parents have more influence over the larger decisions of life, and friends over the day-to-day particulars of living it (Wilks, 1986; Wintre, Hicks, McVey, & Fox, 1988). Among parents, adolescents are more likely to seek, and follow, advice from their mothers than their fathers (Greene & Grimsley, 1990; Reid, Landesman, Treder, & Jaccard, 1989).

Important life decisions reflect values, and adolescents are likely to share these with their parents—values about education, relationships, and work. But values as broad as these do not translate easily into the language of daily affairs. They say little about how one spends an afternoon or which movie to see. With respect to actual behaviors such as these, friends have more influence (Stevens-Long & Cobb, 1983).

Having values in common is not that important to friendship during adolescence. Some similarities are important among friends, certainly, but these are more likely to involve interests and activities such as taste in music and what they enjoy doing, rather than religious beliefs or political views (Kandel, 1978; Tolson & Urberg, 1993).

Deviant Behavior and Peer Pressure

The support of friends remains important with respect to deviant behavior. Adolescents seek out friends who engage in similar activities and, in turn, are influenced by the activities of their friends. In one study of 2,000 adolescents, it was found that after similarities in age, grade in school, sex, and race, friends are most likely to be similar in their use of marijuana. No other single activity or attitude was found to be as likely to be shared by friends as the use of recreational drugs (Kandel, 1978). Similarly, Kathryn Urberg (1992) followed pairs of friends over a two-year period and found that individual friends, and not the social crowd, were the major influence in whether adolescents were likely to smoke.

In part, too, this similarity in the use of recreational drugs reflects adolescents' perceptions of their friends as more deviant than they actually are. Karl Bauman and Lynn Fisher (1986) obtained self-reports from 1,400 seventh-graders whom they followed up in the eighth grade, and another 1,400 ninth-graders whom they surveyed again as tenth-graders. Adolescents were asked to estimate their friends' use of cigarettes, beer, and hard liquor. Then the friends themselves indicated how much they used these substances. The investigators found that adolescents typically overestimated the extent to which their friends engaged in deviant behavior. Adolescents' use of these substances corresponded more closely to their perceptions of what their friends did than with their friends' actual behavior. Adolescents *are* influenced by their friends, but they also appear to select friends based on their perception of similar characteristics—especially as these characteristics relate to deviant behaviors.

Actual pressure from friends to misbehave may be relatively slight. A survey of nearly 700 junior high and high school students found little pressure from friends for misconduct—for example, drug or alcohol use or sexual intercourse—and much actual discouragement by friends. Different crowds exert pressure in different areas of adolescents' lives, of course, and the "druggie-toughs" surveyed in this study experienced more pressure for misconduct than did "jock-populars" or "loners" (Clasen & Brown, 1985).

What are adolescents likely to do if approached by a friend to engage in some deviant activity? Adolescents of either sex feel different pressures. Boys are more likely to agree or disagree because of the anticipated outcome; they will say no because they're not interested or they think they might get in trouble. Peer approval and friendship are more important sources of pressure for girls. Girls are more likely to agree even when they anticipate a negative outcome, citing friendship or peer approval as reasons (Pearl, Bryan, & Herzog, 1990; Treboux & Busch-Rossnagel, 1990).

How much influence parents retain with their teenagers when deviant behaviors or conflicting values arise depends in large measure on the quality of the relationship they have with them. For instance, Andrew Fuligni and Jacquelynne Eccles (1993), studying a sample of over 1,700 sixth and seventh graders, found that adolescents who perceived themselves as having little opportunity to participate in decision making, and who believed their parents to be overly strict, were less likely than other adolescents to seek advice from their parents and more likely to turn to their peers. They were also more likely to sacrifice significant aspects of their own lives, such as keeping up with schoolwork or developing their talents, in order to be popular with friends.

Parents who are overly permissive or authoritarian are least effective. Adolescents are most likely to listen to parents who have involved them since childhood in decision making in the family and have held them responsible for their actions. These parents are also most likely to give reasons for family rules and to maintain an open dialogue with their children. Adolescents from families such as these, with a strongly developed sense of self, are less likely to be pressured by peers to misbehave.

It is easier for adolescents to listen to their parents' views when they are sure of their own autonomy. The quality of the relationship between adolescents and their parents, not the existence of another reference group, determines whether adolescents will remain close to their parents and seek them out for advice in decisions about their lives (Josselson, 1980).

It should be clear at this point that the relative influence of parents and peers cannot be thought of as a simple tug-of-war with the adolescent in the middle. The values of friends frequently overlap with those of parents, minimizing conflict when it occurs. Parents may occasionally even look to an adolescent's friends to determine what is normative when they are uncertain as to what adolescent behaviors are appropriate, for example, when to wear lipstick or when to get a part-time job. Also, the values of parents and peers influence different types of decisions, leading to less conflict than many parents anticipate. Finally, adolescents vary considerably among themselves in the extent to which they are influenced by the attitudes and behaviors of others, whether these be parents or peers (Conger, 1977).

Are adolescents and parents likely to experience conflict? Probably. Does conflict weaken the relationship? Not necessarily. Conflict can help adolescents restructure and strengthen relationships with parents. Parents are likely to participate in this restructuring process as well. Even as they attempt to get teenagers to agree with them, parents also encourage adolescents to think for themselves and to speak their own minds. Honest exchanges such as these frequently lead to the evolution of joint views shared by both (Youniss & Smollar, 1989).

The Generation Gap: Is It Widening?

Adolescents today live in a culture to which their parents have limited access. This is a relatively recent phenomenon, occurring with the emergence of high schools at the turn of the century. Even just 100 years ago, few adolescents continued their education beyond the eighth grade. In 1882, for example, slightly less than one in a thousand graduated from high school. Most got jobs and worked alongside adults. As a consequence, they shared the same experiences and knowledge as their parents (Youniss & Smollar, 1989).

As more adolescents began to attend high school, they acquired knowledge that their parents didn't have, thereby separating the generations. Even though parents experienced themselves as distanced from their children, they were aware that their children needed schooling in order to acquire the skills needed to succeed in a changing culture, one that was becoming increasingly industrialized. In effect, parents at the turn of the century experienced the plight of many ethnic groups today. The education that would help their children find a better place in society would also distance their children from them.

High schools today may contribute to a similar sense of unease among parents. By law, all adolescents must attend high school until they reach a certain age. As our society becomes increasingly diverse ethnically and racially, so do the schools that adolescents attend. High school environments enable adolescents from different social classes and ethnic groups to interact more than they would otherwise. Many parents' fears reflect a concern that their values will be replaced by those of another social or ethnic group.

The mass media—radio, television, and movies—also expose adolescents to values that may not be shared by parents. Most adolescents listen to the same music, wear the same clothes, and have the same role models—those provided by television and movies. Is the gap widening?

A study by H. M. Bahr (1980) provides us with some answers. Bahr interviewed adolescents from a typical American community. What makes his study especially interesting is that adolescents from this same community were interviewed 50 years ago in a similar research effort. As you might expect, there were some differences in the answers of adolescents then and now. But overall, the values of adolescents today are surprisingly similar to those of their grandparents' generation. If anything, Bahr suggests that the generation gap may be smaller now. Teenagers today place more importance on receiving respect for their opinions from parents. They also continue to affirm the importance of time together as a family.

Despite the increasing importance of friends in adolescents' lives, parents continue to remain significant sources of strength and influence. Both parents and peers contribute to adolescents' ability to face changes in yet another area of their lives—school. We will analyze these changes in the next chapter.

SUMMARY

Friendships During Adolescence

Adolescents experiment with new behaviors with their friends, and in doing so, discover new things about themselves. Friends are important sources of self-esteem during adolescence.

Friendships change with age. Those of preadolescents reflect a concern with being accepted. Preadolescents use gossip as a way of affirming group norms and their membership in the group. Adolescent friendships reflect a concern with self-discovery; self-disclosure becomes important to this process.

Friendship Patterns

Patterns of friendship differ with the age and sex of adolescents. Early adolescent girls' friendships focus on the activities that bring friends together. Friendships in mid-adolescence for girls are concerned with the personal qualities of friends more than before. Girls want friends they can confide in and trust. Friendships in late adolescence focus more on personalities. Intimacy continues to grow and more friends are of the opposite sex.

Boys' friendships in early adolescence are

also centered around shared activities. By mid-adolescence, their friendships are as close emotionally as girls' friendships but involve less discussion of feelings.

Adolescents of both sexes experience greater pressure to grow up faster than adolescents of previous generations.

Despite gender differences in close friendships, peer interactions show many of the same patterns for either sex. Most friendships are with peers of the same race.

Interracial friendships form when adolescents live in integrated neighborhoods and attend integrated schools. Classroom climates affect the formation of cross-race friendships, which are likely to develop when students are assigned to small groups to work together in a noncompetitive atmosphere. Interracial friendships face challenges posed by different enculturation experiences. Adolescents of different backgrounds can perceive and react to the same situation differently; misinterpretations and hurt feelings can result.

The Peer Group

The peer group regulates the pace of socialization. Adolescents who either fall too far behind or move too far ahead of their friends are dropped from the group.

Cliques are small groups of close friends. Clique activities provide feedback about the success of social skills.

Crowds are groups of about 20. Adolescents try out new social skills at crowd events, the most important of which involve the opposite sex. The crowd is primarily important in helping adolescents move from same-sex to opposite-sex relationships.

Cliques and crowds change in importance as adolescents age. Crowds are most important in mid-adolescence and decrease thereafter.

Popularity for boys is closely tied to being good in sports; for girls it is related to being a social leader.

Several dimensions of social competence also contribute to popularity: assessing a situation, responding to it, and adopting a process approach to relationships. Popular individuals are better able to see what is going on in a social situation and adapt their behavior accordingly. They are also more responsive to the overtures of others, and they realize that developing friendships takes time.

Dating can begin anywhere between the ages of 12 and 16. Girls start somewhat earlier than boys. The most important determinant of when they start to date is whether their friends are dating.

Even before dating begins, adolescents go through a stage in which they develop crushes. Once dating begins, most adolescents practice multiple dating, going out with many different partners.

Adolescents, Parents, and Peers

Conformity peaks in early adolescence. Adolescents with high social status and a well-developed sense of self are less likely to conform. Authoritative parenting also gives adolescents skills that help them make decisions for themselves.

The values of peers and parents more frequently complement each other than conflict. Most adolescents have friends with values similar to theirs.

When adolescents seek advice from parents and friends, they are more likely to seek parental advice concerning long-term life decisions and the advice of friends in daily matters. With age, adolescents become more comfortable in making their own decisions.

Peers have an important influence on deviant behaviors. Gender differences exist in response to peer pressure; boys consider the anticipated outcome more, and girls consider peer approval and friendship more.

Despite the importance of the peer culture, adolescents and parents share many basic values.

KEY TERMS

Self-disclosure
Enculturation
Clique

Crowd
Social Competence

Conformity
Peer Pressure

SECONDARY SCHOOLS TODAY
Academic Tracking
School Size
School Climate
Teachers' Attitudes

■ *RESEARCH FOCUS   Dependent Variables: Beauty and the Best—Are Looks and Grades Related?*

School Violence
Teaching Peace
Preparing for High School: Junior High or Middle School

ADOLESCENTS AT SCHOOL
Literacy, Television, and Homework
Patterns of Achievement
Gender Differences and Achievement
High School Dropouts

ADOLESCENTS AT THE EDGE
Gifted Adolescents

■ *RESEARCH FOCUS   Case Studies: Educating the Gifted Adolescent*

Adolescents with Learning Disabilities

CULTURE AND GENDER IN THE CLASSROOM: EDUCATION FOR ALL
Gender Stereotypes in Teaching Materials
Multicultural Education
Overcoming the Differences

SUMMARY

KEY TERMS

CHAPTER SEVEN

Adolescents in the Schools

"Oh, no! Here he comes," I muttered.

"Move over, slime ball. Thanks for the place in line."

The kid was huge and his breath was fogging up my glasses. No food was worth this. I stepped out, and he stepped in line. From what I could see of the steam table, I was ahead on this one.

"Aren't you going to fight him?" nudged Sarah.

"Sure, Sarah. You want me to end up in the tossed salad?"

"This is too much!" she rasped. "The morning has gone from bad to awful—I want out!"

"Me too," I nodded. "But I don't think I could find my way. I got lost three times already today. If I'm late to another class, I'll have detention—and it's still the first week! Four minutes to get to classes! What are they training us for, the track team? I can't even open my locker that fast."

"Some ninth grader slammed mine shut this morning—just as I popped the combination."

"Welcome to scrubs-ville, Sarah."

"If this is what it's going to be like, I'm out of here!" she vowed.

Secondary school is a new experience for early adolescents, one that most will never forget. Adolescents leave behind the comfortable familiarity of elementary school: a classroom they know as well as their living room and a teacher they saw more often than their parents. They also leave the comfortable security of being the oldest and biggest students at school. More opportunities are available to students in secondary school—and more is expected of them.

The number of students attending high schools in the United States has increased dramatically over this century. More than two and a third million students graduate from high school each year. A high school education will give them the skills they will need for jobs and college. Courses in computer programming, woodworking and metalworking, conversational French, drafting, journalism, and peer leadership alternate with the basics of math, English, and social studies. In many respects, secondary education is one of our society's biggest success stories. In other respects, it is the focus of national concern and controversy. We look at the successes and failings of our secondary schools in the first section of this chapter.

Not all students have the same interests and not all learn at the same rate. Many schools assign students to academic tracks that reflect their different interests and abilities. Some educators argue that assigning students to academic tracks creates as many problems as it is designed to solve. The practice of tracking and its relationship to academic success are discussed. School variables such as the size of the school and the learning climates of classrooms can also influence adolescents in important ways. We look at these variables in a subsequent section of the chapter.

Some adolescents leave elementary school for a junior high, and others go to a middle school; they spend fifth or sixth, seventh, eighth and sometimes ninth grade here before moving into high school. We consider the research comparing middle schools and junior high schools. Despite obvious differences, these schools have many similarities. Both move at a quicker pace than elementary school. Adolescents move from class to class, with a different teacher in each and sometimes no close friends in any.

In the next section of the chapter, adolescents themselves step into the spotlight. Some achieve and meet the expectations of teachers and parents; others do not. We look first at conditions such as teachers' attitudes and school violence that affect success and failure for all, and then move to a consideration of two extreme populations—the gifted and those with learning disabilities.

Some critics of schools argue that they are white, middle-class institutions dominated by conventional attitudes. We examine how well schools are meeting the needs of female as well as male students and adolescents from ethnically and racially diverse backgrounds. Research into effective schools raises the question of whether changes that are considered necessary in order to reach alienated minorities are also necessary to effectively teach mainstream adolescents.

SECONDARY SCHOOLS TODAY

The growth of secondary education in this country during the last century has been nothing short of phenomenal. Figure 7.1 shows the percentages of individuals under age 19 who graduated from high school over the past 100 years. This society has progressed from graduating fewer than 5% of the population after four years of high school to nearly 75%. Students who take longer than four years to graduate and dropouts who reenter the system bring the overall completion rate to 85% (Huelskamp, 1993). Quite a success story! Yet the successes of secondary education have been punctuated by crises as well.

As more students attend high school, the diversity of the student population has increased (Banks, 1993). In years past, the less successful would not have remained in school. The increasing ethnic diversity of our society is also a source of

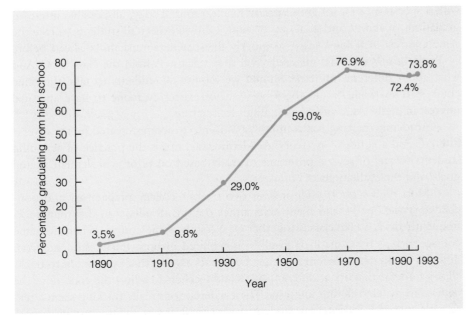

Figure 7.1   Increase in High School Graduates Over the Past 100 Years

Source: Digest of Education Statistics. *(1993). U.S. Department of Education. Washington, DC: U.S. Government Printing Office.*

differences among students. Teachers must reach students of widely differing cultural backgrounds, some of whom have limited knowledge of English or of the dominant culture. Many schools face the need to instruct students from two dozen or more cultural backgrounds.

Secondary schools face an additional crisis. The increase in numbers of students attending high school has not been accompanied by an increase in the number of schools. From 1930 to 1970, for instance, the number of students attending school tripled, but the number of schools remained the same (Garbarino, 1980). Today, there are actually fewer high schools than there were in the mid-70s (*Digest of Education Statistics*, 1993). Thus, high schools are larger today than ever before, and large schools introduce problems of their own. Each of the challenges facing today's schools requires a closer look.

Academic Tracking

One of the biggest problems facing high schools is the tremendous diversity of their students. Generations ago only those who were academically oriented completed high school. Others found jobs and got married. High school was for those with a special interest in, and capacity for, learning. Today, all possible interests, gradations of ability, and goals are present. Can we expect all students to take the same courses? Will some learn so quickly that teachers must move ahead before others have mastered the material? Will slower learners hold the class back? And what about different interests? Should we require all students to take the same courses? If so, what should these be? Can we expect everyone to have an equal interest in math? Auto mechanics? English literature?

Academic tracking is a common solution to problems created by the diverse interests and abilities of students. **Academic tracking** is the practice of assigning students to one of several programs of study based on prior achievement, stated goals, and the evaluations of counselors.

Most high schools offer at least two tracks—college preparatory and non-college (vocational)—and many offer other options. Students in different tracks frequently do not take classes together even for the same course. When the same course, such as basic math or English, is required in both tracks, students from different tracks take different sections. Educators assume that assignment to tracks allows students to work at different paces and teachers to adjust the content of the courses to match differing interests. These assumptions make tracking seem a reasonable approach for teaching students with very different abilities and interests.

However, tracking may in fact contribute to the problems it was designed to correct. Minority and low-income adolescents are more frequently assigned to non-college than to college tracks (Youth Indicators, 1993; Page, 1990). Of the students assigned to noncollege tracks, more lose interest in school and eventually drop out than those assigned to college preparatory tracks. Can assignment to a lower track contribute to a sense of alienation and failure among these students? Research suggests that it does (Snow, 1986).

Analysis of a national sample of over 10,000 high school students reveals that those students assigned to the lower track do more poorly and are less likely to graduate from high school (Gamoran & Mare, 1989). These investigators used achievement scores in mathematics and the probability of graduating as indices of student success. Most of the difference in mathematics achievement between students assigned to college and noncollege tracks was accounted for by preexisting differences. At first glance, these data would appear to support the belief that students assigned to each track differ primarily in ability. However, 20% of the difference could be traced to the assignment to tracks. A difference this size is more than the increase in math achievement scores gained by an average student between his or her sophomore and senior years! It is also larger than the difference between the scores of students in noncollege tracks and the scores of high school dropouts. Tracking has an even greater effect on the probability of staying in school than it does on math scores. Over 50% of the difference in graduation rates between students in college and noncollege tracks could be explained by their track assignment (Gamoran & Mare, 1989).

Secondary-school students are often divided into vocational and college-bound tracks. The mere assignment to one track or the other can profoundly affect students' performance and teachers' expectations.

These and similar data strongly suggest that the practice of tracking adversely affects students who are assigned to lower tracks (Oakes, 1985). Tracking makes it more likely that these students will work toward lower goals, proceed at a slower pace, have fewer opportunities to learn, and achieve less than students in higher tracks. More class time goes to discipline and less to instruction. Even the quality of teaching differs, in addition to what is taught (Page, 1990). Shafer, Olexa, and Polk (1972) conclude that tracking "independently contributes to resentment, frustration, and hostility, finally ending in active withdrawal from the alienating situation or school" (p. 42).

How does tracking contribute to these problems? Reba Page (1990), at the University of California, Riverside, points to the day-to-day experiences of lower-track students, arguing that their courses, rather than training them in job skills, are frequently watered-down versions of college-preparatory classes. She adds that classroom exercises all too frequently communicate a different set of values, in which luck and guessing, rather than hard work and skill, determine success. Page observed nine lower-track classrooms for six months. A particular lesson which involved a "trivia quiz" captured the qualities she had come to recognize in much of lower-track instruction. The quiz was presented to students as a "kinda fun" way of improving their listening skills, one in which they needn't "know" the answers, but simply make "a good guess." Students, however, were not given a strategy to use in coming up with a "good" guess. Nor was the content of the quiz related to their coursework or familiar experiences outside the classroom. Instead, students found themselves participating in a task in which competence had been ruled out and relevance was missing, yet one which they were told would help them in their schoolwork. Disengagement, in the form of problem behavior or lack of apparent motivation, is predictable when effort is unrelated to success and coursework is unrelated to the skills students will need on the job. A vicious cycle is perpetuated when teachers, put off by students' indifference, no longer look for ways of challenging interest and harnessing ability.

One student assigned to the lower track put it this way:

> When you first go to junior high school you do feel something inside—it's like ego. You have been from elementary to junior high, you feel great inside. You say, well, doggone, I'm going to deal with the people here now, I am in junior high school. You get this shirt that says Brown Junior High or whatever the name is and you are proud of that shirt. But then you go up there and the teacher says, "Well, so and so, you're in the basic section, you can't go with the other kids." The devil with the whole thing—you lose something in you—like it just goes out of you. (Schafer, Olexa, & Polk, 1972, p. 47)

Despite the serious problems that exist with tracking, the practice has increased in junior high schools (Snow, 1986), and is even more common in high schools due to differences in career interests and ability levels (Wigdor & Garner, 1982). Educators face a pressing need to find alternatives that work equally well for students in all tracks. Alternatives exist. Students of different ability levels can be placed together in small working groups. This approach, known as cooperative learning, gives students recognition for both their individual performance and that of the group. Power relationships subtly shift, placing the responsibility for learning on students rather than the teacher (C. Banks, 1993). Cooperative learning increases achievement in many students and has eased tensions in multicultural classrooms (Slavin, 1985).

Another powerful alternative is the involvement of parents in the educational process. Parents can be involved in a number of ways: instructing students in the classroom, helping them at home, participating in school governance, and becoming involved in community service. James Comer (1985, 1988), at Yale University, has created a program in which parents, along with teachers, administrators, and staff, are responsible for administering the activities of the school. This program addresses the social and developmental, as well as the educational, needs of students. Comer believes, for instance, that social skills and ties to the community are as important as academic subjects, especially for lower-income students, who often lack these assets. In two inner-city schools using Comer's model, student perform-ance so improved that the schools tied for third and fourth place in the district, with the students testing up to a year above the average for their grade! Attendance also improved dramatically, and behavior problems practically disappeared.

It is easy to understand why such a program could work: teaching becomes more relevant when academic subjects are translated into the daily concerns of students and their families. In turn, what is learned in the classroom receives the support of parents who are committed to educational programs they help plan.

Despite their proven success, alternatives such as cooperative learning and Comer's model will not be beneficial unless teachers and staff are trained to use them effectively. Cooperative learning, for example, is a relatively complex tech-nique to implement, requiring in-service training. Similarly, parental involvement can be cumbersome and can even increase conflict if parents' and teachers' views of education conflict (C. Banks, 1993).

Another alternative combines assignment to noncollege tracks with actual work experience for which students receive academic credit. This approach also addresses the financial difficulties many low-income students face. Innovative use of computers is a promising alternative for students who are "light-sensitive"— that is, who get most of their information through visual media such as television and spend little time reading (Solomon, 1990).

School Size

The size of schools is known to affect behavior at school—inside and outside class. Adolescents from smaller schools have more positive interactions with each other, fewer discipline problems, less truancy, and fewer dropouts. The critical size for a school is about 500 students. Once that number is reached, further increases don't have much effect (Garbarino, 1980).

Small schools can be more flexible in responding to the needs of adolescents. A. S. Bryk and S. W. Raudenbush (1988) analyzed data from a national survey of over 1,000 schools. They found that smaller schools can overcome differences re-lated to social class, academic background, and personal factors more readily than large schools. Programs on drug use, multicultural education, and cooperative learning are easier to set in motion and to change in response to student needs. Students in small schools have more opportunity to participate in activities. The particular type of activity is not important—yearbook staffing, hall monitoring, cheerleading, or peer counseling. Each one gives students a sense of belonging and a way of identifying with school (Coleman, 1993).

Although it is not possible to eliminate large schools, it is possible to create smaller "communities for learning" within them. These smaller environments can be just as responsive to students' needs as small schools are (Epstein, 1990).

School Climate

Unique characteristics of schools may be at least as important as their size (Bryk & Raudenbush, 1988). The relationship between school "input" variables—number of students per classroom, computers per student, or books in the library, for example—and school "output," in the form of student achievement, is not a simple one. Schools with similar resources can differ markedly in their effectiveness. "Process" variables that reflect the qualities of a school, such as differences in social and academic climates between schools or differences in their teaching staffs, must also be entered into the equation. Achievement is determined not so much by how many computers are in a classroom or how many books are in the library, but how effectively these resources are integrated into the instruction. Schools that involve parents, either as classroom aides or tutors or as members of governing committees making school-wide decisions, are more effective, especially in low-income districts where continuity between the home and the classroom needs bridging (C. Banks, 1993). A two-year study of nearly 30 classrooms in nine different schools found that students with a positive sense of school climate not only valued school but felt effective at school; they also had parents who valued education and talked with them about school (Coleman, 1993).

Schools that place as much value in educating students in vocational or lower tracks as those in college preparatory tracks promote higher levels of achievement among all students. Often this requires a redefinition of values among teachers, staff, and parents. Our society has come to define intelligence in terms of verbal and mathematical abilities (see Chapter 4), both of which contribute more heavily to performance in college-preparatory tracks. In emphasizing these abilities, we have slighted others such as interpersonal, mechanical, or musical, which are more evenly distributed among students in all tracks.

Teachers' Attitudes

One factor consistently distinguishes effective schools: the beliefs of the teaching staff that all students are capable of learning. Teachers at effective schools have high expectations. They interact with students more, reward them more, and have friendlier classrooms (Teddlie, Kirby, & Stringfield, 1989). Expecting the most from students and letting them know when they have come through are just as important as the latest in software and the number of books on the shelves. Students in classrooms where progress is monitored and feedback is given as to how well they are doing have higher achievement levels than those not given feedback. New teachers, especially, hold high expectations for their students. Nearly 90% of beginning teachers strongly believe that all their students can learn, and almost 70% feel strongly that they can make a real difference in the lives of students (*Digest of Education Statistics*, 1993).

RESEARCH FOCUS

Dependent Variables: Beauty and the Best—Are Looks and Grades Related?

On a scale of 1 to 10, how important are good looks? Many adolescents would answer "10½!" Activities such as dating, gaining entrance into social groups, and endless comparisons with cultural "10s" can lead many to put physical attractiveness near the top of their lists. But are good looks equally important in everything? Perhaps they help when making an impression on a first date, or in getting noticed to begin with, but surely the value of good looks stops in the classroom, or on the athletic field, or at the tip of one's pencil when taking an exam. Or does it?

Numerous studies report puzzling findings relating physical attractiveness to widely different aspects of personal functioning. Popularity? Naturally. Social competence? Probably. Grade-point average? That may be going too far.

Too far or not, adolescents' grades *are* related to their looks. How is attractiveness related to a student's grades? Do all measures of academic performance pick up this relationship, or only some? And how are we to understand such a relationship?

Richard Lerner and his associates (1990) wanted to know as well. They photographed adolescents and had individuals rate the photos for physical attractiveness on a 5-point scale, with 1 for "very unattractive" and 5 for "very attractive." They also looked at several measures of academic competence: an achievement test (the California Achievement Test, Form C), teacher judgments of classroom performance as reflected in students' overall grade-point averages, adolescents' appraisals of their own abilities, and teachers' appraisals of their abilities. They looked at each measure at three different times over a period ranging from the beginning of the sixth grade to the end of the seventh.

Why did they use more than one measure of academic competence? If the measures don't all show the same relationships, how are we to evaluate which one is most accurate? The answer is that different measures pick up different aspects of behavior. Three criteria distinguish accurate measures: reliability, validity, and sensitivity.

The first consideration with any measure of behavior, or *dependent variable*, is its *reliability*: It should give you the same value each time you use it. If a student takes an intelligence test and retakes it in 3 weeks, one expects the score to be about the same on both occasions. Differences in IQ from one testing to the next reflect factors other than intelligence, that is, *error*. Reliable measures have little error. Second, measures must have *validity*. They must measure what they are designed to measure. Some of the very first intelligence tests were highly reliable but not very valid. Some, for instance, measured how rapidly people could tap their fingers, something that can be measured with little error but that turns out to have little to do with actual intelligence. Third, *sensitivity* is a characteristic of good measures: They are able to detect even small differences where these exist. Current measures of intelligence do more than sort individuals into categories of, say, bright, average, and dull. They offer numerous distinctions within each.

Returning to adolescents' grades and their physical attractiveness, let's consider what Lerner and his associates found. They discovered that students' appearances *are* related to their academic success, but only at the beginning of the school year. This finding suggests that first impressions are important—even in the classroom. At the beginning of the year, before they have much information about a student's ability, teachers' impressions reflect a student's attractiveness. Teachers communicate their expectations to students in subtle ways, and students, in turn, live up to them. Early measures reflect these expectations, both through teachers' impressions, which are present in their grading, and students' self-appraisals, which affect their performance in class and on exams.

With time, differences in ability increasingly contribute to teachers' impressions of students, so that finally neither grade-point averages nor teacher assessments are related to attractiveness. Only by using several response measures could the investigators sort out these many relationships.

Reference: R. M. Lerner, M. Delaney, L. E. Hess, J. Jovanovic, & A. von Eye. (1990). Early adolescent physical attractiveness and academic competence. Journal of Early Adolescence, 10, 4–20.

The most important characteristic of an effective school is teachers who care about their students and have high expectations of them.

School Violence

More important than a school's size or climate or the attitudes of its teachers is its ability to provide an environment in which students feel safe. In the past, safety was simply taken for granted. It no longer can be. Among the top disciplinary problems listed by teachers two generations ago were chewing gum and running in the halls. Today, teachers are concerned about assault, rape, drug abuse, and robbery (see Table 7.1).

Teachers' concerns reflect students' realities. As can be seen in Table 7.2, 33% of tenth-grade males report having been threatened, 11% attacked, and about 11% robbed at school. These figures are even higher for eighth-grade males. Nearly 20% of all high school students report carrying some form of weapon to school for self-protection (Centers for Disease Control, 1991). Differences among ethnic groups and between sexes are large (see Table 7.3).

Violence is a more serious problem in urban than in suburban or rural schools; however, no school is immune to its threat. In a survey of high school principals, 64% of those in urban schools reported that violence had increased over the last five years, but so did 54% of suburban principals and 43% of rural ones (Toch, 1993).

T A B L E   7 . 1

Teachers' Ratings of Top Disciplinary Problems—
Then and Now

1940	1990
Talking out of turn	Drug abuse
Chewing gum	Alcohol abuse
Making noise	Pregnancy
Running in the halls	Suicide
Cutting in line	Rape
Dress-code violations	Robbery
Littering	Assault

Source: T. Toch. (1993). Violence in schools. U.S. News & World
Report, 115, *31–37.*

Even more disturbing are findings suggesting a new attitude among adolescents concerning conflict—and the value of life. In a recent survey of high school students, 20% said they thought it was okay to shoot someone "who has stolen something from you," and 8% said it was okay to shoot someone "who had done something to offend or insult you" (Toch, 1993). These students were not embattled inner-city youth—they were from a suburban Southwestern high school!

What are the sources of these attitudes and behaviors? A number of factors suggest themselves. Violence for many begins in the home: 34% of adults responding to a national survey said they had witnessed a man beating his wife or girlfriend

T A B L E   7 . 2

Percentage of Adolescents Experiencing Violence at School

	8th Grade		10th Grade	
	F	M	F	M
Been involved in physical fights	31.4%	56.5%	25.3%	42.0%
Been robbed	13.5	21.5	10.9	10.8
Been threatened	30.6	44.6	29.2	33.1
Been attacked	10.0	22.5	8.1	11.4
Carried knife	4.5	22.3	5.5	23.8
Carried gun	1.1	2.3	.4	2.9

Source: U.S. Department of Education. (1993). Digest of Education Statistics. *Washington, DC: U.S.*
Government Printing Office.

T A B L E   7 . 3

Percentage of High School Students Carrying a Weapon to School

"During the past 30 days, have you carried a weapon, such as a gun, knife, or club, for self-protection or because you thought you might need it in a fight?"

	Female	Male
Black	16.7	39.4
Hispanic	12.2	41.1
White	5.3	28.6

Source: Centers for Disease Control. (1991). "Weapon-Carrying Among High School Students—United States, 1990," Morbidity and Mortality Weekly Report. Washington, DC: U.S. Government Printing Office.

Note: Weapons other than a gun or a knife are included, making these figures higher than those in Table 7.2; these figures also reflect each time a weapon was carried, whereas in Table 7.2, "once" and "nearly every day" are in the same category.

(*Morbidity and Mortality Weekly Reports*, 1993), and estimates of sexual abuse have been as high as one in four girls and one in ten boys (Finkelhor, 1993). These figures cut across ethnic and class lines, affecting all segments of society (see Chapter 12).

Many adolescents, almost 40%, watch three to five hours of television nightly, hours that are saturated with violence. Before leaving elementary school, children will have watched approximately 8,000 murders and 100,000 violent acts (Toch, 1993). Figures such as these are chilling, given the compelling nature of research demonstrating the effects of viewing aggression (see Bandura, Chapter Two). The ability of television to "teach"—for good or evil—is well established (Beentjes & van der Voort, 1993).

Connecting "copycat" acts of violence with ones portrayed in the media is relatively easy because of their uniqueness. But what of the common, "ordinary" acts of violence in which one person pulls a gun on another—and pulls the trigger? Rather than being seen as the exception, "copycat" violence can be seen as real-life evidence which supports research showing that children will copy acts of violence they have viewed on film in a research laboratory (Bandura, Ross, & Ross, 1963).

Media modeling of violence is not in itself the cause of the increased violence we are presently experiencing as a society. Even more significant are the devastating effects of poverty and discrimination so many adolescents experience, and the very

To investigate whether violent behavior is learned by imitation, Stanford University researcher Albert Bandura had children watch an adult attacking an inflatable "punching bag" doll in a novel way—hitting it with a mallet, for instance, or pummeling it with balls. He found that most children would attack the doll in the same way when they were put in a room with it.

real threats to personal safety both at home and at school. These factors, together with the accessibility of guns, add up to a national problem. Nearly half of a large survey of tenth-grade males, for instance, said they could get a gun if they wanted to; this figure is substantially higher for inner-city youth where violence is most deadly (*Digest of Education Statistics*, 1993).

Teaching Peace

Even though schools suffer the consequences of these conditions, they are also in a position to change them. Morton Deutsch (1993) argues that schools can encourage values and provide experiences that promote constructive, rather than destructive, means of resolving conflict. Four elements are critical to "teaching peace": cooperative learning, training in conflict resolution, putting controversy to constructive use, and creating conflict resolution centers.

Cooperative Learning. Students learn interpersonal skills in cooperative learning classrooms; goals are shared by members of a group, reducing competition. Students are more helpful and caring in these learning environments than in the more traditional, individualistic, and competitive ones.

Conflict Resolution Training. These programs teach students to perceive a conflict as a mutual problem to be solved, one in which all participants can come out ahead, instead of solved competitively, in which some win and others lose. Students also learn to identify potential causes of violence and, knowing its consequences, to discover alternatives (see Chapter 12).

Constructive Controversy. Controversy, in itself, is not undesirable. It can actually stimulate students to think about problems and come up with creative solutions when shown how to do so. One way of doing this is to have students work in small groups in which pairs alternately argue for opposing positions and then reverse their arguments, taking their opponents' position and arguing as earnestly as they can for that. Finally, all work toward reaching a consensus.

Conflict Resolution Centers. Some schools have established mediation programs in which both teachers and students are trained in listening skills and conflict resolution.

Preparing for High School: Junior High or Middle School

Educators are still debating the relative merits of middle schools (fifth or sixth through eighth grade) versus junior high schools (seventh through eighth or ninth grades). Two events focus their concerns: Adolescents enter puberty during these years, and they leave one form of school for another. Puberty introduces intellectual, emotional, and psychological changes as well as physical ones. A change in school settings confronts adolescents with a more impersonal environment than the one they have previously known. Will one type of school ease the stresses of puberty more than the other? Also, which arrangement of grades will best facilitate the transition to high school (Epstein, 1990)?

Because of the secular trend, sixth-graders today are physically more like seventh- and eighth-graders than like school children a year behind them. Sixth-graders are also intellectually and emotionally more mature. Most have begun to use formal thought, and patterns of friendship are changing (see Chapter 6). Students at the highest grades in middle school, those in seventh and eighth grades, are still experiencing pubertal changes and just moving into opposite-sex relationships. Middle schools place students going through similar changes in a single setting. Although some educators argue on this basis that sixth-, seventh-, and

Whether they graduate to a junior high or a middle school, the transition from elementary school is a big step for young adolescents. No longer do they stay in the same classroom with the same teacher; now they have to find their way around campus and manage their time so that they carry out assignments from several teachers.

eighth-graders' needs are best met in a middle school, others voice concerns that by placing sixth-graders with older adolescents, we rush them into more mature forms of behavior. These latter educators want to protect early adolescents from growing up too fast.

In actuality, decisions about middle schools and junior high schools are more likely to be made on the basis of local demographics than educational policy, but since comparisons of these two school settings reveal more similarities than differences, this fact loses much of its importance (Kohut, 1988). Similarities of both types of schools include the curriculum, teaching practices, and extracurricular activities.

Few consistent differences emerge in academic achievement between the two types of schools. Also, attitudes and behaviors among students attending each do not differ consistently. When differences emerge, they usually favor middle schools (Educational Research Service, 1983). Students at middle schools have more positive attitudes about school, and about themselves, their peers, and their teachers than do junior high students. Teachers' attitudes are more positive, too, in many of the comparisons (Kohut, 1988).

ADOLESCENTS AT SCHOOL

Secondary schools challenge students more than elementary schools do. In this section we will look at some of the factors that affect students' performance in school: the relation between television and literacy, patterns of achievement, and gender. Some students fail to meet the challenge and drop out of school.

Literacy, Television, and Homework

It was dark. Everyone was hungry. And they had been driving for hours. Mom called out to the back seat asking when they would reach the interstate. Jake had the map and answered that the interstate was almost 100 miles ahead. "Wait a minute!" said his mother. "It's only 220 miles for the whole trip and we've been driving for 2½ hours. How can that be?!"

Jake isn't alone. Statistics show that almost 50% of adolescents are unable to perform well on such basic tasks as balancing a checkbook or reading a map (Youth Indicators, 1988). Figure 7.2 shows literacy skills for different types of tasks: reading a paragraph and understanding it (prose comprehension), skills such as reading

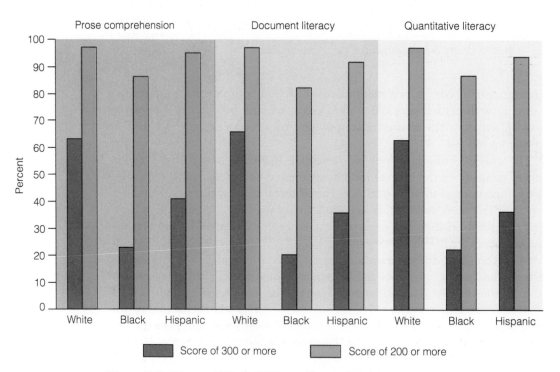

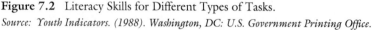

Figure 7.2 Literacy Skills for Different Types of Tasks.
Source: Youth Indicators. (1988). Washington, DC: U.S. Government Printing Office.

a map (document literacy), and balancing a checkbook (quantitative literacy). The levels of these skills are relatively low nationwide. Most adolescents perform well enough when only basic skills are required (scores of 200 or above), but far fewer do well when faced with moderately complex tasks (a score of 300 or above).

Statistics such as these have raised national concerns about the effectiveness of present forms of education. International comparisons do little to allay these concerns. A comparison of mathematical abilities of 13-year-old students from 14 countries including Switzerland, the former Soviet Union, France, and Canada found that American adolescents correctly answered only 55% of the questions on a standardized test, placing them 13th in the field of 14 (see Figure 7.3), nearly 20 points below the highest scoring participants (Youth Indicators, 1993). Within the United States, students showing greatest improvement on recent national tests in mathematics are minority youth—black and Hispanic adolescents (Youth Indi-

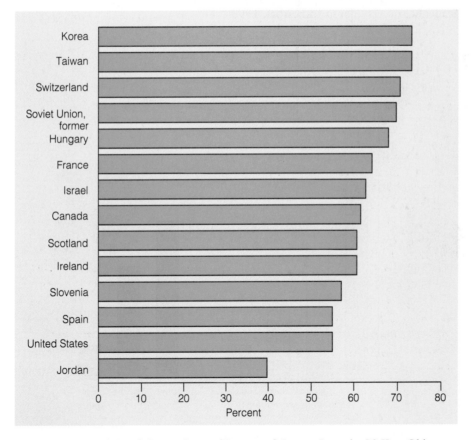

Figure 7.3 International Comparisons of Percent of Correct Items by 13-Year-Olds on a Math Test.

Source: Youth Indicators. (1993). Washington, DC: U.S. Government Printing Office.

cators, 1993). The tremendous diversity due to the sheer numbers of students attending high school and the increasing ethnic variety of the general population certainly contributes to the difficulties in meeting common educational goals.

Another factor related to the lower literacy level of U.S. students is the greater amount of time they spend watching television than doing homework. The less television adolescents watch, the better their writing skills, for instance. This relationship, however, is not easily interpreted. Do adolescents who watch television have poorer writing skills because they are spending time on television that they could otherwise spend on activities that would develop those skills? Or is there some other hidden factor that might account both for their lower literacy skills and the amount of television they watch? The answer may be a bit of both. Figure 7.4 shows that test performance is negatively related to television watching, but also to socioeconomic status. In other words, students who are in the lowest test performance quartile not only watch more television than those in the highest quartile, but they are also lower in socioeconomic status, a factor in itself that predicts academic success (Youth Indicators, 1993).

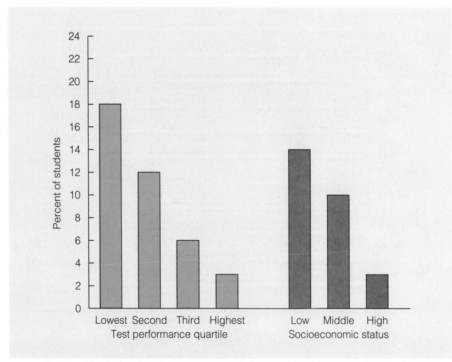

Figure 7.4   Test Performance Scores and Socioeconomic Status of Tenth-Grade Students Who View More Than Five Hours of Television on School Nights.

Source: Youth Indicators (1993). Washington, DC: U.S. Government Printing Office.

Another factor that may contribute to skill level among students is the amount of homework they are assigned. Twenty-two percent of eighth-graders, for example, report having no homework assigned on an average day; 35% spend less than an hour, another 30% spend 1 to 2 hours, and less than 10% spend more than 2 hours.

Once in high school, adolescents spend more time on homework than before, but still less time than watching TV. Fewer spend less than 1 hour a day on homework (26%), and almost twice as many spend more than 2 hours daily. Yet almost 40% still watch television 3 to 5 hours a day, and 36% watch for more than 5 hours! (*Digest of Education Statistics*, 1993) Figure 7.5 shows these patterns.

Which adolescents switch off the TV and do their homework? In the next section, we look at the motivational processes that adolescents bring to the classroom. These can have powerful effects on their levels of achievement.

Patterns of Achievement

The power of positive thinking is getting some scientific backing. The attitude adolescents take toward their successes and failures is an important determinant of

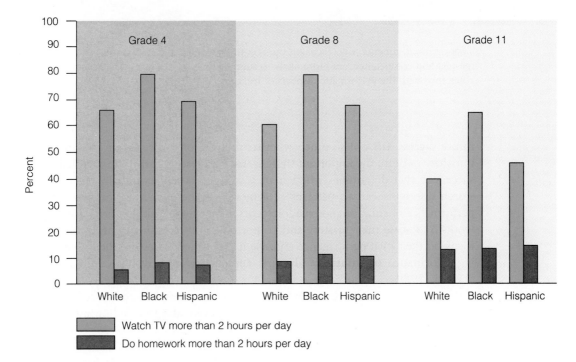

Figure 7.5 Percent of Students Watching Television and Doing Homework More Than Two Hours Per Day.
Source: Youth Indicators. (1988). Washington, DC: U.S. Government Printing Office.

Task-oriented students, who focus on the task to be learned and work to increase their mastery and competence, are more likely to succeed than are students who are primarily concerned with the performance aspects of learning.

future success. It's not so much whether they fail or succeed—we all experience our share of both; the important thing is what adolescents attribute their failure or success to that determines whether they will persist and eventually achieve. Research distinguishes two patterns of achievement behavior: task orientation and performance orientation. Some adolescents focus on the task they are learning and work to increase their mastery and competence; this is **task orientation.** Others focus on their own performance and use it as a way of assessing their ability; this is **performance orientation.** The first approach is adaptive; the second is not (Dweck, 1989).

    Adolescents who are task-oriented enjoy situations that challenge them and work at them even when they are difficult. They even take pride in how much effort they have to put into mastering something new. Adolescents who are performance oriented avoid challenging situations and show little persistence in the face of difficulty. They view any effort they must expend negatively, because having to try hard places their ability in question. If at first they don't succeed, they find something else to do (Dweck, 1989).

Performance-oriented adolescents tend not to pursue challenging material unless they're sure they will succeed. They choose situations that will not reveal what they regard as their lack of ability. These students are likely to prefer tasks that are either very easy or very difficult; failure at the first is unlikely, and failure at the second cannot be taken as a measure of their ability. Even above-average students who are performance oriented will avoid situations that involve risk in preference to those they can perform effortlessly and thereby feel smart. In doing so, however, they miss situations that promote further understanding (Covington, 1983; Dweck, 1986).

The difference between students who stick it out and those who give up is basically one of attitude, which researchers term *attribution of outcome*. Adolescents who persist when they experience failure tend to attribute the outcome of their actions to their efforts. Believing they haven't tried hard enough, they increase their efforts. They are task-oriented (Dweck & Reppucci, 1973; Dweck, 1986).

Those who are disrupted by failure, frequently to the point of giving up, are performance-oriented. Because they interpret failure to mean that they lack the ability for what they have attempted, they defensively withdraw in the face of it. To believe that failure means that one lacks ability is also to believe that trying harder isn't going to help. Rather than trying harder, these students explain their failure as bad luck, or the task's being too difficult. For them, having to try too hard is dangerous; it's just another way of calling their ability into question.

Gender Differences and Achievement

Females frequently respond to success and failure in different ways than do males. Males are likely to attribute their successes to their ability and their failures to lack of effort. What this means, of course, is that males will persist at a problem until, more likely than not, they get it right. Females are more likely to attribute their successes to hard work, luck, or the ease of the task, and their failures to lack of ability, thereby discounting their successes and taking responsibility only for their failures. This interpretation makes females helpless in the face of success; they're not sure how they did it and unsure whether they could do it again. It was luck or an easy grade, they tell themselves, attributing their success to factors other than their own skill. Females are equally helpless in the face of failure. Because they attribute it to their inability, they have little recourse but to give up and try something new (Dweck, 1986, 1989).

Of all adolescents, those who are most likely to show maladaptive achievement behavior are females of high ability. B. G. Licht, T. A. Linden, D. A. Brown, and M. A. Sexton (1984) found a gender difference in response to failure *only* among the brightest students: The performance of the most able females was disrupted and that of males was actually facilitated. Bright females are more likely than males of equal ability, or students of either sex of average ability, to avoid challenge, to attribute their failure to inability, and to withdraw in the face of failure (Dweck, 1989).

Similarly, bright females who experience initial confusion at a task are less likely to do well than less-capable females. Specifically, the brighter the female, the less likely she is to master a task if she encounters initial problems with it. If she experiences no initial confusion, however, her mastery is directly related to ability. A similar pattern does not exist for males. In fact, males are slightly more likely to master tasks when they experience some initial confusion. This is especially true for those of high ability (Dweck, 1986, 1989).

These motivational patterns frequently become evident only when adolescents enter junior high. Prior to this point, course material may not be sufficiently challenging to prompt defensive withdrawal. Mathematics represents a case in point. Girls do as well in math as boys throughout elementary school. Carol Dweck (1986, 1989) notes that achievement in math takes a new turn in junior high, one that is likely to call into play the gender differences in motivational patterns that we have been discussing. Dweck points out that math, unlike verbal tasks, often requires students to determine which solutions are appropriate to which problems. In verbal tasks they can follow the same approach with new material as with the old. Whether a word is "doge" or "dogmatic," if it is unfamiliar, the solution is the same: Look it up in the dictionary. New problems in math often require students to adopt a different approach, and they are likely to make errors at first. The initial confusion that results is more likely to interfere with the performance of girls than that of boys.

A study by J. Byrnes and S. Takahira (1993) points to the importance of cognitive operations, in addition to motivational processes, in explaining gender differences in mathematics. These investigators focused on high school students' performance on the math section of the Scholastic Aptitude Test (SAT), in which males typically outperform females by over 40 points. Students were given five math problems from the SAT. Prior to taking the test, all students completed a measure testing their knowledge of the concepts that would be needed to solve the problems, and immediately after, they indicated which strategies they had used. Even though males did no better on the test assessing mathematical concepts, they outperformed females on the SAT items. Their superiority on these was explained by differences in the way they put to use what they knew.

Attitudes toward math almost surely are important, and girls develop a less positive attitude toward math with age. In a longitudinal study following girls from middle school to high school, P. Klebanov and J. Brooks-Gunn (1992) found that girls' attitudes about math became less positive, even though their grades did not change. These investigators note the importance of socialization in contributing to attitudes toward math, showing that mothers' attitudes toward their daughters' achievement corresponded to how well they did in middle school. By high school, girls' own attitudes toward math became more important, reflecting sex-role stereotypes in which math achievement is perceived as masculine.

Learning in a group can be more interesting than learning on one's own. In a jigsaw classroom, students work in small groups that are balanced for both ability and for gender and ethnic or racial background.

the experiences of the pioneers, the American Indians, and the Mexicans turns this problem into an advantage. The introduction of a multicultural perspective enriches all students' understanding of the issues surrounding westward expansion (C. Banks, 1993; Howard, 1993).

Most minority students face instances of prejudice and discrimination on at least some occasions. Interviews with black adolescents who attended predominantly white high schools revealed a number of ways of coping with their minority status. One way was to be a "model" student. Students who chose this coping style made good grades, studied for college, and participated in school activities. Many also earned the resentment of their black friends for "acting white." One model student had this to say:

> They . . . prefer to be black, they want to just hang around with the blacks, they don't want nothing to do with the whites. . . . I'm not like that. . . . I attended the ski club

and I asked if anyone else wanted to get into it, and you should have seen their faces, it was hysterical. What is this kid talking about, the ski club? It's a bunch of "honkies" gonna be there. (R. L. Miller, 1989, p. 181.)

Other students coped by forming interracial friendships and becoming members of popular crowds at school. Still others became involved in many different school activities. Not all the black adolescents preferred attending an integrated school to a predominantly black school. Some who were bussed from inner-city schools to suburban ones made few friends and felt little connection with the school. When asked why they attended, they mentioned getting a better education and more opportunities (Miller, 1989).

In the classroom, unfamiliar patterns of communication complicate learning for some minority students. The simple matter of asking questions is a case in point for many black students. Teachers ask questions in very different ways than do adults in the community (Brice-Heath, 1982). Teachers use questions to stimulate classroom discussions and to focus ongoing behavior. It's common to ask about things the class has already discussed. Adults typically ask questions only when they want information they do *not* have. They rarely use questions as a way of discussing issues or of channeling ongoing behavior into more desirable forms (as a teacher might, by asking a question of a student who is talking with a classmate to get that student to pay attention). Consequently, students may misunderstand questions regarding material the class has already covered ("What is she asking for? We've gone over that"). Effective intervention depends on discovering differences such as these. The solution in this instance is for everyone—teachers, parents, and students—to be made aware of the different rules that regulate language in class and at home (Slaughter-DeFoe, Nakagawa, Takanishi, & Johnson, 1990).

Other problems arise from lack of familiarity in using standard English, the language used in the classroom. Some minority students—such as Hawaiians, American Indians, and Eskimos—can understand standard English well enough, but still not be at ease speaking it in front of classmates if they speak a dialect at home. Using different languages at home and in school limits opportunities to practice the way they need to speak at school and can cause them to be silent for fear of embarrassing themselves. Even written schoolwork becomes problematic for students who have difficulty translating the ideas they frame easily in the intimate language of their home into standard English. Additional complications arise when corresponding terms are not available in the two languages (Feldman, Stone, & Renderer, 1990).

Overcoming the Differences

The increasing ethnic diversity of our society makes it progressively difficult to characterize students in terms of simple behavioral and motivational profiles. Recognizing the distinctive approaches that characterize different ethnic groups can be a start and can be used to advantage in the classroom. Research on ethnic groups reveals distinct differences along four dimensions of personal interaction: group

Minority students from cultures that value the group more than the individual may pay as much attention to the feelings of others as to the task at hand. This orientation can frustrate teachers but it serves the students well in group-learning situations and in the world outside the classroom.

versus individual orientations, active versus passive coping styles, attitudes toward authority, and expressive versus restrained mannerisms.

Group Versus Individual Orientations.   Some cultures, such as Japan and Mexico, stress affiliation, interdependence, and cooperation. Other cultures, such as the United States, stress individual achievement, independence, and competition. Within the United States ethnic differences emerge along this dimension. Chinese, Hispanic, and black adolescents, for instance, are more group-oriented than those from the dominant culture (Rotheram & Phinney, 1987). These adolescents are more attentive to the feelings and expectations of others than their white counterparts are. An Hispanic or a black adolescent may pay as much attention to the feelings of others as to the demands of the task at hand, an orientation many teachers may not understand or appreciate. However, in learning situations that require students to work together, this orientation will serve these students as well inside the classroom as outside it (Rotheram & Phinney, 1987).

Active Versus Passive Coping Styles.   Cultures characterized by active coping styles stress the importance of controlling one's environment and being productive. Those with passive styles place more emphasis on being than on doing. The sense of the present is greater in the latter and of the future in the former. These differences—like those of group versus individual orientation—can translate into either strengths or weaknesses in the classroom. Adolescents with a "take charge" attitude may find it difficult to wait for others, or to take enough time to explore all the issues. The strength of this approach is the way that it fosters achievement.

The strengths of the passive approach are the freedom it gives students to turn themselves over to the moment and learn what it can teach them. The disadvantages to this coping style are most apparent in classrooms structured according to active coping strategies. Adolescents from cultures with a passive coping style are not likely to ask for help or materials, and if teachers and classmates assume that no help is needed unless asked for, they will not receive the help they need to keep up (Rotheram & Phinney, 1983).

Attitudes Toward Authority.   Clear ethnic differences exist for this dimension. Hispanic and Asian American adolescents, for instance, are likely to have been raised in authoritarian homes (see Chapter 5) and taught to be respectful and not to question those in authority. Certain Native American and many white adolescents have been socialized to make decisions for themselves and are less accepting of authority (Rotheram & Phinney, 1987). It should not be surprising that some students want to be told what to do, and do their best work under those conditions; whereas others want to make decisions for themselves and do not fare well with authoritarian teachers.

Expressive Versus Restrained Mannerisms.   Interactions in some cultures are informal and open, and in others are ritualized and private. The former is more characteristic of black and white adolescents, the latter of Asian American adolescents. Black adolescents express their feelings even more openly than whites; theirs is a "high-intensity" culture, in which feelings are given more open expression. An Asian student might easily misread a black student's expressions of anger as "aggression" or a white student might regard an Asian's reaction to an incident as "timid" simply because each is not familiar with the other's culture.

Adolescents are not very accurate in predicting how those from another culture will react. Differences along each of these dimensions underscore the importance of developing cross-ethnic awareness among adolescents as well as teachers.

Many minority adolescents have difficulty predicting their own experiences as they move from home, to school, to community. Urie Bronfenbrenner (1979) describes the experiences that make up one's reality in terms of overlapping spheres of influence. At the most immediate level, the **microsystem**, are one's first-hand experiences—interactions at home, in the classroom, and with friends. The **mesosystem** arises from interactions among the different microsystems of which one is a part. Minority adolescents frequently experience problems with interactions involving the mesosystem. They may see their parents distrust the system, or teachers communicate less respect for their parents than for those of other students.

Adolescents experience the **exosystem** at the level of their communities. Available housing and the types of schools they attend reflect decisions made at the community level but influence their lives directly. The **macrosystem**, which consists of the underlying social and political climate, is even further removed from adolescents' daily experiences, yet it impinges on their realities in very real ways. Laws concerning compulsory education, the mainstreaming of students with special needs, and the separation of grades into elementary, junior high, and high schools all illustrate the direct ways the macrosystem can affect the lives of adolescents. A less-observable, but no less real, impact of the macrosystem is experienced in the form of beliefs, biases, and stereotypes. The values of the macrosystem can be at odds with those of the home microsystem for adolescents from some minority groups (Spencer, 1985).

John Ogbu (1981; 1992) offers a disturbing analysis of the plight of many minority students. He notes that educational programs have assumed that the problems many minorities experience at school (e.g., poor attendance, high dropout rates, low achievement) should be addressed at the level of the microsystem—by improving the home environment or enriching educational experiences. Ogbu suggests that the problem is generated at the macrosystem level and can only be solved by changes introduced at that level. He attributes poor academic performance and high dropout rates among minorities to a "job ceiling," or discrimination in job opportunities, and to their perception that members of their own families have not been rewarded for their achievements.

If all adolescents progressed through the same *social mobility system,* one in which mobility, or social class, reflects their abilities, then the most effective method of intervention for minorities who are failing would be at the microsystem level, reaching into the home or classroom to bring their abilities and skills up to the level of the others. But *do* all members of our society move through the same mobility system? Is there more than one system, similar to academic tracking, but with respect to economic rather than educational opportunities?

If there is more than one mobility system, what factors other than ability and skill determine the system in which individuals participate? Notice that if we have more than one social mobility system, social class is an *effect* rather than a cause, and minority problems must be addressed at another level. Social status among minorities, argues Ogbu, reflects the realities of a job ceiling: a consistent set of social and economic obstacles preventing equal selection based on ability imposed on certain minorities at birth, that is, a society stratified by ethnic and racial castes as well as by class. The problems of minority groups can be resolved only at the macrosystem level, by addressing social ills such as prejudice and discrimination.

SUMMARY

Secondary Schools Today

More adolescents attend high school now than in any previous generation. A hundred years ago, less than 4% of high school-age adolescents graduated from high school; in the 1990s, 80% to 85% will. As more students remain in high school, differences among them have increased. Ethnic diversity is one source of the differences.

Academic tracking is a common solution to problems created by diverse interests and abilities among students. Tracking itself contributes to differences in achievement and dropout rates among those assigned to college and noncollege tracks. Powerful alternatives to tracking include forming small cooperative learning groups in the classroom and involving parents in the educational process. Work-study programs and use of computer-assisted instruction (CAI) offer additional alternatives.

Both the size of a school and its educational climate are related to its success. Students attending small schools are less likely to drop out; there are also fewer disciplinary problems and less truancy. Teachers' beliefs that all students are capable of learning contribute to their students' success.

Perhaps most important to its success is a school's ability to provide an environment in which students feel safe. Schools suffer from a dramatic increase in violence, which reflects societal attitudes, media modeling, poverty, and discrimination. Schools can promote peace through cooperative learning, training in conflict resolution and constructive controversy, and by establishing conflict resolution centers.

Adolescents at School

Middle schools place fifth- or sixth-, seventh-, and eighth-graders together in a separate school; junior highs place seventh- through eighth- or ninth-graders together. Few consistent differences emerge in comparisons of these two educational settings.

The amount of homework adolescents do and the number of hours they spend watching television affect their achievement. Achievement in even basic skills such as map reading and balancing a checkbook is low for many adolescents. The less television adolescents watch, the better their skills. Most adolescents spend more time watching television than doing homework on any day.

Achievement motivation patterns distinguish adolescents. Task-oriented adolescents focus on the task and work to increase their mastery. Performance-oriented adolescents focus on their performance and use it as a measure of their ability. Task-oriented adolescents are less likely to be disrupted by initial failure, believing it to result from lack of sufficient effort rather than inability.

Gender differences reveal more adaptive motivational patterns for males. Gender-role stereotypes contribute to the less positive attitudes that affect girls' motivation. These differences often do not appear until adolescents enter junior high and encounter work that is challenging enough to prompt defensive withdrawal.

Over the past 20 years, the number of adolescents who drop out of school has decreased for majority and some minority adolescents, while remaining high for others. Even so, more minority students drop out than do those from the dominant culture. Parents' educational level, socioeconomic status, and attitudes toward education are related to dropping out.

School variables that predict dropout rate are a history of difficulty or failure, low self-esteem, assignment to a noncollege track, and behavior problems.

Programs that are effective in helping at-risk students involve parents, provide individualized counseling, and help students meet their financial as well as academic needs, as in work-study programs for which students receive academic credit. Success of a school system's dropout programs is a key measure of the system's quality.

Adolescents at the Edge

Adolescents who score 130 or above on an intelligence test or who have creative, artistic, leadership, or other special talents are defined as gifted. Gifted adolescents fail to fit any stereotype. Educational programs for the gifted offer enrichment, providing them with more experiences than they would ordinarily get, or acceleration, allowing them to advance beyond their grade level.

Adolescents with learning disabilities are of average or above-average intelligence who show a discrepancy between expected and actual performance. They have difficulty in academic tasks that presumably can be traced to a neurological dysfunction.

Learning-disabled high school students can fall five to seven grade levels behind classmates in some subject areas and generally have poor study habits and test-taking skills. Social skills are also affected for many.

Mainstreaming places learning-disabled students in regular classes with their classmates. Frequently this approach is combined with the use of a consulting special education teacher who advises regular teachers on the special needs of these students. At the other extreme, learning-disabled students may be placed in special classes with specially trained teachers. Each of these educational options has different advantages.

Culture and Gender in the Classroom

Some gender-role stereotyping still exists in teaching materials. In textbooks, males are still pictured more frequently than females, appear in more diverse occupations, and need rescuing less frequently. But these differences represent tremendous improvements over the materials in use a generation ago.

The use of male generic language represents another form of bias. Using the masculine pronoun generically predisposes students and their teachers to think of males, not of individuals in general. Their evaluations of the competence of individuals of either sex for different types of work is thereby skewed.

Jigsaw classrooms, where students work in small groups, each contributing a different part of the lesson, foster cooperation and promote better relations among students from different ethnic backgrounds. Presenting material from several cultural perspectives is helpful to minority students who may not always share the perspective assumed in the textbook or other materials used.

Communication problems arise for some minority students when language is used differently at school and at home. Four distinctive approaches characterize different ethnic and racial groups: group versus individual orientations, active versus passive coping styles, attitudes toward authority, and expressive versus restrained mannerisms. Intervention programs that heighten teacher and student awareness of these differences improve the quality of multicultural education.

Most intervention programs have focused on problems minority students may experience at the level of the microsystem, that is, in the home and the classroom. Problems of poorer achievement and higher dropout rates may have to be addressed at the level of the macrosystem. The assurance of equal opportunity for jobs may be the most effective form of intervention.

KEY TERMS

Academic Tracking	Learning Disability	Mesosystem
Task Orientation	Male Generic Language	Exosystem
Performance Orientation	Jigsaw Classroom	Macrosystem
Gifted	Microsystem	

PART THREE

CONTINUITY AND CHANGE IN IDENTITY CONSOLIDATION

You have met a number of adolescents so far in the pages of this book. Each has illustrated in some way the themes of the text, themes that characterize the experiences of adolescents today; the continuity to their lives, the many changes they face, and their cultural diversity.

A strong thread of continuity runs through the lives of adolescents. Despite the dramatic changes that begin with puberty, the achievements of adolescence build on the prior accomplishments of childhood. Issues that focus the experiences of children—such as trust and intimacy in infancy, autonomy in toddlerhood, and competence and mastery during the school years—come up again, in somewhat different form, in adolescence. Adolescents confront the need for trust as they form intimate relationships. Relationships with parents revolve around issues of autonomy and independence. And adolescents' developing sense of self, of identity, reflects their sense of mastery and competence in their dealings with the world around them.

Despite this continuity, the concerns of late adolescents and the developmental issues they face are sufficiently different from those of early adolescents to require special attention. What parent would think of his or her 16-year-old as the same child who, three short years ago, wondered what puberty was all about? What poten-

tial employer does not believe that a high school student is more able to shoulder the responsibilities of a job than a middle school student? What teacher does not expect high school students to be capable of more subtle understanding than 11- or 12-year-olds?

In the various domains of development— formulating an identity, attaining sexual maturity, planning for future work or college, and defining values to live by—late adolescents address different issues than do early adolescents. With respect to achieving a sense of themselves, early adolescents are just beginning to discover the ways they differ from their parents; late adolescents are consolidating these changes into a personal identity. With respect to sexuality, late adolescents are learning to integrate their sexuality into their intimate relationships, whereas early adolescents are still sorting through the significance of pubertal changes for their sense of self.

Differences exist, too, in their extended social worlds. Late adolescents are preparing to leave high school to begin work or enter college, while early adolescents are leaving elementary school for a middle school or junior high. Late adolescents are distinguishing values and beliefs that are unique to them, whereas the beliefs and values of early adolescents are the ones they have acquired from their parents.

Chapter 8 opens Part Three with an examination of identity development in adolescents. Identity gives one a sense of self, and is perhaps one of the most important achievements of adolescence. Prior to adolescence, children's sense of self reflects a simple identification with their parents. Adolescents craft an independent identity by synthesizing elements of their earlier identity into a new whole; this new sense of self is not consolidated until late adolescence or even early adulthood.

The next three chapters in Part Three cover separate aspects of identity. Chapter 9 examines sexuality and the way adolescents integrate gender roles and sexual experiences into a changing sense of self. Chapter 10 looks at adolescents' ability to envision their future occupational identity. As they grow older, more adolescents begin to plan for their own economic security and autonomy. Some enter the work force after graduating from high school; others go on to college to prepare for an eventual career. Just as importantly, late adolescents begin to integrate a personal set of values and beliefs into their emergent identity. Chapter 11 looks at the standards adolescents use in making decisions—at their developing ethics and morality. Many adolescents base their decisions on community standards and conventional ways of behaving, but others move beyond convention to formulate their own ethical standards.

Chapter 12 examines stress and adolescents' coping strategies. Although all adolescents experience some stress, many must handle extreme stress, whose causes often originate within the home. Some of these adolescents run away; many are abused. Juvenile delinquency, substance abuse, suicide, and psychological disorders such as depression are also discussed in this chapter.

Finally, Chapter 13 provides a broad overview of the research methods and issues that have shaped the scientific study of adolescence. Because this presentation relates to the research focus boxes in each chapter, you may wish to read this chapter out of sequence and refer to it often.

IDENTITY: THE NORMATIVE
CRISIS OF ADOLESCENCE
Identity Defined
The Process of Identity Consolidation

VARIATIONS ON A THEME
OF IDENTITY
Identity Statuses
Identity and Personal Expressiveness
Identity Styles

■ RESEARCH FOCUS
*Operationalizing Concepts: You Are
How You Think*

IDENTITY: GENDER AND
ETHNICITY
*Gender Differences in Identity
  Formation*
*Contributions of Ethnicity to Identity
  Development*

THE SELF
Self-Concept: Who Am I?
Self-Esteem: Do I Like Myself?

INTIMACY: THE SELF THROUGH
RELATIONSHIPS
Intimacy with Oneself

■ RESEARCH FOCUS   *Path Analysis:
Too Young for Intimacy?*

Intimacy with Others

INTIMACY AND IDENTITY:
DIFFERENT PATHS TO
MATURITY?
Development in Adolescence
Development in Females
Dimensions of Relatedness
Gender Differences in Relatedness
A New Definition of Maturity

SUMMARY

KEY TERMS

CHAPTER EIGHT

Defining the Self: Identity and Intimacy

"Why are you replacing the spark plugs? You just got new ones," whined Francie.

"Because the firing's off and I've tested everything else," snapped Allie as she grabbed the wipe rag. "It's not the distributor; the fuel-injection checks out. Just because Dad said they're new doesn't mean one of them isn't a dud. It's the only possibility I haven't ruled out. You've got to consider all the possibilities, Francie, you can't accept what people tell you."

"What about the possibility that it's 'unnatural' for a cheerleader to know more about engines than most of the guys on the team?"

"Give me that wrench. They were happy enough when I fixed the bus, weren't they? We made the game in time."

"Tell me again why you're doing this?" Francie asked as she examined a broken nail.

"It's the only way I get to have a car. You know my Dad, 'If you want to own a car, you'll have to know how it works.' "

"Sounds like Ms. Wright. You missed a fresh class yesterday. She said most history books reflect a point of view. You can't just accept what's written. Did you know that the man who said the British were the first to fire at Lexington was actually a British soldier who was being held as a prisoner by the Colonists?"

"So what's the point?"

"The point is he could have been trying to win their favor so they'd let him go. How come you can think of all the possibilities when it comes to this car of yours but not when it comes to Ms. Wright's class?"

"Dunno. Guess I just don't find history that interesting."

By the time most adolescents are old enough to drive a car (let alone repair one), they have sharpened their sense of themselves through countless exchanges such as the one above, in which ambitions and plans mesh with the daily realities of life. **Identity** gives a sense of oneself that transcends any particular moment or circumstance, and establishing one's identity is perhaps among the most important achievements of adolescence. This chapter examines Erikson's original formulation of identity, as well as more recent elaborations of it.

Minority adolescents face an additional task of achieving an ethnic identity, and females, irrespective of cultural or racial background, appear to undertake self-definition in substantially different ways than males do. Intimate relationships are more important in defining the self in females than in males. The variations due to gender and ethnicity have required us to re-examine our view of "normal" development, and even of maturity itself.

IDENTITY: THE NORMATIVE CRISIS OF ADOLESCENCE

"Normative crisis" sounds like an oxymoron, a combination of contradictory terms like "thunderous silence." Doesn't *normative* refer to a standard, a pattern, something that is predictable and regular? And doesn't *crisis* mean something *out of* the ordinary, something that violates the pattern, that *doesn't* happen every day?

In discussing the term "identity crisis," Erik Erikson (1968) noted that, although the term later acquired a distinctive meaning, at the time he first used it, he considered himself to be naming something so familiar as to be taken for granted. He illustrated this point with a story about an old man who vomited each morning but would not see a doctor. Finally, his family convinced him to get a checkup. After examining him, the doctor asked how he was feeling. "Fine," the old man replied. The doctor, impatient with what appeared to be denial of a serious problem, responded, "But your family tells me you vomit every morning!" The old man looked surprised and said, "Sure. Doesn't everybody?"

Erikson's point is that the term "identity crisis" names something that all of us have experienced and may have taken for granted but would have no difficulty recognizing in ourselves and others once it is labeled. Something that is, despite the upset, quite normative (Erikson, 1968).

Similarly, Erikson used the word *crisis* to refer not to some imminent catastrophe but to a developmental turning point in which the individual must choose one course or another simply because it is no longer possible to continue as before (Erikson, 1968).

Perhaps no term is more closely associated with the writing and thinking of Erik Erikson (see Chapter 2) than *identity*. Erikson was, above all else, a clinician whose concepts reflected real-life experiences. In writing about the personality, Erikson noted that "old troubles" return when we are tired or otherwise defenseless, simply because we are what we *were* as well as what we might want to become or presently may be (Coles, 1970; Erikson, 1954).

Erikson believed that, like his patients, adolescents have to confront "old troubles" in arriving at an identity. Consider Erikson's description of Jill, a young woman he knew:

> I had known Jill before her puberty, when she was rather obese and showed many "oral" traits of voracity and dependency while she also was a tomboy and bitterly

ego identity, which has made it possible to empirically test many implications of Erikson's writings.

Identity Statuses

Most of the work we do on our identity takes place in adolescence; however, as Marcia notes with a touch of humor, if identity formation were necessary by the end of adolescence, many of us would never become adults. His point is that achieving a personal identity is not an easy process. Adolescents must be willing to take risks and live with uncertainty.

Some of the uncertainty comes from exploring possibilities and options in life that differ from those chosen by one's parents. Most adolescents expect this exploration to be risky. Few adolescents, however, expect the risks that occur when they

Most, if not all, of these football players probably dream of sports scholarships or even going pro. But as they go through the process of identity formation, they will gradually let go of such fantasies and commit themselves to more realistic futures.

must make commitments based on their exploration. Adolescents form their identities both by taking on new ways of being *and* by excluding others. It is every bit as important to let go of their fantasies and commit themselves to a definite course of action as it is to challenge the familiar by exploring possibilities never even considered by their parents or families. Marcia (1980, 1992) refers to these two dimensions of the identity process as exploration and commitment.

Marcia distinguishes four ways by which adolescents arrive at the roles and values that define their identities. Each of these ways, or identity statuses, is defined in terms of the dimensions of commitment and exploration (see Figure 8.1). Adolescents who are committed to life options arrive at them either by exploring and searching for what fits them best or by foregoing exploration and letting themselves be guided by their parents' values. The first alternative results in the ego reorganization that Erikson characterized as identity formation; the second leaves parental identifications unchallenged and unchanged. Adolescents who have searched for life options that fit them best are termed **identity achieved**; those who adopt their parents' values without question are termed **identity foreclosed** (Kroger, 1988; Marcia, 1980).

Two other paths lead to noncommitment. Some adolescents begin to evaluate life options but don't close off certain possibilities because the decisions are too momentous to risk making a mistake; as a result, they remain uncommitted to any path. These adolescents are in **moratorium**. Others remain uncommitted for the opposite reason: failure to see the importance of choosing one option over any other. They are termed **identity diffused**. Even though adolescents in moratorium begin to question parental ways, like foreclosed adolescents they ultimately do not

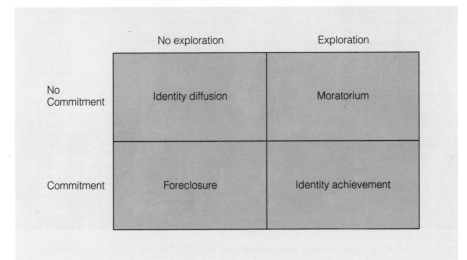

Figure 8.1 Marcia's Identity Statuses.

the foreclosed status and the diffused/avoidant orientation more likely for the identity-diffused.

Berzonsky (1993) reports that individuals adopting an information orientation are not only more open to ideas but are more experientially open in general, their openness extending to alternative values, feelings, fantasies, and even things of an aesthetic nature. In contrast, those adopting a normative orientation are closed to information that might challenge beliefs or values central to their self-definition. These styles, by the way, are as likely to be used by adolescents of one sex as the other.

IDENTITY: GENDER AND ETHNICITY

Gender Differences in Identity Formation

Adolescents find answers to the question "Who am I?" by examining the societal roles they see around them, roles they will soon assume. Erikson considered the most central of these roles to be that of a future occupation. Following close on the heels of this decision come decisions about political and religious beliefs, and the expression of an adult gender role (Erikson, 1968). Occupation, political stance, and ideology—all of these characterized males more than females at the time Erikson formulated this concept. Thirty years ago, relatively few females wrestled with issues of occupation and ideology. Josselson writes:

> At this point in his writing, it becomes most apparent that Erikson, like Freud and most other important psychological theorists, is writing about men. Indeed, all Erikson's psychobiographies analyze identity as it develops in men, and most of his case examples are from male patients. All Erikson had to say about women was that much of a woman's identity resides in her choice of the men she wants to be sought by. (1987, p. 22)

Erikson on Gender Differences.   *Was* Erikson writing primarily about males? If so, how did he think females formulated an identity? Was it, as Josselson summarizes, through the men in their lives?

Erikson did, in fact, believe that the process of identity formulation differs for males and females—in content, timing, and sequence (Patterson, Sochting, & Marcia, 1992). With respect to the content of identity, he considered interpersonal issues, rather than vocational and ideological ones, to be central for females. He also thought the timing of identity resolution is different for males and females, with females keeping their identity options partially open, rather than resolving them as males do, so that they might better complement a potential mate. Erikson also believed that females resolve identity and intimacy issues more or less concurrently, whereas males resolve these issues sequentially (Patterson, Sochting, & Marcia, 1992).

Why would male and female adolescents go about so fundamental a process in different ways? In partial answer, Erikson referred to a "profound difference . . . between the sexes in the experience of the ground plan of the human body" that "predisposes" adolescent males and females to work out their identities in different ways. He believed that women find "their identities in the care suggested in their bodies and in the needs of their issue, and seem to have taken it for granted that the outer world space belongs to the men" (1968, p. 274). Males achieve their identities by exploring this outer world and finding pursuits and beliefs to which they can commit themselves—an occupation and an ideology.

Erikson asserted that a female finds her identity "whatever her work career" when she "commits herself to the love of a stranger and to the care to be given to his and her offspring" (1968, p. 265). When asked by young women whether they can attain an identity before they marry, Erikson answered that "much of a young woman's identity is already defined in her kind of attractiveness and in the selective nature of her search for the man (or men) by whom she wishes to be sought" (1968, p. 283). He argued that she may postpone identity closure with education or a career, but that "womanhood arrives when attractiveness and experience have succeeded in selecting what is to be admitted to the welcome of the inner space 'for keeps' " (1968, p. 283).

Was Erikson right? Do sex differences such as the "ground plan of the human body," for example a female's sense of "inner space" (the womb), primarily shape the process by which one achieves an identity? Do we see the same pattern of concerns and commitments among adolescents today as Erikson saw a generation ago? A number of studies supply us with answers to these questions.

Research on Gender Differences.   Early research on Marcia's identity statuses found differences in the adaptiveness of different statuses for either sex. The identity-achieved and moratorium statuses were found to be most adaptive for males. Both statuses involve a time of soul-searching in which adolescents question and evaluate the options before them. Questioning societal values and choosing among life options are congruent with cultural expectations for males (e.g., self-reliance, decision making, defense of beliefs, risk taking), who are likely to receive more support for pursuing their identities in this way. Males in these statuses were found to be more self-assured, have higher self-esteem, be less anxious, perform better under stress, and be less influenced by others than males in either of the other two statuses (Bourne, 1978a, 1978b; Marcia, 1980).

Similar research painted a different picture for females. Early work with identity statuses found that the foreclosure status was as adaptive for females as the achieved status, and that females in the moratorium status function in many ways like identity-diffused females. Identity-foreclosed females, along with identity-achieved females, were found to enjoy high levels of self-esteem, experience little anxiety, and see themselves as effective (Marcia, 1980). Marcia assumed that foreclosure was adaptive for females, even though it did not lead to self-chosen goals, because it reflected cultural expectations for females.

Identity-achieved females appear to focus on achieving a balance between self-assertion and relatedness. They use strengths drawn from their relationships to fuel their solo efforts.

Recent research, however, finds few differences among male and female adolescents in identity development. In three separate studies, Sally Archer (1989a) interviewed nearly 300 adolescents in the sixth, eighth, tenth, and twelfth grades, using a semistructured interview similar to the one developed by Marcia. With few exceptions, she found equivalent numbers of males and females in each of the identity statuses. When gender differences occurred, males were more likely than females to be in the foreclosure status.

Was Erikson right in assuming that the content of identity differs for males and females? Archer (1989a) examined whether different content domains have greater salience for adolescents of one sex than the other by looking separately at vocational choice, religious beliefs, political ideologies, and gender roles. Few differences appeared within any of the domains. When they did, males were more likely to be foreclosed and females to be diffused in their political beliefs, and females were more likely than males to be identity-achieved or in moratorium concerning family roles. Overall, Archer concluded from her research as follows:

> The minimal finding of gender differences in the processes, domains, or timing of identity activity in these three studies suggests that the traditional theoretical assumptions . . . should be discarded, or at least reconsidered. . . . Taken together the findings from these studies . . . suggest a similar epigenetic underpinning to the formative period of identity development for males and females. (1989a, p. 136)

Do females keep identity options partially open, as Erikson suggested, resulting in differences in the timing of development? The answer to this question is yes—and no. That is, at least two courses appear to be open to females when it comes to resolving identity issues. One involves a process of self-searching and introspection and is typical of females with continuous careers. It is, in other words, the same process followed by Marcia's identity-achieved and moratorium individuals. The other is the more traditional course described by Erikson, in which females define themselves interpersonally through their husbands and children, gaining a sense of their importance and value largely through their relations with others.

A. N. O'Connell (1976) distinguishes the first of these two courses as personal identity and the second as reflected identity. Females who pursue personal identities undergo the most progress in identity development in late adolescence, as do most males. In other words, they do not differ in the timing of their development. Females with reflected identities, however, describe themselves in terms of relational roles until their children start school, and only then begin to develop a personal identity. Contrary to Erikson's assumptions then, a woman's identity does not await confirmation by having children. Instead, having to care for young children appears to require women to postpone work on their personal identity (Patterson, Sochting, & Marcia).

The sequencing of identity formation appears to be more stepwise for males, with identity serving as a foundation for later intimate relationships (see section on Intimacy: The Self Through Relationships). For females, issues of intimacy and identity are more apt to be resolved concurrently (Patterson, Sochting, & Marcia, 1992).

Recent research by Ruthellen Josselson (1988, 1992), based on narrative accounts of women's lives, reveals the importance that relationships have in giving women a sense of themselves. Josselson's interviews indicate that, rather than defining their identities primarily in terms of individual goals and principles, women also include issues of relatedness and responsibility to others. On the basis of this research, Patterson, Sochting, and Marcia (1992) suggest that, in addition to exploration and commitment, a third dimension, relatedness, is important in defining identity statuses for females.

Is this suggestion contrary to Archer's conclusion that the process of identity formation is more similar than different between adolescents of either sex? Archer (1992) offers a tentative resolution to this apparent contradiction. She points to a remarkable "tunnel vision" that she noticed in her interviews with adolescents when it came to seeing the implications that commitments in one domain have for another domain. For instance, an adolescent boy might describe his vocational plans in detail as well as his plans for marriage and children, and yet not connect the two. Thus, potential conflicts, such as who would care for the children if his wife also chose a career or whose career would determine where they would live, simply are not anticipated. Those interviewed by Archer who were most likely to make connections between domains were late adolescent females. A sense of relatedness for females, an awareness of themselves in relation to others, may prompt them to integrate identity domains.

Relatedness may also play a more central role in defining the process of exploration in females than in males. For example, a sense of relatedness may cause females to give greater thought to the implications of adopting one lifestyle over another or of setting aside traditional beliefs, each of which would be a potential outcome of exploration. Mary Belenky and her associates, for instance, cite the concern of young college women that, by taking an intellectual stand, they might isolate themselves from others (Belenky, Clinchy, Goldberger, & Tarule, 1986). The very decision to go to college or pursue a career is, for some women, a repudiation of their family's ways, especially for minority females from traditional backgrounds.

In such cases, relationship implications set limits to exploration. However, it is equally possible that the limits may prompt more creative approaches to identity formation given the greater complexities which they introduce to the task for females (Archer, 1985). Serena Patterson, Ingrid Sochting, and James Marcia (1992), in summarizing the findings of Archer and others on this point, note that females face a need to balance competing occupational and interpersonal commitments, involving them in "meta-decisions" across domains. In contrast, males can resolve these more easily as separate issues.

Taken together, the research on gender differences reveals that the *process* of identity formation is comparable for adolescents of either sex. Adolescents who allow themselves to question, explore, and experience the uncertainty of not knowing—to experience a period of crisis—mature in this process. However, the particular content that adolescents address in finding their own way can differ for either gender. Thus similarities in process do not rule out other gender differences.

Contributions of Ethnicity to Identity Development

Because our sense of self reflects an awareness of how others see us, cultural values as well as individual experiences contribute to the development of identity. What happens when the larger society fails to validate these sources of identity? A generation ago, Erikson (1968) noted that minorities whose groups are devalued by society risk internalizing the negative views of society and can develop negative identities.

Despite the significance of Erikson's observation, comparatively little research had been done on ethnic identity until very recently (Phinney, 1990). Yet the developments that underlie an identity search in majority adolescents are likely to contribute to an awareness of one's ethnicity in minority adolescents. Social networks widen in adolescence, frequently including those from other backgrounds. Intellectual capacities develop, making it possible to view the self from a third-person perspective, heightening one's sense of self. Broader intellectual horizons make it likely that adolescents will recognize the existence of racial and ethnic overtones in local and national issues. All of these factors argue for ethnicity's being a salient factor in adolescent identity development.

Ethnic identity has several components. The first is simply whether one identifies oneself as belonging to an ethnic group. The second component is one's knowledge of and engagement in behaviors characteristic of the ethnic group, for example, the celebration of holidays, patterns of speech and dress, and the types of food one prefers. Feelings about one's ethnic group membership are the third component to ethnic identity—individuals can either value their ethnicity or react negatively to belonging to an ethnic group. The final component is the importance one places on one's ethnic group membership (Phinney, 1990; Phinney & Rosenthal, 1992).

The boundaries that define a group provide its members with a feeling of belonging. When boundaries are clear, they allow adolescents to distinguish between their own and other groups, and result in stronger ethnic identity. Some boundaries are maintained from within by the group, others are imposed on the group by the dominant culture (Isajiw, 1974). Internal boundaries come about through identifying with others in one's group. Adolescents adopt the values, attitudes, and perspectives of their group. Interactions with those outside the group provide a second type of boundary, through which minority adolescents experience the social opportunities and constraints that exist for members of their group—the relative status and value given them by others. The value accorded one's group by society is an important component of ethnic identity.

Adolescents' consciousness of their ethnic identity varies with the situations they are in. Rosenthal and Hrynevich (1985) found that adolescents experience a strong ethnic identity when they are with their family or speaking their parents' native language, but feel part of the dominant culture when with others from that culture, such as when they are at school. They also found that the strength of the inner boundary of the ethnic group relates to adolescents' pride in their ethnic identity. Their measure of this strength was the institutional completeness of the community, the extent to which it provides its own schools, markets, churches, and other institutions. This finding helps explain the previously unexpected discovery that blacks in segregated schools frequently have higher self-esteem than those in integrated schools (Powell, 1985).

In the process of acculturation, external behaviors of minority adolescents frequently become less distinct from those of the majority culture while attitudes and values remain unchanged (see Chapter 1). Doreen Rosenthal and Shirley Feldman (1992) suggest that some components of ethnic identity may be more resistant to change than others because they are more central. Minority adolescents whose behavior closely resembles that of peers from the dominant culture might still have strong ethnic identities in other respects.

These investigators compared first- and second-generation Chinese American and Chinese Australian adolescents on several measures of ethnic identity. As expected, they found that despite differences in knowledge about their culture and in observable behavior between first- and second-generation minorities, the core aspects to their ethnic identities differed little; both first- and second-generation adolescents ascribed the same importance to their ethnic group membership and evaluated their ethnicity equally positively.

William Cross, a professor of African Studies at Cornell University, distinguishes several steps to the process of forming an ethnic identity. In the *pre-encounter* state, individuals identify with the dominant culture. They notice differences between themselves and the dominant culture but do not consider them important. The second stage of identity formation, which happens only for minority adolescents, is the *encounter*. Cross traces the emergence of this stage to one or more vivid incidents in which adolescents experience discrimination. These experiences precipitate an awareness of membership in their ethnic group. This stage is a turning point in the development of an ethnic identity in which minority adolescents turn from the ways and values of the dominant culture and take on those of their ethnic group (Cross, 1980, 1987).

In the stage that follows, which Cross calls the *immersion* stage, adolescents immerse themselves in the ways of their ethnic group, developing a high degree of awareness and valuation of those ways, along with a devaluation of those of the dominant culture. This stage is frequently characterized by social activism or even militancy. Finally, in the *internalization* stage, adolescents become able to appreciate themselves and others as individuals and to recognize differences that don't always correspond to group membership. Attitudes toward others reflect personal characteristics rather than group membership, as in the previous stage. Ethnic identity is less strident, and attitudes toward the dominant culture are less negative (Cross, 1980, 1987).

In the third stage of ethnic identity formation, adolescents immerse themselves in the ways of their ethnic or racial group. Here, three young Native Americans prepare to participate in a pow-wow.

This progression parallels a number of other developmental progressions in which development moves from a focus on the self to a focus on the group, to respect for the individual (Aboud, 1987).

Do minority adolescents first internalize the values of the dominant culture and then question these values as they experience their implications before they adopt the values of the minority culture? For ethnic identity—just as for identity achievement in general—a crisis in which one questions the values one had previously accepted may be central to further development. Gordon Parks, a black photographer, describes such an incident from his boyhood:

> I was only 12 when [a] cousin of mine, Princetta Maxwell, a fair girl with light red hair, came from Kansas City to spend the summer at our house. One day she and I ran, hand in hand, toward the white section of town to meet my mother, who worked there as a domestic. Suddenly three white boys blocked our path. I gripped my cousin's hand and we tried going around them, but they spread out before us.
>
> "Where you going with that nigger, blondie?" one snarled to my cousin.
>
> We stopped. The youngest one eased behind me and dropped to his hands and knees, and the other two shoved me backward. Pain shot through my head as it bumped against the sidewalk, and I could hear Princetta screaming as she ran back toward home for help. I caught spit in my face and a kick in the neck. I jumped up and started swinging, only to be beaten down again. Then came a kick in the mouth. Grabbing a foot, I upended its owner, scrambled up and started swinging again. Then suddenly there was help—from another white boy. Waldo Wade was in there swinging his fists alongside mine. The three cowards, outnumbered by the lesser count of two, turned tail and ran.
>
> Waldo's left eye began puffing up as we walked along nursing our bruises. "How'd it all start?" he finally asked.
>
> "They thought Princetta was white." "Idiots," he answered. "Hell, I know'd she was a nigger all the time." Waldo and I had trapped and fished together all our lives, but only through the delicacy of the situation did I resist busting him in his jaw.
>
> That fight was sort of a turning point. (1990, p. 4)

Stages of Ethnic Identity Development.   Jean Phinney, a psychologist at California State University, Los Angeles, points out that the progression toward an ethnic identity parallels differences among Marcia's (1988) identity statuses. Although Marcia did not initially think of the statuses developmentally, most research suggests that identity achievement is the most mature resolution and diffusion the least, with foreclosure and moratorium as intermediate steps (Josselson, 1982; Orlofsky & Frank, 1986). Phinney (1989a, 1989b, 1990) proposes a stage model of ethnic identity development that parallels Marcia's analysis of identity.

Three distinct stages to ethnic identity development emerge. Just as with Marcia's identity statuses, it is possible for minority adolescents to avoid exploring the implications of their ethnicity and to remain committed to the values of the dominant culture. Adolescents with an **unexamined ethnic identity** have simply internalized the values and attitudes of the dominant culture, in a way similar to that of foreclosed adolescents, and have little understanding of issues related to their ethnicity. Those in an **ethnic identity search**, or moratorium stage, are involved in exploring the meaning of their ethnicity and may experience a growing conflict between the values of the dominant culture and those of their ethnic group. Adolescents with an **achieved ethnic identity** have a clear sense of their ethnicity that reflects feelings of belonging and emotional identification. They have little defensiveness and show confidence in their ethnicity (Phinney, 1989a; Phinney & Rosenthal, 1992).

Phinney (1989a) interviewed tenth-graders from different ethnic backgrounds regarding ethnic identity issues. These adolescents were Asian Americans, blacks, Hispanics, and whites. The interviews contained questions that tapped their exploration of and commitment to their ethnicity. An exploratory question was "Do you ever talk with your parents or other adults about your ethnic background or what it means to be ——?" Commitment was tapped by questions such as "Some people find these questions about their background pretty confusing and are not sure what they really think about it, but others are pretty clear about their culture and what it means to them. Which is true of you?" Adolescents also completed measures of ego identity, self-evaluation, sense of mastery, social and peer relations, and family relations.

As Phinney expected, stages of ethnic identity development correlated positively with the measure of ego identity. Similar correlations existed for measures of a sense of mastery and peer and family interactions. These findings suggest that the stages are indeed developmental, although we can't say that they increase with age. Slightly less than 50% of the minority adolescents had explored the implications of their minority status by the tenth grade. Even though a direct comparison is not possible because different samples are involved, this percentage is still higher than that for eighth-graders found in a previous study (Phinney & Tarver, 1988).

The stages themselves were independent of any particular minority. As shown in Table 8.1, just about the same percentage of adolescents from the three minorities was in each of the three stages of ethnic identity formation. This latter finding suggests that adolescents from different minorities have the same need to come to terms with the personal implications of minority membership. The important element appears not to be the particular minority group the adolescent is from, but the adolescent's stage of development of an ethnic identity. The one exception to this finding comes from white adolescents, who had no sense of their own ethnicity

T A B L E   8 . 1

Percentage of Minority Adolescents in Stages of Ethnic Identity Formation

	Unexamined	Search (Moratorium)	Achieved
Asian Americans	57.1%	21.4%	21.4%
Blacks	56.5	21.7	21.7
Hispanics	52.1	26.9	21.7
Total	55.7%	22.9%	21.3%

Source: *Adapted from J. Phinney. (1989). Stages of ethnic identity development in minority group adolescents.* Journal of Early Adolescence, 9, 34–49.

and saw themselves only as "American." Phinney notes that this ethnocentric attitude is out of touch with our increasingly pluralistic society. By the mid-1990s, minorities will constitute about one-third of all those between the ages of 15 and 25 (Wetzel, 1987).

Somewhat different issues are important for different ethnic groups. Asian American adolescents were more likely to express concerns related to academic achievement, for example, quotas for universities that might exclude them. Black males expressed concern about job discrimination and negative images of black adolescents, and black females mentioned standards of beauty that did not include them, for example, long, flowing hair and "creamy" skin. Hispanic adolescents reported most concern with prejudice (Phinney, 1989a). Despite these concerns, relatively few minority adolescents appear to have internalized negative attitudes toward their group. Only 20% mentioned negative attitudes during the interview, and these were distributed evenly across identity statuses (Phinney, 1989a).

THE SELF

The search for identity is a central task facing all adolescents. Adolescents are brought face to face with this task by two forces, one from within and the other from without. The first force—puberty—radically alters bodies that have become as comfortable as an old shoe. The shoe begins to pinch when adolescents develop the physiques, feelings, and cognitive capacities of adults. The second force, in the form of psychosocial expectations, confirms these inner changes. Adolescents are expected to be more adult—to start making decisions for themselves, to be responsible, to plan for their futures. But despite this alliance of culture with nature, someone within still asks, "Who am I?"

Self-Concept: Who Am I?

Each of us has a theory about ourself; it helps explain the way we feel, what we like or do not like, what we are good at, and why. Developmentalists call this theory the **self-concept**. Just as with other theories, the self-concept is a way of explaining and interpreting the "facts" one experiences in daily life (Epstein, 1973).

Adolescents' ability to relate isolated events in terms of more general principles allows them to pull different experiences together into general assumptions about themselves. A boy who backpacks and bikes, plays ball well, and is on the swim team can think of himself as athletic. A friend who belongs to the drama club, is illustrating the class yearbook, and gets As in her art classes can think of herself as artistic. Both adolescents are making generalizations about themselves from specific experiences.

The capacity for self-reflection that comes with adolescence brings with it a concern about personality in general and thoughts about oneself in particular. Adolescents' observations about themselves begin with specific events (e.g., being on the swim team, or swimming the 100-meter faster than anyone else). These soon take the form of more general beliefs ("I am a good swimmer"). At an even more general level, the adolescent who can say of himself that he is a good swimmer, a strong runner, and a good ball player can integrate these into a sense of himself as athletic. If this adolescent also is a good student and holds down a part-time job, he can formulate even more general self-statements, such as, "I'm competent" and "I'm responsible."

The beliefs an adolescent has about himself or herself determine many of that adolescent's emotional reactions. Which of these beliefs are central to their sense of self? Adolescents can easily know which are most central by the way they react when these ideas are challenged. An adolescent who values her independence, for example, will find herself in frequent arguments whenever someone tells her that she cannot do something. One who values his competence will resent having anyone tell him he is not able to manage a task.

Because so many of the beliefs about the self in adolescence are recently formulated, they lack experiential support. As a consequence, the adolescent's new self-concept is particularly vulnerable to disconfirming evidence. Perhaps because of this, adolescents spend a lot of time and energy gathering evidence in support of their theories of the self. Events that otherwise might be commonplace take on significance if they support adolescents' beliefs about themselves. Getting a driver's license and going out on a first date are examples of experiences that assume this kind of significance, because they validate important beliefs, such as, "I'm adult" or "I'm attractive" (Okun & Sasfy, 1977). Many of the self-statements adolescents include in their self-concepts reflect potential more than actual accomplishments. These discrepancies also explain why the theory of self is at first so vulnerable to disconfirming evidence.

To be healthy, self-concepts need to be self-correcting. When they are, adolescents can face new information about themselves openly. When teenagers feel threatened, they tend to close themselves off to defend their beliefs, incapable of seeing the ways in which their experiences fail to confirm these beliefs. But adolescents who feel secure about themselves are able to revise their beliefs in light of their experiences. Remaining open to new views of the self is especially difficult in adolescence because so much changes, and the need to explain these changes is so great.

The self-concept becomes more abstract, more differentiated, and more adaptive during adolescence. Children derive their sense of themselves from concrete, physical characteristics. Adolescents think of themselves in terms of psychological characteristics such as being impulsive, shy, loud, or witty. Children draw their characters in bold strokes—as either good or bad, right or wrong, strong or weak. Adolescents make finer distinctions; they see subtleties and nuance. They under-

Adolescents' sense of self includes who they have been as well as who they hope to be. Formulating their self-identity requires them to discover what they like, what they are good at, and what they believe in.

stand how a characteristic can be both a strength and a weakness. A 15-year-old might pride himself on his reflectiveness in social situations and his sensitivity with his friends, yet realize that these very same qualities can be his downfall when faced with a taunting classmate, knowing that a less-reflective friend could simply swing a punch at the offender. Self-concepts also become more adaptive as adolescents accumulate more years of decision making. These decisions provide a history of successes and failures. Most have learned that they usually make good decisions, and that even when they make mistakes, they are not devastating.

Self-Esteem: Do I Like Myself?

If the self-concept is a set of beliefs about the self, then **self-esteem** is a measure of how good one feels about these beliefs. A girl who describes herself as athletic, artistic, short, witty, and friendly does not stop there. She evaluates each of these qualities. "Is it really okay to be as athletic as I am? So I'm artistic; but is that as

B O X   8 . 2

Parental Attitudes and Self-Esteem

"I think it's really fun to watch them grow up and mature. It's fun to see them discover things about themselves and their lives. The older ones have boyfriends, and I'm seeing them interact with the boyfriends."—*Mother*

"Sometimes the kids have friends over, and they all start to talk about things. It's nice to see them get along with their siblings as well as their friends. It gives you a good feeling to see them enjoying themselves."—*Father*

"I felt very pleased when my son at sixteen could get a summer job in the city and commute and be responsible for getting there and doing a good job."—*Mother*

"I enjoy that she is following in the family tradition of rowing. I rowed in college, and my brothers did, my father and grandfather did, and she saw a city team and signed up. She does it all on her own and has made a nice group of friends through it."—*Father*

"I like it when they sit around and reminisce about the things they or the family have done in the past. They sit around the table and talk about an outing or a trip we took, saying 'Remember this?' It's always interesting what they remember. This last summer we took a long sightseeing trip, and what stands out in their minds about it is funny. They remember Filene's basement in Boston or a chicken ranch where we stopped to see friends. One father took the scouts on a ski trip. They got stuck in the snow on the highway for hours, and the car almost slid off the road. He said, 'Never again.' I said, 'Don't you realize that because of those things, the boys will probably remember that trip forever. You have given them wonderful memories.'"—*Mother*

"I really enjoy her happiness. She always sees the positive side to a situation. Things might bother her from time to time, but she has a good perspective on things."—*Father*

good as being a 'brain?' Am I too short or just tall enough?" The answers she comes up with contribute to her feelings of adequacy and self-worth. Self-esteem is an adolescent's overall positive or negative evaluation of herself or himself (Simmons & Blyth, 1987).

Foundations of Self-Esteem.   Relationships with parents provide the foundation for self-esteem. When parents are loving, children feel lovable and develop feelings of self-worth. These feelings become established early in life. Infants quickly learn whether the world in which they live will meet their needs; when those around them are responsive, they develop a sense of trust. The establishment of trust in these first, basic relationships permeates all later ones. S. E. Bartle, S. A. Anderson, and R. M. Sabatelli (1989) found that self-esteem among adolescents still reflects their interactions with parents. Adolescents with authoritative parents, who stress self-reliance, shared decision making, and willingness to listen, have higher feelings

---

BOX 8.2 *(continued)*

Parental Attitudes and Self-Esteem

"I can't believe that she has had her first boyfriend and it worked out so well. They met at a competition; and he lives some distance away, so they talk on the phone. He has a friend who lives here, and he comes for a visit sometime and does lots of things with the family. We all like him, and it is nice for her to have a boyfriend like that."—*Mother*

"The joys are seeing them go from a totally disorganized state to a partially motivated, organized state. You can see their adult characteristics emerging."—*Father*

"I enjoy seeing my daughter develop musical ability, seeing her progression from beginning flute to an accomplished player who performs, and seeing how much pleasure she takes in her accomplishment."—*Mother*

"It really gives me a lot of pleasure to see the two of them help each other. They seem to have respect for each other. She is the brain and helps him with school, and he helps her too at times."—*Father*

"I enjoy his maturity. He's so responsible. He tests us, but when we're firm, he accepts that. I'm real proud of him because he looks at the consequences of what he does."—*Father*

"I enjoy his honesty and the relationship he has with his friends. He is real open with his feelings, and his friends look up to him. He's a leader."—*Mother*

"He's not prejudiced. His best friends are of different ethnic groups. People trust him and like him because he's real concerned about people."—*Father*

Source: Adapted from J. B. Brooks. (1991). The process of parenting (3rd. ed.). Mountain View, CA: Mayfield.

---

of self-worth. Interactions with fathers in particular contribute to their self-esteem. Box 8.2 illustrates some of the attitudes parents have about adolescents that can foster self-esteem.

A number of factors outside the home are also associated with self-esteem. Popularity and feeling attractive both contribute to a positive self-image. These are interrelated; adolescents who are popular also think of themselves as better looking. For males, being athletic also contributes to self-esteem, as does higher socioeconomic status (Simmons & Blyth, 1987).

Ethnicity and Self-Esteem.   When we distinguish private aspects of self-esteem, such as pleasure in oneself or pride in one's beliefs, from its more public aspects, such as how intelligent one feels with others or satisfaction with one's physical attributes, different patterns of self-esteem emerge for minority and majority adolescents. Minority adolescents' self-esteem in private domains is as high as that of

Self-esteem is the overall positive or negative evaluation of oneself. Opportunities for responsible work help to build self-esteem.

majority adolescents. For black and Hispanic adolescents, self-esteem has even been found to be higher than for white adolescents (Phinney & Rosenthal, 1992). Yet for the public domain of traits, the self-esteem of minorities is generally lower (Iheanacho, 1988; Martinez & Dukes, 1987).

Gender is an important variable mediating self-esteem in minorities. Self-esteem among adolescent girls who are black, Native American, or Asian has been found to be higher than that for their male counterparts for public aspects of self-esteem (Martinez & Dukes, 1987). These gender differences may reflect the tendency within the dominant culture to attribute more well defined and frequently less positive stereotypes to minority males than to minority females (Eagly & Kate, 1987).

Gender and Self-Esteem. Among majority adolescents, males tend to have higher self-esteem than females. Girls are more likely to negatively evaluate characteristics about themselves they consider to be important. Figure 8.2 shows that in mid-adolescence, for example, nearly one-third of all girls who care either "a great deal" or "pretty much" about their looks are not satisfied with them. Similarly, we see that more than 50% of all ninth-grade girls who are not satisfied with their weight still care about it very much. Self-esteem has nowhere to go but down under conditions such as these (Simmons & Blyth, 1987).

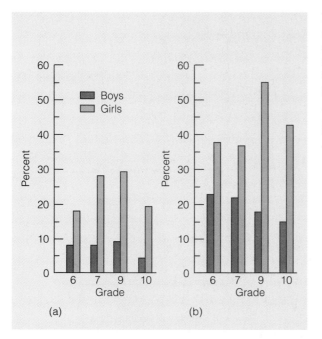

Figure 8.2 Negative Evaluations of (a) Appearance and (b) Weight Among Adolescents Who Rank These Characteristics High for Self-Esteem.

Source: R. G. Simmons & D. A. Blyth. (1987). Moving into adolescence. *New York: Aldine de Gruyter.*

The greater resilience of boys' self-esteem during adolescence shows up in another respect as well. Their self-esteem is less vulnerable in the face of change than is that of girls. All adolescents face some transitions in common: puberty, a change in schools, and, with dating, a reordering of their social world. Some adolescents must also cope with geographical relocations and with family disruption, when parents change jobs or divorce. Having time to gradually get used to one change before having to cope with another makes it easier to adjust to such transitions.

The more changes adolescents must cope with simultaneously, the more likely they are to show the effects of related stress. Grade-point average and participation in school activities drop for both males and females. As shown in Figure 8.3, as the number of life transitions increases, self-esteem also drops in girls. A comparable drop in self-esteem does not occur in boys. The more stability adolescents have in any one area, the better they can cope with changes in others (Simmons & Blyth, 1987).

Consider a hypothetical 14-year-old girl who is midway through puberty and just beginning to date. Her parents are recently divorced, and she lives in a new neighborhood. She has so many things to talk about with her friends, but she never gets to see them. She doesn't know which of the physical changes she's experiencing are "normal" and which are "weird." She feels angry all the time—except when she's depressed. When she tells her counselor at school, he tells her it's because of her hormones. The last person she can talk to is her mother, who feels

Figure 8.3 Drop in Self-Esteem with Number of Life Changes for Adolescent Girls.

Source: R. G. Simmons & D. A. Blyth. (1987). Moving into adolescence. *New York: Aldine de Gruyter.*

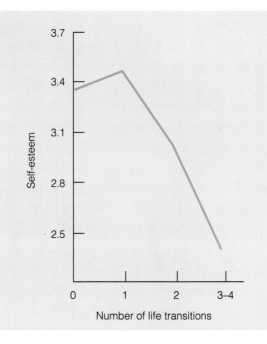

even worse than she does. Her grades have fallen, and she's lost interest in doing things at school. When asked how she feels about herself, she has a hard time thinking of any qualities that she likes.

This adolescent's experiences are extreme, yet the situation she faces is increasingly common for many (see Chapter 5). Under conditions such as these, self-esteem understandably suffers in adolescence.

How do adolescents come up with a sense of themselves that they can live with and like? Puberty forces the issue, but it also sets the stage for new answers. Because of pubertal changes, adolescents find it difficult to think of themselves as they did as children. But they also develop ways of thinking that give them the means to combine aspects of the old self with newly developing ones. Some of these aspects involve others; we turn to intimate relationships next.

INTIMACY: THE SELF THROUGH RELATIONSHIPS

Adolescents of every background have one thing in common: They all will share themselves with others in intimate relationships. Intimacy is often misunderstood.

Like many adults, most adolescents associate it with romance, passion, being to-gether, or being so close one can finish the other's sentences. Yet arguments, like romance, can provide the ground for intimate encounters, passion can involve little sharing of feelings, and always being together may signal a relationship that pro-vides little room for being oneself. As for being able to finish another's sentences, this may mean the other has said nothing new for some time. But perhaps the biggest misunderstanding concerning intimacy is that it occurs only in relationships with others. Intimacy begins with oneself and only then can it be extended to others.

What is intimacy? **Intimacy** is a sharing of innermost feelings and thoughts in an atmosphere of caring, trust, and acceptance.

Intimacy with Oneself

Intimacy, when it concerns oneself, means that one is in touch with inner feelings and needs; that is, one possesses self-awareness. Adolescents' capacity for intimacy should develop under the conditions that make it safe for them to know themselves. We discussed some of these conditions in the context of individuation in Chapter 5. Families that allow members to express their ideas, even when they differ from those of others, communicate that it is safe to disagree. Once adolescents have this safety, they are able to examine how they really feel (Grotevant & Cooper, 1986).

Self-acceptance is also important for intimacy. Adolescents who like them-selves are free to be themselves without trying to change anything. Self-acceptance and self-awareness go hand in hand. Adolescents who have accepted themselves can be aware of desires and feelings that they otherwise might feel a need to deny or distort. Since a common way of distorting needs is to attribute them to others (i.e., projection), self-awareness makes it possible for them to perceive others more accurately as well. In appreciating the complexity of their feelings, they can realize that the feelings of others are similarly complex and can validate those emotions. Self-acceptance creates a self-perpetuating cycle; having been validated, others are able to hear what they are saying and, in turn, validate them (Bell & Bell, 1983).

An important ingredient to self-acceptance is liking oneself. Adolescents who like themselves can let others get close enough to see them as they really are. Adolescents who don't like themselves frequently feel ashamed and are unwilling to let others get close. Often they feel it necessary to put up a front to look better, or to use their relationships to prove to themselves that they are acceptable (Mas-ters, Johnson, & Kolodny, 1988). These approaches block intimacy, either by not being open with the other person or by using that person for one's own needs. Adolescents who feel negative about themselves are likely to handle their feelings of depression and anxiety in ways that block self-knowledge, by escaping into al-coholism or drug abuse, seeking distractions such as television, or finding substi-tutes such as eating. None of these behaviors lends itself to intimacy. Of course,

RESEARCH FOCUS

Path Analysis: Too Young for Intimacy?

Shelly spends all her time with friends—if not with them at school, then on the phone. Shrieks of laughter and silent smiles punctuate their conversations. It's clear who's "in" and who's not when they're with others. Shelly is 16. Her life revolves around her friends.

Yet some experts would question how close Shelly really is to her friends. These developmentalists argue that adolescents can form intimate relationships only after they have established a stable identity—a task several years beyond this 16-year-old. Erik Erikson assumes that adolescents must resolve the psychosocial crisis of identity before they can become intimate with others, that is, that intimacy is *contingent on* identity. Other theorists, such as Carol Gilligan and Ruthellen Josselson, argue that Erikson's developmental model fits the experience of males better than that of females. These theorists note that females' interpersonal skills prepare them to define themselves through their relationships with others, that is, that intimacy *contributes to* identity. Is the connection between identity and intimacy different for adolescent males and females? How might we tell?

Couldn't we simply measure identity achievement and intimacy in a group of adolescents and see whether those who have a better sense of themselves also have closer relationships with others? Let's say we do and discover that our assumption was correct. Does this finding support Erikson? Gilligan and Josselson? Actually, we have no way of knowing. There is no way to tell from this single correlation which factor is responsible for the other.

Would it help to separate the adolescents by sex and look at the degree to which the two measures are correlated for each? Not really. Even if we found a stronger relationship for one group than the other, we still would not know for that group which quality contributed to, or caused, the other—that is, whether identity is necessary for intimacy to develop, or whether intimacy contributes to the development of identity. All we would know is that adolescents who are high in one attribute are also high in the other, and vice versa.

Path analysis is a statistical procedure that allows developmentalists to infer the direction, or path, of an effect from correlational data. To use this procedure, one must obtain measures for the same variables on more than one occasion. Since causes precede their effects, we need this time difference to trace the direction of the relationship. But how is this procedure any better than a single correlation? We're still measuring both factors at the same time, just doing it twice instead of once.

That's true. However, because causes *precede* their effects, we can look for differences in the strength of relationships that differ *only* in which factor precedes the other. If Factor A causes Factor B, these factors should be most strongly correlated when measurements for A precede those for B, that

(continued)

adolescents need not be happy with themselves all the time. As Masters, Johnson, and Kolodny (1988) note:

> Generally, we separate what we like from what we don't like and use this process to try to change. If we are honest in our self-appraisals, the intimate knowledge we develop helps us relate to others. At the same time, a person who *never* looks inward (whether out of fear, laziness, or self-hatred) has such distorted self-perceptions that it is unlikely he or she can contribute fully to a relationship with someone else. (p. 318)

RESEARCH FOCUS (*continued*)

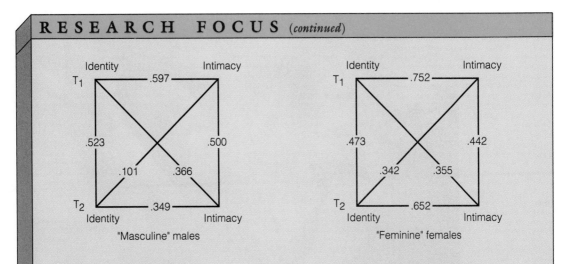

is, between Factor A at Time 1 and Factor B at Time 2. The opposite correlation (Time 1 measures of Factor B with Time 2 measures of Factor A) should be relatively weak. The figure shows these correlations as diagonals stretching from Time 1 (T_1) measures at the top to Time 2 (T_2) measures at the bottom.

But let's get back to Shelly. Are her friendships likely to be as intimate as they seem, or is their closeness illusory, awaiting further identity development? Patricia Dyk and Gerald Adams (1990) conducted the study we have been describing (except their subjects were older than Shelly). These investigators found no simple gender difference in the relationship between identity and intimacy:

Identity predicts intimacy for both sexes. However, when factors such as gender-role typing and empathy are taken into account, different patterns emerge for females and males. In males, and in females high in masculinity, identity predicts intimacy. In highly feminine females, the association between identity and intimacy is more fused, suggesting that intimacy and identity develop together, as Gilligan and Josselson also suggest. Some of these relationships appear in the figure.

Reference: P. H. Dyk & G. R. Adams. (1990). Identity and intimacy: An initial investigation of three theoretical models using cross-lag panel correlations. Journal of Youth and Adolescence, 19, 91–110.

Intimacy with Others

Self-disclosure is important to intimacy. Adolescents who are intimates share their thoughts and feelings with each other (Orlofsky, Marcia, & Lesser, 1973; Schiedel & Marcia, 1985). Not everything they share is personal (often it's just gossip), but much of it is. Intimacy takes time to develop, as adolescents learn to trust each other with increasingly personal aspects of themselves. Self-disclosure has to be

Adolescents have to learn to accept themselves before they are ready for an intimate relationship, which requires having the self-confidence to let someone else know them as they really are.

mutual to be comfortable; one adolescent cannot "tell all" and the other tell nothing. We tend to shy away from people who tell us everything about themselves the moment we meet them. Choosing to disclose things about oneself is a bit like taking off one's clothes. How "undressed" one appears depends on how much others are wearing. Someone in a bathing suit has enough on when lounging poolside, but at a dance would look nearly naked.

Adolescents are willing to share their personal experiences when they can trust that others will respect their confidence. Trust takes time to develop and usually requires some testing of the waters. An adolescent may start by sharing things she would not be devastated to hear repeated, such as what she thinks of a particular teacher, and work her way up to her most private thoughts and feelings, for example, what she really thinks of her stepfather, or the details of her relationship with her boyfriend. This kind of trust requires a commitment to a relationship.

INTIMACY AND IDENTITY: DIFFERENT PATHS TO MATURITY?

To what extent are intimacy and identity related? Can adolescents be close to others without knowing themselves well? Can they develop a sense of themselves apart from their intimate relationships with others? Erikson believed that identity is a

Some theorists believe that females define themselves primarily in the course of their relationships but that males must define themselves before they are capable of close relationships. If they hope to build a lasting relationship, young couples need to be willing to accept changes in their partner's self-definition.

necessary precursor to intimacy. He wrote that "True engagement with others is the result and the test of firm self-delineation" (1968, p. 167). Intimacy assumes developmental significance for Erikson only after identity has been achieved.

This developmental progression, however, is not typical of females. Josselson (1988) writes that development in females takes place on an "interpersonal track" that is not represented in Erikson's scheme. Erikson wrote, for example, about industry (the crisis preceding that of identity) as the development of competence by learning how things are made and how they work. Competence for females is more likely to take the form of increasingly complex interpersonal skills (Marcia, 1980). These two types of skills set a different stage for the drama that unfolds during adolescence than that envisioned by Erikson. Prior developments prepare females to define themselves interpersonally through skills that bring them into relationships with others, whereas the same developments prepare males to define themselves *impersonally* through skills that result in products. Feiring and Lewis

(1991) note that as girls move into adolescence, their social networks relate to their perceived self-competence across a variety of areas, in ways that boys' relationships do not.

Erikson viewed intimacy as a characteristic of relationships with others. But for females, it is also a process by which they define themselves. Rather than postponing identity consolidation until they find a mate, as Erikson suggested, intimacy affords the means by which female adolescents *achieve* self-definition (Gilligan, 1982; Josselson, 1988; Marcia, 1980). Ruthellen Josselson states:

> Intimacy, or interpersonal development, among women *is* identity and resides not in the choice of a heterosexual partner, but in the development, differentiation, and mastery of ways of being with others (not just men) that meet her standards for taking care, that connect her meaningfully to others, and that locate her in an interpersonal network. (1988, p. 99)

If relationships assume a different developmental significance for females, we should expect to see gender differences in levels of intimacy during adolescence. Don Schiedel and James Marcia (1985), both at Simon Fraser University, classified individuals into intimacy statuses that reflected commitment to and depth of relationships, as shown in Table 8.2. They found significantly more females in the higher intimacy statuses than males. In fact, females were nearly twice as likely as males to be in the highest two statuses. Perhaps because the individuals they studied were in late adolescence or early adulthood, the proportion of females high in intimacy did not increase with age. This proportion did increase for males, however, suggesting that males, as Josselson and Carol Gilligan also imply, are not as prepared for relationships as are females.

But what about the relationship between intimacy and identity mentioned earlier? A number of studies support Erikson's suggestion that intimacy is contingent on achieving identity, but find this relationship to be more characteristic of males than females (Dyk & Adams, 1990; Schiedel & Marcia, 1985). Schiedel and Marcia found, for instance, that for males, those in the highest intimacy categories were most likely to be in the identity-achieved or moratorium status. This trend for females was not significant. Further, they found virtually no males who were high in intimacy but low in identity. Identity and intimacy do not, however, appear to be achieved in succession by women; a full one-third of the females who were high in intimacy were low in identity. These findings support Josselson's contention that for females intimacy *is* a means by which identity is resolved.

Does development take the form of increasing autonomy and separation? Most personality theorists have answered yes. Every now and again a few voices raise alternatives, but until recently, these have not been incorporated into mainstream developmental theory. Revisions may be afoot (Gilligan, 1982; Gilligan, Lyons, & Hanmer, 1989; Josselson, 1987, 1988).

David Bakan (1966) distinguishes two aspects of mature functioning. **Agency** captures qualities of assertiveness, mastery, and distinctiveness, and **communion**

TABLE 8.2

Intimacy Statuses in Late Adolescence

Isolate	Relationships consist only of casual acquaintances.
Stereotyped	Relationships are shallow and conventional.
Pseudointimate	Relationships are similar to those of Stereotyped but have commitment to long-term sexual relationship; these defined through conventional roles rather than self-disclosure.
Preintimate	Close, open relationships characterized by mutuality; ambivalence regarding commitment to long-term sexual relationship.
Intimate	Relationships are similar to those of Preintimate but also have commitment to long-term sexual relationship.

Source: D. G. Schiedel & J. E. Marcia. (1985). Ego identity, intimacy, sex role orientation, and gender. Developmental Psychology, 21, 149–160.

reflects qualities of cooperation and union. Bakan considers these two facets of personal functioning to be balanced in the mature person. Developmentalists have traditionally translated these aspects of maturity into a developmental progression moving *from* communion *to* agency, thereby assigning greater maturity to agency. An alternative interpretation of Bakan's view of maturity, but one that equally distorts it, has assigned agency to the masculine personality and communion to the feminine. This approach easily reduces to the first because development in females often falls short of that in males when comparisons use measures that have been standardized with males (e.g., Kohlberg's measure of moral development, the use of rules in games). Most Western cultures implicitly confirm either of these translations through the greater value they place on agentic over communional behaviors. Our society, for example, defines success in terms of individual accomplishment and achievements rather than the quality of a person's relationships.

But is development most accurately thought of as increasing separation and individuation? Ruthellen Josselson (1988) notes that recent research in two areas within psychology—adolescent development and the psychology of women—reveals difficulties in viewing development this way.

Development in Adolescence

Development during adolescence does not require an end to, but rather a modification of, significant relationships with parents. Adolescents achieve a sense of themselves *within* their relationships, not in spite of them (Josselson, 1988). Research with adolescents and their parents such as that of Grotevant and Cooper (1986) finds that attachment and separation are not opposites but are different aspects of the same process. If the task of adolescence is to break ties with parents, then adolescents either accomplish this task or they don't—they either separate *or* remain attached. If the task is for adolescents to renegotiate relationships with parents to achieve greater mutuality and equality, they can separate as persons *and* remain emotionally connected or attached (Josselson, 1988). Any theory that emphasizes separation as developmentally more advanced gives a distorted view of development in which an autonomous self is accepted as the pinnacle of maturity (Josselson, 1988).

Development in Females

A second challenge to the prevailing view of development as progressive separation and individuation comes from attempts to chart female development. These attempts bring a new awareness of the male bias in much developmental theory. Developmentalists have assumed their theories to be universal, that is, to cover issues fundamental to the whole of human experience. Yet theories are not totally objective representations of human nature; they are interpretations that often reflect the personal experiences of the theorists. And most personality theorists have been men. There is a growing recognition that current theories address experiences that are more common among, or even unique to, males (Adelson & Doehrman, 1980; Bettleheim, 1961; Gilligan, 1982, 1986; Josselson, 1988).

Erikson, for instance, thought of identity as an exploration of issues related to vocation, political views, and religion. When females are interviewed about their identity concerns, one hears about their relationships—not about industry, autonomy, or ideology. Autonomy may well serve the function of a "developmental organizer" for most males in our society, but relationships serve this function for most females. Josselson adds, "Because women define themselves in a context of relationship, a developmental orientation that equates growth with autonomy will automatically relegate women to lower rungs of development" (1988, p. 99). She notes in support of this point that the cultural myths that exist in our society make it difficult to view the "achievement of adult commitment, fidelity, intimacy, and care [as] meaningful and heroic" (1988, p. 99).

Carol Gilligan (1986) comments that the adolescent girl especially faces a problem in that, as she affirms her connection with her mother, she sees how disconnected they both are from a society in which the male experience defines reality. Gilligan writes:

> The ability to establish connection with others hinges on the ability to render one's story coherent. Given the failure of interpretive schemes to reflect female experience and given the distortion of this experience in common understandings of care and attachment, development for girls in adolescence hinges . . . on the courage to challenge two equations: the equation of human with male and the equation of care with self-sacrifice. Together these equations create a self-perpetuating system that sustains a limited conception of human development and a problematic representation of human relationships." (1986, p. 296)

proach to identity must give equivalent weight to a person's relatedness to others. Maturity involves movement toward a greater capacity for relationships. Contributing to this capacity are assertion and autonomy. Josselson turns the tables and makes self-in-relationship the more embracing concept of which autonomy and separateness are components.

Does development move from dependence to autonomy, as traditional theory asserts? Does it involve increasingly articulated ways of relating to others? We have seen that adolescents of both genders work out their identities in the context of continuing significant relationships with others, and males as well as females face intimacy as a central issue leading to adulthood. Josselson maintains that each person has a need for separateness *and* attachment, for inclusion *and* exclusion. Each of these creates tensions, but to give in to one and not strive for balance is to forfeit some degree of maturity (Josselson, 1988).

Males, on the other hand, tend to define relationships according to fixed categories and to assume that they'll always remain the same. The difference in the genders' view of relationships may be partly due to differences in identity formation: Males are defined more in terms of what they can do, and females are defined more in terms of how they relate to others.

SUMMARY

Achieving Identity

Achieving an identity is a central task facing adolescents. Identity gives one a coherent, purposeful sense of self.

There are several ways by which adolescents arrive at the roles and values that define their identities. Alternate paths, involving either a personal search or an adherence to old beliefs, lead to commitments. Conversely, alternate paths can lead to noncommitment—some adolescents not being able to choose among alternatives for fear of closing off important options, and others because they fail to see the importance of choosing. These paths lead to four identity statuses: identity-achievement, foreclosure, moratorium, and identity diffusion.

Even though Erikson believed the search for identity to be a central task facing all adolescents, he assumed that females and males approached it differently. The task for males involved making choices and commitments about an occupation, a set of beliefs, and their sex role. Erikson believed females arrived at their identity by committing themselves to a future mate.

Research on gender differences in identity development shows these to be minimal. The process and timing of development suggest more similarities than differences.

Ethnic identity development progresses through several stages. Adolescents with an unexamined ethnic identity internalize the values and attitudes of the dominant culture. Those in an ethnic identity search are exploring the meaning of their ethnicity, and those with an achieved ethnic identity have a clear sense of their ethnicity and emotionally identify with their ethnic group. These stages correlate with ego identity statuses.

The Self

The self-concept becomes more abstract, differentiated, and adaptive during adolescence. The capacity for self-reflection allows adolescents to think of themselves in terms of psychological characteristics; they appreciate subtlety and nuance. Increased experience in making decisions contributes to more adaptive self-concepts.

Self-esteem reflects the overall positive or negative attitude adolescents have about the self. Relationships with parents provide the foundation for self-esteem. Other factors such as popularity and attractiveness also contribute to self-esteem.

Degree of self-esteem varies with ethnicity and gender. Some aspects of self-esteem are higher among minority adolescents than majority ones; others are not. In general, males have higher self-esteem than females during adolescence.

Intimacy: The Self Through Relationships

Intimacy is the sharing of innermost feelings and thoughts in an atmosphere of caring, trust, and acceptance. To be intimate with others, adolescents must first know and accept themselves.

Self-disclosure provides a vehicle for intimacy with others. Intimacy is contingent on achieving identity, but this relationship is more characteristic of males. For females, intimacy is often the means by which identity is resolved.

Developmental Paths to Maturity

Development has traditionally been viewed in terms of increasing autonomy and separation from others. Recent research on adolescent-parent relationships and on female development questions this view.

Relationships between adolescents and parents show that continuing emotional attachment and increasing autonomy coexist and are different aspects of the same process. For females, relationships with others contribute importantly to their sense of self. New definitions of maturity will need to include movement toward a greater capacity to relate to others, as well as increasing autonomy and separateness.

KEY TERMS

Identity
Identification
Identity Formation
Identity-Achieved
Identity-Foreclosed
Moratorium

Identity-Diffused
Personal Expressiveness
Ethnic Identity
Unexamined Ethnic Identity
Ethnic Identity Search
Achieved Ethnic Identity

Self-Concept
Self-Esteem
Intimacy
Agency
Communion

GENDER STEREOTYPES: THE
MEANING OF MASCULINE
AND FEMININE
The Masculine Gender Role
The Feminine Gender Role
Androgyny: A New Alternative

SEXUALITY AND INTIMACY
Love and Romance
Dating and Sexual Activity

■ RESEARCH FOCUS: *Between-*
Subjects Design: Date Rape

SEXUAL ORIENTATION
Homosexuality
Biological and Psychosocial Bases
  of Sexual Attraction

SEXUAL FUNCTIONING: FACT
AND FICTION
The Sexual Response Cycle

■ RESEARCH FOCUS: *Matched-*
Subjects Designs: Initiation of Sexual
Activity

Myths and Misconceptions

TEENAGE PREGNANCY
AND PARENTING
Teenage Mothers
Teenage Fathers
Adolescents and Abortion

SEXUALLY TRANSMITTED
DISEASES
Chlamydia
Gonorrhea
Genital Warts
Genital Herpes
Syphilis
Pubic Lice
Risks and Precautions
HIV Infection and AIDS

■ RESEARCH FOCUS: *Ethics: AIDS*
Prevention Research—What You Can't
Say Can Kill You

SUMMARY

KEY TERMS

CHAPTER NINE

The Sexual Self: Close Relationships in Late Adolescence

"Hey, Raffie," Arnie grinned over the locker door. "You a lucky man this morning, or not?"

"Or not," thought Raffie, as he grabbed his books and gave the door a slam. But he grinned back, "You think you're the only one around here gets lucky?"

"All right!" exclaimed Arnie, giving his friend a "deadarm" and heading for his first class on the run.

Raffie glared at Arnie's back as he disappeared down the hall. What was it with his friends? Did they really have all the sexual adventures they said they had? Was he the only one who was different?

Raffie was 16, and he was worried. Raffie was a virgin.

Now imagine the same scenario between two female adolescents.

"Hey, Rachel," Annie grinned at her friend. "Make anything happen last night, or what?"

"Or what," thought Rachel, but she grabbed her books and grinned back. "You think you're the only 'happening one' around?"

"All right," said Annie, giving her friend an affectionate squeeze. She promised to catch all the details over lunch then ran off to class.

Rachel stared at her friend as she rushed off. "Am I really that different?" she wondered.

Is the second scene harder to imagine than the first? What does the phrase "getting lucky" communicate about a sexual encounter? Are females and males equally likely to think of sex this way? Would Raffie's father have been as embarrassed in his day by sexual inexperience? Is Rachel likely to be? What are the sexual attitudes and practices of adolescents today, and how do these contribute to teenagers' sense of self?

The topic of sexuality raises questions at any age, but especially during adolescence. Researchers have recently begun to supply us with some answers. In other instances, however, they have only begun to ask the questions. Still, knowing what questions to ask can be the first step to understanding, even if these questions are sometimes very personal. Sexuality looms large in adolescence, in part because it takes exciting new turns, and in part because it contributes so heavily to adolescents' sense of themselves.

Ready-made roles, in the form of sex-role stereotypes, await adolescents as they step into adulthood. These gender stereotypes, like ready-made clothes, will fit some adolescents better than others. For still others, they will not fit at all. We will consider stereotypes of masculinity and femininity in the opening section of this chapter, along with the more flexible alternative of androgyny.

Sexuality forms the basis for a new type of emotional intimacy in adolescents' relationships. Adolescent males and females describe their romantic experiences in strikingly similar ways that are also similar to the descriptions of adults. The manner in which sexual feelings are expressed varies with the type of dating relationships adolescents have.

For most adolescents, sexual attraction involves someone of the opposite sex. A small percentage discover they are attracted to those of their own sex. The biological and psychosocial bases of sexual attraction will receive attention in this chapter.

The sexual response cycle is strikingly similar for all individuals, despite differences in gender or sexual orientation. Research reveals four phases of response: excitement, plateau, orgasm, and resolution. We examine similarities in sexual response before discussing myths and misconceptions common among adolescents about their sexual functioning. The chapter ends with a consideration of some consequences of adolescent sexuality: unintended pregnancies and sexually transmitted diseases.

GENDER STEREOTYPES: THE MEANING OF MASCULINE AND FEMININE

Gender-role stereotypes are the cultural expectations concerning which behaviors are appropriate for each sex. These stereotypes play an important role in self-definition as adolescents begin to integrate questions posed by their sexuality into their developing sense of themselves—questions such as "What does it mean to be an adult male or female?" "How much will I have to change the way I think of myself?" "In what ways will I still be the same?"

The Bem Sex-Role Inventory (BSRI) is an instrument that assesses the attitudes of individuals concerning what it is to be masculine and feminine in our society (see Box 9.1). A score of 4.9 on either the feminine or the masculine scale is considered average for that scale, indicating a traditionally masculine or feminine gender role. About half of all individuals who take the inventory score at or above this number on one of the scales (Hyde, 1991).

Agape, or selfless love, is long-suffering and non-demanding, always putting the needs of the other ahead of one's own—for example, "I can't be happy unless I put her happiness above my own."

Levesque found three love styles contribute to relationship satisfaction for adolescents: eros, agape, and ludus. These styles have also been found to be important for adults (Davis & Latty-Mann, 1987). Exhilaration and togetherness, both components of relationship satisfaction for adolescents, also characterize the erotic and storgic love styles. Conversely, pragma and mania correlate negatively to relationship satisfaction. Adolescents are happiest, in other words, in relationships they do not have to see in terms of marriage and other commitments (pragma), and that do not make them lose sleep or feel sick or otherwise depressed (mania).

Dating and Sexual Activity

Attitudes toward sex have changed substantially over the past several generations. One of the most noticeable changes is a weakening of the **double standard**—different standards of sexual conduct for males and females that reflect prevailing societal beliefs. The traditional standard for males is to have numerous sexual contacts prior to marriage. Remaining a virgin is not only unnecessary, it's considered not masculine. On the other hand, the standard for females permits sex only within the context of an exclusive sexual relationship, preferably marriage.

In large measure, changes in the sexual behavior of female adolescents have been responsible for a decrease in the double standard. However, socialization into a double standard of sexual conduct may still be the norm for adolescent males, many of whom still experience subtle pressures to transform their social contacts into sexual encounters and to view females as potential conquests (Byrne, 1983; Sonenstein, 1986).

Some observers of the social scene speak of a new morality, one that emphasizes the authenticity of relationships rather than conformity to social norms, and that judges sexual conduct less by social convention than by the nature of the relationship in which it occurs. Rather than ask whether a sexually involved couple is married, this morality asks if they love each other. A single standard—"permissiveness with affection"—may be coming to characterize the sexual encounters of both sexes, replacing the double standard that has dominated sexual attitudes and behavior in the past (Koch, 1988).

A survey of several hundred college students confirms these trends. The percentage of those who engaged in increasingly intimate sexual behaviors increased with the degree of affection and commitment in the relationship. Figure 9.1 shows these trends.

RESEARCH FOCUS

Between-Subjects Design: Date Rape

It was well past midnight when Carol Ann slipped into the darkened house.

"Is that you, honey?" her mom called out in a sleepy voice.

"Yeah, Mom," she whispered hoarsely as she hurried to the bathroom.

Safe behind the closed door, she tore off her crumpled clothes, turned on the shower, and let the steaming water scald her skin pink.

She felt so dirty. She still didn't know how she had gotten away. She remembered struggling, punching, fighting back. Ugly bruises reddened on her arms and body as she choked back sobs of rage and humiliation. He had tried to rape her!

It had been their third date. He had been so polite and attentive each time before, never out of line. She hadn't been concerned when he suggested a party at a friend's house and turned down a dark road. What could she have said or done to make him think . . . ? And why did *she* feel so responsible? So terribly ashamed?

Carol Ann's experience is not that unusual. A national survey found that 60% of acquaintance rapes among college students occur in a dating situation (Koss, Dinero, Seibel, & Cox, 1988). What kind of male violates the consent of his date? Is it one whose sex drive is so strong that once aroused, he cannot stop himself? Or does date rape first start in the mind—with an attitude?

Rape myths are stereotyped perceptions of rapists and victims that minimize rape as a crime by shifting blame to the victim. As the term implies,

they represent myth, not fact. Are males who endorse such statements more accepting of violations of consent on a date? Would they be more likely to answer "Yes" than "No"? Several of these myths appear below:

- If a girl engages in necking or petting and she lets things get out of hand, it is her fault if her partner forces sex on her.

- Any healthy woman can successfully resist a rapist if she really wants to.

- In the majority of rapes, the victim is promiscuous or has had a bad reputation.

- A woman who is stuck up and thinks she is too good to talk to guys on the street deserves to be taught a lesson.

- When women go around braless, or wearing short skirts and tight tops, they are just asking for trouble.

- Many women have an unconscious desire to be raped, and may then unconsciously set up a situation in which they are likely to be attacked.

- If a woman gets drunk at a party and has intercourse with a man she's just met there, she should be considered "fair game" to other males at the party who want to have sex with her too, whether she wants to or not.

Are beliefs such as these more likely to be held by certain people than by others? What other attitudes are they related to? Do they predict attitudes

(continued)

RESEARCH FOCUS (*continued*)

toward other intimate behaviors such as kissing, necking, petting, or even holding hands? Do attitudes about violations of consent depend on the level of assumed intimacy in the relationship? How could we find out?

Leslie Margolin, Melody Miller, and Patricia Moran (1989) found answers to these and similar questions by having male and female students read a description of a dating situation in which a male tried to kiss a female while they were at a movie together; when she refused, he kissed her anyway. Some of the students read that John and Mary were on a first date, others that they had been going together for two years, and others that they were married. Can you identify the independent variable in this experiment? If you said something like "level of intimacy," you were right. The other variable—gender—is a classification variable. (See Chapter 3, Research Focus: An Experiment and Chapter 4, Research Focus: Correlational Research for definitions of terms.)

These investigators used a *between-subjects design*. In this type of experiment, each subject experiences only one level of the independent variable. Remember that some of the students read that John and Mary were on a first date, others that they were going together, and still others that they were married. When subjects are randomly assigned to one and only one level of an independent variable, it is a between-subjects design. Why might this matter? Why might we care whether they experienced more than one experimental condition?

A major advantage to this type of design is that investigators need not worry that subjects' re-

sponses will reflect the effects of another condition that may still be present. In other words, what if subjects assigned to the "first date" condition had just previously read of a similar incident involving a couple who was married? Could we safely assume that these subjects would be able to separate their reactions to each situation? In a between-subjects design, one need not worry about such matters. Also, since subjects can be assigned at random to conditions, investigators can be reasonably confident that groups do not initially differ until they impose different treatments. Both assumptions involve the issue of internal validity. (See Chapter 5, Research Focus: Internal and External Validity.) To the extent that guarantees exist in experimental research, between-subjects designs offer high guarantees of internal validity.

What did these investigators discover about attitudes toward violations of consent? They found that acceptance of rape myths *is* related to acceptance of violations of consent, regardless of level of intimacy. They also found that males are more accepting of rape myths than are females. Consequently, they were not surprised to find that males also were more supportive of John's right to violate Mary's consent to be kissed.

References: Adapted from M. P. Koss, T. E. Dinero, C. A. Seibel, & S. L. Cox. (1988). Stranger and acquaintance rape: Are there differences in the victim's experience? Psychology of Women Quarterly, 12, *1–24. L. Margolin, M. Miller, & P. B. Moran (1989). When a kiss is not just a kiss: Relating violations of consent in kissing to rape myth acceptance.* Sex Roles, 20, *231–243.*

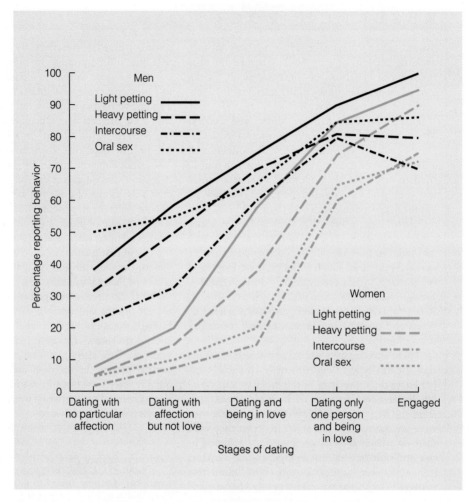

Figure 9.1   Sexual behavior reported by students at each stage of dating.

Source: Adapted from J. P. Roche & T. W. Ramsby. (1993). Premarital sexuality: A five-year follow-up study of attitudes and behavior by dating stage. Adolescence, 28, 67–80.

SEXUAL ORIENTATION

One of the central tasks of adolescence involves achieving a personal identity, and a major component of this is one's sexual identity. Although children label themselves as being one sex or the other from the earliest years on, sexual orientation does not become firmly established until adolescence. It is then that sexual experimentation embellishes and confirms, or disconfirms, these earlier labels. Late

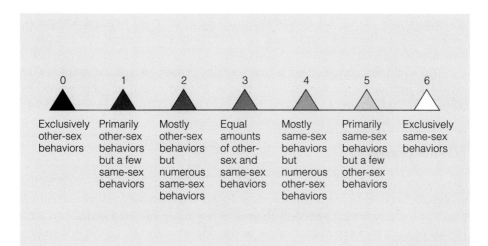

Figure 9.2 Kinsey's continuum of sexual orientation.
Source: Adapted from A. C. Kinsey, W. B. Pomeroy, & C. E. Martin. (1948). Sexual behavior in the human male. *Philadelphia: Saunders.*

adolescence brings the additional task of infusing relationships with emotional intimacy.

Sexual orientation refers to the attraction individuals feel for members of the same or the other sex. Those with a **heterosexual** orientation are attracted to people of the opposite sex, those with a **homosexual** orientation are attracted to members of their own sex, and **bisexually** oriented people are attracted to individuals of both sexes. *Gay* and *straight* are terms commonly used to refer to people who are homosexuals and heterosexuals, respectively; *lesbian* is a term used to refer to gay women.

How many adolescents share each of these orientations? Simple answers are not forthcoming, for a number of reasons. Rather than discrete categories into which individuals neatly sort themselves, sexual orientations are more like segments along a continuum (see Figure 9.2). It is not always clear where one orientation leaves off and another begins. For instance, surveys reveal that 13% of all females have had sex with another female to the point of orgasm, yet only 1% to 3% of females consider themselves to be lesbian. Similarly, from 20% to 37% of adolescent and adult males have had sex to the point of orgasm with another male, yet only 4% are exclusively gay throughout their lives (Kinsey, 1948, 1953; Strong & DeVault, 1994).

This last statistic introduces yet another factor that contributes to the "fuzziness" of these categories. Sexual attraction can change during one's lifetime. For instance, Kinsey found that 10% of the males he interviewed were predominantly homosexual for three or more years; however, only 4% remained so throughout their lifetime.

An additional complication is that sexuality cannot be reduced simply to behavior; it includes attraction and desire as well. One could, in other words, be celibate throughout one's life and still be straight or gay (Strong & DeVault, 1994).

Homosexuality

How is one to think of homosexuality, if having homosexual experiences does not necessarily mean that one is homosexual? In general, homosexuals are individuals who, for some extended period of their lives, are more attracted sexually to individuals of their own sex than to those of the opposite sex. This definition underscores several points. First, sexual attraction is as important in defining sexual orientation as actual behavior; and second, an isolated sexual experience does not mean one is homosexual: sexual orientation reflects a prolonged sexual preference. Furthermore, many individuals are neither exclusively heterosexual nor exclusively homosexual.

Establishing a sexual identity is difficult for most adolescents, but especially so for those who wonder whether or not they're homosexual. Being different is never easy, especially when it places one in a group that is viewed negatively by many segments of society. Fear and denial can prolong the process of establishing a sexual identity. Homosexual males are likely to discover their sexual orientation in adolescence but females may not become aware of their sexual orientation until adulthood (Masters, Johnson, & Kolodny, 1988).

For adolescents of either sex, awareness that they are gay often develops only gradually. Many gay adolescents report having felt vaguely "different" during childhood, but without a sense of what that might mean. These feelings assume sexual significance with puberty and homosexual attractions. Even then, a period of confusion may follow. Even those who are predominantly attracted to people of their own sex may alternately consider themselves to be straight, gay, or bisexual. One study of 75 gay men found that most had noticed being attracted to someone of the same sex by about the age of 10, but had not necessarily considered themselves homosexual. Some did not do so until their 20s or even their 30s (Hamer, Hu, Magnuson, Hu, & Pattatucci, 1993). In large measure, this difficulty reflects the pain gay teenagers experience in identifying themselves as members of a group considered to be deviant by society (Strong & DeVault, 1994).

Gay, lesbian, and bisexual adolescents face a number of additional problems. Academic performance frequently deteriorates, and for many substance abuse is a problem. Significantly more gay than straight adolescents attempt suicide, some studies reporting close to one-third of gay males having done so (Coleman & Ramefedi, 1989). Tracie Hammelman (1993) examined suicidal tendencies in gay

Too few gay adolescents are like the young men and women in this group. Most have no one with whom to share concerns and questions about their developing sexual identity, and they must cope by themselves with the social prejudices against homosexuality.

and lesbian youth and found almost half had thought about suicide at one point or another, and a third had actually made a suicide attempt, most during adolescence, and most mentioned sexual orientation as a reason contributing to the attempt.

Biological and Psychosocial Bases of Sexual Attraction

What determines one's sexual orientation? Are we born straight or gay? Can sexual attraction be traced to formative experiences, such as the type of family one is raised in or a first sexual encounter? We will look first at recent biological explanations, and then at psychological ones.

Biological Factors.   J. Michael Bailey and Richard Pillard (1991) interviewed gay and bisexual men with twin brothers. Twins can be of two types. Identical (monozygotic) twins share the same genetic makeup, having developed from the same cell (zygote). Fraternal (dizygotic) twins develop from separate cells and are no more similar genetically than other siblings. If there is a genetic contribution to sexual orientation, more identical twin brothers should both be homosexual than fraternal twin brothers. This study also included an additional, third group of gay and bisexual men; these men had adoptive brothers, that is, with no shared genetic background. It was expected that the coincidence of homosexuality would be lowest in this third group.

Bailey and Pillard found that over 50% of the identical twins whose brothers were homosexual were themselves homosexual, whereas only 22% of the fraternal twin brothers were, and even fewer, 11%, of the adoptive brothers.

A similar study of sexual orientation in females revealed comparable findings. Forty-eight percent of monozygotic twin sisters of gay women were also lesbian, in contrast to only 16% of dizygotic twin sisters, and 6% of adoptive sisters (Bailey, Pillard, Neale, & Agyei, 1993).

These findings strongly suggest a genetic component to sexual orientation. Additional research suggests that the path of genetic transmission, at least for males, is likely to be through the mother. A higher percentage of maternal uncles of gay men, and cousins who are sons of maternal aunts, are gay than the base rate of homosexuals in the population. Higher rates are not found for paternally related males. Furthermore, a particular site along the X chromosome of the 23rd pair of chromosomes (the pair determining one's sex) has been implicated through research on genetic mapping. The X chromosome is received from the mother (Hamer, Hu, Magnuson, Hu, & Pattatucci, 1993).

Such research should not be taken to mean that all genetic contributions to sexual orientation will relate to the X chromosome or take any single form. It is likely, given the complexity of our genetic makeup, that many avenues of transmission are possible.

Nor is the precise means by which genes might influence sexual orientation known. One possibility is through the hormones that are present in differing amounts in males and females. However, studies of gay males and lesbians and of heterosexuals do not find expected differences in the levels of circulating hormones (Money, 1988).

Hormones might also affect prenatal brain development. One study found that a node of the hypothalamus, which is related to sexual behavior, is smaller in gay males than in heterosexual males (LeVay, 1991). However, since the gay males in this study had all died of AIDS, differences in hypothalamic size might have been due to the disease, or even to their behavior. Additionally, since the researcher analyzing the brain tissues was not "blind" to the sexual orientation of the subjects, this knowledge could have influenced the observations.

It is also possible that individuals may be genetically predisposed to homosexuality but nonetheless develop a heterosexual orientation because of the presence or absence of other contributing factors.

Psychological Factors. Sexual orientation develops within a psychosocial environment. Freud assumed that children are initially bisexual and only gradually develop heterosexual interests. He traced the development of these interests to the child's resolution of the Oedipal or Electra complex in early childhood (see Chapter 2).

Other theorists have suggested that homosexuality in males is due to a domineering, overprotective mother and a passive father (Bieber, 1962). However, one would expect such family influences to affect siblings, and the incidence of homosexuality among brothers of gay males is no higher than in the population at large, with the exception of twins, as discussed above.

Similarly, lesbianism has been traced to traumatic early sexual experiences which turned these women away from males as objects of sexual desire. However, estimates of the frequency of such experiences are considerably higher than the incidence of homosexuality among females (see Chapter 12).

The most immediate context in which sexual behavior can be studied is the very private world of the human sexual response. Like much else related to adolescent sexual functioning, our understanding has been late to develop, and myths and misconceptions consequently abound.

SEXUAL FUNCTIONING: FACT AND FICTION

The Sexual Response Cycle

Sputnik had orbited the earth and Neil Armstrong had one foot on the moon before scientists began to unravel the complexities of the human sexual response. In 1966, two scientists, William Masters and Virginia Johnson, published their signal research on sexual physiology. Like Kinsey before them, they braved a critical social climate—and took one step forward for humankind. Their study of sexual physiology differed from previous research in an important respect: They studied actual sexual encounters between men and women. Their research reflects over 10,000 sexual episodes between more than 300 men and 300 women under conditions of controlled observation.

Masters' and Johnson's research revealed a sexual response cycle consisting of four phases: excitement, plateau, orgasm, and resolution. Two processes underlie the changes of each phase: vasocongestion and myotonia. *Vasocongestion* is an accumulation of blood in the vessels serving the erogenous zones (areas of the body that are particularly sensitive to sexual arousal), and *myotonia* is an increase in muscular tension. The tension is more like a building up of energy in the muscles rather than a state of feeling tense. At each phase of the cycle, striking similarities exist in the response of females and males.

RESEARCH FOCUS

Matched-Subjects Designs: Initiation of Sexual Activity

When do adolescents become sexually active? Is the onset of sexual activity related to hormonal levels? To forces outside the family, such as the sexual activities of friends? To factors within the family, such as parental dating and remarriage, or sexually active siblings?

Research into the biological and social factors that contribute to the initiation of sexual behavior is relatively new. Researchers have just recently begun to identify relevant variables. The larger task of piecing together patterns of mutual influence still remains to be tackled. We know, for instance, that parental variables such as dating and remarriage are important. But what about older siblings? Surely they should have some influence, especially if they are sexually active.

Joseph Rodgers and David Rowe (1988) thought they should. Specifically, they anticipated that adolescents who had older siblings would be more active sexually than would those without older siblings. They also thought that the younger siblings would be more active sexually than their older siblings were at their age. To determine

whether older siblings have an influence, one would need to compare the sexual activity of adolescents with and without older siblings. Simple? Yes, as long as one controls for other variables that might relate to sexual activity. Age is one of these.

Rodgers and Rowe selected two samples of adolescents, one with older siblings and one without. The ages of adolescents in the two samples were *matched*. To match subjects along some variable, one first needs to rank the subjects in each sample according to the matching variable—from oldest to youngest—and then draw pairs of subjects from the two samples that are the same or approximately the same age. Using this procedure, one can be sure that the two groups will be equivalent regarding the matching variable. If age is related to sexual activity (and it is), it will be equated for the two groups. Any differences between groups in sexual activity cannot be due to age.

Matching carries an additional advantage. It reduces the amount of unexplained variability in the groups. This variability is termed *random error*. By reducing random error, one can more easily see the

(continued)

Excitement.   Vasocongestion is responsible for the first signs of *excitement*, or sexual arousal, in both males and females. In males it causes blood to pour into the spongy tissues in the shaft of the penis, making it erect. Masters, Johnson, and Kolodny (1988) note that since an erection is caused by an increase in fluid pressure, it is essentially a "hydraulic event." Vaginal lubrication, one of the first signs of sexual arousal in females, occurs when blood vessels in the pelvic area swell with blood, pressing fluids into the tissues surrounding the vagina (Lips, 1993). In both sexes, the nipples harden and muscular tension increases throughout the body (myotonia).

Plateau.   Continued vasocongestion during the *plateau* phase causes the erection in males to become harder. Drops of lubricating fluid, secreted by the Cowper's glands, appear at the opening of the glans. Because this fluid frequently contains live sperm, withdrawal prior to ejaculation, a birth control practice common among

RESEARCH FOCUS (*continued*)

effects of the independent variable. Another way of describing this advantage is to say that matched designs are more *sensitive* than those in which each subject is randomly assigned. The sensitivity of a design refers to its ability to detect a difference due to the treatment variable if such a difference exists.

Matching sounds like such a good idea that one has to wonder why investigators don't use this method all the time. Yet like other procedures, it has its disadvantages. The most serious drawback is a statistical one concerning the degrees of freedom used when determining the significance of the tests that evaluate the research outcome.

In designs that do not match subjects, the degrees of freedom reflect the number of *subjects*; in matched-subjects designs, they reflect the number of *pairs*. Matching cuts the degrees of freedom in half. This means that one must obtain a larger difference for it to reach statistical significance. The irony to this disadvantage is that matching is most advantageous when one is using few subjects, because it increases the sensitivity of the design. But this is the very condition under which one can least afford to lose degrees of freedom. Before one matches, one needs to be sure that the matching

variable is highly correlated with the measure one is using. Only in this way will it effectively reduce unexplained variability and pay for the loss in degrees of freedom.

Matched designs are slightly more *time-consuming* to conduct than are those involving simple random assignment of subjects. One must first administer the matching variable, then rank subjects before they can be assigned to conditions. Extra *expense* may also be involved. A more serious disadvantage than either of these is the threat to *external validity* that occurs when subjects who can't be matched must be discarded. Any loss of subjects can affect the representativeness of the sample and the ability to generalize to the population from which it was drawn.

What does Rodgers' and Rowe's matched design tell us about the influence of older siblings on adolescent sexuality? Generally, the findings confirmed their predictions. Adolescents who have an older sibling are likely to be sexually active at an earlier age.

References: J. L. Rodgers & D. C. Rowe. (1988). Influence of siblings on adolescent sexual behavior. Developmental Psychology, 24, *722–728.*

---

teenagers, is not an effective means of preventing pregnancy. In females, continued vasocongestion causes the walls of the vagina to swell, creating an *orgasmic platform*, which constricts the size of the vagina, making penis size relatively unimportant for stimulation. Because females require more pelvic congestion than males to reach orgasm, the plateau stage lasts longer in females (Williams, 1983).

Orgasm.   The sensations of *orgasm* result from rhythmic muscular contractions and discharge of tensions resulting from vasocongestion and myotonia. Orgasms can vary in intensity from one time to the next, depending on a host of factors, including mood, fatigue, and so on. Despite similarities in its physiological bases for both sexes, orgasm tends to be a more consistently uniform phenomenon in males than in females (Masters & Johnson, 1966). However, individuals of both sexes describe their experience of orgasm in similar ways. Box 9.3 presents some of these descriptions.

BOX 9.3

Descriptions of the Experience of Orgasm

Research finds that trained judges can't tell which written descriptions of orgasm are given by females and which by males. Can you? (See answers below.)

1. "Like a mild explosion, it left me warm and relaxed after a searing heat that started in my genitals and raced to my toes and head."
2. "Suddenly, after the tension built and built, I was soaring in the sky, going up, up, up, feeling the cool air rushing by. My insides were tingling and my skin was cool. My heart was racing in a good way, and breathing was a job."
3. "Throbbing is the best word to say what it is like. The throbbing starts as a faint vibration, then builds up in wave after wave where time seems to stand still."
4. "When I come it's either like an avalanche of pleasure, tumbling through me, or like a refreshing snack—momentarily satisfying, but then I'm ready for more."
5. "My orgasms feel like pulsating bursts of energy starting in my pelvic area and then engulfing my whole body. Sometimes I feel like I'm in freefall, and sometimes I feel like my body's an entire orchestra playing a grand crescendo."
6. "An orgasm feels like a dive, magnified many times over. First I feel my muscles tensing, then there's a leap into a cool lake, a sense of suspension and holding my breath, and then my whole body feels relaxed and tingling."
7. "Exhilaration is the best word I can find. I feel all pumped up and then, instead of exploding, I am one big wave of happiness and whooshing feeling."
8. "Some orgasms feel incredibly intense and earth-shattering, but other times orgasms feel like small, compact, self-contained moments."
9. "I feel like a cork popping out of a champagne bottle."
10. "There is a warm rush from my toes to my head, with a strong, pulsing rhythm. Then everything settles down like a pink sunset."

1. M   2. F   3. M   4. F   5. F   6. M   7. F   8. M   9. F   10. M

Source: Adapted from W. H. Masters, V. E. Johnson, & R. C. Kolodny. (1988). Human sexuality (3rd ed.). Glenview, IL: Scott, Foresman.

Resolution.   In the *resolution* phase, following ejaculation, the penis becomes flaccid, and males experience a *refractory period*, lasting anywhere from several minutes to several hours, during which stimulation will not produce an erection. Resolution lasts much longer in females, because vasocongestion in the pelvic area dissipates slowly and they can experience *multiple orgasms.*

Myths and Misconceptions

Despite today's relatively open attitudes toward sex, considerable ignorance and myth surround sexual functioning. Interviews with adolescents found that many are surprisingly ignorant about even the basics. A 16-year-old girl remarked, "I wasn't ready for it being so *real*. Because in movies they don't get sweaty and—you know—all this awkward stuff. Like maybe not being that easy to get it in, him not finding quite the right place, it kind of hurting" (Aitken & Chaplin, 1990, p. 24). Most of the boys who had intercourse said they had trouble even finding the vagina. One boy commented, "I wish sex came with instructions. All the time I was thinking about doing it, I was worrying, *How* do you do it?" (p. 24). A surprising number of boys feared there was something wrong with them because they did not know the way a male's body functions sexually. A few, for example, thought that they suffered from impotence when they lost an erection, and many, because they did not know how long it normally takes a male to reach orgasm, believed they were premature ejaculators (Aitken & Chaplin, 1990).

Ignorance concerning sexual functioning is by no means limited to adolescents. Many of their parents are surprisingly uninformed, too. Countless adults cannot accurately name the parts of their own genitals or those of the opposite sex. Masters, Johnson, and Kolodny (1988) noted that "While we cannot imagine a person unable to distinguish between eyes, nose, mouth, and chin, many men and women have no idea of the locations of the female urethra, clitoris, or hymen" (p. 53).

Bigger Is Better.   For adolescent males, concern about the size of their penis is at the top of the list. Many boys don't know what size is normal and are sure theirs is too small. This concern is fueled by large variations from one boy to the next in the timing and rate of growth. Comparisons are inevitable, and as Masters, Johnson, and Kolodny (1988) point out, a male's penis almost always looks shorter to him than someone else's simply because his visual perspective (in looking down) foreshortens it.

Size assumes added importance as a result of the common misconception that penis size is related to sexual adequacy—which is simply untrue. The orgasmic platform corrects for differences in circumference of the penis, and because there are few nerve endings in the upper vagina, length is unimportant. Though one penis can differ noticeably from another in size when flaccid, this difference all but disappears when erect. Masters, Johnson, and Kolodny (1988), in fact, refer to an erection as "the great equalizer."

A common concern among adolescent girls concerns their breasts. Many notice that one breast is slightly larger than the other. Girls may wonder if it's normal for one breast to be smaller than the other (it is), and what they can do about it (nothing short of cosmetic surgery). Boys face a similar concern when they notice that one testicle is higher than the other, which is also quite normal.

Capacity for Sexual Pleasure.   Perhaps the most pervasive cultural myth among adolescents is that males experience more sexual pleasure than females. The fact that females take longer to reach orgasm may contribute to this myth. Once they

Interviews with adolescents reveal that many are surprisingly ignorant about even the basics of sexual intimacy and its consequences.

reach orgasm, however, their capacity to achieve additional orgasms exceeds that of males. Similarities in the phases of the sexual response cycle in either sex, and in the way individuals describe orgasm, suggest similarities in the pleasure each experiences.

Need for Orgasm.   A related misconception is that only males need to reach orgasm. Considerable discomfort can result from reaching the plateau phase and not experiencing orgasm. Both males and females experience this discomfort, the result of blood vessels remaining engorged in the pelvic and genital areas. This vasocongestion underlies orgasm in both sexes, and failure to release the accumulated blood and the muscular tension produces discomfort in both males and females.

Intercourse During Menstruation.   Numerous cultural taboos exist regarding intercourse during menstruation (Delaney, Lupton, & Toth, 1977). Some cultures even isolate menstruating females, fearing that they might contaminate the things with which they come into contact, whether these be people, animals, food, or plants. What dangers might befall a male? Misconceptions range from fears of infection to impotence and loss of virility. There is no factual basis for any of these fears (Delaney, Lupton, & Toth, 1977).

Current attitudes concerning menstruation are less negative than in previous generations, but reference to it as "the curse" is still common. Cultural messages—for example, advertisements and commercials for pads and tampons—communicate in subtle ways that menstruation is an untidy and unsanitary condition, to be "cleaned up" by using "sanitary napkins." Similarly, advertisements for tampons communicate that if a female handles things properly, she can go about her business almost as if she were "normal" (Lips, 1993; Masters, Johnson, & Kolodny, 1988).

Even though attitudes toward menstruation are changing, negative attitudes are likely to persist as long as we have a sexually polarized society in which the attributes of one sex are valued more than those of the other. Gloria Steinem once observed that if men menstruated, cultural views of the menstrual cycle almost surely would be different; in all probability we would see the cycle as a psychobiological advantage. Imagine thinking of the menstrual cycle in terms of peaks of heightened energy and productivity that rise from a baseline of "normal" competence and energy.

Intact Hymen and Virginity.   Another common misconception is that the presence of a hymen indicates virginity. The hymen is actually likely to tear in most girls during childhood with active play or curious exploration (see Chapter 3). Some girls are not even born with a hymen, and in others intercourse only stretches the hymen and does not rupture it (Masters, Johnson, & Kolodny, 1988).

TEENAGE PREGNANCIES AND PARENTING

Teenage Mothers

More than half the teenagers who become pregnant choose childbirth over abortion, and more than 95% keep their infants. What do we know of these mothers?

Kristen Sommer and her associates (1993) compared pregnant adolescents and adults on a number of measures assessing their readiness for parenting. They found that, in general, teenage mothers were less ready for parenting and experienced more stress in this role than adults. Adult mothers, for instance, knew more about infants, such as when a baby is able to hold a bottle or say its first words, and were more responsive and adaptive to their infants' needs.

A study of unmarried teenagers who agreed to interviews 1, 3, 5, and 17 years after giving birth provides important longitudinal information about adolescent mothers who choose to keep their infants. Furstenberg, Brooks-Gunn & Morgan (1987), found that a majority of the teenage mothers they interviewed finished

Teenage pregnancies are due partly to a lack of information and partly to a denial of personal responsibility. Adolescents need help in learning how to make decisions about their sexual behaviors, especially those that could alter the course of their lives.

high school and were regularly employed; though periodically on welfare, most supported themselves and their families. Most also had families no larger than those of their classmates who had children later. The vast majority coped.

Teenage Fathers

There are fewer teenage fathers than teenage mothers because nearly half of the fathers involved in teenage pregnancies are at least 20 years old (Sonenstein, 1986).

What do we know of the fathers who are teenagers? Contrary to stereotypes casting them as exploitive or uncaring, most remain psychologically involved with the mother through the pregnancy and for some time following the child's birth (Strong & DeVault, 1994). Most teenage fathers have less education and lower incomes than do those who postpone parenting, and many find it difficult to provide support for the mother and infant. Many are themselves children of unmarried mothers and grew up in homes without a father present. But most teenage fathers indicate a willingness to learn to be fathers (Strong & DeVault, 1994).

Presently, there are few programs to help teenage fathers learn to be better fathers. Those in existence stress the importance of finishing high school and getting a job. Many provide job training as well as parenting classes, enabling teenage fathers to provide financial as well as emotional support (Strong & DeVault, 1994).

Adolescents and Abortion

Approximately 40% of teenage pregnancies end in abortion (Strong & DeVault, 1994). What conditions affect an adolescent's decision to abort a pregnancy? Adolescents who say they intended to become pregnant are more likely to have the baby. In reviewing this literature, Cheryl Hayes (1987) points out that the issue of intentionality is not a simple one to evaluate. Girls review their intentions only when they discover they are pregnant; for most, conception was unintended, and carrying the baby to term is the decision that reflects intending to be pregnant.

Reasoning such as this makes it sound as if adolescents use abortion as an alternative to contraception. Yet studies following teenagers who have aborted a pregnancy suggest that this is not the case. Adolescents who have aborted one pregnancy are even less likely than those who give birth to have a second pregnancy within 2 years of the first. Repeat abortions are relatively infrequent among teenagers. Approximately 12% of 15-to-17-year-olds who have had an abortion have another, compared to 22% of 18-to-19-year-olds (Hayes, 1987).

Family background variables and peer influences also affect the decision to abort or carry a baby to term. Teenagers from middle-class homes are more likely to abort an unintended pregnancy than those living at the poverty level. White adolescents are also more likely to terminate a pregnancy than are black adolescents. These relationships are difficult to interpret because, as noted earlier, race and socioeconomic status are clearly related. Personal variables such as religious beliefs and parents' attitudes also play a role in a teenage girl's decision to carry a baby to term or to abort. Girls who have strong religious beliefs are less likely to abort a pregnancy, as are those whose parents disapprove of abortion. Peers influence an adolescent's decision, too. Girls with friends who are single teenage parents are more likely to carry the pregnancy to term; those whose friends view abortion positively (and are perhaps less likely themselves to be single parents) are more likely to terminate a pregnancy (Hayes, 1987). Box 9.4 gives a close-up view of decision making prompted by an unintended pregnancy.

Complicating decisions about abortion for many teenagers is the fact that many do not realize at first that they are pregnant. Young adolescents especially are likely to have irregular menstrual cycles, making it difficult to determine when they have missed a period. Still others may attempt to deny they are pregnant until

B O X   9 . 4

Unintended Pregnancy: Personal Decisions About Abortion, Adoption, and Keeping the Baby

Many factors influence an adolescent girl's decision when faced with an unintended pregnancy. Family, friends, and personal beliefs are all important, as the following examples illustrate.

Stephanie

Stephanie hadn't been careless—the contraceptive device she'd used had failed. "I want a baby in what I think is a healthy circumstance," she said. "I don't have a husband. I don't have a man who really wants this child. Russ will see me through an abortion, but he's walking out of my life when it's over."

After the abortion: "I felt abandoned. I wanted a lot of hugging and to know that somebody cared." The father had offered to accompany her to the clinic where she had her abortion and to spend the weekend with her, but he didn't behave lovingly. "Russ couldn't deal with the experience and was quite cruel, really. I suppose he was frightened, but that didn't make it any easier for me. He stayed with me, but when I wanted to be held, he said, "Don't hug me; we're just friends." Considering I'd just gone through an abortion in order not to have this person's child, I thought that was a ludicrous thing to say."

Laura

After eight pregnancy tests and eight personal denials, my father confronted me by asking if I was pregnant. I answered, scared, "Yes."

"My father gave me an ultimatum: to have an abortion or leave the family. I chose to leave.

"Knowing I had to leave the house I went to the crisis pregnancy center. They took care of me.

"I am currently at home again with my three-month-old boy. I am now engaged and looking forward to having my own family soon."

it is no longer possible to hide from the truth. The difficulties adolescents experience in finding out where to go for health services and arranging transportation compound these problems. As a result, teenagers are less likely to have an abortion in early pregnancy than are women who are young adults (Hayes, 1987).

The issues surrounding abortion are magnified as the result of delay, since the timing of an abortion has both health and moral consequences. Early abortions carry less risk to the adolescent. Similarly, issues concerning the taking of a life are less clear-cut before the fetus becomes viable, or even earlier in the pregnancy, before the appearance of signs, such as brain-wave activity, that are used at the other end of the age spectrum in decisions to terminate life support.

Furstenberg, Brooks-Gunn, and Morgan (1987) note that other countries such as England, Sweden, and the Netherlands have rates of adolescent sexuality

BOX 9.4 (*continued*)

Unintended Pregnancy: Personal Decisions About Abortion, Adoption, and Keeping the Baby

Susan

Susan was a freshman in college and was very caught up in her new academic and social activities. Bill (another student) and she had been dating for about three months, when one evening she decided to "take a chance" since she had just finished her menstrual period. When her next period was two weeks overdue, she had a pregnancy test. It was positive.

When Bill first learned of the pregnancy, he became distant, but he did agree to help pay for an abortion. Soon, however, he withdrew completely and had no further contact with Susan. The hardest time for Susan was before the abortion when she found herself crying frequently. She talked a lot with her close girlfriends, who comforted her. After the abortion, she felt that she had made the best decision, but she occasionally wondered how she would feel in future years.

Karen

Karen chose not to have an abortion, but to give her baby up for adoption. When the Bakerfields arrived at the hospital and walked down the corridor, Karen held out her baby to them. The baby was wearing a T-shirt with the inscription, "I love my Mommy and Daddy!" Then the Bakerfields and Karen prayed together, and Karen formally relinquished her child to their care.

"I was so happy to give life to someone else to start a family," Karen said. "That excited me. It still excites me." Karen has told her story to a number of high school audiences, and generally they are puzzled about her decision. What Karen tries to communicate is that love motivated her.

"I never had a father, really, growing up," she said. "By giving my baby to the Bakerfields, I gave her a father. She needed that."

Source: Adapted from P. Insel & W. Roth. 1991. Core concepts in health *(6th Ed.), Mountain View, CA: Mayfield.*

similar to those in the United States, yet they have lower pregnancy rates. One reason, they suggest, is that these countries have identified teenage *pregnancy*, not teenage sexuality, as a social problem. They offer programs that teach teenagers to assume responsibility for their sexuality, and more teenagers in these countries practice contraception effectively. As a consequence, one sees far fewer instances of teenage parenting or abortion.

Better access to clinics, more information, and promotion of contraceptive use in the media are important steps to be taken here at home. Yet teenage pregnancies are likely to remain a problem, especially among minority teens who experience the effects of racial discrimination. The likelihood of future success for most minority adolescents is much lower than for nonminority age-mates. The temptation to compromise future options, which may appear doubtful at best, for the immediate gain of sexual conquest can be hard to resist.

SEXUALLY TRANSMITTED DISEASES

Quite another consequence of teenage sexuality threatens the health of increasing numbers of adolescents. Many **sexually transmitted diseases (STDs)** have reached epidemic proportions. STDs affect approximately 3 million adolescents each year (Strong & DeVault, 1994). Since many STDs are asymptomatic and since many adolescents do not seek treatment, the actual number of adolescents affected is almost surely greater than estimated.

A sexually transmitted disease is an infection that is spread through sexual contact. Some STDs, such as syphilis and HIV infection, can also be acquired through blood transfusions, and a few, at least theoretically, by contact with contaminated toilet seats and bedsheets. They range in seriousness from irritating itches to life-threatening infections. Some are reaching epidemic levels among adolescents. The most serious STDs are HIV infection, syphilis, and gonorrhea. Less-serious infections range from genital herpes, for which there is no known cure, to

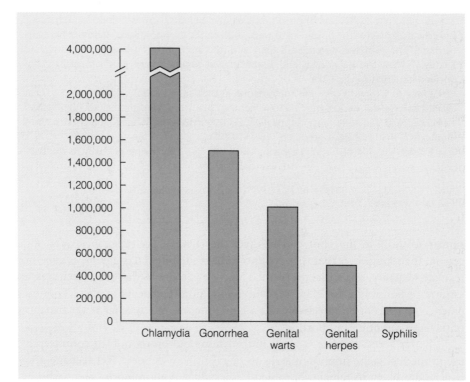

Figure 9.3 Estimated Incidence of Most Common STDs, United States, 1992.
Source: B. Strong and C. DeVault (1994). Human sexuality. *Mountain View, CA: Mayfield.*

pests such as pubic lice, which can be treated with a prescription shampoo. Figure 9.3 shows the incidence of the five most common STDs.

Chlamydia

Chlamydia is a common STD in the United States. It is caused by an organism that acts both like a bacterium and a virus (Strong & DeVault, 1994). Many individuals experience no initial syptoms; approximately 80% of females are asymptomatic, as are 30% to 50% of males. Those who do have symptoms experience urethral itching, painful urination, and usually notice a discharge. Adolescents can easily dismiss each of these. However, the consequences of doing so are serious, especially for females. The infection can spread through the reproductive tract, causing pelvic inflammatory disease (PID). Inflammation of the tiny tubules of the tract leaves scar tissue and increases the risk of ectopic pregnancy (a pregnancy occurring outside the uterus) and sterility in both sexes. Abdominal pain, a symptom of pelvic inflammatory disease, should be treated promptly (Brookman, 1988).

Gonorrhea

The next most common STD is **gonorrhea**, a bacterial infection. Gonorrhea can be transmitted by just about any form of sexual contact: intercourse, oral-genital sex, or even kissing. From 10% to 40% of males and 50% to 80% of females experience either no symptoms or very mild ones. In males, the most noticeable symptom is a watery discharge from the penis. Females also may notice a discharge; and both may experience pain when urinating. The rate of infection with gonorrhea declined in the 1980s, but varies considerably with ethnicity and race, and may be increasing among African Americans, especially teenage girls. In 1991, the rate of infection among African Americans was nearly 40 times higher than among whites. It is also higher among Native Americans and Hispanics (Strong & DeVault, 1994).

Left untreated, the disease spreads through the reproductive system, leaving scar tissue that can block the tubules and cause infertility. Untreated cases of gonorrhea can also affect the joints, causing a type of arthritis, and the heart, affecting the valves.

Early adolescent females may run a special risk because the immature cervix is especially vulnerable to infection by the bacterium causing gonorrhea. Early coital activity also appears to delay cervical development, as does the use of oral contraceptives. Thus early adolescent females who are using oral contraceptives are at greater risk of infection than those using other forms of birth control. Because the long-term consequences of infection for females include a higher risk of cervical cancer, those who have ever had gonorrhea should routinely get Pap smears (Brookman, 1988).

Prompt treatment with penicillin can cure the infection completely. Recently, however, a strain of gonorrhea has developed that is resistant to penicillin. The number of such cases has grown rapidly over a short period (see Figure 9.4).

Adolescents who discover they have gonorrhea should notify any sexual partner who is likely to have been infected or to have passed on the infection (symptoms are usually noticeable within 2 to 10 days of infection). They should also refrain from sexual contact until a checkup indicates that the infection is gone. Both steps are important in preventing the spread of this disease.

Genital Warts

Genital warts (sometimes called HPV for their cause, the human papilloma virus) are painless, dry, light-colored outgrowths on the genitals or rectum. Until recently they were not thought to pose a threat to health. Yet because the presence of warts is associated with other STDs, adolescents who notice them should seek treatment and at the same time be checked for other infections. Recent data suggest also that

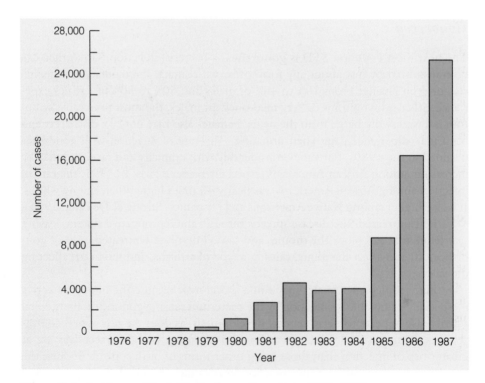

Figure 9.4   Incidence of Penicillin-Resistant Gonorrhea, 1976–1987.

Source: Centers for Disease Control. (1988). Atlanta, GA: U.S. Department of Health and Human Services, Public Health Service, Center for Prevention Services, Division of Sexually Transmitted Diseases.

when left untreated, warts are associated with a higher risk of cervical cancer in females, and other cancers in both sexes. This infection has risen sharply in recent years, increasing more than tenfold over the past several decades (Centers for Disease Control, 1988).

Genital Herpes

Genital herpes infections, caused by the herpes virus, are usually spread by sexual contact. However, the virus can also be spread by hand, after touching an infected area, and can survive for several hours on surfaces such as toilet seats, sauna benches, towels, and in tap water (Strong & DeVault, 1994). Clusters of itching or burning blisters appear, usually on the genitals but also in the rectum, on the cervix, or in the urethra, accompanied by slight fever, headache, and body soreness. The blisters break after several days, leaving small wet sores that dry up in a week or two. Even though the blisters eventually disappear, the virus remains dormant in the body, and outbreaks can reoccur at any time. No cure presently exists for herpes, although medication can diminish the unpleasantness of the symptoms when they first occur and decrease the frequency of recurrences.

Persons with genital herpes are contagious when the blisters appear. Recent data suggest that a partner can be infected even when there are no blisters, although this form of transmission is not as common. The incidence of genital herpes has increased dramatically since the mid-1960s. With approximately 40 million Americans already infected and 200,000 to 500,000 more infected each year, genital herpes has reached epidemic proportions. Because females with herpes are at some risk of developing cervical cancer, even those who have had only a single herpes outbreak should have a Pap smear twice a year. Cervical cancer can be successfully treated when detected early (Centers for Disease Control, 1988).

Syphilis

Sexual contact is the most common way **syphilis** is transmitted, although this bacterial infection can also be transmitted through contaminated blood transfusions, or passed from an infected pregnant woman to her fetus. Symptoms first occur from 2 to 4 weeks following infection. In the *primary stage* of the disease, small, usually painless sores appear on the genitals, rectum, fingers, mouth, or nipples. These typically heal within several weeks, and unsuspecting adolescents may believe that whatever they had is gone.

If not treated, syphilis progresses to a *secondary stage* marked by symptoms including a rash, fever, headache, and sore throat. These symptoms are easily mistaken for flu, especially as they can come and go for several months. During this time highly infectious open sores develop around the genitals and anus. Once these symptoms disappear, the disease enters a *latent stage*. Although adolescents in the latent stage can no longer infect others, the disease continues its course within their bodies. Many who have syphilis remain in this stage and experience no further complications. Others move into a *tertiary stage* in which damage to the heart, eyes, brain, and spinal cord can occur, and blindness, insanity, paralysis, and death can result (Strong & DeVault, 1994).

Despite its highly destructive nature, syphilis is easily treated with penicillin in the primary and secondary stages, and even in later stages is responsive to larger doses over longer periods. Despite the ease of treatment, the rate of infection increased markedly in the 1980s and has continued to rise. Approximately 120,000 to 130,000 people are infected each year. Large numbers of these are minority youth (Strong & DeVault, 1994).

Pubic Lice

Frequently known as "crabs," **pubic lice** are pests that are usually transmitted sexually but can also be transmitted via bedsheets or clothing. Lice live in the pubic hair, causing severe itching as they draw the blood on which they live. Bedding used by an infested person can remain infected for up to a week. A prescription shampoo (marketed as Kwell) kills the lice, but since eggs that drop onto bedding and clothing can survive for 5 or 6 days, clean sheets and clothing are important to prevent a recurrence.

Risks and Precautions

Many adolescents mistakenly believe that other people get sexually transmitted diseases—not them. Well-dressed, neatly groomed teenagers assume they could never get anything like syphilis or gonorrhea, much less AIDS. Assumptions such as these couldn't be further from the truth. STDs are presently as American as apple pie and country music. The facts are simple: Most diseases have reached epidemic proportions, and some, such as gonorrhea, are especially rife among adolescents. Adolescents who are sexually active are likely at some point to get a sexually transmitted disease.

Knowing the Risks.   One need not be promiscuous to run the risk of contracting an STD. Even adolescents who practice serial monogamy, limiting themselves to one sexual partner before becoming active with another, expose themselves to the sexual history of their partner—as well as the sexual history of each of their partner's partners, and so on. Like standing in a hall of mirrors, the regression is infinite. Since many diseases have no symptoms following the initial infection, adolescents who are infected, even if well intentioned, can pass the disease unknowingly to future partners.

less likely to tear during intercourse. However, any cuts or sores in the genitals of either partner expose that person to the virus if the other is infected. Similarly, sores or cuts in the mouth provide exposure to the virus during oral-genital contact (Masters, Johnson, and Kolodny 1988).

2. *Use a latex condom.* If one engages in intercourse, the use of a condom decreases the risk of infection because the virus cannot pass through the latex walls. Even so, using a condom is no guarantee that sex is ever completely safe; a tear in the condom or the escape of semen due to improper condom use can expose the partner to infection. The effectiveness of condoms is also dependent on their being consistently used (Roper, Peterson, & Curran, 1993). Most adolescents who report using condoms do so only intermittently.

    Beliefs play an important role in determining usage. Adolescents who believe condoms are effective are more likely to use them (Hingson, Strunin, Berlin, & Heeren, 1990). Similarly, those who believe themselves to be at greater risk are more likely to use condoms. One survey of condom use asked men to self-identify as either straight, homosexual, or bisexual. Among those identifying themselves as straight yet reporting at least one occurrence of anal sex with men, 64% said they never used condoms; in comparison, only 16% of those who considered themselves homosexual or bisexual said they never used condoms (Centers for Disease Control, 1993a).

3. *Use a spermicide.* Combining a spermicide that contains nonoxynol-9 with use of a condom offers more protection than a condom alone. Nonoxynol-9 has been found to kill HIV. Spermicide alone, however, is not as effective as with a condom.

4. *Be discriminating.* Certain practices and lifestyles increase the risk of infection. Individuals who have had numerous sexual partners and those who have used drugs intravenously are more likely to have been infected.

It is also possible to avoid infection by having an exclusive sexual relationship with a noninfected partner. Of course, both partners must be free of the virus at the outset. A blood test can establish whether an individual is free of the virus; those who are infected with the virus have antibodies in their blood. Because it takes several months for antibodies to develop, a blood test done too soon after the last sexual contact is not conclusive.

How likely are adolescents to follow or even understand any of these precautions? A randomly sampled survey of 1,773 adolescents aged 16 through 19 found that adolescents who have the most sexual partners (more than ten a year) are least likely to use a condom, yet these adolescents have the highest risk of infection (Hingson, Strunin, Berlin, & Heeren, 1990).

All the factors that make it difficult for adolescents to use contraceptives in general apply equally to the precautions they must take against HIV infection. Massive misinformation among adolescents complicates the problem. One study

RESEARCH FOCUS

Ethics: AIDS Prevention Research—What You Can't Say Can Kill You

How much do adolescents know about AIDS? More to the point, how much does what they know affect what they do? Adolescents commonly engage in sexual practices that place them at risk for acquiring AIDS. Would understanding the dangers of these practices decrease the likelihood of engaging in them? Current approaches to prevention assume that it would. Most programs attempt to decrease the frequency of high-risk behaviors among adolescents by increasing their knowledge of the risks involved. The little research that exists suggests that more than an "information blitz" is needed.

Psychological factors, such as denial, and developmental ones, such as the personal fable (the belief that what happens to others will not happen to you) and difficulty in translating abstract information into the concrete business of living (something most adults find difficult as well), all point to the need for personalizing information about AIDS to make it effective.

To determine whether increased information lessens high-risk behavior, one must first find out what adolescents know about AIDS and then what behaviors they engage in. Putting this plan into practice introduces a number of complications. To assess what adolescents know, one must ask questions that link the disease to sexual practices that happen to be common for those their age. In the course of answering the questions, adolescents might suspect they've been infected. Similarly, in

assessing sexual practices, one must ask personal questions about the occurrence and variety of sexual contacts. These questions could cause distress and reactivate feelings that might become unmanageable.

What ethical concerns guide such research? The overriding principle governing any research with humans is to protect the *dignity and welfare* of the subjects who participate in the research. Investigators inform the subjects in their study that their participation is *voluntary* and can be discontinued at any point. They also inform them of anything that could affect their willingness to participate. Once individuals agree to serve as subjects, investigators assume responsibility for protecting them from *physical or psychological distress*. After the data have been collected, the investigators *debrief* the subjects, informing them about the nature of the study and removing any misconceptions that may have arisen. If investigators suspect any undesirable consequences, they have the responsibility to correct them. Any information gained about participants is *confidential*.

Let's look at some research that illustrates these principles. David Sandberg, Mary Jane Rotheram-Borus, Jon Bradley, and Jacqueline Martin (1988) examined the effectiveness of information programs directed at adolescents. These investigators distinguished general knowledge that adolescents might have about AIDS from what they termed "personalized knowledge." Personalized knowl-

(continued)

found that 30% of teenagers living in San Francisco believed that AIDS could be cured. Another 25% thought they could be infected with HIV by casual physical contact such as a handshake or sharing personal items (DiClemente, Zorn, & Temoshok, 1987).

Cultural beliefs can also compound the problems of general misinformation. For instance, one study of working-class Latino males found that most believe they can tell whether a woman is infected simply by her appearance or her social class.

RESEARCH FOCUS (*continued*)

edge refers to their (1) perception of AIDS as a personal threat, (2) beliefs that it can be prevented, and (3) self-perceptions concerning their own ability to minimize the risk of infection.

After assessing each type of knowledge with questionnaires, the investigators interviewed participants to determine their sexual practices. Following data collection, participants were debriefed. The debriefing included semistructured interviews to determine the presence of any anxiety generated during the data collection, and focus groups in which adolescents role-played safe behaviors in a simulated sexual situation—for example, screening—a potential sexual partner or negotiating the use of a condom. The focus groups provided a check for consistency between the self-report data (responses to the questionnaire and interview) and simulated behavior in an analogous setting.

How effective *are* current prevention programs? The level of general information about AIDS was high among these adolescents: 84% correct understanding about means of transmission and 74% about prevention strategies. Personalized knowledge revealed little fear of acquiring AIDS and moderate confidence (4 on a 6-point scale) in their ability to engage in safe behaviors. Few adolescents anticipated problems, for example, in negotiating the use of a condom. However, when asked to role-play these behaviors, adolescents were unable to do so. Only then did they realize their inability to put into effect the behaviors they knew would decrease their risk of infection.

How were possible ethical concerns met in this research? The adolescents who participated did so on a voluntary basis and knew in advance the nature of the research. Debriefing interviews determined whether they had experienced any anxiety. Despite the sensitive nature of the research, adolescents indicated that they felt little anxiety discussing their sexual experiences, and some even said this had been their only chance to discuss their sexual concerns. Most adolescents remarked that the interviews had been personally helpful. The investigators kept the information confidential.

This research highlights the importance of using multiple types of prevention programs in combating the spread of AIDS. Information alone—at least for most adolescents—is not enough. Adolescents need to know what they can handle in a real-life situation—and what they can't. Courses in sex education, to the extent that they focus on information alone, will be less effective than if they give adolescents skills that allow them to incorporate this information into their behavior. Such courses could include role playing as a way of simulating the decision making that takes place in sexual encounters. Training in assertion skills would also be helpful. Can you think of other types of experiences that would be useful?

Reference: D. Sandberg, M. J. Rotheram-Borus, J. Bradley, & J. Martin. (1988). Methodological issues in assessing AIDS prevention programs. Journal of Adolescent Research, 3–4, 413–418.

Few understand that individuals infected with HIV can be symptom-free and appear healthy. Many also believe that casual contact, such as sharing personal items, can lead to infection (Forrest, Austin, Valdes, Fuentes, & Wilson, 1993).

More than misinformation is at work with adolescents. Almost surely adolescents' cognitive immaturity sets limits on their ability to understand the seriousness of the disease or the precautions that need to be taken (Peterson & Murphy, 1990). So, too, does adolescents' sense that they are invulnerable.

SUMMARY

Gender Stereotypes and Identity

Well-defined gender roles exist for both male and female adolescents. The gender role stereotype for males emphasizes independence, action, and self-reliance, but little emotional sensitivity. The gender role stereotype for females emphasizes interpersonal sensitivity but little assertive action. These roles may cause conflict in adolescents of either sex. An androgynous role, combining both male and female personality characteristics represents an alternative to the stereotypes.

Sexuality and Intimacy

Factors that are important to adolescents' satisfaction with relationships are similar to ones important for adults: passion, communication, commitment, emotional support, and togetherness. Love styles which contribute to relationship satisfaction for adolescents are those adults also find most satisfying: eros, agape, and ludus.

Attitudes toward sex are becoming more permissive. Changes in the sexual behavior of females have been primarily responsible for a decrease in the double standard of sexual conduct. Sexual activity changes in predictable ways with intimacy. As the degree of affection and commitment increases, adolescents are more accepting of increasingly intimate sexual behaviors.

Sexual Orientation

Sexual orientation refers to the attraction individuals feel for members of the same or the other sex. Adolescents who are homosexual are, for some extended period of their lives, more attracted sexually to individuals of their own sex than to those of the opposite sex. Gay, lesbian, and bisexual adolescents are more likely to experience problems associated with their sexual orientation and are at greater risk for suicide than are straight adolescents. Research comparing co-incidence of homosexuality among identical and fraternal twins and adoptive siblings suggests a genetic component to sexual orientation.

Sexual Functioning

The sexual response cycle consists of four phases: excitement, plateau, orgasm, and resolution. Similarities in the sexual response for each gender exist for all phases. Two processes, vasocongestion and myotonia, underlie the changes that occur in each phase.

Adolescents have numerous misconceptions about sexual functioning. Many are not aware that the size of the male's penis is not important in sexual functioning, or that females have the same capacity for sexual pleasure as males. Adolescents frequently do not know that individuals of either sex experience discomfort if orgasm does not follow the plateau phase. Adolescents as well as adults fail to distinguish cultural taboos from physical reasons for not engaging in intercourse during menstruation.

Teenage Pregnancies and Parenting

Over 95% of adolescent females who give birth keep their babies. Most unmarried teenage mothers finish high school, are regularly employed, and have no more children than their later-childbearing classmates do. Teenage fathers, though generally willing to be involved, often find it difficult to take on the responsibilities of parenthood.

Approximately 40% of teenage pregnancies end in abortion. Decisions to abort or carry the pregnancy to term are related to whether the pregnancy was intended, socioeconomic status, race, and personal as well as parents' and friends' attitudes.

Sexually Transmitted Diseases

STDs are on the rise among adolescents. Some of these have reached epidemic proportions, and many do not have well-defined symptoms. If treated promptly, most STDs do not have serious health consequences. If left untreated, some can cause sterility and serious complications—even death.

Chlamydia is the most common STD in the United States. It can affect the reproductive system and cause pelvic inflammatory disease in females.

Gonorrhea results from a bacterial infection and has reached epidemic proportions among adolescents. Many individuals experience no symptoms. If not treated, the disease can cause infertility and other medical problems.

Genital herpes is caused by the herpes virus. The incidence of this disease has increased markedly over the past generation, as has genital warts.

Syphilis is a bacterial infection that progresses through three stages. If not treated, it can result in serious medical complications and even death.

Pubic lice, which can cause severe itching, are easily killed by medicated shampoo.

Risks and Precautions

Sexually active adolescents have difficulty realizing that they run a high risk of contracting STDs. Many do not take precautions to prevent these diseases or get treatment when symptoms do appear because of ignorance, shame, or a sense of invulnerability. Preventative programs must change adolescents' personal and cultural beliefs and dispel myths as well as provide information on safe sex practices.

Human immunodeficiency virus (HIV) attacks the immune system. The disease progresses through three stages, the last of which is AIDS. There is no known cure for the disease; individuals die when the immune system fails.

Prevention of HIV infection includes avoiding exchange of body fluids, using condoms and spermicides, and being discriminating in sexual relationships.

KEY TERMS

Gender-Role Stereotypes	Double Standard	Genital Warts
Androgynous	Heterosexual	Genital Herpes
Eros	Homosexual	Syphilis
Storge	Bisexual	Pubic Lice
Ludus	Sexually Transmitted Disease	HIV Infection
Mania	(STD)	AIDS
Pragma	Chlamydia	
Agape	Gonorrhea	

ADOLESCENTS AT WORK
Part-Time Employment
Dropouts and Employment

CHOOSING A VOCATION
Social-Cognitive Theory
Ginzburg: Vocational Stages
Super: Careers and the Self-Concept
Holland: Personality Types and Work

JOINING THE WORKFORCE
Job Availability
Women and Work
Minorities and Work

INTERVENTION PROGRAMS:
STRATEGIES FOR CHANGE
Counselors as Change Agents

■ RESEARCH FOCUS   Quasi-
Experimental Designs: Precollege
Programs for Minority Youth

Irrational Beliefs and Maladaptive
   Myths

ADOLESCENTS AND COLLEGE:
THINKING ABOUT IDEAS
New Solutions to Old Problems:
   Structural Analytical Thinking

■ RESEARCH FOCUS   Factorial
Designs: Career Indecision—Don't

Push Me; I'm Still Thinking

How College Changes the Way
   Adolescents Think
Gender Differences in Intellectual
   Development

■ RESEARCH FOCUS   Theory-Guided
Research: How Sexist Is Our Language?

ADOLESCENTS AS EXPERTS
Experts and Novices
Knowledge of One's Culture:
   Everybody's an Expert

PUTTING KNOWLEDGE
TO WORK
Active Knowledge
Inert Knowledge
Thinking as Problem Solving

CREATIVITY
Characteristics of Creativity
Origins of Creativity in Adolescents

ADOLESCENT DECISION
MAKING
Personal Effectiveness
Dealing with Everyday Problems

SUMMARY

KEY TERMS

CHAPTER TEN

Careers and College

Kip leaned on the horn and cursed his friend's ability to sleep through an alarm. "Late one more time and you'll be docked in pay," Mr. Perkins had said.

Sam flew out the door with a sandwich in his mouth and a sweater half over his head.

"Climb in," shouted Kip, as he threw the car in gear and spun away from the curb.

"Gi-yugh," spat Sam, "I got jelly on this sweater."

"Don't worry, no one will notice."

"Not on the outside, fool. It's inside the sleeve!" griped Sam.

"Serves you right," Kip said. "You're the only one I know eats in his clothes— and I mean inside 'em."

"So what was I supposed to do with the sandwich while I was putting on the sweater?"

Sam changed the subject. "How much longer on this shift?"

"It's a killer, isn't it? Sometimes I wonder if these wheels are worth it," Kip replied.

"Can you see doing this the rest of your life?" Sam asked from under the sweater, turning the sleeve inside out for repairs.

"I'm already tired of working and I've just started," answered Kip, as he wheeled into the last parking space and switched off the ignition. "Let's go. Sooner begun, sooner done, or something like that, as my Dad says."

"You wonder how they do it," Sam replied. "Year after year at the same old job. Is this what it's gonna be like for the next fifty years?"

What it's like for the next 50 years, give or take ten for most people, will depend on a number of things, many of which get sorted out in adolescence. This chapter opens with a look at adolescents in the workplace. Increasing numbers of adolescents work while still in high school. Others start full-time jobs after graduating, and still others will work while they go to college. For those who never finish high school, occupational choices are more limited. We will consider students, dropouts, and work in the opening section of the chapter.

Why do individuals choose one type of work and not another? Explanations for vocational choice differ. Social-cognitive theory looks at environmental variables that influence career decisions—such as parents' occupations and the salience of models in different occupations. The developmental theories of Ginzburg and Super identify stages of occupational choice. Ginzburg, for example, believes that realistic decisions occur fairly late in the process, and Super links occupational choice to the development of the self-concept. Finally, Holland identifies different personality types that are suited to different types of work.

What happens to young workers once they are on the job? Many need additional training beyond high school. Business and industry increasingly find that they must pick up the tab for the education of their newest workers, often having to train them in basic skills such as reading and math. Ironically, many of the nation's newest full-time workers must continue their education on the job. Adolescents in the workforce is the subject of the next section.

Many factors affect adolescents' decisions about the type of work they will do. Not least among these are gender and ethnicity. Some adolescents never even consider certain jobs because they rarely see individuals of their gender or race in them. Even when adolescents do consider a wide variety of jobs, the opportunity structure all too frequently reflects inequities associated with gender, race, and socioeconomic level. Gender and ethnicity are considered as they relate to occupational choice in adolescence. Intervention programs aimed at changing belief structures about career opportunities have been effective in helping adolescents realistically evaluate the opportunities available to them.

Many adolescents will go off to college instead of beginning work. They too will face new experiences; these can change the way they think about themselves, even the way they think about knowledge itself. Is it possible to discover "truth"? Or does truth, like beauty, exist only in the mind of the beholder? Some adolescents attempt to discover absolute truths in their classes; others view truth as relative. Still others achieve ways of reconciling the alternative truths of relativism. This progression takes different forms in male and female adolescents, and we will chart changes in knowing separately for each.

Real-life problem solving is not as straightforward as logicians would have us believe. For instance, adolescents, like everyone else, think most efficiently and in more sophisticated ways in areas that interest them, and problems arising in the context of one's culture are solved more efficiently than similar problems that do not utilize culturally specific knowledge. Cultural knowledge is a form of expertise in which natives think like experts and strangers like novices.

The chapter moves to a discussion of the ways in which knowledge is put to work in daily settings, whether on the job or pursuing a degree. Facts can become easily compartmentalized; adolescents can miss the connection between what they have learned and their other experiences. Psychologists speak of compartmentalized facts as "inert" knowledge. Unlike inert metals or gases, inert knowledge has few uses. We'll consider several ways of addressing this problem.

Next the subject of creativity is discussed. What qualities distinguish creative adolescents from those who don't express their creativity? Can it be cultivated in all adolescents?

The final section of the chapter addresses the way adolescents think through practical problems in daily settings. As with other aspects of reasoning, success increases with age.

ADOLESCENTS AT WORK

Part-Time Employment

Approximately 30% of all 16- and 17-year-old high school students have jobs (Youth Indicators, 1993). Even more adolescents would be working if only they could find jobs. The unemployment rate for 16-to-19-year-olds seeking but unable to find work is just under 30%. Not all adolescents are equally affected by unemployment, however. For minority adolescents, the percentage is much higher. Recent unemployment among white adolescent males was about 18%, for example, but the figure reached 42% among black adolescent males. Unemployment of black adolescents of either sex is more than double that of whites, and unemployment of Hispanics is 50% greater than that of whites their age. These differences persist into early adulthood, as can be seen from Figure 10.1 (Youth Indicators, 1993).

Spending Patterns. Adolescents with jobs spend their money in different ways than they will as adult workers. Most of what they earn they spend on personal items such as clothes, records, and entertainment (see Figure 10.2). Since over half of those who work earn more than $50 a week, adolescents can engage in a fair amount of conspicuous consumption. The price of clothes is high if one buys designer labels—and many adolescents do. Popular name-brand athletic shoes once topped the line at $50 to $70, but are now outstripped in price by footgear such as "airs" that go for well over $100. One might imagine that at those prices, few adolescents would buy name-brand athletic shoes. But increasing numbers of adolescents choose to work in order to spend money on personal items such as these. Jeans, a staple wardrobe item for most adolescents, are also expensive, many starting at $50 a pair and working their way up, depending on extras such as "acid-washes," type of cut, and so on. The cost of an outfit can add up, and we haven't even gotten above the belt in this example.

Adolescents put much of the money they earn toward entertainment. A simple date, such as a movie and hamburger afterward, can cost $20 or more: $12 to $15 for tickets, another $5 or $6 at the concession stand, and a whopping $5 to $10 more for hamburgers and drinks afterward—and this doesn't include the cost of the round-trip gas. Special events, such as rock concerts, can be four to five times as expensive. Even though most adolescents go to concerts infrequently, they go

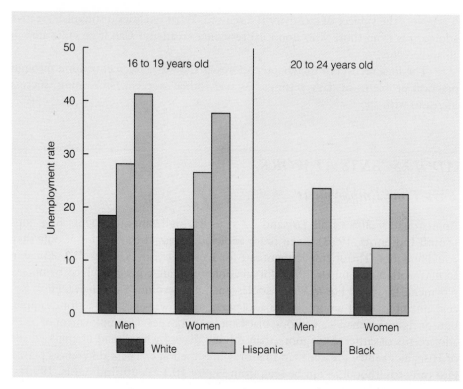

Figure 10.1   Unemployment Among White, Hispanic, and Black Youth.
Source: U.S. Department of Labor, Bureau of Labor Statistics, Employment and Earnings *(January issues); and labor force statistics derived from the* current population survey: A data book, *Vol. 1, Bulletin 2096. In* Youth Indicators. *(1993).* Trends in the well-being of American youth. *Washington, DC: U.S. Government Printing Office.*

to other events, such as school dances or get-togethers after games, regularly—and these all add up. Just spending an evening with a friend or two can be expensive. When adolescents get together, they eat. Two or three adolescents can kill several 2-liter bottles of cola in a night and munch through several bags of chips at $2 a bag.

The above expenses can be minor compared to those for a car. Car expenses are a significant item for many adolescents as Figure 10.2 shows. A sizable number of adolescents—27%—spend from half to all they make on their cars.

A number of adolescents save some of their money for either upcoming education or other long-term plans. High school seniors who are planning to attend a 4-year college are, predictably, more likely to put more of their money into savings

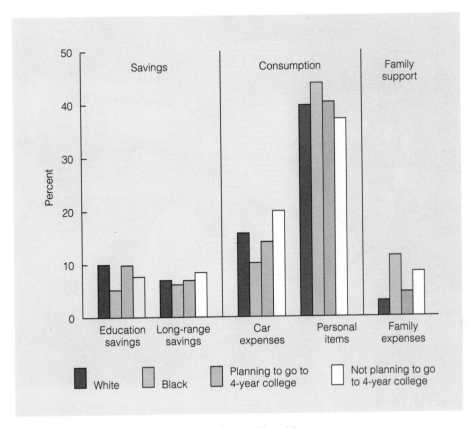

Figure 10.2 How High School Seniors Spend Their Money.

Source: University of Michigan, Institute for Social Research, Monitoring the future, *1991. In Youth Indicators. (1993).* Trends in the well-being of American youth. *Washington, DC: U.S. Government Printing Office.*

for education than those without plans for college. Figure 10.2 also shows that a fairly large number of black adolescents contribute to their families' expenses. Nearly 24% of the black adolescents who work report putting anywhere from half of what they earn to all of it toward their families' expenses. The comparable figure for white adolescents is just under 7% (Youth Indicators, 1993).

Disadvantages of Part-Time Employment. Some researchers question whether part-time employment exposes adolescents to an unrealistic standard of living. They point out that most teenagers are allowed to spend what they earn as discretionary income; as we have seen, only a few contribute to family expenses. As a result, few adolescents are prepared for the realities that confront employed adults, such as

More high school students work today than a generation ago. But their jobs are usually for minimum wage and provide few opportunities to move up to more responsible and challenging positions.

the costs of housing, food, transportation, and health care. Figure 10.3 presents a comparison of spending patterns of people under 25 to overall spending patterns.

Laurence Steinberg, Suzanne Fegley, and Sanford Dornbusch (1993) surveyed 1,800 high school sophomores and juniors concerning part-time employment. By following these students over a year's time, they could look for differences that existed prior to their part-time employment, as well as compare adolescents who worked with those who did not.

These investigators found that adolescents who work are less invested in school than their peers, even before beginning to work, and that working contributes to their disengagement from school, especially if they work more than 20 hours a week. Conversely, adolescents who work moderate hours and then quit their jobs show improved performance in school.

Even though students who work part-time spend less time on homework and do not attend classes as regularly as those who are not employed, working does not result in lower grades. It seems that working students accommodate for the demands on their time by taking less rigorous classes, and some also cheat on

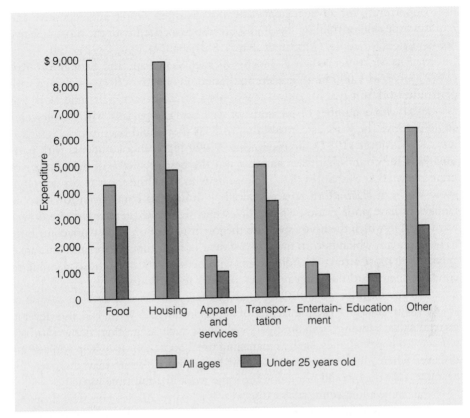

Figure 10.3 Spending Patterns of People 25 Years of Age and Under Compared to All People.

Source: U.S. Department of Labor, Bureau of Labor Statistics, Consumer expenditure survey: Integrated survey, *1990. In Youth Indicators. (1993).* Trends in the well-being of American youth. *Washington, DC: U.S. Government Printing Office.*

homework and exams. For example, more than a third of the students who work said they took easier classes in order to maintain their grade-point average.

Part-time employment may have a number of other, indirect effects. For instance, it is related to higher rates of substance abuse, perhaps because adolescents who work have more discretionary income. Steinberg, Fegley, and Dornbusch found that adolescents who had worked 20 hours or more a week for a year used alcohol and drugs 33% more often than classmates who did not work. In general, adolescents who do not work are better adjusted than those who do, having higher self-esteem, greater self-reliance, and less delinquency.

Perhaps working has so many negative consequences for adolescents because of the types of jobs that they typically fill. For instance, most adolescents are employed in high-turnover positions, with little pay, little authority, and relatively little opportunity for advancement. The work is often simple and repetitive and requires little skill or training. Such jobs are also associated with the most negative consequences for adults (Mortimer, Finch, Shanahan, & Ryu, 1992).

Jeylan Mortimer, Michael Finch, Michael Shanahan, and Seongryeol Ryu (1992) surveyed 1,000 ninth graders and found no negative effects associated with part-time work if it was for only a few hours a week. In fact, part-time work was associated with a number of measures of well-being, especially when adolescents could perceive the work as contributing to skills they could later use.

K. A. Meyer (1987) surveyed nearly 2,000 high school students with part-time jobs and found that class standing was the best predictor of the number of hours they work. She notes that adolescents who work the most hours are often those who can least afford to academically—those who come from low-income families or have poor grades. These adolescents frequently get caught in a downward spiral in which the hours spent on the job instead of on homework contribute to poor grades, which in turn make investment of their time in nonacademic areas appear even more attractive. Adolescents with better grades and those planning to continue their education after high school work fewer hours.

On the brighter side, holding a job can help adolescents develop a sense of responsibility and give them a feeling of being productive. Work can also develop general skills, ranging from interpersonal ones, such as getting along with co-workers, to personal ones, such as managing time. Some jobs may help adolescents discover where their interests lie, even if by exclusion—they may discover, for example, that they would not enjoy the same work in a full-time capacity.

For some adolescents, such a discovery is a luxury. Adolescents who drop out of high school find it difficult to obtain work even under the best of circumstances. Many cannot afford to be choosy. We turn to this group of workers next.

Dropouts and Employment

Adolescents who drop out of high school are more than twice as likely to be unemployed as those who graduate. Since future jobs will require even more education and preparation, dropouts will find it harder to compete for these jobs than in the past. Figure 10.4 shows the rather grim job outlook for high school dropouts: Fewer than 40% of those who drop out find employment. Only 23% of those who remain unemployed continue to look for work, and an even larger number, 40%, neither have jobs nor are looking for them. Quite a few of these jobless dropouts are young mothers taking care of children (Youth Indicators, 1993). Minority students are even more likely to drop out than those from the dominant culture (see Chapter 7). With figures like these, one looks for programs that have been successful in working with adolescents at risk of becoming dropouts. Several successful programs share four features, referred to as the four Cs: cash, concern, computers, and coalitions (Bloch, 1989).

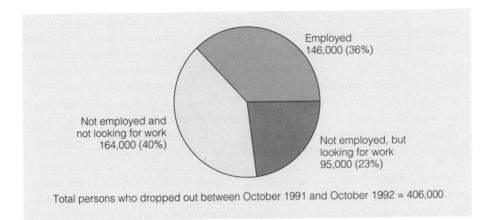

Employed
146,000 (36%)

Not employed and
not looking for work
164,000 (40%)

Not employed, but
looking for work
95,000 (23%)

Total persons who dropped out between October 1991 and October 1992 = 406,000

Figure 10.4 Employment Status of High School Dropouts.

Source: U.S. Department of Labor, Bureau of Labor Statistics, Employment of school-age youth, graduates, and dropouts, *1992. In Youth Indicators. (1993).* Trends in the well-being of American youth. *Washington, DC: U.S. Government Printing Office.*

Schools that are effective in reaching potential dropouts, such as teenage parents, communicate to students that they care. These schools usually support teacher involvement by reducing class workloads so that teachers can have more time to interact with students.

Cash.   High schools that are effective in keeping at-risk adolescents in school establish the connection between having a diploma and earning money. Although the actual amount of money earned by high school graduates versus dropouts is not always large, the likelihood of *having* a job is significantly greater if one has a diploma. Successful programs offering work opportunities that provide on-the-job experience have been particularly successful. Most also give intensive training in basic skills, increasing the likelihood of success both at school and on the job. Many programs also prepare students to take the GED, a test which, when passed, gives them the equivalent of a high school diploma.

Concern.   Effective programs usually have lower student-teacher ratios, smaller campuses, and an atmosphere that communicates the message that any student who wants to can be successful. Teachers have more time to interact with students. Many schools also provide infant care for adolescent mothers returning to school.

Computers.   Many dropouts have a history of school failure and are demoralized by the time they reach high school. Effective programs integrate computers into their instructional programs, using them for individualized instruction in basic skills. Remedial programs in reading and math help break self-defeating cycles in which students avoid work at which they feel inadequate, causing them to fall even further behind.

Coalitions.   Successful schools often involve individuals from the community, such as civic leaders and local businesses and industry, in their programs. Students learn about resources in the community. Parents are an important part of any co- alition, and these programs involve parents in the students' progress (see Chapter 7). Frequently, too, counseling for emotional problems is available to students who need it.

Successful programs increase the motivation of the students enrolled in them. They also help students set realistic goals, or, as Bloch says, narrow "the gap be- tween fantasy and reality." These two benefits are almost surely related. Students' motivation to do well in their courses will increase as they see the relationship between their own success and what they need for specific jobs. More generally, these programs have an impact on students' self-esteem; when one likes oneself, one does not have to have fantasy-level aspirations about a job—reality does quite well (Bloch, 1989).

CHOOSING A VOCATION

At-risk students face one problem in common with other students. Almost all ad- olescents have difficulty discovering the type of work for which they are best suited or would enjoy most. We look first at social-cognitive theory for an explanation of how adolescents select the type of work they will engage in for most of their adult lives, and then at the theories of Ginzburg, Super, and Holland.

Social-Cognitive Theory

Why do individuals choose the occupations they do? Social-cognitive theory, which emphasizes the role of observational learning and modeling, emphasizes complex interactions between the inborn talents, the environmental conditions in which these are played out (e.g., demographic trends affecting the availability of jobs, or social policies regulating equal employment opportunities), the unique learning histories of each person, and the skills with which individuals approach their work (Mitchell & Krumboltz, 1990).

Adolescents observe themselves and note how well their skills, interests, and values match the requirements of the situation. These *self-observation generalizations* have consequences for the types of work they think they might be good at. They are also related to what they are interested in and what they value (Mitchell & Krumboltz, 1990). Let's take a look at how social-cognitive theory puts these constructs together in explaining career choices.

Consider the case of a fictitious adolescent, Carlos, age 17. Carlos grew up in a quiet, ethnically mixed neighborhood; his mother is native-born and his father came to this country as a young boy. Both parents are hardworking; his father is a contractor and his mother a day-care worker. Carlos was quiet in elementary school and received little attention from his predominantly white teachers. He often heard his father say that "white teachers think Mexican kids aren't that smart." He began to perceive his teachers as different from himself, and he emotionally shut down when interacting with them. Nothing in elementary school disproved what he had learned from his father.

In junior high, Carlos' English teacher noticed that his creative stories were well written and that he had an unusually large vocabulary for his age. She displayed his work in the classroom. Carlos felt proud, and his classmates often asked him for help. Carlos began to think that not all teachers are alike—some think he is smart.

Carlos tells himself that he might not tell stories as well as his Grandma, but he knows he's better than the other kids in his class (a self-observation generalization). Carlos enjoys writing and wonders if he's good enough to get paid for doing it for a living. He also questions whether he would enjoy it more than being a contractor. When he has worked for his father, he has always felt competent. He wonders which occupation would be best for him, and decides to take some creative writing courses and talk to his father about a summer job. These concerns reflect *task-approach skills*, such as work habits and one's criteria for evaluating work—for example, "How good am I at this?" "How much would it interest me as an occupation?"

Environmental events such as higher interest rates on loans (and a drop-off in construction) and a TV writer's strike can affect vocational decision making. Even though social-cognitive theory emphasizes individual learning experiences, many of which are planned (such as taking a writing course), it acknowledges the impact of unplanned events like an economic recession and its effect on the construction industry, or a screen writer's strike and national awareness of the importance of writers (Mitchell & Krumboltz, 1990).

Critique of Social-Cognitive Theory.   A strength of social-cognitive theory is its use of learning principles to explain individual choices, yet doing so without portraying individuals as automatons. Social-cognitive theory recognizes that people actively attempt to understand the consequences of their actions and use this un-

Vocational development can be viewed as a progressive narrowing of choices in the search for the best fit between one's goals and self-concept and the opportunities that actually exist.

care workers), health-related occupations (for example, medical assistants and home health aides), and technical occupations (for example, computer scientists and technicians) (U.S. Bureau of the Census, 1993). Table 10.1 presents projections of the fastest-growing and fastest-declining occupations.

Even though most adolescents will replace workers in existing jobs, the qualifications for these jobs will increase as technology and foreign trade affect the

TABLE 10.1

Fastest Growing and Declining Occupations: 1990–2005

	Percent Change 1990–2005		
	Low	Moderate	High
FASTEST GROWING			
Home health aides	78	92	103
Systems analysts and computer scientists	66	79	87
Personal and home care aides	64	77	87
Medical assistants	62	74	85
Human services workers	59	71	82
Radiologic technologists and technicians	58	70	80
Medical secretaries	57	68	79
Psychologists	55	64	72
Travel agents	51	62	70
Correction officers	49	61	74
Flight attendants	45	59	67
Computer programmers	44	56	63
Management analysts	44	52	58
Child care workers	42	49	55
FASTEST DECLINING			
Electrical and electronic equipment assemblers, precision	−55	−48	−46
Electrical and electronic assemblers	−52	−45	−44
Child care workers, private household	−44	−40	−36
Textile draw-out and winding machine operators	−41	−31	−29
Telephone and cable TV line installers and repairers	−36	−30	−26
Machine tool cutting operators and tenders	−36	−29	−26
Cleaners and servants, private household	−30	−25	−21
Machine forming operators and tenders	−32	−25	−21
Switchboard operators	−29	−23	−19
Farmers	−23	−21	−18
Sewing machine operators, garment	−37	−20	−18
Farm workers	−14	−11	−8
Typists and word processors	−17	−11	−6

Source: U.S. Bureau of the Census. (1993). Statistical abstract of the United States: 1993 (113th ed.). Washington, DC: U.S. Government Printing Office.

workplace. Twenty years ago, an auto mechanic had to master only 5,000 pages of service manuals to work on any car on the road, compared to today, when 465,000 pages of service manuals exist for the hundreds of models sold in this country. Equally demanding changes are taking place in service sector jobs:

> The secretary who once pecked away at a manual typewriter must now master a word processor, a computer and telecommunications equipment. Even the cashier at the 7-Eleven store has to know how to sell money orders and do minor maintenance jobs on the Slurpee and Big Gulp machines. ("The forgotten half," 1989, p. 46)

Industry and private companies are picking up some of the expenses involved in training new workers. They spend an estimated $30 billion to $50 billion annually to train new employees. Another $180 billion goes into "informal training" of employees (Committee for Economic Development, 1987).

The newly created jobs will require more skill than did jobs in the past. Peter Coleman (1993) estimates that approximately 40% of new jobs will require more than sixteen years of preparation and training. The greatest challenge facing our nation is to meet the needs of adolescents who will *not* be college graduates (Glover & Marshall, 1993; Hoyt, 1988).

Women and Work

Discrimination in Employment.   Most women of working age are employed— 80% in their mid-20s to mid-40s, and just below 70% in their mid-40s to mid-60s (U.S. Bureau of the Census, 1993). Even though more female adolescents today plan to work in top-level jobs than ever before (Davey & Stoppard, 1993), sex segregation in the workforce is still widespread. More females than males hold low-status, low-paying clerical, sales, and service jobs; the vast majority of high-paying professional jobs are held by males (U.S. Bureau of the Census, 1993). Table 10.2 shows the median weekly earnings for each of six occupational categories and the percentages of males and females employed in each of them.

Although the numbers of males and females graduating from college are about equal, Hoyt (1989) notes that the average college-educated woman is paid less than a man with a high school degree. Even among adolescents, the median annual income for males exceeds that for females. Males aged 16 to 19 make an average of $1,400 more than females their age. This difference increases to almost $1,800 for 20-to-24-year-olds, and reaches $3,400 for 25-to-29-year-olds. The difference over all ages is a stunning $6,448 (Youth Indicators, 1988, 1991; U.S. Bureau of the Census, 1993).

Sex discrimination in the workforce takes shape primarily in the different types of jobs held by individuals of either sex. The terms "pink collar" and "blue collar" refer to occupations that are female- or male-dominated. Females are more likely to work in service occupations—clerical and salesclerk positions, or child care— and males as craftsmen, machine operators, technicians, farmers, or laborers.

T A B L E   1 0 . 2

Occupations and Median Weekly Earnings
of Males and Females, 1992

Occupational categories	Male		Female	
	% of total employed	Median weekly earnings	% of total employed	Median weekly earnings
Managerial and professional (e.g., business executives, doctors, nurses, lawyers, teachers, engineers)	52.7%	$777	47.3%	$562
Technical, sales, and administrative support (e.g., health technicians, sales representatives, sales clerks, bank tellers, teacher aides)	36.1	519	63.9	365
Service (e.g., child care workers, police officers, firefighters, food service workers, janitors, hairdressers)	40.9	330	59.1	248
Precision production, craft, and repair (e.g., mechanics, construction workers, carpenters)	91.4	503	8.6	336
Operators, fabricators, laborers (e.g., machine operators, truck drivers, bus drivers, freight handlers)	75.0	393	25.0	279
Farming, forestry, fishing (e.g., farmers, loggers, fishers)	84.1	269	15.9	223

Source: U.S. Bureau of the Census. (1993). Statistical abstract of the United States: 1993 *(113th ed.). Washington, DC: U.S. Government Printing Office.*

The trends are changing, however. Occupational planning among high school seniors is not as sex-typed as in previous years. M. Gerstein, M. Lichtman, and J. U. Barokas (1988) compared the occupational plans of a national sample of 28,000 high school seniors in 1980 with a comparable sample in 1972, and found that the number of adolescent females planning for a profession had substantially increased, whereas the number of males had decreased slightly (see Table 10.3). Nearly 30% of the females indicated an intention to enter a profession such as accountant, artist, nurse, or social worker (Professional 1 category). The 30% figure is considerably higher than in prior years and is slightly higher than that for male adolescents. The percentage of adolescent females planning to become lawyers, college professors, doctors, dentists, or scientists (Professional 2) nearly doubled over the same time period and is equal to that for males. In all, nearly half of female high school seniors planned for professional occupations.

TABLE 10.3

Occupational Plans in 1972 and 1980 for All Seniors—Men and Women

Plan	All seniors (%)[a]			Men (%)			Women (%)		
	1972	1980	Percentage difference	1972	1980	Percentage difference	1972	1980	Percentage difference
Professional 2 (e.g. attorney, physician, scientist)	11.9	13.5	+1.6	16.6	13.3	−3.3	7.8	13.7	+ 5.9
Professional 1 (e.g. accountant, architect, artist, engineer, nurse, social worker)	19.8	27.6	+7.8	19.1	25.4	+6.3	20.5	29.4	+ 8.9
Technical	6.0	9.3	+3.3	7.8	11.6	+3.8	4.5	7.0	+ 2.5
Teacher	11.5	3.8	−7.7	6.7	1.6	−5.1	15.7	5.6	−10.1
Manager/Proprietor	4.4	10.9	+6.5	7.0	13.2	+6.2	2.1	8.8	+ 6.7
Craftsman/Operator	13.2	9.5	−3.7	24.9	16.9	−8.0	3.1	2.0	− 0.9
Clerical/Sales	18.2	12.3	−5.9	3.1	3.9	+0.8	31.3	19.2	−12.1
Service	8.1	5.3	−2.8	4.7	3.2	−1.5	11.1	7.0	− 4.1
Farmer/Laborer	3.5	3.2	−0.3	6.8	5.8	−1.0	0.7	0.7	0.0
Military	1.7	2.4	+0.7	3.1	3.6	+0.5	0.6	1.3	+ 0.7
Housewife	1.5	2.4	+0.9	0.1	0.1	0.0	2.7	4.1	+ 1.4

[a]*Percents based on number responding to this question. Excludes missing data.*

Source: *M. Gerstein, M. Lichtman, & J. U. Barokas. (1988). Occupational plans of adolescent women compared to men: A cross-sectional examination.* Career Development Quarterly, 36, 222–230.

Table 10.3 also shows a large decrease in the percentage of females planning to become teachers, secretaries, and salesclerks, and those planning to enter service jobs—all of which are traditionally female-dominated occupations. The percentage of high school females planning for professional occupations or thinking of entering male-dominant occupations increased from just over half in 1972 to over two-thirds in 1980 (Gerstein, Lichtman, & Barokas, 1988).

Advancement Opportunities.   Despite statistics such as these, females will find it difficult to get the jobs they want. Kenneth Hoyt (1989), at Kansas State University's Manhattan campus, notes that the upward mobility of entrants to the labor force will be limited by the large numbers of baby boomers already there (see Chapter 1). Hoyt (1988) points out that 75% of those who will be working in the year 2000 presently hold jobs. Shifts in patterns of employment are not likely until these baby boomers reach retirement age. The relatively large numbers of middle-

Even though more female adolescents today aspire to high-level jobs than in previous generations, they will still have to battle many assumptions about women's ability to make hard decisions and close multimillion-dollar deals.

aged "boomers" also cuts down on advancement opportunities for youth who are starting work now, since they will still be in the workforce when the latter are ready to move up to more advanced positions (Fullerton, 1987).

More females are employed today than previously, and the number of attractive new jobs (i.e., those requiring more skill and offering better pay) is relatively small. By far the largest number of available jobs are low paying and offer little opportunity for advancement. The upshot is a situation in which relatively stiff competition exists. Under similar conditions in the past, we have seen the privileged group, in this case white males, close ranks to protect its interests. Unless effective social initiatives continue, external barriers to advancement for females in the year 2000 may be worse than today (Subich, 1989).

The problem for females is not so much getting work as it is getting *quality* work (Subich, 1989). Females still have difficulty entering certain occupational areas and getting jobs from which they can advance. Until recently, career counselors focused primarily on external barriers to equal employment, that is, active or passive discrimination. Such barriers will continue to exist until eradicated by social movements; however, internal barriers in the form of self-limiting expectations are also present. Subich comments that an immediate advantage to focusing on these barriers is to place the forces of change in the hands of the individual. Change through broad social movements such as legislation will of course remain important (Subich, 1989).

Self-Limiting Expectations.   One of the primary internal barriers adolescent females face when they begin a job is the value they assign to their work. Studies
find that women place less value on their work than do men (Major & Forcey,
1985). As a consequence, women expect to be paid less—and are. An office worker
who sees the importance to a company of maintaining files and records (invoices,
shipments, etc.) will value the work he or she does and expect to be paid accordingly. This person might argue, with reason, that the company's income depends
on how effectively records are kept. Those who consider their work to be important
are likely to show initiative and creativity—important for pay increases and advancement to higher positions. Most, if not all, of the self-limiting expectations
females have are learned (Major & Forcey, 1985).

A number of factors distinguish females who expect to pursue nontraditional
occupations (the ones that also pay more) from those who stay in traditional types
of work. The influence of significant others, including role models, is important.
So, too, is the anticipated cost of education (Davey & Stoppard, 1993). Information about the availability of jobs and the many types of jobs that exist is also
vitally important. But for such information to have an effect, adolescent females
must see it as relevant to their own career plans—that is, that *they* can be a botanist,
beautician, electrician, skip loader, teacher, or business owner (Subich, 1989).

Many of the problems women face in the workforce are shared by minorities.
We turn to a consideration of minorities in the workforce next.

Minorities and Work

Whitney Young, a prominent black leader, once remarked, "The trouble is that
blacks are so visible. You hire one secretary and it looks like a whole lot of integration." As Young reminds us, we are still at the "token" stage with respect to
the full range of job opportunities open to minority adolescents. One black or
Hispanic in the office may look like a lot of integration, but that token minority
person is usually a secretary, not the boss.

Minority youth start out with career aspirations as high as those of youth
from the dominant culture. But they encounter numerous social, cultural, and
personal barriers to success. Despite the landmark legislation in the 1960s and
1970s that paved the way for equity in employment, progress has been slow. At
least one expert in the field has concluded that "minority persons in the labor force
are worse off today than they were in 1968" (Hoyt, 1989, p. 208). Hoyt (1989)
grimly adds that the picture is not likely to get better in the near future; upward
mobility in the workforce will continue to be limited for minorities. Table 10.4
shows the percentages of blacks and whites employed in different types of occupations, along with the median weekly earnings in each. We find many more white
workers in the two highest paid categories (Managerial/professional and Technical,
sales and administrative support) and, if we exclude the infrequent category of
"farming, forestry, and fishing," more black workers are in the two lowest paid
categories (Service and Operators, fabricators, and laborers).

TABLE 10.4

*Percentage Breakdown by Occupational Category
for Black and White Workers*

Occupational categories	Median weekly wage	Blacks	Whites
Managerial and professional	$670	18.6%	30.6%
Technical, sales, and administrative support	442	26.5	30.7
Service	289	22.5	10.6
Precision production, craft, and repair	420	9.0	12.2
Operators, fabricators, laborers	336	21.6	13.0
Farming, forestry, fishing	246	1.9	3.0

Source: U.S. Bureau of the Census. (1993). Statistical abstract of the United States: 1993 (113th ed.). Washington, DC: U.S. Government Printing Office.

Poverty.   The high incidence of poverty among minority adolescents is a common link among the factors that affect their eventual employment; among the most important factors are staying in school, receiving quality education, and making informed decisions about their futures (Hoyt, 1989). The rate of poverty can be four times as high among minorities as among whites ("Still 'separate,' " 1988). Poverty in relation to education is much like oil in relation to water—the two don't mix. Low-income students are nearly four times as likely to drop out of high school as their upper-income counterparts (Wetzel, 1987), and those who remain in school are more likely to be tracked in noncollege-preparatory and vocational courses (Orum, 1986; see also Chapter 7).

Poverty is also related to lower academic performance. Low-income students are not as likely to achieve at the same levels as middle-income and upper-income students (Wetzel, 1987), nor are the educational programs they receive of the same quality as those provided to middle- and upper-income youth. Poverty is unevenly distributed, tending to be centralized in urban and inner-city schools, where minority students make up most of the student body. In 23 of the 25 largest cities in the United States, for example, minorities make up most of the students (Hoyt, 1989).

Programs.   Some programs are more important to occupational success than others. Math and science courses provide a gateway to many of the higher level jobs. Preparation in both of these areas is generally poorer among minority students (Hall & Post-Kammer, 1987). Black students, for instance, take fewer math courses and do more poorly in them than white students (Reyes & Stanic, 1985). They also have less actual experience with science either inside the classroom (e.g., watching chicks hatch, growing a plant from seed, studying an ant colony) or outside it (e.g., trips to museums and science fairs) and, not surprisingly, can think of fewer

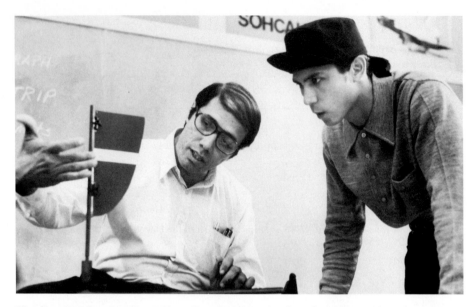

The film *Stand and Deliver* is the story of a high school math teacher in East Los Angeles who dared to believe in his students and to demand that they believe in themselves. Motivated by his high expectations and his refusal to give up on them, these adolescents not only stayed in school but also passed the advanced placement exam in calculus.

uses for science (Kahle, 1982). Almost two-and-a-half times as many white as black males in college major in math or science (Trent, 1983). With the exception of Asian Americans, all minorities are underrepresented in science, math, and engineering (Brooks, 1990; Hall & Post-Kammer, 1987), and these are the fields preparing students for the high-level jobs of the future (Arbona, 1989; Hall & Post-Kammer, 1987).

Planning.   Many minority adolescents simply don't know about the many types of career options that exist and are unaware of the financial aid that is potentially available to them. Most also do not receive adequate help with career planning. Many students choose their courses with little knowledge of the requirements they'll need for different types of jobs. Even more immediately, few know what courses they will need if they want to go to college, or what courses will best prepare them for trade or technical schools. In one study, when students were asked who had been the most help to them in planning their programs, most said either their friends or their parents—not counselors and teachers (Boyer, 1983). Since parents and friends of minority parents are less likely to have attended college themselves, these students are not likely to receive the information they need.

Preparation.   Many of the newly created jobs will require some postsecondary education. Yet minority high school students are not entering college at levels that allow them to earn the qualifications for these more desirable jobs. The proportion of black students going on to college, for instance, decreased slightly over the 15-year period ending in 1986 (Hoyt, 1989). Though black women are nearly as likely as white women to earn a bachelor's degree, black men are not close to parity (American Council on Education, 1988).

Positions.   Most minority youth are all too aware of the barriers to equal employment, and both blacks and Hispanics adjust their expectations accordingly. Thus Hispanic students have just as high career *aspirations* as do whites, but lower expectations of achieving them (Arbona, 1989). Similarly, black students are aware of the existence of barriers (Howell, Frese, & Sollie, 1984). Perhaps no statistic speaks more clearly to this issue than unemployment rates: unemployment among blacks who graduated from high school in 1986 was higher than among whites who dropped out of school (Wetzel, 1987).

INTERVENTION PROGRAMS: STRATEGIES FOR CHANGE

Adolescent females, minority students, and the counselors who work with them need to increase their awareness of the problems these youth face in making career decisions.

Counselors as Change Agents

Because the opportunity structure for minority adolescents, and for females, is not the same as that for white, middle-class males (see Chapter 7), counselors may have to become active "change agents" in order to effectively prepare students for jobs (Brooks, 1990; Ogbu, 1992). Linda Brooks (1990) suggests that counselors leave their offices and meet with parents, teachers, and local businesses to combat the inequities that minority youth face. Many minority adolescents are not as well prepared as their nonminority counterparts for the careers that have traditionally been held by white males. Many have fallen below competitive levels in basic skills such as reading and math. Counselors may need to act as student advocates, working with teachers and schools to develop effective intervention programs that prepare minority youth for the full range of careers open to others.

An example of one such program is currently under way at California State University, Los Angeles (Wapner, 1990). The university established a contractual agreement with a local, predominantly Hispanic, junior high school. All students who participate in a "precollege program" in the sciences are guaranteed admittance to the university. Junior high school teachers, counselors, university professors, and administrators meet with students and parents to familiarize them with the program. Students receive tutoring in basic math and reading skills while taking

RESEARCH FOCUS

Quasi-Experimental Designs: Precollege Programs for Minority Youth

What is this nation's largest untapped natural resource? Minority youth.

The number of minority youth of college age is increasing. Yet minority youth continue to be underrepresented in colleges and universities. Many factors contribute to this pattern. Dropout rates from high school are higher among minority students than those in the dominant culture. Also, talented minority students are less likely to be noticed because they are not as likely to be placed in college preparatory courses. Fewer minority youth leave higher education prepared for the more prestigious careers requiring a mathematical or scientific background. Is there anything to be done to change these patterns?

Precollege programs select minority students with academic potential and offer them courses that build in the basic skills necessary for college work. Because precollege programs upgrade academic skills, they also lessen the likelihood of dropping out of high school and increase the likelihood that minority youth can compete successfully at the college level. In addition to the courses themselves, which are taught by university and high school instructors, these intervention programs offer tutorial help, advising, career counseling, and programs to raise students' level of awareness of career possibilities.

Do these programs work? Definitive answers are not available, although follow-up studies suggest that the programs have been successful in meeting their goals. Why, if we have data, can't we say definitely whether these programs are effective?

The data come from *quasi-experimental studies*. These designs lack the controls that allow one to state with confidence that the changes one observes are due to the conditions that have been studied. Often, research in this area takes the form of a *one-group pretest-posttest design*. In this type of study, one would measure basic skills and specific achievements prior to the program (pretest) and then again after the program (posttest). Any changes from pretest to posttest are attributed to participation in the program. A number of problems exist with this type of design.

Because there is no control condition—that is, a comparable group of students who do not participate in the program—we don't know how to interpret the findings. Suppose, for instance, one finds that posttest scores are no better than pretest scores. Can we conclude that the program is ineffective? Not necessarily. It's always possible that performance could have declined during that time, and that only because of the program did scores remain the same. Similarly, increases in performance on the posttest do not lend themselves to a

(continued)

science courses in junior high and, later, high school. Programs such as this one have been started at a number of universities across the country (Kammer, Fouad, & Williams, 1988).

Before counselors can assume the role of active change agents, many need to face their own biases. A counselor who accepts a talented minority girl's statement that she is interested in working with children as an aide or a helper in a classroom or playground, without suggesting other career opportunities that also involve helping people (e.g., medicine, psychology, social work), reveals an insensitivity to the existence of very real gender or culturally based conflicts (Brooks, 1990).

Would it be too intrusive to direct this student to consider other career options? Brooks argues that counselors *must* begin directing minority and female

---

RESEARCH FOCUS (*continued*)

simple interpretation. Several potential *confounds* exist. These can be due to maturation, testing, history, instrument decay, or statistical regression.

Maturation effects reflect any systematic changes that occur over time. These can be long-term, such as the developmental changes in intelligence discussed in Chapters 4 and 9, or short-term, such as changes due to fatigue, boredom, or practice. *Testing* effects reflect any changes that might occur due to familiarity with the tests. Since pretests usually involve the same type of question as posttests and frequently measure knowledge about the same subject matter, testing effects are likely. *History* effects refer to events that occur during the time between testings that can affect the behavior being measured. Television might run a series of public service spots featuring a famous minority athlete who promotes the value of a college education at the same time as the intervention program. *Instrument decay* reflects changes in the measures used; these are especially likely when people serve as "instruments"; for example, counselors or teachers, where we might expect them to become more practiced over time or in other ways to have their standards change.

Statistical regression can occur when students are selected for a program because they are atypical, because their scores are either especially low or high. When they are retested, as they are on the posttest, most scores will change somewhat simply

because the two tests are not perfectly correlated (no two tests ever are). Students who are selected because of especially low scores will look like they have improved due to the program. In actuality, because they were at the bottom of the distribution, their scores could *only* go up. Of course, by the same token, students with especially high scores on a pretest would show a drop in performance on the posttest. In each case scores "drift" or regress toward the mean of the distribution, since that is where most scores are to be found. Each of the above confounds is a threat to the internal validity of the research. (See Chapter 5, Research Focus: Internal and External Validity.)

With the above in mind, what can we say about the success of precollege programs? Phyllis Kammer, Nadya Fouad, and Ruth Williams (1988) surveyed students who had participated in one such program between 1977 and 1983. They found the dropout rate to be significantly lower than that for minorities in the public schools in the same area. Furthermore, a majority of the students who had already graduated from high school had either entered or said they planned to enter some form of postsecondary education.

Reference: P. P. Kammer, N. Fouad, & R. Williams. (1988). Follow-up of a pre-college program for minority and disadvantaged students. Career Development Quarterly, 37, 40–45.

---

students' attention to areas other than the role-traditional ones in which they express an initial interest. Those who have doubts as to the appropriateness of such actions should consider what the same counselor would be likely to do if a talented white male student expressed interest in becoming a teacher's aide or helper (Brooks, 1990).

Irrational Beliefs and Maladaptive Myths

Students frequently approach career decisions with maladaptive beliefs and myths (Mitchell & Krumboltz, 1987). These can be about themselves ("I'm not very

BOX 10.1

Myths That Interfere with Adaptive Career Decision Making

- "I have to know exactly what I want to do before I can act."
- "Choosing a career involves making just one decision."
- "If I change my mind once I've picked a career, I'm a failure."
- "If I can only be good in nursing [construction, management, etc.], then I will be content."
- "Work satisfies all of a person's needs."
- "If I work hard enough, I can be successful at anything."
- "How good I am at my job determines my worth as a person."

Source: L. K. Mitchell & J. D. Krumboltz. (1987). The effects of cognitive restructuring and decision-making training on career indecision. Journal of Counseling and Development, 66, *171–174.*

smart"), a profession ("You have to be self-confident to be a nurse"), or the conditions that lead to satisfaction with a career ("I wouldn't be happy in a profession unless I made a lot of money at it"). Box 10.1 identifies types of myths that keep many people from trying interesting careers.

Cognitive Restructuring.   The social-cognitive approach to counseling students with career indecision recommends intervention programs that confront them with their irrational beliefs. Confrontation results in cognitive restructuring and makes more adaptive decision making possible. A female, for instance, may think that her parents "would have nothing to do with her" if she didn't become an elementary school teacher. Because she has little interest in teaching, she finds it difficult to plan for college or think about a career.

Intervention in the form of cognitive restructuring would encourage her to look at the evidence supporting the belief that her parents would sever their relationship if she did not become a teacher (she might find little to support this belief). A counselor might then give her the "assignment" of talking to her parents about her future. She discovers they are concerned only that she will be able to support herself in a secure job. She is also assigned the task of interviewing five women in different professions and asking them the most satisfying and frustrating aspects of their work. She finds that accounting, career guidance, and being a teacher (surprise!) are all attractive alternatives. She decides to apply to college (Mitchell & Krumboltz, 1987).

Mitchell and Krumboltz (1987) report that cognitive restructuring helps reduce students' anxiety when thinking about career planning, consequently making it easier for them to think about their futures. It is also more effective than other programs in maintaining the behaviors that help students explore career options.

At present we need much more information about the effectiveness of the many programs that exist to help minority youth and adolescent females combat the internal and external barriers they face in attaining career goals. What is clear so far is that most teachers, parents, counselors, and students need to expand their thinking beyond role-traditional careers for minorities and females.

ADOLESCENTS AND COLLEGE: THINKING ABOUT IDEAS

With age, adolescents get better at solving life's problems. Is this simply because they can bring more experiences to bear on any decision? Or do their experiences contribute to new ways of thinking, ways that allow them to see that what they presently face often has much in common with problems they solved in the past?

New Solutions to Old Problems: Structural Analytical Thinking

What form might thinking take if it were to move beyond the formal thinking that emerges in early adolescence? Remember, formal thought enables adolescents to stretch their minds beyond a physical world defined by their senses to a world of possibilities that exists first and foremost in their minds, a process that enables them to think of all the possible forms a problem could assume. Formal thought is thought that generates a system, a set of all possible alternatives.

M. L. Commons and F. A. Richards (1982) suggest a way of thinking that allows individuals to relate two or more systems. Just as formal thinking generates a single system, **structural analytical thinking** identifies parallels between several systems by noting relations that are common to each.

Does structural analytical thinking sound like something only philosophers and metaphysicians engage in? Don't be too quick to say yes. You have already used this way of thinking yourself when reading Chapter 4. Piaget himself has provided us with an example of structural analytical thought: he had to think in a structural analytical way to envision the characteristics of formal thinking. Piaget had to see, in other words, how each of several quite different problems required the same operations for their solution. Whether determining what form life might take on a newly discovered planet or which combination of chemicals produces a yellow liquid, one must isolate the relevant variables, generate all the possible combinations, and systematically test each combination. To see each problem as a reflection of formal thinking, one must think at a structural analytical level.

Structural analytical thinking has a distinct advantage over formal thinking: It gives one a perspective from which to view the problems one is attempting to

RESEARCH FOCUS

Factorial Designs: Career Indecision—Don't Push Me; I'm Still Thinking

The way she described it, she felt like a diver, her toes on the edge of the high board and the pool a blue square beneath her. People were climbing up the ladder, crowding behind her, telling her to jump. But she'd forgotten how to swim.

The counselor had heard it before. He met so many students throughout the year, mostly juniors and some seniors. All were panicked at the thought of jumping off—graduating and beginning a career. What makes it hard for some individuals to make career decisions while others find it relatively easy? Is there anything to be done to help those who have difficulty deciding on a career?

Career indecision is associated with numerous maladaptive beliefs and myths. Students believe that they have to be "absolutely certain" before they can do anything, that "planning for a career involves just one decision," that their parents will "never understand" if they don't become a teacher, social worker, carpenter, brain surgeon, and so on. Do these myths interfere with adaptive decision making? Or does the problem lie in the decision-making steps themselves? Most career counselors assume the latter, and train students in the skills they need to make career decisions. Although the most common intervention approach to career counseling, this type of decision-making training has had only modest success.

An alternative approach, cognitive restructur-ing, addresses the irrational beliefs students have about career decisions. This method confronts students with their irrational beliefs and thus enables them to replace these with adaptive ones. Lynda Mitchell and John Krumboltz (1987) compared the effectiveness of cognitive restructuring and decision-making training as methods of dealing with career indecision. They included a third condition, in addition to cognitive restructuring and decision-making training, in which students received no career counseling—that is, a *no-treatment control*.

These investigators used a factorial design that included, in addition to counseling conditions, the sex of the students as a variable. In a *factorial design,* two or more independent variables, or factors, are completely *crossed* so that each level of one variable is combined with each level of all the other variables. This design appears in schematic form below. Factorial designs provide information about the effect of each independent variable alone, called a *main effect,* and information about the effect of a variable when another variable is present, called an *interaction*.

An interaction exists when the effect of a variable changes when a second variable is present. We might find, for instance, that both types of counseling are equally effective for female students, but for males, one type works better than the other. The existence of an interaction means that we must

(*continued*)

solve. Unlike formal thinking, which is limited to solving problems within the systems that define them, structural analytical thinking makes it possible to mentally step outside any particular system and consider another approach.

Propositional and Dialectical Reasoning. Stepping outside a system and seeing things from another perspective touches all areas of adolescents' lives, not just the intellectual. Not every adolescent (or even every adult) can do this; it requires reasoning in a new way. Klaus Riegel (1973) distinguishes this reasoning, which he terms dialectical reasoning, from the propositional reasoning that develops with formal thinking. Both types of reasoning start with a set of premises, or assumptions

RESEARCH FOCUS (*continued*)

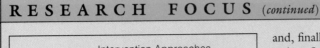

Intervention Approaches		
Cognitive Restructuring	Decision-Making Training	No-Treatment Control
Females		
Males		

qualify what we say about a variable. Is decision-making training just as effective as cognitive restructuring? It depends. If the students being counseled are females, then it is. But if males are being counseled, then it is not.

Going back to Mitchell and Krumboltz's experiment, let's see what they did and what they found. Students in the cognitive restructuring condition participated in a 5-week program in which they identified maladaptive beliefs and their effect on behavior and completed actual "assignments" requiring them to test the accuracy of these beliefs. Students in the decision-making training condition also participated in a 5-week program in which they learned decision-making skills; defining the problem, clarifying their objectives, then generating and systematically eliminating alternative solutions,

and, finally, committing themselves to a course of action. Students in the control condition received no treatment.

How effective were the programs? Cognitive restructuring helped to reduce anxiety about career decisions more so than did decision-making training. This was true even though students' maladaptive attitudes did not change significantly. Since anxiety is almost always associated with career indecision, its reduction through cognitive restructuring is important. A 1-month follow-up revealed that the cognitive restructuring group continued to explore career possibilities more than the other groups. A scale designed to assess decision-making skills revealed that all groups had good skills and did not differ in this respect. This latter finding is especially important, because career decision counseling often focuses on decision-making skills—something at which most students are already quite good. Finally, the type of intervention program interacted with the gender of the students. Males who received training in decision-making skills used these skills less than did the females who were trained in them, or than students of either sex who were trained in cognitive restructuring.

References: P. C. Cozby. (1989). Methods in behavioral research *(4th ed.). Mountain View, CA: Mayfield. L. K. Mitchell & J. D. Krumboltz. (1987).* The effects of cognitive restructuring and decision-making training on career indecision. *Journal of Counseling and Development, 66, 171–174.*

that are accepted as true. As these assumptions are put to the test, in the course of thinking through numerous life problems, they are either supported or refuted.

In **propositional reasoning,** these premises are never questioned, even though any number of situations may reveal them as wrong. In dialectical reasoning, the premises are put into question if, over time, actions based on them are not supported. What does it mean to question our most basic assumptions? We must be able, if only for the moment, to assume another perspective, another view of reality. We must be able to move beyond our world view to frame questions about the assumptions that underlie it. **Dialectical reasoning** provides a means by which we can gain a perspective on the system we use to define our world.

Although a job can help older adolescents develop structural analytical thinking and dialectical reasoning, the college experience provides more systematic opportunities for cognitive growth. These students will be prepared for a wider array of career possibilities than their counterparts who start working full-time right after high school.

Formal and Structural Analytical Thinking Compared. Consider two adolescent females as each realizes that even though her parents have always told her that she was free to do or be whatever she wanted, they do not accept her plans for her life. Each has introduced to her parents a young man she intends to marry and has found that they do not approve of her choice.

Connie is upset and confused. She can think of only two explanations for her parents' reaction. Either she is wrong or her parents are wrong. Either her parents *are* willing to accept the choices she makes, but this choice is so outrageous that no parent could support it, or her parents have been living a lie—it's not all right with them for her to be anything she wants to be if that means being different from them. She reacts with hurt and anger and can think of nothing to say to them or to her fiancé.

Janice recognizes her hurt and anger at her parents and begins to think about the differences in their values and hers. She recognizes that people's values influence their actions, but that in acting, people change events, and these changes frequently lead to new awareness and new values. Her parents' affirmation of her freedom to be herself has allowed her to be the person she is—a person who is quite different from them. Janice knows that because her parents have valued her, they valued her

foresees his own future as an authority and stakes his claim to the intellectual terrain. . . . [His] perception of the multiplicity of truth becomes a tool in the process of his separation and differentiation from others. His opinion distinguishes him from all others and he lets them know it. (1986, p. 64)

Adolescent females take a different first step. Those who begin the intellectual journey move from subjective knowledge (realizing that truth is relative) to procedural knowledge (assuming responsibility for what they know) to constructive knowledge (being aware that knowledge is constructed by each knower). Not all complete this journey.

Subjective Knowledge: Agreeable Dissent.   Adolescent females with **subjective knowledge** appreciate that the multiplicity of truth frees them from traditional authority; but they are cautious about embracing an intellectual position. Unlike males, who have been rewarded for testing the status quo, females have been rewarded for being quiet, predictable, and agreeable. Speaking up, taking a stand, or disagreeing with others runs counter to all they have learned. Female adolescents repeatedly express concern that, in taking an intellectual stand, they will isolate themselves from others. Thus their relationships constrain them from forming and defending ideas that would distinguish or separate them from other people. They experience few expectations about, and get little support for, this type of intellectual risk taking (Belenky, Clinchy, Goldberger, & Tarule, 1986).

Rather than speaking out, many maintain a surface conformity while they covertly examine issues. "They become the polite listeners, the spectators who watch and listen but do not act." (Belenky, Clinchy, Goldberger, & Tarule, 1986, p. 66). Belenky and her associates note the intellectual loneliness of these female adolescents:

> The tragedy is that [they] still their public voice and are reluctant to share their private world; ultimately this hinders them from finding mentors who might support their intellectual and emotional growth. [They] can be silently alienated . . . , knowing somehow that their conformity is a lie and does not reveal the inner truth or potential they have recently come to value. (p. 67)

In speaking up, males lay claim to an "intellectual terrain" that has been staked out for centuries as theirs. There is no equivalent intellectual domain for females, and few means are identified for their use in defining one. Instead of "reason"—the ultimate analytic tool—females have been told their strength lies in intuition, which in relation to reason is like a divining rod compared to a surveyor's level. Instead of mapping out ideas, many learn to wait for the gentle tug of mind in an otherwise silent trek across an uncharted terrain.

In becoming skilled listeners of themselves and others, some women come to see the contradictions of their stance. Their observations make it possible for them to develop the more critical thought that characterizes the next step they take.

RESEARCH FOCUS

Theory-Guided Research: How Sexist Is Our Language?

Masculine words such as "he" and "man" have been used generically in English for centuries to refer to individuals of either sex. In contrast, when comparable words such as "she" or "woman" are used, the listener knows that the person being referred to is female. But how generic are these masculine words? Are listeners equally likely to think of a woman as a man when they hear "he"? Or do they do a quick semantic shuffle and mentally note that the word could also refer to females?

The question is an interesting one, but the answer has been difficult to obtain. It's hard to observe "quick semantic shuffles," especially when these are mental. In this case, theory suggests a way to get some answers. Sik Hung Ng (1990) used the concepts of proactive inhibition and release from proactive inhibition, concepts derived from a theory of learning and memory, to determine how words are linguistically coded in memory.

We know that words are coded both for their specific meaning and for category membership. Thus the word "poodle" would be coded in terms of the animal's specific characteristics (e.g., curly hair, intelligence, pointed snout), but also in terms of the category "dog." This is true for "man" as well. "Man" would be coded in terms of specific characteristics (e.g., adult, human), and also in terms of the category "male." But are words such as "he" and "man" assimilated just as easily into the feminine category as the masculine one? Linguistically speaking, that is, are they truly generic?

The concept of proactive inhibition suggests a way of finding out. *Proactive inhibition* refers to interference caused by prior learning when remembering new material. The interference is greatest when the old and new material are similar. In other words, one's ability to learn something new is inversely related to how much similar material one has previously learned. Proactive inhibition tells us that memory for a new word will not be as good if one has already memorized other words from the same category (i.e., if the new word shares the same linguistic category) than if the word is different from others one has memorized (belongs to a different linguistic category). *Release from proactive inhibition* occurs when the new word is from a dif-

(continued)

Procedural Knowledge: Stepping Out Intellectually.   Women who step out intellectually—with **procedural knowledge**—assume responsibility for discovering things for themselves. Some do this by mastering the facts in an area, whether it be political economics, nursing, or managing a home. Others adopt a more subjective approach to what they are learning, approaching ideas for what they have to say about their lives. The understanding these women gain is more intimate and personal than that of the first group. Only the first approach is characteristic of Perry's males. For those who adopt it, doubting becomes an important way of putting ideas "on trial" and bull sessions provide a forum in which individuals attack each other's position to hone the cutting edge of their logic. Belenky and her associates (1986) note that

> women find it hard to see doubting as a "game"; they tend to take it personally. Teachers and fathers and boyfriends assure them that arguments are not between *persons* but between *positions*, but the women continue to fear that someone may get hurt. (p. 105).

ferent category; the release takes the form of better memory for the distinctive than the similar item. These twin concepts provide a means for discovering the linguistic category of any word. If the linguistic code for "his" and "man" is truly a masculine one, these words will not be remembered as easily following a list of other masculine words (proactive inhibition) as after a list of feminine ones (release from proactive inhibition).

Adolescents were randomly assigned to one of two conditions in which they listened to pairs of feminine words (queen-Linda, nun-Mary, girl-Iris, mom-Ruth) or masculine ones (king-Ivan, son-Lewis, boy-Ross, dad-Mike). After each list, they heard two additional pairs (man-Robin and his-Chris). Unlike the names in the masculine or feminine list, both Robin and Chris are unisex names. Will "man" and "his" be as easy to remember after the list of masculine pairs as after the feminine? If so, these words are genuinely generic.

Theory tells us that we first need to check for a buildup of proactive inhibition over the initial list of pairs, that is, to look for poorer recall of the last words than the first ones. As expected, this oc-curred. Next, we need to determine whether proactive inhibition continued for the generic words when they followed the masculine list, and whether release from proactive inhibition occurred following the feminine list. Both of these occurred as well.

These findings tells us that the words "man" and "his" are coded as masculine words in memory and are not truly generic. The author notes that if they were generic, then their usage in sentences such as the following should not appear incongruous: "Throughout most of history, men have always breast-fed their babies." But sentences such as these do jar and prompt a rereading to discover what is amiss.

The problem adolescents face is not one of having to make sense of incongruities such as the above. The more serious problem occurs when they experience no incongruity—when language so structures experience that half of *human*kind can be excluded.

Reference: S. H. Ng. (1990). Androcentric coding of man *and* his *in memory by language users.* Journal of Experimental Social Psychology, 26, 455–464.

Conversations for females serve the function of bull sessions for males. Belenky and her associates give an example of a young Ethiopian college student who explained in one such conversation with an American friend why her country had adopted communism. They note the following:

> These young women did not engage in metaphysical debate. They did not argue about abstractions or attack or defend positions. No one tried to prove anything or to convert anyone. The Ethiopian articulated her reality, and the American tried to understand it. They did not discuss communism in general, impersonal terms, but in terms of its origins and consequences among a particular group of real people. (p. 114)

Though more advanced than subjective knowledge, procedural knowledge operates within a system of knowledge that cannot examine itself. Women who think in either of these ways

> can criticize a system, but only in the system's terms, only according to the system's standards. Women at this position may be liberals or conservatives, but they cannot

be radicals. If, for example, they are feminists, they want equal opportunities for women within the capitalistic structure; they do not question the premises of the structure. When these women speak of "beating the system," they do not mean violating its expectations but rather exceeding them. (Belenky, Clinchy, Goldberger, & Tarule, 1986, p. 127)

For females to move beyond these forms of knowing, they need more than formal thought.

Constructive Knowledge: Examining the Self.   Women who move into **constructive knowledge** report a period of self-examination in which they experience being out of touch with parts of themselves. "During the transition into a new way of knowing, there is an impetus to allow the self back into the process of knowing, to confront the pieces of the self that may be experienced as fragmented and contradictory" (Belenky, Clinchy, Goldberger, & Tarule, 1986, p. 136). These women ask themselves questions such as, "Who am I?" and, "How will I approach life?"

Questions such as these echo the concerns of Perry's young men who experienced the need for commitment in their relativistic thought. Belenky and her associates note that these women experience a "heightened consciousness and sense of choice" about the ways they examine their world and who they will become. They become aware of the fact that given a different perspective or even a different point in time, they could come up with different answers to the same questions (Belenky, Clinchy, Goldberger, & Tarule, 1986). This awareness leads to the central truth of constructed knowledge: that knowledge is constructed and hence relative, and the knower is an intrinsic part of the process. This position allows these females to examine a set of beliefs from a perspective outside that system. Something like structural analytical thinking almost surely is present at this point.

In addition to their general approach to knowledge, how much adolescents know about the subject they are studying affects how they think about it and how much they will remember of what they learn. We turn to research on expert knowledge next.

ADOLESCENTS AS EXPERTS

Experts and Novices

On the subject of expert knowledge, research supports the age-old observation that the rich get richer. The more adolescents know in a given area, the easier it is for them to learn even more. A classic study supports this observation. Chess masters and novices briefly saw boards from chess games in progress and attempted to reproduce what they had seen. The masters could reproduce the entire board of play easily; novices could not. However, when each viewed boards with pieces

Research supports the observation that the rich get richer, at least with respect to increasing expert knowledge. Students who know a lot about a subject organize information about it differently and make better use of it than do students who know less.

placed at random, the masters were no better than the novices (de Groot, 1965). The masters were only better when they could bring their knowledge to bear on the situation. Are chess masters uniquely gifted? And do adolescents ever function like experts?

They do—inside the classroom and out. Just as chess masters can remember more of the board in play, adolescents who are *experts* in a subject have better memory for what they've read on the subject than do novices. How much adolescents will remember of what they read is much more closely related to their background knowledge about the material than their ability (Lee, 1990).

M. T. H. Chi (1985), at the University of Pittsburgh, found that students who know a lot about a subject organize information differently than those who do not. Specifically, students with "expert" knowledge are more likely to organize what they know according to high-level, abstract categories. Those who know less not only have fewer facts at their disposal but also organize them less efficiently. Consider a science class in which students have just completed a section on desert ecology. The teacher has asked them to name all the insectivores. The more knowledgeable students will have classified life forms in a way that allows them to pull out this information, abstractly according to functions, such as eating habits. Less knowledgeable students distinguish organisms in terms of their immediately obvious features, such as size or shape (Boster & Johnson, 1989).

Deane Schiano and her colleagues (1989) classified high school students according to their skill in an area and compared the strategies each type of student used in solving problems. These investigators looked for differences between skilled and unskilled adolescents in the way they organized information and used strategies. This research, just as Chi's, found that more knowledgeable students organize information in higher level categories, an approach which in turn allows them to adopt more efficient strategies when solving problems. Adolescents who are unskilled sort problems on the basis of perceptual similarities. Skilled students look for similarities in the relationships among problems. Students who are skilled are better able to abstract prototypes of the problems involved; less skilled adolescents are limited to visual comparisons of the alternatives at hand (Schiano, Cooper, Glaser, & Zhang, 1989).

Jill Larkin, at Carnegie-Mellon University, studied the way expert and novice college students approach problems. Once again, Larkin (1985) found that students of either type tend to adopt different approaches. Those who know more—the experts—approach problems in terms of general principles that reflect what they know of the elements involved. In organic chemistry, for example, one must be able to say what reactions will result when two or more chemicals are combined under different conditions. The number of potential outcomes under different conditions can be quite large.

Larkin finds that students who are knowledgeable rely little on memorized combinations. Instead, they abstract properties of the chemicals that would affect their combination with other elements and use these properties to predict possible reactions. Similarly, expert students in physics solve problems by first classifying them according to general principles and then applying specific equations appropriate to that domain of problem. Novices, lacking the knowledge that would allow them to classify problems in this way, apply formulas that are suggested by specific expressions in the problems and often end up pursuing the wrong course. Larkin's observations confirm those of Chi and others who find that experts organize information into more abstract categories, which in turn allows them to apply more efficient strategies (Larkin, 1985).

Expert knowledge offers a way of explaining the noticeable differences in thought that often characterize adolescents. Some parallels exist between this approach and Piaget's stage theory of intellectual development. Both experts and formal thinkers are systematic in their approach to a problem. Experts define a domain of knowledge in terms of abstract categories—for example, eating habits—and classify specific instances accordingly. Does this sound like formal thought? Both approaches require a high degree of abstraction in defining the parameters of the domain and then a systematic ordering of particular instances within that domain.

Knowledge of One's Culture: Everybody's an Expert

We have seen that what adolescents know can affect how easily they can learn even more. The examples of expertise considered thus far have involved academic knowledge, the type gained in the classroom. All adolescents are experts in one other area: their own culture. This expertise makes it easy to assimilate information that is consistent with what they know based on their experiences. Information that is inconsistent is not easy to learn, since they must change the way they understand things in order to accommodate a new perspective. Consequently, it is difficult to learn concepts and facts that violate one's cultural perspective or are incongruent with one's experiences.

Anderson Franklin, at the City University of New York, put these observations to the test in a simple experiment. Franklin (1985) assumed that black adolescents would have an advantage over white adolescents in remembering words common to the black culture but not common outside it. Franklin interviewed 75 urban black teenagers to obtain commonly used slang terms. He constructed lists of categories of words using the terms they supplied, together with words common to both blacks and whites.

As shown in Figure 10.5, black adolescents remember more words than do white adolescents. In fact, if one did not know how the list of words had been derived, one might assume that black adolescents have better memories than do whites. Based on similar comparisons, some investigators have assumed that whites are more intelligent than blacks and other minorities because they score higher on measures common to intelligence tests. In doing so, these investigators have failed to take into account that minorities may not be familiar with the items included in the tests (see Chapter 4). Franklin noticed that black adolescents were also better at recalling items that were equally familiar to the white students. Blacks were more

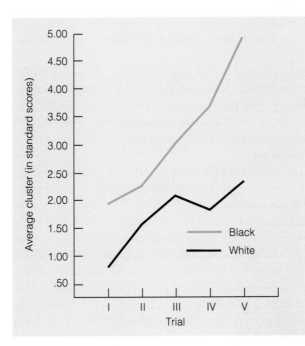

Figure 10.5 Clustered Recall of Words by Black and White Adolescents.

Source: A. J. Franklin. (1985). The social context and socialization variables as factors in thinking and learning. In S. F. Chipman, J. W. Segal, & R. Glaser (Eds.), Thinking and learning skills *(Vol. 2). Hillsdale, NJ: Erlbaum.*

likely to categorize items into related clusters, a strategy that vastly improves memory when it is used. The presence of unfamiliar items may have led the white adolescents to believe that the words were unrelated. Familiarity with all the words, which was the case only for the black adolescents, had allowed them to see that the words could be easily categorized (Franklin, 1985).

PUTTING KNOWLEDGE TO WORK

Active Knowledge

Aside from the fact that some students are experts in a particular subject and some are not, important differences still remain in the amount of knowledge adolescents bring to a subject. Just as with experts, the more they know, the easier it is for them to learn even more. Differences in what adolescents know can affect their ability to understand, remember, and put new information to use. How much they know will also determine the types of strategies they use in learning new material.

Consider an example from a high school health class in which students are learning about the cardiovascular system. The teacher has just told them that arteries are thick and elastic, and veins are thin. Students who know nothing else about either type of blood vessel may have difficulty remembering which is thin and which is thick unless they do something to hold on to these facts. Most will rely on rote memorization. Students with some knowledge of arteries and veins—who know, for example, that arteries carry blood away from the heart and veins carry it back—may be able to relate that information to the need for arteries to be elastic, to expand and contract with each pulse of blood (Bransford, Stein, Shelton, & Owings, 1981).

But what about those students who do not know anything about the cardiovascular system? Is it possible for them to learn material without blindly memorizing facts? The answer depends a lot on the techniques teachers use. Simple presentations of facts are more likely to result in memorization, whereas class experiences that require students to put information to use generate the type of learning that results in understanding.

Let's say the teacher in the above example gives the class the task of designing an artificial artery. As students consider possible materials from which to construct the artery, they are likely to encounter the issue of whether the materials should be rigid or elastic, thick or thin, and so on. The teacher might feed relevant information into the discussion as decisions are being made, indicating, for example, that the heart pumps blood in spurts, that considerable pressure occurs, or that blood travels "uphill" from the heart to the head as well as laterally and "downhill." Students will arrive at the need for elasticity themselves. They will see its function in accommodating surges of blood and as a constricting valve that closes after each surge, preventing blood from flowing back to the heart (Bransford, Stein, Shelton, & Owings, 1981; Bransford, Vye, Adams, & Perfetto, 1989).

BOX 10.2

Applying Strategies in Problem Solving

The same strategy applies to the solution of each of the problems below.

Military Campaign

A general wishes to capture a fortress located in the center of a country. There are many roads radiating outward from the fortress. All have been mined so that while small groups of men can pass over the roads safely, a large force will detonate the mines. A full-scale direct attack is therefore impossible. The general's solution is to divide his army into small groups, send each group to the head of a different road, and have the groups converge simultaneously on the fortress. (Gick & Holyoak, 1980)

Inoperable Tumor

Suppose you are a doctor faced with a patient who had a malignant tumor in his stomach. It is impossible to operate on the patient, but unless the tumor is destroyed the patient will die. There is a kind of ray that may be used to destroy the tumor. If the rays reach the tumor all at once and with sufficiently high intensity, the tumor will be destroyed. At lower intensities the rays are harmless to healthy tissue, but they will not affect the tumor either. What type of procedure might be used to destroy the tumor with the rays, and at the same time avoid destroying the healthy tissue? (Duncker, 1945)

Sources: Adapted from K. Duncker. (1945). On problem solving. Psychological Monographs, 58 *(Whole No. 270). M. L. Gick & K. J. Holyoak. (1980). Analogical problem solving.* Cognitive Psychology, 12, *306–355.*

Inert Knowledge

Having access to background knowledge has a potent effect on how and what one learns and remembers. Yet some adolescents fail to use the information they possess.

What adolescents know all too often exists as **inert knowledge:** facts and concepts they can recite but not use. Is this because the information they learn in school is so exotic it is irrelevant to the daily problems they face? Not always. More to the point, inert knowledge refers to the inability to draw on knowledge in just those situations in which it is potentially useful (Whitehead, 1929).

Why might adolescents be unable to use what they know? The ways in which they acquire information can make access to it difficult. Facts that have been memorized do not transfer readily to new situations. M. L. Gick and K. J. Holyoak (1980) presented students with a problem of an inoperable tumor, to be solved using the same strategy they'd just memorized concerning a military campaign. As shown in Box 10.2, the same strategy can be used to solve two completely different problems, yet even though the tumor problem directly followed the military one, 80% of the students didn't realize the military solution could be used as a strategy to destroy the tumor. When given a hint that the military tactics were applicable to the second situation, 90% solved the problem.

BOX 10.3

Finding Commonalities Among Problems

Physics	Algebra
What is the acceleration (increase in speed each second) of a train if its speed increased uniformly from 15 miles per second at the beginning of the 1st second to 45 miles per second at the end of the 12th second?	Every typist goes through a warm-up period during which his/her typing rate constantly increases until reaching a typical typing rate. Jane starts typing at a rate of 40 words per minute, and after 12 minutes reaches her typical typing rate of 58 words per minute. What is the constant increase in her typing rate during her warm-up period?

Sample protocols of students:

Student 1:   This is pretty similar to the things we did with a straight line in physics. Maybe I can use something from that.

Experimenter: How is it similar?

Because it's just like her going faster, she's not moving in a straight line; it's just how many words she types. So it's just like meters per second. Acceleration equals . . . I'm using the acceleration formula. Her acceleration would be 8⅙ words per minute.

Student 2:   Subtract the initial words per minute from the final words per minute to get 18. Divide that by the number of minutes to get 1.5. So you get 1.5 words per minute.

Source: Adapted from M. Bassok. (1990). Transfer of domain-specific problem-solving procedures. Journal of Experimental Psychology: Learning, Memory, and Cognition, 16, 522–533.

Adolescents frequently have difficulty overlooking content-specific details to see underlying commonalities among problems. Memory seems to be triggered more by the content of what one is doing than by the procedures one is carrying out. Some courses lead to better transfer than others. Students do better, for instance, in applying what they have learned in algebra to their physics problems than vice versa (Bassok & Holyoak, 1989). One of the things they appear to learn in algebra is to disregard the content and focus on the procedure. When the procedure one is following becomes the content (by focusing on it), spontaneous transfer to problems with a similar procedure is likely. Miriam Bassok (1990) found that high school students could interchange solutions to physics and algebra problems (see Box 10.3) but only when everything about the problems was the same. When seemingly small changes were made, students needed many hints before they thought to apply a previously learned solution.

Thinking as Problem Solving

J. D. Bransford and his colleagues (1989) suggest that we think of learning as problem solving and thinking, rather than as simply remembering. They make the point that problems of learning, such as inert knowledge, do not reflect either a poor memory or limitations to one's ability to learn; they are simply failures to apply the proper strategies when facing a new problem. The task becomes one of knowing what it means to understand something. These authors suggest a five-step approach for overcoming some of the difficulties that lead to inert knowledge. The names of these five steps are combined to form the acronym **IDEAL.**

Basic to this approach is learning to *identify* when a problem exists, that is, to recognize when one does not understand something just read or heard. The next step is to *define* the problem. Why didn't I understand? Was it a momentary lapse in attention? Or was it because I didn't have some relevant information? One can *explore* alternative solutions to the problem. One might reread the passage or get additional information. In either case, one must *act,* and then *look* to see if these actions have improved comprehension. Notice that learning becomes an active rather than a passive process (Bransford, Vye, Adams, & Perfetto, 1989). Procedures that increase one's engagement with the material decrease the likelihood that what one learns will become inert.

Many of the problems of inert knowledge can be resolved by teaching thinking skills. Even so, individuals of some ages may not find it easy to think about their thinking. Remember that this ability develops during adolescence. Adolescents almost surely will find it easier than young children to search their memories or monitor their learning. Each of these activities is more abstract than simply putting information to use. Both involve getting information about information or knowing what one knows, and formal thought is necessary in either case.

If inert knowledge is the failure to see the relationship between what one knows and the problems one faces, creativity is just the opposite. Creativity allows us to put knowledge together in novel and unexpected ways.

CREATIVITY

Characteristics of Creativity

Creative adolescents have a high *tolerance for ambiguity.* Ambiguity exists whenever one is uncertain regarding a course of action or the meaning of an event. Creative adolescents enjoy the risks that come with uncertainty, even when it involves a certain amount of disorder. They welcome people and ideas that are different from their own. Instead of closing themselves or others off when faced with uncertainty, they remain open-minded (Dacey, 1989b).

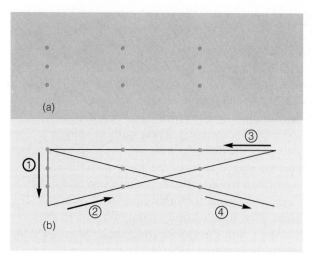

Figure 10.6 (a) The Nine-Dot Problem. Connect the nine dots in this figure with four straight lines, without taking the pen or pencil off the page. (b) Solution.

Source: J. S. Dacey. (1989). Fundamentals of creative thinking. Lexington, MA: D. C. Heath.

John Dacey (1989b) studied creativity by having individuals write a story about a simple picture, instructing them to try to create a story no one else would. Although nearly three-quarters of the more than 1,000 stories were the same, creative stories were highly dissimilar. They revealed a restless imagination and a disdain for "following the rules" by telling an ordinary story. Rules are the antithesis of ambiguity. When there are rules, one knows what to do. Creative adolescents enjoy *stimulus freedom*. They can bend the rules when the rules interfere with their creative ideas, and they do *not* assume that rules must exist unless they are in evidence. Less-creative age-mates may even make up rules in ambiguous situations to reduce their fear of being wrong. Dacey considers the fear of being wrong to be the most powerful inhibitor of creativity (Dacey, 1989b).

Not seeing rules where none exist is a necessary condition for creativity. The solution to the problem shown in Figure 10.6 depends on it. One must be able to "leave the field" of the rectangle described by the dots. Adolescents who have been coloring outside the lines since kindergarten have no trouble eventually coming up with a solution (Dacey, 1989b). The ability to leave the field is analogous to the ability of structural analytical thinkers to mentally step outside the logical system they are using in order to gain a new perspective on it.

Creative adolescents are both *analytic* and *intuitive*. They combine intuitive leaps of imagination with careful analyses of outcomes compared to their expectations. Another characteristic is *open-mindedness*. Creative adolescents are less likely to prejudge new situations or try to fit unfamiliar information into comfortable categories. Finally, they are both *reflective* and *spontaneous*. They can deliberate on the spontaneous flashes that come to them (Dacey, 1989b).

Origins of Creativity in Adolescents

Dacey (1989a) compared families with a creative adolescent or a creative parent with those in which no member of the family was creative. He found that parents

Creative adolescents are both reflective and spontaneous. They are less likely to conform to accepted practice and more likely to try new ways of doing things than their less creative peers. These two teenagers in the Bronx used their spray cans to transform a crumbling concrete wall next to an empty lot.

of a creative adolescent frequently use a style of parenting not previously identified (see Chapter 5). Unlike authoritative, authoritarian, and permissive parents, these parents show high interest in their adolescent's activities yet set very few rules governing behavior. The mean number of rules in noncreative families is six, while creative families average one rule! Rather than rules, parents provide strong models through their own behavior and use family discussions to establish behavioral expectations. Like authoritative parents, they expect adolescents to make decisions for themselves. These parents give frequent feedback on their children's behavior, but rarely punish. Their teenagers comment that their parents' disappointment in them is a stronger motivation to do well than any system of punishment or rewards.

Humor is an important element in creative families. Jokes and "kidding around" are common. When asked what they value, members of creative families rank humor higher than those of other families, often placing it well above characteristics such as popularity or high intelligence. Creative adolescents rank getting high grades or having a high IQ moderately low.

Dacey (1989a) notes that many creative adolescents experience more trauma in life than average children. He suggests that the need to cope with trauma stimulates creative approaches. Creative adolescents see themselves as working harder than their peers. This quality contradicts the stereotype of the creative individual who spontaneously generates novel ideas and approaches. Spontaneity is there, but creative people follow up in a deliberate and disciplined way.

ADOLESCENT DECISION MAKING

Intellectual changes during adolescence have very real implications for daily living. How effective do adolescents perceive themselves to be? What are they willing to attempt? How motivated are they to pursue different goals? How successful will they be? The answers to these and similar questions reflect their burgeoning intellectual skills.

Personal Effectiveness

Feelings of personal effectiveness reflect how much control adolescents feel they have in a situation, which stems directly from their ability to predict the outcome. The ability to predict is an intellectual skill. "If I tell Gina that the junior she has a crush on asked me out, she'll flirt with my boyfriend." Or, "if I work all the different types of algebra problems in this chapter, I'll be able to pass the test on it." Adolescents who know the consequences their actions will have are in a better position to control what happens to them by doing or not doing certain things. Predicting outcomes involves the same type of analytic thinking (if . . . then . . .) adolescents use in the classroom: inductive and deductive reasoning.

Adolescents can think about outcomes of their actions probabilistically, a development that accompanies formal thought. They also realize that events can have more than one cause (e.g., "Gina might also flirt with my boyfriend because she thinks he's cute") and that the same event can contribute to different outcomes (e.g., "Gina might even spend more time with me . . ."). In addition to intellectual skills, how much adolescents believe in themselves also affects their approach to any situation; in this case, by the type of outcomes they anticipate. Those who perceive themselves as effective anticipate positive outcomes. They mentally rehearse adaptive solutions, which help them find their way through problems more effectively (Bandura, 1989; Zimmerman, Bandura, & Martinez-Pons, 1992).

The type of outcome adolescents anticipate also affects their motivation to engage in an activity. In other words, the goals they set reflect their appraisal of their ability to meet them. Those who doubt themselves are likely to give up when they face some difficulty; adolescents who believe in themselves work harder. Belief in self has other effects as well; it can determine how much stress one can tolerate. Those who think they can cope with something do not anticipate all the possible negative outcomes that others with self-doubts imagine. As a consequence, they don't have to deal with the negative emotional side effects such fantasies may produce (Bandura, 1989).

Bandura points out that, at times, inaccurate self-assessments can actually *help* adolescents when making decisions. Optimistic evaluations of competence—if not too far off the mark—can help for all the reasons just reviewed. A less optimistic, if truer, judgment can be self-limiting, failing to motivate adolescents to stretch beyond their present performance.

Feelings of competence or incompetence can be general or quite specific. Are some adolescents more likely to react to failure at one thing with general feelings of inadequacy? M. E. Poole and G. T. Evans (1988) had adolescents rate their competence in several life skill areas (e.g., use of time, setting goals, making choices, social awareness). In general, adolescents view themselves as being competent at the things they value, though not always as much as they might desire. Important gender differences exist in self-perceptions. Females view themselves as less competent than males overall and as competent in fewer areas, even though an objective measure that all adolescents completed showed females doing slightly better (Poole & Evans, 1988). Do female adolescents' lower ratings of themselves limit their actual competence in any way? At the very least, we might expect their lower ratings to affect the goals they set for themselves.

Dealing with Everyday Problems

Most of the thinking adolescents do is directed at solving the problems of life— *their* lives. Most of these take the form of "daily hassles," that is, interpersonal problems such as an argument with parents or a misunderstanding with friends. Several skills help adolescents negotiate successful resolutions to interpersonal problems. Not unexpectedly, older adolescents are better at these than younger ones (Berg, 1989; Mann, Harmoni, & Power, 1989).

Any of three general strategies can be attempted when a problem arises. Adolescents can alter their behavior so that it better fits their environment, they can attempt to change the environment so that it better fits their behavior, or they can select another environment (Sternberg, 1985). A number of additional steps are important. The first is simply to plan to take action. Also helpful is to get more information, and to change one's perception of the problem. Sometimes redefining the problem, looking at it in a different way, is all that is needed to emotionally defuse it.

Each of these steps underscores the importance of flexibility when faced with a problem, and flexibility increases with age. When asked, "What does a good decision maker do when making a decision?" older adolescents are more likely to mention generating options, and they are better at doing this themselves. They are also more likely to take into consideration the consequences of following any of the options and to check the advice or information they get (Mann, Harmoni, & Power, 1989).

Cynthia Berg (1989) asked adolescents to evaluate the effectiveness of the above strategies when faced with a problem such as the following:

> Your parents have become more strict in what time you must be home at night. On Friday and Saturday nights you have to be home by 12:00. You and your friends want to go out to a movie on Friday night that will not be over until 12:30, so you won't be home until 1:00. You find out from the movie theater that the movie will be

The demands of school and homework are relatively inflexible compared to the negotiated settlements that can be reached with friends and parents.

showing at the theater for one more week. Rate how good each of the answers is in allowing you to see the movie and be home by 12:00. [The curfew for fifth-, eighth-, and eleventh-graders was 9:30, 10:30, and 12:00, respectively.]

Ask your friends if they have a strict time that they must be home at night. (Get more information)

Decide that seeing the movie is really not worth causing problems with your parents. (Redefine the problem)

Wait to see the movie on Saturday afternoon. (Alter behavior)

Persuade your parents that the new rule is not fair. (Change the environment)

Spend Friday night at the house of a friend who does not have to be home so early. (Pick another environment)

Plan how you could both see a movie and be home by 12:00. (Plan a course of action) (p. 618)

Older adolescents choose more effective strategies than younger ones, and females do so more than males. As obstacles are introduced or removed, less-effective problem solvers are likely to radically alter their approach. The best problem solvers change their strategies relatively little. This difference suggests that interpersonal problem solving is a skill that, once learned, adolescents can apply across a variety of settings. Supporting this interpretation is Berg's finding that using strategies effectively is related to adolescents' own evaluations of their practical intelligence, as well as that of their teachers' and parents', and to their actual achievement (in the form of grades and achievement test scores).

The effectiveness of strategies varies with the setting in which problems arise. Adolescents believe, for example, that the problems they encounter at school (e.g., getting into a special class, resolving a grade discrepancy) are best handled either by redefining their perception of the problem or by simply selecting another environment. An adolescent who receives a C on an essay that she feels deserves a B might think the teacher is biased against her. Most adolescents in high school realize that the best way to resolve grade discrepancies is to find out what the teacher wanted (i.e., redefine the problem from an interpersonal one to an academic one) or try to get another teacher next time (select another environment).

When problems arise outside of school, planning and getting more information are seen as most effective. Opting for different approaches in either setting itself reveals knowledge of effective strategies. School settings are relatively inflexible compared to the environments where one can negotiate settlements, such as with friends or parents. Older adolescents are more likely to realize this difference than younger ones (Berg, 1989).

In all, whether it be thinking through academic arguments and abstract ideas or facing everyday decisions, adolescents use increasingly sophisticated strategies.

SUMMARY

Adolescents at Work

Almost 40% of all 16- and 17-year-old students have part-time jobs, and more want to work than can find jobs. Students who work part-time spend less time on schoolwork and with families, but they develop a sense of responsibility and feel productive. Unemployment among minority adolescents is higher than among majority youth.

Most adolescents spend their money on personal items such as clothes, entertainment, and cars. Smaller numbers save for education or other long-term plans.

High school dropouts are more than twice as likely to be unemployed as graduates; the majority of dropouts are unemployed. Minority students are more likely to drop out than those from the dominant culture.

Programs that are successful in preventing at-risk students from dropping out communicate the importance of having a degree for making money. These programs create an atmosphere of caring and involvement, provide individualized instruction through computerized programs, and involve the community and parents.

Choosing a Vocation

Social-cognitive theory emphasizes the interrelationships among inborn abilities, one's particular environment and unique learning history, and each person's skills in explaining vocational choices.

Developmental theories trace occupational choices over stages. Ginzburg views vocational development as a progressive narrowing of choices that at first reflect only fantasy, then tentative career choices, and, with increasing age, realistic choices.

Super assumes that people choose occupations that reflect the way they see themselves. Because the self-concept changes with age, so will occupational plans. In the growth stage, adolescents develop a realistic self-concept; in the exploration stage, they begin to make choices related to future work. Individuals settle into their work as early adults in the establishment stage, maintaining their occupational position through middle adulthood in the maintenance stage. The decline stage involves retirement.

Holland classifies individuals into six personality types; different work environments either complement or oppose the qualities that make up any type. Realistic types prefer orderly, structured work. Investigative types prefer work that involves analytic skills. Artistic types do best in unstructured situations that let them express their creativity. Social types have good interpersonal skills. Enterprising types enjoy work that brings them into contact with others in ways in which they can express their assertiveness. Conventional types prefer to work under the direction of others.

Joining the Workforce

Most adolescents who find full-time employment work in service jobs as salespeople, waiters, or waitresses. They can get entry-level training for occupations through high school vocational programs.

More female adolescents plan to work in professional jobs than before. Sex segregation still exists in the workforce, and advancement opportunities for females are limited. Female adolescents also have internal barriers to advancement that take the form of lower expectations for pay and lower valuation of their work; these barriers are learned.

Minority adolescents face problems similar to those of females; in addition, poverty contributes heavily to the problems they face. Minority adolescents' career aspirations are as high as those of majority adolescents, but their lower expectations reflect social barriers to equal employment opportunities.

Intervention Programs: Strategies for Change

Because of inequities in the opportunity structure for minority adolescents and females, counselors may need to become active "change agents" to prepare these students for the full range of jobs that exists. Effective intervention programs work with local businesses, parents, and teachers as well as the students. Counselors often must first address their own biases.

Students frequently approach career decisions with maladaptive beliefs and myths. Intervention programs based on cognitive restructuring effectively address these as the first step to vocational counseling.

Adolescents and College: Thinking About Ideas

Some developmentalists believe a new form of thinking develops in late adolescence. Structural analytical thinking builds on the achievements of formal thought and allows adolescents to find parallels among different views of a problem.

Dialectical reasoning is necessary for structural analytical thought, just as propositional reasoning is necessary for formal thought. In propositional reasoning, the premises are not questioned even when they are not supported. In dialectical reasoning, one questions the premises if, over the course of time, actions based on them are not supported.

William Perry has identified three major forms of thought in college men. (a) Dualistic thinkers approach problems in a straightforward manner and look for the "right" answer. They operate within a single frame of reference that allows them to view ideas as either right or wrong. (b) Relativistic thinkers are aware that what they previously accepted as facts are actually interpretations that make sense within a given frame of reference. They are aware that more than one frame of reference exists and that each represents a legitimate point of view. (c) Relativists who commit themselves to a point of view create new meaning through anchoring their beliefs in a committed style of life.

Female adolescents do not think in ways captured by Perry's intellectual progressions. (a) Subjective knowers covertly examine issues while maintaining a surface conformity to traditional ideas. (b) Procedural knowers own the responsibility of discovering things for themselves, but their thought is limited by the confines of formal thinking. (c) Constructive knowers are aware that knowledge is constructed and hence relative, and that the knower is an intrinsic part of the process. They can examine their beliefs using structural analytical thought.

Adolescents as Experts

Adolescents who know a lot about a subject organize information more efficiently and use more abstract, high-level categories than novices. This approach allows them to use more efficient strategies when solving problems.

A form of expertise that does not involve academic learning comes from knowledge of one's culture. All adolescents are experts in their own culture. This expertise makes it easy for them to assimilate information consistent with cultural experiences, but difficult to learn material that runs counter to their experiences.

Putting Knowledge to Work

Even adolescents who are not experts can remember material more easily if they have had to put the information to some use when learning it than if they have simply memorized it. Frequently students are unable to draw on knowledge in situations in which it is potentially useful. Such information exists as inert knowledge.

Approaching learning as problem solving prompts adolescents to adopt study skills that allow them the best use of what they have learned. IDEAL is an acronym for a set of thinking skills that teaches students to identify problem areas and adopt an active approach.

Creativity

Creative adolescents are distinguished by their tolerance of ambiguity. They can remain open-minded in the face of uncertainty. They can bend the rules when they interfere with their creative approach and do not assume any rules unless they are evident. Creative adolescents are most likely to come from families with another creative individual. Their parents show high interest in their activities and set few rules governing their behavior. Humor is an important element in creative families.

Adolescent Decision Making

Adolescents' intellectual skills contribute to their sense of personal effectiveness. The control they feel in situations stems directly from their ability to predict outcomes, which involves the same types of analytic thinking used in the classroom.

Most of the intellectual skills put to use outside the classroom are directed at solving interpersonal problems. Adolescents get better at this with age.

KEY TERMS

Fantasy Stage
Tentative Stage
Realistic Stage
Growth Stage
Exploration Stage
Establishment Stage
Maintenance Stage
Decline Stage
Realistic Personality Types
Investigative Personality
  Types

Artistic Personality Types
Social Personality Types
Enterprising Personality
  Types
Conventional Personality
  Types
Inductive Reasoning
Deductive Reasoning
Structural Analytical
  Thinking

Propositional Reasoning
Dialectical Reasoning
Dualistic Thinking
Relativistic Thinking
Commitment in Relativism
Subjective Knowledge
Procedural Knowledge
Constructive Knowledge
Inert Knowledge
IDEAL

THE VALUES OF ADOLESCENTS
Values and Identity
A Developing Morality

SOCIAL-COGNITIVE THEORY
AND MORAL DEVELOPMENT
Internalizing Standards
Considering Intentions
Questioning Values
Acting Morally
Critique of Social-Cognitive Theory

KOHLBERG AND MORAL
DEVELOPMENT: MORALITY
AS JUSTICE
Preconventional Moral Reasoning
Conventional Moral Reasoning:
    Internalizing Standards
Postconventional Moral Reasoning:
    Questioning Values

RESEARCH FOCUS   Surveys: Death
of a High School Basketball Star

Critique of Kohlberg's Theory

GILLIGAN: AN ETHIC OF CARE
Level 1: Caring for Self (Survival)
Transition: From Selfishness to
    Responsibility
Level 2: Caring for Others (Goodness)
Transition: From Conformity to Choice
Level 3: Caring for Self and Others
    (Truth)
Critique of Gilligan's Theory
Comparison of Gilligan's and
    Kohlberg's Approaches

FREUD: MORALITY AND
THE SUPEREGO
Critique of Freud's Theory

ADOLESCENTS' RELIGIOUS
BELIEFS
Importance of Religion

RESEARCH FOCUS   Within-
Subjects Design: Forgiveness

SUMMARY

KEY TERMS

488

CHAPTER ELEVEN

Facing the Future: Values in Transition

White-lipped and shaking, Sarah replaced the receiver with exaggerated care, as if each movement could restore order to her world.

"So what's the word? Are you or aren't you?" asked Gina in a voice tight with urgency.

"I'm not," replied her friend.

"So, then, what's the problem?"

"I'm not sure," began Sarah, "but until now I don't think any of this has been real to me."

"You mean," interrupted Gina, "that a minute ago you weren't afraid you might be pregnant?"

"Hey, I was. I just didn't feel anything. But when I heard that the test was negative, I felt empty . . . sad . . . and happy and angry . . . all at once. It's strange. When I thought I might be pregnant, I felt nothing, but now that I know I'm not, I have all these feelings."

Gina looked at her friend with concern. "How could you have taken care of a baby?"

"I sure can't imagine myself as a mother," agreed Sarah, with a wry look on her face.

"You would've had to forget about plans for college and working with abused children."

"That's a laugh!" Sarah answered bitterly. "How can I put those two parts of myself together—the one that thought about giving the baby away or even getting an abortion, and the other that wants to help children whose parents hurt them?"

"You have a responsibility to yourself as well," offered Gina.

"Sure, but how do I balance that against my responsibility to someone else? Would it have been responsible to give the baby away if I couldn't have taken care of it properly? Or was it wrong to have even thought of it?"

"Was Eddie any help in thinking about this?" asked Gina.

"We were both too numb to think very clearly," answered Sarah. "But the few times we talked, we seemed to be discussing different problems altogether."

"I can relate to that!" snapped Gina. "At times J.J. doesn't even seem to speak the same language."

"Eddie talked about whether the fetus was a person, and whether it had the same rights that we had. It sounded so impersonal. All I could think of was whether I could take care of it and still take care of myself," Sarah replied quietly, as she broke another toothpick and absently added it to the pile in front of her.

Many adolescents find themselves face to face with problems like Sarah's and Eddie's. In this chapter, we will look at the standards adolescents use in making decisions—decisions that increasingly affect others as well as themselves. Changing roles, untrodden rights, and uncharted responsibilities create a compelling need for a system of values to guide decisions. Beliefs that have worked all through childhood come up again for review in adolescence. Many will withstand close scrutiny; others will not. All will be tested against a developing system of values as adolescents face the challenge of defining themselves.

Self-definition means that adolescents must distinguish values and beliefs that are unique to them from those they acquired from their parents. Many begin by scrutinizing their families' values to see which ones they will accept for themselves. Some adolescents forego this process and continue to live by standards set by others. The development of values is an integral part of one's identity.

What criteria distinguish moral concerns from social convention? From religious beliefs? Some developmentalists consider early experiences within the family to be pivotal to later moral development, while others stress the importance of interactions with peers. Do females and males approach moral issues differently? Are there progressions in religious development as there are in moral development? Developmentalists, as well as the families they study, frequently arrive at different answers to questions such as these. Their answers will structure our discussion of moral development.

THE VALUES OF ADOLESCENTS

The values of adolescents have changed little in the last 10 years. Most adolescents indicate that work, marriage and family, and leisure time are most important. Despite similarities in these basic values over time, adolescents have become less idealistic. Over one-quarter of high school seniors in 1972, for instance, said that correcting inequalities was very important to them, yet just one-tenth shared this belief in the mid-1980s (Youth Indicators, 1988). Figure 11.1 shows some of these trends.

Most adolescents hold attitudes that are in substantial agreement with those of their parents. Close to 90% of adolescents and their parents have similar attitudes concerning the value of an education, and nearly 75% agree with parents on big questions such as what to do with one's life. Similarly, high agreement exists con-

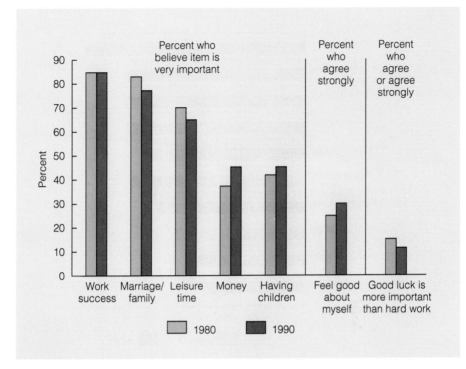

Figure 11.1   Values of Adolescents, 1980 and 1990.

Source: Youth Indicators. (1993). Trends in the well-being of American youth. *Washington, DC: U.S. Government Printing Office.*

cerning religion, racial issues, and roles of women. As Figure 11.2 shows, agreement in each of these areas between adolescents and parents has increased since the 1970s (Youth Indicators, 1993).

More similarities than differences also exist in the values held by adolescent females and males. High school seniors of both sexes consider work important, and just as many males as females value having strong friendships. Differences appear only when it comes to having children and making money: Females are more likely than males to indicate that having children is important, and males are more likely to place a higher value on having a lot of money. In other respects, the values of each are remarkably similar (Youth Indicators, 1993).

Values and Identity

Adolescents' values shape their sense of themselves. Erik Erikson believed values are an important component of our identity. A sense of identity allows us to make

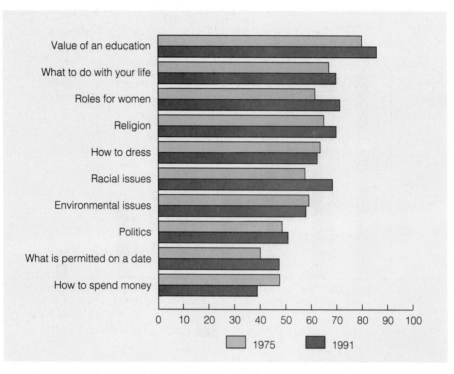

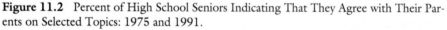

Figure 11.2   Percent of High School Seniors Indicating That They Agree with Their Parents on Selected Topics: 1975 and 1991.

Source: Youth Indicators. (1993). Trends in the well-being of American youth. *Washington, DC: U.S. Government Printing Office.*

countless daily decisions, to take ourselves for granted, as Ruthellen Josselson (1987) puts it. Like much of the way we function, our identity remains largely unavailable for inspection—until we hit a snag.

Developmental "snags" await us all. They take the form of age-related changes in the expectations that we and others hold up to ourselves. Erikson (1956, 1968) refers to these changes as psychosocial crises. Crises arise when physical maturation, together with changing personal and cultural expectations, lead individuals to re-examine their sense of who they are and what they are about. "Taking oneself for granted," because it flows from one's identity, is precisely what most adolescents find hardest to do: Most of them are continually revising their sense of themselves (see discussion of identity statuses in Chapter 8).

Prior to adolescence, the elements that contribute to identity are ascribed (Josselson, 1987). For example, children have few choices in such matters as where they live, go to school, worship, and so on. Adolescents can begin to explore possibilities that differ from those chosen by their parents. Some will continue to

The parents of today's teenagers aren't as different as their children sometimes think. The things that adolescents today say matter the most—family life, work, and friends—are essentially the same things that these 1950s adolescents also valued the most highly.

live out the patterns established by their parents. This is still a choice, although adolescents who follow this path may not be aware of making a decision as such. The decision facing *all* adolescents is whether they will decide things for themselves or live with decisions made by others. Being aware that one has choices, and considering the various possibilities, can make adolescents uncomfortably aware of themselves. Erikson considers this discomfort to be central to one's experience of crisis. By crisis he does not mean that adolescents' lives are in pieces, but simply that until identity decisions are firmly behind them, they cannot "take themselves for granted."

Because identity reflects one's values, the stance toward values taken by adolescents in each of the identity statuses described in Chapter 8 will differ.

Identity Achievement. Adolescents who have begun to discover the ways in which they differ from their families are more tolerant of differences in others than those who have not experienced a period of crisis. Openness in examining one's own

Identity-achieved and moratorium adolescents do not automatically define themselves according to convention, and they are tolerant of others who are unconventional.

beliefs goes hand in hand with accepting different beliefs in others. Perhaps because of the high value that identity-achieved adolescents place on discovering themselves, even at the risk of displeasing others, they are unwilling to hold others to conventional standards of right or wrong (Marcia, 1988).

Does this description sound too good to be true? Keep in mind that conscientious and principled behavior is not necessarily what most adults label as "good." Adolescents in search of themselves are likely to question and experiment. They may dress flamboyantly, act outrageously, and generally adopt a "show me" attitude. They may not follow in their parents' footsteps or be ready to settle down when others their age have already found their way. The positive side to this picture is that these adolescents develop a sense of who they are and translate that image into effective strategies for living, including close relationships with others. The independence they achieve reflects an internal struggle, one that frees them for change, not an external one in which they must sever ties with others.

Identity Foreclosure. Identity-foreclosed adolescents are more rule-bound and authoritarian than identity-achieved adolescents. They have a strong sense of duty and feel that others, just as they, should obey the rules. Their respect for rules and tradition is reflected in the conventional standards they hold for their own and others' behavior. These adolescents tend to be critical of those whose behavior or ideas differ from their own or who are unconventional in other ways (Josselson, 1987).

Foreclosed adolescents derive their feelings of self-esteem from the approval of others. Accordingly, the opinions of others remain important to them; these adolescents are highly sensitive to social cues concerning the appropriateness of their behavior. Actions or beliefs that might cause conflict will be rejected. Security, not independence, is their overriding concern (Marcia, 1980).

Moratorium. Moratorium adolescents, like foreclosed adolescents, seek others to complete themselves. However, instead of seeing others as sources of security, they look to them as models. Like identity-achieved adolescents, they realize that their own values are not any more "right" than those of others, but unlike identity-achieved adolescents, who experiment until they find their own way, moratorium adolescents set out on a "kind of crusade, determined to discover what is 'really right'" (Josselson, 1987). Josselson points out that theirs is an impossible quest, made all the harder because they hold back from experiences that would define them, always leaving a back door open through which to escape if they make a wrong choice. Josselson writes:

> Often, we unconsciously arrange for someone to function as a kind of savings bank. We deposit our old self in them for safekeeping, trusting them to hold it for us if we decide to come back to claim it. Many of the moratorium women spoke of this process. In describing the ways in which they thought their parents expected them to be, they were describing old selves, ways they used to be. They could, then, have the luxury of experiencing their growth as an external battle, between themselves and their parents, rather than inside themselves. In addition, they knew that their parents were holding the old selves for them, just in case they ever decided to return, which is exactly what many of them did. (1987, p. 138)

Perhaps because moratorium adolescents live with so much indecision themselves, they are tolerant of differences in others. Their ability to question, and to tolerate the uncertainty of not having all the answers, a characteristic they share with identity-achieved adolescents, allows them to transcend the thinking of the group and move beyond social convention. Adolescents who have not examined

When they were younger, these skateboarders probably enjoyed the thrill of skateboarding where they weren't supposed to if they knew they wouldn't be caught. Now, because their moral reasoning is more mature, they are more likely to limit their skateboarding to legal sites.

their values—foreclosed adolescents—are more likely to live lives of conformity and be bound by the expectations of others (Josselson, 1987; Marcia, 1980).

Identity Diffusion.   Identity-diffused adolescents, rather than confront issues head-on, tend to avoid them (Berzonsky, 1992). These adolescents are, in large measure, defined by the absence of strong commitments of their own and by their dismissal of the importance of commitment in others. Their actions, rather than reflecting beliefs or values, are likely to reflect the demands of the situation or the moment. These adolescents are neither rule-bound and authoritarian as are foreclosed adolescents nor truly tolerant as are identity-achieved and moratorium adolescents. Tolerance of differences in both of the latter implies a tension arising out of their differences that is not present in diffused adolescents, since others' ways do not conflict with clear-cut beliefs of their own.

A Developing Morality

Adolescents and children differ in important ways with respect to a developing morality. Adolescents evaluate others' actions in terms of internalized standards; children do not. Adolescents take the intentions of others into consideration; children judge actions in terms of their consequences. Adolescents can question values; children adopt a fixed standard of right and wrong. How are we to understand these developmental changes?

Answers differ, depending on who is speaking. In the sections that follow, we will consider four approaches to the development of morality: Social-cognitive theory, derived from the environmental model; Kohlberg's and Gilligan's approaches, reflecting organismic assumptions; and Freud's psychoanalytic interpretation.

SOCIAL-COGNITIVE THEORY AND MORAL DEVELOPMENT

Why do adolescents internalize the standards of their communities? Why do they become law-abiding citizens? Social-cognitive theorists look to principles of learning for explanations.

Internalizing Standards

Those who adopt the social-cognitive approach assume that rewards and punishments regulate behavior. These incentives are initially effective in young children only when other people, such as parents and teachers, are around to administer them. As children imitate adult models, they also tell themselves when they have been "good" or "bad," administering their own rewards and punishments (Mischel & Mischel, 1976).

Community standards determine which behaviors are to be rewarded and which ones punished. In learning the consequences of their behavior, children also acquire the standards of the group. These internalized controls tend to be concrete at first. Children learn specific actions and their consequences; they learn to say "thank you," for example, or not to interrupt. In time they also acquire the principles behind these actions. Being polite, for instance, can take the form of a "thank you," or considering others' feelings by not interrupting. Thus, social-cognitive theory offers an explanation for internalizing the standards of one's community.

Considering Intentions

How does social-cognitive theory explain age-related changes in moral thought? Children at first do not take the intentions of others into consideration; they judge actions in terms of their consequences. This literal focus is one of the "facts" that any theory of moral development must address. Social-cognitive theorists point out that the experiences of children make this type of reasoning likely. Adults rarely give children reasons for doing things, often simply relying on physical restraints. Because physical rewards and punishments are common with young children, they are more likely to attend to the rewards or punishments that follow what they do than to the reasons that directed their actions (Mischel & Mischel, 1976).

Parental reactions to damage and messes probably contribute to children's literal focus. Most parents become more upset over big messes than small ones, even though both can be equally unintentional. Consider a child who, keeping out of his mother's way as she fixes dinner, attempts to pour himself a glass of milk. His grip slips as he positions the milk carton, and he watches transfixed as a stream of milk sends the cup scudding, flooding the countertop with milk. Is this mother likely to comment on his thoughtfulness at not disturbing her? Probably not. This child, like most, will be scolded for making a mess. It makes sense that children fail to understand that intentions can enter into one's evaluation of a situation when their intentions are so imperfectly considered.

Questioning Values

Social-cognitive theory also explains the questioning of values that occurs in adolescence. Parents and teachers expect adolescents to start thinking for themselves, to evaluate ideas on their merit instead of accepting the endorsement of authorities. Social-cognitive theorists argue that we subtly reward adolescents for questioning the very ideas we taught them to uncritically accept as children. Similarly, learning experiences explain the relativistic form of thought that emerges in many adolescents as they near their twenties. Exposure to new values challenges them to consider their own values as one of a number of possible belief systems.

Acting Morally

How likely are adolescents to act in ways that reflect their moral understanding? It depends on the incentives. *Incentives* are the rewards and punishments for acting in particular ways. Martin Ford and his associates (1989) asked adolescents to indicate how they would respond in a situation involving conflict (e.g., giving a friend exam questions versus abiding by the school's honor code) if they could be sure that nothing bad would happen to them if they acted irresponsibly, and then to imagine what they would do if there were negative social consequences (e.g., getting grounded, peer disapproval). As expected, adolescents were considerably more likely to choose the socially responsible alternative when there would be negative consequences for not doing so; the results are shown in Figure 11.3. The emotions motivating their choice reflected both external consequences, like fear of negative

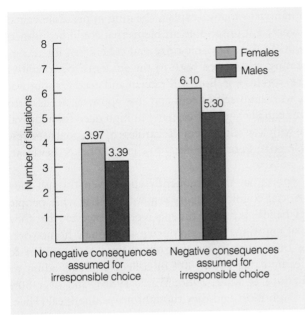

Figure 11.3 Mean Number of Situations in Which Adolescents Choose to Act Responsibly.

Source: M. E. Ford, K. R. Wentzel, D. Wood, E. Stevens, & G. A. Siesfeld. (1989). Processes associated with integrative social competence: Emotional and contextual influences on adolescent social responsibility. Journal of Adolescent Research, 4, *405–425.*

sanctions, and internalized ones, such as anticipated guilt and empathic concern. Choices were more likely to be motivated by self-interest or concern with peer approval when negative consequences were not anticipated (Ford, Wentzel, Wood, Stevens, & Siesfeld, 1989).

Factors other than incentives also affect the likelihood of action. Adolescents are more likely to imitate the actions of prestigious people than of those whom they don't regard as important. Models who are nurturant are also more likely to be imitated, perhaps because we like them more than less-nurturant people and want to be like them. Models who are similar to us in one or more ways are also likely to be imitated, again perhaps because we can imagine being like them (Mischel & Mischel, 1976).

Critique of Social-Cognitive Theory

How well does this approach explain particular forms of moral behavior? We can look at how well it explains two forms of behavior: cheating at school and shoplifting.

Cheating. Cheating in most students is motivated by the fear of failing or the need for approval. However, whether adolescents with those motives will actually cheat is influenced by situational variables such as the normative behavior of classmates, incentives either for being honest or for cheating, the amount of risk, and characteristics of models for honesty and dishonesty.

Both personality and situational variables explain cheating in preadolescents. In one experiment, students worked at unsolvable problems that could be finished only if they cheated. Some worked for a tangible prize and others just for recognition. The likelihood of cheating was related both to the students' personalities and to the incentives they were working for. Both self-esteem and need for approval predicted cheating. Students with high self-esteem and low approval needs were least likely to cheat. Those with equally high self-esteem but high need for approval were as likely to cheat as those with low self-esteem. Regardless of personal motives, students working for a tangible prize were more likely to cheat (Lobel & Levanon, 1988).

High school students report that they frequently cheat even though they consider it wrong to do so. Social-cognitive theory reminds us that what people do is not necessarily what they believe is right. Students report, however, that they engage in less-serious forms of cheating, such as copying someone's homework, more frequently than serious ones, such as cheating on exams (McLaughlen & Ross, 1989). Similarly, studies find that about 30% of college students admit to cheating on exams (Lanza-Kaduce & Klug, 1986; Ward, 1986), and over 50% admit to plagiarizing, even though most said they thought it was unethical (Hale, 1987).

Among college students, cheating becomes more likely as the school term progresses and as students become more concerned with their grades, that is, as the incentives increase (Gardner, Roper, Gonzalez, & Simpson, 1988). These same investigators found that students with low exam grades are also more likely to cheat than are those who are doing better in their courses, although not all surveys find a relationship between students' overall grade-point averages and cheating (Houston, 1986).

Situational factors, such as sheer opportunity, are also important. Gardner and his colleagues (1988) found that, on the average, students cheated on half the questions they answered when completing a study guide assignment. When allowed to correct their own midterms, not knowing that scores had already been recorded, almost 30% of another group of students cheated (Ward, 1986). Houston (1986) similarly found that conditions such as the size of the room and student-to-proctor ratios predicted amount of cheating.

Shoplifting.   Other forms of deviant behavior similarly lend themselves to explanations through social-cognitive principles. Shoplifting, for example, is more likely when conditions of unemployment and low income make incentives more desirable and when individuals believe that their need justifies their actions (Ray & Briar, 1988; Turner & Cashdan, 1988). Whether rationalizations such as need or unemployment make it possible for individuals to engage in deviant behavior without guilt appears to depend on whether they believe these motives apply to the situation at hand. Survey data regarding both cheating and shoplifting suggest that students can engage in these behaviors with less guilt if they believe there are extenuating circumstances (Agnew & Peters, 1986).

The frequency with which one engages in deviant behavior may alter one's perceptions of the deterrents that exist. A comparison of expert and novice shoplifters, for instance, found that novices are deterred by feelings of guilt, fear, and the possibility of getting caught. Experts, on the other hand, report being deterred primarily by strategic problems, such as whether an item is too big to conceal. Then again, those who engage in these activities to the point of becoming experts may experience little guilt to begin with (Weaver & Carroll, 1985).

Little mention has been made about conscience in this discussion. Social-cognitive theory suggests that many internalized controls are not necessarily related to moral values or to conscience; they simply reflect conditioning. Adolescents become helpful or law-abiding in order to avoid the anxiety they associate with doing otherwise. Conscience, when it does apply to behavior, is merely the set of standards one internalizes with the learning process (Seiber, 1980). For social-cognitive theorists, there is no inner voice other than the echo of the voices around them.

KOHLBERG AND MORAL DEVELOPMENT: MORALITY AS JUSTICE

What makes one moral? Is it simply that one internalizes the standards of one's community? Is it ever possible for individuals to function at a higher level than the society in which they live? Where does a sense of justice come from if it is not present in the social order? Lawrence Kohlberg's theory of moral reasoning addresses these questions.

Kohlberg's (1976, 1984) theory bases its assumptions about moral development on the organismic model, stressing the importance of the inner forces that organize development. The most important of these forces is a sense of justice, which underlies the highest forms of moral thought.

Kohlberg's theory traces moral reasoning over a number of discrete stages. Movement from one stage to the next is prompted by the need to resolve conflict. This conflict arises when one realizes that others view things differently. Individuals gain insight into the perspectives of others through increases in role-taking skills. As they become able to put themselves in the place of another, they can see things as that person does. Cognitive maturity—the ability to think about and balance the competing demands produced by examining several perspectives—also contributes to moral development. Kohlberg assumes that one's level of cognitive development places limits on the sophistication of moral thinking (Kohlberg, 1976, 1984).

Kohlberg traces moral development over three levels of moral reasoning, with two stages at each level. The levels reflect the stance adolescents take in relation to the standards of their community. Not all standards reflect moral issues. Some standards exist as laws, others simply as conventions or customary ways of behaving.

It is the law, for example, that one not take another person's life; it is customary that one not giggle when hearing of another's death. Both of these reflect a common value, the sacredness of life. But only when adolescents reach the postconventional level of moral reasoning do they distinguish social convention, whether codified as laws or customs, from the values these conventions reflect. And only then, according to Kohlberg, can they distinguish conventional concerns from moral ones. Box 11.1 presents Kohlberg's levels of moral development and corresponding stages of moral reasoning.

BOX 11.1

Kohlberg's Stages of Moral Reasoning

Preconventional Level of Moral Reasoning
Stage 1: Obedience
Perspective	Only one's own
Motive	To satisfy one's needs; avoid punishment
Standards	The rules of others
Criteria	Consequences

Stage 2: Instrumental
Perspective	One's own and a second person's
Motive	To satisfy one's needs and those of the other
Standards	The rules of others
Criteria	Fairness

Conventional Level of Moral Reasoning
Stage 3: Conformist, or "Good Boy, Nice Girl"
Perspective	A third person's
Motive	To receive approval from others
Standards	Internalized rules
Criteria	Living up to expectations

Stage 4: Social Accord, or "Law and Order"
Perspective	The community's
Motive	To uphold the law
Standards	Rules codified as laws
Criteria	Compliance with the law

Postconventional Level of Moral Reasoning
Stage 5: Social Contract
Perspective	Society's, as seen by someone from another society
Motive	To maintain the social order
Standards	Laws as agreements among those governed
Criteria	Justice

Stage 6: Universal Principles
Perspective	Any society's as seen by humankind
Motive	To ensure human rights for all
Standards	Personal principles
Criteria	Universal moral values

Children at the level of **preconventional moral reasoning** want only to satisfy their needs and not get punished while doing so. At this level, they have not internalized the standards of their community even though they know what these standards are. They abide by the rules only when someone else is around. The "rule enforcers," and not the rules, constrain their actions. In the absence of the former, anything goes as long as you don't get caught (Kohlberg, 1984).

By adolescence, most adopt the standards of their community and reach the level of **conventional moral reasoning.** Simply observing the behavior of individuals at the first of Kohlberg's two levels does not reveal underlying differences. Kohlberg stresses the importance of the motives behind actions, not just the actions themselves, when evaluating moral conduct. Those at the conventional level want to live up to the standards of their group, and are not motivated simply by the desire to avoid punishment. These standards have become their own; they are no longer other people's rules. In one sense, though, their behavior still lacks internal control, because the standards they live by are set by others rather than by themselves.

Only at the level of **postconventional moral reasoning** do adolescents and young adults develop genuine inner controls over behavior; the principles by which they live are self-derived standards rather than the conventions of their community. Motives, as well, reflect a sense of obligation to live within a code that is determined by one's principles. Thus, Kohlberg distinguishes levels of moral development in terms of both a progressive internalization of standards for behavior and motives for living according to these standards (Hoffman, 1980; Kohlberg, 1984).

Preconventional Moral Reasoning

Stage 1: Obedience.   Individuals at this stage (usually children) assume that everyone sees things as they do, not realizing that their view of a situation is just one of several possible perspectives. Consequently, they experience little or no conflict in their interactions with others. Their actions reflect only a need to satisfy their own desires, without getting punished for doing so. Stage 1 morality is not reflective; individuals do not take motives and intentions into consideration (they do not understand others' feelings and points of view easily). They judge behavior simply in terms of its consequences. Actions that are rewarded must have been good; those that were punished, bad. Turn to the dilemma presented in Box 11.2 before reading on, then consider how a stage 1 adolescent might respond to this situation.

What should Rachel do? Kohlberg reminds us that it is the reasoning rather than the answer itself that reveals the stage at which an adolescent is functioning. Adolescents at stage 1 might not report Elsie to the school counselor, fearing that the counselor would discover that they, too, had used drugs and that punishment would result. Conversely, they might report her, fearing that they would be punished if they didn't. There is nothing in this reasoning to indicate conflict over which course of action is *right;* decisions are based on the potential impact the actions have for oneself.

B O X   1 1 . 2

Rachel's Dilemma

> Rachel didn't know what to do. Elsie looked so whacked out she could hardly put one foot in front of the other. Was it lack of sleep? (Elsie *did* party a lot.) Or was she actually on something? They had experimented with marijuana together, and Rachel suspected that Elsie had tried other drugs. Elsie had once started to talk about her friends and the parties they went to. It sounded like they did a lot of drugs. Elsie had gotten nervous when Rachel asked her about this. She'd changed the subject, and Rachel never heard any more about it. Elsie no longer wanted to get together with Rachel and their old friends, even referring to them as "small time" once. Rachel could see even from here that Elsie's eyes looked funny, like she was having a hard time focusing, even though it was only second-period gym class. She was perspiring, too, and the air conditioning was on. Should she tell her counselor that she thought Elsie was on drugs? Elsie and she had once promised each other they would never betray their confidence about smoking marijuana. And if she reported Elsie, her parents would almost surely find out that she also had experimented with drugs. She could forget about that life-guard job this summer. They'd never let her out of their sight. Then again, drugs could kill.

Stage 2: Instrumental, or Considering Intentions.   As adolescents become better able to put themselves in the place of another person, they can see things as the other person would. Adopting the other's perspective gives them two points of view, and, in turn, the likelihood that they will experience conflict. Which perspective is right? They can understand the reasons for the other person's actions and know that the other can understand theirs—that each of them can consider the intentions of the other. Adolescents who reason at this level don't have to rely on others' reactions to evaluate behavior. They can look at the motives behind an action. Even though fairness is central to reasoning at this stage, morality is still preconventional, because adolescents consider only the actions and intentions of those they are with and not the rules or laws of the group, whether the school or community.

What would Rachel do? First consider the reasoning that would lead a stage 2 adolescent to believe Rachel should not report Elsie. This adolescent knows it's the rule to report anyone using drugs. However, Elsie and Rachel had made an agreement never to tell on each other. It's only fair for Rachel to live up to that promise. Besides, if she reported Elsie, she'd almost surely get caught herself. Best to let everyone take care of themselves in this case. The reasoning that might lead an adolescent to say that Rachel should report Elsie is similarly self-serving. Rachel might be rewarded in some way for reporting her friend; even if the authorities found out that she, too, had experimented with drugs, they would not punish her as severely as if she didn't indicate her respect for the rules by reporting those who she knew were breaking them.

Conventional Moral Reasoning: Internalizing Standards

Stage 3: Conformist, or "Good Boy, Nice Girl." The self-reflection that comes with formal thought makes it possible for adolescents to see themselves as they imagine others would. This third-person perspective forms the basis for taking the norms of their group, in the form of concern with what others think of them, into consideration, and here adolescents move into conventional reasoning. This concern about the opinions of others adds a new dimension to morality: the need to live up to the expectations of others. Kohlberg believes that stage 3 reasoning is dominant during adolescence, and even common in adulthood (Kohlberg, 1984). The prevalence of stage 3 reasoning helps to explain adolescents' sensitivity to the approval of peers. Rather than thinking through a situation in terms of the claims of those involved, adolescents are likely to be swayed by the opinions of their friends.

How would stage 3 adolescents reason about Rachel's dilemma? Reasoning that leads to not reporting Elsie would focus on loyalty among friends—how would she look turning in a friend? Reasoning that leads to reporting her would focus on what her teachers and parents would think of her for *not* reporting Elsie. The decision turns on which reference group the adolescent considers: that of friends and peers, or that of teachers and parents.

Stage 4: Social Accord, or "Law and Order." As the ability to think more abstractly increases, adolescents begin to see themselves as members of an invisible but nonetheless real community. As such, they realize the need to evaluate actions by the community's standards. Kohlberg believes that reasoning at the fourth stage is frequently the highest that most people reach.

Rachel's dilemma takes on new proportions for adolescents at stage 4. On the one hand, friendship demands that she not betray Elsie to the authorities; her duty is to be loyal to her friend. On the other hand, Rachel has a duty to live within the law and to see that others do as well. After all, if everyone "did their own thing," the system would break down. Stage 4 reasoning is usually adequate for most situations. It breaks down, however, when laws conflict with human values. When this occurs, adolescents must develop a way to see their society in relation to the needs of others.

Postconventional Moral Reasoning: Questioning Values

Stage 5: Social Contract. Kohlberg believes that adolescents move into stage 5 only when they have been exposed to other value systems, usually in late adolescence. Individuals who come to respect others' ways of life find it difficult to continue seeing their own as more valid. Once adolescents recognize that their society's

RESEARCH FOCUS

Surveys: Death of a High School Basketball Star

Research is simply one way of answering a question. "What would happen if . . . ?" or "Why did this occur?" Some questions are prompted by developmental theory; others arise spontaneously from observations of the everyday world. The study that follows illustrates the interplay of both theory and observation.

A developmentalist noticed that a better-than-average basketball team in a small rural community had lost all of its games the season after its star player died of leukemia. Did the team's performance reflect the disruption caused by grief over the loss of a valued player and teammate? More generally, is grief especially difficult for adolescents? More so than for adults or children? How does the experience of grief relate to the developmental issues adolescents face?

One model of grieving proposes that in coping with loss, adolescents face many of the same issues they normally face in meeting the developmental tasks of their age group (Fleming & Adolph, 1986). Early adolescents face the task of emotionally separating from parents. Death also confronts

them with separation. Middle adolescents face issues of competence, mastery, and control, yet death is an event over which they, or anyone else, have little control. Late adolescents face the twin tasks of intimacy and commitment. These issues, like earlier ones, are compounded by the loss of someone with whom they have been close. How do adolescents react to the death of a friend? Might we anticipate the intensity of their reactions by knowing something about the conflicts they ordinarily experience? Would doing so place professionals and those who care in a better position to help?

To answer these and similar questions, Joan McNeil, Benjamin Silliman, and Judson Swihart (1991) surveyed reactions of students to their peer's death. *Surveys* obtain information from large numbers of people through either interviews or questionnaires. In either case, survey information relies on subjects' personal reports. The use of personal reports has its strengths and weaknesses. A major strength of this approach is the chance it offers to study behavior that cannot easily be observed. Because grief is often a very private emo-

(continued)

conventions are in some sense arbitrary, they are forced to look beyond the conventions themselves to the function they serve. When they do, they discover that laws derive their importance because they represent agreements among people who live together, not because they are "right" in and of themselves. Members of a society enter into a contract with others in the society in which they agree to live within its laws, foregoing some individual freedoms, for the mutual benefit of all.

Stage 5 adolescents might reason that Rachel should not report Elsie because the way she has chosen to live her life reflects her values, and values are relative. They might add that Rachel is obliged to act in a way that protects each person's rights, including Elsie's, and might remind us that Rachel and Elsie had entered into a contractual agreement concerning their use of drugs. Reasons for reporting Elsie would stress that, as members of society, Rachel and Elsie have implicitly agreed to keep the laws of their community and that these laws must be upheld for the greater good of all.

R E S E A R C H   F O C U S (*continued*)

tion, most of our information relies on self-report data. A weakness to relying on individuals' reports is the opportunity for distortion, either by deliberately changing information (as might occur in surveys on drug use among adolescents) or by failing to remember events as they really happened. Our memories are notably better for pleasant events or occasions in which we come off looking good.

These researchers developed both *closed and open-ended questions.* The first provide alternative answers from which students can choose. For example, "The death of Tom affected me: (a) Not at all; (b) Somewhat; (c) Quite a bit; (d) Very much." The second leaves the form of the answer open to the respondent: "How were you affected by the death of Tom?" The first type of question is easier to score, but the second type is helpful in generating ideas.

How did the death of this student affect his peers? Even though most students knew he had leukemia, many reacted to the news of his death with shock and anger. Questionnaire items distinguished the reactions of close and more distant friends. Close friends thought about death more

frequently, had more difficulty talking about death, and indicated their lives had been changed in some way. However, all students indicated some difficulty in coping with the death. These investigators observed:

> Acceptance of death was most difficult for this group, perhaps because beyond the loss of friendship was a profound sense of vulnerability and mortality. In a familiar paradox, great difficulty handling death predicted greater attitude change, mostly in increased reverence for life and compassion toward others. Even some "distant" acquaintances were brought face-to-face with the inevitable limitations of life at a developmental stage when death is usually held at arm's length. (McNeil, Silliman, & Swihart, 1991, p. 142)

References: J. N. McNeil, B. Silliman, & J. J. Swihart. (1991). Helping adolescents cope with the death of a peer: A high school case study. Journal of Adolescent Research, 6, 132–145. S. J. Fleming & R. Adolph. (1986). Helping bereaved adolescents: Needs and responses. In C. A. Corr & J. N. McNeil (Eds.), Adolescence and death. New York: Springer, pp. 97–118.

Stage 6: Universal Principles.   This stage provides adolescents with yet another perspective: seeing past the mutual agreements shared by members of a society to the values these agreements reflect. The social contracts we enter into reflect underlying values such as truth, justice, honor, and the value of life itself. The step that adolescents take in order to gain a perspective on their society removes them from the claims of time and circumstance. Kohlberg asserts that all societies throughout history have recognized these values—that they are, in fact, universal ethical principles. Those who reason at this final stage understand that societal conventions are imperfect reflections of these values and, consequently, individuals must look beyond conventions, and even laws, to their own principles when arriving at moral decisions (Kohlberg, 1984).

Why might Rachel not report Elsie to the counselor? Stage 6 reasoning stresses the honor among friends that would require Rachel to keep her word with Elsie. Conversely, those who reason that Rachel should report Elsie would be likely

In the course of moral development, adolescents come to see themselves not only as members of the community but also as able to challenge community decisions that they feel are wrong. These high school students are attending a school board meeting to protest the dropping of a class.

to mention the value of Elsie's life, which is threatened by her use of drugs. They might add that even if they were in Elsie's place, they would expect to be turned in by anyone else who opposes the use of life-threatening drugs. This last reason illustrates a point that Kohlberg makes about stage 6 individuals. He describes them as able to imagine themselves in the place of every other person in a situation and to impartially evaluate the rights of each. The image of the stage 6 person is that of the blindfolded figure of Justice who weighs the claims of each without knowing which person has made which claim. This ability is truly an idealized form of role-taking, and very few people function at this level (Kohlberg, 1984).

Critique of Kohlberg's Theory

Kuhn, Langer, Kohlberg, and Haan (1977) report clear developmental trends in moral reasoning. Preconventional reasoning decreases with age, and the use of higher levels increases. These investigators found that movement to higher stages depends on reaching a level of cognitive development that will support higher forms of moral thought. Thus, concrete operational thought is associated with conventional reasoning, and formal operational thought is necessary for postconventional reasoning. Even so, formal thought is not a guarantee that one will reach Kohlberg's highest levels. In one sample of 256 people, over three-quarters showed some formal thought, but less than one-quarter reasoned at a principled level. These data suggest, as Kohlberg asserts, that one's general reasoning ability will set a limit to one's level of moral reasoning (Kuhn, Langer, Kohlberg, & Haan, 1977).

Do most adolescents and adults reason at stages 3 and 4, as Kohlberg asserts? J. R. Snarey (1985) reviewed nearly 50 studies that had used Kohlberg's scale, and found that 75% of the individuals who were interviewed reasoned entirely at the conventional level or at a combination of conventional and preconventional levels. Less than 10% functioned at higher levels. Similarly, Schweder, Mahapatra, and Miller (1987) reported that only 15% of the children and adults they interviewed treated conventional rules (such as those governing table manners or forms of greeting) as if they could be changed. These data suggest that most people do not distinguish moral issues from social conventions.

Joan Miller and David Bersoff (1989) of Yale University question this conclusion. They find that adults and children alike consider the usefulness of social conventions before deciding whether they could be changed. Nearly 80% thought it wrong to violate conventions that are useful (those that maintain order, such as using properly marked exits), but less than 15% felt it wrong to violate ones with little usefulness (such as standards of dress). Rules with little utility were accepted only for private settings. Violating the same restrictions in a public setting was not considered wrong, whereas violating a moral rule was considered wrong irrespective of the setting—and by individuals of all ages (Miller & Bersoff, 1989).

Both morals and conventions set forth rules for behavior; however, each relates rules to behavior in different ways. Elliot Turiel (1983), a psychologist at the University of California, Berkeley, maintains that even very young children distinguish moral rules from conventional ones. Conventional rules reflect accepted ways of doing things. As these change, so do the rules. Standards of dress and speech reflect these flexible relationships. The rules relating moral concerns to behavior are inflexible. Moral rules reflect a concern for the well-being of others and do not change with climates of opinion.

Turiel interviewed preschoolers and found 80% agreement that it would be all right to engage in certain conventional actions if there were no rules against them (e.g., wear socks that don't match, call the teacher by her first name). Nearly 90% of the same children said that moral issues, such as hurting another child or taking something that wasn't theirs, would not be all right even without any rules against such behaviors (Nucci & Turiel, 1978).

Similarly, Tisak and Turiel (1988) found that first-graders regarded transgressions of conventional rules to be less important than moral ones. Asked to predict whether a classmate would choose a highly unconventional behavior (wearing pajamas to school) or a minor moral one (stealing an eraser) as punishment for losing a bet, these children guessed their peers would steal the eraser, but agreed that they *should* come to school in pajamas. These data indicate that even young children distinguish moral from conventional concerns; Kohlberg assumes that one makes this distinction only with the fifth stage of reasoning.

If even the youngest children can distinguish moral issues, how can we explain the developmental progression that Kohlberg has noted? Martin Hoffman (1980) answers that we socialize children in either of two very different ways. One way stresses being obedient and following the rules; the other emphasizes altruism and a concern for others. Hoffman points out that it is possible for young children to comply with both sets of demands because the behaviors called for by either usually apply in different settings. However, older children frequently experience conflict between the demands for living by the rules and their prosocial concerns. Hoffman suggests that the emergence of truly moral concerns in adolescence is actually a resurgence of earlier prosocial ones that had been channeled into conventional behavior in middle childhood in the course of acquiring society's norms (Hoffman, 1980; 1988.)

Kohlberg's theory, despite the debate it has occasioned, enjoys wide support. His theory has an intrinsic elegance. Each of the six stages is a logical extension of the preceding one, and the progression is systematically related to new role-taking skills and cognitive maturity. But there may be another reason to account for the popularity of this theory. Kohlberg has given us a sympathetic view of human nature. He accounts for our ability to control our behavior in terms of the development of an inner sense of justice, rather than the "carrot and stick" approach of social-cognitive theory.

Carol Gilligan questions whether justice is the highest arbiter of moral issues. She finds that an ethic of care, rather than a morality of justice, is more characteristic of females. She points out that Kohlberg developed his theory based on interviews with only males. Like many developmentalists before him, Kohlberg equated the male perspective with development in general (see Chapter 2).

GILLIGAN: AN ETHIC OF CARE

Carol Gilligan (1982, 1988a, 1988b, 1989a, 1989b), of Harvard University, gives a fresh perspective on moral development, one that balances male-oriented theories such as Kohlberg's and Freud's with insights gained from interviews with females. Gilligan finds that most females think of morality more personally than males do; they adopt an **ethic of care**. They speak of morality in terms of their responsibilities to others rather than as the rights of individuals. Their moral decisions are based on compassion as well as reason, and they stress care for others as well as fairness.

Gilligan traces these approaches to differences in the way females and males define themselves in relation to others. While males tend to view themselves as separate from others, females see themselves in terms of their relationships with others. These themes of separation and connectedness translate into different approaches to morality. The assumption that one is separate from others highlights the need for rules to regulate the actions of each person with respect to the other; the assumption that one is connected to others emphasizes the responsibility each has to the other (Gilligan, 1982).

Gender differences also exist in the way individuals think of responsibility (see Chapter 2). Males tend to think of responsibility as *not* doing something that would infringe on the rights of others, such as not hurting them. Females think of responsibility in terms of *meeting* the needs of others, that is, as something to be done. Both males and females are concerned with not hurting others, yet each sex thinks of this in a different way. Gilligan points out that, given differences such as these, attempts to chart moral development as a single sequence are bound to give us only half the picture.

Gilligan traces moral development in females through three levels, each of which reflects a different resolution to the conflict between responsibility to self and responsibility to others. Movement from one level to the next occurs in two transitional periods. At the first level, the primary concern is with oneself. Transition to the next level occurs when one sees caring only for oneself as selfish and at odds with responsibility to others. At the second level, females equate morality with goodness and self-sacrifice—caring for others. Transition to the third level occurs when they experience problems in their relationships that result from excluding themselves from their own care. At the third level, they equate morality with care for both themselves and others.

Level 1: Caring for Self (Survival)

The primary concerns at this level of moral development are pragmatic: What's best for me? The motivation is survival. Actions are guided by self-interest and self-preservation. Gilligan says of this perspective that "the woman focuses on taking care of herself because she feels that she is all alone. From this perspective, *should* is undifferentiated from *would*, and other people influence the decision only through their power to affect its consequences" (Gilligan, 1982, p. 75). Gilligan notes that the issue of "rightness" is considered only when one's own needs are in conflict and force the individual to consider which need is more important. Otherwise there is little conflict over making the "right" decision.

Why might individuals function at this level? Gilligan believes that a preoccupation with one's needs reflects feelings of helplessness and powerlessness. These feelings have their origin in being emotionally cut off, or *disconnected*, from others. The young women she interviewed who were at this level had frequently experienced disappointing relationships in which they had been hurt by others. These women often chose to hold themselves apart from others rather than experience further pain. Feeling alone and cut off from others, they were left with the sense that they had to look to their own needs, since no one else would (Gilligan, 1982).

This first level is similar to Kohlberg's preconventional level of moral reasoning. In neither level do individuals consider others except for their possible reactions to what they do, that is, except as potential consequences for their actions. Conflict is also absent in both levels and self-interest rather than the need to make the "right" decision, dictates what one does.

Because females define themselves in relation to others and males define themselves as separate from others, the course of their moral development is different, according to the research of psychologist Carol Gilligan.

Transition: From Selfishness to Responsibility

Individuals begin to move beyond the first level when they experience a discrepancy between the way they are and the way they feel they ought to be, that is, between self-concern and responsible concern for others. A certain amount of self-worth is needed in order to move through this transitional phase. One must feel sufficiently good about oneself in order to see oneself as having the capacity for good and to be included in the social group (Gilligan, 1982).

Level 2: Caring for Others (Goodness)

Gilligan assumes that females move to a second level of moral development when they internalize social conventions. The progression is similar to that described by Kohlberg for movement from preconventional to conventional reasoning. Gilligan notes that in the first level,

> morality is a matter of sanctions imposed by a society of which one is more subject than citizen, [and in the second] moral judgment relies on shared norms and expectations. The woman at this point validates her claim to social membership through the

adoption of societal values. Consensual judgment about goodness becomes the overriding concern as survival is now seen to depend on acceptance by others. (1982, p. 79)

Transition: From Conformity to Choice

The equation of morality with conventional feminine goodness is a step toward repairing the failed relationships that led to a preoccupation with the self at the first level. But this equation creates a second imbalance that itself is in need of repair. Conventional images of feminine goodness center around the care of others. They also involve self-sacrifice. Females at the second level of morality purchase membership in the larger community at the cost of caring for themselves. The price of membership is costly and introduces tensions that, for some, will prompt movement to the third level. These individuals realize that excluding themselves from their own care creates as many problems as excluding others had done previously; in other words, goodness results in as much hurt as selfishness (Gilligan, 1986). This realization is an important step in moving to an ethic of care that includes themselves as well as others. Gilligan, like Kohlberg before her, believes that many females do not take this step and do not develop beyond conventional forms of thought.

Level 3: Caring for Self and Others (Truth)

To move into the third level, females must move beyond the conventional wisdom that tells them to put the needs of others above their own. In doing so, they must reformulate their definition of care to include themselves as well as others. As females reconsider their relationships with others, they once again must consider their own needs. Questions such as, "Is this selfish?" again arise. Because these occur in the context of relationships with others, they also prompt a re-examination of the concept of responsibility.

When one moves beyond conventional forms of wisdom, one finds there is no one to turn to for answers but oneself. Females at this level cannot rely on what others might think; they must exercise their own judgment. This judgment requires that they be honest with themselves. Being responsible for themselves, as well as for others, means they must know what their needs actually are. As Gilligan asserts, "The criterion for judgment thus shifts from goodness to truth when the morality of action is assessed not on the basis of its appearance in the eyes of others, but in terms of the realities of its intention and consequence" (Gilligan, 1982, p. 83). The bottom line is simple: To care for oneself, one must first be honest with oneself and acknowledge the reasons behind one's actions.

Individuals at this level adopt an inclusive perspective that gives equal weight to their responsibility to themselves and to others. Care extends to all. To exclude the self would introduce pain that could otherwise be avoided, and their commitment to minimizing pain requires a new balance of concern for self with responsibility for others.

Although Gilligan and Kohlberg document developmental sequences that parallel each other in many respects, a critical difference separates these two accounts. Kohlberg believes that his sequence is a path universally trodden by all individuals as they move into adulthood. He assumes that this sequence takes the form it does because it reflects developments in cognitive maturity that have a strong biological component (see the discussion of Piaget in Chapter 2). Gilligan is not equally convinced that the sequence she documents in adolescent girls and young women is developmentally necessary. She does not believe the sequence to be "rooted in childhood," as does Kohlberg. She suggests, instead, that it is a response to a crisis, and that the crisis is adolescence itself (Gilligan, 1989a).

Gilligan proposes that leaving childhood is problematic for girls in ways that it is not for boys. The problem lies with the culture each enters. Adolescence introduces the expectation that children will assume the conventions of their society, whether these be adult gender roles, the knowledge that forms the basis of cultural wisdom, or behaviors that fit prescribed definitions of "goodness" and "rightness." Why should this expectation present more problems for girls?

Gilligan's answer is powerful. The most visible figures populating the landscape of adulthood are males—whether plumbers, politicians, poets, or philosophers—and their collective experiences form its norms. Girls risk losing themselves as they relax the intimate bonds of childhood to embrace a larger world of experience. Gilligan writes:

> As the river of a girl's life flows into the sea of Western culture, she is in danger of drowning or disappearing. To take on the problem of her appearance, which is the problem of her development, and to connect her life with history on a cultural scale, she must enter—and by entering disrupt—a tradition in which "human" has for the most part meant male. Thus a struggle often breaks out in girls' lives at the edge of adolescence. (1989b, p. 4)

The problem is pervasive because it is woven into the very fabric of cultural thought. Even formal education, Gilligan suggests, presents a challenge to female identity: "In learning to think in the terms of the disciplines and thus to bring her thoughts and feelings into line with the traditions of Western culture, . . . she also learn[s] to dismiss her own experience" (Gilligan, 1989b, p. 2).

Gilligan traces the crisis of connection for girls to their ability to find a "voice" with which to speak and a context in which they will be heard. The culture they are entering has not been equally responsive to the voices of women and men, "or at least has not been up to the present. The wind of tradition blowing through women is a chill wind, because it brings a message of exclusion. . . . The message to women is: keep quiet and notice the absence of women and say nothing" (Gilligan, 1989a, p. 26).

Critique of Gilligan's Theory

What evidence is there for gender differences in moral concerns? D. Kay Johnston (1988) asked 11- and 15-year-olds to generate solutions to two of Aesop's fables involving moral issues. Specifically, she wanted to know whether gender differences exist in the spontaneous use of justice and care orientations, and whether both orientations are available to adolescents of each sex. The two fables appear in Box 11.3, along with characteristic modes of solution by male and female adolescents. We see from this material that gender is related to moral orientation. Boys were much more likely to spontaneously adopt a justice than a care approach to both of the fables. Girls, however, were fairly evenly divided in their adoption of either approach. Judgments about the "best" solution showed that boys still strongly preferred (3:1) a justice solution to one of the fables; girls strongly favored a care solution as "best" to both of the fables.

These findings are interesting because they show, in addition to the expected gender difference, that each type of moral solution is available to adolescents of either sex. Gender differences in moral solutions take the form of choosing one approach over another, rather than thinking of only one type of solution. We see also that males as a group tend to rely more on the justice orientation, and that females are likely to adopt either a justice or a care approach. Johnston suggests that females can shift perspectives more easily than boys. In learning the socially

Young people, male and female, with a justice orientation are more likely to protest inadequate funding for AIDS research, while those with a care orientation are more likely to express their concern by providing a helping hand to people with AIDS.

BOX 11.3

Two Moral Orientations to Fable Dilemmas

The Porcupine and the Moles

It was growing cold, and a porcupine was looking for a home. He found a most desirable cave but saw it was occupied by a family of moles.

"Would you mind if I shared your home for the winter?" the porcupine asked the moles.

The generous moles consented and the porcupine moved in. But the cave was small and every time the moles moved around they were scratched by the porcupine's sharp quills. The moles endured this discomfort as long as they could. Then at last they gathered courage to approach their visitor. "Pray leave," they said, "and let us have our cave to ourselves once again."

"Oh no!" said the porcupine. "This place suits me very well."

The Dog in the Manger

A dog, looking for a comfortable place to nap, came upon the empty stall of an ox. There it was quiet and cool and the hay was soft. The dog, who was very tired, curled up on the hay and was soon fast asleep.

A few hours later the ox lumbered in from the fields. He had worked hard and was looking forward to his dinner of hay. His heavy steps woke the dog who jumped up in a great temper. As the ox came near the stall the dog snapped angrily, as if to bite him. Again and again the ox tried to reach his food, but each time he tried the dog stopped him.

Examples of Care Orientation
- Wrap the porcupine in a towel.
- If there's enough hay, split it.

valued moral perspective, justice, they have acquired a second perspective in addition to their own. Since the perspective voiced by society is the one boys tend to spontaneously use, boys are less likely to develop a second approach. Johnston suggests that the flexibility evidenced by these adolescent girls might characterize any minority to the extent that individuals must approach social situations from both the dominant and the minority perspective.

Gilligan and Attanucci (1988) found similar evidence for both perspectives among a sample of college-age adults. They compared the reactions of females and males to a hypothetical situation in which they had to decide whether to report someone who had violated a school rule (involving drinking in medical school). Twice as many of the males as females adopted a justice orientation; of those voicing a care orientation, all were female. Gilligan and Attanucci conclude that while a care orientation is not necessarily the approach adopted by all females, it is more

B O X   1 1 . 3 (*continued*)

Two Moral Orientations to Fable Dilemmas

Examples of Justice Orientation
- The porcupine has to go. It's the mole's house.
- It's a question of ownership and nobody else has the right to it.

Solutions

	Porcupine/Moles			
	Spontaneous		Best	
	Female	Male	Female	Male
Justice	15	21	6	17
Care	10	7	18	5
Both	5	1	5	6
Uncodable	0	1	1	2

	Dog in Manger			
	Spontaneous		Best	
	Female	Male	Female	Male
Justice	12	22	3	13
Care	15	5	24	13
Both	3	1	3	3

Source: D. K. Johnston. (1988). Adolescents' solutions to dilemmas in fables: Two moral orientations—two problem solving strategies. In C. Gilligan, J. V. Ward, & J. M. Taylor. (Eds.), Mapping the moral domain. *Cambridge, MA: Harvard University Press.*

characteristic of women than men. They also point out that concerns about both justice and care are common to individuals of either sex. However, because people tend to focus a problem one way or the other, they lose one perspective as they employ the other to frame the relevant issues.

When individuals are asked to describe moral dilemmas they have experienced in their own lives and indicate the extent to which they have adopted justice or care resolutions, females again are more likely to adopt a care orientation and males to use a justice orientation in resolving personal dilemmas (Ford & Lowery, 1986). Is this because more of the females' dilemmas involve actual issues of care, that is, because they are relationship dilemmas? A content analysis revealed no differences in the types of dilemmas reported by either sex. This finding adds support to Gilligan's contention that females are more likely to see relationship issues in moral dilemmas than are males.

Comparison of Gilligan's and Kohlberg's Approaches

Some dilemmas may yield themselves more easily than others to a care perspective. Many of Kohlberg's dilemmas, for instance, are relatively impersonal. Onlookers are asked to think about courses of action that might be taken by people they have never met. Is reasoning under such conditions more likely to be abstract and to stress justice rather than care for others? Lonky, Roodin, and Rybasch (1988) compared the reasoning of people who were asked to respond to dilemmas from the position of someone actually experiencing the dilemma versus those who read about a dilemma as experienced by someone else. They found that when people are asked to imagine the dilemma as their own, they are more likely to adopt a care orientation. Evaluating dilemmas as experienced by someone else favors the adoption of a justice orientation. These data suggest that both orientations are available to each sex, and that which guides reasoning will depend on how the situation is presented.

Gilligan views the developmental sequence which she catalogs as complementing that of Kohlberg's, not as an alternative (Gilligan & Attanucci, 1988). She points out, however, that the care orientation would have been missed had she and others not studied females as systematically as Kohlberg studied males.

Lawrence Walker (1984), after reviewing numerous studies of moral reasoning, concludes that there are more similarities than differences in the reasoning of females and males on Kohlberg's measures. When differences do emerge, they tend to favor males at each of his developmental levels except the first. Although Walker's conclusion that there are no significant gender differences is statistically correct, it is misleading to dismiss the differences that exist as unimportant. Given that Kohlberg's model is a developmental one, the finding that gender differences favor males at older ages, presumably as development progresses, but not at the earliest ages, suggests that when differences occur they reflect differences in the maturity of moral thought, and that males are more likely than females to evidence greater maturity. It is Gilligan's and others' contention (Baumrind, 1986; Gilligan and Attanucci, 1988) that differences associated with gender reflect other factors, such as level of education, working status, and the insensitivity of Kohlberg's measure to moral issues as they are defined by females.

FREUD: MORALITY AND THE SUPEREGO

Freud's theory of moral development derives from his more general theory of personality development. Like other psychoanalytic theorists, Freud looked to sources within the organism to explain developmental changes. He assumed that the strong biological forces he identified must be balanced by equally strong social constraints that develop only with age.

Freud believed that responsibility for moral behavior resides with the **super-ego**, the last of the three facets of the personality to develop (see Chapter 2). The superego embraces the cultural standards of right and wrong that make up the **conscience**. Prior to the development of the conscience (at about age 5), Freud assumed that children are governed only by the desire to win parental affections and the fear of being rejected for wrongdoing. Like social-cognitive theorists and Kohlberg, Freud believed that an internalized code or ethic is not present in early childhood.

Freud (1961) assumed that the libido—the life force within each individual—seeks genital expression in childhood, and that the object of the child's sexual desires is the very person who is closest in so many other ways. For the boy, this person is the mother; for the girl, the father. Sexual desire for the parent of the opposite sex makes the parent of the same sex a rival. The emotional triangle that results creates unbearable anxiety in the child. Freud believed that children repress their sexual desires to reduce the anxiety they experience, and identify with the same-sex parent. **Identification** is the process by which the child internalizes or appropriates the values and behaviors of the parent. These values form the superego and serve as the basis for an internalized set of standards for behavior.

Freud assumed the situation differed for male and female children. Freud reasoned that girls are not as motivated as boys to resolve Oedipal tensions, because they have already suffered an incalculable loss: They were not born with a penis. Rather than fearing castration (castration anxiety), they long for a penis (penis envy). Since girls literally have less to lose than boys, they do not experience the same anxiety that motivates boys to identify with the same-sex parent. Also, the figure with whom the girl identifies, the mother, is not as powerful or threatening as the father. As a consequence, Freud believed that girls' superegos are not as strong or as demanding as those of boys.

The final step in moral development occurs in adolescence when puberty threatens the surface tranquility achieved through repression and identification. New sexual desires assail the fragile bulwark the child has erected against Oedipal turmoil. Freud assumed that adolescents' only defense against the onslaught of their own sexuality, and the incestuous threat this poses, is to emotionally distance themselves from their parents. In doing so, they have to toss out the parental figures they had internalized in childhood. Adolescence becomes a time for reworking the parental standards that have been uncritically accepted as part of these figures (Josselson, 1980, 1987).

Critique of Freud's Theory

Freud's theory of personality development and his assumptions about moral development are widely accepted. His theory continues to influence vast numbers of clinical practitioners and is taught in college courses around the world. Many of his concepts—such as the unconscious, projection, and repression—have entered the popular vocabulary. Nevertheless, the bulk of support for this theory comes from clinical evidence based on small numbers of individuals and is often heavily interpreted (Hoffman, 1980).

Carol Tavris and Carole Wade (1984) point to the absence of systematic, objective support for Freud's twin concepts of castration anxiety and penis envy, concepts that are central to his explanation of moral development in males and females, respectively. Regarding the concept of penis envy, they note that women as well as men value the male role more highly, but point out that males have enjoyed more power, greater opportunities, and more privileges than women. Do women envy men for their penis? Or do they desire the social advantages that go with having one?

Freud believed that the absence of castration anxiety in females and the presence, in its stead, of penis envy resulted in a weaker superego in females and differences in their moral behavior. Freud wrote:

> I cannot evade the notion (though I hesitate to give it expression) that for women the level of what is ethically normal is different from what it is in men. Their superego is never so inexorable, so impersonal, so independent of its emotional origins as we require it to be in men. Character traits which critics of every epoch have brought up against women—that they show less sense of justice than men, that they are less ready to submit it to the great exigencies of life, that they are more often influenced in their judgment by feelings of affection or hostility—all these would be amply accounted for by the modification in the formation of their super-ego which we have inferred. (1961, pp. 257–258)

These assumptions concerning the basis for gender differences in moral behavior have not received empirical support. Research on the internalization of moral standards does not find males to have stronger superegos than females. Nor do differences in behavior, when they occur, favor males. They are, if anything, as likely to favor females (Ford et al., 1989; Lobel & Levanon, 1988; see Hoffman, 1980, for a review).

Research has similarly failed to support any other of Freud's assumptions related to the development of morality. For instance, adolescence is not a period of emotional turmoil for most teenagers. Also, large surveys of normal adolescents do not find they are preoccupied with sex or with controlling their impulses. Nor do most adolescents have weak egos, nor have they cut emotional ties with their parents (see Chapter 5).

Internalizing Standards.   How does Freud explain the facts that other theories of moral development have addressed? Like social-cognitive theorists (as well as Kohlberg and Gilligan for conventional standards of morality), Freud assumes that individuals acquire their values and their sense of right and wrong by internalizing society's norms. The conditions that prompt children to internalize parental standards differ for each theory, however. Freud traces internalization to resolution of the Oedipal complex and identification with the parent of the same sex. Social-cognitive theory speaks of the child's ability to reinforce itself, rather than having to receive praise or punishment at the hands of others. Both theories must address the central problem with internalization as an explanation for moral conduct: If one's culture is the ultimate source of moral authority in an individual's life, how does a person ever reach a level higher than that which characterizes the society? Gilligan and Kohlberg both view the internalization of social conventions as an intermediate step in moral development. Gilligan believes that females take this step when they experience a discrepancy between their self-concern and concern for others. Kohlberg traces this step to increases in cognitive maturity.

Considering Intentions. For Freud, the emergence of the superego explains the child's shift from evaluating behavior in terms of its consequences to the motives that underlie it. Social-cognitive theorists, in contrast, explain this shift in terms of the social-learning experiences of the child, but frequently fail to take into consideration the child's own motives and intentions, or the expectation that adolescents will begin to think for themselves. Kohlberg attributes this shift to new levels of cognitive maturity and role-taking skills. Gilligan's analysis of morality begins with individuals who have already made this transition.

Questioning Values. And how, finally, might Freud explain the flexibility that characterizes the moral thought that develops in some with late adolescence? Rather than refer to changing social expectations, increasing cognitive maturity, or the need to repair relationships, psychoanalytic thought attributes flexibility in moral judgments to the work of the ego in balancing the demands of the id and superego. Individuals who remain relatively inflexible are those dominated by a threatening superego. The ability to evaluate a situation, to develop coping strategies, and to delay gratification of one's impulses are all functions of the ego and characterize mature moral functioning.

ADOLESCENTS' RELIGIOUS BELIEFS

Do adolescents think of God the same way children do? Or do the intellectual developments that occur in adolescence affect their views of God and religion just as they affect their views of so many other things? James Fowler (1976, 1981) suggests that they do. He identifies stages of religious belief that parallel the stages of moral development discussed earlier.

Children's views of God reflect the concrete nature of the way they think in general. To them, God is someone with a human form who sits celestially enthroned above them. They accept the teachings and stories of their religion literally and do not question them, other than to try to fit them into their current ways of understanding: "How can God be everywhere at the same time?" (Fowler, 1981).

In a few years, because cognitive development affects all aspects of life, this adolescent may start to question some of the religious beliefs she accepts today.

The ability to think abstractly that comes with adolescence also transforms their religious beliefs. More abstract qualities of God can be appreciated, such as righteousness, compassion, and mercy. Just as adolescents begin to question other sources of authority in their lives, they begin to question religious beliefs. "If God is all-powerful, why is there suffering and evil in the world?" The answers adolescents arrive at reflect an increasingly personalized faith much as Kohlberg's final stages of postconventional morality reflect commitment to personally arrived at principles (Fowler, 1981).

Even so, religious beliefs reflect more than adolescents' ability to think in certain ways. The processes of exploration and commitment that are central to identity formation also contribute to differences in religiosity. The ability to think abstractly may make it possible for adolescents to entertain questions such as why God would tolerate suffering, but having the ability is not enough in itself to determine that they will.

The same willingness to consider the unfamiliar, whether in terms of a career or a lifestyle, is also at the heart of religiosity. Will adolescents give themselves the freedom to *think* about their religion? Some will, others will not. Adolescents can remain committed to traditional religious beliefs without ever examining them. These adolescents can be said to be foreclosed in their religiosity. Conversely, adolescents can explore their beliefs, asking questions to which they do not have simple or familiar answers, and be identity achieved (Markstrom-Adams, 1992).

that an ethic of care characterizes females' approach to moral decisions; this ethic emphasizes compassion and a sense of responsibility to others in contrast to the justice orientation of Kohlberg, which emphasizes reliance on rules and reason.

Gilligan traces gender differences in moral reasoning to differences in ways of viewing the self. Females define themselves in relation to others; from this comes a sense of responsibility of each to the other. Males define themselves as separate from others; the assumption of separateness highlights the need for rules to regulate the actions of each with respect to the other.

Gilligan traces moral development in females through three levels, each reflecting a different resolution to their conflict between responsibilities to themselves and to others. In level 1 the primary concern is care for oneself. Females soon see this as selfish and move to level 2, in which they equate morality with care of others. Only as they encounter problems that result from excluding themselves as legitimate recipients of their own care do they move to level 3, in which they equate morality with care both of themselves and of others.

Research finds that while a care orientation is not necessarily the approach adopted by all women, it is more characteristic of women than men. Studies find that both females and males share concerns about justice and care but that individuals tend to focus on one orientation to the exclusion of the other in thinking through a dilemma.

Freud: Morality and the Superego

Freud placed the responsibility for moral behavior in the superego, an aspect of the personality that embraces cultural standards of right and wrong. The superego develops when the young child identifies with the same-sex parent. Freud assumed the superego of females to be weaker than that of males because they are not as motivated to resolve Oedipal tensions and identify with a less-threatening parental figure.

Despite the usefulness of Freud's theory to clinicians, his assumptions concerning gender differences in moral development have not been supported by research.

Adolescents' Religious Beliefs

The intellectual changes that occur in adolescence make it possible for adolescents to view God in new ways and to question beliefs they once accepted uncritically. As with identity status, processes of exploration and commitment determine the form beliefs will take.

For nearly 60% of adolescents, religion is very to moderately important in their lives.

KEY TERMS

Preconventional Moral Reasoning	Postconventional Moral Reasoning	Superego
Conventional Moral Reasoning	Ethic of Care	Conscience
		Identification

STRESS AND COPING

■ RESEARCH FOCUS
Confidentiality: Troubled
Relationships—"You Sound Just Like
Your Mother!"

What Is Stress?
How Adolescents Cope with Stress
Learning Effective Coping Strategies

ALIENATION AND THE FAILURE
TO COPE

■ RESEARCH FOCUS   Statistical Tests
of Significance: Stress in Mexican
American Adolescents

Runaways
Abuse and Neglect
Sexual Abuse

JUVENILE DELINQUENCY
Age Differences in Delinquency
Gender Differences in Delinquency
Ethnic Differences in Delinquency
Delinquency and Social Class
The Face of Delinquency
Gangs
Youth and Violence

ADOLESCENTS AND DRUGS
What Is Dependence?
Alcohol
Cigarettes
Marijuana
Stimulants
Depressants
Narcotics
Hallucinogens
Anabolic Steroids

DEPRESSION
Three Depressive Disorders
Masked Depression

SUICIDE
Gender and Ethnic Differences
Warning Signs
Risk Factors
Counseling and Prevention

SCHIZOPHRENIA
Warning Signs
Distinguishing Features
Prognosis

SUMMARY

KEY TERMS

CHAPTER TWELVE

Atypical Development in Adolescence

"No, don't! . . ." Abbie bolted upright in a sweat. She sat in the dark, the dream swirled around her, its sharp pain softening with each panting breath.

"Too much!" she cried, slipping her feet over the side of the bed and starting for the bathroom.

As her foot hit the dresser, she hissed angrily. "Why isn't anything where it's supposed to be?" she exploded, blindly feeling for the light switch and finding nothing.

Then she remembered where she was. This wasn't her room. She was in her stepsister's bedroom at her father's house. Her mom had thrown her out. She had forgotten the reason for the fight; they had thrown things, said things.

As the heavy reality of her world closed in on her, she slipped to the floor sobbing—the angry words, fists, and ashtrays flying, her friends so far away, her father nervous, on edge, his wife distant and formal—and no place to call her own. She suddenly felt that she could bear none of it anymore.

Adolescents face many pressures. Abbie is one of those with more than her share. Most adolescents will cope in one fashion or another; Abbie may, too. Relatively few will fail to cope. In this chapter we will address the problems of those for whom coping has become the ultimate test: the alienated and abused, delinquents, adolescents with emotional disorders, the drug abusers, the severely depressed, the suicidal, and those who become schizophrenic.

STRESS AND COPING

Bones mend and cuts heal, but worries fray the edges of the mind. Sometimes it's all one can do to keep from unravelling totally. Adolescence offers no immunity to life's stresses; in fact, the body's response to stress is remarkably similar at all ages. The only thing that changes is the way individuals cope with stress as they grow older.

RESEARCH FOCUS

Confidentiality: Troubled Relationships—
"You Sound Just Like Your Mother!"

"You sound just like your mother," he shouted, "always changing the subject when things get hot."

"And what if I do," she objected. "Mom and Dad have been married for 19 years—I could do a lot worse."

"And fighting for 18 of them—probably because he never gets a chance to finish a sentence. She keeps changing the subject before he can make his point."

"That's a cheap shot! Maybe we should stop seeing each other until this blows over."

"There you go again. Do you think that not seeing each other is going to settle anything? C'mon, stop avoiding things and talk to me."

Does this teenager fight the way her parents do? Do we inherit patterns of coping from our parents, passing them on from one generation to the next along with the shape of our noses and the color of our eyes? Do parents who deal with conflicts by avoiding them, for instance, have adolescents who use the same approach with *their* boyfriends or girlfriends? How might we find out?

This is a sensitive area of research. To obtain data, investigators must ask adolescents to answer difficult questions about their own and their parents' relationships. Often the answers aren't pretty: petty quarrels, verbal aggression, family violence, failed relationships. These are matters most of us would like to forget, and nearly all of us, if we *do* tell others, want to be sure the information will be held in confidence. How do investigators treat issues of confidentiality? More generally, what ethical considerations guide their treatment of subjects?

The American Psychological Association, like most professional organizations, provides guidelines governing the ethical conduct of research with human subjects. The overriding concern is to respect the dignity and welfare of those who participate in the research. Other considerations follow from this concern. Subjects are informed, for instance, that their participation is voluntary and that they are free to leave at any time. They are also assured that their answers will be held in confidence.

How can an investigator keep answers confidential and still make public the findings of the re-

(continued)

What Is Stress?

Hans Selye (1982), a pioneer in stress research, defines **stress** as the body's specific and nonspecific responses to a demand or event. Depending on the event, the response can differ widely: shivering when cold, perspiring when hot, heart pounding when in danger. Selye labels the nonspecific response the **general adaptation syndrome**, or **GAS**. This response consists of three stages. In the *alarm reaction*, initial shock is followed by a mobilization of defenses. Mobilization is possible for only so long, and symptoms such as nervous tension, headache, and irritability soon develop. In the *adaptation* phase, the body accommodates to the additional demands, and stress symptoms diminish or even disappear. These reappear in the final stage of *exhaustion*, as the body loses its ability to accommodate further.

RESEARCH   FOCUS (*continued*)

search? The key to this problem is *anonymity*. Investigators code the information subjects give them to prevent the identification of individuals. A common procedure gives subjects numbers to use instead of their names. If an investigator anticipates the need to disclose information, she or he must inform subjects in advance so that they can decide whether to participate under those conditions.

What conditions might cause an investigator to disclose confidential information? Information suggesting that a subject may be dangerous to himself or herself or to others is sufficient cause to violate confidentiality. Threatened suicide or attacks against others are examples. In other instances, investigators may be forced by the courts to reveal information concerning illegal activities. Research on gangs or delinquent activities serve as examples.

Barclay Martin (1990) looked for similarities in the ways adolescents and their parents resolve conflict. Late adolescents responded to questionnaires on the frequency of overt conflict between their parents, on the ways their parents were most likely to resolve conflicts, and on the way they resolved conflicts with their own boyfriend or girlfriend. Martin protected his subjects' confidentiality by as-

signing each subject a code number to use instead of a name.

As expected, Martin found that conflict styles are similar across generations, especially when avoidant styles are used. Martin suggests that because the latter approaches do not deal with conflicts directly, needs and feelings will persist. Also, adolescents don't have the chance to learn the skills that will enable them to cope with conflicts when they arise in their own relationships.

Martin also suggests that adolescents may select partners who are similar to their parents in the way they resolve conflicts—for example, those who also use avoidant styles—either because this style is familiar and comfortable or for deeper psychodynamic reasons. In either case, they are more likely as a couple to perpetuate the difficulties in the relationship experienced by their parents than if they were to select a partner who approached conflict more directly.

Reference: B. Martin. (1990). The transmission of relationship difficulties from one generation to the next. Journal of Youth and Adolescence, 13, 181–199.

Selye refers to the chemical messengers that organize behavior as messengers "of peace" and "of war." The former coordinate behavioral responses when we are not stressed. The latter ready the body for fight or flight when stressed (Selye, 1982). Adolescents have the option of interpreting many situations in ways that would make either reaction possible. Consider an example in which someone bumps into a boy's locker, knocking it shut. The adolescent can either swing around ready for a fight, or he can simply ignore the incident. If he chooses to fight, chemical messengers will flood his body with adrenaline, pump blood into his muscles, stop his stomach from digesting his lunch, and heighten his awareness to all incoming stimuli. His blood pressure and heart rate will soar. These adaptations prepare him for a fight if one should occur, but they are also, to use Selye's words, "biologically suicidal" when called upon too frequently.

Adolescents can also ignore potential stressors. In the above example, doing so would allow other chemical messengers to coordinate the adolescent's reactions, permitting him to reopen the locker, continue a conversation with a friend, and get on with digesting his lunch. The quality of life is determined not simply by the presence or absence of stressors, but by the way adolescents interpret and cope with them. In other words, it's not *what* happens, but *how* one reacts to what happens that ultimately matters.

How Adolescents Cope with Stress

The above example highlights the distinction between stress and coping. A stressor is an event; coping is what one does about it. R. S. Lazarus and S. Folkman (1984) define **coping** as "efforts to manage specific external and/or internal demands that are appraised as taxing or exceeding the resources of the person" (p. 141). Adolescents can cope in either of two general ways. Problem-focused coping attempts to change the stressful situation; this approach is primarily offensive. Emotion-focused coping is directed at minimizing the impact of the stress and is primarily defensive. When adolescents cope in the first of these two ways, they are likely to look for additional information or come up with an alternative, less stressful approach to the problem. The process is an active one in which they evaluate information, make decisions, and confront the problem. Emotion-focused coping is *re-*active rather than active. The focus, as the term suggests, is on minimizing the emotional damage of stress, not on changing the stressor. This approach more frequently takes the form of defensive measures such as wishful thinking, denial, or seeking comfort from others.

The ways adolescents cope reflect more general aspects of their personalities. H. W. Krohne and J. Rogner (1982) characterize coping reactions as a continuum, with repression at one extreme and sensitization at the other. Responses in the middle range of this continuum are the most adaptive; those at either extreme are usually maladaptive. Adolescents who cope as "repressors" will usually fail to process or deal with negative information. In contrast, "sensitizers" will typically focus only on the negative. Neither approach is adaptive. Adolescents need to be aware of situations that are potentially threatening, but they also need to be able to see means of resolving them. Michael Berzonsky (1992, 1993) distinguishes individuals in terms of their openness to information, whether in coping with stressors or resolving identity issues (see Chapter 8). Those who seek out experiences that are relevant to the decisions or problems they face (information-oriented) are most likely to adopt a problem-focused approach to coping. Conversely, those who are relatively closed to new information, relying instead on the standards of others (normative-oriented), are more likely to use emotion-focused approaches, as are individuals who procrastinate and do nothing when faced with stress (avoidant-oriented).

Adolescents who live in gang-ridden neighborhoods experience a high degree of stress. Some try to cope by looking for solutions to the problem; others try to minimize the emotional damage by joining a gang themselves or by emotionally withdrawing.

Many of the stressors adolescents face occur daily. Those at school take a number of forms. Among the most common are aggression (whether actual or threatened), fear of theft, and racial tensions. Seventy percent of the students in one survey (Armacost, 1989) said they feared their belongings would be stolen. Academic pressures were also stressful; over 40%, for example, said it was stressful to have a job and also keep up with schoolwork. Nearly 70% mentioned stresses related to the academic track they were in at school, with those in the highest tracks experiencing the most stress. Additional stressors take the form of conflicts with peers and dating anxieties. Adolescents also experience stress resulting from career and educational goals, peer pressures, and parental expectations (Adwere-Boamah & Curtis, 1993; Kohn & Milrose, 1993).

The concerns of adolescents remain relatively similar across racial and socioeconomic groups and over time. For instance, Joseph Adwere-Boamah and Deborah Curtis (1993) found that a predominantly low-income sample of African-American and Hispanic students ranked the same concerns as most and least serious as did a sample containing mainly white students who were surveyed five years earlier. For all these junior and senior high school students, the most important concerns were career, grades, and future schooling, and the least important were problems relating to drugs, cigarettes, or alcohol. The fact that low-income minority students place career goals and grades as their highest concerns underscores the importance of specific interventions in school counseling programs. Making clear to minority students all the academic and career paths that are available (see Chapter 10).

Even though adolescents agree which events are stressful, the coping responses that work for one adolescent will not necessarily work for another. Thomas Reischl and Barton Hirsch (1989) studied different methods of coping among students. They found that highly social students cope in ways that utilize their social skills; they seek help from friends, maintain relationships, and continue social activities like studying and eating together. Students who are academically oriented cope in academic ways, by taking classes they enjoy, taking less difficult courses, and keeping up with their schoolwork. Each type copes effectively, but differently.

Unpredictable and infrequent events are most stressful. This is true whether they are limited to a single point in time (e.g., an accident) or are life-reorganizing (e.g., parents' divorce). Stressors that adolescents see as normal, such as developmental changes, are less stressful than equally major but non-normative events. Although daily hassles, such as conflicts with parents or friends, are least stressful of all, they can affect self-image, especially in adolescent females. Perhaps males compartmentalize their experiences more than females do (Adwere-Boamah & Curtis, 1993); or perhaps because females' sense of self is more relationally determined, conflicts with others affect more aspects of the self (Tolan, Miller, & Thomas, 1988).

The perception of stressful events changes with age. G. E. Davis and B. E. Compas (1986) find that for early adolescents unpleasantness is the single most important factor contributing to whether they perceive a situation to be stressful. Late adolescents evaluate possible stressful events in more complex ways, such as appraising their potential impact on their lives.

Almost surely, too, skill in coping with stressful events improves with age. Some evidence for this comes from a series of studies by Paul Kohn at York University. Kohn and Milrose (1993) found that high school girls report more hassles, or minor irritants, than boys do. College females also report feeling more hassled than males do, but they, unlike high school girls, do not experience more stress than males do (Kohn, Lafreniere, & Gurevich, 1990).

The concerns of adolescents also differ with gender. Concerns that loom largest for boys are not among those mentioned first by girls. Boys, for instance, indicate more concern with sexual impulses and extracurricular activities than girls do. Girls express more concern than boys do with physical appearance (Adwere-Boamah & Curtis, 1993).

Positive as well as negative events can be stressful. Being elected class president, making the debating team or the cheerleading squad, or getting the job one applied for are all stressful even though each is desirable. Stress exists whenever adolescents must respond to new demands and events, and both positive and negative events can require adolescents to adapt in new ways.

A growing number of schools are succeeding in curbing violence with programs that train students in conflict mediation skills. Here, junior high school students in Oakland, California, are role-playing conflict resolution.

Learning Effective Coping Strategies

Coping with stress, like most of the activities adolescents engage in, requires skill; therefore, some are better at it than others. Luckily, as with other skills, adolescents can be taught to cope with stress. D. Meichenbaum's **stress-inoculation training** program teaches adolescents ways to cognitively restructure stressful situations, making them less stressful and improving the chances of coping successfully (Cameron & Meichenbaum, 1982; Meichenbaum, 1988; Meichenbaum & Deffenbacher, 1988). Three elements make up this program. Adolescents learn to identify and appraise stressful situations, anticipate their own reactions, and manage the resulting emotions.

Appraising the Situation. Misinterpretations easily arise from personal blind spots that can cause adolescents to overestimate or underestimate potential stressors. Overestimates can turn what could have been a harmless episode into an interpersonal disaster, whereas underestimates can expose adolescents to potential harm. Only by appraising a situation correctly can adolescents predict the most likely set of events. Accurate prediction, in turn, puts them in a place where they can better influence the course of events. Appraisal becomes more accurate as adolescents learn to think of alternative interpretations for situations.

A. A. Hains and M. Szyjakowski (1990) trained adolescents to challenge self-defeating interpretations. This training requires adolescents to put their new intellectual skills to use: thinking of all the possibilities in a situation, thinking logically, and thinking abstractly by analyzing a situation in terms of its underlying elements. (These features of thought are discussed in detail in Chapter 4.) As adolescents bring new intellectual capacities to bear on problems, they're better able to revise their reading of ongoing situations and react appropriately. Frequently the most appropriate step is to get more information to find out which interpretation is the most reasonable. Sometimes this step can be as simple as asking the other person, "Did you really mean . . . ?"

Adolescents (like individuals of all ages) are likely to make an **attributional error** in which they overestimate the importance of *dispositional stressors* (presumed traits such as aggressiveness or anger) and underestimate the importance of *situational stressors* (such as tensions due to relationships or threats of personal violence). A girl who is dissatisfied with her boyfriend because she sees him as aggressive and angry (dispositional stressors) may think there is little possibility of improving their relationship. By tracing his anger to situational factors—strife at home or hazing at school, for example—it becomes possible for her to think of ways to improve their relationship (McAdams, 1990).

Adolescents frequently commit a second error when they notice only information that confirms their appraisal of a situation, or *confirmatory information*. An adolescent who expects a teacher to be unsympathetic or overly demanding is likely to act in a hostile way toward that teacher, provoking a reaction that confirms the expectation. Cameron and Meichenbaum (1982) recommend that adolescents look for, and even generate, behavior that disconfirms predisposing expectations. The above adolescent might, for example, thank the teacher in advance for her attention and time, thus creating a positive atmosphere in which she will be more likely to listen to the problem sympathetically.

Responding to the Situation.   Sometimes the response can be as simple as getting information or advice, or suggesting a talk with a friend. At other times the most effective action can be *no* action, like not shooting back an angry reply to a friend or parent. In most cases, skills related to assertiveness, communication, negotiation, and compromise are involved. Even adolescents who have these skills don't always think to use them. Under the stress of the moment they may not use an approach that has worked for them in the past, or they may fail to recognize which skills are called for. Sometimes, too, adolescents fail to respond effectively, because other, less-adaptive responses are more dominant. Nonassertive adolescents might fail to speak up, for instance, simply because of concerns that inhibit assertive action.

The most effective responses are those that prevent stressful situations from occurring. Individuals create, as well as respond to, their environments. This fact makes preventive actions possible. Adolescents can pick up on social cues that bring out the best in others. Adolescents who develop these skills are more likely to bring out friendly, helpful behavior in others and less likely to cause the hostile or aggressive behaviors that typify stressful interactions.

Managing Emotions.   Even after successfully handling a stressful encounter, adolescents must still deal with the emotions caused by the situation. Adolescents differ widely in how quicky they get over feelings of anger or frustration. Although not as much is known about this aspect of coping as the others, mentally rehearsing one's successes, or failures, will either facilitate or interfere with the process of "unwinding" (Cameron & Meichenbaum, 1982; Meichenbaum & Deffenbacher, 1988). Adolescents who have been trained in a stress-inoculation program involving the above three components (appraising, responding, and managing) have lower anxiety, less anger, and higher self-esteem (Hains & Szyjakowski, 1990).

Differences in *instrumentality* relate to these dimensions of coping. Adolescents who are instrumental are assertive, independent, and task-oriented. These qualities affect their appraisal of situations, their ability to act, and their emotions. Instrumentality also is positively related to self-esteem; as such it serves as a buffer against stress. L. C. Towbes, L. H. Cohen, and K. Glyshaw (1989) found that high school females who are high in instrumentality experience less anxiety in the face of negative events. Junior high females benefit from instrumentality only at low levels of stress. Instrumentality is unrelated to stress in boys, perhaps because, since it figures more centrally in their sex role definition, it may be less of an option (Towbes, Cohen, & Glyshaw, 1989).

The majority of adolescents cope successfully with the stress, and relatively few have serious chronic problems. Those who cope and those who do not increasingly diverge over the adolescent years (Kazdin, 1993).

ALIENATION AND THE FAILURE TO COPE

Some of the most common stressors in adolescence reflect the absence rather than the presence of something. Adolescents frequently feel cut off from themselves and others, emotionally distanced from their world, observers rather than participants in their own reality. Feelings of **alienation**—a sense of estrangement and loss—can be common in adolescence. These feelings are to be expected, given the many changes adolescents experience; however, when alienation becomes the predominant focus of an adolescent's experience, he or she is in trouble.

The most interesting times in life are those characterized by innovation and change, yet both are stressful and bring the potential for crisis and dislocation (Wapner, 1990). Adolescents live in very interesting times; they face enormous changes. Each change introduces a new realm of experience; each also represents a loss. Many adolescents experience sadness at the passing of their childhood. The success of cartoonists such as Bill Watterson comes in part from restoring the

RESEARCH FOCUS

Statistical Tests of Significance: Stress in Mexican American Adolescents

Lupe noticed the woman's eyes scan the sinkful of dirty dishes, move to the cluttered countertop, and finally rest on her father's shirt draped over the top of the door to the bedroom. A sock lay beneath it on the floor.

"She probably thinks we live like this," she fumed. She hated it when someone from the county came to their house. She knew what they thought. But her brother was sick, and she was relieved the visiting nurse could come.

"If only Mama were here instead of with Grandma in Mexico," she thought. Her mother kept things spotless! Never a dirty dish in sight, always something good on the stove. She didn't know how she did it. In ways they had it hard. Pop didn't make that much money, and their house was no showplace—even when it was clean. And then there was the neighborhood. Pop said it wasn't safe. But she wouldn't trade places with anyone.

Lupe was 13 and, according to some standards, already carried a heavy load of responsibilities. On-call babysitter, sometime translator, part-time cleaning lady, and full-time adolescent.

Stress? Definitely. All adolescents experience some stress; some experience more than others. Do minority adolescents have more than their share?

Ruth Zambrana and Victor Silva-Palacios (1989) looked for answers among recent immigrants enrolled in an English as a second language course. They administered a stress inventory to 244 Mexican American adolescents. All indicated that the most stressful situations were those relating to their families, for example, having parents get sick or not having enough money to pay all the bills. The next most stressful situations involved language problems and ethnic issues at school, such as not understanding the teacher or having kids make fun of the way they spoke.

Zambrana and Silva-Palacios noticed that the stress scores of the females were somewhat higher than those of the males. Could they conclude from this difference that females were more affected by these events than males? How much higher would the females' scores have to be to support this conclusion? After all, each adolescent is an individual, and one can always expect slight variances simply as a result of individual differences. Unexplained variability that is not due to the variable being in-

(continued)

Calvin and Hobbes   by Bill Watterson

Part of the appeal of the *Calvin and Hobbes* cartoons for adults is nostalgia for the innocence of childhood. Copyright 1991 Watterson. Reprinted with permission of Universal Press Syndicate. All rights reserved.

RESEARCH FOCUS (*continued*)

vestigated is termed *random error*. (See Chapter 9, Research Focus: Ethics.)

To determine whether a difference between two groups is due to random error or whether it reflects the variable being studied, one uses a *test of significance*. Common tests are chi-square, t-tests, and F-tests. If the value obtained is larger than a tabled value for the same number of subjects, one can reject the assumption that random error was responsible and attribute the difference to the independent variable. Probability theory tells us that the likelihood that random error is responsible for the difference decreases with increases in the number of subjects in each group. The number of subjects is reflected in the *degrees of freedom*. With larger degrees of freedom, one needs a smaller difference to reject the assumption that random error was responsible.

Zambrana and Silva-Palacios' statistical test for gender was significant. Females experienced a number of events as being more stressful than did males, especially events that involved family, loss, or change. Recall from Chapter 8 that female adolescents are affected more negatively by multiple changes than are males. The stress experienced by these adolescent girls might also have been related to their need to establish affiliative connections and

their difficulty doing so because of language and cultural differences (Gilligan, 1982).

Gender differences in reactions to events highlight one of the central features of stress: Stress is psychological in nature and cannot be traced to objective events in any simple way. Will an event be stressful? It depends on how it is perceived. Just as beauty is in the mind of the beholder, so is stress.

As another illustration of this point, many of the situations that nonminority adolescents might find stressful, such as having to take care of younger brothers and sisters, were not perceived as stressful by the minority adolescents. Cultural expectations about extended families and child-care responsibilities rendered these situations normative rather than stressful. On the other hand, adolescents in immigrant families acquire the ways of their new culture more rapidly than their parents do, creating intercultural tensions in addition to the intergenerational tensions that all adolescents experience. (Szapocznik & Kurtines, 1993; Zetlin, 1993).

References: C. Gilligan. (1982). In a different voice. Cambridge, MA: Harvard University Press. R. E. Zambrana & V. Silva-Palacios. (1989). Gender differences in stress among Mexican immigrant adolescents in Los Angeles, California. Journal of Adolescent Research, 4, 426–442.

Hobbes to the Calvin in each of us. Many adolescents also feel cut off from themselves as well as their parents, as they struggle to define their values and goals.

Feelings of cultural estrangement can also contribute to feelings of alienation. Adolescents are expected to assume more adult ways but are not given the same privileges as adults nor the same freedom to define the standards by which they will live. Many feel disenfranchised and powerless—pressured to conform to customs of dress, speech, and behavior that are not their own.

Change leaves adolescents with more questions than answers. What are they to hold on to? To let go of? What really matters? Does anything matter if everything can be questioned? When nothing matters, adolescents feel they have lost everything they have valued. Though most adolescents at times feel alienated, only a few act out their feelings of separateness, powerlessness, and isolation.

Loss is central to alienation, and it is always the loss of something important. Reactions to this loss can range from hostility to sadness to indifference—from anger to a defensive "What does it matter anyway?" The alienated who cannot replace their loss with the sense of a competent self, linked to a social order that gives meaning to their lives, surround the void without filling it.

Runaways

For some adolescents, the loss is of something they never had. Approximately 1.5 million adolescents run away from home before they reach the age of 18 (Farber, 1987). Some run away in the hopes of finding excitement, independence, or their own maturity, but most are running *from* something—frequently from neglect or abuse. Until recently, the number of abused runaways was thought to be quite small, no more than about 5%. Recent studies of runaways suggest that most have been abused or neglected (Morrow & Sorell, 1989). Table 12.1 shows the types

Most runaway adolescents were physically mistreated at home; although life on the street may offer companionship with other homeless youth who understand their experiences, the conditions are seldom any safer or healthier.

TABLE 12.1

Problems Reported by Adolescents in Runaway and Homeless Youth Centers

Type of Problem	Total	Female	Male
Family problems[a]			
Emotional conflict at home	41%	43%	39%
Parent too strict	21	24	18
Parental physical abuse	20	23	18
Parental neglect	20	19	21
Parent drug or alcohol problems	18	19	17
Family mental health problems	11	12	11
Parental domestic violence	10	10	10
Parental unemployment	9	9	9
Wants to live with other parent	6	7	6
Parental sexual abuse	7	9	2
Physical or sexual abuse by other family member	5	6	3
Physical or sexual abuse by nonfamily member	4	5	2
No parent figure	4	4	5
Parent is homosexual	1	2	1
None of the above	16	13	19
Individual problems[a]			
Poor self image	49%	51%	46%
Depressed	43	48	36
School attendance or truancy	33	33	33
Bad grades	31	30	33
In trouble with justice system	19	13	27
Drug abuse	15	13	17
Alcohol abuse	13	13	13
Possibly suicidal	12	15	8
Cannot get along with teachers	13	10	17
Learning disability	7	5	10
Custody change	5	5	5
Pregnant or suspects pregnancy	4	7	0
Other health problems or handicap	4	4	4
Homosexual or sexual identity issue	2	2	3
Prostitution	1	2	1
Venereal disease	1	1	0
None of the above	19	19	20

[a]*Because multiple responses are permitted, totals exceed 100 percent.*

Source: K. Maguire, A. L. Pastore, & T. J. Flanagan (Eds.), (1993). Sourcebook of criminal justice statistics 1992. *U.S. Department of Justice, Bureau of Justice Statistics. Washington, DC: U.S. Government Printing Office.*

of problems reported by adolescents in runaway and homeless youth centers: 62% of the females and 46% of the males had experienced some form of physical or sexual abuse, or parental neglect. Abuse in general is more frequent among adolescents than is widely known; 24% of all fatalities resulting from abuse are of adolescents, for example, and 41% of serious injuries resulting from abuse involve those between ages 12 and 17 (Farber, 1987).

Despite the uniqueness of individuals when looked full in the face, the profile of runaways is disturbingly similar: low self-esteem, depression, poor interpersonal skills, insecurity, anxiousness, impulsiveness, and little sense of control over life's events. Most do poorly in school, and many run into trouble with the law. Almost all experience conflict within their families, and for a majority this includes abuse. One-quarter have attempted suicide. With an average age of 15, runaways can be from any socioeconomic level; there is little difference in the numbers from blue-collar and white-collar homes.

Running away is clearly not the answer to their problems. It is equally clear that these adolescents are unable to face their problems and come up with any reasonable solution at the moment. Running away is almost never well planned. Two-thirds, for example, leave home with less than a dollar in their pocket. Many stay with friends or relatives, some seek out youth shelters, and others remain homeless. Most return within the first week, and 40% the same day. Nearly 90% will run away again in the future (Farber, 1987).

Homelife for most runaways is chaotic. The problems from which they are running (and to which almost all will return) have usually existed for years, yet the solutions remain as distant as ever. The dynamics of family life that would offer an answer to the problems are the very same ones that foster the personal development of its members. Thus, most runaways lack a sense of who they are or what they can become, in large part because the development of their sense of self and of their potential has not been supported within their families. Runaways are in need of programs that give them the interpersonal skills they did not develop within their families: skills in communicating thoughts and feelings, negotiating conflict, and in making responsible decisions (see Chapter 5).

Edward Farber (1987) notes that many more services are available to abused youth than to runaways; society tends to see the former as victims and the latter as merely unruly. Yet in a study of runaways, Farber and his associates found these adolescents had experienced the same amount of violence as had a similar group of adolescents identified as abused. Seventy-eight percent of the runaway adolescents studied had been physically mistreated within the past year (Farber, Kinast, McCoard, & Faulkner, 1984). Although estimates vary from one study to the next, most likely 25% of runaways have been sexually abused at home. Rather than being the problem itself, running away is a symptom of other problems. One cannot expect such troubled adolescents to return home without first addressing the problems of family conflict and violence they would face upon their return.

Abuse and Neglect

The actual number of adolescents who are abused is unknown; however, some estimates place this figure at nearly half of all reported cases of abuse of children 18 or under (Doueck, Ishisaka, & Greenaway, 1988). Cases of adolescent abuse and neglect are likely to follow one of three patterns: a continuation of earlier child abuse, a change in the type of punishment used by parents, and neglect related to the onset of adolescence (Doueck, Ishisaka, & Greenaway, 1988).

Continuation of Earlier Abuse. The abuse some adolescents experience continues a pattern of earlier child abuse within the family. The following fictional case study illustrates this type of abuse:

> Mr. and Mrs. B have been married 15 years. Mrs. B is 34 years old and Mr. B is 38. They have 4 children: Tom, 14; Richard, 12; Sheila, 9; and Laura, 5. Mr. B works on and off at odd jobs doing maintenance and/or janitorial work. He is currently unemployed. His relationship with his wife and family has been a stormy one. Periodically he physically assaults her or beats one of the children. After particularly violent episodes, he leaves the house and is not heard from for several days. They live in a small, two-bedroom home in a rural county and seldom see relatives or friends. Both Mr. B and Mrs. B have been in alcohol treatment centers on at least two separate occasions. The children have few friends at school, spending most of their time alone. Tom is in a special class for behavior problem children. Richard and Sheila are in special education programs. Recently, Tom was picked up by the police for shoplifting. He has run away several times over the past 2 years and was expelled from school for vandalism. (Doueck, Ishisaka, & Greenaway, 1988, p. 136)

Tom comes from a family with many long-standing problems: violence between parents, alcoholism, financial instability, few social supports, and physical isolation from others. The abuse he presently suffers is not much different from that experienced when he was younger or the abuse currently experienced by his younger brother and sister, and reflects the inadequate coping skills of the parents and the generally dysfunctional nature of the family.

Abusive Punishment. A second type of abuse, a change in the type of punishment used, is illustrated in this second fictional case study:

> John is a 16-year-old boy who appears physically strong and socially confident. . . . When he dressed down for physical education, his teacher noticed bruises on John's back, arms, and legs. . . . The teacher reported the incident to protective services. During an interview with the parents, the protective services worker was told by John's father, a 39-year-old contractor, that John had always been a problem child who needed guidance and correction. Frequently, the correction consisted of a "good spanking like my father did to me!" John's mother supported these practices and said that lately they weren't working because John was still misbehaving: smoking, staying out at night, using drugs, shoplifting, hanging out with the wrong crowd, and disobeying his father. She stated that, most recently, John got into an argument with his

father over the length of John's hair. A fist fight ensued between John and his father, who used a strap in an attempt to "knock some sense into the child!" (Doueck, Ishisaka, & Greenaway, 1988, p. 137)

In this second type of abuse, parents who have used physical punishment since childhood have increased the intensity of the punishment in an attempt to control adolescent misbehavior. Families in which this form of mistreatment occurs are typified by controlling, rigid parents who become even more controlling, to the point of abuse, when faced with adolescent bids for greater autonomy and independence and the loss of their own control (Doueck, Ishisaka, & Greenaway, 1988).

Neglect Precipitated by Adolescence.   A third type of mistreatment is brought about by the onset of adolescence itself. An example is illustrated by the following fictional case account:

> Lois is a 14-year-old girl who lives with her divorced father, age 41. Her parents divorced when she was 9, with her mother leaving town. Lois's father described Lois as his sole means of emotional support during the early years of his divorce. [Following a serious illness] he quit his job . . . and changed careers. Lately he has been spending two nights a week outside the home. During these nights away, he leaves money for Lois to "buy whatever she needs." He states, "Now that she is 14, she is capable of caring for herself." The family situation came to the attention of the local mental health agency when Lois called their hotline and said that she was all alone in the world and was going to commit suicide." (Doueck, Ishisaka, & Greenaway, 1988, p. 137)

In this type of neglect, the parent mistakenly concludes that since the child has reached adolescence, she is able to be on her own and care for herself. The parent's conduct appears to be related to midlife concerns of his own.

Each of the three examples illustrates common factors related to child or adolescent abuse and neglect. Most abusive parents have had inadequate parenting models themselves and have inadequate parenting skills. (Kelly & Grace, 1990). They appear to be less able to deal with stress, more depressed, passive, and withdrawn. Long-term unemployment of the father, alcoholism in either parent, and social isolation are also common (Moeller & Bachmann, 1993).

Physical and emotional abuse of adolescents is not limited to low-income families. A study of nearly 700 predominantly white women revealed that abuse had occurred at all income levels, although multiple forms of abuse (e.g., both physical and emotional abuse, or physical and sexual abuse) were more common in lower-income families (Moeller & Bachmann, 1993). Also, rates of abuse appear not to have changed substantially with time. The ages of the subjects in this particular study ranged from 16 to 76, a span of 60 years, and younger subjects reported no more abuse than older ones.

Sexual Abuse

Recent epidemiological studies indicate that sexual abuse is not as rare as was once thought. Some studies estimate that one of every four girls and one of every ten boys has suffered some form of sexual abuse (Finkelhor, 1993). Contrary to current social prejudices, sexual abuse appears to be as common at higher socioeconomic levels as lower ones. For instance, even though the *reported* incidence is greater for lower-income homes, community surveys find sexual abuse to be equally represented in higher-income families, suggesting the operation of class-biased stereotypes among health care professionals. Also, in no racial or ethnic subgroup is sexual abuse uncommon (Finkelhor, 1993).

The risk for sexual abuse increases sharply in pre-adolescence (Finkelhor & Baron, 1986). Two characteristics of families are associated with increased risk of sexual abuse: inadequate supervision of children's activities and the presence of physical or psychological abuse or neglect (Finkelhor, 1993).

Most victims of sexual abuse are female. Eight times out of ten the abuser is a male. Almost as often the abuser is a member of the immediate family or a relative. Table 12.2 shows the percentages of sexual abuse committed by individuals in various relationships to the victim. Despite figures showing greater overall incidence of abuse by biological fathers than stepfathers, stepfathers are disproportionately (because their numbers are lower) more likely to sexually abuse daughters in the family (Gordon, 1989; Habenicht & Futcher, 1990). In a majority of cases

T A B L E   1 2 . 2

Males and Females Sexually Abused by Different
Types of Offenders

	Victim	
Offender	Male	Female
Biological father	26.2%	37.8%
Stepfather	16.2	22.5
Biological mother	10.0	5.0
Stepmother	2.3	0.6
Other relative	5.4	13.4
Nonrelative	11.5	10.3
Other (e.g., day care)	28.5	10.3

Source: K. C. Faller. (1989). Characteristics of a clinical sample of sexually abused children: How boy and girl victims differ. Child Abuse and Neglect, 13, *281–291.*

TABLE 12.3

Long-Term Physical and Psychological Consequences for Female Victims of Childhood Abuse (Physical, Emotional, and/or Sexual)

Self-Perception of Physical Health

Characteristics of Physical Health	Percentages for Women Reporting Childhood Abuse	Percentages for Women Reporting No Abuse
Frequent feelings of fatigue	45.4	27.0
Obesity	30.1	15.3
Severe PMS	19.4	11.0
Frequent gynecologic problems	15.2	4.6
Excessive drug use	5.4	0.3
Alcoholic	2.5	0.0
Satisfied with physical health	62.3	71.4
Frequent headaches	27.6	19.8
Trouble sleeping	26.5	17.5
Frequent vaginal infections	14.7	9.7
Frequent stomachaches	12.1	8.8
Often miss work due to illness	5.6	2.0
Underweight	4.8	4.6
Drug overdose	1.4	0.0

(continued)

the abuse starts early. In over 300 confirmed abuse victims, more than 50% were sexually abused before they were 6 years old. Less than 20% first became victims as adolescents (Faller, 1989).

Criteria for Sexual Abuse. Criteria for distinguishing abusive sexual contact from exploratory behavior between young siblings or playmates stress the exploitive nature of the contact. Exploitation exists when one of the members is considerably older than the other or uses force or threats. D. H. Finkelhor and G. T. Hotaling (1984) recommend the following criteria for determining abuse:

1. If the victim is under 13 and the perpetrator is 5 or more years older, or the victim is age 13 to 16 and the perpetrator is 10 or more years older, sexual contact is abusive.

numbers of minority youth come from lower-income homes, and factors common to poverty are related to delinquency apart from ethnic status. Unemployment, poorer academic and vocational preparation, and fewer social and family resources are just a few of these factors. In addition, much middle-income (nonminority) delinquency is never reported; families are able to intervene, and youth authorities are more willing to release offenders to their parents' custody.

Even so, some types of delinquent activity vary with social class. Middle-income youth are less likely to commit violent crimes (e.g., aggravated assault, rape, robbery) or crimes against property (e.g., auto theft, burglary) than are lower-income youth. Status offenses and minor delinquent acts such as creating a public nuisance, drunkenness, and disorderly conduct are as common among middle-income as lower-income adolescents.

The Face of Delinquency

Are there common characteristics of adolescents who engage in delinquent activities? Is delinquency a social problem? A personal decision? A bit of both? Are there typical patterns to delinquent adolescents' interactions at school, with peers, or parents? Questions such as these raise a host of complex issues.

Identifying Delinquency.   Most delinquency is never reported; much of it is simply never observed. When it is, observers may turn a blind eye to avoid retaliation, as may the victims themselves when victims are involved. A 1991 survey revealed that nearly 1.2 million crimes involving violence against adolescents were not reported (U.S. Department of Justice, 1991). Of the delinquents who reach the attention of the police, over one-third do not go to court. Many offenders are let go with a warning, others are released to parents, others may be held in temporary custody, still others may be referred to welfare or other social agencies.

One self-report study of delinquency found that of 2,000 12-to-18-year-olds surveyed, 93% had engaged in at least one act of delinquency during the past year that, if detected, could have resulted in being processed by the juvenile justice system. Eighty-eight percent of the adolescents had committed status offenses (e.g., truancy, use of alcohol). Although as many as 82% admitted to committing criminal offenses (e.g., petty theft, use of drugs, vandalism), only 9% had engaged in serious delinquent acts such as robbery (LeBlanc, 1983). A more recent study of largely middle-class 13-to-17-year-olds confirms these trends (Simons, Robertson, & Downs, 1989).

Rather than label any adolescent who has engaged in delinquency a delinquent, only those repeatedly brought to the system's attention by police or parents, or those who engage in activities that would be regarded as criminal at any age, are considered to be delinquents. Problems still remain in separating cause from effect. Do poor peer relations, for example, contribute to delinquency, or is a delinquent who is impulsive and aggressive likely to have poor relationships with others? The answer may involve a combination of factors.

Academic Skills.   Delinquents characteristically fall behind their peers in achievement at school. In schools having more than one track, they are less likely to be in the academic track, are more likely to drop out, and less likely to be involved in school activities. Many are learning-disabled, falling two or more grades behind their peers, and many have poor verbal skills (Perlmutter, 1987; Quay, 1987).

Self-Esteem.   Delinquents typically have low self-esteem and poor self-images. They are less apt than their peers to see themselves as competent and successful (Arbuthnut, Gordon, & Jurkovic, 1987). Lack of success in school and in other areas of their lives—family relations, for instance—probably contributes to the relationship between low self-esteem and delinquency (Henggeler, 1989). Delinquent activities can also enhance self-esteem, especially for those in lower-income groups, if the acts receive peer approval (Rosenberg, Schooler, & Schoenbach, 1989).

Family Relations.   Delinquents come from homes characterized by violence, and many are victims of child abuse and/or neglect. Poor communication, excessively harsh punishment, and parental strife are common (Cernkovich & Giordano, 1987; Henggeler, 1989; Huesmann, Lefkowitz, Eron, & Walder, 1984). Parental rejection, experienced as a lack of warmth, affection, or love, is consistently related to delinquency (Simons, Robertson, & Downs, 1989).

Social Skills.   Delinquents are more aggressive than their peers and more likely to rely on physical than verbal means to settle disagreements (Goldstein, Sprafkin, Gershaw, & Klein, 1980). Among a group of fifth-graders followed to the end of high school, aggression toward peers significantly predicted juvenile delinquency (Kupersmidt & Coie, 1990). The same study found that children who were rejected by their peers were also more likely to have had some police contact or problems with school, such as truancy, suspension, or dropping out. A number of studies suggest that delinquents have poorer problem-solving skills than peers, although A. A. Hains and E. B. Ryan (1983) have suggested that this difference may reflect a failure to see the need to consider alternative solutions rather than a lack of ability to generate them.

Self-Control.   Delinquents are more impulsive and less likely to rely on internalized constraints for behavior than their peers. They tend to evaluate situations in terms of their needs and evaluate their actions in terms of how likely they are to get away with something. Many express little guilt for their actions, and some appear to believe they are being punished not for what they did, but because they got caught (Arbuthnut, Gordon, & Jurkovic, 1987). As individuals, delinquent adolescents can cause considerable harm to others and themselves. As a group, their presence in a community can be disastrous.

Gangs

Perhaps one of the most significant factors contributing to the number of delinquent acts committed by adolescents is their membership in a gang. T. Thornberry, M. Krohn, A Lizotte, and D. Chard-Wierschem (1993) found that rates of delinquency were approximately four to five times higher for gang members. Because these investigators followed the same adolescents over several years, they could compare rates of delinquency for these adolescents prior to joining a gang. The researchers found these adolescents did not have higher rates than other adolescents; furthermore, once they left the gang, their rates typically dropped. Only when they were in a gang did they have a high rate of delinquency.

The nature of gangs has changed over the last generation. In previous generations gangs arose from the spontaneous associations of neighborhood males, and gang activities were primarily oriented toward defending the neighborhood territory or "turf." Membership was almost exclusively limited to males and to

Although today's gangs are still neighborhood-based and their activities still involve defending "turf," they are more likely to be linked to organized crime and the sale of drugs than in the past.

those of the same ethnic group. Rumbles with rival gangs defined the territories of each and gave status to gang members. The leader of the gang carried a gun, but most members did not (Kratcoski & Kratcoski, 1986). Today, gang members have sophisticated weapons and use them freely. As one former gang member from Detroit remarked,

> When I grew up we had it out with our hands. Maybe we'd steal a car and go for a ride. Now they steal a car and rip somebody off or shoot somebody. I'm afraid to walk down the street at night. I've never seen it like this. (Kratcoski & Kratcoski, 1986)

Today's gangs are still formed from neighborhood associations, and gang activities still involve defense of turf, but gangs are more likely to be linked with organized crime than in the past, and making money, primarily through the sale of narcotics, is one of their major activities.

Other types of crime include murder, rape, burglary, extortion and the illegal sale of guns. Offshoots of gangs from larger cities have appeared locally across the country again with the sale of narcotics as a primary activity.

What attractions do gangs hold for their members? It has been suggested that gangs serve as surrogate families, offering an intense intimacy, emotional support, protection, and a feeling of belonging (Henggeler, 1989; Vigil, 1988). Research has found, for instance, that parents of gang members do not monitor their children's activities closely, and families are less cohesive (Henggeler, 1989). Parental absence, either in the form of long work hours, a single parent, or simple neglect, is also more common. In general, positive role models are less in evidence. Gang membership is also believed to confer a sense of identity, something especially important in adolescence. Members dress alike and adopt unique identifying behaviors they share with their gang, even being tattooed with gang insignia. The violence, too, can be an attraction, providing feelings of power and excitement to members.

Jean-Marie Lyon, Scott Henggeler, and James Hall (1992) found only partial support for the above assumptions. In a study comparing gang and non-gang members on a number of measures, these investigators found no difference between the two groups in measures of family relations such as parental acceptance, or in peer relationships such as emotional bonding in friendships. In fact, friendships among gang members were more aggressive and less mature than those of non-members. The constant need of gang members to prove themselves to maintain their status within the gang also argues against emotional intimacy.

Youth and Violence

Violence is not restricted to inner-city youth or gangs; it extends to the suburbs and middle-income families. Across all ethnic groups, homicide is the second leading cause of injury-related deaths in children and adolescents; teenagers are two and a half times more likely to be victims of a violent crime than is someone 20 years or older (Hammond & Yung, 1993). Minority males are most at risk: Native

Americans are more than twice as likely to die violently as white males their age, Hispanic males are three to four times more likely, and African-American males are nine times more likely than their white counterparts to die violently. In the 10-year period from 1978 to 1988, homicide accounted for over 40% of the deaths of black males aged 15 to 24 (Hammond & Yung, 1993).

Patterns emerge in the midst of this violence. Blacks are most likely to be killed at home, by a friend or an acquaintance, and be killed by a gun. Hispanics are more likely to be killed on the street, and to die from a stabbing. Across all ethnic groups, the most commonly given reason for violent crimes such as these is retaliation or revenge (Hammond & Yung, 1993).

In examining factors related to assaultive violence among black adolescents, W. Rodney Hammond and Betty Yung, at Wright State University, summarize a number of contributing misperceptions and myths. Those who are most aggressive, for instance, are more likely to interpret accidents as intentional and malicious. They are also more likely to endorse aggression as a means of settling disputes. A survey of inner-city adolescents (Price, Desmond, & Smith, 1991) revealed that black adolescents tend to believe that blacks are most likely to be shot by the police, and for this reason, that limiting ownership of guns would be unfair to them. Blacks believe they are safer with a gun in the house; they do not know that blacks who are shot are most likely to be shot by a friend or acquaintance in their own homes (Hammond & Yung, 1993).

Adolescents in all segments of society risk becoming desensitized to violence. Evening programs on television are saturated with murders, rapes, kidnappings, and petty thuggery, and box-office stars offer images of buffed and bare-chested bodybuilders with semi-automatic weapons. Both television programs and movies model graphic acts of violence as well as provide violent role models with whom adolescents can identify. Much popular music, whether rock or rap, provides an undercurrent of violent imagery, both in lyrics such as those found in "gangsta rap," and in the sensational behavior of the artists (Leland, 1993). An anecdote offers an interesting, if chilling, example of the way in which television and the movies contribute to our images of violence. A niece reported she had recently been in a bank when it was held up by two armed men. She noted that on hearing "Everyone down," people knew immediately what to do—lie face down on the floor, not crouch or kneel, and not look at the robbers' faces—because they had all seen this on the screen. However, after the robbers left, no one knew what to do—the TV and movie cameras always cut to the getaway and chase.

Some have argued that recent media attention to inner-city violence, in particular that associated with gangs, may reflect a subtle racism within society, confirming the dominant society's preconceptions of minority youth. Comparable treatment of youth who make it out of the inner city, by studying hard, getting good grades, and holding down jobs or going on to college, is harder to find (Horowitz, 1993).

Social factors contributing to violence cannot be discounted. The poverty and hopelessness confronting inner city youth, their daily exposure to community

Do violent scenes in the movies and on television desensitize adolescents to violence or make them more likely to act violently?

and family violence, and the reality of job discrimination and racism for minority adolescents are powerfully related to violence. In the end, however, some adolescents choose violence and others do not. Most who engage in violent crimes have law-abiding siblings with whom they have eaten at the same family table and shared relatives, friends, and life experiences (Horowitz, 1993; Kennedy & Baron, 1993; Witkin, 1991).

Among social factors contributing to violence, the most important, in all probability, is the accessibility of firearms. Not only handguns, but sophisticated semi-automatic weapons are readily available to those who would have them. The most frequently used weapon in the United States is a gun. Studies tracking the relationship of gun regulations to patterns of violent crime find them to be predictably related. A six-year study conducted in Seattle and Vancouver, for instance, found that as gun regulations became more restrictive, the risk of injury or death by guns decreased (Garland & Zigler, 1993; Sloan et al, 1988).

ADOLESCENTS AND DRUGS

As Ferris Bueller says, "Life moves pretty fast. If you don't stop and look around once in a while, you could miss it." He's right. If anything, it's faster now than

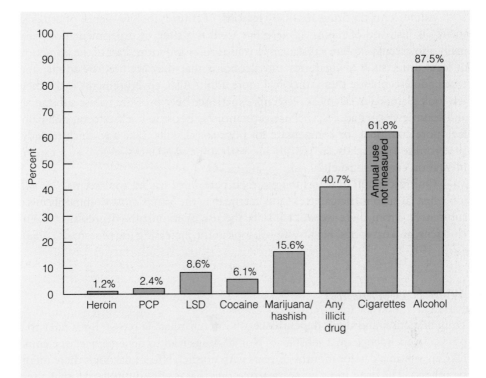

Figure 12.2 High School Seniors Reporting Having Ever Used Selected Drugs.
Source: Youth Indicators. (1993). Trends in the well-being of American Youth. *Washington, DC: U.S. Government Printing Office.*

ever before: instant banking, express mail, 1-hour faxing, 24-hour markets, fast foods, and five-lane expressways. Stimulants, tranquilizers, sedatives, and alcohol fit neatly into the pace of our lives—they instantaneously pick us up, settle us down, mellow us out, or just blur the edges.

Today's adolescents expect fast results, and drugs are part of society's response to that expectation. Millions of Americans find it impossible to get started in the morning without coffee or a cigarette or to relax in the evening without a drink. Millions more take medication for pain, pills to sleep, laxatives to correct faulty diets, pills to suppress appetites, and vitamin supplements when they fail to eat enough. Adolescents see quick pick-me-ups and instant remedies modeled everywhere around them. It is little wonder that by their senior year in high school, 91% of adolescents have tried alcohol, 44% have used marijuana/hashish, 26% have used stay-awake pills, and 33% of all adolescent females have used diet pills (Johnston, O'Malley, & Bachman, 1989; Youth Indicators, 1993). Figure 12.2 shows the number of high school seniors reporting use of various drugs.

Adolescents try drugs for many reasons, of course; the prevalence of drugs in society is just one of them. Adolescence itself is a time of experimentation, and many adolescents explore substances as well as roles and ideas. Part of the attraction of legal drugs such as cigarettes and alcohol is that they are used by adults; and when adolescents use them, they feel more adult. Also, advertisements make their use look glamorous. Many adolescents experience peer pressure to use substances and countless other adolescents use substances to boost low self-esteem, dull pain, feel more confident, or compensate for poor social skills. Like any quick remedy, the promise far exceeds the payoff, and with some substances, even casual experimentation carries substantial risk.

Our discussion of drugs follows their pattern of use by adolescents. We will look first at alcohol, cigarettes, and marijuana, the three most commonly used substances. From there we will consider the use of stimulants, depressants, hallucinogens, and narcotics. Finally, we will look at the increasing use of steroids (*DSM-IIIR*, 1987).

What Is Dependence?

Drug addiction and **drug dependence** are interchangeable terms. Both refer to a physical dependence on a substance. Not all drugs lead to dependence; one could take an aspirin a day for months or years with no such effect (although there might be others). The drug must be *psychoactive*: one that is self-administered, that alters one's mood, and comes to control behavior in such a way that one is no longer free *not* to use it (Surgeon General's Report, 1988). Dependence on a drug always involves developing a tolerance for it; the body requires increased amounts of the drug to achieve the same effect. Dependence also results in withdrawal symptoms whenever use is discontinued. Drug dependence can interfere with school, work, and relationships (*DSM-IIIR*, 1987). The criteria for dependence appear in Box 12.1.

Alcohol

Alcohol is usually the first drug adolescents try; most do so before they reach high school. Many people do not think of alcohol as a drug, because its use is so embedded in the context of everyday life, but it is a powerful central nervous system (CNS) depressant. Its effect on the nervous system is to restrain inhibitions, making the person feel more spontaneous. Many people become more talkative, confident, and socially at ease after they have had a drink.

Alcohol's effect on the central nervous system is in direct relation to its concentration in the blood. As the blood-alcohol level rises, activities controlled by the CNS are increasingly affected. Movements become uncoordinated, thoughts disorganized, reactions slowed, and mood frequently turns negative. Even small

BOX 12.1

Criteria for Drug Dependence

Drug dependence has occurred when at least three of the following factors are present:

- One uses more of the substance or for a longer time than intended.
- Attempts to stop or cut down are unsuccessful.
- Significant amounts of time are devoted to getting the substance, using it, or recovering from it.
- Use interferes with performance at school, work, or with one's relationships.
- Tolerance develops such that one needs more of the substance to achieve the same effect.
- Withdrawal symptoms occur if one discontinues use of the substance.
- One gives up or reduces social, recreational, or occupational activities because of substance use.
- One continues to use the substance in the face of problems occasioned by it, e.g., family disputes over cocaine use, aggravation of an ulcer by drinking.
- One will take the substance to relieve withdrawal symptoms.

Source: Adapted from Diagnostic and statistical manual of mental disorders *(3rd ed., rev. ed.). (1987). Washington, DC: American Psychiatric Association.*

amounts of alcohol may be enough to affect complex activities requiring coordination and judgment. Continued use of alcohol leads to dependence (Westermeyer, 1986).

Despite, or perhaps because of, its powerful effects, almost all high school seniors have tried alcohol; 64% use it with some regularity. Even though the number of adolescents who drink daily is low (4.2%), 35% engage in periodic episodes of heavy drinking, in which they are likely to have five or more drinks in a row at least once in a 2-week period. These episodes are more frequent among males, largely due to the frequency with which they drink beer (Johnston, O'Malley, & Bachman, 1989). Not all adolescents are equally at risk for abusing alcohol. Hispanic adolescents, and particularly Dominican adolescents, are especially at risk (Bettes, Dusenbury, Kerner, James-Ortiz, & Botvin, 1990). Conversely, black high school seniors have been found to have lower frequencies of alcohol use than white classmates (Benson & Donahue, 1989).

The abuse of alcohol is associated with numerous complications. Alcohol is absorbed into all tissues of the body, affecting everything from the central nervous system, to internal organs, to the skeletal muscles. Excessive use of alcohol can damage the liver, produce gastritis, affect kidney functioning, lead to sensory disturbances; it can cause blackouts, memory loss, coma—and ultimately even death (Westermeyer, 1986). Its destruction to the bodies of chronic abusers is paralleled by the destruction it causes in the lives of those around them. Approximately 1.5

BOX 12.2

Students Against Driving Drunk (SADD)

Students Against Driving Drunk (SADD) is designed to improve adolescents' knowledge about alcohol in order to save their lives—and the lives of others. The program has three components.

1. It provides a series of lessons that present the facts about drinking and driving, permitting students to make informed decisions.
2. It mobilizes students to help each other, through peer pressure, to face up to the potential dangers of mixing driving with alcohol or drugs.
3. It promotes a dialogue between adolescents and their parents through the SADD Contract. Under this agreement, both students and their parents pledge to contact each other should they ever find themselves in a potential DUI (driving under the influence) situation.

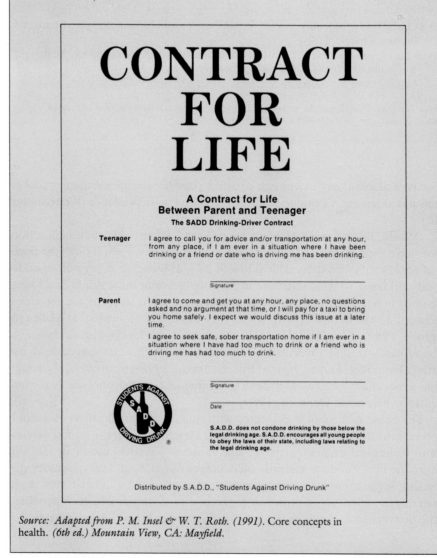

CONTRACT FOR LIFE

**A Contract for Life
Between Parent and Teenager**
The SADD Drinking-Driver Contract

Teenager   I agree to call you for advice and/or transportation at any hour, from any place, if I am ever in a situation where I have been drinking or a friend or date who is driving me has been drinking.

_____
Signature

Parent   I agree to come and get you at any hour, any place, no questions asked and no argument at that time, or I will pay for a taxi to bring you home safely. I expect we would discuss this issue at a later time.

I agree to seek safe, sober transportation home if I am ever in a situation where I have had too much to drink or a friend who is driving me has had too much to drink.

_____
Signature

_____
Date

S.A.D.D. does not condone drinking by those below the legal drinking age. S.A.D.D. encourages all young people to obey the laws of their state, including laws relating to the legal drinking age.

Distributed by S.A.D.D., "Students Against Driving Drunk"

Source: Adapted from P. M. Insel & W. T. Roth. (1991). Core concepts in health. (6th ed.) Mountain View, CA: Mayfield.

a sense of mastery. It is usually inhaled but can also be injected or smoked as "crack." Recent use of cocaine among high school seniors has dropped dramatically. Despite a spreading of the drug to new communities, this decline is most likely the result of media coverage of the hazards associated with its use. Adolescents have become increasingly aware that even one-time use can kill. Many adolescents appear to have been motivated not to even try cocaine, and many of those who have used it have stopped. Of the 6.1% of seniors who said they had ever tried cocaine, only 1.3% had used it in the last month (Youth Indicators, 1993).

Depressants

Substances called **depressants** reduce or lower the activity of the central nervous system. Alcohol is the most common of these; other depressants used by adolescents include inhalants, barbiturates, and tranquilizers. These substances decrease anxiety and produce a sense of euphoria. Since they depress the activity of vital centers in the nervous system, their use can be dangerous or even fatal in higher doses. Barbiturates, for example, are especially dangerous when combined with alcohol (Kaufman, Shaffer, & Burglass, 1985).

Inhalants. Inhaling fumes from substances such as glue, gasoline, paint thinner, lighter fluid, nail polish remover, and other solvents can produce feelings of mild intoxication and elation. The use of **inhalants** can also result in disorientation, nausea, pulmonary crisis, psychosis, and even coma. Inhalants are especially toxic substances that can damage numerous tissues within the body, including those of the brain, kidneys, liver, and bone marrow. Perhaps because inhalants are readily accessible (many are found around the house), they are among the first substances to be tried by many adolescents. Although the use of inhalants increased in the mid 1980s, it has dropped off in the last several years (Johnston, Bachman, & O'Malley, 1989).

Barbiturates. Street names for barbiturates include "yellow jackets" (Nembutal), "reds" (Seconal), and "tueys" (Tuinal). Literally thousands of different types of barbiturates are manufactured for medical use; many of these end up on the street. **Barbiturates** give adolescents a sense of euphoria and lessened inhibitions; their use can also result in intense mood swings, paranoia, and suicidal thoughts. Almost all barbiturates are highly addictive. Their use has been declining over the past 15 years. Only 3.2% of high school seniors reported using them in the past year, compared with nearly 11% in 1975 (Johnston, O'Malley, & Bachman, 1989; Kaufman, Shaffer, & Burglass, 1985).

Quaaludes. Commonly known as "ludes," **Quaaludes** produce effects similar to those of barbiturates, though they are not actually barbiturates. Their addictive potential is high. The use of this drug by adolescents has been steadily declining over the past decade. Only 1.3% of high school seniors reported having used it in the past year (Johnston, O'Malley, & Bachman, 1989).

Tranquilizers.   **Tranquilizers** include such drugs as Valium, Librium, Equanil, and Miltown. They decrease anxiety and increase feelings of well-being and relaxation; they can also produce psychological and physiological dependence. As with other depressants, their use has declined over recent years. Fewer than 5% of high school seniors reported using them in 1988 (Johnston, O'Malley, & Bachman, 1989).

Narcotics

Narcotics include heroin, morphine, and opium. *Heroin* is a derivative of *morphine,* which itself is derived from opium; *opium* comes from the seeds of poppies. Heroin produces its most intense effects when injected into the bloodstream ("mainlining"), although it can also be injected under the skin ("popped") or sniffed. Users report an intense initial euphoria followed by a more prolonged period of calm and well-being that lasts for several hours. Weakness, sweating, nausea, and vomiting are also common among users. Relatively few adolescents try heroin; 1.2% of high school seniors surveyed had ever tried it (Youth Indicators, 1993).

All narcotics are highly addictive, and tolerance develops rapidly. The extreme pleasure experienced initially by users lessens with continued use, making it necessary for them to increase the dosage to obtain the same effect. The risk of an overdose increases as the dosage is increased. This risk is even greater than might be imagined, because the difference between a dose that would produce a "high" and a lethal dose is often relatively small.

Narcotics are actually not as toxic to the body as alcohol and barbiturates; however, their use carries greater secondary risk. Since heroin is almost always injected, infection from shared contaminated needles is a major risk. Hepatitis, tetanus, and AIDS are associated with the practice of sharing unsterilized needles. Users can also inject an air bubble into their vein, which can be fatal. Once dependence is established, the cost of the drug can run as high as several hundred dollars a day, a habit that for most can only be supported by crime.

Hallucinogens

The experience obtained from using hallucinogens is unlike that from using any other substances. **Hallucinogens** primarily affect thought and perception. One person described the experience as follows: "Closing my eyes, I saw millions of color droplets, like rain, like a shower of stars, all different colors" (Goode, 1984). It is common for adolescents to experience ordinary objects as fascinating, time as slowing, emotions as magnified, and the sense of self as profoundly changed. *LSD* and *mescaline* are common hallucinogens. Marijuana can also produce hallucinogenic effects.

Anabolic Steroids

Anabolic steroids are synthetic male hormones widely used by athletes to improve their muscular development and athletic performance. (Anabolic is the term for a metabolic process that builds up tissue.) An estimated half a million adolescent athletes use anabolic steroids. Considerable controversy surrounds their use because steroids have a number of negative side effects. Anabolic steroids increase aggressiveness and hostility, cause liver damage, raise blood pressure, and are associated with the development of several types of cancer. The only effects that adolescents may notice immediately are a slight change in their mood; they become more irritable and aggressive. However, the lure of enhanced performance and the "body beautiful" may seduce many to use steroids and disregard the potential hazards of their long-term use.

Most adolescents will experiment with at least some drugs before they reach adulthood. A positive note is that most will not abuse them. However, even casual experimentation with some substances carries substantial risks. How best can society protect adolescents from the potential hazards of experimentation? Is the most effective approach to bombard them with information concerning the dangers of drugs such that they never take that first sip, puff, or pop? Given the pleasurable effects of drugs and the powerful pressures to use them, as well as the excitement of daring the forbidden, scare programs are not likely to keep most adolescents from experimenting. Candid discussions that acknowledge the pleasurable effects of drugs as well as their potential for abuse promise a better safeguard for adolescents. Establishing trust through open communication makes it possible for adolescents to approach adults when they need information, or even help.

DEPRESSION

Emotions color experience and give meaning to life. For most individuals they are anchored in reality, tethered to the situations that prompt them. Some individuals are pulled past reality to an inner world of thoughts and feelings that bears little resemblance to the situations that occasion them. These individuals suffer from **affective disorders**, disturbances that affect their mood. Mood is an enduring emotional state that varies along a continuum of depression to elation (*DSM-IIIR*, 1987). Individuals who suffer from affective disorders live much of their lives at the extremes of this continuum.

Three Depressive Disorders

From time to time everyone feels sad. Those who live with **depression** feel a crushing weight of hopelessness and despair. They may have any of three major forms

Nearly half of all adolescents report experiencing some of the symptoms that characterize depression: sadness, crying spells, pessimism, and feelings of unworthiness.

of depression. Adolescents with *major depressive disorder* experience severe periods of depression lasting several weeks or more. These are accompanied by some or all of the following symptoms: difficulty concentrating, loss of pleasure, slowed speech and movements, and "vegetative signs" such as sleepiness, loss of appetite, and weight changes. Adolescents suffering from *dysthymia* have a less severe form of depression but one that generally lasts much longer. The third form, *adjustment disorder with depressed mood,* is brought on by stress and is relatively brief (Petersen, Compas, Brooks-Gunn, Stemmler, Ey, & Grant, 1993).

Feelings of sadness, loneliness, and despair become common by mid-adolescence. Nearly half of all adolescents report experiencing some of the symptoms that characterize depression—sadness, crying spells, pessimism, and feelings of unworthiness. Even so, fewer than 10% of adolescents are diagnosed with depression (Weiner, 1980).

Adolescents who suffer from depression share with adult depressives feelings of low self-esteem, pervasive sadness, hopelessness, and helplessness (Craighead & Green, 1989). A self-defeating cycle exists in which low self-esteem contributes to depression, which in turn fuels negative feelings about the self (Rosenberg, Schooler, & Schoenbach, 1989). More females than males experience depression.

A change in the sex ratio of those suffering from depression occurs during puberty (Rutter, 1986). This change could reflect hormonal influences, or may reflect identification with culturally defined gender roles. The female gender role includes more socially undesirable characteristics than does the male gender role. This difference could easily affect the self-esteem of adolescent females as they identify with the culturally defined role. L. W. Craighead and B. J. Green (1989) found differences in self-esteem to account for approximately half of the variability in depression among normal adolescents.

Masked Depression

Depression is often masked in early adolescence (Weiner, 1980). Several symptoms signal *masked depression*, the most frequent being fatigue, poor concentration, and hypochondriasis (excessive concern with illness or health). Continual fatigue can reflect inner struggles with feelings that adolescents cannot put to rest or talk about with others. Similarly, difficulties in concentration can result from concerns they do not yet feel secure enough to articulate, and preoccupations with their health, or a seeming lack of it, may reflect fears of inadequacy or incompetence.

Each of these symptoms can be mistakenly interpreted as a natural part of adolescence. Fatigue is expected, given the accelerated growth of puberty and the demands of school, friends, and family. Similarly, poor concentration can easily be mistaken for problems with schoolwork ranging from boredom to being overwhelmed, and excessive concern with one's body is natural, given the changes that take place during puberty. Treatments that take into consideration the underlying source of an adolescent's depression will be more effective in combatting these symptoms than those that are directed at the symptoms themselves: the fatigue, poor concentration, or excessive concern with health (Weiner, 1980).

Irving Weiner (1980) suggests that adolescents may not be able to admit feelings of inadequacy and still accomplish the developmental tasks they face— achieving emotional independence, finding a sense of self, developing heterosexual relationships, and so on. Any one of these would be difficult under the best of conditions, and can be impossible with feelings of inadequacy. Early adolescents may also be more caught up in *doing* things than in reflecting about them (Weiner, 1980). In either case, depression, or attempts to keep it at bay, are likely to at first assume a physical form in early adolescence.

SUICIDE

An alarming number of adolescents report thinking about suicide. In a national survey of over 12,000 high school students in 1991, 29% said that they had thought seriously about attempting suicide at some point during the past year, 19% indicating they had even made specific plans (Maguire, Pastore, & Flanagan, 1993).

By comparison, the percentage who actually attempt suicide is relatively low, 7%, and still fewer actually commit suicide. However, adolescence stands out as a time in life that is especially hazardous with respect to suicide. Suicide is the third leading cause of death among 15- to 19-year-olds, being responsible for 14% of all deaths in that age group (National Center for Health Statistics, 1991). The number of suicide attempts peaks between ages 15 and 24 (Schuckit & Schuckit, 1989).

The rate of suicide for 15- to-19-year-olds has more than tripled over the past three decades (National Center for Health Statistics, 1991). Approximately every 90 minutes a young person completes a suicide (Bolton, 1989). Startling as these figures are, they probably underestimate the actual number of deaths by suicide because they don't include the many deaths recorded as accidents (e.g., single person car crashes, drownings, overdoses), which in many cases are misclassified suicides. The picture darkens further with the addition of attempted suicides. For every completed suicide, anywhere from 8 to 20 more adolescents unsuccessfully attempt it; of these, up to 10 percent will later succeed (*Report of the Secretary's Task Force on Youth Suicide*, 1989).

Though startling in themselves, these figures assume a more ominous note when compared with suicide rates for other age groups. Figure 12.3 shows that the overall rate of suicide for the total population has changed little over this same time period, while that for young persons has increased substantially.

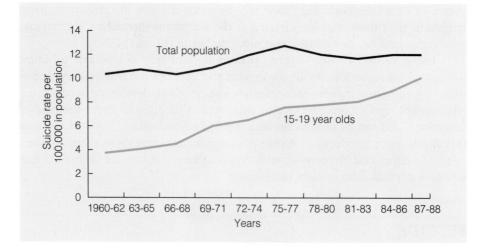

Figure 12.3 Suicide Rates per 100,000 in Population for Total Population and for 15–19-Year-Olds.

Source: A. F. Galton & E. Zigler. (1993). Adolescent suicide prevention: Current research and social policy implications. American Psychologist, 48, *169–182.*

Gender and Ethnic Differences

Males are four times more likely than females to complete a suicide, despite the fact that females attempt suicide three times as often as males (Berman & Jobes, 1991). In part, this difference can be traced to the different methods chosen by males and females. Males are most likely to use a gun or attempt to hang themselves, both of which are more immediately lethal than ingesting harmful substances, the method most commonly used by females (Garland & Zigler, 1993). Among completed suicides, for both sexes, using a gun is the most frequent method. Although at first glance, these gender differences would seem to suggest less ambivalence about dying among males, other factors are probably more important. Males, in general, are more impulsive and violent than females, qualities that are reflected in the methods they choose. Impulsivity may be a critical factor in most suicides, and males, because they are likely to choose a violent method, will be successful more frequently (Garland & Zigler, 1993). Also, females may be able to use interpersonal supports more easily than males, who typically find it more difficult to reveal neediness or ask for help (Garland & Zigler, 1993).

Ethnic differences exist as well in suicidal thoughts and behavior. Table 12.5 summarizes the responses of over 11,000 high school students to questions concerning suicide. Black students reported fewer suicidal thoughts or attempts than either white or Hispanic students. Conversely, Hispanic students reported substantially more suicide attempts and were somewhat more likely to think about suicide than either of the other groups (Maguire, Pastore, & Flanagan, 1993).

T A B L E   1 2 . 5

Percentages of Black, Hispanic, and White High School Students Reporting Suicidal Thoughts and Behavior

Ethnicity	Suicidal Thoughts	Made Suicide Plans	One or More Suicide Attempts	Attempt(s) Requiring Medical Attention
Black	20.4	13.5	6.5	1.4
Hispanic	30.4	19.5	12.0	2.4
White	28.1	16.1	7.9	2.1

Note: Questions asked whether students had seriously thought about attempting suicide at any time in the past year, whether they had made a specific plan, how many attempts they had made, and whether any of these required treatment by a doctor or nurse.

Source: Centers for Disease Control. (1991, September 20). Attempted suicide among high school students—United States, 1990. Morbidity and Mortality Weekly Report, Washington, DC: U.S. Government Printing Office.

Among all ethnic groups, the rate of suicide is highest for Native Americans. However, large differences exist between different tribes. The rate of suicide among Navajos, for instance, is close to that nationally, whereas the rate among Apaches is more than three times as high (Garland & Zigler, 1993). As a rule, tribes which are more traditional tend to have lower suicide rates, perhaps because they provide a greater sense of community and their members experience more support (Wyche, Obolensky, & Glood, 1990).

Suicide used to be most common among older white males with mental health problems. Currently, the rate of suicide in that segment of the population is decreasing, while increasing among the young, many of whom do not have the same history of problems. As a consequence, previous prevention and treatment approaches may not be useful in identifying potential youth suicides.

Prevention is just one link in a chain beginning with detection. A report of the Secretary's Task Force on Youth Suicide observes that the rate at which adolescents are committing suicide is unprecedented, but concludes that we know less about youth suicide than most other health problems. Past research on suicide has focused on the relation between suicide and mental disorders. The extent to which we can extend this relationship in any simple fashion to youth suicide remains to be seen (*Report of the Secretary's Task Force on Youth Suicide*, 1989).

Warning Signs

Although every case of suicide is unique, a number of common warning signs exist. These include sudden changes in behavior, changes in patterns of sleeping or eating, loss of interest in usual activities or withdrawal from others, experiencing a humiliating event, feelings of guilt or hopelessness, an inability to concentrate, talk of suicide, or giving away one's most important possessions (Blumenthal & Kupfer, 1988). The presence of any one of these is a cause for concern; the presence of several is a clear signal that an adolescent is in danger.

Risk Factors

A variety of factors are associated with an increased risk of suicide. Most of these characterize the person at risk, although some, such as substance abuse or exposure to suicidal behavior can also involve elements of the family or the larger culture. Even though most suicides are associated with one or more of these risk factors, about one-third of youth suicides are associated with no risk factors at all; these youths come from loving and supportive homes.

S. J. Blumenthal and D. J. Kupfer (1988) classify risk factors into potentially overlapping domains. As the overlap among domains increases, so does the risk of suicide, as illustrated in Figure 12.4. According to this approach,

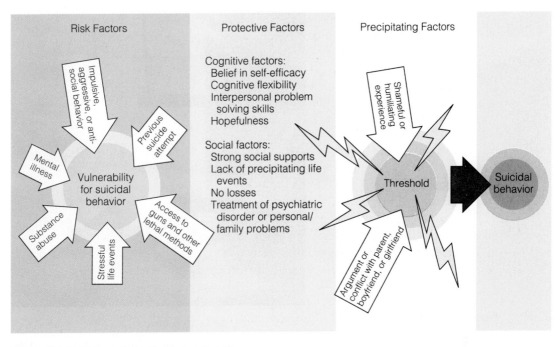

Figure 12.4 Factors Contributing to Suicide.

Source: Adapted from S. J. Blumenthal & D. J. Kupfer. (1988). Overview of early detection and treatment strategies for suicidal behavior in young people. Journal of Youth and Adolescence, 17, 1–23.

the breakup of a relationship might be a final humiliating experience that triggers a depressive episode in a young person with a family history of affective disorder. Such an individual may also have poor social supports, which interact with the other identified risk factors to increase the individual's vulnerability for suicide. (Blumenthal & Kupfer, 1988, p. 4)

Cognitive factors that help to protect adolescents from the threat of suicide are feelings of self-efficacy, problem solving skills, and hopefulness. Similarly, social factors decreasing the risk of suicide are the presence of strong social supports, the lack of precipitating life events, and getting treatment or help for personal or family problems.

Mental Illness.   Mental illness plays a significant role in almost all adolescent suicides (Garland & Zigler, 1993). Several diagnostic categories in particular are especially implicated; suicide is particularly high for those with affective disorders and schizophrenia (Blumenthal & Kupfer, 1988; Garland & Zigler, 1993). Antisocial behavior is also closely linked to suicidal behavior. The Secretary's Task Force notes that "antisocial behavior and depressive symptoms appear to be a particularly

One-third of youth suicides are not associated with known risk factors; these adolescents come from loving and supportive homes, and the parents find themselves at a loss to explain why their child would attempt suicide.

lethal combination" (*Report of the Secretary's Task Force on Youth Suicide,* 1989, p. 20).

Prior Attempt. Perhaps one of the most serious risk factors for suicide is having made a prior attempt. Anywhere from 50% to 80% of all actual suicides by adolescents have been preceded by a previous attempt (Shafii, Carrigan, Whittinghill, & Derrick, 1985). Suicidal remarks or other warning signs among such adolescents assume added significance.

A common cultural stereotype of adolescent suicide attempts holds that these are shallow and impulsive bids for attention. Neither assumption is true. Adolescents who are suicidal are in personal pain and have usually sought a number of solutions to their present problems. Suicidal adolescents usually attempt to communicate their distress in a number of ways, and thoughts of suicide are often a last resort (Weiner, 1980). The poem in Box 12.3 is a poignant illustration of this point.

Personality Traits. Three personality characteristics are especially linked to suicide: aggression, impulsiveness, and a sense of hopelessness, the most significant characteristic (*Report of the Secretary's Task Force on Youth Suicide,* 1989).

Substance Abuse. Abuse of alcohol or other substances, either by adolescents themselves or by someone in their families, is associated with increased risk of suicide (Windle, Miller-Tutzauer, & Domenico, 1992). Thirty percent to 40% of adolescents who attempt suicide have parents who abuse alcohol (*Report of the*

BOX 12.3

A Poem Written by a 15-Year-Old Boy Two Years Prior to Committing Suicide

To Santa Claus and Little Sisters

Once . . . he wrote a poem.
And called it "Chops."
Because that was the name of
    his dog, and that's what it was
    all about.
And the teacher gave him
    an "A"
And a gold star.
And his mother hung it on the
    kitchen door, and read it to
    all his aunts . . .
Once . . . he wrote another
    poem.
And he called it "Question
    Marked Innocence."
Because that was the name of
    his grief and that's what it
    was all about.
And the professor gave him an "A"
And a strange and steady look.
And his mother never hung it
    on the kitchen door, because
    he never let her see it . . .
Once, at 3 a.m. . . . he tried
    another poem . . .
And he called it absolutely
    nothing, because that's what it
    was all about.
And he gave himself an "A"
And a slash on each damp wrist,
And hung it on the bathroom
    door because he couldn't reach
    the kitchen.

Sources: A. Russell Lee, M.D., Director of Family Therapy Training, Pacific Medical Center, San Francisco, California, and Contra Costa, California, Mental Health Services; and Charlotte P. Ross, Executive Director, Suicide Prevention and Crisis Center, San Mateo County, Burlingame, California.

Secretary's Task Force on Youth Suicide, 1989). Many adolescents who attempt suicide get drunk first, perhaps to muster the courage they need. Although alcohol dulls psychological pain, it is a depressant and may contribute to suicidal impulses. As a substance that can be easily abused, it can also interfere with long-term constructive approaches to problem solutions. The combined effects of alcohol and other substances, such as barbiturates, amphetamines, and cocaine can be especially deadly.

Other forms of substance abuse are also significantly related to suicide. Death rates among adolescents who are heavy drug users are anywhere from two to eight times higher than among those their age in the general population. Approximately half of these deaths are estimated to be suicides.

Psychosocial Circumstances.   Adolescents who attempt or commit suicide commonly experience more life stress, more losses, and more changes within the family than those who do not. Frequently a humiliating event precipitates the suicide attempt, such as a crisis or an interpersonal problem involving parents or peers. Family life is more likely to be chaotic, relationships with parents are frequently problematic, and parental strife is more common. Suicidal adolescents generally have fewer social supports and personal resources while facing these added stresses (Blumenthal & Kupfer, 1988).

Lethal Means.   The availability of lethal methods, particularly firearms, appears to be a factor affecting suicide rates. The increase in the rate at which adolescents commit suicide by shooting themselves has risen three times faster than the rates for other methods. This increase has paralleled the increased availability of guns to teenagers, both in their own homes (Brent, Perper, Goldstein, Kolko, Allan, Altman, & Zelenak, 1988) and in society in general (Garland & Zigler, 1993). Since firearms are the most frequent means in the United States by which adolescents commit suicide, the importance of determining the impact of gun-control legislation cannot be overestimated. Guns account for the majority of suicides—among females as well as males (*Report of the Secretary's Task Force on Youth Suicide,* 1989).

Biochemical Imbalance.   Evidence suggests involvement of brain neurotransmitters (chemicals involved in communication between one nerve cell and another) in suicidal behavior. The two neurotransmitters involved are serotonin and dopamine. Specifically, investigators find lower levels of the by-products of these neurotransmitters (5-hydroxyindoleacetic acid, or 5-HIAA, and homovanillic acid, or HVA) in the cerebrospinal fluid (*Report of the Secretary's Task Force on Youth Suicide,* 1989).

Exposure to Suicidal Behavior.   Coverage of a suicide by the news media has been shown to affect local suicide rates, especially among adolescents. Also, adolescents who have a friend or family member who has attempted or committed suicide are more likely to attempt suicide (Garland & Zigler, 1993).

ticipate and manage the emotions prompted by stress. Differences in instrumentality among adolescents capture these dimensions of coping and predict adaptive responses.

Alienation and the Failure to Cope

Feelings of alienation are common in adolescence. These can be triggered by pubertal changes, identity issues, and feelings of cultural estrangement.

Many alienated adolescents are runaways. These youths are frequently abused or neglected. As a group they suffer from low self-esteem, depression, poor interpersonal skills, insecurity, anxiousness, impulsiveness, and lack of a sense of personal control over their lives. Homelife for most is chaotic and characterized by violence.

Three homelife patterns distinguish adolescents who are abused and neglected. The abuse may be a continuation of abusive patterns that started in childhood, it may reflect a change in the type of discipline used when they reach adolescence, or it may be occasioned by the onset of adolescence itself. Abusive parents are likely to have had inadequate parenting models and have inadequate parenting skills.

Most adolescents who are sexually abused are female. Most of the perpetrators are males, and most are members of the immediate family or are relatives. Most sexual abuse starts in childhood.

Juvenile Delinquency

Juvenile delinquency involves illegal behavior committed by a minor. Status offenses are behaviors that are illegal when engaged in by minors, but legal for adults. Index offenses are behaviors that are criminal at any age.

The incidence of adolescents committing either type of offense has increased sixfold since 1955. The type of delinquent act varies with age. There is little evidence suggesting that minor forms of delinquency predict a later shift to more serious crime. The pattern instead suggests a small subgroup of delinquents who start early and account for a relatively large proportion of criminal activity.

Gender, ethnic, and social class differences exist in delinquency. Females are nearly twice as likely as males to commit status offenses, and males are more likely to commit index offenses. Large ethnic differences exist, but these are difficult to separate from social class differences and racial bias within the juvenile justice system.

Adolescents who become delinquent usually experience problems in school, have low self-esteem, come from homes characterized by violence and abuse, have poor social skills, are more aggressive with peers, and are more impulsive.

Juvenile gangs have changed over the last generation. They are more likely to be linked to organized crime than in the past, and are associated with more violent crimes and the sale of narcotics. The threat of violence is not limited to gang members. Teenagers are two and a half times more likely to be victims of violent crime than those 20 years or older. Homicide is the second leading cause of injury-related deaths in children and adolescents. Those most at risk are minority males.

Adolescents and Drugs

Physical drug dependence occurs with psychoactive substances when they control behavior so that the individual cannot easily discontinue their use. Dependence on a drug involves developing a tolerance for it such that increased amounts are necessary to achieve the same effect, resulting in withdrawal when use is discontinued. Adolescents are likely to first try alcohol, then cigarettes, and then marijuana.

Alcohol depresses the activity of the central nervous system; it loosens inhibitions and makes individuals feel more spontaneous. As blood-alcohol level rises, activities controlled by the central nervous system are increasingly affected. Almost all high school seniors have tried alcohol and nearly 64% do so with some regularity.

Cigarettes contain nicotine, which is both a stimulant and a depressant. Most adolescents who smoke start before they reach high school. Nearly 20% of high school seniors smoke daily. Most adolescents who start to smoke have tried unsuccessfully to stop. The use of cigarettes and alcohol is associated with the use of other, illicit substances.

Marijuana is a mild hallucinogen that affects thought, perception, reaction time, and coordination. Long-term heavy use carries a number of potential health risks. Of all illicit drugs, marijuana is the most frequently used by adolescents.

Stimulants excite the central nervous system, boost energy, elevate mood, and depress appetite. They include amphetamines, cocaine, and the crystal form of cocaine known as crack. Serious health hazards attend their use.

Depressants reduce or lower the activity of the central nervous system. Alcohol is the most common depressant; others include inhalants, barbiturates, and tranquilizers. The use of each of these by adolescents has declined in recent years.

Narcotics include heroin, morphine, and opium. Heroin is a derivative of morphine, which is derived from opium, which comes from the seeds of poppies. Tolerance develops rapidly with narcotics; the risk of an overdose increases correspondingly. Other serious risks attend the use of narcotics. Hallucinogens primarily affect thought and perception. LSD, mescaline, and marijuana are common hallucinogens.

Anabolic steroids are synthetic hormones that improve muscular development and athletic performance. They are widely used by athletes. Steroids increase aggressiveness and hostility, and their use is associated with numerous health risks.

Most adolescents will experiment with some drugs before they reach adulthood; most will also not use them frequently. Even casual experimentation with some substances carries substantial risks. Candid discussions that acknowledge the pleasurable effects of drugs as well as their potential dangers promise to be the most effective ways of providing help to adolescents.

Depression

Depression is an affective disorder that can take a number of forms. Adolescents with major depressive disorder suffer episodes of debilitating depression that can last for several weeks or more. Those with dysthymia experience less-severe but longer-lasting symptoms. Those with adjustment disorder with depressed mood experience brief bouts of depression brought on by stress. Adolescents who suffer from depression have feelings of low self-esteem, sadness, hopelessness, and helplessness. Depression can be masked by physical symptoms in early adolescence.

Suicide

The rate of suicide among adolescents has nearly tripled over the past three decades. Males are four times more likely than females to complete a suicide. Suicide is the third most common cause of death among those 15 to 19 years old.

Warnings signs include sudden changes in behavior, changes in sleeping or eating patterns, loss of interest in usual activities or withdrawal from others, experiencing a humiliating event, feelings of guilt or hopelessness, inability to concentrate, talk of suicide, or giving away important possessions.

Factors that place adolescents at risk of suicide are mental illness, substance abuse, life stresses and chaotic family lives, biochemical imbalances, the availability of lethal means, and prior suicide attempts.

The most effective treatment programs work with the family as well as the suicidal adolescent.

Schizophrenia

Schizophrenia is a disorder characterized by disturbances of thought, perception, and emotion. It is most likely to occur first in adolescence or early adulthood. Warning signs include becoming shy and withdrawn or aggressive.

The most distinguishing feature to schizophrenia is a disturbance of thought that takes the form of loosely associated and shifting ideas. Approximately one-quarter of adolescents who have been hospitalized for schizophrenia recover and another quarter improve with relapses.

KEY TERMS

Stress
General Adaptation
   Syndrome (GAS)
Coping
Stress-Inoculation Training
Attributional Error
Alienation
Juvenile Delinquency
Status Offenses

Index Offenses
Drug Dependence
Marijuana
Stimulants
Amphetamine
Cocaine
Depressants
Inhalants
Barbiturates

Quaaludes
Tranquilizers
Narcotics
Hallucinogens
Anabolic Steroids
Affective Disorders
Depression
Schizophrenia

RESEARCH STRATEGIES
Number of Subjects
Degree of Control

ISSUES AND DESIGNS IN
DEVELOPMENTAL RESEARCH
Cross-Sectional Designs
Longitudinal Designs
Sequential Designs
Path Analysis

RESPONSE MEASURES IN
DEVELOPMENTAL RESEARCH
Dependent Variables
Types of Response Measures

RESEARCH ISSUES
Internal and External Validity
Theory-Guided Research
Operationalizing Concepts
Sampling
Bias and Blind Controls
Tests of Significance
Ethics

RESEARCH DESIGNS
Between-Subjects Designs
Within-Subjects Designs
Matched-Subjects Designs
Factorial Designs

CHAPTER THIRTEEN

Studying Adolescence: Research Methods and Issues

Even the best minds can arrive at the wrong conclusions unless they base them on sound observations. For instance, Robert Solso and Homer Johnson (1994) note that medieval scholars believed that a shaft of wheat, if left undisturbed in an open box for several days, would turn into mice. Had these scholars also observed bins with lids on them, they could have avoided this mistaken conclusion. It's possible, of course, that they did *and still concluded that wheat turned into mice—the bins may have had some holes in them. Clearly, observation alone carries no guarantees.*

The opening section of this chapter introduces a number of research strategies. Research strategies differ in terms of the numbers of individuals studied and the degree of control the investigator exerts. A number of different strategies will be examined in terms of their relative effectiveness.

Developmental research, in which age is a variable, faces the need to separate the effects of age from variables that may vary with age. Three research designs—cross-sectional, longitudinal, and sequential—are compared for their effectiveness in achieving this end.

The chapter moves to a discussion of response measures and research issues, including internal versus external validity, operationalizing concepts, sampling, and ethics.

The last section of the chapter compares the relative advantages and disadvantages of between-subjects, within-subjects, matched-subjects, and factorial designs.

Finally, the Research Focus boxes that appear in each of the preceding chapters of the book present the different types of research that developmentalists employ in studying adolescents. Each box introduces a particular research problem concerning adolescents, then analyzes the research procedures that were used. Together, these boxes illustrate distinctions that are basic to an understanding of the methodology used by developmentalists.

RESEARCH STRATEGIES

Research strategies are procedures that scientists follow to safeguard against making faulty observations. Our discussion of these procedures will be organized in terms of two dimensions: (1) the number of subjects that are studied and (2) the degree of control the investigator has over conditions that could affect the observations. With respect to the first of these dimensions, strategies differ markedly. Researchers can limit their observations to a single individual, as in research involving case studies, or they can collect observations from as many as hundreds or even thousands of people in survey research. Differences are equally large with respect to the degree of control. At one extreme is naturalistic observation in which researchers record behavior in natural, everyday surroundings. At the other extreme are experiments in which behavior is observed under the controlled and often highly artificial conditions of the laboratory. Between these extremes lie correlational research and quasi-experiments. Clearly, we are talking about very different procedures in each case. Each type of research carries a particular set of advantages, and each has its own problems.

Number of Subjects

Case Studies.   In a **case study**, the investigator studies a single case extensively in order to arrive at a picture of the individual. The case is usually a person, although sometimes it might be a new program in a school, such as a jigsaw classroom (see Chapter 7), or even a school or work setting itself if it is unique in some way. Many clinical observations reflect the case study method. This method presents a detailed picture of the person. Freud, for example, saw many of his patients daily. The richness of the observations this method supplies is, in fact, one of its advantages. For instance, the case study of Grace, the highly gifted 13-year-old who was admitted to college (see Chapter 7, Research Focus: Case Studies), was based on extensive interviews with both Grace and her parents and weekly meetings with the director of the gifted program she participated in. Additional input came from sources such as Grace's grades in her college courses and observations of her developing relationships with peers. This strategy is useful, as the case study of Grace illustrates, for studying cases or conditions that are highly unusual and can't be studied in large numbers. One can gain insights through case studies leading to hypotheses that can be tested using other types of research.

Disadvantages to this approach concern the *generalizability* of the findings and the *objectivity* of the observations. How confident can we be that observations collected from a single individual are representative of others? This objection becomes especially critical when the individual is atypical. The concern, in fact, has been raised with respect to Freud's theory of psychosexual development (see Chapter 2). How reasonable is it to formulate a general theory of development

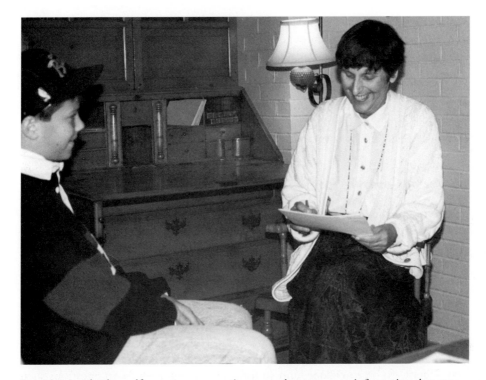

Interviews and other self-report measures give researchers access to information that cannot be easily observed. Roberta Simmons, shown here interviewing a young adolescent, used this technique in her research into adolescent development. With Dale Blyth and other colleagues, she provided important insights into the social and academic effects of early and late maturation.

based on the study of limited numbers of individuals, most or even all of whom suffered from psychological problems important enough to warrant psychoanalysis? Also, since the developmentalist collecting the observations works closely with the individual or program being observed, there is always the danger of losing one's objectivity, and reading more into the behavior than is actually there.

Surveys. *Surveys* allow one to study large numbers of people through **self-report** measures supplied by *interviews* or *questionnaires*. In self-reports, the subjects supply the information about themselves; the investigator does not observe their behavior directly. A distinct strength of this approach is the opportunity it provides to study behavior that could not be observed easily otherwise. For instance, A. L. Greene (1990) asked adolescents to describe what they thought their lives would be like as adults, what life events they would have experienced by different ages (see Chapter 1, Research Focus: Interviews). The interview format allowed Greene not only to study something which would have been difficult, if not impossible, to directly observe—expectations—but also to get adolescents to project themselves into the future and talk about behavior and events that had not even happened yet. Similarly, information about adolescents' sexual attitudes or practices is obtained almost exclusively through surveys. So, too, is most information about drug use. A weakness to relying on individuals' reports about themselves is the opportunity for distortion, either through deliberately changing information or by failing to remember events as they actually happened. Memory is significantly better for pleasant events than for unpleasant ones.

Degree of Control

Research strategies also differ in the *degree of control* the investigator has over conditions that could affect the observations. Procedures vary from those that exercise no control, such as archival research or naturalistic observations, to those with a high degree of control over extraneous conditions—experiments. Between these extremes lie quasi-experimental designs and correlational procedures.

Archival Research. **Archival research** uses data that already exist to answer questions posed by the investigator. Archival data exist in many forms, the most extensive source being the census. What percentage of adolescents live with a single parent? How many work at part-time jobs? What percentage of adolescents finish high school, go on to college, and so forth? To obtain answers to questions such as these, developmentalists can use census data and need not collect their own. Because census data are collected from large groups of individuals, they have the additional advantage of being representative of the population.

Other archival sources exist in the form of public records, such as birth certificates, marriage license applications, and applications for housing or welfare (Cozby, Worden, & Kee, 1989). One investigator checked marriage license applications for place of residence to identify changes in patterns of cohabitation prior to marriage and found that 53% of the couples gave the same address in 1980 in comparison to only 13% in 1970 (Gwartney-Gibbs, 1986).

Numerous public and private organizations maintain extensive archives; hospitals, housing and welfare agencies, newspapers, and libraries are just a few examples. What diseases are most common among adolescents? Records maintained by local health agencies provide answers. Are males more prone to accidents than females? Hospital emergency room records indicate that they are. Do more adolescents live in poverty today than 20 years ago? State and federal welfare agencies supply answers. For more on archival research, see Chapter 1, Research Focus: Archival Research.

Naturalistic Observation. Perhaps the purest form of research is to directly observe subjects in their natural settings. Developmentalists using **naturalistic observation** as an approach do not disrupt the natural flow of events; they simply watch and record behavior. Dian Fossey's research on the mountain gorilla of central Africa is perhaps the most widely known example of this type of research. Pure though it may be, this research is often extremely difficult to carry out. Fossey's research illustrates this point well. Mountain gorillas live in the rain forest, making it impossible to observe them from a distance. Yet if she attempted to get closer, the gorillas would notice her and either flee or attack. Her solution was to become a *participant observer*, observing their behavior by moving among them as just another member of the group. How does one do this? For Fossey this meant acting like a gorilla until they accepted her as one. Fossey describes beating her chest, vocalizing like a gorilla, and sitting for hours chewing on wild celery. The gorillas eventually accepted her, making it possible for her to live among them and observe their behavior.

Dexter Dunphy (1963) used much the same procedure to study adolescent peer groups. He observed them at school, after school, at social functions, or just hanging out together (see Chapter 6, Research Focus: Naturalistic Observation). Like Fossey, he became a participant observer, moving among the adolescents he was studying until they accepted him as one of the group. He found two distinct types of groups: the clique and the crowd. Cliques and crowds meet different needs in adolescents' lives. Crowd activities provide a setting in which adolescents experiment with new social behaviors; cliques provide feedback about the success of these behaviors.

Naturalistic observation is most helpful when the investigator does not know much about the domain being studied. As Dunphy's research illustrates, naturalistic observation allows one to discover patterns in the observed behavior. These patterns frequently suggest hypotheses that can be tested with other forms of research. Although it gives richly detailed descriptions of behavior, naturalistic observation does not offer explanations for why the behavior occurs. Developmentalists arrive at explanations only when they can rule out competing alternatives. To do this, they must be able to control extraneous conditions that could affect the behavior. Only experiments provide this type of control.

Erikson's Psychohistorical Approach.   Erik Erikson developed a unique style of research that combined the tools of clinical analysis with those of field work. His insights into human development reflected the psychoanalytic training he had received in working with Sigmund and Anna Freud. Erikson applied these skills to an analysis of the relationship between the individual and the group. His observations of individuals from different groups—whether Amerian teenagers or the Sioux and Yurok—convinced him that human development takes place within a social community. His willingness to study individuals in their natural communities contributed to his insights concerning the psychosocial nature of human development. This approach is discussed in Chapter 2, Research Focus: Erikson's Psychohistorical Approach.

Quasi-Experimental Designs.   **Quasi-experimental designs** work with existing groups, introduce a treatment, and look to see whether differences follow. This type of research differs from archival research and naturalistic observation in that the researcher intervenes in, or steps into, the flow of behavior. These designs differ from experiments in that investigators do not randomly assign subjects to the groups. Instead, they work with intact groups. Examples are groups of students in different academic tracks; social groups such as "the populars," "the brains," "the jocks"; and so on. Quasi-experimental research is common in applied settings in which developmentalists may want to observe the effects of a treatment but don't have control over all the conditions that might affect their observations.

The disadvantage to quasi-experimental designs is that one can't be sure that differences actually reflect the treatment. They may reflect differences that were present in the groups before the treatment was introduced. For instance, research evaluating the effectiveness of precollege programs for minority youth, discussed in Chapter 10, Research Focus: Quasi-Experimental Design, works with existing groups of adolescents, those whose parents agreed to the conditions for enrolling their children in such a program. Why do these students do better than their peers at the same schools? The benefits of the program are not the only possible answer. These adolescents may differ also in the value their parents place on education or on getting ahead, attitudes that led them to enroll their children in such programs in the first place and that could well influence their academic performance apart from participation in a precollege program. The presence of alternative explanations for observed differences is known as **confounding**.

Other potential confounds exist in quasi-experimental research. *Maturation* refers to systematic changes over time, apart from those due specifically to the treatment under study. For instance, minority adolescents enrolled in a precollege program may become more serious about their studies simply because as they get older, they also get closer to having to support themselves and see the need of a good education. This realization could be all that is needed to spur them in their studies.

Another type of confound common to quasi-experimental research is a **testing effect**. The performance of adolescents enrolled in special programs may improve simply because they have been tested so often that they are better at taking tests than others whose performance is not being monitored so closely. Testing effects include both specific and general knowledge. For instance, pretests might include the same types of questions, covering the same information, as those included on tests given at the conclusion of the program. Adolescents enrolled in such programs would then be more familiar with these items and do better on tests including them. Also general test-taking skills are acquired with frequent test taking. Students learn, for instance, whether to guess, how to manage their time, and how to stay on top of anxiety that might otherwise interfere with their performance.

Similarly, a **history effect** refers to confounding resulting from events that occur during the time in which adolescents are enrolled in the program and which can affect the behavior being measured. For instance, network channels might run a series of public service spots featuring well-known minority personalities who promote the value of a college education.

Statistical regression is yet another confound that can occur. This confound enters the picture when students are selected because of their initial differences, either because they are behind or ahead of their classmates. For instance, students selected for a precollege program are more likely to have low scores on initial measures of their performance. When these students are retested at the conclusion of the program, the scores for most will be higher, but not necessarily because they have profited from the program. When they are tested at the end of the program, most scores will change somewhat simply because the two tests are not perfectly correlated. This change is to be expected since no tests ever are perfectly correlated. But for students who were initially at the bottom of the distribution, test scores can only go up. Since such a change is expected by those administering such programs, it is usually not questioned.

However, if one were to place another group of students who initially scored at the top of the distribution in such a program, their second test scores would drop, and for the same reason. Just as with the other students, there is only one direction in which their test scores could change, and for these students that would be down. In each case, scores on the second test "drift" toward the mean of the distribution, since this is where most of the scores are. In other words, to the extent that performance on the first test is unrelated to performance on the second test, chance influences the score a student gets. What score would a student be most likely to "draw" by chance? A score that occurs most frequently in the distribution—in other words, a score that is close to the mean, where most of the scores lie.

Experiments. **Experiments** start with equivalent groups of subjects and treat each group differently. If the groups differ at the conclusion of the experiment, we can assume the difference is due to the way they were treated. To be confident about this assumption, we need to be sure that the groups are comparable at the outset. Given the myriad ways in which adolescents differ from each other, such an assumption might seem an impossible requirement.

Is it? Do investigators have a way of insuring initial equivalence among their groups? The key to the solution is that the groups need not be identical, only equivalent. Rather than requiring that subjects be the same in each of the groups, an admittedly impossible requirement, we need only require that they not differ in any *systematic* way. They will, of course, differ in countless respects, but if each person has the same chance of being assigned to each group, and if enough people are assigned to each group, differences among people will soon be balanced across the groups. **Random assignment**—assigning subjects in such a way that each has the same chance as every other of being assigned to any condition—distributes individual differences more or less evenly across the groups.

Let's say we want to determine the influence of a television model on adolescents' choice of reading materials. Specifically, we want to see whether adolescents will choose magazines that are described as appropriate to their gender and

To assess the relation between body image distortion and eating disorders, J. Kevin Thompson and his colleagues set up an experimental laboratory situation. They created an adjustable light beam apparatus that subjects adjust to what they believe is the width of their cheeks, waist, hips, and thighs. The estimated width divided by the actual width gives a ratio that represents to amount of body image distortion.

avoid those that are described as inappropriate. We can pretest a variety of magazines and select those for our experiment that appeal equally to either sex. In one part of the experiment, twenty 15-year-old girls will be randomly assigned to either of two groups. Each group is shown one of two videotapes in which the model describes several magazines. One videotape describes the magazines as appropriate for males; the other describes the same magazines as appropriate for females.

We could then have the girls wait for the next part of the experiment in another room with those magazines plus others on a table. We would record the amount of time they spent looking at the "target" magazines. Let's say we found that the girls spent more time looking at the magazines that were identified as appropriate for them. Since the only difference between the groups was the way the magazines were described, we could assume that the televised sequences had affected their behavior.

We said that an experiment treats two or more groups of individuals differently and looks for measured differences in their behavior. The treatment assigned to either group is called the **independent variable**. The independent variable in this experiment is the televised sequence viewed by each group. The measure of the effect of the independent variable is called the **dependent variable**. In a sense, the way individuals react "depends" on how they are treated. The dependent var-

T A B L E   1 3 . 1

Comparison of Experimental and Non-Experimental Research Strategies

	Non-Experimental	Experimental
Control	non-manipulative	manipulative
Subjects	not randomly assigned to conditions	randomly assigned to conditions
Variables	classification variables	independent variables
Conclusions	X co-varies with Y	X causes Y

iable in this experiment is magazine choice. Which magazine the girls chose to look at depended on the way they had been treated.

We see the experimental approach illustrated in the research described in Chapter 3, Research Focus: An Experiment. Jerry Klein and Iris Litt (1983) wanted to determine whether aspirin would inhibit the production of hormones responsible for cramping during menstruation. Female subjects were randomly assigned to either an aspirin or a no-aspirin condition to determine whether taking aspirin for three days prior to their expected periods would lessen discomfort due to cramping.

Because subjects had been assigned to groups at random, giving each subject the same chance as every other of being assigned to one group or the other, these investigators could be confident that the two groups were equivalent. When enough subjects are assigned to groups in this way, the likelihood of any systematic differences between groups is very low, and any resulting differences in discomfort between subjects in the two groups can be attributed to the aspirin.

Correlational Research. The experimental approach described above is often difficult to achieve in developmental research. Age is not a variable that can be manipulated. Individuals come to the laboratory with one age or another; they can't be assigned one. Instead of working with an independent variable, one that can be assigned at random to different groups, **correlational research** works with **classification variables**. Developmentalists classify individuals according to age, or some other variable, and then see whether that variable is related to other differences. The use of classification variables is illustrated in Chapter 4, Research Focus: Correlational Research. Table 13.1 presents the ways in which experimental differs from non-experimental research.

Let's say we want to know whether adolescents become more conscious of the sex-appropriateness of their behavior with age. We could show a group of 10-year-olds, a group of 15-year-olds, and a group of 20-year-olds video materials similar to those described above. Assume for the moment that we find that sex-appropriate choices of magazines increase with age. Is this because adolescents become more aware of the sex-appropriateness of their behavior with age? They may, in fact, but this is just one of several alternative conclusions.

These adolescents already differ in at least one respect: their age. They probably differ in other ways, too. Their age may be related to another condition that is causing the relationship we noticed. An author of several books on methodology (Underwood, 1957) tells of a teacher in a private boy's school who observed that the best students all had very good vocabularies. This teacher suggested to a colleague that the school should require all students to take a course in developing their vocabularies. After a moment's thought, the colleague answered that he had noticed a relationship between the height of these students and the length of their trousers, but he doubted whether the school could increase their height by lengthening their pants.

We also have no way of knowing, in this hypothetical study of ours, if the relationship we observed is due to age itself. All we observed was a difference that corresponded to age. This difference could be an age change, something we would see in anyone the same age, regardless of their culture or the historical period in which they lived; or it could be either of two alternatives that are frequently confused with age in developmental research: cohort differences and time of measurement effects.

ISSUES AND DESIGNS IN DEVELOPMENTAL RESEARCH

Developmentalists face the central problem of separating genuine age changes from changes due to cohort differences or time of measurement differences (Schaie, 1974).

Age changes are the biological and experiential changes that always accompany aging; these occur in all cultures and all points in history. We assume that age changes have a biological basis (although we are not always able to identify it); therefore, these changes should be universal—that is, they should occur in all people no matter what their social or cultural background. A good example of an age change is the loss of high frequency tones in hearing. If we notice that adolescents in all cultures become more aware of the sex-appropriateness of their behavior with age, we might be willing to say this awareness is a genuine age change. Even so, the difference could reflect either of two alternatives: cohort differences and time of measurement differences.

The only way we can observe age changes is to observe individuals of different chronological ages. The problem is that people who differ in chronological age also differ in other ways, namely, in their social and historical backgrounds. These differences don't always have to affect the way they respond to the measures we are taking, but they might. People of the same age belong to the same *cohort* group. Cohorts are more likely to have similar cultural experiences than people of different ages. Adolescents today live in relatively plentiful times, usually grow up in urban or suburban settings, and can remember no wars. Adolescents born in 1930 grew up in the shadow of the Depression and lived with World War II. Differences such as these appear in all sorts of attitudes and behaviors and can easily be confused with age changes and are termed **cohort differences**.

If we return now to our hypothetical study, we can see how changing gender and work roles might lead to behavior that is less sex-stereotyped than before, with the consequence that older adolescents, who are further removed from these changes, may show more stereotyped behavior.

It is always possible, of course, to test a single group of 10-year-olds and then wait until they reach 15 and test them again, then wait and retest them again at 20. We wouldn't have any cohort differences, but we could have **time of measurement differences**. These differences reflect social conditions, currents of opinion, and historical events that are present when we make our observations and can affect attitudes and behavior. When we study age changes by repeatedly observing the same group of individuals over time, we can mistake time of measurement changes for age changes. It's always possible, for example, that researchers today are more aware of sexist attitudes and more likely to notice adolescents who label some things as appropriate only for one sex.

Developmentalists need to distinguish differences due to cohort effects and time of measurement from genuine age changes. We can evaluate the adequacy of three common developmental designs by their ability to do just this.

Cross-Sectional Designs

The **cross-sectional design** (discussed in Chapter 4, Research Focus: Cross-Sectional and Sequential Designs) is one of the most common designs in developmental research. This design calls for testing several groups of individuals, each of a different age, at the same time. Going back to our hypothetical study, we would measure sex-appropriate choices for adolescents at each of three ages: 10, 15, and 20. There is but a single time of measurement in this design, but several cohort groups (Figure 13.1).

It is difficult to interpret cross-sectional data, because differences between the groups can reflect either age changes or cohort differences. Until fairly recently, however, we were unaware of this weakness in the design and used it regularly, mainly because it simplified data collection. We can obtain information about developmental differences relatively quickly, certainly in a matter of days as opposed to decades. The relative strengths and weaknesses of this design receive attention in the Research Focus box.

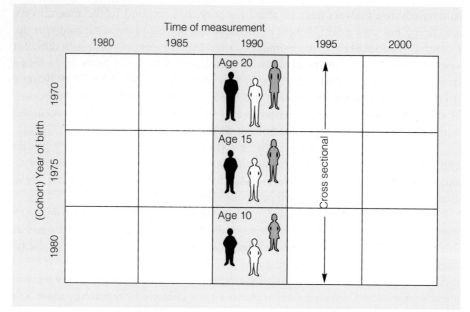

Figure 13.1   Cross-Sectional Design.

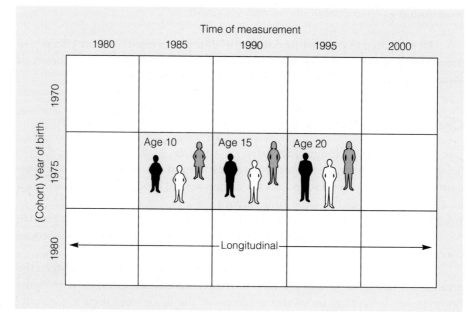

Figure 13.2   Longitudinal Design.

Source: Adapted from J. Stevens-Long & M. Commons. (1992). Adult life: Developmental processes *(4th ed.). Mountain View, CA: Mayfield.*

Longitudinal Designs

Longitudinal design studies a single cohort group of individuals over time, repeatedly observing its members as they age. Thus we have a single cohort group but several times of measurement. We illustrated this design when we sampled a group of 10-year-olds, tested them, then retested them when they reached 15, and again at 20 (Figure 13.2). By following the same individuals over time, we can see patterns to development that we might miss with cross-sections. And since we are comparing individuals with themselves at each age, we minimize the problem of having equivalent samples.

This design, too, is seriously flawed, however, because it confounds age changes and time of measurement differences. It is impossible, in other words, to separate the effects of age from those due to time of measurement. This difficulty is discussed in Chapter 3, Research Focus: Longitudinal Design. The design suffers from other problems as well. Longitudinal research is very expensive because a large research staff is needed to maintain the elaborate records that must be kept to stay in touch with the individuals and maintain information about them over the years. Longitudinal research is also time-consuming. We must wait while individuals age—and there is no guarantee that we'll outlive them.

A more serious problem than either of these is the nearly inevitable loss of individuals with time. People move away, die, or for other reasons are not available for study. This loss is called **subject mortality** and is almost always systematically related to age. Thus, the individuals who remain are not representative of those their age in the population, because the less healthy and otherwise less fortunate are generally the first to leave the sample.

Each of these designs has its own problems of interpretation, which we can see by looking at some of the research on age-related changes in intelligence. Cross-sectional studies for many years charted a marked decline in intellectual functioning after about age 30. Warner Schaie (1974), a researcher at the University of Southern California, cautions that most of this decline actually reflects cohort or generational differences. Our society has changed significantly within our lifetimes, and individuals today have different experiences than those born 20 or 30 years ago. Longitudinal research supports Schaie's argument. When we track the intellectual functioning of an individual over time, we fail to see any real decline until advanced old age.

Sequential Designs

A third design, the **sequential design** (discussed in Chapter 4, Research Focus: Cross-Sectional and Sequential Designs) is the most successful in isolating age changes from cohort and time of measurement differences. This design tests several different cohort groups at several different times. In a way, the sequential design

How does intelligence change with age? Are personality traits constant over time? Do sibling relationships go through predictable changes at various stages of the life cycle? To answer these kinds of developmental questions, researchers use longitudinal studies of the same individuals, such as these two brothers, over a number of years.

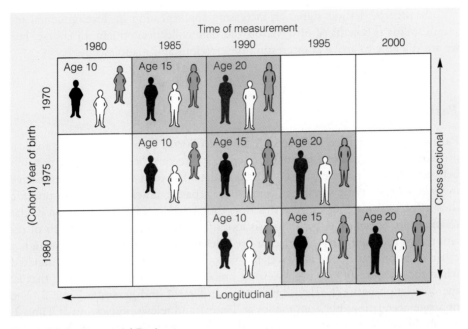

Figure 13.3 Sequential Design.
Source: Adapted from J. Stevens-Long & M. Commons. (1992). Adult life: Developmental processes
(4th ed.). Mountain View, CA: Mayfield.

is a number of longitudinal studies, each starting with a different age group, as
shown in Figure 13.3.

Let's suppose we want to see whether intelligence changes with age. By looking at the blocks that form the diagonals in Figure 13.3, we can compare 10-year-
olds with 15-year-olds and 20-year-olds. The means for each of these diagonals
will reflect age differences in intellectual functioning as well as cohort differences
and time of measurement differences.

By taking an average of the scores for the blocks in the top row, we get a
mean for the 1970 cohort. By averaging the scores for the blocks in the middle
row, we get a mean for the 1975 cohort. And by averaging the scores for the blocks
in the bottom row, we get a mean for the 1980 cohort. Differences among these
three means provide an estimate of the amount of variability in intellectual functioning that is contributed by cohorts.

We can also estimate the effect of time of measurement. We can compare
performance measured in 1985 (the blocks in the second column), for example,
with performance measured in 1995 (the blocks in the fourth column). Thus, by
using appropriate statistical techniques, we can isolate cohort and time of measurement effects and subtract these out; differences that remain reflect age changes.

Sequential designs signal an increasing sophistication in developmental research. Many problems of observation and data collection remain, of course, but we are still able to arrive at interesting observations about adolescents.

Path Analysis

Path analysis (discussed in Chapter 8, Research Focus: Path Analysis) is a statistical procedure that allows one to infer the path, or direction of effect in a relationship between variables representing correlational data. For path analysis, one must have measures for the same variables taken at two separate times. Since causes precede their effects in time, we can use this time difference to trace the direction of the relationship. Specifically, path analysis looks for differences in the strength of relationships according to which factor precedes the other. If television viewing is a cause of poor grades, for instance, the factors should be most highly correlated when the measure of television viewing precedes the measure for grades, that is, the correlation between television viewing at Time 1 and grades at Time 2. The opposite correlation, between grades at Time 1 and television viewing at Time 2, should be relatively weak. By using path analysis, developmentalists can look for causal relationships between classification variables.

RESPONSE MEASURES IN DEVELOPMENTAL RESEARCH

Dependent Variables

All research is based on observation. Dependent variables (discussed in Chapter 7, Research Focus: Dependent Variables) are the measures researchers use in making these observations. The dependent variable is always some aspect of a person's behavior, feelings, or thoughts. Developmentalists attempt to trace behavior to its causes. Does watching violence on television cause children to be more aggressive? Or get poorer grades? In each case, aggressiveness or grades is the dependent variable. Each is a measure of the effect of the independent variable watching violence on television.

What qualities does one look for in a dependent variable? First, the variable should be **reliable**; random variation should create little difference in a person's score from one occasion to the next. Second, the variable should be **valid**. The validity of a measure refers to whether it measures what it was designed to measure. Early intelligence tests, for instance, often included highly reliable but not very

Behaviorist John Watson's experiments in the 1910s to condition phobic reactions in "Little Albert" would not have met the guidelines for ethical research later drawn up by the American Psychological Association. After Watson had transferred Little Albert's conditioned fear of white rats to several other objects, including human hair and Santa Claus masks, he simply sent the three-year-old home with his artificially created fears intact. (Courtesy of Professor Benjamin Harris.)

each will learn at a slightly different rate due to individual differences. Individual differences contribute heavily to random error.

To determine whether a difference between groups is due to random error or whether it reflects the variable being studied, one uses a **test of significance** (discussed in Chapter 12, Research Focus: Statistical Tests of Significance). Common tests are chi-square, t-tests, and F-tests. If the value that is obtained is larger than a tabled value for the same number of subjects, we can rule out random error as responsible for the difference and attribute it to the independent variable, in this case, whether students kept a log. The likelihood of random error being responsible for the difference decreases with increases in the number of subjects in each group. The number of subjects is reflected in the **degrees of freedom**. With larger degrees of freedom, one needs a smaller difference to reject the assumption that random error was responsible.

Ethics

What ethical concerns guide research? Like most professional organizations, the American Psychological Association provides guidelines governing the ethical conduct of research with human subjects (see Research Focus: Ethics in Chapter 9 and

Research Focus: Confidentiality in Chapter 12). The overriding principle governing any research with human participants is to protect the *dignity and welfare* of the subjects who participate in the research. Other considerations follow from this concern. Participants are told, for instance, that their participation is *voluntary* and that they are free to leave at any point. They are also informed of anything in the research that could affect their willingness to participate.

Once participants agree to serve as subjects, investigators assume responsibility for protecting them from *physical or psychological distress*. After the data have been collected, the investigators *debrief* subjects, informing them about the nature of the study and removing any misconceptions that may have arisen. If investigators suspect any undesirable consequences, they have the responsibility for correcting these. Any information gained about participants is *confidential*.

RESEARCH DESIGNS

Between-Subjects Designs

In a **between-subjects research design**, each subject experiences only one level of the independent variable. The Research Focus box, Between-Subjects Design, in Chapter 9 describes an experiment in which subjects read a description of a dating situation in which a male tried to kiss a female while they were at a movie together and, when she refused, kissed her anyway. Some of the subjects read that it was a first date; others read that they were married. The independent variable here is the couple's level of intimacy. Thus some students experienced one level of the independent variable, "first date," and other students experienced another level, "married."

Why might we care whether subjects experience no more than one experimental condition? A major advantage to their not doing so is that investigators need not worry that subjects' responses will reflect the effects of any other condition that may still be present. What if subjects assigned to the "first date" condition had just previously read of a similar incident involving a couple who was married? Could we safely assume that these subjects would be able to separate their reactions to each situation? In a between-subjects design, one need not worry about such matters.

There is a second advantage to this design. Because subjects can be assigned at random to conditions, investigators can be reasonably confident that groups don't initially differ before they experience the different treatments. Both advantages address the issue of internal validity (discussed in Chapter 5, Research Focus: Internal and External Validity). Between-subjects designs are high in internal validity.

Within-Subjects Designs

In a **within-subjects research design**, each subject experiences all of the experimental conditions. This design can be compared to the between-subjects design above, in which each subject would experience only one condition. Within-subjects designs are *economical*; they require fewer subjects, because the same subjects react to all conditions. They are also *sensitive*. A design is sensitive to the extent that it can pick up, or detect, differences due to the experimental treatment when these exist. Within-subjects designs are sensitive because they use the same subjects in all conditions, thus reducing variability due to individual differences.

Despite these advantages, this type of design has a number of serious disadvantages. **Carryover effects** can occur in which the effect of one treatment is still present when the next is given. In addition to carryover effects, there can be **order effects** with this design. These reflect systematic changes in performance over time due to factors such as practice, fatigue, boredom, and so on. Both carryover and order effects introduce the potential for confounding, in that the difference between treatments can be explained in more than one way.

Matched-Subjects Designs

The Research Focus box, Matched-Subjects Design, in Chapter 9 describes research in which subjects in each of two groups were *matched* for age. To match subjects along some variable, one first needs to rank the subjects in each sample according to the matching variable—e.g. from oldest to youngest—and then draw pairs of subjects that are the same or approximately the same age from the two samples. Using this procedure, one can be sure that the two groups will be equivalent with regard to the matching variable. If age is related to the independent variable, age is then equated for the two groups; that is, any differences between the groups cannot be due to age.

A **matched-subjects research design** carries an additional advantage. It reduces random error, or the amount of variability between groups that does not result from the independent variable. By reducing random error, one can more easily see the effects of the independent variable. Another way of describing this advantage is to say that matched designs are more sensitive than those in which each subject is randomly assigned to a condition.

Given the importance of these advantages, one might wonder why investigators don't routinely match subjects in all their experiments. Yet like other procedures, matching has its disadvantages. The most serious of these is a statistical one, concerning the degrees of freedom used when determining the significance of the tests that evaluate the research outcome. In designs that do not match, the degrees of freedom reflect the number of *subjects*. In matched-subjects designs, they reflect the number of *pairs*. Matching cuts the degrees of freedom in half. This means that one must obtain a larger difference for this to reach statistical significance. The irony to this disadvantage is that matching is most advantageous when one is using few subjects, because it increases the sensitivity of the design. But these are the very conditions under which one can least afford to lose degrees of freedom. Investigators should determine that the matching variable is highly correlated with the measure they are using before matching. Only in this way will matching effectively reduce unexplained variability and pay for the loss in degrees of freedom.

A second disadvantage is less serious. Matching designs are somewhat more *time-consuming* to conduct than are those involving simple random assignment of subjects. One must first administer the matching variable and then rank subjects before they can be assigned to conditions. Extra *expense* may also be involved. A more serious disadvantage than either of these is the threat to *external validity* that occurs when subjects who cannot be matched must be discarded. Any loss of subjects can affect the representativeness of the sample and the ability to generalize to the population from which it was drawn. Finally, investigators run the risk of *sensitizing* subjects to the treatment by first pretesting them along a matching variable. Subjects who are sensitized become aware of the treatment in ways that other subjects are not. Because they are sensitized to a variable, subjects may respond to it in ways they might not had their awareness not been initially raised.

Factorial Designs

In a **factorial design** two or more independent variables, or factors, are completely *crossed*, so that each level of one variable is combined with each level of all the other variables. Factorial designs provide information about the effect of each of the independent variables alone, called a **main effect**, and information about the effect of a variable when another variable is present, called an **interaction**. An interaction exists when the effect of a variable changes when a second variable is present.

The Research Focus box, Factorial Designs, in Chapter 10 describes an experiment testing the effectiveness of two types of career counseling with male and female college students. To illustrate an interaction, we might find that both types of counseling are equally effective for females, but that one type works better than the other for males. The existence of an interaction means that we must qualify what we say about a variable. Is Type X counseling effective? It depends. If the students being counseled are females, then it is. But if males are being counseled, then it is not.

SUMMARY

Research Strategies

Research strategies are procedures that social scientists follow to avoid making faulty observations. Research strategies can be broadly distinguished in terms of two dimensions: the number of subjects studied and the degree of control the investigator has over conditions that could affect the observations.

In terms of number of subjects, research can study a single case, as in a case study, or can embrace large numbers of subjects, as in surveys. Case studies have the advantage of giving richly detailed data that can lead to hypotheses for future research, but suffer from problems of generalizability and objectivity. Surveys, which rely on self-report measures obtained either through interviews or questionnaires, allow investigators to study behavior that is not open to direct observation, but carry the risk of distortion.

In terms of degree of control, both archival research, which utilizes existing records, and naturalistic observation, which involves observation of behavior as it occurs in a natural setting, involve no control by the investigator over conditions that might affect the observations, thereby reducing the chance of artifact due to intervention. Erikson's psychohistorical approach applies clinical skills in a fieldwork setting. These designs do not allow the investigator to make causal inferences concerning the relationships observed.

Quasi-experimental designs involve more intervention, or control, than the previous methods, but less than experiments. Potential confounds in quasi-experimental designs are maturation, testing and history effects, and statistical regression.

Experiments offer the greatest control over possible confounds. In an experiment, the experimenter randomly assigns subjects to groups, which are then exposed to different treatments. Random assignment, by distributing individual differences across groups, ensures that the groups are initially equivalent and allows the investigator to attribute any observed differences to the way the groups are treated.

Developmental Issues

Developmental research, in which age is a variable, faces problems of confounding. Longitudinal designs, in which a single cohort is repeatedly tested at different times of measurement, reveals patterns of developmental change, but is time-consuming, expensive, and potentially confounds age changes with time of measurement differences. Cross-sectional research, in which several age cohorts are tested at a single time of measurement, takes less time to complete, but may miss developmental patterns and potentially confounds age changes with cohort differences. Sequential designs, in which several cohorts are each tested at several times of measurement, allow investigators to estimate time of measurement and cohort effects, and to isolate these from age changes.

Response Measures

The advantages and disadvantages of a number of response measures were considered: direct observation, self-reports, and projective measures.

Research Issues

Research is internally valid to the extent that it provides an unambiguous answer to the questions it was designed to address. External validity exists when the findings of a particular study can be generalized to other populations and contexts.

Concepts can be operationally defined by

defining them in terms of the operations that are used in their measurement. Operational definitions make it possible for investigators working in different laboratories to study the same concept.

Research Designs

In a between-subjects research design, each subject experiences only one level of the independent variable. In a within-subjects research design, each subject experiences all of the experimental conditions. The latter design is economical and sensitive, but runs the risk of carryover and order effects. Matched-subjects designs reduce variability due to individual differences by matching subjects along a third variable, but also reduce degrees of freedom by half, risk sensitizing subjects to the intent of the study by pretesting them, and jeopardize external validity by not including subjects who cannot be matched. Factorial designs combine two or more independent variables and provide information about interactions.

KEY TERMS

Case Study
Self-Report
Archival Research
Naturalistic Observation
Quasi-Experimental Designs
Confounding
Testing Effect
History Effect
Statistical Regression
Experiment
Random Assignment
Independent Variable
Dependent Variable
Correlational Research
Classification Variable
Age Changes

Cohort Differences
Time of Measurement
    Differences
Cross-Sectional Designs
Longitudinal Designs
Subject Mortality
Sequential Designs
Path Analysis
Reliability
Validity
Sensitivity
Direct Observation
Projective Measures
Internal Validity
External Validity
Operational Definition

Population
Sample
Bias
Double-Blind Controls
Test of Significance
Degrees of Freedom
Between-Subjects Designs
Within-Subjects Designs
Carryover Effects
Order Effects
Matched-Subjects Designs
Factorial Designs
Main Effect
Interaction

Glossary

Academic tracking The assignment of students to one of several courses of study in high school on the basis of criteria such as academic interests and goals, past achievement, and ability.

Accommodation Piaget's term for the process by which cognitive structures are altered to fit new events or experiences.

Acculturation A socialization process by which members of a minority adopt the customs of the dominant group, while maintaining a separate cultural identity.

Achieved ethnic identity The final stage in ethnic identity formation; a clear sense of one's ethnicity that reflects feelings of belonging and emotional identification.

Active listening A way of listening that reflects the message and feelings back to the speaker.

Affective disorders Disorders whose primary symptoms reflect a disturbance of mood, such as depression.

Agape In John Lee's typology of styles of love, selfless, long-suffering, and non-demanding love.

Age changes Biological and experiential changes that accompany aging, irrespective of cultural or historical context.

Agency An aspect of mature functioning characterized by assertiveness, mastery, and distinctiveness; the complement of communion.

AIDS Acquired immune deficiency syndrome: A sexually transmitted disease resulting from a virus that attacks the immune system; can also be transmitted through contaminated blood transfusions or from an infected pregnant woman to her fetus.

Alienation Indifference where devotion or attachment formerly existed; estrangement.

Amphetamine A central nervous system stimulant; sometimes known as speed.

Anabolic steroids Synthetic hormones widely used by athletes to improve muscular development and performance.

Androgens Male sex hormones.

Androgynous Characterizing a personality in which there are both masculine and feminine attributes.

Anorexia An eating disorder characterized by severely limiting the intake of food; most common in females.

Archival research The use of existing data, such as public records, to provide answers to research questions.

Artistic personality types In Holland's typology of vocational interests, individuals who prefer work requiring imagination and creativity.

Assimilation Piaget's term for the process by which new events and experiences are adjusted to fit existing cognitive structures.

Asynchrony Differences in the timing of pubertal changes within an adolescent, or from one adolescent to the next.

Attributional error An overestimation of the importance of dispositional stressors or an underestimation of the importance of situational ones.

Authoritarian parenting Parenting that stresses obedience, respect for authority, and traditional values.

Authoritative parenting Parenting that stresses self-reliance and independence; parents are consistent, maintain an open dialogue, and give reasons when disciplining.

Autonomy Being independent and responsible for one's actions.

Axioms The unquestioned assumptions that form the basis of a theory.

Barbiturates Central nervous system depressants; most are highly addictive.

Between-subjects design A research design in which each subject experiences only one level of the independent variable, or one experimental condition.

Bias Distortion of the effect of a variable due to research design or researcher expectations.

Bisexuality Sexual attraction toward individuals of both sexes.

Bulimia An eating disorder characterized by binging and then purging; most common in females.

Carryover effects In within-subjects research designs, the effects of previous conditions that persist when subsequent conditions are given.

Case study Intensive observation of a single subject, such as an individual or a program.

Centration Piaget's term for the tendency to focus on one aspect of an object to the exclusion of others; thought to characterize preoperational thinking.

Cervix The opening to the uterus.

Child labor laws Laws that specify minimum ages for various types of work.

Chlamydia A sexually transmitted disease, caused by a bacterium, that can affect the reproductive tract, possibly leading to pelvic inflammatory disease.

Circumcision Surgical removal of the prepuce covering the glans of the penis.

Classification variable A variable, such as age, that cannot be manipulated, as can an independent variable.

Climacteric Gradual decline in functioning of the reproductive organs in middle age.

Clique A peer group made up of one's best friends, usually including no more than five or six members.

Clitoris That part of the external genitals in females that is the primary source of sexual stimulation.

Cocaine A stimulant from the coca plant; also known as crack in crystallized form.

Cohort A group of people born during the same historical period or undergoing the same historical influences.

Cohort differences Experiential differences between groups of people born at different periods in time; these differences can be confounded with age changes.

Commitment in relativism The third of Perry's three forms of thought: committing oneself to a point of view from which one can derive meaning.

Communion An aspect of mature functioning characterized by cooperation and union; the complement of agency.

Compulsory education laws Legislation making school attendance mandatory for children and adolescents until they graduate or reach a minimum age.

Concrete operational thought Piaget's third stage of intellectual development, thought to characterize middle childhood, during which knowledge is gained through mental operations.

Conditional response (CR) The learned response to the conditional stimulus in respondent conditioning.

Conditional stimulus (CS) The previously neutral stimulus to which the conditional response occurs by virtue of the stimulus' association with the unconditional stimulus in respondent conditioning.

Conformity The tendency to go along with the standards and norms of one's group.

Confounding The presence of factors other than the variable that can account for observed differences.

Connectedness A quality of family interactions thought to be important for individuation; it reflects openness to and respect for others' opinions.

Conservation The realization that something remains the same despite changes in its appearance.

Constructive knowledge The third of Belenky and associates' three forms of thought in females: an awareness that knowledge is constructed; the ability to examine one's beliefs.

Continuity-discontinuity issue Disagreement as to whether the same set of laws is sufficient to explain behavior at all developmental levels and for all species (continuity assumption) or whether lawful relationships change with age and across species (discontinuity assumption).

Conventional moral reasoning Kohlberg's second level of moral reasoning, in which moral thinking is guided by internalized social standards.

Conventional personality types In Holland's typology of vocational interests, individuals who prefer highly structured environments and well-defined tasks.

Coping Strategies for managing stressful situations that tax personal resources.

Correlational research A procedure in which subjects are assigned to groups on the basis of pre-existing characteristics.

Cowper's glands Glands in males that secrete a lubricating fluid that facilitates passage of sperm through the urethra.

Cross-sectional design A research design in which several age cohorts are compared at a single time of measurement.

Crowd A peer group, averaging 20 members and formed from several cliques of the same age group.

Crystallized intelligence The specific knowledge and skills acquired through schooling and acculturation.

Cultural assimilation A socialization process by which members of a minority lose their distinctive characteristics as they assume the customs and beliefs of the dominant group.

Cultural pluralism The coexistence of minority and majority groups within a society such that each participates fully in its political and economic systems while retaining cultural diversity.

Decline stage Super's fifth stage of vocational development, in which one retires.

Deductive reasoning Reasoning from the general to the particular.

Degrees of freedom The number of scores in a set that are free to vary given certain constraints, such as a known mean.

Dependent variable The measure of the effect of the independent variable in an experiment.

Depressants Substances that reduce or lower the activity of the central nervous system.

Depression An affective disorder which may take any of three major forms, all of which are characterized by a disturbance of mood; the three forms are major depressive disorder, dysthymia, and adjustment disorder with depressed mood.

Development The orderly set of changes that occur over the lifespan.

Developmental tasks Age-related norms that reflect social expectations for normal development.

Dialectical reasoning Reasoning that questions the premises on which it is based when tests of the premises are not supported.

Diffuse/avoidant orientation A style of information processing characterized by procrastinating and avoiding decisions.

Direct observation A response measure in which behavior is observed and recorded as it occurs.

Double-blind control Research procedure in which neither the researcher nor the subjects knows which subjects have been assigned to which experimental condition.

Double standard Referring to the different standards of sexual conduct for males and females.

Drug dependence Physical dependence on a substance, such that one develops a tolerance and experiences withdrawal when use is discontinued; also known as drug addiction.

Dualistic thinking The first of Perry's three forms of thought: the belief that truth is independent of one's frame of reference.

Ego The executive aspect of the personality in Freudian theory, which seeks to satisfy impulses in socially acceptable ways.

Egocentrism The failure to realize that one's perspective is not shared by others.

Emergence The appearance of new structures or functions that cannot be reduced to earlier and simpler forms.

Encoding The process by which information is transferred from one form to another in memory.

Enculturation Acquiring the norms of one's social group.

Endocrine system The system of the body that includes the glands that produce hormones and those parts of the nervous system that activate, inhibit, and control hormone production.

Enterprising personality types In Holland's typology of vocational interests, individuals who prefer work involving interpersonal skills and assertiveness, such as management, law, or sales.

Epididymis A mass of coiled tubes near the top of each testis that receives the sperm produced by the testes.

Epigenesis The emergence of new complexities in development that cannot be predicted from, or reduced to, earlier forms.

Epigenetic principle Erikson's assumption that an internal ground plan governs the timing or period of ascendence for each new development.

Equilibration Piaget's term for the balance between assimilation and accommodation that is responsible for the growth of thought.

Eros In John Lee's typology of styles of love, intense, romantic, passionate love.

Establishment stage Super's third stage of vocational development, in which one settles into one's work.

Estrogens Female sex hormones.

Ethic of care Gilligan's description of a morality based on responsiveness to and care for others; complements Kohlberg's morality based on individual rights and justice.

Ethnic identity An awareness of belonging to an ethnic group that shapes one's thoughts, feelings, and behavior.

Ethnic identity search The intermediate stage in ethnic identity formation; exploration of the meaning of one's ethnicity.

Exosystem Contexts occurring at the level of the community, such as types of schools and housing.

Experiment A research procedure in which subjects are randomly assigned to groups which are then treated differently.

Exploration stage Super's second stage of vocational development, in which one begins to make choices related to future work.

External validity The generalizability of research conclusions to other populations and contexts.

Factorial design An experiment in which two or more independent variables, or factors, are completely crossed, so that each level of one variable is combined with each level of all the other variables.

Fallopian tubes The tubes that feed into either side of the uterus from the ovaries; also called oviducts.

Family paradigm The core beliefs held by members of the family about their environment.

Fantasy stage Ginzburg's first stage of vocational development, characterized by focus on highly visible aspects of vocations and no assessment of personal qualifications.

Female circumcision The excision of the clitoris, the primary source of sexual stimulation, and of the inner labia and sewing shut most of the outer labia in girls.

Fluid intelligence Reasoning and problem-solving skills acquired independently from formal education.

Formal operational thought Piaget's fourth stage of intellectual development, thought to characterize adolescence and adulthood, during which mental operations are extended to include thoughts in addition to concrete objects.

Gender differences Culturally determined differences in masculinity and femininity.

Gender-role stereotypes The cultural expectations concerning behaviors that are appropriate for each sex.

General adaptation syndrome (GAS) A three-stage response to a stressor in which the body mobilizes its defenses (alarm reaction), accommodates to the additional demands imposed by the stressor (adaptation), and finally loses the ability to further accommodate (exhaustion).

Genital herpes A sexually transmitted disease characterized by recurring outbreaks of itching or burning blisters; caused by a virus that remains dormant in the body.

Genital warts A sexually transmitted disease caused by the human papilloma virus.

Gifted Characteristic of individuals who place above a predetermined cut-off point on intelligence scales or who demonstrate special talents in diverse areas.

Glans The part of the clitoris or penis that is most sensitive to stimulation.

Gonads The sex glands; the ovaries in females and the testes in males.

Gonorrhea A sexually transmitted disease caused by a bacterium.

Growth The result of a metabolic process in which proteins are broken down and used to make new cells.

Growth spurt A period of rapid growth during puberty.

Growth stage Super's first stage of vocational development characterized by little discovery about vocations.

Habituation Decreased responsiveness to a stimulus with repeated exposure to it.

Hallucinogens Psychoactive substances that can produce altered states of awareness, e.g., a distorted sense of time, hallucinations.

Heterosexuality Sexual preference for individuals of the other sex.

History effect Events extraneous to a research project that can affect the behavior being measured and confound the research results.

HIV infection Impairment of the immune system by the human immunodeficiency virus (HIV), leading to AIDS (acquired immune deficiency syndrome).

Homosexuality Sexual preference for individuals of the same sex.

Hormones Chemical messengers that are secreted directly into the bloodstream and are regulated by the endocrine system.

Hypothalamus A center within the brain that regulates hormonal activity and regulatory activities such as eating, drinking, and body temperature.

I-message A message that tells the listener how his or her actions make one feel.

Id The primitive aspect of the personality in Freudian theory, which seeks immediate gratification of biological impulses.

IDEAL The acronym for a five-step approach to overcoming problems of learning.

Identification The child's uncritical incorporation of parental ways and beliefs.

Identity The part of one's personality of which one is aware and is able to see as a meaningful and coherent whole.

Identity achievement The resolution of conflict over identity through the personal formulation of occupational goals and religious and political commitments.

Identity diffusion A failure to develop a strong sense of self coupled with a failure to experience much discomfort or conflict over the issues of identity resolution.

Identity foreclosure A resolution of the problem of identity through the assumption of traditional, conventional, or parentally chosen goals and values without the experience of crisis or conflict over identity issues.

Identity formation In adolescence, a synthesizing of elements of one's earlier identity into a new whole; involves individuation.

Imaginary audience The experience of being the focus of attention; assumed to be due both to adolescents' ability to think about thought in others and to their confusing the concerns of others with their preoccupation with themselves.

Independent variable The variable that is manipulated in an experiment, by randomly assigning subjects to levels of it.

Index offenses Behaviors that are criminal at any age, such as homicide or burglary.

Individuality A quality of family interactions thought to be important for individuation, reflecting the ability to express one's ideas and say how one differs from others.

Individuation The process of distinguishing one's attitudes and beliefs from those of one's parents.

Inductive reasoning Reasoning from the particular to the general.

Inert knowledge Facts and concepts that one can recite but not use.

Information orientation A style of information processing characterized by actively searching for and evaluating information.

Inhalants Central nervous system depressants; obtained by inhaling fumes from substances such as glue, gasoline, paint thinner, and other solvents.

Intelligence The ability to profit from experience and adapt to one's surroundings; measured by intelligence tests.

Interaction An interaction exists when the effect of a variable changes when another variable is present.

Internal validity The extent to which a research study unambiguously answers the questions it was designed to address.

Intimacy The ability to share oneself with another; characterized by self-disclosure and mutuality.

Investigative personality types In Holland's typology of vocational interests, individuals who prefer work requiring intellectual curiosity, best suited for careers in science and math.

Jigsaw classroom A classroom organized into small, ethnically balanced working groups in which each student contributes a different part of the lesson.

Juvenile delinquency Illegal actions committed by a minor.

Juvenile justice Legislation instituting separate legal proceedings for juveniles and adults.

Laws Relationships that are derived from axioms and that can be proven to be true or false.

Learning disability Difficulty with academic tasks

that is not due to emotional or sensory problems and presumably reflects neurological dysfunction.

Libido The psychic energy Freud assumed is expressed through different body zones and motivates much of behavior.

Longitudinal design A research design in which a single cohort group is followed over time, tested at several times of measurement.

Long-term memory A relatively permanent memory of unlimited capacity, in which information is organized according to meaning.

Ludus In John Lee's typology of styles of love, game-playing, uncommitted love.

Macrosystem The underlying social and political climate at the level of society.

Main effect In a factorial research design, the effect of each independent variable alone.

Maintenance stage Super's fourth stage of vocational development, in which one maintains one's occupational skills and position.

Male generic language Use of the pronoun "he" to refer to an individual of either sex, and use of words such as "man" or "mankind" to refer to all people.

Mania In John Lee's typology of styles of love, possessive, obsessive, insecure love.

Marijuana A mild hallucinogen from the plant *Cannabis sativa*; the psychoactive substance is THC.

Masturbation Self-stimulation of the genitals.

Matched-subjects design A research design in which groups are initially equated by matching subjects according to a variable that correlates highly with the dependent variable.

Menarche The occurrence of a girl's first menstrual period.

Menopause A cessation of menstrual periods in middle age.

Mental operations Piaget's term for actions that can be carried out in one's head and then reversed or undone.

Mesosystem Social contexts involving interactions of several microsystems, such as when parents meet teachers.

Metamemory The awareness of one's memory and of those factors that affect it.

Microsystem One's immediate social contexts, involving first-hand experiences, such as interactions at home or in the classroom.

Minority A social group, distinguished by physical or cultural characteristics, that often receives differential treatment.

Model A set of assumptions about reality in general and about human nature in particular from which theories proceed.

Moratorium The experience of conflict over the issues of identity formation prior to the establishment of firm goals or long-term commitments.

Narcotics Highly addictive opiates, i.e., opium and its derivatives, morphine and heroin.

Naturalistic observation The observation and recording of subjects' behavior in their natural setting.

Nature-nurture controversy The controversy concerning the primary source of development: nature (heredity) or nurture (environment).

Negative reinforcement An event that increases the frequency of the behavior on which its removal is made contingent.

Nocturnal emission A spontaneous ejaculation of seminal fluid during sleep; sometimes called a wet dream.

Normative orientation A style of information processing characterized by reliance on social norms and the expectations of relatives and friends.

Obesity An eating disorder in which one is 20% above the mean (average) weight for one's height.

Object permanence Piaget's term for the infant's recognition that objects exist even when they cannot be seen.

Observational learning A form of learning through which one acquires new behaviors by observing others.

Oedipal complex A Freudian concept in which the young boy is sexually attracted to his mother, and the young girl to her father.

Operant conditioning A simple form of learning in which the probability of a behavior is affected by its consequences.

Operational definition The definition of a concept in terms of the procedures used to measure it.

Order effects In within-subjects research designs, systematic changes in performance over time due to factors such as practice and fatigue.

Ovaries Structures within the female reproductive system flanking the uterus that house the immature eggs and produce female sex hormones.

Ovum (plural **ova**) The female sex cell, also called the egg; the male equivalent is sperm.

Path analysis A statistical procedure that indicates the direction, or path, of effect with correlated variables.

Peer group A group of individuals of the same age; a social group that regulates the pace of socialization.

Peer pressure Experienced pressure to think and act like one's friends.

Penis The part of the external genitals in males that is the primary source of sexual stimulation.

Performance orientation A motivational pattern in which students focus on their own performance, using it as a way of assessing their ability.

Permissive parenting Parenting that uses little punishment, is accepting, makes few demands for responsibility, and exercises little control.

Personal expressiveness A dimension of identity formation that distinguishes between seeking practical from personally fulfilling options.

Personal fable The feeling of being special; thought to derive from the imaginary audience.

Pituitary An endocrine gland located beneath the hypothalamus that is part of a feedback system regulating the hormonal control of puberty.

Population The entire group of individuals in which an investigator is interested.

Positive reinforcement An event that increases the frequency of the behavior on which its occurrence is made contingent.

Postconventional moral reasoning Kohlberg's third level of moral reasoning, in which moral thinking is guided by self-derived principles.

Pragma In John Lee's typology of styles of love, pragmatic, rational, patient, and practical love.

Preconventional moral reasoning Kohlberg's first level of moral reasoning, characterized by the absence of internalized standards.

Preoperational thought Piaget's second stage of intellectual development, thought to characterize toddlerhood and early childhood, during which experience is represented symbolically.

Prepuce A thin skin covering the glans of the clitoris or penis.

Primary sex characteristics Sex differences in the reproductive system that develop during puberty.

Procedural knowledge The second of Belenky and associates' three forms of thought in females: independent thought that is nonetheless limited to a single frame of reference.

Projective measure Ambiguous stimuli, such as inkblots or uncaptioned pictures, that subjects are asked to describe; in doing so, they may reveal subconscious feelings and thoughts.

Propositional reasoning Reasoning from a set of premises that themselves are not questioned even when not supported by tests derived from them.

Prostate gland A structure at the base of the urethra in males that is involved in producing semen.

Pseudostupidity The inability to see the obvious by making a simple task more complicated than it is; thought to derive from the ability to think hypothetically and consider a problem from all possible perspectives.

Pubic lice Pests that are usually transmitted sexually; sometimes called "crabs."

Quaaludes Central nervous system depressants with effects similar to barbiturates; potentially addictive.

Quasi-experimental design A research design in which subjects are not randomly assigned to conditions, but pre-existing groups are used, causing problems of confounding.

Random assignment The assignment of subjects to groups in such a way that each subject has an equal chance of being assigned to any condition.

Realistic personality types In Holland's typology of vocational interests, individuals who prefer situations that are explicitly defined and require few interpersonal skills; suited for work as farmer, mechanic, computer programmer.

Realistic stage Ginzburg's third stage of vocational development, characterized by exploration of and commitment to a vocational path.

Reductionism Explaining complex behaviors by reducing them to their simpler components.

Reflective abstraction A process of thought in Piagetian theory in which aspects of behavior become abstracted so that they can be applied in other contexts.

Rehearsal A control process used to prolong items in short-term memory by repeating them.

Relativistic thinking The second of Perry's three forms of thought: awareness of more than one frame of reference by which ideas can be evaluated.

Reliability The extent to which the same observations are obtained each time a measure is used.

Repression A Freudian defense mechanism that operates by relegating distressful thoughts and feelings to the unconscious.

Respondent conditioning A simple form of learning in which simple behaviors are brought under the control of environmental stimuli that are associated with biologically significant events.

Reversibility Piaget's term for the ability to mentally undo or reverse an action in one's head.

Role clarity An understanding among family members about each one's role.

Sample A subgroup drawn from the population that is the subject of research.

Schemes Piaget's term for the precursors of concepts; ways of representing experience through one's actions.

Schizophrenia A psychotic disorder characterized by disturbances of thought and perception.

Scrotum The sac that hangs just beneath the penis and houses the testes.

Secondary sex characteristics Differences between females and males in body structure and appearance, other than differences in the reproductive system; include differences in skeletal structure, hair distribution, and skin texture.

Secular trend The earlier onset of puberty, faster growth, and larger size reached by adolescents today than in the past.

Self-concept The individual's awareness of the self as a person; a theory about the self that explains personal experience.

Self-disclosure The sharing or exchange of personal information; considered a primary basis for the development of intimacy.

Self-esteem The individual's overall positive or negative evaluation of herself or himself.

Self-report Information supplied by research subjects themselves, usually in response to interview or survey questions.

Semen A milky white fluid in which sperm are suspended.

Seminal vesicles Structures within the male reproductive system in which sperm are stored.

Sensitivity The extent to which the dependent variable can pick up very small differences due to the independent variable.

Sensorimotor thought Piaget's first stage of intellectual development, assumed to characterize infancy, during which knowledge is based on perception and reflexes.

Sensory memory A brief memory, usually lasting for less than a second, that preserves information during processing.

Sequential design A research design in which several different cohort groups are tested at several times of measurement; essentially, a number of longitudinal studies, each starting with a different age group.

Sex differences Biological and physiological differences distinguishing the sexes.

Sexual dimorphism The physical differences that distinguish adult females and males.

Sexually transmitted disease (STD) An infection that is spread through sexual contact.

Shaft The part of the clitoris or penis that becomes erect during sexual stimulation.

Short-term memory A brief memory, limited in capacity to about seven items.

Smegma A thick secretion that collects around the glans and under the prepuce.

Social competence Accurately assessing and maintaining a social encounter.

Social personality types In Holland's typology of vocational interests, individuals who prefer work involving them with people, such as counseling or teaching.

Social understanding Assumed to develop gradually with the ability to assume another's perspective and eventually to coordinate one's own with others' perspectives.

Sperm The male sex cell; the female equivalent is the ovum.

Spermarche A boy's first ejaculation of seminal fluid.

Stage A level of development that is assumed to be qualitatively different from the earlier level from which it evolves. Stages are assumed to occur in a fixed sequence and to occur universally within a species.

Statistical regression A potential confound in quasi-experimental research in which extreme pretest scores drift toward the mean of the post-test distribution.

Status offenses Behaviors that are illegal when engaged in by minors but legal for adults, such as truancy and drinking alcohol.

Stimulants Substances that excite the central nervous system.

Storge In John Lee's typology of styles of love, companionate love based on friendship.

Stress The body's specific and nonspecific responses to a demand or stimulus that disrupts its balance.

Stress-inoculation training A coping strategy that teaches ways to cognitively restructure stressful situations by identifying the stressful elements, anticipating one's reactions, and managing the emotions they occasion.

Structural analytical thinking A stage of cognitive development characterized by the ability to relate two or more systems of thought.

Subject mortality In longitudinal studies, the loss of subjects over time.

Subjective knowledge The first of Belenky and associates' three forms of thought in females: covert examination of issues while maintaining a surface conformity to traditional ideas.

Superego The aspect of the personality in Freudian theory that represents the internalized standards and values of society.

Syphilis A sexually transmitted disease, caused by a bacterium, that can also be transmitted through blood transfusions or from a pregnant woman to her fetus; progresses over several stages.

Task orientation A motivational pattern in which students focus on the task they are learning and work to increase their mastery and competence.

Tentative stage Ginzburg's second stage of vocational development, in which vocational choice is directed more by interests than capacities.

Test of significance Use of a statistical table to determine whether a difference in scores between experimental groups is due to random error or to the effects of the independent variable.

Testes Structures within the male reproductive system contained in the scrotum that produce sperm and male sex hormones.

Testing effect Knowledge and skills acquired by taking similar tests over the course of a research project; a potential confound in research.

Theory A set of testable statements derived from the axioms of a model.

Time of measurement differences Differences due to social conditions, currents of opinion, and historical events that can affect observations in longitudinal research; such differences are confounded with age changes.

Tranquilizers Central nervous system depressants; potentially addictive.

Unconditional response (UCR) The unlearned response to the unconditional stimulus in respondent conditioning.

Unconditional stimulus (UCS) The stimulus that elicits the unconditional response in respondent conditioning.

Unexamined ethnic identity The initial stage in ethnic identity formation; a lack of awareness of the issues related to one's ethnicity; a simple internalization of the values of the dominant culture.

Urethra The urinary canal, leading from the bladder to the urethral opening.

Uterus A muscular enclosure at the top of the vagina that holds the fetus during pregnancy.

Vagina The muscular tube in females leading from the labia at its opening to the uterus.

Validity The extent to which the dependent variable measures what it was designed to measure.

Vas deferens Long coiled tubes that carry sperm to the seminal vesicles, where they are stored.

WAIS-R An intelligence scale for adults that is individually administered.

Within-subjects design A research design in which each subject experiences all levels of the independent variable.

You-message A message communicating what you think of another person.

Youth An age group spanning the years from early adolescence to early adulthood.

References

Aboud, F. E. (1987). The development of ethnic self-identification and attitudes. In J. S. Phinney and M. J. Rotheram (Eds.), *Children's ethnic socialization*. Beverly Hills, CA: Sage Publications.

Adams-Price, C., & Greene, A. L. (1990). Secondary attachments and adolescent self-concept. *Sex Roles, 22*, 187–198.

Adelson, J., & Doehrman, M. J. (1980). The psychodynamic approach to adolescence. In J. Adelson (Ed.), *Handbook of adolescence*. New York: Wiley.

Adwere-Boamah, J., & Curtis, D. A. (1993). A confirmatory factor analysis of a four-factor model of adolescent concerns revisited. *Journal of Youth and Adolescence, 22*, 297–312.

Agnew, R., & Peters, A. A. (1986). The techniques of neutralization: An analysis of predisposing and situational factors. *Criminal Justice and Behavior, 13*, 81–97.

Aiken, L. R. (1987). *Assessment of intellectual functioning*. Boston: Allyn & Bacon.

Aitken, D., & Chaplin, J. (1990). Sex miseducation. *Family Therapy Networker, 14*, 24–25.

Alan Guttmacher Institute. (1981). *Teenage pregnancy: The problem that hasn't gone away*. New York: Author.

Alexander, C. S., Somerfield, M. R., Ensminger, M. E., Johnson, K. E., & Kim, Y. J. (1993). Consistency of adolescents' self-report of sexual behavior in a longitudinal study. *Journal of Youth and Adolescence, 22*, 455–471.

Allen, J. P., Weissberg, R. P., & Hawkins, J. A. (1989). The relation between values and social competence in early adolescence. *Developmental Psychology, 25*, 458–464.

Allen, L., & Majidi-Ahi, S. (1989). Black American children. In J. T. Gibbs, L. N. Huang, & Associates (Eds.), *Children of color*. San Francisco: Jossey-Bass.

American Council on Education. (1988). *Minorities in higher education*. Washington, DC: American Council on Education.

Ammons, P., & Stinnett, N. (1980). The vital marriage: A closer look. *Family Relations, 29*, 37–42.

Apter, D., & Vilko, R. (1977). Serum pregnenolone, progesterone, 17-hydroxyprogesterone, testosterone and 5 alpha. *Journal of Clinical Endocrinology and Metabolism, 45*, 1039–1048.

Arbona, C. (1989). Hispanic employment and the Holland typology of work. *Career Development Quarterly, 37*, 257–268.

Arbuthnut, J., Gordon, D. A., & Jurkovic, G. J. (1987). Personality. In H. C. Quay (Ed.), *Handbook of juvenile delinquency*. New York: Wiley.

Archer, S. L. (1985). Career and/or family: The identity process for adolescent girls. *Youth and Society, 16*, 289–314.

Archer, S. L. (1989a). Gender differences in identity development: Issues of process, domain, and timing. *Journal of Adolescence, 12*, 117–138.

Archer, S. L. (1989b). The status of identity: Reflections on the need for intervention. *Journal of Adolescence, 12*, 345–359.

Archer, S. L. (1992). A feminist's approach to identity research. In G. R. Adams, T. P. Gullotta, & R. Montemayor (Eds.). *Adolescent identity formation*. Newbury Park, CA: Sage.

Arehart, D. M., & Smith, P. H. (1990). Identity in adolescence: Influences of dysfunction and psychosocial task issues. *Journal of Youth and Adolescence, 19*, 63–72.

Arey, L. B. (1956). *Developmental anatomy.* Philadelphia: Saunders.

Aries, P. (1962). *Centuries of childhood.* New York: Knopf.

Armacost, R. L. (1989). Perceptions of stressors by high school students. *Journal of Adolescent Research, 4,* 443–461.

Armistead, L., Wierson, M., & Forehand, R. (1990). Adolescents and maternal employment: Is it harmful for a young adolescent to have an employed mother? *Journal of Early Adolescence, 10,* 260–278.

Artman, L., & Cahan, S. (1993). Schooling and the development of transitive inference. *Developmental Psychology, 29,* 753–759.

Asher, S. R. (1983). Social competence and peer status: Recent advances and future directions. *Child Development, 54,* 1427–1434.

Assh, S. D., & Byers, E. S. (1990). Effects of behavioral exchanges and cognitions on the relationship satisfaction of dating and married persons. *Canadian Journal of Behavioral Science, 22,* 223–235.

Atkinson, R. C., & Shiffrin, R. M. (1968). Human memory: A proposed system and its control processes. In K. W. Spence & J. T. Spence (Eds.), *Advances in the psychology of learning and motivation research and theory* (Vol. 2). New York: Academic Press.

Bahr, H. M. (1980). Changes in family life in Middletown, 1924–77. *Public Opinion Quarterly, 44,* 35–52.

Bailey, J. M., & Pillard, R. C. (1991). A genetic study of male sexual orientation. *Archives of General Psychiatry, 48,* 1089–1096.

Bailey, J. M., Pillard, R. C., Neale, M. C., & Agyei, Y. (1993). Heritable factors influence sexual orientation in women. *Archives of General Psychiatry, 50,* 217–223.

Bakan, D. (1966). *The duality of human existence.* Boston: Beacon Press.

Bakan, D. (1971). Adolescence in America: From idea to social fact. *Daedalus, 100,* 979–995.

Bandura, A. (1977). *Social learning theory.* Morristown, NJ: General Learning Press.

Bandura, A. (1980). Self-referent thought: A developmental analysis of self-efficacy. In J. H. Flavell and L. D. Ross (Eds.), *Cognitive social development: Frontiers and possible futures.* New York: Cambridge University Press.

Bandura, A. (1989). Regulation of cognitive processes through perceived self-efficacy. *Developmental Psychology, 25,* 729–735.

Bandura, A., Ross, D., & Ross, S. A. (1963). Imitation of film-mediated aggressive models. *Journal of Abnormal and Social Psychology, 66,* 3–11.

Banks, C. A. McGee. (1993). Restructuring schools for equity: What we have learned in two decades. *Phi Delta Kappan, 75,* 42–48.

Banks, J. A. (1993). Multicultural education: Development, dimensions, and challenges. *Phi Delta Kappan, 75,* 22–28.

Bardwick, J. M., & Douvan, E. (1971). Ambivalence: The socialization of women. In V. Gornick & B. K. Moran (Eds.), *Women in sexist society.* New York: Basic Books.

Barkley, T. J., & Procidano, M. E. (1989). College-age children of divorce: Are effects evident in early adulthood? *Journal of College Student Psychotherapy, 4,* 77–87.

Baron, J. B., & Sternberg, R. J. (1987). *Teaching thinking skills: Theory and practice.* New York: Freeman.

Barrera, M., Jr., Chassin, L., & Rogosch, F. (1993). Effects of social support and conflict on adolescent children of alcoholic and nonalcoholic fathers. *Journal of Personality and Social Psychology, 64,* 602–612.

Barth, R. P., Fetro, J. V., Leland, N., & Volkan, K. (1992). Preventing adolescent pregnancy with social and cognitive skills. *Journal of Adolescent Research, 7,* 208–232.

Bartle, S. E., Anderson, S. A., & Sabatelli, R. M. (1989). A model of parenting style, adolescent individuation and adolescent self-esteem: preliminary findings. *Journal of Adolescent Research, 4,* 283–298.

Basseches, M. (1984). *Dialectical thinking and adult development.* Norwood, NJ: Ablex.

Bassok, M. (1990). Transfer of domain-specific problem-solving procedures. *Journal of Experimental Psychology: Learning, Memory, and Cognition, 16,* 522–533.

Bassok, M., & Holyoak, K. J. (1989). Interdomain transfer between isomorphic topics in algebra and physics. *Journal of Experimental Psychology: Learning, Memory, and Cognition, 15,* 153–166.

Bauman, K. E., & Fisher, L. A. (1986). On the measurement of friend behavior in research on friend influence and selection: Findings from longitudinal studies of adolescent smoking and drinking. *Journal of Youth and Adolescence, 15,* 345–353.

Baumrind, D. (1971). Current patterns of parental authority. *Developmental Psychology Monographs, 4,* 1–103.

Baumrind, D. (1975). Early socialization and adolescent competence. In S. E. Dragastin & G. E. Elder (Eds.), *Adolescence in the life cycle.* New York: Hemisphere Publishing.

Baumrind, D. (1986). Sex differences in moral reasoning: Response to Walker's (1984) conclusion that there are none. *Child Development, 57,* 511–521.

Baumrind, D. (1991a). The influence of parenting style on adolescent competence and substance use. *Journal of Early Adolescence, 11,* 56–95.

Baumrind, D. (1991b). Effective parenting during the early adolescent transition. In P. A. Cowan & E. M. Heatherington (Eds.), *Family transitions* (pp. 111–164). Hillsdale, NJ: Erlbaum.

Beentjes, J. W. J., & van der Boort, T. S. A. (1993). Television viewing versus reading: Mental effort, retention, and inferential learning. *Communication Education, 42,* 191–205.

Belenky, M. F., Clinchy, B. M., Goldberger, N. R., & Tarule, J. M. (1986). *Women's ways of knowing.* New York: Basic Books.

Bell, D. C., & Bell, L. G. (1983). Parental validation and support in the development of adolescent daughters. In H. D. Grotevant & C. R. Cooper (Eds.), *Adolescent development in the family.* San Francisco: Jossey-Bass.

Bell-Scott, P. (1987). Introduction. In *Consortium for research on black adolescence: Topical summaries and annotated bibliographies of research* (pp. 5–9). Storrs, CT: University of Connecticut, School of Family Studies.

Bem, S. L. (1974). The measurement of psychological androgyny. *Journal of Consulting and Clinical Psychology, 42,* 155–162.

Benbow, C. P., & Stanley, J. C. (1980). Sex differences in mathematical ability: Fact or artifact? *Science, 210,* 1262–1264.

Benbow, C. P., & Stanley, J. C. (1982). Consequences in high school and college of sex differences in mathematical reasoning ability: A longitudinal perspective. *American Educational Research Journal, 19,* 598–622.

Benbow, C. P., & Stanley, J. C. (1983). Sex differences in mathematical reasoning ability: More facts. *Science, 222,* 1029–1031.

Benin, M. H., & Edwards, D. A. (1990). Adolescents' chores: The difference between dual- and single-earner families. *Journal of Marriage and the Family, 52,* 361–373.

Benson, P. L., & Donohue, M. J. (1989). Ten-year trends in at-risk behaviors: A national study of black adolescents. *Journal of Adolescent Research, 4,* 125–139.

Berg, C. (1989). Knowledge of strategies for dealing with everyday problems from childhood through adolescence. *Developmental Psychology, 25,* 607–618.

Berman, A. L., & Jobes, D. A. (1991). *Adolescent suicide: Assessment and intervention.* Washington, DC: American Psychological Association.

Berndt, T. J. (1982). The features and effects of friendships in early adolescence. *Child Development, 53,* 1447–1461.

Berzonsky, M. D. (1989). Identity style: Conceptualization and measurement. *Journal of Adolescent Research, 4,* 268–282.

Berzonsky, M. D. (1992). A process perspective on identity and stress management. In G. R. Adams, T. P. Gullotta, & R. Montemayor (Eds.). *Adolescent identity formation.* Newbury Park, CA: Sage.

Berzonsky, M. D. (1993). Identity style, gender, and social-cognitive reasoning. *Journal of Adolescent Research, 8,* 289–296.

Berzonsky, M. D., & Sullivan, C. (1992). Social-cognitive aspects of identity style: Need for cognition, experiential openness, and introspection. *Journal of Adolescent Research, 7,* 140–145.

Betancourt, H., & Lopez, S. R. (1993). The study of culture, ethnicity, and race in American psychology. *American Psychologist, 48,* 629–637.

Bettelheim, B. (1961). The problem of generations. In E. Erikson (Ed.), *The challenge of youth.* New York: Doubleday.

Bettes, B. A., Dusenbury, L., Kerner, J., James-Ortiz, S., & Botvin, G. J. (1990). Ethnicity and psychosocial factors in alcohol and tobacco use in adolescence. *Child Development, 61,* 557–565.

Bieber, I. (1962). *Homosexuality: A psychoanalytic study.* New York: Basic Books.

Bird, G. W., & Kemerait, L. N. (1990). Stress among

early adolescents in two-earner families. *Journal of Early Adolescence, 1,* 344–365.

Bjorklund, D. F. (1989). *Children's thinking.* Pacific Grove, CA: Brooks/Cole.

"Blacks in college: Trend reverses." (1990, April 17). *Los Angeles Times.*

Blasi, A. (1988). Identity and the development of the self. In D. K. Lapsley & F. C. Power (Eds.), *Self, ego, and identity.* New York: Springer-Verlag.

Bloch, D. P. (1989). Using career information with dropouts and at-risk youth. *Career Development Quarterly, 38,* 160–171.

Block, J. H. (1978). Another look at sex differentiation in the socialization behaviors of mothers and fathers. In J. Sherman & F. Denmark (Eds.), *Psychology of women: Future directions of research.* New York: Psychological Dimensions.

Blos, P. (1967). The second individuation process of adolescence. In R. S. Eissler et al. (Eds.), *Psychoanalytic study of the child* (Vol. 22). New York: International Universities Press.

Blos, P. (1979). *The adolescent passage.* New York: International Universities Press.

Blum, R., et al. (1992). American Indian–Alaska Native youth health. *Journal of the American Medical Association, 267,* 1637.

Blumenthal, S. J., & Kupfer, D. J. (1988). Overview of early detection and treatment strategies for suicidal behavior in young people. *Journal of Youth and Adolescence, 17,* 1–23.

Blyth, D. A., Hill, J., & Thiel, K. S. (1982). Early adolescents' significant others: Grade and gender differences in perceived relationships with familial and nonfamilial adults and young people. *Journal of Youth and Adolescence, 11,* 425–450.

Bolton, F. G., Jr., & MacEachron, A. E. (1988). Adolescent male sexuality: A developmental perspective. *Journal of Adolescent Research, 3,* 259–273.

Bolton, I. M. (1989). Perspectives of youth on preventive intervention strategies. *Report of the Secretary's Task Force on Youth Suicide. Vol. 3.* Washington, DC: U.S. Government Printing Office.

Boster, J. S., & Johnson, J. C. (1989). Form or function: A comparison of expert and novice judgments of similarity among fish. *American Anthropologist, 91,* 866–889.

Bourne, E. (1978a). The state of research on ego identity: A review and appraisal. Part I. *Journal of Youth and Adolescence, 7,* 223–257.

Bourne, E. (1978b). The state of research on ego identity: A review and appraisal. Part II. *Journal of Youth and Adolescence, 7,* 371–392.

Boyer, E. (1983). *High school: A report on secondary education in America.* New York: Harper & Row.

Boyes, M. C., & Chandler, M. (1992). Cognitive development, epistemic doubt, and identity formation in adolescence. *Journal of Youth and Adolescence, 21,* 277–304.

Bransford, J. D., Stein, B. S., Shelton, T. S., & Owings, R. A. (1981). Cognition and adaptation: The importance of learning to learn. In J. Harvey (Ed.), *Cognition, social behavior and the environment.* Hillsdale, NJ: Erlbaum.

Bransford, J. D., Vye, N. J., Adams, L. T., & Perfetto, G. A. (1989). Learning skills and the acquisition of knowledge. In A. Lesgold & R. Glaser (Eds.), *Foundations for a psychology of education.* Hillsdale, NJ: Erlbaum.

Brent, D. A. Perper, J. A., Goldstein, C. E., Kolko, D. J., Allan, M. J., Allman, C. J., & Zelenak, J. P. (1988). Risk factors for adolescent suicide: A comparison of adolescent suicide victims with suicidal in-patients. *Archives of General Psychiatry, 45,* 581–588.

Brice-Heath, S. (1982). Questioning at home and at school: A comparative study. In G. Spindler (Ed.), *The school achievement of minority children: New perspectives.* Hillsdale, NJ: Erlbaum.

Bronfenbrenner, U. (1979). Contexts of child rearing. *American Psychologist, 34,* 844–850.

Brookman, R. R. (1988). Sexually transmitted diseases. In M. D. Levine & E. R. McArney (Eds.), *Early adolescent transitions.* Lexington, MA: D. C. Heath.

Brooks, J. (1991). *The process of parenting.* Mountain View, CA: Mayfield.

Brooks, L. (1990). Counseling special groups: Women and ethnic minorities. In D. Brown, L. Brooks, & Associates (Eds.), *Career choice and development.* San Francisco: Jossey-Bass.

Brooks-Gunn, J. (1991). Maturational timing variations in adolescent girls, Consequences of. In R. M. Lerner, A. C. Petersen, & J. Brooks-Gunn (Eds.). *Encyclopedia of adolescence* (Vol. 2, pp. 614–618). New York: Garland.

Brooks-Gunn, J., & Ruble, D. N. (1982). The development of menstrual-related beliefs and behaviors during early adolescence. *Child Development,* *53,* 1557–1566.

Brooks-Gunn, J., & Ruble, D. N. (1983). The experience of menarche from a developmental perspective. In J. Brooks-Gunn & A. C. Petersen (Eds.), *Girls at puberty.* New York: Plenum Press.

Brooks-Gunn, J., & Ruble, D. N. (1986). Men's and women's attitudes and beliefs about the menstrual cycle. *Sex Roles, 14,* 287–299.

Brooks-Gunn, J., & Warren, M. P. (1985). Measuring physical status and timing in early adolescence: A developmental perspective. *Journal of Youth and Adolescence, 14,* 163–189.

Brown, A. L., & DeLoache, J. S. (1978). Skills, plans, and self-regulation. In R. S. Siegler (Ed.), *Children's thinking: What develops?* Hillsdale, NJ: Erlbaum.

Brown, B. B. (1989). The role of peer groups in adolescents' adjustment to secondary school. In T. J. Berndt & G. W. Ladd (Eds.), *Peer relationships in child development.* New York: Wiley.

Brown, B. B., & Lohr, M. J. (1987). Peer group affiliation and adolescent self-esteem: An integration of ego-identity and symbolic-interaction theories. *Journal of Personality and Social Psychology, 52,* 47–55.

Brown, D. (1990). Summary, comparison, and critique of major theories. In D. Brown, L. Brooks, & Associates (Eds.), *Career choice and development.* San Francisco: Jossey-Bass.

Bryk, A. S., & Raudenbush, S. W. (1988). Toward a more appropriate conceptualization of research on school effects: A three-level hierarchical linear model. *American Journal of Education, 97,* 65–108.

Buchanan, C. M., Maccoby, E. E., & Dornbusch, S. M. (1992). Adolescents and their families after divorce: Three residential arrangements compared. *Journal of Research on Adolescence, 2,* 261–291.

Buhrmester, D. (1990). Intimacy of friendship, interpersonal competence, and adjustment during preadolescence and adolescence. *Child Development, 61,* 1101–1111.

Bukowski, W. M., Newcomb, A. F., & Hoza, B. (1987). Friendship conceptions among early adolescent: A longitudinal study of stability and change. *Journal of Early Adolescence, 7,* 143–152.

Butcher, J. (1986). Longitudinal analysis of adolescent girls' aspirations at school and perceptions of popularity. *Adolescence, 21,* 133–143.

Bybee, J., Glick, M., & Zigler, E. (1990). Differences across gender, grade level, and academic track in the content of the ideal self-image. *Sex Roles, 22,* 349–358.

Byrne, D. (1983). Sex without contraception. In D. Byrne & W. A. Fisher (Eds.), *Adolescent sex and contraception.* Hillsdale, NJ: Erlbaum.

Byrnes, J. P., & Takahira, S. (1993). Explaining gender differences on SAT-math items. *Developmental Psychology, 29,* 805–810.

California Council on Criminal Justice. (1989). *State task force on gangs and drugs.* Sacramento, CA: Author.

Camarena, P. M., Sarigiani, P. A., & Petersen, A. C. (1990). Gender-specific pathways to intimacy in early adolescence. *Journal of Youth and Adolescence, 19,* 19–32.

Cameron, R., & Meichenbaum, D. (1982). The nature of effective coping and the treatment of stress related problems: A cognitive-behavioral perspective. In L. Goldberger & S. Breznitz (Eds.), *Handbook of stress.* New York: Free Press.

Campbell, D. (1974). *The Strong-Campbell interest inventory.* Palo Alto, CA: Stanford University Press.

Campione, J. C., & Brown, A. L. (1978). Toward a theory of intelligence: Contributions from research with retarded children. *Intelligence, 2,* 279–304.

Cavior, N., & Dokecki, P. R. (1973). Physical attractiveness, perceived attitude similarity, and academic achievement as contributors to interpersonal attraction among adolescents. *Developmental Psychology, 9,* 44–54.

Centers for Disease Control. (1991a). The HIV/AIDS epidemic: The first 10 years. *Morbidity and Mortality Weekly Report, 40,* 357–369.

Centers for Disease Control. (1991b). Mortality attributable to HIV infection/AIDS—United States, 1981–1990. *Morbidity and Mortality Weekly Report, 40,* 41–44.

Centers for Disease Control. (1991c). Pilot study of a household survey to determine HIV seroprevalence. *Morbidity and Mortality Weekly Report, 40,* 1–4.

Centers for Disease Control. (1991d). Weapon-carrying among high school students—United States, 1990. *Morbidity and Mortality Weekly Report, 40,* 623.

Centers for Disease Control. (1992a). 1993 revised classification system for HIV infection and expanded surveillance case definition for AIDS among adolescents and adults. *Morbidity and Mortality Weekly Report, 41,* 1–19.

Centers for Disease Control. (1992b). Selected behaviors that increase risk for HIV infection, other sexually transmitted diseases, and unintended pregnancy among high school students—United States, 1991. *Morbidity and Mortality Weekly Report, 41,* 845–850.

Centers for Disease Control. (1993a). Condom use and sexual identity among men who have sex with men—Dallas, 1991. *Morbidity and Mortality Weekly Report, 42,* 7–17.

Centers for Disease Control. (1993b). Emergency department response to domestic violence—California, 1992. *Morbidity and Mortality Weekly Report, 42,* 617–619.

Centers for Disease Control. (1993c). *HIV/AIDS Surveillance Report, 5* (3).

Cernkovich, S. A., & Giordano, P. C. (1987). Family relationships and delinquency. *Sociological Quarterly, 20,* 131–145.

Cheek, D. B. (1974). Body composition, hormones, nutrition, and adolescent growth. In M. M. Grumbach, G. D. Grave, & F. E. Mayer (Eds.), *Control of the onset of puberty.* New York: Wiley.

Children's Defense Fund. (1988). *Teens and AIDS: Opportunities for prevention.* Washington, DC: Author.

Chi, M. T. H. (1985). Interactive roles of knowledge and strategies in the development of organized sorting and recall. In S. F. Chipman, J. W. Segal, & R. Glaser (Eds.), *Thinking and learning skills* (Vol. 2). Hillsdale, NJ: Erlbaum.

Chiu, M. L., Feldman, S. S., & Rosenthal, D. A. (1992). The influence of immigration on parental behavior and adolescent distress in Chinese families residing in two Western nations. *Journal of Research on Adolescence, 2,* 205–239.

Chodorow, N. (1978). *The reproduction of mothering.* Los Angeles: University of California Press.

Chomsky, N. (1957). *Syntactic structures.* The Hague: Mouton.

Cicirelli, V. G. (1980). A comparison of college women's feelings toward their siblings and parents. *Journal of Marriage and the Family, 78,* 111–118.

Clark, B. (1988). *Growing up gifted* (3rd ed.). New York: Macmillan.

Clasen, D. R., & Brown, B. B. (1985). The multidimensionality of peer pressure in adolescence. *Journal of Youth and Adolescence, 14,* 451–468.

Clausen, J. A. (1975). The social meaning of differential physical and sexual maturation. In S. E. Dragastin & G. H. Elder (Eds.), *Adolescence in the life cycle.* New York: Wiley.

Coleman, E., & Remadedi, G. (1989). Gay, lesbian, and bisexual adolescents: A critical challenge to counselors. *Journal of Counseling and Development, 68,* 36–40.

Coleman, J. C. (1980). Friendship and the peer group in adolescence. In J. Adelson (Ed.), *Handbook of adolescence.* New York: Wiley.

Coleman, J. S. (1961). *The adolescent society.* New York: Free Press.

Coleman, J. S. (Chairman). (1974). *Youth: Transition to adulthood. Report on the panel for youth, President's Science Advisory Committee.* Chicago: University of Chicago Press.

Coleman, P. (1993). Testing the school system: Dropouts, accountability, and social policy. *Curriculum Inquiry, 23,* 329–342.

Coles, Robert. (1970). *Erik Erikson: The growth of his work.* Boston: Little, Brown.

Comer, J. P. (1985). The Yale–New Haven Primary Prevention Project: A follow-up study. *Journal of the American Academy of Child Psychiatry, 24,* 154–160.

Comer, J. P. (1988). Educating poor minority children. *Scientific American, 259,* 42–48.

Committee for Economic Development, Research and Policy Committee. (1987). *Work and change: Labor market adjustment policies.* New York: Author.

Commons, M. L., & Richards, F. A. (1982). A general model of stage theory. In M. L. Commons, F. A. Richards, & S. Armon (Eds.), *Beyond formal operations: Late adolescent and adult cognitive development.* New York: Praeger.

Conger, J. J. (1977). *Adolescence and youth.* New York: Harper & Row.

Constantine, L. L. (1987). Adolescent process and family organization: A model of development as a function of family paradigm. *Journal of Adolescent Research, 2,* 349–366.

Constantinople, A. (1973). Masculinity-femininity: An exception to a famous dictum? *Psychological Bulletin, 80,* 389–407.

Cook, W. L. (1993). Interdependence and the interpersonal sense of control: An analysis of family relationships. *Journal of Personality and Social Psychology, 64,* 587–601.

Cooper, C. R., Grotevant, H. D., & Condon, S. M. (1983). Individuality and connectedness in the family as a context for adolescent identity formation and role-taking skill. In H. D. Grotevant & C. R. Cooper (Eds.), *Adolescent development in the family.* San Francisco: Jossey-Bass.

Côté, J. (1992). Was Mead wrong about coming of age in Samoa? An analysis of the Mead/Freeman controversy for scholars of adolescence and human development. *Journal of Youth and Adolescence, 21,* 499–527.

Cotman, C. W., & McGaugh, J. L. (1980). *Behavioral neuroscience.* San Francisco: Academic Press.

Covington, M. V. (1983). Strategic thinking and the fear of failure. In S. F. Chipman, J. Segal, & R. Glaser (Eds.), *Thinking and learning skills: Current research and open questions* (Vol. 2). Hillsdale, NJ: Erlbaum.

Cozby, P. C. (1993). *Methods in behavioral research* (5th ed.). Mountain View, CA: Mayfield.

Craighead, L. W., & Green, B. J. (1989). Relationship between depressed mood and sex-typed personality characteristics in adolescents. *Journal of Youth and Adolescence, 18,* 467–474.

Cross, W. E., Jr. (1980). Models of psychological nigrescence: A literature review. In R. L. Jones (Ed.), *Black psychology.* New York: Harper & Row.

Cross, W. E., Jr. (1987). A two-factor theory of black identity: Implications for the study of identity development in minority children. In J. S. Phinney & M. J. Rotheram (Eds.), *Children's ethnic socialization.* Beverly Hills: Sage Publications.

Crouter, A. C., & Crowley, M. S. (1990). School-age children's time alone with fathers in single- and dual-earner families: Implications for the father-child relationship. *Journal of Early Adolescence, 10,* 296–312.

Csikszentmihalyi, M., & Larson, R. (1984). *Being adolescent.* New York: Basic Books.

Cutler, G. B., Jr., Comite, F., Rivier, J., Vale, W. W., Loriaux, D. L., & Crowley, W. F., Jr. (1983). Pituitary desensitization with a long-acting luteinizing-hormone-releasing hormone analog. In J. Brooks-Gunn & A. C. Petersen (Eds.), *Girls at puberty.* New York: Plenum Press.

Dacey, J. S. (1989a). Discriminating characteristics of the families of highly creative adolescents. *Journal of Creative Behavior, 23,* 263–271.

Dacey, J. S. (1989b). *Fundamentals of creative thinking.* Lexington, MA: D. C. Heath.

D'Amico, R. (1984). Does employment during high school impair academic progress? *Sociology of Education, 57,* 152–164.

Daniel, W., Jr. (1983). Pubertal changes in adolescence. In J. Brooks-Gunn & A. C. Petersen (Eds.), *Girls at puberty.* New York: Plenum Press.

Darling, C. A., & Hicks, M. W. (1982). Parental influence on adolescent sexuality: Implications for parents as educators. *Journal of Youth and Adolescence, 11,* 231–245.

Davey, F. H., & Stoppard, J. M. (1993). Some factors affecting the occupational expectations of female adolescents. *Journal of Vocational Behavior, 43,* 235–250.

Davis, G. E., & Compas, B. E. (1986). Cognitive appraisal of major and daily stressful events during adolescence: A multidimensional scaling analysis. *Journal of Youth and Adolescence, 15,* 377–388.

Davis, K. E., & Latty-Mann, H. (1987). Love styles and relationship quality: A contribution of validation. *Journal of Social and Personal Relations, 4,* 409–428.

deAnda, D., Becerra, R. M., & Fielder, E. P. (1988). Sexuality, pregnancy, and motherhood among Mexican-American adolescents. *Journal of Adolescent Research, 3,* 403–412.

de Groot, A. D. (1965). *Thought and choice in chess.* The Hague: Mouton.

DeLamater, J., & MacCorquodale, P. (1979). *Premarital sexuality: Attitudes, relationships, behavior.* Madison, WI: University of Wisconsin Press.

Delaney, J., Lupton, M. J., & Toth, E. (1977). *The curse: A cultural history of menstruation.* New York: New American Library.

Deutsch, M. (1993). Educating for a peaceful world. *American Psychologist, 48,* 510–517.

Dewey, J. (1896). The concept of the reflex arc in psychology. *Psychological Bulletin, 3,* 357–370.

DiBlasio, F. A., & Benda, B. B. (1992). Gender differences in theories of adolescent sexual activity. *Sex Roles, 27,* 221–236.

DiClemente, R. J., Zorn, J., & Temoshok, L. (1987). The association of gender, ethnicity, and length of residence in the Bay Area to adolescents' knowledge and attitudes about acquired immune deficiency syndrome. *Journal of Applied Social Psychology, 17,* 216–230.

Digest of Education Statistics. (1993). U.S. Department of Education. Washington, DC: U.S. Government Printing Office.

Dillard, A. (1974). *Pilgrim at Tinker Creek.* New York: Harper's Magazine Press.

Dodge, K. A. (1983). Behavioral antecedents of peer social status. *Child Development, 54,* 1386–1399.

Dornbusch, S. M., Carlsmith, L., Gross, R. T., Martin, J. A., Jenning, D., Rosenberg, A., & Duke, D. (1981). Sexual development, age, and dating: A comparison of biological and sociological influences upon the set of behaviors. *Child Development, 52,* 179–185.

Dornbusch, S. M., Ritter, P. L., Leiderman, P. H., Roberts, D. F., & Fraleigh, M. J. (1987). The relation of parenting style to adolescent school performance. *Child Development, 58,* 1244–1257.

Dornbusch, S. M., Ritter, P. L., Mont-Reynaud, R., & Chen, Z. (1990). Family decision making and academic performance in a diverse high school population. *Journal of Adolescent Research, 5,* 143–160.

Doueck, H. J., Ishisaka, A. H., & Greenaway, K. D. (1988). The role of normative development in adolescent abuse and neglect. *Family Relations, 37,* 135–139.

Douvan, E., & Adelson, J. (1966). *The adolescent experience.* New York: Wiley.

DSM-IIIR: Diagnostic and statistical manual of mental disorders (3rd ed., rev. ed.) (1987). Washington, DC: American Psychiatric Association.

DuBois, D. L., & Hirsch, B. J. (1990). School and neighborhood friendship patterns of Blacks and Whites in early adolescence. *Child Development, 61,* 524–536.

Duke-Duncan, P. (1991). Body image. In R. M. Lerner, A. C. Petersen, & J. Brooks-Gunn (Eds.). *Encyclopedia of adolescence* (Vol. 2, pp. 90–94). New York: Garland.

Dunphy, D. C. (1963). The social structure of urban adolescent peer groups. *Sociometry, 26,* 230–240.

Dweck, C. S. (1986). Motivational processes affecting learning. *American Psychologist, 41,* 1040–1048.

Dweck, C. S. (1989). Motivation. In A. Lesgold & R. Glaser (Eds.), *Foundations for a psychology of education.* Hillsdale, NJ: Erlbaum.

Dweck, C. S., & Reppucci, N. D. (1973). Learned helplessness and reinforcement responsibility in children. *Journal of Personality and Social Psychology, 25,* 109–116.

Dyk, P. H., & Adams, G. R. (1990). Identity and intimacy: An initial investigation of three theoretical models using cross-lag panel correlations. *Journal of Youth and Adolescence, 19,* 91–110.

Eagley, A. H., & Kate, M. E. (1987). Are stereotypes of nationalities applied to both women and men? *Journal of Personality and Social Psychology, 53,* 451–462.

Eccles, J. E., Buchanan, C. M., Midgley, C., Fuligni, A. J., & Flanagan, C. (1991). Individuation reconsidered: Autonomy and control during early adolescence. *Journal of Social Issues, 47,* 53–68.

Educational Research Service. (1983). *Organization of the middle grades: A summary of research.* Arlington, VA: Author.

Eisert, D. C., & Kahle, L. R. (1986). The development of social attributions: An integration of probability and logic. *Human Development, 29,* 61–81.

Eitzen, D. S. (1975). Athletics in the status systems of male adolescents: A replication of Coleman's *The adolescent society. Adolescence, 10,* 267–276.

Elkind, D. (1967). Egocentrism in adolescence. *Child Development, 38,* 1025–1034.

Elkind, D. (1978). Understanding the young adolescent. *Adolescence, 13,* 127–134.

Elkind, D. (1978). *A sympathetic understanding of the child: Birth to sixteen* (2nd ed.). Boston: Allyn & Bacon.

Elkind, D. (1980). Strategic interactions in early adolescence. In J. Adelson (Ed.), *Handbook of adolescence.* New York: Wiley.

Elkind, D. (1984). *All grown up and no place to go: Teenagers in crisis.* Reading, MA: Addison-Wesley.

Elkind, D. (1985). Egocentrism redux: Reply to D. Lapsley and M. Murphy's Developmental Review paper. *Developmental Review, 5,* 218–226.

Enright, R. D., Santos, M. J., & Al-Mabuk, R. 1989. The adolescent as a forgiver. *Journal of Adolescence, 12,* 95–110.

Entwisle, D. R., & Alexander, K. L. (1990). Beginning school math competence: Minority and majority comparisons. *Child Development, 61,* 454–471.

Epstein, J. (1990). What matters in the middle grades—Grade span or practices? *Phi Delta Kappan, 71,* 438–444.

Epstein, S. (1973). The self-concept revisited, or a theory of a theory. *American Psychologist, 28,* 405–416.

Erikson, E. H. (1950). *Childhood and society.* New York: Norton.

Erikson, E. H. (1954). Problems of infancy and early childhood. In G. Murphy and A. J. Bachrach (Eds.). *An outline of abnormal psychology.* New York: Modern Library.

Erikson, E. H. (1956). The problem of ego identity. *Journal of the American Psychoanalytic Association, 4,* 56–121.

Erikson, E. H. (1959). Identity and the life cycle: Selected papers. *Psychological Issues Monograph, Series 1, No. 1.* New York: International Universities Press.

Erikson, E. H. (1963). *Childhood and society* (2nd ed.). New York: Norton.

Erikson, E. H. (1968). *Identity, youth and crisis.* New York: Norton.

Fairburn, C. G., & Cooper, P. J. (1982). Self-induced vomiting and bulimia nervosa: An undetected problem. *British Medical Journal, 284,* 1153–1155.

Faller, K. C. (1989). Characteristics of a clinical sample of sexually abused children: How boy and girl victims differ. *Child Abuse and Neglect, 13,* 281–291.

Farber, E. (1987). The adolescent who runs. In B. S. Brown & A. R. Mills (Eds.), *Youth at high risk.* (DHHS Publication No. ADM 87–1537). Washington, DC: U.S. Government Printing Office.

Farber, E., Kinast, C., McCoard, W., & Faulkner, D. (1984). Violence in families of adolescent runaways. *Child Abuse and Neglect, 8,* 295–299.

Fauber, R., Forehand, R., Thomas, A. M., & Wierson, M. (1990). A mediational model of the impact of marital conflict on adolescent adjustment in intact and divorced families. *Child Development, 61,* 1112–1123.

Faust, M. S. (1983). Alternative constructions of adolescent growth. In J. Brooks-Gunn & A. C. Petersen (Eds.), *Girls at puberty.* New York: Plenum Press.

Federal Bureau of Investigation. (1987). *Uniform crime reports.* Washington, DC: U.S. Department of Justice.

Feiring, C., & Lewis, M. (1991). The transition from middle childhood to early adolescence: Sex differences in the social network and perceived self-competence. *Sex Roles, 24,* 489–509.

Feiring, C., & Lewis, M. (1993). Do mothers know their teenagers' friends? Implications for individuation in early adolescence. *Journal of Youth and Adolescence, 22,* 337–354.

Feldman, C. F., Stone, A., & Renderer, B. (1990). Stage, transfer, and academic achievement in dialect-speaking Hawaiian adolescents. *Child Development, 61,* 472–484.

Feldman, S. S., Mont-Reynaud, R., & Rosenthal, D. A. (1992). When East moves West: The acculturation of values of Chinese adolescents in the U.S. and Australia. *Journal of Research on Adolescence, 2,* 147–173.

Fine, M. A. (1989). A social science perspective on stepfamily law: Suggestions for legal reform. *Family Relations, 38,* 53–58.

Finkelhor, D. (1993). Epidemiological factors in the clinical identification of child sexual abuse. *Child Abuse and Neglect, 17,* 67–70.

Finkelhor, D., & Baron, L. (1986). High-risk children. In D. Finkelhor et al. (eds.). *Sourcebook on child sexual abuse* (pp. 60–88). Beverly Hills, CA: Sage.

Finkelhor, D. H., & Hotaling, G. T. (1984). Sexual abuse in the national incidence study of child abuse and neglect: An appraisal. *Child Abuse and Neglect, 8,* 23–33.

Fisk, W. R. (1985). Responses to "neutral" pronoun presentations and the development of sex-biased responding. *Developmental Psychology, 21,* 481–485.

Flavell, J. H. (1963). *The developmental psychology of Jean Piaget.* Princeton, NJ: Van Nostrand.

Flavell, J. H. (1992). Cognitive development: Past, present, and future. *Developmental Psychology, 28,* 998–1005.

Flavell, J. H., Green, F. L., & Flavell, E. R. (1986). Development of knowledge about the appearance-reality distinction. *Monographs of the Society for Research in Child Development, 51* (Serial No. 212).

Flavell, J. H., Miller, P. H., & Miller, S. A. (1993). *Cognitive development* (3rd ed.). Englewood Cliffs, NJ: Prentice Hall.

Fleming, S. J., & Adolph, R. Helping bereaved adolescents: Needs and responses. In C. A. Corr & J. N. McNeil (Eds.), *Adolescence and death* (pp. 97–118). New York: Springer. (1986).

Flewelling, R. L., & Bauman, K. E. (1990). Family structure as a predictor of initial substance use and sexual intercourse in early adolescence. *Journal of Marriage and the Family, 52,* 171–181.

Ford, M. E., Wentzel, K. R., Wood, D., Stevens, E., & Siesfeld, G. A. (1989). Processes associated with integrative social competence: Emotional and contextual influences on adolescent social responsibility. *Journal of Adolescent Research, 4,* 405–425.

Ford, M. R., & Lowery, C. R. (1986). Gender differences in moral reasoning: A comparison of the uses of justice and care orientations. *Journal of Personality and Social Psychology, 50,* 777–783.

Forehand, R., Thomas, A. M., Wierson, M., Brody, G., & Fauber, R. (1990). Role of maternal functioning and parenting skills in adolescent functioning following parental divorce. *Journal of Abnormal Psychology, 99,* 278–283.

The forgotten half. (1989, June 26). *U.S. News & World Report,* pp. 45–53.

Forrest, K. A., Austin, D. M., Valdes, M. I., Fuentes, E. G., & Wilson, S. R. (1993). Exploring norms and beliefs related to AIDS prevention among California Hispanic men. *Family Planning Perspectives, 25,* 111–117.

Fowler, J. W. (1976). Stages in faith: The structural-developmental approach. In T. Hennessey (Ed.), *Values and development.* New York: Paulist Press.

Fowler, J. W. (1981). *Stages of faith: The psychology of human development and the quest for meaning.* San Francisco: Harper & Row.

Frankel, K. A. (1990). Girls' perceptions of peer relationship support and stress. *Journal of Early Adolescence, 10,* 69–88.

Franklin, A. J. (1985). The social context and socialization variables as factors in thinking and learning. In S. F. Chipman, J. W. Segal, & R. Glaser (Eds.), *Thinking and learning skills* (Vol. 2). Hillsdale, NJ: Erlbaum.

Freeman, D. (1983). *Margaret Mead and Samoa: The making and unmaking of an anthropological myth.* Cambridge, MA: Harvard University Press.

Freeman, D. (1987). Holmes, Lowell D.: Quest for the real Samoa: The Mead/Freeman controversy and beyond. *American Anthropologist, 89,* 392–395.

Freud, A. (1969). Adolescence as a developmental disturbance. In G. Caplan & S. Lebovici (Eds.), *Adolescence.* New York: Basic Books.

Freud, S. (1925). The dissolution of the oedipal complex. In J. Strachey (Ed.), *The standard edition of the complete psychological works of Sigmund Freud* (Vol. 19). London: Hogarth Press, 1961.

Freud, S. (1925). Some psychical consequences of the anatomical distinction between the sexes. In J. Strachey (Ed.), *The standard edition of the complete psychological works of Sigmund Freud* (Vol. 19). London: Hogarth Press, 1961.

Freud, S. (1954). *Collected works, standard edition.* London: Hogarth Press.

Frisch, R. E. (1983). Fatness, puberty, and fertility: The effects of nutrition and physical training on menarche and ovulation. In J. Brooks-Gunn & A. C. Petersen (Eds.), *Girls at puberty.* New York: Plenum Press.

Frisch, R. E. (1991). Puberty and body fat. In R. M. Lerner, A. C. Petersen, & J. Brooks-Gunn (Eds.). *Encyclopedia of adolescence* (Vol. 2, pp. 884–892). New York: Garland.

Fuligni, A. J., & Eccles, J. S. (1993). Perceived parent-child relationships and early adolescents' orientation toward peers. *Developmental Psychology, 29,* 622–632.

Fullerton, H., Jr. (1987). Projections 2000: Labor force projections—1986 to 2000. *Monthly Labor Review.* Washington, DC: U.S. Department of Labor.

Furman, W., & Buhrmester, D. (1992). Age and sex differences in perceptions of networks of personal relationships. *Child Development, 63,* 103–115.

Furstenberg, F. F. (1988). Child care after divorce and remarriage. In E. M. Hetherington & J. D. Arasteh (Eds.), *Impact of divorce, single-parenting, and stepparenting on children.* Hillsdale, NJ: Erlbaum.

Furstenberg, F. F., Jr., Brooks-Gunn, J., & Morgan, S. P. (1987). *Adolescent mothers in later life.* New York: Cambridge University Press.

Gaddis, A., & Brooks-Gunn, J. (1985). The male experience of pubertal change. *Journal of Youth and Adolescence, 14,* 61–69.

Galambos, N. L., & Maggs, J. L. (1990). Putting mothers' work-related stress in perspective: Mothers and adolescents in dual-earner families. *Journal of Early Adolescence, 10,* 313–328.

Gamoran, A., & Mare, R. D. (1989). Secondary school tracking and educational inequality: Compensation, reinforcement, or neutrality? *American Journal of Sociology, 94,* 1146–1183.

Garbarino, J. (1980). Some thoughts on school size and its effects on adolescent development. *Journal of Youth and Adolescence, 9,* 19–31.

Garcia, J. (1993). The changing image of ethnic groups in textbooks. *Phi Delta Kappan, 75,* 29–35.

Gardner, H. (1983). *Frames of mind.* New York: Basic Books.

Gardner, W. M., Roper, J. T., Gonzalez, C. C., & Simpson, R. G. (1988). Analysis of cheating on academic assignments. *Psychological Record, 38,* 543–555.

Garland, A. F., & Zigler, E. (1993). Adolescent suicide prevention: Current research and social policy implications. *American Psychologist, 48,* 169–182.

Gavazzi, S. M., & Sabatelli, R. M. (1990). Family system dynamics, the individuation process, and psychosocial development. *Journal of Adolescent Research, 5,* 500–519.

Gavin, L. A., & Furman, W. (1989). Age differences in adolescents' perceptions of their peer groups. *Developmental Psychology, 25,* 827–834.

Ge, X., Conger, R. D., Lorenz, F. O., Elder, G. H., Montague, R. B., & Simons, R. L. (1992). Linking family economic hardship to adolescent distress. *Journal of Research on Adolescence, 2,* 351–378.

Geller, L. G. (1985). *Word play and language learning for children.* Urbana, IL: National Council of Teachers of English.

Gerber, R. W., & Newman, I. M. (1989). Predicting future smoking of adolescent experimental smokers. *Journal of Youth and Adolescence, 18,* 191–201.

Gerstein, M., Lichtman, M., & Barokas, J. U. (1988). Occupational plans of adolescent women compared to men: A cross-sectional examination. *Career Development Quarterly, 36,* 222–230.

Gibbs, J. T. (1989). Black American adolescents. In J. T. Gibbs, L. N. Huang, & Associates (Eds.), *Children of color.* San Francisco: Jossey-Bass.

Gick, M. L., & Holyoak, K. J. (1980). Analogical problem solving. *Cognitive Psychology, 12,* 306–355.

Giles-Sims, J., & Crosbie-Burnett, M. (1989a). Stepfamily research: Implications for policy, clinical interventions, and further research. *Family Relations, 38,* 19–23.

Giles-Sims, J., & Crosbie-Burnett, M. (1989b). Adolescent power in stepfather families: A test of normative-resource theory. *Journal of Marriage and the Family, 51,* 1065–1078.

Gilligan, C. (1982). *In a different voice: Psychological theory and women's development.* Cambridge, MA: Harvard University Press.

Gilligan, C. (1986). Exit-voice dilemmas in adolescent development. In A. Foxley, M. S. McPherson, & G. O'Donnell (Eds.), *Development, democracy, and the art of trespassing: Essays in honor of Albert O. Hirschman.* Notre Dame, IN: University of Notre Dame Press.

Gilligan, C. (1988a). Adolescent development reconsidered. In C. Gilligan, J. V. Ward, J. M. Taylor, & B. Bardige (Eds.), *Mapping the moral domain.* Cambridge, MA: Harvard University Press.

Gilligan, C. (1988b). Exit-voice dilemmas in adolescent development. In C. Gilligan, J. V. Ward, J. M. Taylor, & B. Bardige (Eds.), *Mapping the moral domain.* Cambridge, MA: Harvard University Press.

Gilligan, C. (1989a). Preface: Teaching Shakespeare's sister. *Making connections: The relational worlds of adolescent girls at Emma Willard School.* Cambridge, MA: Harvard University Press.

Gilligan, C. (1989b). Prologue. In C. Gilligan, N. P. Lyons, & T. J. Hanmer (Eds.), *Making connections: The relational worlds of adolescent girls at Emma Willard School*. Cambridge, MA: Harvard University Press.

Gilligan, C., & Attanucci, J. (1988). Two moral orientations: Gender differences and similarities. *Merrill-Palmer Quarterly, 34,* 223–237.

Gilligan, C., Lyons, N. P., & Hanmer, T. J. (Eds.). (1989). *Making connections.* Troy, NY: Emma Willard School.

Ginsburg, H., & Opper, S. (1988). *Piaget's theory of intellectual development* (3rd ed.). Englewood Cliffs, NJ: Prentice-Hall.

Ginzburg, E. (1972). Toward a theory of occupational choice: A re-statement. *Vocational Guidance Quarterly, 20,* 169–176.

Ginzburg, E. (1990). Career development. In D. Brown, L. Brooks, & Associates (Eds.), *Career choice and development.* San Francisco: Jossey-Bass.

Glick, P. C. (1989). Remarried families, stepfamilies, and stepchildren: A brief demographic profile. *Family Relations, 38,* 24–27.

Glover, R. W., & Marshall, R. (1993). Improving the school-to-work transition of American adolescents. *Teachers College Record, 94,* 588–609.

Goldstein, A. P., Sprafkin, R. P., Gershaw, N. J., & Klein, P. (1980). *Skill-streaming the adolescent.* Champaign, IL: Research Press.

Goode, E. (1984). *Drugs in American society* (2nd ed.). New York: Knopf.

Goossens, L. (1984). Imaginary audience behavior as a function of age, sex, and formal operations. *International Journal of Behavioral Development, 1,* 77–93.

Gordon, M. (1989). The family environment of sexual abuse: A comparison of natal and stepfather abuse. *Child Abuse and Neglect, 13,* 121–130.

Gordon, T. (1972). *Parent effectiveness training.* New York: New American Library.

Grandjean, A. C. (1988). Eating versus inactivity. In K. Clark, R. Parr, & W. Castelli (Eds.), *Evaluation and management of eating disorders.* Champaign, IL: Life Enhancement Publications.

Gray, W., & Hudson, L. (1984). Formal operations and the imaginary audience. *Developmental Psychology, 20,* 619–627.

Greene, A. L. (1990). Great expectations: Constructions of the life course during adolescence. *Journal of Youth and Adolescence, 19,* 289–306.

Greene, A. L., & Grimsley, M. D. (1990). Age and gender differences in adolescents' preferences for parental advice: Mum's the word. *Journal of Adolescent Research, 5,* 396–413.

Greif, G. L., & DeMaris, A. (1990). Single fathers with custody. *Families in Society, 71,* 259–266.

Gross, B. (1990). Here dropouts drop in—and stay! *Phi Delta Kappan, 71,* 625–627.

Grotevant, H. D., & Cooper, C. R. (1986). Individuation in family relationships. *Human Development, 29,* 82–100.

Gunnings, T. S., & Simpkins, G. A. (1972). A systematic approach to counseling disadvantaged youth. *Journal of Non-White Concerns in Personnel and Guidance, 1,* 4–8.

Gwartney-Gibbs, P. A. (1986). The institutionalization of premarital cohabitation: Estimates from marriage license applications, 1970 and 1980. *Journal of Marriage and the Family, 48,* 423–434.

Habenicht, D. J., & Futcher, W. G. (1990). Psychological profile of the female adolescent incest victim. *Child Abuse and Neglect, 14,* 429–438.

Hains, A. A., & Ryan, E. B. (1983). The development of social cognitive processes among juvenile delinquents and nondelinquent peers. *Child Development, 54,* 1536–1544.

Hains, A. A., & Szyjakowski, M. (1990). A cognitive stress-reduction intervention program for adolescents. *Journal of Counseling Psychology, 37,* 79–84.

Hale, J. L. (1987). Plagiarism in classroom settings. *Communication Research Reports, 4,* 66–70.

Hale, S. (1990). A global developmental trend in cognitive processing speed. *Child Development, 61,* 653–663.

Hale, S., Fry, A. F., & Jessie, J. (1993). Effects of practice on speed of information processing in children and adults: Age sensitivity and age invariance. *Developmental Psychology, 29,* 880–892.

Hall, C. S. (1954). *A primer of Freudian psychology.* Cleveland: World Publishing.

Hall, E., & Post-Kammer, P. (1987). Black mathematics and science majors: Why so few? *Career Development Quarterly, 35,* 206–219.

Hall, G. S. (1904). *Adolescence: Its psychology and its relations to physiology, anthropology, sociology, sex, crime, religion, and education* (Vol. 1). New York: Appleton-Century-Crofts.

Hallinan, M. T., & Teixeira, R. A. (1987). Opportunities and constraints: Black-white differences in the formation of interracial friendships. *Child Development, 58,* 1358–1371.

Hamer, D. H., Hu, S., Magnuson, V.-L., Hu, N., & Pattatucci, A. M. L. (1993). A linkage between DNA markers on the X-chromosome and male sexual orientation. *Science, 261,* 321–326.

Hammelman, T. L. (1993). Gay and lesbian youth: Contributing factors to serious attempts or considerations of suicide. *Journal of Gay and Lesbian Psychotherapy, 2,* 77–89.

Hammond, W. R., & Yung, B. (1993). Psychology's role in the public health response to assaultive violence among young African-American men. *American Psychologist, 48,* 142–154.

Hanawalt, B. A. (1986). *The ties that bound: Peasant families in medieval England.* New York: Oxford University Press.

Harris, L. (1988). *Public attitudes toward teenage pregnancy, sex education, and birth control.* New York: Planned Parenthood of America.

Hartup, W. W. (1993). Adolescents and their friends. In B. Laursen (Ed.), *New directions for child development* (pp. 3–22). San Francisco: Jossey-Bass.

Harvey, O. J., & Rutherford, J. (1960). Status in the informal group. *Child Development, 31,* 377–385.

Hass, A. (1979). *Teenage sexuality: A survey of teenage sexual behavior.* New York: Macmillan.

Hatcher, R., Hatcher, S., Berlin, M., Okla, K., & Richards, J. (1990). Psychological mindedness and abstract reasoning in late childhood and adolescence: An exploration using new instruments. *Journal of Youth and Adolescence, 19,* 307–326.

Hauser, S. T., Borman, E. H., Jacobson, A. M., Powers, S. I., & Noam, G. G. (1991). Understanding family contexts of adolescent coping: A study of parental ego development and adolescent coping strategies. *Journal of Early Adolescence, 11,* 96–124.

Havighurst, R. J. (1952). *Developmental tasks and education.* New York: Longman.

Havighurst, R. J. (1972). *Developmental tasks and education.* New York: David McKay.

Hawkins, J., Pea, R. D., Glick, J., & Scribner, S. (1984). "Merds that laugh don't like mushrooms": Evidence for deductive reasoning by preschoolers. *Developmental Psychology, 20,* 584–594.

Hayes, C. D. (Ed.). (1987). *Risking the future: Adolescent sexuality, pregnancy, and childbearing.* (Vol. 1). Washington, DC: National Academy Press.

Hein, K. (1989). Commentary on adolescent acquired immunodeficiency syndrome: The next wave of the immunodeficiency virus epidemic? *Journal of Pediatrics, 114,* 144–149.

Hein, K. (1991). Fighting AIDS in adolescents. *Issues in Science and Technology, 7(3),* 67–72.

Hein, K., & Futterman, D. (1991). Medical management in HIV-infected adolescents. *Journal of Pediatrics, 119,* 518–520.

Held, T. (1986). Institutionalization and deinstitutionalization of the life course. *Human Development, 29,* 157–162.

Hendrick, C., & Hendrick, S. (1986). A theory and method of love. *Journal of Personality and Social Psychology, 50,* 392–402.

Hendrick, C., & Hendrick, S. (1991). Dimensions of love: A sociobiological interpretation. *Journal of Social Clinical Psychology, 10,* 206–230.

Hendrick, C., Hendrick, S., & Adler, N. L. (1988). Romantic relationships: Love, satisfaction, and staying together. *Journal of Personality and Social Psychology, 54,* 980–988.

Henggeler, S. W. (1989). *Delinquency in adolescence.* Newbury Park, CA: Sage Publications.

Hetherington, E. M. (1989). Coping with family transitions: Winners, losers, and survivors. *Child Development, 60,* 1–14.

Hetherington, E. M., Cox, M., & Cox, R. (1982). Effects of divorce on children and parents. In M. E. Lamb (Ed.), *Nontraditional families.* Hillsdale, NJ: Erlbaum.

Hetherington, E. M., Hagan, M. S., & Anderson, E. R. (1989). Marital transitions: A child's perspective. *American Psychologist, 44,* 303–312.

Higham, E. (1980). Variations in adolescent psychohormonal development. In J. Adelson (Ed.), *Handbook of adolescent development.* New York: Wiley.

Hill, J. P., & Holmbeck, G. N. (1987). Disagreements about rules in families with seventh-grade girls and boys. *Journal of Youth and Adolescence, 16,* 221–246.

Hingson, R. W., Strunin, L., Berlin, B., & Heeren, T. (1990). Beliefs about AIDS, use of alcohol and drugs, and unprotected sex among Massachusetts adolescents. *American Journal of Public Health, 80,* 295–299.

Hirsh, R. H., Paolitto, D. P., & Reimer, J. (1979). *Promoting moral growth: From Piaget to Kohlberg.* New York: Longman.

Hoffman, M. L. (1980). Moral development in adolescence. In J. Adelson (Ed.), *Handbook of adolescent psychology.* New York: Wiley.

Hoffman, M. L. (1988). Moral development. In M. H. Bornstein & M. E. Lamb (Eds.), *Developmental psychology: An advanced textbook.* Hillsdale, NJ: Erlbaum.

Hogan, R. (1980). The gifted adolescent. In J. Adelson (Ed.), *Handbook of adolescence.* New York: Wiley.

Hogan, R., Viernstein, M. C., McGinn, P. V., Daurio, S., & Bohannon, W. (1977). Verbal giftedness and sociopolitical intelligence. *Journal of Educational Psychology, 50,* 135–142.

Hogan, R., & Weiss, D. (1974). Personality correlates of superior academic achievement. *Journal of Counseling Psychology, 21,* 144–149.

Holland, J. L. (1961). Creative and academic performance among talented adolescents. *Journal of Educational Psychology, 52,* 136–147.

Holland, J. L. (1985a). *Making vocational choices: A theory of vocational personalities and work environments* (2nd ed.). Englewood Cliffs, NJ: Prentice-Hall.

Holland, J. L. (1985b). *Manual for the Vocational Preference Inventory.* Odessa, FL: Psychological Assessment Resources.

Holland, J. L. (1987). Current status of Holland's theory of careers: Another perspective. *Career Development Quarterly, 36,* 24–30.

Hood, K. E. (1991). Menstrual cycle. In R. M. Lerner, A. C. Petersen, & J. Brooks-Gunn (Eds.). *Encyclopedia of adolescence* (Vol. 2, pp. 642–646). New York: Garland.

Horn, J. L., & Cattell, R. B. (1967). Refinement and test of the theory of fluid and crystallized ability intelligences. *Journal of Educational Psychology, 57,* 253–270.

Horner, M. (1968). Toward an understanding of achievement-related conflicts in women. *Journal of Social Issues, 28,* 157–175.

Horney, K. (1937). *The neurotic personality of our time.* New York: Norton.

Horney, K. (1967). *Feminine psychology.* New York: Norton.

Horowitz, F. D., & O'Brien, M. (1986). Gifted and talented children. *American Psychologist, 41,* 1147–1152.

Horowitz, M. (1993, December). In search of Monster. *Atlantic,* pp. 28–37.

Horst, H. J., Bartesh, W., & Derksen-Thedens, I. (1977). Plasma testosterone, sex hormone-binding globulin-binding capacity and percent binding of testosterone and 5a-dihydrosterone in prepubertal, pubertal, and adult males. *Journal of Clinical Endocrinology and Metabolism, 45,* 522–527.

Houston, J. P. (1986). Survey corroboration of experimental findings on classroom cheating behavior. *College Student Journal, 20,* 168–173.

Howard, G. R. (1993). Whites in multicultural education: Rethinking our role. *Phi Delta Kappan, 75,* 36–41.

Howat, P. M., & Saxton, A. M. (1988). The incidence of bulimic behavior in a secondary and university school population. *Journal of Youth and Adolescence, 17,* 221–231.

Howell, F. M., Frese, W., & Sollie, C. R. (1984). The measurement of perceived opportunity for occupational attainment. *Journal of Vocational Behavior, 25,* 325–343.

Hoyt, K. B. (1988). The changing workforce: A review of projections—1986 to 2000. *Career Development Quarterly, 37,* 31–39.

Hoyt, K. B. (1989). The career status of women and minority persons: A 20-year retrospective. *Career Development Quarterly, 37,* 202–212.

Huang, L. N., & Yin, Y. (1989). Chinese American children and adolescents. In J. T. Gibbs, L. N. Huang, & Associates (Eds.), *Children of color.* San Francisco: Jossey-Bass.

Hu-DeHart, E. (1993). The history, development, and future of ethnic studies. *Phi Delta Kappan, 75,* 50–54.

Huelskamp, R. M. (1993). Perspectives on education in America. *Phi Delta Kappan, 74,* 718–721.

Huesmann, L. R., Lefkowitz, M. M., Eron, L. D.,

& Walder, L. D. (1984). Stability of aggression over time and generations. *Developmental Psychology, 20*, 1120–1134.

Huizinga, D., & Elliott, D. S. (1987). Juvenile offenders: Prevalence, offender incidence, and arrest rates by race. *Crime and Delinquency, 33*, 206–223.

Humphrey, L. L. (1989). Observed family interactions among subtypes of eating disorders using structural analysis of social behavior. *Journal of Consulting and Clinical Psychology, 57*, 206–214.

Hunt, J. M. (1961). *Intelligence and experience*. New York: Ronald Press.

Husbands, C. L. (1970). Some social and psychological consequences of the American dating system. *Adolescence, 5*, 451–462.

Hyde, J. S. (1981). How large are cognitive gender differences? A meta-analysis using *w2* and *d*. *American Psychologist, 36*, 892–901.

Hyde, J. S. (1988). *Half the human experience* (4th ed.). Lexington, MA: D. C. Heath.

Hyde, J. S. (1990). *Understanding human sexuality* (4th ed.). San Francisco: McGraw-Hill.

Iheanacho, S. O. (1988). Minority self-concept: A research review. *Journal of Instructional Psychology, 15*, 3–11.

Inderbitzen-Pisaruk, H., Clark, M. L., & Solano, C. H. (1992). Correlates of loneliness in midadolescence. *Journal of Youth and Adolescence, 21*, 151–167.

Inhelder, B., & Piaget, J. (1958). *The growth of logical thinking from childhood to adolescence*. New York: Basic Books.

Insel, P., & Roth, W. T. (1994). *Core Concepts in Health* (7th ed.). Mountain View, CA: Mayfield.

Irion, J. C., Coon, R. C., & Blanchard-Fields, F. (1988). The influence of divorce on coping in adolescence. *Journal of Youth and Adolescence, 17*, 135–145.

Irving, L. M. (1993). The relationship between childhood sexual abuse and subsequent onset of bulimia nervosa. *Child Abuse and Neglect, 17*, 305–314.

Isajiw, W. W. (1974). Definitions of ethnicity. *Ethnicity, 1*, 111–124.

Jahnke, H. C., & Blanchard-Fields, F. (1992). A test of two models of adolescent egocentrism. *Journal of Youth and Adolescence, 22*, 313–326.

Jensen, A. R. (1969). How much can we boost IQ and scholastic achievement? *Harvard Educational Review, 39*, 1–123.

Jensen, A. R. (1985). The nature of the black-white difference on various psychometric tests: Spearman's hypothesis. *The Behavioral and Brain Sciences, 8*, 193–263.

Joebgen, A. M., & Richards, M. H. (1990). Maternal education and employment: Mediating maternal and adolescent emotional adjustment. *Journal of Early Adolescence, 10*, 329–343.

Johnson, B. M., Shulman, S., & Collins, W. A. (1991). Systematic patterns of parenting as reported by adolescents: Developmental differences and implications for psychosocial outcomes. *Journal of Adolescent Research, 6*, 235–252.

Johnson, C., Steinberg, S., & Lewis, C. (1988). Bulimia. In K. Clark, R. Parr, & W. Castelli (Eds.), *Evaluation and management of eating disorders*. Champaign, IL: Life Enhancement Publications.

Johnston, D. K. (1988). Adolescents' solutions to dilemmas in fables: Two moral orientations—two problem solving strategies. In C. Gilligan, J. V. Ward, & J. M. Taylor (Eds.), *Mapping the moral domain*. Cambridge, MA: Harvard University Press.

Johnston, L. D., O'Malley, P. M., & Bachman, J. G. (1989). *Drug use, drinking, and smoking: National survey results from high school, college, and young adult populations, 1975–1988* (DHHS Publication No. ADM 89–1638). Washington, DC: U.S. Government Printing Office.

Jones, M. C. (1957). The late careers of boys who were early- or late-maturing. *Child Development, 28*, 113–128.

Jones, M. C. (1958). A study of socialization patterns at the high school level. *Journal of Genetic Psychology, 93*, 87–111.

Jones, M. C. (1965). Psychological correlates of somatic development. *Child Development, 36*, 899–911.

Jones, M. C., & Bayley, N. (1950). Physical maturing among boys as related to behavior. *Journal of Educational Psychology, 41*, 129–148.

Jones, M. C., & Mussen, P. H. (1958). Self-conceptions, motivations and attitudes of early- and late-maturing girls. *Child Development, 29*, 491–501.

Josselson, R. L. (1980). Ego development in adolescence. In J. Adelson (Ed.), *Handbook of adolescent psychology*. New York: Wiley.

Josselson, R. L. (1982). Personality structure and identity status in women as viewed through early memories. *Journal of Youth and Adolescence, 11*, 293–299.

Josselson, R. L. (1987). *Finding herself: Pathways to identity development in women*. San Francisco: Jossey-Bass.

Josselson, R. L. (1988). The embedded self: I and thou revisited. In D. K. Lapsley & F. C. Power (Eds.), *Self, ego, and identity*. New York: Springer-Verlag.

Josselson, R. L. (1992). *The space between us*. San Francisco: Jossey-Bass.

Kagan, J. (1971). A conception of early adolescence. *Daedalus, 100*, 997–1012.

Kahle, J. B. (1982). Can positive minority attitudes lead to achievement gains in science? Analysis of the 1977 National Assessment of Educational Progress, Attitudes Toward Science. *Science Education, 66*, 539–546.

Kail, R. (1991). Developmental change in speed of processing during childhood and adolescence. *Psychological Bulletin, 109*, 490–501.

Kail, R. (1992). Processing speed, speech rate, and memory. *Developmental Psychology, 28*, 899–904.

Kammer, P. P., Fouad, N., & Williams, R. (1988). Follow-up of a pre-college program for minority and disadvantaged students. *Career Development Quarterly, 37*, 40–45.

Kandel, D. B. (1975). Stages in adolescent involvement in drug use. *Science, 190*, 912–914.

Kandel, D. B. (1978). Similarity in real-life adolescent friendship pairs. *Journal of Personality and Social Psychology, 36*, 306–312.

Kandel, D. B., & Lesser, G. S. (1969). Parent-adolescent relationships and adolescent independence in the United States and Denmark. *Journal of Marriage and the Family, 31*, 348–358.

Kandel, D. B., & Yamaguchi, K. (1985). Developmental patterns of the use of legal, illegal, and medically prescribed psychotropic drugs from adolescence to young adulthood. In C. L. Jones & R. J. Battjes (Eds.), *Etiology of drug abuse: Implications for prevention. NIDA Research Monograph 56* (DHHS Publication No. ADM 85-1335).

Washington, DC: U.S. Government Printing Office.

Kane, M. J. (1988). The female athletic role as a status determinant within the social system of high school adolescents. *Adolescence, 23*, 253–264.

Kangas, J., & Bradway, K. (1971). Intelligence at middle age: A thirty-eight year follow-up. *Developmental Psychology, 5*, 333–337.

Kann, L., Warren, W., Collins, J. L., Ross, J., Collins, B., & Kolbe, L. J. (1993). Results from the national school-based 1991 Youth Risk Behavior Survey and progress toward achieving related health objectives for the nation. *Journal of the U.S. Public Health Service, 108*, 47–55.

Kantner, J. F., & Zelnik, M. (1972). Sexual experience of young unmarried women in the United States. *Family Planning Perspectives, 4*, 9–18.

Kaufman, J. F., Shaffer, H., & Burglass, M. E. (1985). The biological basics: Drugs and their effects. In T. E. Bratter & G. G. Forrest (Eds.), *Alcoholism and substance abuse*. New York: Free Press.

Kazdin, A. E. (1993). Adolescent mental health: Prevention and treatment programs. *American Psychologist, 48*, 127–141.

Keating, D. P. (1980). Thinking processes in adolescence. In J. Adelson (Ed.), *Handbook of adolescent psychology*. New York: Wiley.

Keating, D. P., & Bobbitt, B. L. (1978). Differences in cognitive-processing components of mental ability. *Child Development, 49*, 155–167.

Keith, J. G., Nelson, C. S., Schlabach, J. H., & Thompson, C. J. (1990). The relationship between parental employment and three measures of early adolescent responsibility: Family-related, personal and social. *Journal of Early Adolescence, 10*, 399–415.

Keller, M., & Wood, P. (1989). Development of friendship reasoning: A study of interindividual differences in intraindividual change. *Developmental Psychology, 25*, 820–826.

Kelly, M. L., & Grace, N. (1990). Acceptability of positive and punitive discipline methods: Comparisons among abusive, potentially abusive, and nonabusive parents. *Child Abuse and Neglect, 14*, 219–226.

Keniston, K. (1970). Youth: A "new" stage of life. *American Scholar, 39*, 631–654.

Kennedy, L. W., & Baron, S. W. (1993). Routine activities and a subculture of violence: A study of violence on the street. *Journal of Research in Crime and Delinquency, 30,* 88–112.

Kenny, A. M., Guardaado, S., & Brown, L. (1989). Sex education and AIDS education in the schools: What states and large school districts are doing. *Family Planning Perspective, 21,* 56–64.

Kett, J. F. (1977). *Rites of passage.* New York: Basic Books.

Kingston, M. H. (1977). *The woman warrior.* New York: Vintage Books.

Kinsey, A. C., Pomeroy, W. B., & Martin, C. E. (1948). *Sexual behavior in the human male.* Philadelphia: Saunders.

Kinsey, A. C., Pomeroy, W. B., Martin, C. E., & Gebhard, P. H. (1953). *Sexual behavior in the human female.* Philadelphia: Saunders.

Kirby, D. (1984). *Sexuality education: An evaluation of programs and their effect.* Santa Cruz, CA: Network Publications.

Kitano, H. H. L., & Daniels, R. (1988). *Asian Americans: Emerging minorities.* Englewood Cliffs, NJ: Prentice-Hall.

Klebanov, P. K., & Brooks-Gunn, J. (1992). Impact of maternal attitudes, girls' adjustment, and cognitive skills upon academic performance in middle and high school. *Journal of Research on Adolescence, 2,* 81–102.

Klein, J. R., & Litt, I. F. (1983). Menarche and dysmenorrhea. In J. Brooks-Gunn & A. C. Petersen (Eds.), *Girls at puberty.* New York: Plenum Press.

Klein, S. S. (1985). *Handbook for achieving sex equity through education.* Baltimore, MD: Johns Hopkins University Press.

Klerman, L. V. (1988). The delivery of health services to early adolescents. In M. D. Levine & E. R. McArney (Eds.), *Early adolescent transitions.* Lexington, MA: D. C. Heath.

Knobil, E. (1980). The neuroendocrine control of the menstrual cycle. *Recent Progress in Hormone Research, 36,* 53–88.

Koch, P. B. (1988). The relationship of first intercourse to later sexual functioning concerns of adolescents. *Journal of Adolescent Research, 3,* 345–362.

Kochman, T. (1987). The ethnic component in black language and culture. In M. J. Rotheram &

J. S. Phinney (Eds.), *Children's ethnic socialization: Pluralism and development* (pp. 219–238). Beverly Hills: Sage Publications.

Kohlberg, L. (1976). Moral stages and moralization: The cognitive developmental approach. In T. Lickona (Ed.), *Moral development and behavior.* New York: Holt, Rinehart & Winston.

Kohlberg, L. (1984). *The psychology of moral development.* New York: Harper & Row.

Kohlberg, L., & Kramer, R. (1969). Continuities and discontinuities in childhood and adult moral development. *Human Development, 12,* 93–120.

Kohn, P. M., Lafreniere, K., & Gurevich, M. (1990). The Inventory of College Students' Recent Life Experiences: A decontaminated hassles scale for a special population. *Journal of Behavioral Medicine, 13,* 619–630.

Kohn, P. M., & Millrose, J. A. (1993). The Inventory of High-School Students' Recent Life Experiences: A decontaminated measure of adolescents' hassles. *Journal of Youth and Adolescence, 22,* 43–55.

Kohut, S., Jr. (1988). *The middle school: A bridge between elementary and high schools* (2nd ed.). Washington, DC: National Education Association.

Koss, M. P., Dinero, T. E., Seibel, C. A., & Cox, S. L. (1988). Stranger and acquaintance rape: Are there differences in the victim's experience? *Psychology of Women Quarterly, 12,* 1–24.

Krasnoff, A. G. (1989). Early sex-linked activities and interests related to spatial abilities. *Personal and Individual Differences, 10,* 81–85.

Kratcoski, P. C., & Kratcoski, L. D. (1986). *Juvenile delinquency.* Englewood Cliffs, NJ: Prentice-Hall.

Krisberg, B., Schwartz, I., Fishman, G., Eisiloits, Z., Guttman, E., & Joe, J. (1987). The incarceration of minority youth. *Crime and Delinquency, 29,* 333–364.

Kroger, J. (1986). The relative importance of identity status interview components: A replication and extension. *Journal of Adolescence, 9,* 337–354.

Kroger, J. (1988). A longitudinal study of ego identity status interview domains. *Journal of Adolescence, 11,* 49–64.

Kroger, J. (1992). Intrapsychic dimensions of identity during late adolescence. In G. R. Adams, T. P.

Gullotta, and R. Montemayor (Eds.), *Adolescent identity formation.* Newbury Park, CA: Sage.

Krohne, H. W., & Rogner, J. (1982). Repression-sensitization as a central construct in coping research. In H. W. Krohne & L. Laux (Eds.), *Achievement, stress, and anxiety.* Washington, DC: Hemisphere.

Kuhn, D., Langer, J., Kohlberg, L., & Haan, N. S. (1977). The development of formal operations in logical and moral judgment. *Genetic Psychology Monographs, 95,* 97–188.

Kuhn, T. S. (1962). *The structure of scientific revolutions.* Chicago: University of Chicago Press.

Kulin, H. E. (1991a). Puberty, hypothalamic-pituitary changes of. In R. M. Lerner, A. C. Petersen, & J. Brooks-Gunn (Eds.). *Encyclopedia of adolescence* (Vol. 2, pp. 900–907). New York: Garland.

Kulin, H. E. (1991b). Puberty, endocrine changes at. In R. M. Lerner, A. C. Petersen, & J. Brooks-Gunn (Eds.). *Encyclopedia of adolescence* (Vol. 2, pp. 897–899). New York: Garland.

Kulin, H. E. (1991c). Spermarche. In R. M. Lerner, A. C. Petersen, & J. Brooks-Gunn (Eds.). *Encyclopedia of adolescence* (Vol. 2, pp. 1091–1092). New York: Garland.

Kupersmidt, J. B., & Coie, J. D. (1990). Preadolescent peer status, aggression, and school adjustment as predictors of externalizing problems in adolescence. *Child Development, 61,* 1350–1362.

Kurdek, L. A. (1990). Effects of child age on the marital quality and psychological distress of newly married mothers and stepfathers. *Journal of Marriage and the Family, 52,* 81–85.

Labouvie-Vief, G. (1980). Beyond formal operations: Uses and limits of pure logic in life-span development. *Human Development, 23,* 141–161.

LaFromboise, T. D., & Low, K. G. (1989). American Indian children and adolescents. In J. T. Gibbs, L. N. Huang, & Associates (Eds.), *Children of color.* San Francisco: Jossey-Bass.

Lanza-Kaduce, L., & Klug, M. (1986). Learning to cheat: The interaction of moral-development and social learning theories. *Deviant Behavior, 7,* 243–259.

Lapsley, D. K., FitzGerald, D. P., Rice, K. G., & Jackson, S. (1989). Separation-individuation and the "new look" at the imaginary audience and per-sonal fable: A test of an integrative model. *Journal of Adolescent Research, 4,* 483–505.

Lapsley, D. K., Milstead, M., Quintana, S. M., Flannery, D., & Buss, R. R. (1986). Adolescent egocentrism and formal operations: Tests of a theoretical assumption. *Developmental Psychology, 22,* 800–807.

Lapsley, D. K., & Murphy, M. (1985). Another look at the theoretical assumptions of adolescent egocentrism. *Developmental Review, 5,* 201–217.

Larkin, J. H. (1985). Understanding, problem representations, and skill in physics. In S. F. Chipman, J. W. Segal, & R. Glaser (Eds.), *Thinking and learning skills* (Vol. 2). Hillsdale, NJ: Erlbaum.

Larson, R., & Lampman-Petraitis, C. (1989). Daily emotional states as reported by children and adolescents. *Child Development, 60,* 1250–1260.

Laswell, M., & Lobsenz, N. M. (1980). *Styles of loving.* Garden City, NY: Doubleday.

Lazarus, R. S., & Folkman, S. (1984). *Stress, appraisal and coping.* New York: Springer-Verlag.

LeBlanc, M. (1983). Delinquency as an epiphenomenon of adolescence. In R. R. Corrado, M. LeBlanc, & J. Trepanier (Eds.), *Current issues in juvenile justice.* Toronto: Butterworth.

Ledoux, S., Choquet, M., & Manfredi, R. (1993). Associated factors for self-reported binge eating among male and female adolescents. *Journal of Adolescence, 16,* 75–91.

Lee, J. A. (1973). *The colors of love.* Ontario, Canada: New Press.

Lee, J. A. (1988). Love styles. In R. J. Sternberg & M. L. Barnes (Eds.), *The psychology of love.* New Haven: Yale University Press.

Lee, S. H. (1990). Influence of metacognitive knowledge and aptitude on problem solving. *Journal of Educational Psychology, 82,* 306–314.

Leland, J. (1993, November 29). Criminal records: Gangsta rap and the culture of violence. *Newsweek,* pp. 60–66.

Leland, N. L., & Barth, R. P. (1993). Characteristics of adolescents who have attempted to avoid HIV and who have communicated with parents about sex. *Journal of Adolescent Research, 8,* 58–76.

Lempers, J. D., & Clark-Lempers, D. S. (1992). Young, middle, and late adolescents' comparisons of the functional importance of five significant relationships. *Journal of Youth and Adolescence, 21,* 53–96.

Lempers, J. D., & Clark-Lempers, D. S. (1993). A functional comparison of same-sex and opposite-sex friendships during adolescence. *Journal of Adolescent Research, 8,* 89–108.

Leon, G. R., Perry, C. L., Mangelsdorf, C., & Tell, G. J. (1989). Adolescent nutritional and psychological patterns and risk for the development of an eating disorder. *Journal of Youth and Adolescence, 18,* 273–282.

Lerner, R. M. (1976). *Concepts and theories of human development.* Menlo Park, CA: Addison-Wesley.

Lerner, R. M. (1986). *Concepts and theories of human development* (2nd ed.). New York: Random House.

Lerner, R. M., Delaney, M., Hess, L. E., Jovanovic, J., & von Eye, A. (1990). Early adolescent physical attractiveness and academic competence. *Journal of Early Adolescence, 10,* 4–20.

LeVay, S. (1991). A difference in hypothalamic structure between heterosexual and homosexual men. *Science, 253,* 1034–1037.

Lever, J. (1976). Sex differences in the games children play. *Social Problems, 23,* 478–487.

Lever, J. (1978). Sex differences in the complexity of children's play and games. *American Sociological Review, 43,* 471–483.

Levesque, R. J. R. (1993). The romantic experience of adolescents in satisfying love relationships. *Journal of Youth and Adolescence, 22,* 219–251.

Levitt, M. J., Guacci-Franco, N., & Levitt, J. L. (1993). Convoys of social support in childhood and early adolescence: Structure and function. *Developmental Psychology, 29,* 811–818.

Levitt, R. A. (1981). *Physiological psychology.* New York: Holt, Rinehart & Winston.

Licht, B. G., & Dweck, C. S. (1984). Determinants of academic achievement: The interaction of children's achievement orientations with skill area. *Developmental Psychology, 20,* 628–636.

Licht, B. G., Linden, T. A., Brown, D. A., & Sexton, M. A. (1984, August). *Sex differences in achievement orientation: An "A" student phenomenon?* Paper presented at the meeting of the American Psychological Association, Toronto, Canada.

Lips, H. M. (1988). *Sex and gender.* Mountain View, CA: Mayfield.

Lips, H. M. (1993). *Sex and gender: An introduction* (2nd ed.). Mountain View, CA: Mayfield.

Lobel, T., & Levanon, I. (1988). Self-esteem, need for approval, and cheating behavior in children. *Journal of Educational Psychology, 80,* 122–123.

Lonky, E., Roodin, P. A., & Rybasch, J. M. (1988). Moral judgment and sex-role orientation as a function of self and other presentation modes. *Journal of Youth and Adolescence, 17,* 189–195.

Lovitt, T. C. (1989). *Introduction to learning disabilities.* Boston: Allyn & Bacon.

Lucas, B. (1988). Family patterns and their relationship to obesity. In K. L. Clark, R. B. Parr, & W. P. Castelli (Eds.), *Evaluation and management of eating disorders.* Champaign, IL: Life Enhancement Publications.

Lyon, J. M., Henggler, S., & Hall, J. A. (1992). The family relations, peer relations, and criminal activities of Caucasian and Hispanic-American gang members. *Journal of Abnormal Child Psychology, 20,* 439–449.

Maguire, K., Pastore, A. L., & Flanagan, T. J. (1993). *Sourcebook of criminal justice statistics 1992.* U.S. Department of Justice, Bureau of Justice Statistics. Washington, DC: U.S. Government Printing Office.

Major, B., & Forcey, B. (1985). Social comparisons and pay evaluations: Preferences for same-sex and same-job wage comparisons. *Journal of Experimental Social Psychology, 21,* 393–405.

Malina, R. M. (1990). Physical growth and performance during the transitional years (9–16). In R. Montemayor, G. R. Adams, & T. P. Gullotta (Eds.), *From childhood to adolescence.* Newbury Park, CA: Sage.

Mann, L., Harmoni, R., & Power, C. (1989). Adolescent decision-making: The development of competence. *Journal of Adolescence, 12,* 265–278.

Marcia, J. E. (1966). Development and validation of ego identity status. *Journal of Personality and Social Psychology, 3,* 551–558.

Marcia, J. E. (1980). Identity in adolescence. In J. Adelson (Ed.), *Handbook of adolescent psychology.* New York: Wiley.

Marcia, J. E. (1988). Common processes underlying ego identity, cognitive/moral development, and individuation. In D. K. Lapsley & F. C. Power (Eds.), *Self, ego and identity: Integrative approaches.* New York: Springer-Verlag.

Margolin, L., Miller, M., & Moran, P. B. (1989). When a kiss is not just a kiss: Relating violations of consent in kissing to rape myth acceptance. *Sex Roles, 20,* 231–243.

Markstrom-Adams, C. (1992). A consideration of intervening factors in adolescent identity formation. In G. R. Adams, T. P. Gulotta, & R. Montemayor (Eds.), *Adolescent identity formation.* Newbury Park, CA: Sage.

Martinez, R., & Dukes, R. L. (1987). Race, gender and self-esteem among youth. *Hispanic Journal of Behavioral Sciences, 9,* 427–443.

Martin, B. (1990). The transmission of relationship difficulties from one generation to the next. *Journal of Youth and Adolescence, 19,* 181–199.

Martorano, S. C. (1977). A developmental analysis of performance on Piaget's formal operations tasks. *Developmental Psychology, 13,* 666–672.

Masters, W. H., & Johnson, V. E. (1966). *Human sexual response.* Boston: Little, Brown.

Masters, W. H., Johnson, V. E., & Kolodny, R. C. (1988). *Human sexuality* (3rd ed.). Boston: Little, Brown.

Matuschka, P. R. (1985). The psychopharmacology of addiction. In T. E. Bratter & G. G. Forrest (Eds.), *Alcoholism and substance abuse.* New York: Free Press.

Maynard, R. C. (1990, August 5). An example of how Afro-American parents socialize children. *The Oakland Tribune.*

Mayr, E. (1982). *Growth of biological thought: Diversity, evolution, and inheritance.* Cambridge, MA: Harvard University Press.

Mazor, A., & Enright, R. D. (1988). The development of the individuation process from a social-cognitive perspective. *Journal of Adolescence, 11,* 29–47.

McAdams, D. P. (1990). *The person: An introduction to personality psychology.* San Diego: Harcourt Brace Jovanovich.

McCary, J. L., & McCary, S. P. (1982). *McCary's human sexuality* (4th ed.). Belmont, CA: Wadsworth.

McLanahan, S. S., Astone, N. M., & Marks, N. (1988, June). *The role of mother-only families in reproducing poverty.* Paper presented at the Conference on Poverty and Children, Lawrence, KS.

McLanahan, S. S., & Booth, K. (1989). Mother-only families: Problems, prospects, and politics. *Journal of Marriage and the Family, 51,* 557–580.

McLaughlin, D., & Whitfield R. (1984). Adolescents and their experience of parental divorce. *Journal of Adolescence, 7,* 155–170.

McLaughlin, R. D., & Ross, S. M. (1989). Student cheating in high school: A case of moral reasoning versus "fuzzy logic." *High School Journal, 72,* 97–104.

McNeil, J. N., Silliman, B., & J. J. Swihart. (1991). Helping adolescents cope with the death of a peer: A high school case study. *Journal of Adolescent Research, 6,* 132–145.

Mead, M. (1928). *Coming of age in Samoa: A psychological study of primitive youth for Western Civilization.* New York: Morrow.

Mead, M. (1930). *Growing up in New Guinea.* New York: Morrow.

Mechanic, D. & Hansell, S. (1989). Divorce, family conflict, and adolescents' well-being. *Journal of Health and Social Behavior, 30,* 105–116.

Meichenbaum, D. H. (1985). *Stress inoculation training.* New York: Pergamon.

Meichenbaum, D., & Deffenbacher, J. L. (1988). Stress inoculation training. *Counseling Psychologist, 16,* 69–90.

Meyer, K. A. (1987). The work commitment of adolescents: Progressive attachment to the work force. *Career Development Quarterly, 36,* 140–147.

Michel, A. (1986). *Down with stereotypes? Eliminating sexism from children's literature and school textbooks.* Washington, DC: UNESCO.

Miller, B. C., Christopherson, C. R., & King, P. K. (1993). Sexual behavior in adolescence. In T. P. Gullotta et al. (Eds.), *Adolescent sexuality.* Newbury Park, CA: Sage.

Miller, B. C., & Fox, G. L. (1987). Theories of adolescent heterosexual behavior. *Adolescent Research, 2,* 269–282.

Miller, G. (1989). Foreword. In J. T. Gibbs, L. N. Huang, & Associates (Eds.), *Children of color.* San Francisco: Jossey-Bass.

Miller, G. A., Galanter, E., & Pribram, K. H. (1960). *Plans and the structure of behavior.* New York: Holt, Rinehart & Winston.

Miller, J. (1976). *Toward a new psychology of women.* Boston: Beacon Press.

Miller, J. (Ed.). (1973). *Psychoanalysis and women.* New York: Brunner/Mazel.

Miller, J. G., & Bersoff, D. M. (1989). When do American children and adults reason in social conventional terms? *Developmental Psychology, 24*, 366–375.

Miller, K. E. (1990). Adolescents' same-sex and opposite-sex peer relations: Sex differences in popularity, perceived social competence, and social cognitive skills. *Journal of Adolescent Research, 5*, 222–241.

Miller, R. L. (1989). Desegregation experiences of minority students: Adolescent coping strategies in five Connecticut high schools. *Journal of Adolescent Research, 4*, 173–189.

Minuchin, S., Rosman, B., & Baker, L. (1978). *Psychosomatic families. Anorexia nervosa in context.* Cambridge, MA: Harvard University Press.

Mischel, W., & Mischel, H. N. (1976). A cognitive social-learning approach to morality and self-regulation. In T. Lickona (Ed.), *Moral development and behavior: Theory, research, and social issues.* New York: Holt, Rinehart & Winston.

Mitchell, L. K., & Krumboltz, J. D. (1987). The effects of cognitive restructuring and decision-making training on career indecision. *Journal of Counseling and Development, 66*, 171–174.

Mitchell, L. K., & Krumboltz, J. D. (1990). Social learning approach to career decision making: Krumboltz's theory. In D. Brown, L. Brooks, & Associates (Eds.), *Career choice and development.* San Francisco: Jossey-Bass.

Moeller, T. P., & Bachmann, G. A. (1993). The combined effects of physical, sexual, and emotional abuse during childhood: Long-term health consequences for women. *Child Abuse and Neglect, 17*, 623–640.

Moffitt, T. E., Caspi, A., Belsky, J., & Silva, P. A. (1992). Childhood experience and the onset of menarche: A test of a sociobiological model. *Child Development, 63*, 47–58.

Money, J. (1988). Commentary: Current status of sex research. *Journal of Psychology and Human Sexuality, 1*, 5–16.

Montemayor, R., & Brownlee, J. R. (1987). Fathers, mothers, and adolescents: Gender-based differences in parental roles during adolescence. *Journal of Youth and Adolescence, 16*, 281–291.

Montemayor, R., & Van Komer, R. (1985). The development of sex differences in friendship patterns and peer group structure during adolescence. *Journal of Early Adolescence, 5*, 285–294.

Moore, D. S., & Erickson, P. I. (1985). Age, gender, and ethnic differences in sexual and contraceptive knowledge, attitudes, and behavior. *Family and Community Health, 8*, 38–51.

Moran, G. F. (1991). Colonial America, Adolescence in. In R. M. Lerner, A. C. Petersen, & J. Brooks-Gunn (Eds.), *Encyclopedia of adolescence* (Vol. 1). New York: Garland.

Morrow, K. B., & Sorell, G. T. (1989). Factors affecting self-esteem, depression, and negative behaviors in sexually abused female adolescents. *Journal of Marriage and the Family, 51*, 677–686.

Morrow, L. (1988, August 8). Through the eyes of children. *Time*, pp. 26–45.

Mortimer, J. T., Finch, M., Shanahan, M., & Ryu, S. (1992). Work experience, mental health, and behavioral adjustment in adolescence. *Journal of Research on Adolescence, 2*, 25–57.

Mosher, F. A., & Hornsby, J. R. (1966). On asking questions. In J. Bruner, R. R. Olver, & R. Greenfield (Eds.), *Studies in cognitive growth.* New York: Wiley.

Munroe, R. (1955). *Schools of psychoanalytic thought.* New York: Dryden Press.

Mussen, P. H., & Jones, M. C. (1957). Self-conceptions, motivations and interpersonal attitudes of late- and early-maturing boys. *Child Development, 28*, 243–256.

Muuss, R. E. (1975). Adolescent development and the secular trend. In R. E. Muuss (Ed.), *Adolescent behavior and society: A book of readings.* New York: Random House.

Muuss, R. E. (1990). *Adolescent behavior and society* (4th ed.). New York: Random House.

Nagata, D. K. (1989). Japanese American children and adolescents. In J. T. Gibbs, L. N. Huang, & Associates (Eds.), *Children of color.* San Francisco: Jossey-Bass.

National Center for Health Statistics. (1968–1991). *Vital statistics of the United States: Vol. 2. Mortality—Part A* [for 1966–1988]. Washington, DC: U.S. Government Printing Office.

National Institute on Drug Abuse. (1985). National household survey on drug abuse. In the Surgeon General's report, 1988, *The health consequences of smoking: Nicotine addiction.* U.S. Department of

Health and Human Services. Washington, DC: U.S. Government Printing Office.

Needle, R. H., Su, S. S., & Doherty, W. J. (1990). Divorce, remarriage, and adolescent substance use: A prospective longitudinal study. *Journal of Marriage and the Family, 52,* 157–169.

Neisser, U. (1967). *Cognitive psychology.* New York: Appleton-Century-Crofts.

Neisser, U. (1976). *Cognition and reality.* San Francisco: Freeman.

Nelson, M. R. (1988). Issues of access to knowledge: Dropping out of school. In L. N. Tanner (Ed.), *Critical Issues in Curriculum, 87th yearbook of the National Society for the Study of Education.* Chicago: University of Chicago Press.

Newman, J. (1985). Adolescents: Why they can be so obnoxious. *Adolescence, 20,* 635–645.

Ng, S. H. (1990). Androcentric coding of MAN and HIS in memory by language users. *Journal of Experimental Social Psychology, 26,* 455–464.

Nolin, M. J., & Petersen, K. K. (1992). Gender differences in parent-child communication about sexuality. *Journal of Adolescent Research, 7,* 59–79.

Norton, E. M., Durlak, J. A., & Richards, M. H. (1989). Peer knowledge of and reactions to adolescent suicide. *Journal of Youth and Adolescence, 18,* 427–437.

Nucci, L. P., & Turiel, E. (1978). Social interactions and the development of social concepts in preschool children. *Child Development, 49,* 400–407.

Oakes, J. (1985). *Keeping track: How schools structure inequality.* New Haven, CT: Yale University Press.

O'Brien, S. F., & Bierman, K. L. (1988). Conceptions and perceived influence of peer groups: Interviews with preadolescents and adolescents. *Child Development, 59,* 1360–1365.

O'Connell, A. N. (1976). The relationship between life-style and identity synthesis and re-synthesis in traditional, neotraditional and nontraditional women. *Journal of Personality, 44,* 675–688.

Offer, D. (1969). *The psychological world of the teenager.* New York: Basic Books.

Offer, D., Ostrov, E., & Howard, K. I. (1981). *The adolescent.* New York: Basic Books.

Ogbu, J. U. (1981). Black education: A cultural-ecological perspective. In H. P. McAdoo (Ed.), *Black families.* Beverly Hills: Sage Publications.

Ogbu, J. U. (1992). Understanding cultural diversity and learning. *Educational Researcher, 21,* 5–14.

Okun, M. A., & Sasfy, J. H. (1977). Adolescence, the self-image and formal operations. *Adolescence, 12,* 373–379.

Omizo, M. M., Omizo, S. A., & Suzuki, L. A. (1988). Children and stress: An exploratory study of stressors and symptoms. *School Counselor, 35,* 267–274.

Orlofsky, J., & Frank, M. (1986). Personality structure as viewed through early memories and identity status in college men and women. *Journal of Personality and Social Psychology, 5,* 580–586.

Orlofsky, J., Marcia, J. E., & Lesser, I. M. (1973). Ego identity status and the intimacy versus isolation crisis of young adulthood. *Journal of Youth and Adolescence, 27,* 211–219.

Ornstein, P. A., Naus, M. J., & Liberty, C. (1975). Rehearsal and organizational processes in children's memory. *Child Development, 26,* 818–830.

Orthner, D. (1990). Parental work and early adolescence: Issues for research and practice. *Journal of Early Adolescence, 10,* 246–259.

Orum, L. S. (1986). *The education of Hispanics: Status and implications.* Washington, DC: National Council of La Raza.

Osherson, D. N., & Markman, E. M. (1975). Language and the ability to evaluate contradictions and tautologies. *Cognition, 3,* 213–226.

Osipow, S. H. (1983). *Theories of career development* (3rd ed.). Englewood Cliffs, NJ: Prentice-Hall.

Overton, W. F., Ward, S. L., Noveck, I. A., Black, J., & O'Brien, D. P. (1987). Form and content in the development of deductive reasoning. *Developmental Psychology, 23,* 22–30.

Owings, J., & Stocking, C. (1985). *High school and beyond: Characteristics of high school students who identify themselves as handicapped.* Washington, DC: National Center for Education Statistics, U.S. Department of Education.

Page, R. N. (1990). Games of chance: The lower-track curriculum in a college-preparatory high school. *Curriculum Inquiry, 20,* 249–281.

Palinscar, A. S., & Brown, A. L. (1984). Reciprocal teaching of comprehension-monitoring activities. *Cognition and Instruction, 1,* 117–175.

Papini, D. R., Farmer, F. L., Clark, S. M., & Snell, W. E., Jr. (1988). An evaluation of adolescent patterns of sexual self-disclosure to parents and friends. *Journal of Adolescent Research, 3,* 387–401.

Papini, D. R., Snell, W. E., Belk, S. S., & Clark, S. (1988, April). *Developmental correlates of women's and men's sexual self-disclosures.* Paper presented at the meeting of the Southwestern Psychological Association, Tulsa, OK.

Pardeck, J. A., & Pardeck, J. L. (1990). Family factors related to adolescent autonomy. *Adolescence, 25,* 311–319.

Paris, S. G. (1973). Comprehension of language connectives and propositional logical relationships. *Journal of Experimental Child Psychology, 16,* 278–291.

Parker, J. G., & Gottman, J. M. (1989). Social and emotional development in a relational context. In T. J. Berndt & G. W. Ladd (Eds.), *Peer relationships in child development.* New York: Wiley.

Parks, G. (1990). *Voices in the mirror: An autobiography.* New York: Doubleday.

Parsons, T. (1961). An outline of the social system. In T. Parsons, E. Shils, K. D. Naegele, & J. R. Pitts (Eds.), *Theories of society* (Vol. 1, pp. 30–79). New York: Free Press.

Pasley, B. K., & Ihenger-Tallman, M. (1989). Boundary ambiguity in remarriage: Does ambiguity differentiate degree of marital adjustment and integration? *Family Relations, 38,* 46–52.

Patterson, S. J., Sochting, I., and Marcia, J. E. (1992). The inner space and beyond: Women and identity. In G. R. Adams, T. P. Gullotta, and R. Montemayor (Eds.), *Adolescent identity formation.* Newbury Park, CA: Sage.

Paulson, S. E., Koman, J. J., III, & Hill, J. P., III. (1990). Maternal employment and parent-child relations in families of seventh graders. *Journal of Early Adolescence, 10,* 278–295.

Pavlov, I. P. (1927). *Conditioned reflexes.* London: Oxford University Press.

Pearl, R., Bryan, T., & Herzog. (1990). Resisting or acquiescing to peer pressure to engage in misconduct: Adolescents' expectations of probable consequences. *Journal of Youth and Adolescence, 19,* 43–55.

Perkins, D. N. (1987). Knowledge as design: Teaching thinking through content. In J. B. Baron & R. J. Sternberg (Eds.), *Teaching thinking skills: Theory and practice.* New York: Freeman.

Perlmutter, B. F. (1987). Delinquency and learning disabilities: Evidence for compensatory behaviors and adaptation. *Journal of Youth and Adolescence, 16,* 89–95.

Perry, W. G. (1970). *Forms of intellectual and ethical development in the college years.* San Francisco: Holt, Rinehart & Winston.

Peskin, H. (1967). Pubertal onset and ego functioning. *Journal of Abnormal Psychology, 72,* 1–15.

Peskin, H. (1973). Influence of the developmental schedule of puberty on learning and ego development. *Journal of Youth and Adolescence, 2,* 273–290.

Peskin, H., & Livson, M. (1972). Pre- and postpubertal personality and adult psychological functioning. *Seminars in Psychiatry, 4,* 343–353.

Petersen, A. C., Compas, B. E., Brooks-Gunn, J., Stemmler, M., Ey, S., & Grant, K. (1993). Depression in adolescence. *American Psychologist, 48,* 155–168.

Petersen, A. C., & Crockett, L. (1985). Pubertal timing and grade effects on adjustment. *Journal of Youth and Adolescence, 14,* 191–206.

Petersen, A. C., Crockett, L., Richards, M., & Boxer, A. (1988). A self-report measure of pubertal status: Reliability, validity, and initial norms. *Journal of Youth and Adolescence, 17,* 117–134.

Petersen, A. C., & Taylor, B. (1980). The biological approach to adolescence. In J. Adelson (Ed.), *Handbook of adolescent psychology.* New York: Wiley.

Peterson, C. C., & Murphy, L. (1990). Adolescents' thoughts and feelings about AIDS in relation to cognitive maturity. *Journal of Adolescence, 13,* 185–187.

Phelps, L., Johnston, S. S., Jimenez, D. P., Wilczenski, F. L., Andrea, R. K., & Healy, R. W. (1993). Figure preference, body dissatisfaction, and body distortion in adolescence. *Journal of Adolescent Research, 8,* 297–310.

Phinney, J. (1989a). Stages of ethnic identity development in minority group adolescents. *Journal of Early Adolescence, 9,* 34–49.

Phinney, J. (1989b, March). *A three-stage model of ethnic identity development in adolescence.* Paper presented at the Third Annual Conference on Ethnic Identity, Tempe, AZ.

Phinney, J. (1990). Ethnic identity in adolescents and adults: Review of research. *Psychological Bulletin, 108*, 499–514.

Phinney, J., & Rosenthal, D. A. (1992). Ethnic identity in adolescence: Process, context, and outcome. In G. Adams, R. Montemayor, & T. Gulotta (Eds.), *Advances in adolescent development* (Vol. 4). Newbury Park, CA.: Sage Publications.

Phinney, J. S., & Rotheram, M. J. (1987). Children's ethnic socialization: Themes and implications. In M. J. Rotheram & J. S. Phinney (Eds.), *Children's ethnic socialization: Pluralism and development.* Beverly Hills: Sage Publications.

Phinney, J., & Tarver, S. (1988). Ethnic identity search and commitment in black and white eighth graders. *Journal of Early Adolescence, 8*, 265–277.

Piaget, J. (1952). *The child's conception of number.* New York: Humanities Press.

Piaget, J. (1952). *The origins of intelligence in children.* New York: International Universities Press.

Piaget, J. (1954). *The construction of reality in the child.* New York: Basic Books.

Piaget, J. (1965). *The moral judgment of the child.* New York: Free Press.

Piaget, J. (1971). *Biology and knowledge.* Chicago: University of Chicago Press.

Pittman, R. B., & Haughwout, P. (1987). Influence of high school size on dropout rate. *Educational Evaluation and Policy Analysis, 9*, 337–343.

Place, D. M. (1975). The dating experience for adolescent girls. *Adolescence, 10*, 157–174.

Pleck, J. H., Sonenstein, F. L., & Swain, S. O. (1988). Adolescent males' sexual behavior and contraceptive use: Implications for male responsibility. *Journal of Adolescent Research, 3*, 275–284.

Pollack, S., & Gilligan, C. (1982). Images of violence in Thematic Apperception Test stories. *Journal of Personality and Social Psychology, 42*, 159–167.

Poole, M. E., & Evans, G. T. (1988). Adolescents' self-perceptions of competence in life skill areas. *Journal of Youth and Adolescence, 18*, 147–173.

Postman, N. (1982). *The disappearance of childhood.* New York: Delacorte.

Powell, G. J. (1985). Self-concepts among Afro-American students in racially isolated minority schools: Some regional differences. *Journal of the American Academy of Child Psychiatry, 24*, 142–149.

Powers, S. I., Hauser, S. T., Schwartz, J. M., Noam, G. G., & Jacobson, A. M. (1983). Adolescent ego development and family interaction: A structural-developmental perspective. In H. D. Grotevant & C. R. Cooper (Eds.), *Adolescent development in the family.* San Francisco: Jossey-Bass.

Price, J., Desmond, S., & Smith, D. (1991). A preliminary investigation of inner city adolescents' perceptions of guns. *Journal of School Health, 61*, 255–259.

Proulx, J., & Koulock, D. (1987). The effect of parental divorce on parent-adolescent separation. *Journal of Youth and Adolescence, 16*, 473–480.

Purcell, P., & Stewart, L. (1990). Dick and Jane in 1989. *Sex Roles, 22*, 177–185.

Putallaz, M. (1983). Predicting children's sociometric status from their behavior. *Child Development, 54*, 1417–1426.

Quay, H. C. (1987). Intelligence. In H. C. Quay (Ed.), *Handbook of juvenile delinquency.* New York: Wiley.

Raja, S. N., McGee, R., & Stanton, W. R. (1992). Perceived attachments to parents and peers and psychological well-being in adolescence. *Journal of Youth and Adolescence, 21*, 471–485.

Ramirez, O. (1989). Mexican American children and adolescents. In J. T. Gibbs, L. N. Huang, & Associates (Eds.), *Children of color.* San Francisco: Jossey-Bass.

Rauste-von Wright, M. (1989). Body-image satisfaction in adolescent girls and boys: A longitudinal study. *Journal of Youth and Adolescence, 18*, 71–83.

Ray, J., & Briar, K. H. (1988). Economic motivators for shoplifting. *Journal of Sociology and Social Welfare, 15*, 177–189.

Reese, H. W., & Overton, W. F. (1970). Models of development and theories of development. In L. R. Goulet & P. B. Baltes (Eds.), *Life-span developmental psychology: Research and theory.* New York: Academic Press.

Reid, M., Landesman, S., Treder, R., & Jaccard, J. (1989). "My family and friends": Six- to twelve-year-old children's perceptions of social support. *Child Development, 60,* 896–910.

Reischl, T. M., & Hirsch, B. J. (1989). Identity commitments and coping with a difficult developmental transition. *Journal of Youth and Adolescence, 18,* 55–69.

Reiss, D., Oliveri, M. E., & Curd, K. (1983). Family paradigm and adolescent social behavior. In H. D. Grotevant & C. R. Cooper (Eds.), *Adolescent development in the family.* San Francisco: Jossey-Bass.

Report of the Secretary's Task Force on Youth Suicide. (1989). *Vol. 1: Overview and recommendations* (DHHS Publication No. ADM 89-1621). Washington, DC: U.S. Government Printing Office.

Restak, R. (1984, November). Master clock of the brain and body. *Science Digest,* pp. 54–104.

Reyes, L. H., & Stanic, G. M. (1985, April). *A review of the literature on Blacks and mathematics.* Paper presented at the meeting of the American Educational Research Association, Chicago.

Reyes, O., & Jason, L. A. (1993). Pilot study examining factors associated with academic success for Hispanic high school students. *Journal of Youth and Adolescence, 22,* 57–71.

Rice, K. G., Cole, D. A., & Lapsley, D. K. (1990). Separation-individuation, family cohesion, and adjustment to college: measurement validation and test of a theoretical model. *Journal of Counseling Psychology, 37,* 195–202.

Riegel, K. F. (1973). *Dialectic operations: The final period of cognitive development.* Princeton, NJ: Educational Testing Service.

Riley, M. W. (1986). The dynamisms of life stages: Roles, people, and age. *Human Development, 29,* 150–156.

Roche, J. P., & Ramsby, T. W. (1993). Premarital sexuality: A five-year follow-up study of attitudes and behavior by dating stage. *Adolescence, 28,* 67–80.

Rodgers, J. L., & Rowe, D. C. (1988). Influence of siblings on adolescent sexual behavior. *Developmental Psychology, 24,* 722–728.

Rogow, A. M., Marcia, J. E., & Slugowski, B. R. (1983). The relative importance of identity status interview components. *Journal of Youth and Adolescence, 12,* 387–400.

Rollins, J. (Ed.). (1981). *Hidden minorities: The persistence of ethnicity in American life.* Washington, DC: University Press of America, 1981.

Roper, W. L., Peterson, H. B., & Curran, J. W. (1993). Commentary: Condoms and HIV/STD prevention—Clarifying the message. *American Journal of Public Health, 83,* 501–503.

Rosenberg, M., Schooler, C., & Schoenbach, C. (1989). Self-esteem and adolescent problems: Modeling reciprocal effects. *American Sociological Review, 54,* 1004–1018.

Rosenthal, D. A., & Feldman, S. S. (1992). The nature and stability of ethnic identity in Chinese youth: Effects of length of residence in two cultural contexts. *Journal of Cross-Cultural Psychology, 23,* 213–227.

Rosenthal, D. A., & Hrynevich, C. (1985). Ethnicity and ethnic identity: A comparative study of Greek-, Italian-, and Anglo-Australian adolescents. *International Journal of Psychology, 20,* 723–742.

Roth, P. (1969). *Portnoy's complaint.* New York: Random House.

Rotheram, M. J., & Phinney, J. S. (1983). *Intercultural attitudes and behaviors of children.* Paper presented at the meeting of the Society for Intercultural Evaluation, Training and Research, San Germignano, Italy.

Rotheram, M. J., & Phinney, J. S. (1987). Ethnic behavior patterns as an aspect of identity. In J. Phinney & M. Rotheram (Eds.), *Children's ethnic socialization: Pluralism and development.* Beverly Hills: Sage Publications.

Rotheram-Borus, M. J., & Phinney, J. S. (1990). Patterns of social expectations among black and Mexican-American children. *Child Development, 61,* 542–556.

Ruble, D. N., & Brooks-Gunn, J. (1982). The experience of menarche. *Child Development, 53,* 1557–1566.

Rutter, M. (1986). The developmental psychopathology of depression. In M. Rutter, C. E. Isard, & P. B. Read. (Eds.), *Depression in young people.* New York: Guilford Press.

Sandberg, D., Rotheram-Borus, M. J., Bradley, J., & Martin, J. (1988). Methodological issues in assessing AIDS prevention programs. *Journal of Adolescent Research, 3,* 413–418.

Satter, E. (1988). Should the obese child diet? In K. Clark, R. Parr, & W. Castelli (Eds.), *Evaluation and management of eating disorders*. Champaign, IL: Life Enhancement Publications.

Scarr, S., & Weinberg, R. A. (1983). The Minnesota adoption studies: Malleability and genetic differences. *Child Development, 34*, 260–267.

Schachter, S., & Singer, J. (1962). Cognitive, social and physiological determinants of emotional state. *Psychological Review, 69*, 379–399.

Schafer, W. E., Olexa, C., & Polk, K. (1972). Programmed for social class: Tracking in high school. In K. Polk & W. E. Schafer (Eds.), *Schools and delinquency*. Englewood Cliffs, NJ: Prentice-Hall.

Schaie, K. W., & Willis, S. L. (1993). Age difference patterns of psychometric intelligence in adulthood: Generalizability within and across ability domains. *Psychology and Aging, 8*, 44–55.

Schiano, D. J., Cooper, L. A., Glaser, R., & Zhang, H. C. (1989). Highs are to lows as experts are to novices: Individual differences in the representation and solution of standardized figural analogies. *Human Performance, 2*, 225–248.

Schiedel, D. G., & Marcia, J. E. (1985). Ego identity, intimacy, sex role orientation, and gender. *Developmental Psychology, 21*, 149–160.

Schuckit, M. A., & Schuckit, J. J. (1989). Substance use and abuse: A risk factor in youth suicide. In *Report of the Secretary's Task Force on Youth Suicide. Vol. 2*. Washington, DC: U.S. Government Printing Office.

Schweder, R. A., Mahapatra, M., & Miller, J. (1987). Culture and development. In J. Kagan (Ed.), *The emergence of moral concepts in young children*. Chicago: University of Chicago Press.

Sebald, H. (1981). Adolescents' concept of popularity and unpopularity, comparing 1960 and 1976. *Adolescence, 16*, 187–193.

Seiber, J. E. (1980). A social learning approach to morality. In M. Windmiller, N. Lambert, & E. Turiel (Eds.), *Moral development and socialization*. Boston: Allyn & Bacon.

Seixas, P. (1993). Historical understanding among adolescents in a multicultural setting. *Curriculum Inquiry, 23*, 301–327.

Selman, R. L. (1976). Social-cognitive understanding. In T. Lickona (Ed.), *Moral development and behavior*. New York: Holt, Rinehart & Winston.

Selman, R. L. (1980). *The growth of interpersonal understanding*. New York: Academic Press.

Selman, R. L., & Byrne, L. F. (1974). A structural-developmental analysis of levels of role taking in middle childhood. *Child Development, 45*, 803–806.

Selye, H. (1982). Stress: Eustress, distress, and human perspectives. In S. B. Day (Ed.), *Life stress* (Vol. 3). New York: Van Nostrand Reinhold.

Sessa, F. M., & Steinberg, L. (1991). Family structure and the development of autonomy during adolescence. *Journal of Early Adolescence, 11*, 38–55.

Shafii, M., Carrigan, S., Whittinghill, J. R., & Derrick, A. (1985). Psychological autopsy of completed suicide in children and adolescents. *American Journal of Psychiatry, 142*, 1061–1064.

Sherman, J. A. (1978). *Sex-related cognitive differences: An essay on theory and evidence*. Springfield, Ill.: Thomas.

Shing, M., & Winer, G. A. (1990). Understanding perceptual processes: Responses to a weight-illusion task. *Developmental Psychology, 26*, 121–127.

Shulman, S., Seiffge-Krenke, I., & Samat, N. (1987). Adolescent coping style as a function of perceived family climate. *Journal of Adolescent Research, 2*, 367–381.

Siegler, R. S. (1991). *Children's thinking*. Englewood Cliffs, NJ: Prentice-Hall.

Silverberg, S. B., & Steinberg, L. (1990). Psychological well-being of parents with early adolescent children. *Developmental Psychology, 26*, 658–666.

Silverstein, B., Perdue, L., Peterson, B., & Kelly, E. (1986). The role of the mass media in promoting a thin standard of bodily attractiveness for women. *Sex Roles, 14*, 519–532.

Simmons, R. G., & Blyth, D. A. (1987). *Moving into adolescence*. New York: Aldine de Gruyter.

Simons, R. L., Robertson, J. F., and Downs, W. R. (1989). The nature of the association between parental rejection and delinquent behavior. *Journal of Youth and Adolescence, 18*, 297–310.

Simpson, G. E., & Yinger, J. M. (1985). *Racial and cultural minorities* (5th ed.). New York: Plenum Press.

Skinner, B. F. (1938). *The behavior of organisms: An experimental analysis*. New York: Appleton-Century-Crofts.

Skinner, B. F. (1953). *Science and human behavior.* New York: Macmillan.

Skinner, B. F. (1961). *Cumulative record* (rev. ed.). New York: Appleton-Century-Crofts.

Slaughter-Defoe, D. T., Nakagawa, K., Takanishi, R., & Johnson, D. J. (1990). Toward cultural/ecological perspectives on schooling and achievement in African- and Asian-American children. *Child Development, 61,* 363–383.

Slavin, R. E. (1985). Cooperative learning: Applying contact theory in desegregated schools. *Journal of Social Issues, 41,* 45–62.

Sloan, J., Kellermann, A., Reay, D., Ferris, J., Koepsell, T., Rivara, F., Rice, C., Gray, L., & LoGerfo, J. (1988). Handgun regulation, crime, assaults, and homicides. *New England Journal of Medicine, 319,* 1256–1262.

Slonim-Nevo, V. (1992). First premarital intercourse among Mexican-American and Anglo-American adolescent women. *Journal of Adolescent Research, 7,* 332–351.

Small, M. Y. (1990). *Cognitive development.* San Diego, CA: Harcourt Brace Jovanovich.

Smetana, J. (1988). Concepts of self and social convention: Adolescents' and parents' reasoning about hypothetical and actual family conflicts. In M. R. Gunnar (Ed.), *21st Minnesota Symposium on Child Psychology.* Hillsdale, NJ: Erlbaum.

Smetana, J. G., & Berent, R. (1993). Adolescents' and mothers' evaluations of justifications for disputes. *Journal of Adolescent Research, 8,* 252–273.

Smetana, J. G., Braeges, J. L., & Yau, J. (1991). Doing what you say and saying what you do: Reasoning about adolescent-parent conflict in interviews and interactions. *Journal of Adolescent Research, 6,* 276–295.

Smith, E. A., & Udrey, J. R. (1985). "Coital & noncoital sexual behaviors of white & black adolescents." *American Journal of Public Health, 75,* 1200–1203.

Smith, T. E. (1990). Parental separation and the academic self-concepts of adolescents: An effort to solve the puzzle of separation effects. *Journal of Marriage and the Family, 52,* 107–118.

Smolak, L., Levine, M. P., & Gralen, S. (1993). The impact of puberty and dating on eating problems among middle school girls. *Journal of Youth and Adolescence, 22,* 355–368.

Snarey, J. R. (1985). Cross-cultural universality of social-moral development: A critical review of Kohlbergian research. *Psychological Bulletin, 97,* 202–232.

Snow, R. E. (1986). Individual differences and the design of educational programs. *American Psychologist, 41,* 1029–1039.

Sokolov, E. M. (1963). Higher nervous functions: The orienting reflex. *Annual Review of Physiology, 25,* 545–580.

Solomon, G. (1990). Using technology to reach at-risk students. *Electronic Learning, 9,* 14–15.

Solso, R. L., & Johnson, H. H. (1994). *Experimental psychology* (5th ed.). New York: HarperCollins.

Sommer, K., Whitman, T. L., Borkowski, J. G., Schellenbach, C., Maxwell, S., & Keogh, D. (1993). Cognitive readiness and adolescent parenting. *Developmental Psychology, 29,* 389–398.

Sonenstein, F. L. (1986). Risking paternity: Sex and contraception among adolescent males. In A. B. Elster & M. E. Lamb (Eds.), *Adolescent fatherhood.* Hillsdale, NJ: Erlbaum.

Sorenson, R. C. (1973). *Adolescent sexuality in contemporary America: Personal values and sexual behavior, ages thirteen to nineteen.* New York: World.

Sowell, T. (1978). Race and IQ reconsidered. In T. Sowell (Ed.), *American ethnic groups.* The Urban Institute.

Spencer, M. B. (1985). Racial variations in achievement prediction: The school as a conduit for macrostructural cultural tension. In H. McAdoo & J. McAdoo (Eds.), *Black children: Social, educational, and parental environments.* Beverly Hills: Sage Publications.

Spires, H. A., Gallini, J., & Riggsbee, J. (1992). Effects of schema-based and text structure-based cues on expository prove comprehension in fourth graders. *Journal of Experimental Education, 60,* 307–320.

Spreen, O. (1988). *Learning disabled children growing up.* New York: Oxford University Press.

Steinberg, L. (1987a). The impact of puberty on family relations: Effects of pubertal status and pubertal timing. *Developmental Psychology, 23,* 451–460.

Steinberg, L. (1987b). Recent research on the family at adolescence: The extent and nature of sex differences. *Journal of Youth and Adolescence, 16,* 191–197.

Steinberg, L. (1989). Reciprocal relation between parent-child distance and pubertal maturation. *Developmental Psychology, 24,* 122–128.

Steinberg, L., Elmen, J. D., & Mounts, N. S. (1989). Authoritative parenting, psychosocial maturity, and academic success among adolescents. *Child Development, 60,* 1424–1436.

Steinberg, L., Fegley, S., & Dornbusch, S. (1993). Negative impact of part-time work on adolescent adjustment: Evidence from a longitudinal study. *Developmental Psychology, 29,* 171–180.

Sternberg, R. J. (1981). Intelligence and nonentrenchment. *Journal of Educational Psychology, 73,* 1–16.

Sternberg, R. J. (1984). Mechanisms of cognitive development: A componential approach. In R. J. Sternberg (Ed.), *Mechanisms of cognitive development.* New York: Freeman.

Sternberg, R. J. (1985). *Beyond I. Q.: A triarchic theory of human intelligence.* New York: Cambridge University Press.

Sternberg, R. J., & Rifkin, B. (1979). The development of analogical reasoning processes. *Journal of Experimental Child Psychology, 27,* 195–232.

Sternberg, S. (1966). High-speed scanning in human memory. *Science, 153,* 652–654.

Stevens-Long, J. (1992). *Adult life* (4th ed.). Mountain View, CA: Mayfield.

Stevens-Long, J., & Cobb, N. J. (1983). *Adolescence and early adulthood.* Palo Alto, CA: Mayfield.

Stevenson, H. W., Chen, C., & Uttal, D. H. (1990). Beliefs and achievement: A study of black, white, and Hispanic children. *Child Development, 61,* 508–523.

Stiles, D. A., Gibbons, J. L., Hardardottir, S., & Schnellmann, J. (1987). The ideal man or woman as described by young adolescents in Iceland and the United States. *Sex Roles, 17,* 313–320.

Still "separate," still "unequal." (1988, March 14). *U.S. News & World Report,* pp. 10–11.

Streitmatter, J. (1993). Identity status and identity style: A replication study. *Journal of Adolescence, 16,* 211–215.

Strong, B., & DeVault, C. (1994). *Human sexuality.* Mountain View, CA: Mayfield.

Subich, L. M. (1989). A challenge to grow: Reaction to Hoyt's article. *Career Development Quarterly, 37,* 213–217.

Super, D. E. (1981). A developmental theory: Implementing a self concept. In D. H. Montross & C. J. Shinkman (Eds.), *Career development in the 1980s: Theory and practice.* Springfield, IL: Thomas.

Super, D. E. (1984). Career and life development. In D. Brown, L. Brooks, & Associates (Eds.), *Career choice and development.* San Francisco: Jossey-Bass.

Surgeon General's Report. (1988). *The health consequences of smoking: Nicotine addiction.* U.S. Department of Health and Human Services. Washington, DC: U.S. Government Printing Office.

Switzer, J. Y. (1990). The impact of generic word choices: An empirical investigation of age- and sex-related differences. *Sex Roles, 22,* 69–82.

Szapocznik, J., & Kurtines, W. M. (1993). Family psychology and cultural diversity: Opportunities for theory, research, and application. *American Psychologist, 48,* 400–407.

Tanner, J. M. (1968). Earlier maturation in man. *Scientific American, 218,* 21–27.

Tanner, J. M. (1972). Sequence, tempo and individual variation in growth and development of boys and girls aged twelve to sixteen. In J. Kagan & R. Coles (Eds.), *Twelve to sixteen: Early adolescence.* New York: Norton.

Tanner, J. M. (1974). Sequence and tempo in the somatic changes in puberty. In M. M. Grumbach, G. D. Grave, & F. E. Mayer (Eds.), *Control of the onset of puberty.* New York: Wiley.

Tanner, J. M. (1991). Menarche, secular trend in age of. In R. M. Lerner, A. C. Petersen, & J. Brooks-Gunn (Eds.). *Encyclopedia of adolescence* (Vol. 2, pp. 637–641). New York: Garland.

Tavris, C., & Wade, C. (1984). *The longest war: Sex differences in perspective* (2nd ed.). San Diego: Harcourt Brace Jovanovich.

Teddlie, C., Kirby, P. C., & Stringfield, S. (1989). Effective vs. ineffective schools: Observable differences in the classroom. *American Journal of Education, 97,* 221–236.

Terman, L. M. (1925). *Genetic studies of genius. Vol. 1: Mental and physical traits of a thousand gifted children.* Stanford, CA: Stanford University Press.

Thomas, R. M. (1979). *Comparing theories of child development.* Belmont, CA: Wadsworth.

Thornberry, T. P., Krohn, M. D., Lizotte, A. J., &

Chard-Wierschem, D. (1993). The role of juvenile gangs in facilitating delinquent behavior. *Journal of Research in Crime and Delinquency, 30*, 55–87.

Thornburg, H. D. (1975). Adolescent sources of initial sex information. In R. E. Grinder (Ed.), *Studies in adolescence: A book of readings in adolescent development* (3rd ed.). New York: Macmillan.

Thornburg, H. D. (1981). Sources of sex education among early adolescents. *Journal of Early Adolescence, 1*, 171–184.

Thornton, M. C., Chatters, L. M., Taylor, R. J., & Allen, W. R. (1990). Sociodemographic and environmental correlates of racial socialization by black parents. *Child Development, 61*, 401–409.

Tidwell, R. (1988). Dropouts speak out: Qualitative data on early school departures. *Adolescence, 23*, 939–954.

Tillman, R. (1986). *The prevalence and incidence of arrest among adult males in California.* Sacramento, CA: State of California Department of Justice.

Tisak, M. S., & Turiel, E. (1988). Variation in seriousness of transgressions and children's moral and conventional concepts. *Developmental Psychology, 74*, 352–357.

Tittle, C. K. (1986). Gender research and education. *American Psychologist, 41*, 1161–1168.

Tobias, A. L. (1988). Bulimia: An overview. In K. Clark, R. Parr, & W. Castelli (Eds.), *Evaluation and management of eating disorders.* Champaign, IL: Life Enhancement Publications.

Tobin-Richards, M. H., Boxer, A. M., & Petersen, A. C. (1983). The psychological significance of pubertal change: Sex differences in perceptions of self during early adolescence. In J. Brooks-Gunn & A. C. Petersen (Eds.), *Girls at puberty.* New York: Plenum Press.

Toch, T. (1993). Violence in schools. *U.S. News & World Report, 115*, 31–37.

Tolan, P., Miller, L., & Thomas, O. (1988). Perception and experience of types of social stress and self-image among adolescents. *Journal of Youth and Adolescence, 17*, 147–163.

Tolson, J. M., & Urberg, K. A. (1993). Similarity between adolescent best friends. *Journal of Adolescent Research, 8*, 274–288.

Towbes, L. C., Cohen, L. H., & Glyshaw, K. (1989). Instrumentality as a life-stress moderator for early versus middle adolescents. *Journal of Personality and Social Psychology, 67*, 109–119.

Trautman, P. D. (1989). Specific treatment modalities for adolescent suicide attempters. In *Report of the Secretary's Task Force. Vol. 3.* Washington, DC: U.S. Government Printing Office.

Trautman, P. D., & Rotheram, M. J. (1986). Reported in Trautman, P. D. (1989). Specific treatment modalities for adolescent suicide attempters. In *Report of the Secretary's Task Force. Vol. 3.* Washington, DC: U.S. Government Printing Office.

Treboux, D., & Busch-Rossnagel, N. A. (1990). Social network influences on adolescent sexual attitudes and behaviors. *Journal of Adolescent Research, 5*, 175–189.

Trent, W. T. (1983). *Race and sex differences in degree attainment and major field distributions for 1975–76 to 1980–81* (Report No. 339). Baltimore, MD: Johns Hopkins University, Center for Social Organization of Schools.

Tschirgi, J. E. (1980). Sensible reasoning: A hypothesis about hypotheses. *Child Development, 51*, 1–10.

Turiel, E. (1983). *The development of social knowledge: Morality and convention.* Cambridge, England: Cambridge University Press.

Turner, C. B., & Cashdan, S. (1988). Perception of college students' motives for shoplifting. *Psychological Reports, 62*, 855–862.

Underwood, B. J. (1957). *Psychological research.* New York: Appleton-Century-Crofts.

Unger, R. (1979). Toward a redefinition of sex and gender. *American Psychologist, 34*, 1085–1094.

Urberg, K. A. (1992). Locus of peer influence: Social crowd and best friend. *Journal of Youth and Adolescence, 21*, 439–450.

U.S. Bureau of the Census. (1980). *School enrollment current population reports, Series P-20.* Washington, DC: U.S. Government Printing Office.

U.S. Bureau of the Census. (1984). *Current population reports, Series P-25, No. 952, Projections of the population of the United States by age, sex, and race: 1983–2080.* Washington, DC: U.S. Government Printing Office.

U.S. Bureau of the Census. (1986). *Statistical ab-*

stract of the United States: 1987 (107th ed.). Washington, DC: U.S. Department of Commerce.

U.S. Bureau of the Census. (1992). *Current population reports, Series P-20, No. 468, Marital status and living arrangements: March 1992.* Washington, DC: U.S. Government Printing Office.

U.S. Bureau of the Census. (1992a). *Current population reports, Series P-20, No. 467, Household and family characteristics.* Washington, DC: U.S. Government Printing Office.

U.S. Bureau of the Census. (1992b). *Current population reports, Series P-25, No. 1104, Projections of the population of the United States by age, sex, and race: 1983–2080.* Washington, DC: U.S. Government Printing Office.

U.S. Bureau of the Census. (1992c). *Current population reports, Series P-60, No. 185, Poverty in the U.S.: 1990.* Washington, DC: U.S. Government Printing Office.

U.S. Bureau of the Census. (1993a). *Current population reports, P25-1104, Population projections of the United States by age, sex, race, and Hispanic origin: 1993 to 2050.* Washington, DC: U.S. Government Printing Office.

U.S. Bureau of the Census. (1993b). *Statistical abstract of the United States: 1993* (113th edition). Washington, DC: U.S. Government Printing Office.

U.S. Department of Education. (1988). *Ninth annual report to Congress on the implementation of the Education of the Handicapped Act.* Washington, DC: OSERS.

U.S. Department of Justice. (1991). *Criminal victimization, 1990* (Special Report No. NCJ-122743). Washington, DC: Bureau of Justice Statistics.

Vigil, J. D. (1988). *Barrio gangs.* Austin: The University of Texas Press.

Visher, E. B., & Visher, J. S. (1989). Parenting coalitions after remarriage: Dynamics and therapeutic guidelines. *Family Relations, 38,* 65–70.

Wagner, R. K., & Sternberg, R. J. (1986). Tacit knowledge and intelligence in the everyday world. In R. J. Sternberg & R. K. Wagner (Eds.), *Practical intelligence: Nature and origins of competence in the everyday world.* New York: Cambridge University Press.

Walker, L. J. (1984). Sex differences in the devel-

opment of moral reasoning: A critical review. *Child Development, 55,* 677–691.

Walker, L. J. (1986). Sex differences in the development of moral reasoning: A rejoinder to Baumrind. *Child Development, 57,* 522–526.

Walker, L. S., & Greene, J. W. (1986). The social context of adolescent self-esteem. *Journal of Youth and Adolescence, 15,* 315–322.

Wallerstein, J. S. (1989). *Second change.* New York: Ticknor & Fields.

Wallerstein, J. S., Corbin, S. B., & Lewis, J. M. (1988). Children of divorce: A ten-year study. In E. M. Hetherington & J. D. Arasteh (Eds.), *Impact of divorce, single-parenting, and stepparenting on children.* Hillsdale, NJ: Erlbaum.

Walters, J. M., & Gardner, H. (1986). The theory of multiple intelligences: Some issues and answers. In R. J. Sternberg & R. K. Wagner (Eds.), *Practical intelligence: Nature and origins of competence in the everyday world.* New York: Cambridge University Press.

Wapner, M. L. (1980). Personal communication.

Wapner, M. L. (1990). Personal communication.

Ward, D. A. (1986). Self-esteem and dishonest behavior revisited. *Journal of Social Psychology, 126,* 709–713.

Ward, S. L., & Overton, W. F. (1990). Semantic familiarity, relevance, and the development of deductive reasoning. *Developmental Psychology, 26,* 488–493.

Warren, M. P. (1983). Physical and biological aspects of puberty. In J. Brooks-Gunn & A. C. Petersen (Eds.), *Girls at puberty.* New York: Plenum Press.

Wason, P. C., & Johnson-Laird, P. N. (1972). *Psychology of reasoning: Structure and content.* Cambridge, MA: Harvard University Press.

Waterman, A. S. (1992). Identity as an aspect of optimal psychological functioning. In G. R. Adams, T. T. Gullotta, & R. Montemayor (Eds.). *Adolescent identity formation.* Newbury Park, CA: Sage.

Waterman, A. S. (1993). Two conceptions of happiness: Contrasts of personal expressiveness (Eudaimonia) and hedonic enjoyment. *Journal of Personality and Social Psychology, 64,* 678–691.

Wattenberg, B. J. (1987). *The birth dearth.* New York: Pharos Books.

Weaver, F. M., & Carroll, J. S. (1985). Crime perceptions in a natural setting by expert and novice shoplifters. *Social Psychology Quarterly, 48,* 349–359.

Wechsler, D. (1981). *WAIS-R Manual: Wechsler Adult Intelligence Scale—Revised.* San Antonio, TX: Psychological Corporation.

Weddle, K. D., McKenry, P. C., & Leigh, G. K. (1988). Adolescent sexual behavior: Trends and issues in research. *Journal of Adolescent Research, 3,* 245–257.

Weiner, I. B. (1980). Psychopathology in adolescence. In J. Adelson (Ed.), *Handbook of adolescent psychology.* New York: Wiley.

Weis, D. (1983). Affective reactions of women to their initial experience of coitus. *Journal of Sex Research, 19,* 209–237.

Wentzel, K. R., & Erdley, C. A. (1993). Strategies for making friends: Relations to social behavior and peer acceptance in early adolescence. *Developmental Psychology, 29,* 819–826.

Westermeyer, J. (1986). *A clinical guide to alcohol and drug problems.* New York: Praeger.

Wetzel, J. (1987). *American youth: A statistical snapshot.* Washington, DC: William T. Grant Foundation.

Whitehead, A. N. (1929). *The aims of education.* New York: Macmillan.

Whiteside, M. F. (1989). Family rituals as a key to kinship connections in remarried families. *Family Relations, 38,* 34–39.

White, K. L., Speisman, J. C., & Costos, D. (1983). Young adults and their parents: Individuation to mutuality. In H. D. Grotevant & C. R. Cooper (Eds.), *Adolescent development in the family.* San Francisco: Jossey-Bass.

White, L. K., & Booth, A. (1985). The quality and stability of remarriages: The role of stepchildren. *American Sociological Review, 50,* 689–698.

Wigdor, A. K., & Garner, W. R. (Eds.). (1982). *Ability testing: Uses, consequences, and controversies.* Washington, DC: National Academy Press.

Wilks, J. (1986). The relative importance of parents and friends in adolescent decision making. *Journal of Youth and Adolescence, 15,* 323–334.

Williams, J. H. (1983). *Psychology of women* (2nd ed.). New York: Norton.

Williams, J. M., & White, K. A. (1983). Adolescent

status systems for males and females at three age levels. *Adolescence, 18,* 381–389.

Wilson, S. M., & Medora, N. P. (1990). Gender comparisons of college students' attitudes toward sexual behavior. *Adolescence, 25,* 615–627.

Windle, M., Miller-Tutzauer, C., & Domenico, D. (1992). Alcohol use, suicidal behavior, and risky activities among adolescents. *Journal of Research on Adolescents, 2,* 317–330.

Winer, G. A., Craig, R. K., & Weinbaum, E. (1992). Adults' failure on misleading weight-conservation tests: A developmental analysis. *Developmental Psychology, 28,* 109–120.

Winer, G. A., & McGlone, C. (1993). On the uncertainty of conservation: Responses to misleading conservation questions. *Developmental Psychology, 29,* 760–769.

Wintre, M. G., Hicks, R., McVey, G., & Fox, J. (1988). Age and sex differences in choice of consultant for various types of problems. *Child Development, 59,* 1046–1055.

Wirth, L. (1945). The problem of minority groups. In R. Linton (Ed.), *The science of man in the world crisis.* New York: Columbia University Press.

Witkin, G. (1991, April 8). Kids who kill. *U.S. News and World Report,* pp. 26–32.

Women on Words and Images. (1975). *Dick and Jane as victims: Sex stereotyping in children's readers* (Expanded ed.). Princeton, NJ: Woman on Words and Images.

Wyche, K., Obolensky, N., & Glood, E. (1990). American Indian, Black American, and Hispanic American youth. In M. J. Rotheram-Borus, J. Bradley, & N. Obolensky (Eds.), *Planning to live: Evaluating and treating suicidal teens in community settings* (pp. 355–389). Tulsa: University of Oklahoma Press.

Wyshak, G., & Frisch, R. E. (1982). Evidence for a secular trend in age of menarche. *New England Journal of Medicine, 306,* 1033–1035.

Yamaguchi, K., & Kandel, D. B. (1984). Patterns of drug use from adolescence to young adulthood: III. Predictors of progression. *American Journal of Public Health, 74,* 673–681.

Yau, J., & Smetana, J. G. (1993). Chinese-American adolescents' reasoning about cultural conflicts. *Journal of Adolescent Research, 8,* 419–438.

Yoder, J. D., & Kahn, A. S. (1993). Working toward

an inclusive psychology of women. *American Psychologist, 48,* 846–850.

Youniss, J. (1980). *Parents and peers in social development.* Chicago: University of Chicago Press.

Youniss, J., & Smollar, J. (1989). Adolescents' interpersonal relationships in social context. In T. J. Berndt & G. W. Ladd (Eds.), *Peer relationships in child development.* New York: Wiley.

Youth Indicators. (1988). *Trends in the well-being of American youth.* Washington, DC: U.S. Government Printing Office.

Youth Indicators. (1991). *Trends in the well-being of American youth.* U.S. Department of Education. Washington, DC: U.S. Government Printing Office.

Youth Indicators. (1993). *Trends in the well-being of American youth.* Washington, DC: U.S. Government Printing Office.

Zabatany, L., & Hartmann, D. P. (1990). The psychological functions of preadolescent peer activities. *Child Development, 61,* 1067–1080.

Zambrana, R. E., & Silva-Palacios, V. (1989). Gender differences in stress among Mexican immigrant adolescents in Los Angeles, California. *Journal of Adolescent Research, 4,* 426–442.

Zelnik, M., & Kantner, J. P. (1980). Sexual activity, contraceptive use and pregnancy among metropolitan-area teenagers: 1971–1979. *Family Planning Perspectives, 12,* 230–237.

Zelnik, M., & Kim, Y. J. (1982). Sex education and its association with teenage sexual activity, pregnancy and contraceptive use. *Family Planning Perspectives, 14,* 117–126.

Zelnik, M., & Shah, F. K. (1983). First intercourse among young Americans. *Family Planning Perspectives, 15,* 64–70.

Zetlin, A. G. (1993). Everyday stressors in the lives of Anglo and Hispanic learning handicapped adolescents. *Journal of Youth and Adolescence, 22,* 327.

Zimmerman, B. J., Bandura, A., & Martinez-Pons, M. (1992). Self-motivation for academic attainment: The role of self-efficacy beliefs and personal goal-setting. *American Educational Research Journal, 29,* 663–676.

Author Index

Aboud, F. E., 358
Adams, G. R., 371, 374
Adams-Price, C., 279
Adelson, J., 212, 266–267, 376
Adler, N. L., 390
Adolph, R., 506–507
Adwere-Boamah, J., 533, 534
Agnew, R., 500
Agyei, Y., 402
Aiken, L. R., 167, 169
Aitken, D., 135, 139, 407
Al-Mabuk, R., 524–525
Alexander, C. S., 133
Alexander, K. L., 314
Allan, M. J., 580
Allen, J. P., 276, 281
Allen, L., 241
Allen, W. R., 15
Allman, C. J., 580
American Council on Education, 457
Ammons, P., 390
Anastasi, A., 173
Anderson, E. R., 244
Anderson, S. A., 225, 364
Andrea, R. K., 123
Apter, D., 109
Arbona, C., 447–448, 456–457
Arbuthnut, J., 556
Archer, S. L., 345, 346, 354, 355
Arehart, D. M., 225
Arey, L. B., 106
Aries, P., 30, 62
Armacost, R. L., 533
Armistead, L., 251
Artman, L., 158
Asher, S. R., 277
Assh, S. D., 390
Astone, N. M., 247
Atkinson, R. C., 179
Attanucci, J., 516, 518
Austin, D. M., 426

Bachman, J. G., 561, 563, 565–570
Bachmann, G. A., 544, 549
Bahr, H. M., 287
Bailey, J. M., 401, 402
Bakan, D., 26, 32, 374, 375
Baker, L., 128
Bandura, A., 58, 59, 302, 482
Banks, C. A., 292, 296–298, 327
Banks, J. A., 326
Bardwick, J. M., 80
Barkley, T. J., 245
Barokas, J. U., 451–452
Baron, J. B., 164, 203
Baron, L., 545
Baron, S. W., 560

Barrera, M., Jr., 234
Bartesh, W., 94
Barth, R. P., 130, 136, 138–140, 423
Bartle, S. E., 225, 364
Basseches, M., 465
Bassok, M., 478
Bauman, K. E., 244, 284
Baumrind, D., 69, 213, 218–221, 518
Bayley, N., 117
Becerra, R. M., 138
Beentjes, J. W. J., 302
Belenky, M. F., 355, 468–472
Belk, S. S., 136
Bell, D. C., 235–236, 369
Bell, L. G., 235–236, 369
Belsky, J., 116
Benbow, C. P., 177
Benda, B. B., 131
Benin, M. H., 251
Benson, P. L., 563
Berent, R., 213, 216, 220
Berg, C., 483–485
Berlin, B., 425
Berlin, M., 150–151
Berman, A. L., 575
Berndt, 256, 264, 266
Bersoff, D. M., 509
Berzonsky, M. D., 347–351, 496, 532
Betancourt, H., 12, 17
Bettes, B. A., 563
Bettleheim, B., 376
Bieber, I., 403
Bierman, K. L., 280
Bird, G. W., 251
Bjorkland, D. F., 196
Black, J., 197–198
Blanchard-Fields, F., 196, 244–245
Bloch, D. P., 316, 438
Block, J. H., 119, 122
Blos, P., 212
Blumenthal, S. J., 576, 577, 580
Blyth, D.A., 123, 242, 354–368
Blyth, J., 242
Bobbitt, B. L., 181
Bohannon, W., 320
Bolton, F. G., Jr., 388
Bolton, I. M., 574
Booth, A., 250
Booth, K., 246–247, 314
Borman, E. H., 234
Boster, J. S., 473
Botvin, G. J., 563
Bourne, E., 352
Boxer, A. M., 97, 103, 123
Boyer, E., 456
Boyes, M. C., 193
Bradley, J., 426–427

Braeges, J. L., 218
Bransford, J. D., 479
Brent, D. A., 580
Briar, K. H., 500
Brice-Heath, S., 328
Brody, G., 244
Bronfenbrenner, U., 330
Brookman, R. R., 415, 419
Brooks, J. B., 342, 364–365
Brooks, J., 227, 237
Brooks, L., 457–459
Brooks-Gunn, J., 96, 108, 110–113, 118–119, 123, 312, 409, 412, 572
Brown, A. L., 179, 204
Brown, B. B., 271, 275, 282, 285
Brown, D., 443
Brown, D. A., 311
Brown, L., 138
Brownlee, J. R., 217
Bryan, T., 285
Bryk, A. S., 297, 298
Buchanan, C. M., 213, 244–247
Buhrmester, D., 259, 265–267, 277
Bukowski, W. M., 267
Burglass, M. E., 568, 569
Busch-Rossnagel, N. A., 285
Buss, R. R., 196
Butcher, J., 275–276
Byers, E. S., 390
Byrne, D., 395
Byrne, L. F., 194–195
Byrnes, J. P., 312

Cahan, S., 158
Camarena, P. M., 263–264, 265
Cameron, R., 535–537
Campbell, D., 447
Campione, J. C., 204
Carlsmith, L., 278
Carrigan, S., 578
Carroll, J. S., 501
Cashdan, S., 500
Caspi, A., 116
Cattell, R. B., 171
Cavior, N., 276
Centers for Disease Control, 300, 302, 416, 417, 420, 422, 423, 425, 575
Cernkovich, S. A., 556
Chandler, M., 193
Chaplin, J., 135, 139, 407
Chard-Wierschem, D., 557
Chassin, L., 234
Chatters, L. M., 15
Cheek, D. B., 103
Chen, C., 314–315
Chen, Z., 225
Chiu, M. L., 239

Chi, M. T. H., 473
Chipman, S. F., 475
Chodorow, N., 80–83, 379
Chomsky, N., 49
Choquet, M., 124, 126–127
Clark, S., 136
Cicerelli, V. G., 242
Clark, B., 320
Clark, M. L., 277
Clark-Lempers, D. S., 257, 264–267
Clasen, D. R., 283, 285
Clausen, J. A., 118
Clinchy, B. M., 355
Clinchy, M., 468–472
Cobb, N. J., 11, 156, 280, 284
Cohen, L. H., 537
Coie, J. D., 556
Cole, D. A., 229
Coleman, E., 400
Coleman, J. S., 24, 274–275
Coleman, P., 297, 298, 315, 316, 450
Colemen, J. C., 267, 272, 275
Coles, R., 78–79, 338
Collins, B., 132–133
Collins, J. L., 132–133
Collins, W. A., 220
Comer, J. P., 296
Commons, M. L., 461, 598, 601
Compas, B. E., 534, 572
Condon, S. M., 232, 282
Conger, J. J., 247, 286
Constantine, L. L., 236
Constantinople, A., 10
Cook, W. L., 220
Coon, R. C., 244–245
Cooper, C. R., 209, 229, 232, 234, 238, 282, 369, 375
Cooper, L. A., 473–474
Cooper, P. J., 126
Corbin, S. B., 244
Costanzo, P. R., 281
Costos, D., 231
Cote, J., 60
Cotman, C. W., 95
Covington, M. V., 311
Cox, M., 244
Cox, R., 244
Cox, S. L., 396
Cozby, P. C., 319, 463, 590
Craig, R. K., 160
Craighead, L. W., 572, 573
Cristopherson, C. R., 132
Crockett, L., 97, 103, 119
Crosbie-Burnett, M., 248–250
Cross, W. E., Jr., 357
Crouter, A. C., 251
Crowley, M. S., 251
Curd, K., 237–239
Curran, J. W., 423, 425
Curtis, D. A., 533, 534
Cutler, G. B., Jr., 95

Dacey, J. S., 479–481
Daniel, W., Jr., 93
Daniels, R., 314
Darling, C. A., 130

Darwin, C., 59, 61
Daurio, S., 320
Davey, F. H., 450, 454
Davis, G. E., 534
Davis, K. E., 395
de Groot, A. D., 473
deAnda, D., 138
Deffenbacher, J. L., 535, 537
Delaney, J., 408–409
Delaney, M., 299
DeLoache, J. S., 179
DeMaris, A., 248
Derrick, A., 578
Desmond, S., 559
Deutsch, M., 303
DeVault, C., 19, 132–134, 136, 399, 400, 410, 411, 414, 415, 417, 418, 420, 423
Dewey, J., 49
DiBlasio, F. A., 131
DiClemente, R. J., 425
Digest of Educational Statistics, 293, 298, 303, 309, 313
Dillard, A., 205
Dinero, T. E., 396
Dirksen-Thedens, I., 94
Dodge, K. A., 276
Doehrman, M. J., 376
Doherty, W. J., 244, 245, 248
Dokecki, P. R., 276
Domenico, D., 578
Donahue, M. J., 563
Dornbusch, S. M., 220, 222, 225, 244–248, 278, 436–437
DuBois, D. L., 268–269
Doueck, H. J., 543, 544
Douvan, E., 80, 212, 266–267
Downs, W. R., 555, 556
DSM-IIIR, 125, 562, 563, 571, 582, 584
Duke, D., 278
Duke-Duncan, P., 123
Dukes, R. L., 366
Duncker, K., 477
Dunphy, D. C., 271, 273–274, 591
Durlak, J. A., 581
Dusenbury, L., 563
Dweck, C. S., 177, 310–313
Dyk, P. H., 371, 374

Eagly, A. H., 366
Eccles, J. E., 212, 213, 220
Eccles, J. S., 285
Educational Research Service, 305
Edwards, D. A., 251
Eisert, D. C., 213
Eisiloits, Z., 553
Eitzen, D., 276
Elder, G. H., 247
Elkind, D., 35, 137, 189–191, 195, 256, 581
Elliot, D. S., 552
Enright, R. D., 229, 231, 524–525
Ensminger, M. E., 133
Entwisle, D. R., 314
Epstein, J., 297, 304
Epstein, S., 361
Erickson, P. I., 133
Erikson, E. H., 77–81, 191, 224, 256, 279, 337,

338, 340–344, 351, 352, 354, 356, 370, 373–374, 382, 467, 491, 492, 591
Eron, L. D., 556
Evans, G. T., 483
Ey, S., 572

Fairburn, C. G., 126
Faller, K. C., 545, 548
Farber, E., 540, 542
Farmer, F. L., 136
Fauber, R., 244–245
Faulkner, D., 542
Faust, M. S., 102
Federal Bureau of Investigation, 551
Fegley, S., 436–437
Feiring, C., 373–374
Feldman, C. F., 328
Feldman, S. S., 239, 357
Ferris, J., 560
Fetro, J. V., 136, 138
Fielder, E. P., 138
Finch, M., 438
Flavell, E. R., 444
Fine, M. A., 249
Finkelhor, D. H., 302, 545, 548
Fisher, L. A., 285
Fishman, G., 553
Fisk, W. R., 325
FitzGerald, D. P., 137, 195–196
Flanagan, C., 213
Flanagan, T. J., 541, 551, 573, 575
Flannery, D., 196
Flavell, J. H., 152, 154, 156, 158, 444
Fleming, A., 200
Fleming, S. J., 506–507
Flewelling, R. L., 244
Folkman, S., 532
Forcey, B., 454
Ford, M. E., 498–499, 520
Ford, M. R., 517
Forehand, R., 244–245, 251
Forrest, K. A., 426
Fossey, D., 590
Fouad, N., 458–459
Fowler, J. W., 521, 522
Fox, G. L., 131
Fox, J., 284
Fraleigh, M. J., 220
Frank, M., 359
Frankel, K. A., 256, 263–264
Franklin, A. J., 475–476
Freeman, D., 60
Frese, W., 457
Freud, A., 74–75, 78, 212
Freud, S., 45, 51, 52, 53, 70–75, 77–80, 84, 212, 403, 510, 518–521, 527
Frisch, R. E., 93, 109, 113–114
Fry, A. F., 180, 183
Fuentes, E. G., 426
Fuligni, A. J., 212, 213, 220, 285
Fullerton, H., Jr., 453
Furman, W., 265–267, 277, 280–281
Furstenberg, F. F., Jr., 244, 409, 412
Futcher, W. G., 545, 550
Futterman, D., 420

Gaddis, A., 112–113
Galambos, N. L., 251
Galanter, E., 50
Gallini, J., 204
Gamoran, A., 294, 314
Garbarino, J., 293, 297
Garcia, J., 326
Gardner, H., 147, 185–189, 317
Gardner, W. M., 500
Garland, A. F., 560, 574–577, 580
Garner, W. R., 296
Gaucci-Franci, N., 259
Gavazzi, S. M., 225
Gavin, L. A., 280–281
Ge, X., 247
Gebhard, P. H., 131–132
Geller, L. G., 204
Gerber, R. W., 566
Gershaw, N. J., 556
Gerstein, M., 451–452
Gibbons, J. L., 123
Gibbs, J. T., 240–241
Gick, M. L., 477
Giles-Sims, J., 248–250
Gilligan, C., 64–71, 80, 83–84, 370, 374, 376,
    497, 510–514, 516–518, 520, 521, 526,
    527, 538, 539
Ginzburg, E., 432, 443–444
Ginzburg, H., 158
Giordano, P. C., 556
Glaser, R., 474–475
Glick, J., 159
Glick, P. C., 248
Glood, E., 576
Glover, R. W., 450
Glyshaw, K., 537
Goldberger, N. R., 355, 468–472
Goldstein, A. P., 101, 556
Goldstein, C. E., 580
Gonzalez, C. C., 500
Goode, E., 566, 567, 570
Goossens, L., 196
Gordan, D. A., 556
Gordon, M., 545
Gordon, T., 215
Gottman, J. M., 260–263
Grace, N., 544
Gralen, S., 124
Grandjean, A. C., 128
Grant, K., 572
Grave, G. D., 103
Gray, L., 560
Gray, W., 196
Green, B. J., 572, 573
Green, F. L., 444
Greenaway, K. D., 543, 544
Greene, A. L., 22, 23, 259, 279, 284, 589
Gregory, D., 197
Greif, G. L., 248
Grimsley, M. D., 284
Gross, B., 316–317
Gross, R. T., 278
Grotevant, H. D., 209, 229, 232, 234, 238, 282,
    369, 375
Grumbach, M. M., 103
Guacci-Franco, N., 241

Guardado, S., 138
Gunnings, T. S., 448
Gurevich, M., 534
Guttman, E., 553
Gwartney-Gibbs, P. A., 590

Haan, N. S., 163, 508, 509
Habenicht, D. J., 545, 550
Hackel, E., 59
Hagan, M. S., 244
Hains, A. A., 536, 537, 556
Hale, J. L., 500
Hale, S., 180, 183, 190
Hall, C. S., 53, 73
Hall, E., 455–456
Hall, G. S., 59, 60, 61, 131
Hall, J. A., 558
Hallinan, M. T., 268–269
Hamer, D. H., 400, 402
Hammelman, T. L., 400
Hammond, W. R., 558, 559
Hanawalt, B. A., 30
Hanmer, T. J., 374
Hansell, S., 245
Hardardottir, S., 123
Harmoni, R., 483
Harris, L., 138
Hartmann, D. P., 256
Hartup, W. W., 257, 268, 278
Harvey, O. J., 281
Hass, A., 132
Hatcher, R., 150–151
Hatcher, S., 150–151
Hauaghwout, P., 315
Hauser, S. T., 234–236
Havighurst, R. J., 20, 36, 37, 55, 77
Hawkins, J., 158
Hawkins, J. A., 281
Hayes, C. D., 136–137, 139–140, 411, 412
Healy, R. W., 123
Heeren, T., 425
Hein, K., 420
Held, T., 35
Hendrick, C., 390
Hendrick, S., 390
Henggeler, S. W., 552–554, 556, 558
Herzog, 285
Hess, L. E., 299
Hetherington, 243–250
Hicks, M. W., 130
Hicks, R., 284
Higham, E., 93
Hill, J. P., III, 217, 251
Hingson, R. W., 425
Hirsch, B. J., 268–269, 534
Hirsch, R. H., 192
Hoffman, M. L., 503, 510, 520
Hogan, R., 317, 320
Holland, J. L., 317, 444, 446–447
Holmbeck, G. N., 217
Holyoak, K. J., 477, 478
Homer, 30
Hood, K. E., 109
Horn, J. L., 171
Horner, M., 69
Horney, K., 75–77

Horowitz, F. D., 317, 322
Horowitz, M., 559, 560
Horst, H. J., 94
Hotaling, G. T., 548
Houston, J. P., 500
Howard, G. R., 327
Howard, K. I., 212
Howat, P. M., 124–125
Howell, F. M., 457
Hoyt, K. B., 447, 450, 452, 454–455
Hoza, B., 267
Hrynevich, C., 356
Hu, N., 400, 402
Hu, S., 400, 402
Hu-DeHart, E., 326
Huang, L. N., 239
Hudson, L., 196
Huelskamp, R. M., 292, 314
Huesmann, L. R., 556
Huizinga, D., 552
Humphrey, L. L., 127
Husbands, C. L., 280
Hyde, J. S., 18, 19, 131, 132, 177, 386, 387

Iheanacho, S. O., 366
Ihenger-Tallman, M., 249
Inderbitzen-Pisaruk, H., 277
Inhelder, B., 152
Insel, P., 104, 106, 412–413, 564, 565
Irion, J. C., 244–245
Irving, L. M., 549
Isajiw, W. W., 356
Ishisaka, A. H., 543, 544

Jaccard, J., 282, 284
Jackson, S., 137, 195–196
Jacobson, A. M., 234–236
Jahnke, H. C., 196
James-Ortiz, S., 563
Jason, L. A., 315
Jenning, D., 278
Jensen, A. R., 175–176
Jessie, J., 180, 183
Jimenez, D. P., 123
Jobes, D. A., 575
Joe, J., 553
Joebgen, A. M., 250
Johnson, B. M., 220
Johnson, C., 127
Johnson, D. J., 328
Johnson, J. C., 473
Johnson, K. E., 133
Johnson, V. E., 223, 369, 370, 400, 403–407,
    409, 424
Johnson-Laird, P. N., 160, 162
Johnston, D. K., 515–517
Johnston, L. D., 561, 563, 565–570
Johnston, S. S., 123, 125
Jones, M. C., 117
Josselson, R. L., 226, 229, 283, 286, 351, 355,
    359, 370, 373–381, 492, 495, 496, 519
Jovanovic, J., 299
Jurkovic, G. J., 556

Kagan, J., 62
Kahle, J. B., 213, 456

Kahn, A. S., 84
Kail, R., 180, 183
Kammer, P. P., 458–459
Kandel, D. B., 212, 284, 567
Keith, J. G., 251
Kane, M. J., 275
Kann, L., 132–134
Kate, M. E., 366
Kaufman, J. F., 568, 569
Kazdin, A. E., 537
Keating, D. P., 63, 163, 181
Kee, 590
Keller, M., 260
Kellermann, A., 560
Kelly, E., 124
Kelly, M. L., 544
Kemerait, L. N., 251
Keniston, K., 33
Kennedy, L. W., 560
Kenny, A. M., 138
Kerner, J., 563
Kett, J. F., 32
Kim, Y. J., 133
Kinast, C., 542
King, P. K., 132
Kingston, M. H., 5
Kinsey, A. C., 131–132, 399, 403
Kirby, D., 139
Kirby, P. C., 298
Kitano, H. H. L., 314
Klebanov, P. K., 312
Klein, J. R., 110–111
Klein, P., 556
Klein, S. S., 325
Klerman, L. V., 419
Klug, M., 500
Knobil, 95
Koch, P. B., 135, 395
Kolbe, L. J., 132–133
Kochman, T., 11
Koepsell, T., 560
Kohlberg, L., 163, 375, 497, 501–503, 505,
  507–514, 518–522, 525, 526
Kohn, P. M., 533, 534
Kohut, S., Jr., 305
Kolko, D. J., 580
Kolodny, R. C., 223, 369, 370, 400, 404, 406,
  407, 409, 424
Koman, J. J., III, 251
Koss, M. P., 396, 397
Koulock, D., 243, 245
Krasnoff, A. G., 177
Kratcoski, L. D., 558
Kratcoski, P. C., 558
Krisberg, B., 553
Kroger, J., 344, 346, 347
Krohn, M. D., 557
Krohne, H. W., 532
Krumboltz, J. D., 441–443, 459–460,
  462–463
Ku, 135
Kuhn, D., 163, 508, 509
Kuhn, T. S., 43
Kulin, H. E., 92, 95, 96, 106, 112
Kupersmidt, J. B., 556
Kupfer, D. J., 576, 577, 580

Kurdek, L. A., 250
Kurtines, W. M., 539

Labouvie-Vief, G., 349
Lafreniere, K., 534
LaFromboise, T. D., 241, 314
Lampman-Petraitis, C., 258
Landsman, S., 282, 284
Langer, J., 163, 508, 509
Lanza-Kaduce, L., 500
Lapsley, D. K., 137, 195–196, 229
Larkin, J. H., 474
Larson, R., 258
Latty-Mann, H., 395
Lazarus, R. S., 532
Leavitt, R. A., 108
LeBlanc, M., 555
Ledoux, S., 124, 126–127
Lee, J. A., 390–394
Lee, S. H., 473
Lefkowitz, M. M., 556
Leiderman, P. H., 220
Leigh, G. K., 135
Leland, J., 559
Leland, N. L., 130, 136, 138–139, 423
Lempers, J. D., 257, 264–267
Leon, G. R., 124
Lerner, R. M., 43, 45, 46, 48, 59, 299
Lesser, G. S., 212
Lesser, I. M., 371
Levanon, I., 500, 520
LeVay, S., 402
Lever, J., 69
Levesque, R. J. R., 390, 391, 395
Levine, M. P., 124
Levitt, J. L., 106, 241, 259
Levitt, M. J., 241, 259
Levitt, R. A., 106
Lewis, C., 125, 127
Lewis, J. M., 244
Lewis, M., 373–374
Liberty, C., 10
Licht, B. G., 311
Lichtman, M., 451–452
Linden, T. A., 311
Lips, H. M., 10, 17, 177, 325–326, 404, 409
Litt, I. F., 110–111
Livson, M., 119
Lizotte, A. J., 557
Lobel, T., 500, 520
LoGerfo, J., 560
Lonky, E., 518
Lopez, S. R., 12
Lorenz, F. O., 247
Lovitt, T. C., 322–324
Low, K. G., 241
Lowery, C. R., 517
Lucas, B., 128, 129
Lupton, M. J., 408–409
Lyon, J. M., 558
Lyons, N. P., 374

Maccoby, E. E., 244–247
MacEachron, A. E., 388
Maggs, J. L., 251
Magnuson, V.-L., 400, 402

Maguire, K., 541, 551, 573, 575
Mahapatra, M., 509
Majidi-Ahi, 241
Major, B., 454
Malina, R. M., 102
Manfredi, R., 124, 126–127
Mangelsdorf, C., 124
Mann, L., 483
Marcia, J. E., 281, 340, 342–344, 346–347, 351,
  352, 354–355, 359, 371, 373–375, 494–496
Mare, R. D., 294
Margolin, L., 397
Markman, E. M., 153
Marks, N., 247
Markstrom-Adams, C., 522
Marshall, R., 450
Martin, B., 531
Martin, C. E., 131–132, 399
Martin, J., 426–427
Martin, J. A., 27
Martinez, R., 366
Martinez-Pons, M., 482
Martorano, S. C., 160
Masters, W. H., 223, 369, 370, 400, 403–407,
  409, 424
Matuschka, P. R., 567
Mayer, F. E., 103
Maynard, R. C., 13
Mayr, E., 164
Mazor, A., 229, 231
McAdams, D. P., 536
McCary, J. L., 104, 106, 109
McCary, S. P., 104, 106, 109
McCoard, W., 542
McGaugh, J. L., 95
McGee, R., 259
McGinn, P. V., 320
McGlone, C., 160
McKenry, P. C., 135
McLanahan, S. S., 246–247, 314
Mare, R. D., 314
McLaughlen, R. D., 500
McLaughlin, D., 245
McNeil, J. N., 506–507
McVey, G., 284
Mead, M., 60
Mechanic, D., 245
Meichenbaum, D. H., 535–537
Meyer, K. A., 438
Michel, A., , 325
Midgley, C., 213
Miller, B. C., 131, 132
Miller, G., 239
Miller, G. A., 50
Miller, J., 77, 509
Miller, J. G., 509
Miller, K. E., 265, 279
Miller, L., 534
Miller, M., 397
Miller, P. H., 152, 154, 158
Miller, R. L., 328
Miller, S. A., 152, 154, 158
Miller-Tutzauer, C., 578
Millrose, J. A., 533, 534
Milstead, M., 196
Minuchin, S., 128

Mischel, H. N., 497–499
Mischel, W., 497–499
Mitchell, L. K., 441–443, 459–460, 462–463
Moeller, T. P., 544, 549
Moffitt, T. E., 116
Money, J., 402
Mont-Reynaud, R., 225, 239
Montague, R. B., 247
Montemayor, R., 217, 267–268
Moore, D. S., 133
Moran, P. B., 31, 397
Morgan, S. P., 409, 412
Morrow, K. B., 540, 549
Morrow, L., 251
Mortimer, J. T., 438
Munroe, R., 76
Murphy, L., 426
Murphy, M., 195
Mussen, P. H., 117
Muuss, R. E., 114, 271

Nagata, D. K., 239–240
Nakagawa, K., 328
National Center for Health Statistics, 574
National Household Survey, 567
Naus, M. J., 180
Neale, M. C., 402
Needle, R. H., 244–245, 248
Neisser, U., 51, 189
Nelson, C. S., 251
Nelson, M. R., 314, 316
Newcomb, A. F., 267
Newman, I. M., 566
Newman, J., 196
Ng, S. H., 470–471
Noam, G. G., 234–236
Nolan, M. J., 130
Norton, E. M., 581
Noveck, I. A., 197–198
Nucci, L. P., 509

Oakes, J., 295
Obolensky, N., 576
O'Brien, D. P., 197–198
O'Brien, M., 317, 322
O'Brien, S. F., 280
O'Connell, A. N., 354
Offer, D., 212
Ogbu, J. U., 330, 457
Okla, K., 150–151
Okun, M. A., 362
Olexa, C., 295–296
Oliveri, M. E., 237–239
O'Malley, P. M., 561, 563, 565–570
Opper, S., 158
Orlofsky, J., 359, 371
Ornstein, P. A., 180
Orthner, D., 250–251
Orum, L. S., 455
Osherson, D. N., 153
Osipow, S. H., 446
Ostrov, E., 212
Overton, W. F., 43, 46, 48, 197–199
Owings, J., 323

Page, R. N., 294–295
Palinscar, A. S., 204
Paolitto, D. P., 192
Papini, D. R., 136
Pardeck, J. A., 225
Pardeck, J. L., 225
Paris, S. G., 159
Parker, J. G., 260–263
Parks, G., 359
Parr, R. B., 124
Parsons, T., 16
Pasley, B. K., 249
Pastore, A. L., 541, 551, 573, 575
Pattatucci, A. M. L., 400, 402
Patterson, S. J., 340, 351, 354–355
Paulson, S. E., 251
Pavlov, I. P., 47
Pea, R. D., 158
Pearl, R., 285
Perdue, L., 124
Perfetto, G. A., 479
Perkins, D. N., 203
Perlmutter, B. F., 556
Perper, J. A., 580
Perry, C. L., 124
Perry, W. G., 349, 465–472
Peskin, H., 118–119
Peters, A. A., 500
Petersen, A. C., 94, 96, 97, 103, 111, 115, 119, 123, 124, 226–227, 263–264, 266, 572
Petersen, K. K., 130
Peterson, B., 124
Peterson, C. C., 426
Peterson, H. B., 423, 425
Phelps, L., 123, 124
Phinney, J. S., 12, 270, 329–330, 356, 359–361, 366
Piaget, J., 60, 61, 62, 63, 64, 77, 146, 152, 154–163, 196, 461, 474
Pillard, R. C., 401, 402
Pittman, R. B., 315
Place, D. M., 278
Pleck, J. H., 135–136, 139
Polk, K., 295–296
Pollack, S., 68, 70–71
Pomeroy, W. B., 131–132, 399
Poole, M. E., 483
Post-Kammer, 455–456
Postman, N., 32, 34
Powell, G. J., 357
Power, C., 483
Powers, S. I., 234–236
Pribram, K. H., 50
Price, J., 559
Procidano, M. E., 245
Proulx, J., 243, 245
Purcell, P., 324
Putallaz, M., 276

Quay, H. C., 556
Quintana, S. M., 196

Raja, S. N., 259
Ramefedi, G., 400
Ramsby, T. W., 398
Raudenbush, S. W., 297–298

Rauste-von Wright, M., 120–121
Ray, J., 500
Reay, D., 560
Reese, H. W., 43, 46, 48
Reid, M., 282, 284
Reimer, J., 192
Reischl, T. M., 534
Reiss, D., 237–239
Renderer, B., 328
Report of the Secretary's Task Force on Youth Suicide, 574, 576, 578, 580
Repucci, N. D., 311
Restak, R., 95
Reyes, L. H., 455
Reyes, O., 315
Rice, C., 560
Rice, K. G., 137, 195–196, 229
Richards, F. A., 461
Richards, J., 150–151
Richards, M., 97, 103
Richards, M. H., 250, 581
Riegel, K. F., 462
Rifkin, B., 15
Riggsbee, J., 204
Riley, M. W., 34
Ritter, P. I., 220, 225
Rivara, F., 560
Roberts, D. F., 220
Robertson, J. F., 555, 556
Roche, J. P., 398
Rogers, J. L., 404, 405
Rogner, J., 532
Rogosch, F., 234
Rogow, A. M., 346
Rollins, J., 15, 17
Roodin, P. A., 518
Roper, J. T., 500
Roper, W. L., 423, 425
Rosenberg, A., 278
Rosenberg, M., 556, 572
Rosenthal, D. A., 239, 356, 357, 359, 366
Rosman, B., 128
Ross, D., 302
Ross, J., 132–133
Ross, S. A., 59, 302
Ross, S. M., 59, 500
Roth, P., 131
Roth, W., 412–413
Roth, W. T., 104, 106, 564, 565
Rotheram, M. J., 329–330, 582
Rotheram-Borus, M. J., 12, 270, 426–427
Rowe, D. C., 404, 405
Ruble, D. N., 110–113
Rutherford, J., 281
Rutter, M., 573
Ryan, E. B., 556
Rybasch, J. M., 518
Ryu, S., 438

Sabatelli, R. M., 225
Samat, N., 234
Sandberg, D., 426–427
Santos, M. J., 524–525
Sarigiani, P. A., 263–264, 266
Sasfy, J. H., 362
Satter, E., 129

Saxton, A. M., 124–125
Scarr, S., 175
Schachter, S., 115
Schaie, K. W., 170–171, 174, 177, 599
Schiano, D. J., 473–474
Schiedel, D. G., 371, 374, 375
Schlabach, J. H., 251
Schnellmann, J., 123
Schoenbach, C., 556, 572
Schooler, C., 556, 572
Schuckit, J. J., 574
Schuckit, M. A., 574
Schwartz, I., 553
Schwartz, J. M., 234–236
Schwartz, R., 421
Schweder, R. A., 509
Scott-Jones, D., 139
Scribner, S., 159
Sebald, H., 275
Segal, J. W., 475
Seibel, C. A., 396
Seiber, J. E., 501
Seiffge-Krenke, I., 234
Seixas, P., 326
Selman, R. L., 194–195
Selye, H., 530, 531, 584
Sessa, F. M., 247
Sexton, M. A., 311
Shaffer, H., 295–296, 568, 569
Shafii, M., 578
Shakespeare, W., 30, 197
Sherman, J. A., 178
Shanahan, M., 438
Shiffrin, R. M., 179
Shulman, S., 220, 234–236
Siegler, R. S., 179, 180, 183
Siesfeld, G. A., 498–499, 520
Silliman, B., 506–507
Silva, P. A., 116
Silva-Palacios, V., 538, 539
Silverberg, S. B., 251–252
Silverstein, B., 124
Simmons, R. G., 364–368
Simons, R. L., 123, 247, 555, 556
Simpkins, G. A., 448
Simpson, G. E., 12, 17
Simpson, R. G., 500
Singer, J., 115
Skinner, B. F., 47, 48, 55, 56, 57
Slater, J., 318–319
Slaughter-DeFoe, D. T., 328
Slavin, R. E., 296
Sloan, J., 560
Slonim-Nevo, V., 134
Slugowski, B. R., 346
Small, M. Y., 194
Smetana, J. G., 213, 216, 218, 220, 239–240, 252
Smith, D., 559
Smith, E. A., 132
Smith, P. H., 225
Smith, T. E., 243, 244, 245
Smolak, L., 124
Smoller, J., 286
Snarey, J. R., 509
Snell, W. E., 136

Snow, R. E., 294, 296
Sochting, I., 340, 351, 354–355
Sokolov, E. M., 49
Solano, C. H., 277
Sollie, C. R., 457
Solomon, G., 297
Somerfield, M. R., 133
Sommer, K., 409
Sonenstein, F. L., 135–136, 139, 395, 410
Sorenson, R. C., 13
Sorell, G. T., 540, 549
Sowell, T., 176
Speisman, J. C., 231
Spencer, M. B., 330
Spires, H. A., 204
Sprafkin, R. P., 556
Spreen, O., 323
Stanic, G. M., 455
Stanley, J. C., 177
Stanton, W. R., 259
Steinberg, L., 210, 222, 225, 247, 251–252, 436–437
Steinberg, S., 125, 127
Stemmler, M., 572
Sternberg, L., 483
Sternberg, R. J., 146, 163, 164, 180, 183, 184, 189, 203
Stevens, E., 498–499, 520
Stevens-Long, J., 11, 156, 222, 223, 280, 284, 598, 601
Stevenson, H. W., 314–315
Stewart, L., 324
Stiles, D. A., 123
Stinett, N., 390
Stocking, C., 323
Stone, A., 328
Stoppard, J. M., 450, 454
Streitmatter, J., 350
Stringfield, S., 298
Strong, B., 19, 132–134, 136, 399, 400, 410, 411, 414, 415, 417, 418, 420, 423
Strunin, L., 425
Su, S. S., 244, 245, 248
Subich, L. M., 453–454
Super, 432, 443, 445–446
Surgeon General's Report, 562, 565, 566
Swain, S. O., 135–136, 139
Swihart, J. J., 506–507
Switzer, J. Y., 325–326
Szapocznik, J., 539
Szyjakowski, M., 536, 537

Takahira, S., 312
Takanishi, R., 328
Tanner, J. M., 24, 98, 113–114
Tarule, J. M., 355, 468–472
Tarver, S., 360
Tavris, C., 74, 76, 520
Taylor, B., 94, 103, 115, 119
Taylor, R. J., 15
Teddlie, C., 298
Teixeira, R. A., 268–269
Tell, G. C., 124
Temoshok, L., 425
Terman, L. M., 317, 320
Thiel, K. S., 242

Thomas, A. M., 244–245
Thomas, O., 534
Thomas, R. M., 71
Thompson, C. J., 251
Thornberry, T. P., 557
Thornburg, H. D., 112
Thornton, M. C., 15, 132
Tidwell, R., 314–315
Tillman, R., 553
Tisak, M. S., 509
Tittle, C. K., 324
Tobias, A. L., 125, 127, 128
Tobin-Richards, M. H., 123
Toch, T., 300–302
Tolan, P., 534
Tolson, J. M., 284
Toth, E., 408–409
Towbes, L. C., 537
Trautman, P. D., 581, 582
Treboux, D., 285
Treder, R., 282, 284
Trent, W. T., 456
Tschirgi, J. E., 160–162
Turiel, E., 509
Turner, C. B., 500
Turner, S. L., 139

U.S. Bureau of the Census, 9, 11, 24, 30, 240–241, 449, 450–451, 455
U.S. Department of Education, 301, 322
U.S. Department of Justice, 555
Udrey, J. R., 132
Underwood, B. J., 596
Unger, R., 9
Urberg, K. A., 284
Uttal, D. H., 314–315

Valdes, M. I., 426
Van Komer, R., 267–268
van der Voort, T. S. A., 302
Viernstein, M. C., 320
Vigil, J. D., 558
Vilko, R., 109
Visher, E. B., 248–249
Visher, J. S., 248–249
Volkan, K., 136, 138–139
von Eye, A., 299
Vye, N. J., 479

Wade, C., 74, 76, 520
Wagner, R. K., 189
Walder, L. D., 556
Walker, L. J., 69, 518
Walker, L. S., 259
Wallerstein, J. S., 244
Walters, J. M., 188
Wapner, 172
Wapner, M., 14, 22, 70, 78, 110, 120, 229, 457, 467
Wapner, M. L., 348, 537
Ward, D. A., 500
Ward, S. L., 197–199
Warren, M. P., 93, 96, 108
Warren, W., 132–133
Wason, P. C., 160, 162
Waterman, A. S., 346

Wetzel, J., 361
Wattenberg, B. J., 9
Weaver, F. M., 501
Wechsler, 164–174
Weddle, K. D., 135
Weinbaum, E., 160
Weinberg, R. A., 175
Weiner, I. B., 572, 573, 578, 581, 583, 584
Weis, D., 135
Weiss, D., 320
Weissberg, R. P., 276, 281
Wentzel, K. R., 498–499, 520
Westermeyer, J., 563
Wetzel, J., 455, 457
Whitehead, A. N., 477
White, K. A., 275
White, K. L., 231
White, L. K., 250
Whiteside, M. F., 250
Whitfield, R., 245

Whittinghill, J. R., 578
Wierson, M., 244–245, **251**
Wigdor, A. K., 296
Wilks, J., 284
Williams, J. H., 405
Williams, J. M., 275
Williams, R., 458–459
Willis, S. L., 171, 174, **177**
Wilson, S. R., 426
Wilszenski, F. L., 123
Windle, M., 578
Winer, G. A., 160
Wintre, M. G., 284
Wirth, L., 12
Witkin, G., 560
Women on Words and Images, 324
Wood, D., 498–499, **520**
Wood, P., 260
Worden, J. W., 590
Wyche, K., 576

Wyshak, G., 114

Yamaguchi, K., 567
Yau, J., 21, 239–240
Ying, Y., 239
Yinger, J. M., 12, 17
Yoder, J. D., 84
Youniss, J., 213, 286
Youth Indicators, 36, 284, 294, 306–309,
    434–439, 490–492, 523, 550–552, 561,
    565, 567, 569, 570
Yung, B., 558, 559

Zabatany, L., 256
Zambrana, R. E., 538, 539
Zelenak, J. P., 580
Zhang, H. C., 473–474
Zigler, E., 560, 574–577, 580
Zimmerman, B. J., 42
Zorn, J., 425

Subject Index

Abortion, 411–413
Abstraction, reflective, 61
Abstract thinking, 148, 150–151, 190, 196, 197, 213
Abuse
  substance, 576–578, 560–569 passim
  youth, 540–548
Academic tracking, 292, 293–297, 298, 314, 455
Acceleration, academic, 321–322
Accommodation, 62, 155
Acculturation, 16–17, 270, 357
Achieved identity, 344–354 passim, 374, 493–496
  ethnic, 359–360
Achievement, academic, 309–311
  active coping style and, 330
  delinquency and, 554
  dropouts and, 314
  ethnic identity and, 361
  failure at, 310–313, 322–324
  gender differences and, 311–313
  interracial friendship and, 268
  learning disability and, 322–324
  looks and, 299
  parenting style and, 220, 222
  part-time employment and, 436–438
  popularity and, 275–276
  tracking and, 294–296
  See also Education
Active coping styles, 329–330
Active knowledge, 476
Active listening, 211
Active organism, theories on, 49, 61–62
Activity, obesity and, 128
Adaptation, 62, 530
Addiction, drug, 560, 561, 563, 567, 568
Adjustment disorder with depressed mood, 570
Adolescence,
  abuse brought about by, 544
  creation of, 32–33
  as crisis, gender difference in, 514
  defining, 17–27
  developmental tasks in, 20–25, 36–38
  early, 7, 20, 91, 264, 266, 272–273, 280, 443, 534
  late, 7, 20, 264–266, 267, 444, 534
  pre-, 259–261, 263
  uni-age and, 34–36
  as unique age, 36–38
Adoption, 412–413
Adulthood, 30–35, 37
  developmental tasks in, 36–38
  drugs and, 562
  early, 33
  late, 33–34
  middle, 33
  uni-age and, 34–36

See also Parents
Adult status hypot⸱⸱⸱ ⸱, 119, 122
Affective disorders, 569
Afro-Americans. *See* Blacks
Age
  autonomy and, 225
  conformity and, 280–282
  dating, 278–280
  delinquency and, 549–550
  ethnic identity and, 360
  flexibility and, 483–484
  friendships changing with, 259–267
  in history, 30–34
  intelligence and, 169–174
  memory and, 180–183, 185
  menarche, 108–109
  old, 33–34
  parenting style and, 220
  population trends in, 7–9, 30
  runaways, 540
  self-concept and, 362
  of sexual intercourse, 132–134, 244
  status offenses and, 548
  and stepfamilies, 249
  suicide and, 572
  thinking skills and, 158–159, 162
  uni-age, 34–36
  as a variable, 595–596
  See also Adolescence; Adulthood; Aging; Childhood; Youth
Age changes, 120–121, 594–595, 599–601
Age-grading, 29, 35
Agency, 374–375
Aggression, 70, 554, 576
  See also Abuse; Violence
AIDS (acquired immune deficiency syndrome), 419–427, 568
Alarm reaction, 530
Alcohol, 576, 560–563, 565, 567
Alienation, 537–540
Ambiguity, tolerance for, 479
American Psychological Association, 59, 530, 607
Amphetamines, 566
Anabolic steroids, 569
Anal stage, 53
Androgens, 19, 93, 101
Androgyny, 11, 388–389
Anonymity, in research, 531
Anorexia, 125–127
Anovulatory cycles, 109
Archival research, 14–15, 590
Arguing, 192–193, 216, 227
Artistic personality types, 447
Asian Americans
  courses of study, 456
  dropout, 314

ethnic identity, 357, 360–361
  families, 239–240
  heterosexual behavior of, 133
  intelligence tests and, 174
  parenting styles, 220–222
  restrained mannerisms and, 330
  self-esteem of, 366
Aspirin, experiment with, 110–111
Assertiveness training, 140
Assimilation, 62, 155
  cultural, 14–16, 176
Asymptomatic, carriers of AIDS, 420
Asynchrony, 116–117
Athletics, popularity and, 275–276
Attachment, 378
  See also Connectedness
Attitudes
  sexual, 130–132
  See also Beliefs; Values
Attractiveness. *See* Physical attractiveness
Attributional errors, 536
Attribution of outcome, 311
Authoritarian parenting, 218–222, 284, 330
Authoritative parenting, 218–222, 281–282, 285, 364, 481
Authority
  ethnic differences and, 330
  parenting styles and, 218
  stepfamilies and, 249–250
Autonomy, 68, 81, 224–229
  deviant behavior and, 286
  divorced families and, 247
  dual-earner families and, 252
  family type and, 238
  identity and, 81, 381
  parents and, 212, 224–225, 226, 218–222
Avoidance, in families, 235
Axioms, 43

Barbiturates, 567
Bartholin's glands, 105
Beauty, 124
  See also Physical attractiveness
Behaviorism, radical, 56–58
Beliefs
  abortion, 441
  about careers, 459–461
  family core, 236
  religious, 491, 521–526
  self-concept and, 362–363
  self-defeating, 454, 459–461
  See also Values
Bem Sex-Role Inventory, 386–387, 608
Between-subjects design, research, 396–397
Bias, research, 126–127, 606
  male, 75–77, 83–84, 351, 373–376, 380–381, 514, 520

Biochemistry
schizophrenia and, 582
suicide and, 578
Biological definition of adolescence, 18–19, 55,
59–60, 70–75
See also Physical changes; Puberty
Biological focus
theoretical, 28
See also Age
Blacks
abortion and, 411
alcohol, drinking less of, 561
cultural knowledge and, 475–476
delinquency, 551–552
dropout, 313–314
education, 240, 308, 327–328, 454–455
ethnic identity of, 357–361
expressiveness and, 330
families, 240–241
friendships, 268–270
intelligence tests and, 175–176
life-course projections, 23
parenting styles, 220–221
pregnancy and parenting and, 411
self-esteem of, 366
sexual behavior of, 133–134
socialization of, 13, 14–15
spending by, 435
violence and, 557
vocational choice and, 447–448
in workforce, 240, 454
Blind controls, in research, 126–127, 606
Body. *See* Physical. . .
Body image
of adolescents, 27, 122–123
of adults, 27, 122, 222
of anorexics, 127
of parents, 222
self-image and, 128
Boys. *See* Males
Breasts
development, 98, 101, 118
size, 407
Bulimia, 125–127
Bull sessions, 470–471

California State University,
Los Angeles, 457
Calm, continuity and, 212
Care
ethic of, 69, 510–518
tending and, 378
Careers, 24, 223
counseling for, 448, 453, 457–459
family dual, 250–252
indecision about, 462–463
planning, 456
Carryover effects, research, 524–525, 609
Cars
spending on, 434–435, 437
See also Driving
Case studies, 318–319, 588–589
Castration anxiety, 73, 519–520
Centration, 155
Cephalocaudal direction, of growth, 120
Cervix, 105, 415, 417

Change
age changes in research and, 120–121, 596–597
continuity and, 27–28, 213–218
counselors as "change agents," 457–459
in family structures, 243–250
in parent-adolescent relationship, 210–218
self-esteem and, 367–368
turmoil and, 210–212
in values, 490–491
in work roles, 250
See also Physical changes; Transition
Cheating, 499–500
Childhood, 30–32, 34
abuse in, 543
arguing in, 192–193
autonomy and, 225–226
developmental tasks in, 37
egocentrism in, 155, 190, 196
emotions, 192
labor, 26
language and, 50, 155
memory in, 180–183
moral development and, 497–498, 503,
509–510, 519–521
prodigies, 188
rules, use of in, 64, 509–510
self-esteem and, 362
stepfamilies and, 248, 250
thinking in, 148–156
uni-age and, 34–35
vocational aspirations and, 443
Child labor laws, 26
Chinese Americans, 357
See also Asian Americans
Chlamydia, 414–415
Cigarettes, 560, 563–565
Circumcision, 107
female, 107
Class, social
abortion and, 411
black family, 240–241
delinquency and, 550, 552–553
eating disorders and, 127
social mobility system and, 330
timing of maturation and, 118–122
Classes, thought and, 156
Classical conditioning, 47
See also Respondent conditioning
Classification variables, 150, 595
Classroom
jigsaw, 326
See also Cooperative learning; Education
Climacteric, 222–223
Cliques, 271–274, 591
Clitoris, 105, 107
Clothing, 35, 433, 437
Cocaine, 561, 566–567
Coding
in research, 23, 221
See also Encoding
Cognitive development
college and, 465–467
cognitive maturity, 501
gender differences in, 467–472
imaginary audience and, 190
in late adolescence, 461–465

moral development and, 501, 503–510
Piaget's stage theory of, 61–64, 154–163
sexuality and, 130, 137–138
See also Intelligence; Knowledge
Cognitive restructuring, 460–461
Cohorts, in research, 30, 597
cohort differences, 172–173, 597
College
college preparatory track, 294–295
precollege programs, 457–459
thinking during, 465–472
See also Education
Commitment
to ethnic identity, 428–429
in identity, 341
identity status and, 344, 349
intimacy and, 372
to occupation, 444
in relativism, 467, 472
Communication
electronic, 34, 124, 306–309
See also Television
in family, 214–215, 136
multicultural education and, 328
with suicidal adolescents, 576, 579
See also Language
Communion, 374–375
Community standards, 497, 501–503
Competence
gender and, 326, 373–374
job, 326
parenting style and, 220
personal effectiveness and, 482–483
social, 259–261, 276–278, 499
Complexity, biological, 28
Compromise, 53
Compulsory education laws, 26
Computer-assisted instruction (CAI), 297,
316–317
Concentration, 570–571
Concrete operational thought, 63, 130, 156,
195–196, 508
Conditional response (CR), 47
Conditional stimulus (CS), 47
Conditioning, 501
operant, 47–48
See also Respondent conditioning
Condoms, 135–136, 424–427
Confidentiality, in research, 426–427, 530–531,
608
Confirmatory information, on stress, 536
Conflict
family, 127–128, 129, 213–218, 220, 233–234,
243–244, 249, 252, 285–286
with friends, 265
moral development and, 501, 511
resolving, 128, 303–304, 530–531, 536–537
about sexuality, 129, 137
See also Divorce
Conformity, 280–282
female surface, 469
morality and, 505, 513
Confounding, in research, 120–121, 458–459,
525, 592–593, 596–599, 604
Connectedness
gender differences and, 66–69, 82–83, 379, 510

individuality and, 229–234, 375–376
morality and, 510, 511
Conscience, 73, 501, 519
Conservation, 155
Constructive knowledge, 469, 472
Context, organismic theory and, 51
Continuity, 44, 45
 calm and, 212
 change and, 27–28, 213–218
Continuity-discontinuity issue, 44–45
Contraception, 135–136, 419, 424–425, 427
Control group, 110–111
Controls, research, 110–111, 126–127, 462, 588, 590–596, 606
Conventional moral reasoning, 501–503, 505, 508–510, 512
Conventional personality types, 447
 See also Conformity
Coping, 244–245, 329–330, 482, 529, 531–537
Correlational research, 150–151, 590, 595–596
Correlation coefficients, 150
Counseling
 career, 448, 453, 457–459
 peer, 139
 for stepfamilies, 249
 suicide, 579–580
Counselors, as change agents, 457–459
Counterbalancing, in research, 525
Cowper's glands, 105, 402
"Crabs," 418
Crack, 566–567
Creativity, 317, 479–481
Crime, 548, 549–552, 556
Crisis, 80–81, 338, 342, 492, 514
Crossed variables, in research, 462, 610
Cross-sectional designs, 172–173, 597–598
Crowds, 271–275, 591
Crushes, 279
Crystallized intelligence, 171–174
Cultural assimilation, 14–17
Cultural diversity, 11–17
 education and, 326–330, 474–476
 in heterosexual behavior, 133–134
 intelligence and, 164, 174–176
 knowledge and, 474–476
 sexual taboos, 408–409
 teenage pregnancy and, 130, 135, 137–138, 409–413
 See also Ethnic differences; Gender differences; Socioeconomic status
Cultural pluralism, 17, 361
Cultural systems, 12

Danger, perception of, 70–71
Dating, 278–280
 friends and, 265
 multiple, 279–280
 parents and, 223, 251, 278
 rape, 396–398
Death, 506–507
Decision-making, 220, 222, 226–229, 348–349, 482–483
 abortion, 409, 411–412
 career, 462–463
 divorced families and, 247

parenting style and, 220, 285, 481
 self-concepts and, 364
 sexual, 129–135, 140
 social-cognitive approach and, 443
 stepfamilies and, 249–250
Decline stage, vocational, 446
Deductive reasoning, 196–197
Degree of control, in research, 588, 590–596
Degrees of freedom, in research, 539, 607, 609–610
Delinquency, juvenile, 548–558
Demandingness, parenting style of, 221
Democratic parenting, 221
Dependence, drug, 560, 561, 568
Dependent variables, 111, 229, 594–595, 602
Depressants, 567
Depression, 569–571
 of bulimics, 127
 in divorced families, 244–245
 masked, 571
 schizophrenia and, 581
 suicide and, 575–576
Developmental psychology, 59, 382–383, 372–376, 402–407
 See also Cognitive development; Lifespan developmental perspective; Models; Research; Theories
Developmental stages. *See* Stages; Transition
Developmental tasks, 20–25, 36–39, 55
Deviance hypothesis, 119
Deviant behavior, 284–286, 499–501, 548–558
Dialectical reasoning, 462–463
Diet, 114, 124
Dieting, 124
Differentiation
 bias as, 606
 biological, 28
 object relations and, 405–406
 See also Cultural diversity; Gender differences; Individuation; Sex differences
Diffuse orientation, 348
Direct-effects models, 115
Direct observation, 221, 603
Disagreements
 family, 217, 233–234, 234–236, 281–282
 See also Conflict
Discipline, stepfamilies and, 248–250
Discrimination
 against minorities, 240–241, 327–328, 361
 sexual, 324–326, 470–471, 450–453
Diseases
 mental, 575–576, 580–582 (*see also* Depression)
 sexually transmitted, 130, 135, 414–427
Disposition stressors, 536
Distortion
 in families, 234
 in surveys, 589–590
Divorce, 223, 243–248
Dopamine, 581
Double-blind controls, in research, 127
Double standard, sexual, 395
Dragons, 5
Driving, drugs and, 562, 563, 564
Dropouts, high school, 313–317, 438–440, 455, 459
Drugs, 284–285, 558–569

AIDS and, 419–427, 568
 dependence on, 560, 561, 568
 for dysmenorrhea, 110–111
 gangs selling, 556
 suicide and, 576–578
Dual-earner families, 250–252, 389
Dualistic thinking, 465–466
Dysmenorrhea, 110–111
Dysthymia, 570

Eating disorders, 124–129
Economical research designs, 524, 609
Economics
 developmental tasks and, 24, 36–38
 gang, 556
 parents' middle age and, 223
 single parents and, 9, 246–248
 spending, 433–435
 stepfamilies and, 249
 See also Employment; Income; Poverty
Education, 291–333
 careers and, 24
 compulsory, 26
 dropouts' parents and, 313, 314
 generation gap and, 286–287
 for jobs, 448–450, 455–456
 laws about, 26–27
 menarche in, 110–111
 minority, 240–241, 294, 296, 326–330, 455–456, 458–459
 moral development and, 514
 parental involvement, 296–297, 298, 316
 postindustrial technology and, 33
 printing and, 32
 savings for, 434–435
 sex, 138–140
 thinking in, 200–205, 362, 363
 in urban centers, 32
 See also Achievement, academic; Schools
Education Consolidation and Improvement Act (1981), 317
Ego, 53, 73, 404, 406
 family and development of, 234–236
 identity formation and, 341, 429
 moral development and, 521
Egocentrism, 155, 194, 404–405
Ego-ideal, 73
Ejaculation, 19, 99, 112–113
Electronic technology, 34, 124, 297, 306–309, 316–317
Embeddedness, 378
Emergence, 62
Emotions, 229
 dating and, 265
 depressive, 244–245, 569–571
 eating disorders and, 128
 friends and, 256, 263–266
 of gifted, 321
 new, 192
 parents and, 24, 185–187, 406
 self-concept and, 361
 sexuality and, 137–138
 stress management of, 537
Empathy, 81–83
Employment, 448–457
 advancement opportunities, 452–453

Employment *continued*
changed roles in, 250–252
discrimination in, 240–241, 450–451
divorced families and, 247
dropouts and, 316, 438–440
female, 240–241, 250–252, 433, 450–452, 460–461
industrialization and, 26, 32
irrational beliefs and maladaptive myths about, 459–461
job availability, 448–450
minority, 240–241, 454–457, 460–461
part-time, 433–438
retirement from, 33–34, 36, 452
See also Careers; Labor
Encapsulations, 407
Encoding, 181–182, 403
Encounter, in ethnic identity formation, 357
Enculturation, 270
Endocrine system, 91, 92–96
Engineering courses, 456
Enmeshment, 128
Enrichment, academic, 321–322
Enterprising personality types, 446–448
Entertainment, spending on, 433–434
Environmental forces, 45, 49, 61, 442
See also Environmental theories
Environmental theories, 55–59, 61
models for, 44, 45–48, 50, 53–55
of personality, 403–404
Epididymis, 105
Epigenesis, 45
Epigenetic principle, 80
Epithelial cells, 107
Equilibration, 62
Erections, 107, 223, 404, 407
Error, research, 299
random, 404–405, 538–539, 606–607, 609–610
Establishment stage, vocational, 446
Estrogens, 93, 104, 109, 141, 223, 530
Ethic of care, 69, 510–518
Ethics
research, 426–427, 530–531, 607–608
See also Morality
Ethnic differences, 11–17
in delinquency, 551–552
dropout, 313–314
families and, 239–241
in friendship, 268–270
parenting styles and, 220–222
schools and, 292–293, 326–330
self-esteem and, 365–366
in sexual activity, 133–134
vocational choice and, 447–448
See also Ethnic identity; Minorities; Whites
Ethnic identity, 240–241, 356–361
Ethnic identity search, 359–361
Ethnicity
intergenerational conflict, 239
Evolution, 59–60
Excitement, sexual, 404
obesity and, 128–129
Exhaustion, 530
Exosystem, 330
Expectancies, 403

self-limiting, 454, 536
Expense, in matching, 405, 610
Experimental group, 110
Experiments, 110–111, 587, 593–595, 606
Experts, 472–476, 501
Exploitation, sexual abuse as, 545–548
Exploration stage, vocational, 445
Expressive mannerisms, 330
External validity, research, 217, 221, 405, 604–605, 610

Factorial designs, research, 462–463, 610
Failure, academic, 311–312, 320, 322–323
Fairy tales, 150–151
Fallopian tubes, 105
Families, 209–253
abuse in, 543–548
changing structures, 243–250
characteristics of, 9
communication in, 136–137, 139, 226–227, 580
conflict in, 128, 217, 231–236, 244–245, 247, 252, 281–282, 286
consensus-sensitive, 213–214
coordination, 213–214
creativity and, 480–481
of delinquents, 553, 554
of dropouts, 314
dual-earner, 250–252
eating disorders and, 128–129
environment-sensitive, 213–214
impact of, 205–207
individuation and, 221, 229–236
intimacy and, 369
minority, 239–241, 435
modeling in, 205–207
moral development and, 590
preparing for, 24
process in, 236
psychodynamic theories and, 76
roles, 35, 239, 241, 248–249, 250, 251
runaways' , 540–542
social interaction and, 205–207
step-, 243, 248–250, 545
structure, 243–250
suicide and, 574, 578, 580
supportive, 234, 235–236, 259
in transition, 243–252
types of, 213–214
See also Marriage; Parents; Siblings
Family paradigm, 236–239
Fantasy stage, vocational, 443–444
Fat, body, 109
fat spurt, 99
female, 99, 110, 124, 125
obesity, 128–129
Fathers
divorced, 244, 247–248
in dual-earner families, 251
self-esteem and, 365
sexual abuse by, 545
sexual information from, 110–111, 113
step-, 248, 249–250, 545
Fatigue, 571–572
Females, 5–6, 376

achievement by, 289, 311–313
autonomy and, 225
black, 361, 457
body image of, 120–121, 122–123
career counseling for, 453, 457–459
cognitive development by college, 467–472
contraception by, 136, 137–138
dating, 278–279
delinquent, 550–551
depression among, 570–571
deviant behavior, 285
dieting, 124
from divorced families, 248–249
double standard and, 395
drugs used by, 564, 565
dual-earner families and, 251
early and late maturing, 118–119
eating disorders, 125
employment of, 240–241, 250–252, 450–454, 460–461
femininity and, 137, 375, 388
friendships, 110, 112, 113, 264–265
future projections of, 23
head of household, 244, 245–247, 314
heterosexual behavior of, 132–135, 399, 402–403
Hispanic, 241, 220–222, 538–539
homosexuality and, 399–401
identity formation, 351–356
income of, 450
instrumentality in, 537
intelligence testing of, 176–179
interpersonal focus of, 67–70, 83–84, 373–374, 380–381
intimacy for, 373–374, 433
masturbation by, 131–132
menarche feelings of, 109–112
menopause, 222–223
moral development of, 510–518
Oedipal complex in, 73–74
organismic theories and, 64–70
parenting styles with, 221
personal effectiveness of, 483
physical development, 97, 102, 103
popularity, 275, 276
psychodynamic theories and, 73–74, 80–83
puberty, 18–19, 24, 28, 94–123 passim
reproductive system, 104–105
rules and, 64, 69
schizophrenic, 581
self-esteem of, 366–368
sexual abuse of, 545–548
sexual functioning and, 406–409
sexual response cycle, 403–406
sisters and menarche, 110
STDs and, 415, 417, 419
stress among, 538–539
suicide means, 579
in teaching materials, 324–326
values of, 491
vocational choice and, 444–445, 447–448
in workforce, 240–241, 250–252, 450–452
See also Mothers; Sex roles
Femininity, 137, 375, 388
See also Gender stereotypes
Fights, family, 217

Filipino Americans, 314
Flexibility, 483, 521
Fluid intelligence, 171–174
Follicle-stimulating hormone (FSH), 95, 105, 106–107, 109
Food, 114
Forgiveness, 524–525
Formal operational thought, 156–158, 162–163, 195–196, 201 passim
  experts and, 474
  moral reasoning and, 508
  personal effectiveness and, 483
Friends, 213, 255–289
  career planning with, 456
  continuity and, 418–419
  dating and, 278–279
  deviant behavior and, 284–286
  divorce and, 245, 247
  interracial, 268–270, 328
  menarche and, 110, 112, 113
  moral reasoning and, 505
  sexual information from, 138
  values and, 284
Frisbee, analysis of, 202–203

Games, 64, 69
Gangs, 555–556
Gender differences, 5–6, 376
  black families and, 240–241
  body image and, 122–123
  in delinquency, 550–551
  in depression, 570–571
  education and, 311–313, 324–326
  failure and, 311–312
  in friendship, 267–268
  future projections and, 23
  in heterosexual behavior, 132–133, 134–135
  in identity formation, 351–356
  in intellectual development, 467–472
  in intelligence tests, 176–179
  in intimacy, 370, 373–374
  in mathematics, 177–178, 312–313
  in moral development, 510–511, 515–520
  in observational skills, 151
  organismic theories and, 64–70
  in personal effectiveness, 483
  in physical development, 97–98, 100, 103
  psychodynamic theories and, 73–74, 80–84
  in schizophrenia, 581
  self-esteem and, 366–368
  vs. sex differences, 9–11
  in sexual information, 109–113
  sports and, 275–276
  in stress, 538–539
  in thinking, 467–472
  in timing of maturation, 117–119
  vocational choice and, 444–445, 447–448
  See also Females; Male bias; Males
Gender stereotypes, 10, 137, 251, 324–326, 386–389
  See also Sex roles
General adaptation syndrome (gas), 530
Generalizability, of observations, 588
Generalizations, in self-observation, 441
Generational differences
  generation gap, 286–287

in research, 599
Genital herpes, 414, 417
Genitals, 104–105, 105–108, 407
  See also Penis; Vagina
Genital stage, 53
Genital warts, 416
Germinal epithelial cells, 107
Giftedness, 317–322
Girls. *See* Females
Glands, 92, 95
Glans, 105, 107
Goals, 482–483
God, 521, 522
Gonadostat, 96
Gonadotropin-releasing hormone (GnRH), 95
Gonadotropins, 95, 99–101
Gonads, 95, 96
Gonorrhea, 414, 415–416, 418
Goodness, 512, 513
Gossip, 259, 260–261
Grades. *See* Achievement, academic
Grandparents, 36
Grieving, 506–507
Group identity, 356
  See also Ethnic identity
Group orientation, 329
Growth
  cephalocaudal direction of, 120
  of genitals, 107
  in puberty, 18–19, 28, 91–92, 99–103 passim, 113–114
Growth hormones, 102
Growth spurt, 19, 102–103
Growth stage, vocational, 445–446
Guns, 556, 578

Habituation, 49
Hair, 99
  facial, 97, 100
  pubic, 98, 99
  underarm, 99
Hallucinogens, 568
  See also Diseases; Physical changes
Heredity, 44, 175
Heroin, 568
Herpes, genital, 414, 477
Heterosexuality, 399, 400, 402, 403, 420
High school, 291–333
  climate, 298, 315
  dropouts, 313–315, 438–440, 455, 459
  drugs in, 560
  generation gap and, 286–287
  "input," 298
  "output," 298
  "process," 298
  size, 297, 315
  See also Education
Hispanics
  alcohol drinking, 561
  career counseling, 457
  delinquent, 551
  dropout, 313–314, 315
  ethnic identity, 366
  families, 241
  friendships, 270
  math tests, 307

parenting styles, 220, 222
  stress among, 538–539
  unemployment, 433, 434
  vocational choice and, 447–448
  in workforce, 457
Historical perspective
  in lifespan approach, 30
  psychohistorical approach, 78–79, 591
History, aging through, 30–36
History effects, in research, 459
HIV (human immunodeficiency virus), 419–427
Holding, 378
Homework, television and, 306–309
Homosexuality, 400–401, 402, 403, 420, 425
Hopelessness, suicide and, 576
Hormones
  anabolic steroid, 569
  in menstrual fluids, 110
  in puberty, 18, 28, 92–110 passim, 108–111, 115
  sex, 93–95, 97–103 passim, 108–110
Humor, 481
Hymen, 105, 409
Hypochondriasis, 571
Hypothalamus, 94–95, 96
Hypothetical thinking, 148, 152, 161

I-messages, 253
Id, 53, 73
Ideal
  date, 280
  self-images, 257–258
Identification, 340, 337–360, 378–380
Identity, 79–80, 191, 343–346
  achieved/foreclosed/diffused/moratorium, 344, 372, 382, 340–367 passim, 493–496
  body image and, 121
  ethnic, 356–361, 291, 359–361
  formation, 341, 351–352
  group, 344–346
  intimacy and, 371–372
  midlife and, 222–223
  occupation and, 351–352, 444
  relativism and, 466, 467
  self and, 341–381
  sexual, 400–401
  styles, 347–351
  unexamined/search/achieved ethnic, 359–361
  values and, 491–497
Ideology, 25, 351
Image. *See* Body image; Self-images
Imaginary audience, 190–191, 195–196
Imitation, 58–59
Immersion, in ethnic identity formation, 357
"Impression management," 259–260
Impulsiveness, suicide and, 576
Incentives, moral, 498–499
Incest, 545–548
Income
  academic tracking and, 294
  black family, 240–241
  delinquency and, 552–553
  of dropouts' families, 314–315, 455
  female, 450, 453–454
  single-parent family, 245–246, 314
  See also Poverty

Inconsistency, in parenting, 220
Independence, 24, 220, 225, 247
  See also Autonomy
Independent variable, 111, 150, 593–594,
  606–607, 609–610
Index offenses, 550
Indians. *See* Native Americans
Individualistic perspective, 69
Individuality, 32
  connectedness and, 229–304, 221, 375–376
  peers and, 280
Individual orientation, 329
Individuation, 225–236, 372–376, 372–381
  families and, 229–235, 375–376
  gender differences and, 83–84
Inductive reasoning, 196–197, 482
Industrialization, 26–27, 32
Industry, 80
Inert knowledge, 477–479
Infancy
  developmental tasks in, 37
  language and, 50–51
  reflection and, 61–62
  self-esteem and, 364–365
  sensorimotor thought of, 154–155
Inferiority, female, 74, 75, 76
Information
  job, 454
  sexual, *see* Sexual information
Information orientation, 348
Information processing, 179–183, 197
  control features, 179, 180
  structural features, 179–180
  See also Thinking
Inhalants, 569
Initiative, 80
Instrumentality, 504, 537
Instrument decay, in research, 475, 459
Integrity, 80
Intellectualization, 74–75
Intelligence, 146–147, 164–189
  age and, 169–174, 176, 184–185, 312
  componential, 183–185
  crystallized, 171–174
  defining, 164
  fluid, 171–174
  learning disability and, 322–324
  Piaget on, 61–64, 146, 154–163
  practical, 189
  primary abilities and, 170–171
  tests, 146, 163–179, 189, 299, 317
  See also Cognitive development; Knowledge
Intentions, considering, 497–498, 504, 521
Interaction
  interpersonal, *see* Interpersonal focus
  in research, 458–459
Internalization
  of ethnic identity, 357
  of standards, 497, 501, 503, 505, 519, 520–521
Internal validity, research, 217, 604–605, 606,
  609
Interpersonal focus
  of females, 67–70, 82–83, 373, 374, 381
  theories with, 58–59, 65–70, 77–84
  See also Connectedness; Social skills
Intervention programs

employment-related, 457–461
  suicide-related, 579–580
  See also Counseling
Interviewer bias, 22
Interviews, 22–23, 506–507, 589, 603
Intimacy, 80, 81, 340, 368–375
Intuition, 480
Invariant sequencing, in cognitive development,
  64
Investigative personality types, 447–448
Irony, 204–205
Isolation, 69

Japanese Americans, 174–175, 314
Jefferson County High School, Louisville,
  Kentucky, 316
Jigsaw classrooms, 326–328
Jobs. *See* Employment
Junior high, 292, 304–305
Justice, 26–27, 501–510, 515–517, 524–525
Juvenile delinquency, 548–556
Juvenile justice, 26–27

Kissing, 132
Knowledge, 469–479
  See also Education; Information processing;
    Sexual information
Knowledge-acquisition
  components, of intelligence, 184–185

Labia, outer, 107
Labia, inner, 107
Labor
  child, 26
  industrialization and, 26, 32
  See also Employment
Language
  in classroom, 325–326, 328
  male generic, 325–326
  Native Americans and, 241
  organismic theories and, 49
  sexist, 470–471
Latency stage, 53
Laws
  child labor, 26
  education, 26, 317
  equal employment, 455
  gun-control, 578
  juvenile justice, 26–27
  theoretical, 43, 45
"Leading crowd," 271, 276
Learning, 55
  cooperative, 296–297, 303, 304
  observational, 58–59, 441
  See also Education
Learning disabilities, 322–324
"Leave It to Beaver," 35
"Liaisons," 274
Libido, 53, 72–73, 519
Lice, pubic, 415, 418
Lifespan developmental perspective, 6–7, 27–30,
  445–446
  See also Developmental tasks
Life stages. *See* Stages
Liking, self, 369
Listening, active, 214

Literacy
  age and, 32, 34
  television and, 306–309
  See also Education
Literature courses, 196
Living arrangements
  developmental tasks and, 38–39
Logical-mathematical abilities, 187–188
  See also Logical thinking; Math
Logical thinking, 152–154, 158–163, 196, 197
Longitudinal designs, 120–121, 601
Long-term memory, 179–180, 181–183
Loss, 537–542, 506–507
Love, 390–395
LSD, 568
Luteinizing hormone (LH), 95, 106, 108, 109

Machine, environmental model and, 45–47
Macrosystem, 330
Magazines, dieting and, 124
Main effect, in research, 462, 610
Mainstreaming, 323–324
Maintenance stage, vocational, 446
Male bias, 75–76, 80–84, 376, 444
Male generic language, 325–326
Males, 5–6, 376
  achievement by, 311–313
  autonomy and, 225
  black, 23, 366, 457
  body image of, 120–121, 123
  climacteric in, 223
  cognitive development by college, 461–472
  condom use, 135–136
  delinquent, 550–551
  depression among, 570–571
  deviant behavior, 284–286
  dieting and, 124, 125
  from divorced families, 247, 248–249
  double standard and, 395
  drugs used by, 561, 563, 564
  early and late maturing, 117–118
  friendships of, 266–267
  future projections and, 23
  in gangs, 555
  gonorrhea and, 427
  heterosexual behavior of, 132–135
  Hispanic, 241, 538–539
  homosexuality and, 400–401
  identity formation, 378–380
  income of, 450
  instrumentality in, 537
  intelligence testing of, 176–179
  intimacy for, 573–574
  masculinity and, 374, 388
  masturbation by, 131–132
  moral development of, 510–511, 515–521
  Oedipal complex in, 73–74
  organismic theories and, 65–70
  parenting styles with, 221
  personal effectiveness of, 483
  physical development, 97–98, 101, 105–108
  popularity, 275–276
  psychodynamic theories and, 73–74, 80–83
  puberty, 18–19, 24, 28, 97–101 passim,
    103–107, 112–123 passim
  reproductive system, 105–107

rules and, 64, 68, 69
schizophrenic, 580–581
self-esteem of, 365–368
sexual abuse by, 545–548
sexual functioning and, 406–409
sexual pressure on, 140
sexual response cycle, 328
stress among, 538–539
suicide means, 578
in teaching materials, 324–326
unemployment, 460
values of, 491
vocational choice and, 444, 447–478
in workforce, 450–452
See also Fathers; Sex roles
Manipulation, of research variables, 111
Marijuana, 284, 559–560, 564–565, 568
Marriage, 24, 35, 248–250, 278, 409
See also Divorce
Masculinity, 137, 375, 388
See also Gender stereotypes
Masochism, 74, 76
Masturbation, 131–132
Matching, in research, 404–405, 609–610
Mathematical abilities, 187–188, 196, 197
gender differences in, 176–178, 312
international comparisons, 307–308
minorities and, 307, 455–456
Maturation, in research, 459
Early vs late, 116–122, 123
See also Asynchrony
Maturity, 380–381
cognitive, 501
Meaning, metaphors and, 204–205
Media
age portrayals in, 35
on beauty, 124
electronic, 34, 124, 306–309
schools and, 296
values in, 287
violence and, 302, 557
Mediated-effects models, 115–116
Melting pot, 6, 12
Memorization, 476
Memory, 179–183
Men. *See* Males
Menarche, 102, 105, 107–113, 116, 123
Menopause, 222
Menstruation, 18–19, 28, 97, 98
dysmenorrhea with, 110–111
first (menarche), 102, 105,
107–113, 123
intercourse during, 408–409
Mental illness, 575–576, 580–582
See also Depression
Mental operations, 156
See also Thinking
Mescaline, 568
Mesosystem, 330
Metacomponents, of intelligence, 183–185
Metamemory, 183
Metaphors, 204–205
Mexican Americans, 241, 270, 538–539
Microsystem, 330
Middle class
abortion, 411

black family, 240–241
delinquent, 552–553
eating disorders, 125, 128
timing of maturation and, 118, 122
Middle school, 304
Midlife, 33, 36–38, 222–223, 251
Minorities, 11–17
abortion and, 409–413
career counseling for, 458–459
cultural knowledge, 474–476
defined, 11–12
discrimination against, 241, 327–328, 360, 413
dropout, 313–314, 438–439
education and, 241, 294, 296, 326–331,
454–457, 458–459
employment of, 241, 454–457, 459–461
ethnic identity of, 356–361
families, 239–243, 435–436, 437
intelligence tests and, 176
interracial friendships with, 268–270, 328
math abilities, 307, 455–456
self-esteem and, 365–366
sexual activity and, 133–134
socialization, 13, 14–17, 239–241
stress among, 538–539
teenage pregnancy and, 409–413
unemployment, 433, 435
vocational choice and, 447–448
See also Asian Americans; Blacks; Ethnic differences; Hispanics; Native Americans
Modeling, 499
family, 234–235, 242
Models, 41, 42–55
defined, 42–43
direct-effects, 115
environmental, 44, 45–48, 50, 53–55
mediated-effects, 115–116
psychodynamic, 45, 51–55
See also Theories
Monogamy
AIDS and, 426
serial, 134–135, 418
Mood, 569
Morality, 25–26, 53, 497–521
cognitive development and, 64
as ethic of care, 510–518
gender differences in, 69, 84
as justice, 501–510, 515–517
sexual, 129, 137
superego and, 518–521
See also Values
Moratorium, 344–345, 340–356 passim, 374,
495–496
Morphine, 568
Mothers
adolescent, 409–410, 438
autonomy and, 225
divorced, 243–244, 245–250
dropout, 438
in dual-earner families, 250–251
ego development, 236
employed, 250–252
menarche, 110–111, 113
psychodynamic theories and, 81
sexual information from, 138
step-, 249

Motivation, gender differences in, 311–313
Multicultural perspective, 327–328
Mutuality, 235
connectedness and, 232, 238
of understanding, 194–196
relatedness and, 378
Myotonia, 403–405

Naming, children, 30–32
Narcotics, 556, 568
Native Americans
dropout, 313–314
Erikson and, 78–79
families, 241
self-esteem of, 365–366
Naturalistic observations, 274, 588,
590–591
Nature-nurture controversy, 44, 45, 48
Negative reinforcement, 48, 57
Neglect, 543–544
Neighborhood, interracial friendship and,
268–270
Neurotransmitters, brain, 578
Nicotine, 564
Nocturnal emission ("wet dream"), 112–113
Nonoxynol-9, 425
Normative orientation, 348
No-treatment control, in research, 462
Nurse cells, 28, 107
Nutrition, 113–114

Obedience, 503–504
Obesity, 128–129
Objectivity, of observations, 590
Object permanence, 154
Objects, thought and, 156
Observational learning, 58–59, 441
Observations
direct, 221, 605
naturalistic, 274, 588, 590–591
research, 151, 221, 588, 590–591, 602
self-, 151, 441
Occupation
choosing, 440–448
females', 452–454
identity formation and, 351–352, 444–445
See also Careers; Work
Oedipal complex, 52, 73–74, 76, 212, 519, 520,
521
Old age, 33–34
One-group pretest-posttest design, 458–459
Open-mindedness, 479, 480–481, 508
Operant conditioning, 47–48, 441, 442
Operationalizing concepts, in research, 348–349,
605
Opium, 568
Oral sex, 132
Oral stage, 53
Order effects, research, 525, 609
Organismic theories, 45, 48–51, 55, 59–70
of moral development, 501
Organized activity, theories on, 49–50, 62
Orgasm, 19, 106, 223, 405, 406
multiple, 405
need for, 408
Orgasmic platform, 405, 408

Others
  caring for, 512, 513–514
  intimacy with, 371–372
  perception of, 151
  responsibility to, 66–67
  self with, 66–67, 337–381
  understanding, 194–196
Ova, 28, 104–105, 106–107
Ovaries, 104
Overprotection, 128
Ovulation, 109

Pairs, research, 405, 609–610
Parents, 24, 210–223
  abortion and, 411
  abuse by, 543–544
  authoritarian, 218–222, 285, 330, 481
  authoritative, 218–225, 281–282, 285, 364, 481
  autonomy and, 212, 218, 225, 229
  bodily images of, 27, 222
  career planning with, 456
  communication with, 136–137, 139, 580
  conformity and, 280, 281–282
  coping strategies from, 530–531
  creativity and, 480–481
  dating and, 218, 223, 278
  of delinquents, 550, 551
  democratic, 221
  developmental tasks of, 36–38
  deviant behavior and, 285
  divorced, 243–250
  dropouts and, 314, 315, 440
  eating disorders and, 127
  ego development, 234–235
  employment, 250–252
  generation gap and, 286–287
  grand-, 36, 38
  identity consolidation and, 340–341
  individuation and, 121, 136, 225–228, 230–239 passim
  joys of parenting adolescents, 230–231
  media images of, 35
  middle-aged, 222–223
  minority, 240–241, 455
  obesity and, 128–129
  Oedipal complex and, 73–74, 212
  parenting styles, 218–224, 221
  permissive (laissez-faire), 218–222, 285, 481
  puberty changes and, 110–112
  racial socialization by, 14, 15
  reinforcement and, 57
  self-esteem and, 222, 251, 259, 362–363
  sexual decision making and, 35
  sexual information from, 136–137, 138, 139, 407
  single, 9, 242, 244, 245–248
  step-, 248–250, 545
  styles of, 218–222, 281–282, 286, 329–330, 481
  suicide and, 575, 580
  support from, 235, 282
  values and, 284, 442, 491, 498
  See also Fathers; Mothers
Passionate experience, 378, 379–380
Passive coping styles, 329–330

Path analysis, 370–371, 602
Patriarchy, family, 241
Peers, 271–287
  abortion and, 411
  adolescents and parents and, 280–287
  body image and, 123
  deviant behavior and, 284–286
  drugs and, 560
  gossiping and, 259–261
  interactions, 267–268
  moral development and, 505–506, 522
  peer pressure, 282–286, 560
  sexual information from, 139
  of suicidal adolescents, 579–580
  values and, 282–284
  See also Friends
Pelvic inflammatory disease (PID), 415
Penis, 105, 107, 404–405
  changes in puberty, 99, 100, 107
  penis envy, 73–74, 76, 519
  size of, 407
  See also Erections
Pension plans, 33
Perception, 48, 50–51
  of others, 151
  of stress, 532–533
Performance components, of intelligence, 184–185
Performance orientation, 310–312
Permeability, connectedness and, 230, 232
Permissive (laissez-faire) parenting, 218–222, 285, 481
Personal effectiveness, 482–485
Personal expressiveness, 346
Personal fable, 189–192, 579
Personal focus
  theories with, 56–57, 61–64, 75–77
  See also Self
Personality
  age and, 445–446
  cheating and, 500
  dating and, 279–280
  friends and, 266–267
  healthy, 77–79
  popularity and, 275
  suicide and, 576
  theory, 377
  three facets of, 53, 71
  timing of maturation and, 116–122
  vocational choice and types of, 446–448
  as whole, 75–77
Petting, 132
Phallic stage, 53
Physical attractiveness
  dieting and, 124
  grades and, 299
  popularity and, 275–276
  self-esteem and, 365
Physical changes, 27, 97–113
  continuity of self and, 363
  from drugs, 562–571 passim
  of parents, 27
  of puberty, 17–19, 21, 24, 97–103, 115–123
  sexual behavior and, 400
  See also Body image; Growth

Physical dependence, on drugs, 560, 561, 567, 568
Physical sexual functioning, 403–409
Physical superiority, of gifted, 320
Pituitary, 94–95, 96
Placebo, 111, 127
Plateau, sexual, 404–405, 407
Pleasure capacity, sexual, 407–408
Pluralism, cultural, 7, 17, 360
Political stance, identity and, 351–352, 355
Popularity, 275–278
Population
  adolescent, 7, 239, 240, 241
  aging, 30
  AIDS, 424
  high school graduate, 291–292, 293
  minority, 11, 239, 240, 360
  old, 33–34
  pyramids, 7, 8, 9
  in research, 258, 605
  runaway, 540–542, 543
  rural/urban, 32–33
  teenage abortion, 411
  teenage mothers keeping babies, 409–410
Positive reinforcement, 48, 57
Positive thinking, 309–311
Postconventional moral reasoning, 502, 503, 505–507, 508–509, 522, 525
Poverty
  abortion and, 411
  delinquency and, 552–553
  minority, 240–241, 455
  single parents and, 9, 246
Practical intelligence, 189
Preadolescence, 236–261, 263
Preconventional moral reasoning, 503–505, 508–510, 512, 525
Prediction
  stress and, 535–536
  in thinking, 482
Pre-encounter, in ethnic identity formation, 357
Pregnancy
  AIDS and, 420
  contraception, 135–138, 411–413
  ectopic, 415
  smoking during, 564
Preoperational thought, 155
Prepuce, 105, 107
Preschoolers, language, 48–49
President's Science Advisory Committee, 25
Primary sex characteristics, 97
Printing press invention, 32, 34
Proactive inhibition, 470–471
Probabilities, thinking of, 482
Probes, 22, 180
Problem solving, 348–349, 477, 479
Procedural knowledge, 468, 469–472
Process
  family, 236
  of identity formation, 356
  in relationships, 276, 278
  school, 299
Prodigies, 188
Projective measures, 70–71, 603
Prolactin, 107
Prostaglandins, 109

Prostate gland, 106
Pseudostupidity, 189–190
Psychoactive drugs, 560
Psychoanalytic theories, 212
    models for, 45, 51–55
    of morality, 518
Psychohistorical approach, 78–79, 588
Psychological definition, of adolescence, 21–24
Psychological impact
    of divorce, 243–245, 245–248
    of puberty, 115–123
    See also Personality
Psychological perspective, in lifespan approach,
    28–29
Psychology. *See* Developmental psychology; Person-
    ality; Psycho. . .
Psychometric approach, 146, 179
Psychosocial circumstances, suicide and, 578
Psychosocial crises, 492–493
Psychosocial stages, of development, 80
Puberty, 17–19, 20, 21, 28, 91–104
    depression and, 569–571
    friendship, 267–268
    gifted and, 321
    identity and, 351
    physical changes of, 17–19, 20, 21, 97–103,
        115–124
    psychological impact of, 115–124
    school type and, 306
    self-esteem and, 367–368
    timing of, 94–96, 116–118
Pubic lice, 414, 415
Punishment
    abusive, 543–544
    internalizing standards and, 497
    juvenile justice, 550–552

Quaaludes, 567
Qualitative differences, in cognitive development,
    63
Quasi-experimental designs, 458–459, 588,
    591–593, 606
Questionnaires, 22, 508–509, 589, 603
Questions
    closed-ended, 507
    open-ended, 507

Race. *See* Ethnic differences; Minorities; Whites
Random assignment, 111, 593–595, 600–601
Random error, 404–405, 539, 607–608, 609–610
Rape, 396–397
Rapport, 22
Realistic personality types, 446–448
Realistic stage, vocational, 443–444
Reality, appearance vs., 197
Reasoning
    deductive, 197, 198–199, 482
    about forgiveness, 525
    inductive, 196–197, 482
    moral, 501–510, 512–513, 518, 522, 525
Rebellion, parenting style and, 220
Reductionism, 44–46
Reinforcement, 56
Reflection
    self-, 194, 361, 362, 480
Reflective abstraction, 62

Refractory period, sexual, 406
Rehearsal, memory and, 180
Reinforcement, 48, 56–57, 270, 521
Rejection, 234, 259–261
Relatedness, 355, 377–381
Relationship, 380–381, 530–531
    See also Connectedness; Interpersonal focus
Relativism, 466–467, 469, 472
Reliability, research, 221, 349, 602
Religion, 521–526
Remarriage, 248–250
Representativeness, in sampling, 258
Repression, 72
Reproductive system
    female, 104–105
    male, 105–108
    midlife, 222
    See also Pregnancy
Research, 506, 587–612
    on abstract thinking, 150–151
    on adolescent expectations, 22–23
    on adolescent sexuality, 403
    on AIDS prevention, 426–427
    on body image, 120–121
    on career indecision, 462–463
    on cliques and crowds, 274, 591–592
    on danger perception, 70–71
    on date rape, 396–397
    on death, 506–507
    on dysmenorrhea treatment, 110–111
    on eating disorders, 126–127
    on emotions, 258
    on fairy tales, 150–151
    on family fights, 217
    on gifted, 321–322
    on identity status, 351–356
    on intelligence, 172–173
    on intimacy, 370–371
    on minority education, 458–459
    on parenting styles, 221
    on problem solving, 348–349
    on racial socialization, 14–15
    on relationship difficulties, 530–531
    on sexist language, 470–471
    on sexual initiation, 404–405
    on Sioux, 78–79
    on stress, 538–539
Resolution
    conflict, 530–531
    sexual, 406
Respondent conditioning, 47
Response measures, research, 603
Responsibility
    autonomy and, 225, 245–248
    morality and, 498–499, 511, 512, 513
    to self and others, 66–67
    social, 26
Responsive parenting style, 221
Restrained mannerisms, 330
Retirement, 33–34, 36, 452
Reversibility, 155
Rewards, 498
    See also Reinforcement
Rigidity, family, 128
Rituals, in stepfamilies, 250
Role clarity, 248–249, 250

Roles, 28–29, 35, 278–279, 351
    family, 35, 240–241, 242, 248–249, 250, 251
    work, 250–252, 351
    See also Sex roles
Romance, *See also* Love
Rorschach inkblot test, 603
Rules
    age and, 64
    creativity and, 479–480, 481
    gender differences and, 64, 68, 69
    identity foreclosure and, 494
    moral reasoning and, 508–510
Runaways, 540–542, 548

Sampling, research, 258, 605–606
Sarcasm and satire, 205
Savings, 434–435
Scatterplots, 150
Schemes, 155
Schizophrenia, 575, 580–582
Schools
    college, 461–472
    junior high, 292, 304
    middle, 304
    sex education in, 138–139
    See also Education; High school Science courses,
        196, 197, 200–204, 455–456
Scrotum, 108
Secondary school. *See* High school
Secondary sex characteristics, 20–21, 97
Secular trend, 113–114, 267
Self
    caring for, 511, 513–514
    conformity and, 281–282
    identity and, 361–368
    intimacy with, 369–370
    multifaceted, 342–351
    organismic theories and, 66–67, 68–69
    with others, 66–67, 337–381
    responsibility to, 66–67
    sense of, 224–243, 340, 356
    See also Identity; Individuality; Self. . .
Self-acceptance, 369
Self-assertion, 230, 232
Self-awareness, 233, 364, 369
Self-concepts, 243, 361–363, 445–446
    See also Self-esteem; Self-images
Self-control, of delinquents, 554
Self-defeating beliefs/interpretations, 443, 536,
    570
Self-disclosure
    in friendships, 259, 261–263, 264–265, 266,
        267
    intimacy and, 371–372
Self-esteem, 363–368
    of blacks, 240–241
    body image and, 122–123
    of bulimics, 125
    cheating and, 499–500
    of delinquents, 554
    depression and, 569–571
    divorce and, 244
    foreclosed identity and, 495
    friends and, 257–259
    instrumentality and, 537
    obesity and, 128

Self-esteem *continued*
  parents and, 218, 220, 259, 364–365
Self-images, 365
  body image and, 128
  ideal, 256–257
  See also Self-esteem
Selfishness, 512, 513
Self-limiting expectations, 454
Self-observation, 151, 441
Self-reflection, 195, 362
Self-reports, research, 23, 506–507, 589–592, 603
Semen, 106
Seminal vesicles, 107
Sensitivity, research, 299, 405, 603, 609, 610
Sensitizing subjects, research, 610
Sensorimotor thought, 154–155
Sensory memory, 179–180
Separateness, 374–380
  conformity and, 280–281
  gender differences and, 65–66, 70, 78–79, 80, 511
  individuality and, 230–231, 232, 234
  morality and, 511
Sequential designs, 172–173, 599–602
Serial search 180
Serotonin, 578
Sertoli cells, 28, 107
Sex differences, 18–19
  in friendship, 267–268
  vs. gender differences, 9–11
  in identity formation, 351–356
  in moral thought, 26
  organismic theories on, 64–70
  See also Females; Males; Sex roles
Sex flush, 404–405
Sex glands, 95
Sex hormones, 93–96, 102, 106–107, 108–112, 223 passim
Sexism, 324–326, 450–453, 470–471
Sex organs. *See* Genitals
Sex roles, 21–23, 129–130, 386–389
  correlational research on, 595–596
  depression and, 508–509, 570–571
  employment and, 240–241, 250–251, 454, 460
  minority, 240–241
  in teaching materials, 324–325
Sex segregation, in workforce, 450–451, 452–454
Sexual abuse, 542, 545–548
Sexual attitudes
  parents and, 130–131
Sexual attraction
  biological factors in, 401–402
  psychological factors in, 403
Sexual desires
  Freud on, 74, 519
  See also Oedipal complex
Sexual dimorphism, 19, 92
Sexual functioning, 403–409
Sexual information, 138–140
  age of access to, 35
  AIDS and, 422–423, 425, 426–427
  about contraception, 130, 136–137, 138–140, 413, 426–427
  decision making and, 129–130
  gender differences in, 110–113

about sexual functioning, 406–409
  teenage pregnancies and, 412–413
Sexual intercourse, 403–409
  abuse, 547
  age of, 132–135, 244
  decision making about, 129–135 passim
  first, 132–135, 244
  oral, 132
  premarital, 133
  taboos, 408–409
Sexuality, 24, 385–427
  of delinquents, 55
  heterosexuality, 399–400, 402
    AIDS and, 420–423, 425
  homosexuality, 399–403
    AIDS and, 420, 423, 424
  middle age and, 222–223
Sexually transmitted diseases (STDs), 414–427
Sexual orientation, 398–400
Sexual attraction, 399–403
Sexual response cycle, 403–406
Shaft, 105–107
Shoplifting, 500–501
Short-term memory, 179–181
Siblings, 242–243
  of dropouts, 314
  menarche and, 110
  sexual activity and, 404–405
  step-, 248–250
Single adults, 24
Single-blind controls, in research, 127
Sioux, 78–79
Sisters, menarche and, 110
Situational stressors, 586
Skepticism, 193
Smegma, 107
Smoking, 284, 563–564
Social accord, 505
Social and conventional system, of understanding, 195
Social-cognitive theories, 59, 441–443, 460–461, 497–501, 519, 520–521
Social competence, 259–261, 276–278
  friends and, 277–278
Social contract, 505–506
Social desirability, 22
Social-informational level, of understanding, 194
Social injustices, to gifted, 320
Socialization
  double standard and, 395
  minority, 13, 14–17, 239–241
  moral development and, 510
  peer group and, 271–272, 278
Social mobility system, 331
Social personality types, 447
Social responsibility, 25
Social roles. *See* Roles
Social skills
  of delinquents, 556
  of learning-disabled, 323
  peer group and, 271, 276–278
  runaways', 542
Social systems, 12
Social understanding, 194–196
Socioeconomic status

abortion and, 411–413
  of dropouts, 314
  runaway, 542
  self-esteem and, 365
  timing of maturation and, 118, 122
  See also Class, social; Income
Sociological definition, of adolescence, 26–27
Sociological perspective, in lifespan approach, 29
Special education classes, 324
Special education consultants, 323–324
Specialization, vocational, 444
Spending patterns, 433–435
Sperm, 105–108
Sperm cells, 28, 107
Spermarche, 108, 112–113
  See also Nocturnal emission
Spermicide, 425
Sphinx, 30
Spontaneity, 53, 480, 481
Sports, 35, 275–276
Stages
  of AIDS, 420–421
  clique/crowd, 272–274
  of cognitive development (Piaget), 62–63, 154–163
  of ethnic identity development, 357–360
  of heterosexual behavior, 132–133
  of moral development, 501–510
  organismic, 50
  psychodynamic, 53, 73–75
  psychosocial (Erikson), 80, 81
  of syphilis, 417–418
  uni-age and, 34–36
  vocational, 443–444, 445–446
  See also Transition
Stage termination hypothesis, 119
Standards
  community, 497, 503
  double, 395
  internalizing, 497, 502, 505, 519, 520–521
  See also Morality; Values
Statistical regression, in research, 459
Status offenses, 550, 552–553
Status, social
  gender differences and, 11
  minority, 12
  timing of maturation, 116–122
  See also Socioeconomic status
Step-families, 243, 248–250, 545
Stereotypes
  ethnic, 366
  gender, 9, 137, 251, 324–326, 386–389
  "perfect" body, 24
Steroids, anabolic, 569
Stimulants, 565–567
Stimulus freedom, 480
Stress, 529–537
  confirmatory information and, 536
  coping with, 529, 532–537
  divorce and, 244–245
  of dropouts' families, 314
  parents' middle age and, 222–223
  personal effectiveness and, 482–483
Stress-inoculation training, 535–537
Strong-Campbell Interest Inventory, 447
Structural analytical thinking, 461–465, 472, 480

Students Against Driving Drunk, 562–563
Study skills, 204
Subjective knowledge, 469
Subjects, research
 confidentiality for, 426, 530–531, 608
 debriefed, 426, 608
 dignity and welfare of, 426, 530, 608
 experimental and control groups of, 110–111
 number of, 405, 588–590, 607, 609
 protected from physical or psychological distress, 426, 608
 random assignment of, 111, 593–595
 sensitizing, 610
 subject mortality, 121, 604
 voluntary, 426, 530, 608
Substance use
 divorce and, 244
 suicide and, 578–580
 See also Drugs
Suicide, 542, 573–582
 prevention programs, 581–582
Superego, 53, 73–75, 519–521
Support
 divorce and, 245
 families and, 220, 234–236, 259, 282
 from friends, 265
 groups for, 249
 from peer group, 271
Surveys, 22–23, 506–507, 589–592
Survival, 511
Symbols, 155
Symptomatic carriers, 421
Syphilis, 414, 417–418
Systematic differences, in research, 111, 593

Task orientation, 310–312
Tasks, developmental, 20–26, 36–38, 55
Technology, 30–32, 33, 35
 computer, 297, 316–317
Telegraphy, 34
Television, 34, 124, 306–309
Tentative stage, vocational, 443–444
Testes, 101, 105–108
Testing effects, in research, 459
Testosterone, 101, 106
Test-retest reliability, 349
Tests
 intelligence, 163–174, 187–189, 299, 317
 math, 312–313
 Rorschach inkblot, 603
 Thematic Apperception, 70–71, 603
Tests of significance, in research, 530–531, 606–607
Thematic Apperception Test (TAT), 70–71, 603
Theories, 41–55, 374–381
 defined, 43–45
 Holland on, 447
 organismic, 45, 48–51, 53, 54, 59–70, 501
 personality, 374

social-cognitive, 59, 441–443, 460–461, 497–501, 519, 520
 See also Environmental theories; Psychodynamic theories; Stages; Theory-guided research, 470–471, 605
Thinking, 148–163, 189–205 passim, 213, 461–472 passim
 concrete, 156, 194, 508
 deductive reasoning, 197, 198, 199, 482
 inductive reasoning, 196–197, 482
 as problem solving, 478, 479
 structural analytical, 461–465, 472, 480
 See also Cognitive development; Formal operational thought; Intelligence
Time consumption, by research, 221, 405, 610
Times of measurement, in research, 120, 172–173, 596, 599
Timing
 of abortions, 411–412
 of parents' middle age, 222–223
 of puberty, 94–96, 116–122
Tracking, academic, 293–297, 314, 455
Training
 job, 450
 See also Education
Tranquilizers, 568
Transition
 adolescence as, 38, 60
 from conformity to choice, 513
 families in, 243–252
 from selfishness to responsibility, 512
 values in, 490–526
Trauma, creativity and, 481
Truancy, 550
Trust
 in friendships, 260, 264
 intimacy and, 371–372
 psychosocial crisis of, 80
 self-esteem and, 364
Turmoil, change and, 210–212
Twins, 44

Unconditional forgiveness, 524–525
Unconditional response (UCR), 47, 84
Unconditional stimulus (UCS), 47, 84
Unconscious, 71–72
Understanding, 194–196, 228
Unemployment, youth, 433, 434, 439, 457
Unexamined ethnic identity, 359–360
Uni-age, 34–36
Unisex, 34–36
Universality, 63, 507
Urban centers
 industrialization and, 32
 poverty in schools of, 455
Urethra, 107
Uterus, 104, 105

Vagina, 104, 105, 404–405
Vaginal lubrication, 404
Validation, personal, 235
 eye-to-eye, 378, 379
Validity (research), 299, 602–603
 construct, 349
 external, 217, 221, 405, 604–605, 610
 internal, 217, 604–605, 606, 608
Values, 7, 36, 287, 490–526
 ethnic identity and, 359
 peer pressure and, 282–284
 questioning, 498, 505–506, 521
 vocational choice and, 443
 See also Beliefs; Cultural diversity; Morality
Vas deferens, 105
Vasocongestion, 403–406, 408
Violence
 abusive, 543–544
 criminal, 549, 553
 gender and, 68–69
 school, 300–303
 youth and, 556–558
Virginity, 409
Vocation
 choosing, 440–448
 See also Careers; Occupation
Vocational Preference Inventory, 447
Vocational track, 294
Voice change, 99, 101

WAIS-R, 164–170, 174
Warts, genital, 416–417
Wechsler Adult Intelligence Scale (WAIS), 164–170
Whites, 11–12
 abortion and, 411
 alcohol drinking, 561
 delinquent, 551–552
 dropout, 438
 ethnic identity and, 360–361
 interracial friendship, 268–269
 math and science and, 456
 sexual activity of, 133–134
 spending, 435
 unemployment, 433, 434
 vocational choice and, 447–448
Within-subjects design, research, 524–525, 609
Women. *See* Females
Work
 roles, 250–252, 351
 See also Employment; Vocation
Working class, 26, 32–33
 black family, 241
 timing of maturation and, 118, 122
Work-study programs, 316

You-messages, 214–215
Youth, 33
 See also Adolescence

PHOTO CREDITS

Chapter 1

CO, © Skjold Photos; page 6, © David Toy; page 10, © Elizabeth Crews; page 16, © Joel Gordon; page 18, © David Madison 1992; page 21, © Jim West/Impact Visuals; page 25, © Barbara Rios/Photo Researchers, Inc.; page 29, © Stock, Boston; page 31, © The Bettmann Archive; page 38, © Elizabeth Crews.

Chapter 2

CO, © Roberta Hershenson; page 44, © David Toy; page 52, © Jonathan A. Meyers/JAM Photography; page 54, Jonathan A. Meyers/JAM Photography; page 56, © Ken Heyman/Woodfin Camp & Associates; page 58, © Skjold Photos; page 68, Courtesy Carol Gilligan; page 72, © The Bettmann Archive; page 75, © UPI/The Bettmann Archive; page 77, © UPI/The Bettmann Archive; page 82, Courtesy Nancy Chodorow; page 83, © John Ficara/Woodfin Camp & Associates.

Chapter 3

CO, © Craig Aurness/Woodfin Camp & Associates; page 98, © Gale Zucker/Stock, Boston; page 100, © Joan Liftin/Actuality, Inc.; page 102, left and right, © Lynne Jaeger Weinstein/Woodfin Camp & Associates; page 112, Courtesy Christine DeVault; page 117, © Elizabeth Crews; page 122, © Dagmar Fabricius/Stock, Boston; page 125, © William Thompson/The Picture Cube; page 134, © Lawrence Migdale/Stock, Boston; page 140, © Laima Druskis.

Chapter 4

CO, © Elizabeth Crews; page 147, © Nita Winter; page 153, © Comstock; page 157, © Will & Demi McIntyre/Photo Researchers, Inc.; page 159, © Suzanne Arms; page 163, © Suzanne Arms; page 168, © Elizabeth Crews; page 175, © Tony Stone Images/Marleen Ferguson; page 178, © Elizabeth Crews; page 182, © Elizabeth Crews; page 186, top, © Skjold Photos; page 186, bottom, © Richard Hutchings/PhotoEdit; page 187, © Elizabeth Crews; page 191, © Suzanne Arms; page 193, © Billy Barnes/Jeroboam; page 201, © Paul Conklin/PhotoEdit.

Chapter 5

CO, © Alan Carey/Photo Researchers, Inc.; page 211, top, © Alan Hutchings/Photo Researchers, Inc.; page 211, bottom, © Jane Scherr/Jeroboam; page 219, © Skjold Photos; page 224, © Jeffry W. Myers/Stock, Boston; page 228, © Suzanne Arms; page 233, © Michael Weisbrot/Stock, Boston; page 240, © Frank Siteman/Jeroboam; page 242, © Skjold Photos; page 246, © Suzanne Arms/Jeroboam.

Chapter 6

CO, © Polly Brown/Actuality, Inc.; page 257, © Skjold Photos; page 260, Suzanne Arms; page 262, © Rhoda Sidney/PhotoEdit; page 265, © Bob Daemmrich/The Image Works; page 266, © Skjold Photos; page 269, © CLEO Photo/Jeroboam; page 272, © Rhoda Sidney/PhotoEdit; page 277, © CLEO Photo/Jeroboam; page 279, © Suzanne Goldstein/Photo Researchers, Inc.; page 282, © Skjold Photos; page 283, © Elizabeth Crews.

Chapter 7

CO, © Suzanne Arms; page 295, © Elizabeth Crews; page 300, © Skjold Photos; page 303, Courtesy of Professor Albert Bandura; page 305, © PhotoEdit; page 310, © Frost Publishing Group; page 321, © Suzanne Arms/Jeroboam, Inc.; page 325, © Suzanne Arms; page 327, © Jeffry W. Myers/Stock, Boston; page 329, © Elizabeth Crews.

Chapter 8

CO, © Mary Kate Denny/PhotoEdit; page 339, © Suzanne Arms; page 341, © Bob Daemmrich/The Image Works; page 343, © Comstock; page 345, © Robert V. Eckert, Jr./The Picture Cube; page 347, © Elaine Rebman/Photo Researchers, Inc.; page 350, © Comstock; page 353, © Jonathan A. Meyers/JAM Photography; page 358, © Joel Gordon; page 363, © Sam Forencich; page 366, © Hiroji Kubota/Magnum Photos; page 372, © Joan Liftin/Actuality, Inc.; page 373, © Jim Weiner/Photo Researchers, Inc.; page 380, © Skjold Photos; page 381, © Brian Palmer/Impact Visuals.

Chapter 9

CO, © The Picture Cube; page 389, © Elizabeth Crews; page 401, © Tom McKitterick/Impact Visuals; page 408, © Joan Liftin/Actuality, Inc.; page 410, left, © Katherine McGlynn/The Image Works, right, © Children's Defense Fund; page 424, © Roger Mastroianni.

Chapter 10

CO, © Miro Vintoniv/Stock, Boston; page 436, © Audrey Gottlieb/Monkmeyer Press; page 439, © Joel Gordon; page 442, © Alan Carey/The Image Works; page 448, © Billy E. Barnes/Stock, Boston; page 453, © Joel Gordon; page 456, © The Image Works; page 464, © Michael Newman/PhotoEdit; page 468, © K. Horan/Stock, Boston; page 473, © Loren Santon/Tony Stone Images; page 481, Courtesy of Jim Prigoff and Henry Chalfant; page 484, © Dave Shaffer/Jeroboam, Inc.

Chapter 11

CO, © Lionel Delevigne/Stock, Boston; page 493, © The Bettman Archive; page 494, © Jane Scherr/Jeroboam; page 496, © D. Fineman/Sygma; page 508, Courtesy of Nancy Cobb; page 512, © Bob Daemmrich/Stock, Boston; page 515, © Tom McKitterick/Impact Visuals; page 522, © Skjold Photos.

Chapter 12

CO, 1994 Mark Constantini/San Francisco Examiner;

page 533, © 1994 Mark Constantini/San Francisco Examiner; page 535, © 1994 Mark Constantini/San Francisco Examiner; page 540, © Dorothy Greco/The Image Works; page 551, © Bart Bartholomew/Black Star; page 552, © Ellis Herwig/The Picture Cube; page 555, © Eugene Richards/Magnum Photos; page 558, © The Motion Picture and TV Photo Archive; page 563, © Spencer Grant/Stock, Boston; page 566, © Keith Haring/Stock, Boston; page 570, © Jim Whitmer/Stock, Boston; page 581, © Skjold Photos.

Chapter 13
CO, © Bob Daemmrich/The Image Works; page 589, Courtesy of Richard L. Simmons; page 594, Courtesy of Robert Cohen; page 600, top and bottom, © Elizabeth Crews; page 604, Drawing from Levy, S. J. (1985) "Dreams, fairy tales, animals and cars." *Psychology & Marketing, 2,* 67–81. Copyright 1985 by John Wiley & Sons, Inc. Reprinted by permission of John Wiley & Sons, Inc.; page 607, Courtesy of Professor Benjamin Harris.

TEXT CREDITS

Chapter 1
Table 1.1. Reprinted by permission of Random House, Inc.

Chapter 2
Box 2.1, reprinted by permission of the publishers from *In a Different Voice* by Carol Gilligan, Cambridge, Mass.: Harvard University Press. Copyright © 1982 by Carol Gilligan. **Figure 2.2,** Ulric Neisser, *Cognitive Psychology,* © 1967, p. 73, adapted by permission of Prentice-Hall, Englewood Cliffs, New Jersey. **Table 2.2,** J.H. Flavell, P.H. Miller, & S.A. Miller, *Cognitive Development,* 3rd edition. Copyright © 1993 by Prentice-Hall, Inc.

Chapter 3
Figures 3.3 and **3.5,** W.A. Daniel, Jr., "Pubertal Changes in Adolescence," in J. Brooks-Gunn & A.C. Petersen (Eds.), *Girls at Puberty: Biological and Psychosocial Perspectives.* Reprinted by permission of Plenum Publishing Corporation.

Chapter 4
Figure 4.5, S.C. Martorano, "A Developmental Analysis of Performance on Piaget's Formal Operations Tasks," from *Developmental Psychology,* 13, 666–72. Copyright 1977 by the American Psychological Association. Reprinted by permission.

Chapter 5
Box 5.4 and **Figure 5.1** adapted with permission from Cooper, C.R., Grotevant, H.D., & Condon, S.M., "Individuality and Connectedness in the Family as a Context for Adolescent Identity Formation and Role-Taking Skill," in Grotevant, H.D. & Cooper, C.R. (eds.), *Adolescent Development in the Family: New Directions in Child Development,* No. 22, © 1983 by Jossey-Bass, Inc., Publisher.

Chapter 6
Figure 6.2, © 1989, The Society for Research in Child Development, Inc. Reprinted by permission of the publisher.

Chapter 7
Figure 7.7, © 1990, The Society for Research in Child Development, Inc. Reprinted by permission of the publisher.

Chapter 8
Figures 8.2, 8.3, reprinted with permission from Roberta G. Simmons and Dale A. Blyth, *Moving Into Adolescence: The Impact of Pubertal Change and School Context* (New York: Aldine de Gruyter) Copyright © 1987 by the authors.

Chapter 9
Table 9.1 Reprinted with permission of Plenum Publishing Corporation.

Chapter 10
Table 10.3 Gerstein, M., Lichtman, M. & Barokas, J.U., *The Career Development Quarterly,* 36, 222–30. © 1988 AACD. Reprinted by permission. Research Focus Kammer, P.P., Fouad N., and Williams R., *The Career Development Quarterly,* 37, 40–45 © 1988 AACD. Reprinted by permission. **Figure 10.5** A.J. Franklin, 1985, "The Social Context and Socialization Variables as Factors in Thinking and Learning," in S.F. Chipman, J.W. Segal, & R. Glaser (Eds.), *Thinking and Learning Skills,* Vol. 2. Reprinted by permission of Lawrence Erlbaum Associates, Inc.

Chapter 11
Box 11.3 Reprinted by permission of the publishers from *Mapping the Moral Domain,* edited by Carol Gilligan, Jane Victoria Ward and Jill McLean Taylor, Cambridge, Mass: Harvard University Press. Copyright © 1983 by the President and Fellows of Harvard College.

Chapter 12
Box 12.1 From *The American Psychiatric Association: Diagnostic and Statistical Manual of Mental Disorders, Third Edition, Revised,* Washington, D.C, American Psychiatric Association. 1987. Reprinted by permission.